W9-AXJ-715

SCHOOLCRAFT COLLEGE LIBRARY
3 3013 00059 4667

Roger Pearson, Ph.D.
The Institute for the Study of Man

ROBERT E. KRIEGER PUBLISHING COMPANY
MALABAR, FLORIDA
1985

Original Edition 1985

Printed and Published by
ROBERT E. KRIEGER PUBLISHING COMPANY, INC.
KRIEGER DRIVE
MALABAR, FLORIDA 32950

Printed in the United States of America

Library of Congress Cataloging in Publication Data

Pearson, Roger, 1927-
Anthropological glossary.

1. Anthropology—Dictionaries. I. Title.
GN11.P43 1985 306'.03'21 85-195
ISBN 0-89874-510-1

10 9 8 7 6 5 4 3 2

AUTHOR'S INTRODUCTION

Anthropology has been defined as the study of 'the origin and evolution of man, culture and society'. As such it embraces an extremely broad field of enquiry, and anthropologists need to be conversant with a wide range of technical terms and an enormous spectrum of data regarding diverse peoples, languages, concepts and artifacts. The potential utility of a conveniently alphabeticized compendium of anthropological information is readily apparent.

This *Anthropological Glossary* is an attempt to supply such a compendium, by providing readers with a concise handbook for on-the-spot reference. The idea came to the author while he was compiling the brief twenty-one page glossary included as an appendix in his *Introduction to Anthropology* (Holt, Rinehart and Winston, 1974). However, as the reader will observe, the text not only grew as he worked upon it, it slowly allowed itself to become transformed into what can best be described as a companion to anthropological studies – an alphabetically organized introduction to the study of 'the origin and evolution of man, culture and society'.

The reason for this expansion beyond the strict limits of an ordinary glossary is one with which any student who enjoys anthropology will readily sympathize. There is a fascination about anthropology which is implicit in the meaning of the original Greek word *anthropologia* – a complimentary epithet used when describing persons who were possessed of lofty vision, and whose thoughts rose above their own mundane needs and desires, enabling them to see man and his environment as an integral part of the larger universe. The key to achieving this elevated state of mind is a dispassionate and unbiased thirst for knowledge about the individual human organism, about the diverse peoples and races of the world, and about man's place in the total cosmic environment. The quest for such knowledge not only raises the individual above the problems of his or her immediate environment, but also brings with it a refined and exquisite form of pleasure – a form of intellectual aesthetics experienced when a sense of *anthropologia* permits the observer to become detached from selfish interests and to contemplate instead the grand drama of the cosmic forces at work. It was a sense of *anthropologia* that enabled the heroes of Greek antiquity to face with dignity such perils as causality – known to them as *Moirae* or 'fate', and perceived in mythological terms as a web of causal forces spun by three sisters named significantly, in the cognate Norse mythology, as 'Was', 'Is', and 'Will Be' – ordained for them, free from any false hubris rooted in phantasies about the power of man to act in opposition to the laws of nature. Similarly, the study of anthropology helps us to understand how Alexander Pope felt when he wrote the famous words: 'whatever is, is right'. To the scientist, there is beauty in everything that exists, and the key to finding that beauty is to be able to perceive the forces of causality in even the most seemingly trivial of data. Caught up in this spirit, the author has allowed himself to include many snippets of information of the sort that has made anthropology so fascinating for him. He hopes and believes that many of those who dip into this book will share his fascination for anthropological trivia of all kinds.

One final word: when anthropology was in its infancy, the world was still privileged to play host to a number of very elementary societies, comprising small, technologically impoverished bands of hunters and food-gatherers, whose life-styles reflected those of our earlier hominid forebears during the greater part of the evolutionary history of our species. The accounts of these cultures, prepared by early ethnographers, have been invaluable in helping us to reconstruct the social and cultural evolution of our species. Although these pristine examples of man's archaic past have now almost universally disappeared, the evidence which they provided is so important that it is still customary to describe such societies in the present tense, as though we were seeing them through the eyes of the ethnographers who first recorded their habits and customs. Accordingly, the author has adhered to the convention known as 'the ethnographic present', and has used the present tense to describe the social and cultural characteristics of such peoples, many of whom have long since passed away.

The Institute for the Study of Man
Washington, D.C.

FOREWORD

By
C. Scott Littleton

In the course of the last hundred and fifty-odd years, a dedicated legion of anthropological field workers has brought to light an impressive body of evidence as to the well-nigh limitless range and diversity of the human condition. That evidence is certainly well-represented in *Anthropological Glossary*. Professor Pearson has combed the literature with a fine-toothed, albeit judicious, comb, and has assembled a fascinating collection not only of "trivia," as he modestly describes it, but of informative mini-essays on a remarkable variety of subjects. For example, on pages 241-42 the reader will discover a concise yet remarkably comprehensive essay on ancient Sumer, one that puts the language, religion, and other important aspects of this most ancient of Western civilizations into their proper focus. Other mini-essays of this sort can be found in the entries "CULTIVATION," "RACE," and "WAR," to mention but a few.

It should be emphasized that the majority of the entries are short and very much to the point. But that is precisely what is called for in a book of this sort. The student needs a ready reference to these topics, and Professor Pearson has certainly provided it. The decision to combine tribal and ethnic names with conceptual categories and the basic concepts of the discipline was a good one, I think, for it allows the reader to move easily from one entry to another, unhindered by a complex – and, for the beginner, inevitably confusing – set of subcategories and cross-references. Thus, on page 150, for example, one can find such diverse entries as "LAGUNA" (a North American Indian group), "LAMA" (a Tibetan Buddhist monk and "teacher") and "LAMARCKISM" (the discredited evolutionary theory, predicated on the presumed inheritance of acquired characteristics, that was put forward by the French naturalist Jean Baptiste de Lamarck at the end of the 18th century). These facts and/or mini-essays, as I've termed them, should prove invaluable to students in the early stages of mastering anthropology.

At the same time, *Anthropological Glossary* can serve as a primary reference work for the professional; that is, it's a handy compendium of specific facts that will prove invaluable in the preparation of class lectures, etc. The author's selections are balanced, and no undue weight seems to have been given to any one of the several major sub-disciplines (cultural anthropology, physical anthropology, archaeology, linguistics, etc.), contemporary schools of anthropological thought, or regions of the planet. Indeed, as the reader will quickly discover, Pearson consistently, and with good reason, avoids purely theoretical entries, as well as the names of theorists, preferring to concentrate instead on those concepts and categories that are firmly rooted in ethnographic facts. This, I think, was a wise choice.

I would be less than candid if I neglected to say that I would have preferred to see the inclusion of a few maps, as well as some charts and diagrams, and perhaps even a few selected photographs. But this is a minor fault, and could easily be rectified in future editions. The book has a great many things going for it that more than make up for the lack of a visual dimension; not the least of these is its readability. Like the author's highly regarded introductory textbook, which is now unfortunately out of print, the current work is written in a straightforward and thoroughly readable style. Considering the atrocious, jargon-ridden exposition one generally encounters in works of this sort, this in itself is a major achievement!

In sum, I very much admire Professor Pearson's enterprise, to say nothing of his vast erudition, in putting together such an extensive reference book. Indeed, I predict that, a few years hence, dog-eared copies of *Anthropological Glossary* will be found at the elbows of anthropologists everywhere, professionals as well as students, and that it will have become, as they say, "a classic."

Occidental College
Los Angeles, California

A

ABACUS, a counting device comprising a number of beads mounted on parallel rods, first used in ancient Sumeria.
ABADIR, a title meaning, literally, 'powerful father', employed by the Carthaginians to refer to their principal deities.
ABBEVILLIAN, a pre-Acheulian hand axe industry centered in Europe, which dates from the Mindel glacial era. Abbevillian tools are also found in parts of Africa, where they are usually referred to as Chellean.
ABDOMEN, the abdomen first appears in the Arthropoda (q.v.) as a posterior group of segments which are only slightly specialized. In mammalia (q.v.), by contrast, the abdomen constitutes a most important region of the body containing the intestines, liver, kidneys and virtually all the viscera other than the heart and lungs.
ABELAM, a North Papuan people who are dependent on horticulture, food-gathering, hunting and some animal husbandry.
ABELLION, a Celtic god, equivalent to and cognate with the Roman Apollo.
ABIOGENETIC, originating from non-living matter, without genetically-determined form.
ABIPON, a South American Indian people living in Paraguay and adjacent territories, where they are dependent on hunting and food-gathering supplemented by some fishing. The Abipon speak a Guaycuri language.
ABNAKI, an Eastern Woodland, Algonquian American Indian people located in northern Maine.
ABOR, a Mongoloid people who occupy the mountain valleys north of the Upper Brahmaputra valley. The Abor speak a Tibeto-Burman language, and depend for their subsistence on cultivation, animal husbandry, fishing and hunting.
ABORIGINAL, a term used to refer to the original or indigenous inhabitants of a country, such as the Semangs of Malaya, to distinguish them from subsequent immigrant populations.
ABORTION, a primitive birth control technique, involving deliberate inducement to ensure the premature birth of a fetus, is practised in many societies. The methods used vary from the application of tight binding-clothes to the abdomen, to prevent it from swelling naturally, to such crude measures as walking on the woman's extended abdomen.
ABRACADABRA, a medieval corruption of the ancient Gnostic (q.v.) magico-religious formula, formerly inscribed upon amulets worn by Gnostic devotees on the chest. Literally translated, the original phrase meant 'Do not hurt me!'
ABSOLUTE DATING, the determination of the approximate age of a fossil or artifact by the use of scientific means, as distinct from 'relative dating' (q.v.). Such methods include amino-acid dating, potassium-argon dating, radiocarbon dating, and uranium-lead dating. Other absolute dating techniques combine some degree of the relative dating approach. These include dendrochronology, obsidian-hydrogen dating, and varve-counting. (See DATING SYSTEMS).
ABU SIMBEL, two temples carved from the rock cliffs by Pharaoh Rameses II around 1250 B.C. The site of the Abu Simbel temples is now covered by the waters of the Aswan High Dam, but the main parts of the Abu Simbel monument were skillfully cut into blocks and re-erected on a new site, safely above the waters of the dam, by means of funds contributed internationally.
ABYDOS, an archeological site in Upper Egypt, 200 miles north of Luxor, which was closely associated with the god Osiris. The most famous temples were erected during the 19th dynasty, although some date from the first dynasty.
ABYSS, the Babylonians believed that the universe evolved from a primeval chaos or abyss, and the ancient Egyptians similarly equated the concept of the underworld with a gigantic bottomless abyss.
ACCLIMATIZATION, changes in the physiological functions of an organism which enable it to adjust to new climatic conditions. Such changes do not involve any modification of the genetic heritage.

ACCULTURATION, a process of cultural adjustment occurring when two distinct cultures come into contact. The complete adoption of the norms and conditions of one people by another usually leads to the absorption of the adopting peoples into the dominant culture.
ACEPHALOUS SOCIETY, a society lacking in formal political offices or statuses, sometimes described as equalitarian.
ACHAEANS, the name by which the Greeks of the Homeric period described themselves. Today the Achaeans are frequently referred to as Myceneans, after the famous archeological site of Mycenae (q.v.). Excavations at Mycenae, Tiryns and Pylos, have revealed exquisite painted pottery, highly artistic metal work, ornamental frescoes, and clay tablets inscribed with the linear B script which the Myceneans subsequently introduced into Crete following their conquest of Knossos.
ACHAEMENID, the family name of the Persian dynasty descended from Achaemenes, an Aryan king who united the Persian tribes and laid the foundations of the Persian empire. At the peak of its power the Indo-European Achaemenid empire extended from the Indus Valley to Egypt and Anatolia, embracing Palestine and Babylonia. The attempt by the Achaemenid emperor Xerxes to conquer Greece was defeated by the Greeks following the destruction of the Persian fleet at Salamis in 480 B.C., and in 331 B.C. the Achaemenid Empire was overthrown by the Macedonian Alexander the Great.
ACHEULIAN, an improved biface core tool technique associated with Swanscombe man. Dating from the later, more highly evolved phase of the Lower Paleolithic, Acheulian techniques extended over Western Europe, Africa, and Southwest Asia, and were characterized by elegant hand axes and a wide range of flake tools.
ACHOLI, an African people resident in Northern Uganda.
ACHOMAWI, a Northeastern California Hokan-speaking people, dependent on food-gathering, hunting and fishing.
ACHONDROPLASTIC DWARFISM, an aberrant form of physical development implying extremely short limbs, which is inherited as a dominant gene.
ACNA. a Mayan moon-goddess.
ACOMA, a North American Indian, Western Pueblo people who speak a Keresan language. The Acoma were primarily dependent on horticulture and hunting, but have practiced some animal husbandry since the introduction of domestic animals by the Spaniards.
ACQUIRED CHARACTERISTICS (INHERITANCE OF), the Lamarckian theory of genetic inheritance maintained that variations arising in individuals as a response to environmental influences were genetically transmitted to their offspring. It is now known that no such transmission takes place in any organisms which reproduce sexually unless the gametes (q.v.) are themselves modified by such variations, as is the case when mutations (q.v.) arise as a result of exposure to radiation or other forces. (see MUTATION and NATURAL SELECTION).
ACROPOLIS, the fortified center of a Greek city, usually situated on the highest geographical prominence, wherein the palace of the king and the chief temples were located.
ADAPTATION, the response of an organism to its environment involving some kind of adjustment which will enhance its chances of leaving more numerous descendants. Cultural systems may also adapt to environmental needs.
ADAPTATION, ENVIRONMENTAL, a term used by anthropologists to refer to the process by which a species becomes genetically adjusted to the problem of survival in a given environment. Natural selection (q.v.) works to ensure the adaptation of any population to its environment, providing that environmental changes are not so drastic or abrupt that they prevent adaptation from taking place.
ADAPTATION, EVOLUTIONARY, evolutionary adaptation occurs when genetic differences arise due to mutations (q.v.) within a species, some of which improve the chances that an individual organism will survive to produce more

live offspring than are produced by other individuals lacking these specific genetically-transmissible characteristics. Through succeeding generations, any inbreeding population will therefore tend to adapt to the prevailing environmental conditions as a result of over-reproduction and a process of natural selection (q.v.) which favours the reproduction of those individuals whose genetic equipment favours their survival under the prevailing environmental conditions.

ADAPTIVE RADIATION, one of the principal effects of the evolutionary process (q.v.) has been the tendency for many divergent forms of living species, each adapted for different modes of survival in a distinctive environment, to evolve from a single, originally less-specialized, simpler species.

ADENA, a Woodland culture formerly covering most of the eastern half of North America. The Woodland culture (q.v.) emerged approximately 1000 B.C., and contributed to the later Hopewell culture, with which it coexisted for some time.

ADOBE, a term used for sun-dried mud bricks widely manufactured in Central America for use in the construction of houses, temples and pyramids. Adobe bricks lack the durability of kiln-baked bricks, and need constant repair or replacement.

ADOLESCENCE, that period in which the individual male or female is in transition from childhood to adulthood. In less structured societies adolescence may be characterized by a degree of status uncertainty and this frequently results in psychological tensions. In many traditional societies, by contrast, adolescent uncertainty is avoided by puberty and initiation rituals (q.v.). Such 'rites of passage' (q.v.) clearly define the status of the individual adolescent, who is generally treated as a child prior to the initiation but is awarded the status of an adult immediately thereafter, with all the rights and privileges of adulthood.

ADONIS, a handsome Greek youth with whom Aphrodite fell in love. After being killed by a boar in a hunting accident, Adonis descended into the Underworld, where he was obliged to spend every Autumn and Winter, but was permitted to return to the earth to live with Aphrodite during Spring and Summer. The story of Adonis and Aphrodite, explaining the cycle of the seasons, is parallel to the Babylonian nature myth of the God Tammuz, the Babylonian god of vegetation (q.v.) and Ishtar, the Babylonian goddess of fertility.

ADOPTION, most human societies provide for the adoption of children, by persons who are not their parents, under certain specifically-defined circumstances. The purpose of adoption, whereby an individual becomes the socially or legally recognized son or daughter of persons who are not his natural parents, may range from the need to provide a home, sustenance and legal identity for an orphaned child to the need (as in ancestor-worshipping societies) for parents without offspring to acquire an heir. In societies dominated by kinship systems, such children are normally close relatives of the adopting party, as when a brother is obligated to adopt and care for the children of a deceased sibling. The North American Plains Indians on the other hand, frequently permitted the adoption of orphans by persons not directly related to them provided there was a physical resemblance between the child and a dead relative. As might be expected customs concerning adoption vary dramatically from one society to another in accordance with the prevailing social mores.

ADULTERY, although wife-lending is common in many primitive societies, adultery is regarded as a serious offense in almost all kinship-oriented societies, being frequently punishable by death or physical torture.

ADZE, a hafted tool, usually made from stone in Neolithic cultures and from metal in metal age cultures. It is principally used for wood-working and differs from an axe in that the cutting edge of the blade is set at right angles to the haft, instead of parallel to the haft.

AEGYPTOPITHECUS, a pre-hominid known as 'Egyptian ape' identified from fossil remains which have been found by E. L. Simons in the Fayum (q.v.) area of Egypt. These belong to the Upper Oligocene and are dated around 28 million years ago. They are important since the fossil remains indicate that Aegyptopithecus hominoids were probably ancestral to Dryopithecines, and that they are closely related to the common ancestors of both man and the surviving apes (except possibly the gibbon).

AEOLIS, the eponymous ancestor of the Aeolian royal family who was traditionally credited with the invention of sails, and appears to have been deified by the Greeks as a god who controlled the winds.

AEON, a Phoenician god who controlled or personified the passing of time.

AESIR, the twelve councilors or companions of Odin in Asgard, in whose honour the Yuletide rituals were held. The number '12' is common to many bodies of councilors in cultures of Indo-European origin (e.g. Homeric Greece) and is still the traditional number of members on the jury in the Anglo-Saxon jury system. (See NORSE RELIGION).

AFALOU MAN, North African fossils found in a rock shelter in Algeria, and regarded as closely related to the Cro-Magnons of Europe. Containing the parts of some 50 skeletons in association with Upper Paleolithic artifacts, the site was discovered by C. Arambourg in 1928.

AFAR, a Cushitic people of East Africa almost wholly dependent on animal herding and minimal fishing and food-gathering.

AFFINAL EXCHANGE, a custom whereby two separate kinship groups enter into a mutual obligation to provide wives for each other's sons, thus ensuring enduring kinship and genetic relationship through the generations. Marriage by exchange is still commonly practiced by pygmies and is also to be found in more advanced societies.

AFFINAL RELATIONSHIP, marital relationship, as distinct from relationship by consanguinity or birth.

AFRICAN RELIGION, the religions of the many different Niger-Congo peoples of sub-Saharan Africa all combine some degree of ancestor-worship with the recognition of a number of nature gods. Among the latter they mostly recognize a High God whose relation to the other gods is similar to that of an African tribal chief to the village chiefs and ordinary members of a tribe. Sacrifice plays an important role in the propitiation of both the nature gods and the ancestral spirits, but few African societies have organized priesthoods, except for those, such as the Baganda, who appoint priestlike guardians of tombs and shrines. In most instances the tribal chieftain, being descended from deified ancestors, controls the tribal worship, aided in some cases by a younger brother who specializes in ritual detail, or by wizard-priests, where these exist. Generally speaking, the attitude of most Niger-Congo people towards the ancestral spirits is one of fear rather than reverence, and most religious activities are aimed at avoiding the animosity of the gods, or at badgering them into providing the tribe or the individual communicant with special benefits, with the aid of magical formulas and rituals. Indeed, many Bantu peoples believe that it is possible to conceal from the gods acts and deeds which might arouse their displeasure, on the principle that that which the gods are ignorant of cannot displease them. Divination is widespread, most disasters being attributed to either witchcraft or the wrath of supernatural beings, and witchdoctors are regularly consulted to ascertain which of these causes is applicable, and to advise on appropriate countermeasures.

AFRO-ASIATIC LANGUAGES, a large phylum of languages combining two major groups: the Hamitic group, localized in North Africa, and the Semitic group, which was originally localized in the Arabian peninsula but subsequently spread out over much of the Middle East and a large part of Africa. It is possible that the entire Afro-Asian family of languages may have formerly originated in the Arabian peninsula, and that the Hamitic group may have been carried into Africa by early waves of nomadic pastoralists and sedentary cultivators who entered Africa as early as the 7th and 6th millennia B.C. (See HAMITIC LANGUAGES and also SEMITES).

AFTERLIFE, the belief that some part of a man may live on after death is very widespread among both primitive and civilized peoples. The first evidence to date of a belief in an afterlife appears among the Classic Neanderthals of Europe, who not only buried their dead but placed personal or useful objects in the grave along with the body of the deceased. This practice would seem to indicate a belief in the survival of a soul (q.v.) after death, on the grounds that the objects placed in the grave would be needed by the soul, or else that the spirit or soul would be jealous if these objects were retained and used by the survivors. (See also GRAVE GOODS).

AGAIDUKA (LEMHI RIVER SHOSHONI), a Shoshone-(Uto-Aztec) speaking North American Indian people of the Coastal Great Basin, dependent on fishing, food-gathering and hunting.

AGE GRADE, a group of males of approximately the same age who are initiated into tribal society at the same time and therefore share the same social status. Although membership is normally restricted to males, in some societies females may also be grouped into age grades or sets. Among the Masai of East Africa, especially, the age grade is associated with military functions, all the young men of particular age being initiated into their grade at the same series of rites of passage (q.v.), after which they live together in a military kraal 'camp' for a set period of time, before being replaced by younger age grades. Only after their military service is completed are they permitted to marry and enter into the normal social and political life of the community. Age grades have a 'horizontally' bonding effect, uniting the 'vertical' clan-based divisions of tribal societies by enrolling young men from different clans into the same grade.

AGE SET, any group of persons of similar age who cooperate for specific purposes.

AGGLUTINATING LANGUAGE, a term used to refer to any language possessing numerous dependent morphemes arranged in recognized sequences to make words. Such words can consequently be of considerable length. The Eskimo and Finno-Ugric languages are examples of agglutinating languages.

AGGLUTINATION, any process whereby separate chemical or biological components tend to adhere to each other. In biology the term is used to describe the tendency of the red blood corpuscles to cluster together when blood from two incompatible groups is mixed.

AGGRESSION, considerable debate has taken place among anthropologists as to whether men possess an innate or instinctive tendency towards aggression or whether aggression is a purely learned or culturally-determined pattern of behaviour. Undoubtedly the behaviour of different peoples varies considerably in this respect, and cultural traditions play a large part in shaping the personality and behaviour of individuals. However, the limits of learned behaviour are biologically determined and an innate biological tendency towards aggressive behaviour as a defense mechanism or as a means of achieving a desired objective would seem to be inherent in the glandular and physiological make-up of all hominid races, though possibly stronger in some than in others.

AGING, longevity and the rate of aging vary considerably from one people to another, and would appear to be influenced by both genetico-racial factors and by environmental life habits.

AGNATE, a person related by descent through the male line.

AGNATHA, an early class of vertebrates (q.v.), today represented by the fish-like lampreys which – though equipped with vertebrae (q.v.) – lack jaws and fins. Agnatha were probably ancestral to all other vertebrates.

AGNI, the Vedic god of fire, synonymous with the ancient Sanskrit word for fire. Fire played an important role in early Indo-European ritual.

AGNI HOTRI, the name given to the Aryan priests who served Agni, the Indo-Aryan god of fire.

AGONISTIC DISPLAY, a term frequently used by primatologists (q.v.) to refer to threatening gestures used by one or more primates against other members of the same group.

AGRICULTURE, an advanced method of cultivation implying the possession of domesticated animals and some knowledge of fertilizing techniques or crop rotation.

AHAGGAREN, Hamitic-speaking Tuareg people of North Africa, dependent primarily on animal husbandry with some horticulture and hunting.

AHMOSE, the Thebean prince who drove the Hyksos out of Egypt, around 1580 B.C., and established the 18th dynasty – the first dynasty of a reinvigorated Egypt known as the 'New Kingdom'.

AHU, a Polynesian term for a stone platform or altar used in religious ceremonies, known by the modified name of Tuahu among New Zealand Maories. (See also MARAE).

AHURA MAZDA, the Persian god of Light and Truth, 'the Lord of Knowledge,' who led the powers of Goodness against Ahriman, the 'Spirit of Evil and Darkness'.

AIMOL, a Mongoloid people who speak a Tibeto-Burman language and live in the forested mountains separating the Indian sub-continent from Burma and are dependent on horticulture, hunting and some animal husbandry.

AINU, the so-called 'hairy Ainu', well-known for their hirsute character, are still found on the islands of Hokkaido and Sakhalin to which they are indigenous. It would seem, though, that they were formerly much more widely distributed throughout Eastern Asia and the Japanese islands. Physiologically and linguistically they are generally identified with the Paleo-Asians of Northeastern Siberia.

AIR PHOTOGRAPHY, vertical photographs taken from the air frequently reveal changes in the coloration of soil or patterns of vegetation which may indicate the presence of hitherto undetected archeological material beneath the surface of the soil.

AJIE, a Melanesian (Malayo-Polynesian) people from New Caledonia, largely dependent on horticulture, fishing and some animal husbandry.

AKAR, the Egyptian equivalent of hell.

AKHA, a Sinitic (Tibeto-Burman)-speaking people, largely dependent on horticulture with some hunting, food-gathering and animal husbandry.

AKHENATON (Armenotope IV), one of the Pharaohs of the 18th dynasty of Egypt whose queen was the famed Nefertiti. Akhenaton attempted to weaken the power of the priesthood, which was organized around the worship of Amen-Ra and the older pantheon of gods, by introducing a monotheistic religion of Sun-worship in the name of the God Aton. To support this endeavor he removed his capital from Thebes to a new site at Tell-el-Amarna. All his efforts proved unsuccessful, however, for after his death his successor Tutankhamen returned to the tradition of polytheism centered around the worship of Amen-Ra.

AKKAD, the capital city founded by Sargon, king of the Semitic Akkadians around 2370 B.C. The Akkadians brought the entire northern part of Sumeria, including Babylon, under their rule, but retained much of the Sumerian culture, in particular the use of the cuneiform script.

AKKADIANS, the Semitic inhabitants of Akkad (q.v.).

ALACA HÜYÜK, an important archeological site in Central Anatolia which has revealed a large number of tombs, some of which date from the 4th millennium B.C. Most important, however, are some 13 tombs dating around 2500 B.C. These contain a number of Indo-European royal burials, replete with weapons, gold and copper sun discs, animal standards, and miscellaneous ritual vessels. Later Alaca Hüyük artifacts are undoubtedly Hittite.

ALACALUF, a South American Indian people living in Southern Chile whose language is related to that of the Ona and Yahgan. The Alacaluf are dependent on fishing with some hunting and food-gathering.

ALBANIANS, a people of distinctive Indo-European speech who preserved clan and tribal traditions into the present century.

ALBINISM, a mutant form found with varying degrees of frequency among all races of man and also among many animals. Albinism is caused by the absence of pigmentation. Being genetically the result of a recessive gene, its incidence varies considerably from population to population. It has no direct genetic relationship to the standard racial variations of lightness or darkness of skin colour.

ALBUMIN, the basic protein in blood serum.

ALCHEMY, sometimes described as the forerunner of chemistry, alchemy appears to have originated in the Hellenistic city of Alexandria, on the northern coast of Egypt, during the first century A.D. It derived from a combination of ancient Chaldean and Egyptian magical rituals with Greek philosophical speculation, mathematics and such metallurgical knowledge as had accumulated during the Copper, Bronze and Iron Ages. From Alexandria, alchemy spread throughout the Middle East, North Africa and much of Europe, and was later adopted and widely practiced by Muslim alchemists throughout the Mohammedan world. Above all, alchemists sought to discover the formula for eternal life, and for the transmutation of base metals into gold.

ALEUTS, sometimes described as 'Western Eskimos', the Aleuts inhabit the Aleutian Isles and depend on fishing supplemented by hunting and some minimal food-gathering.

ALFHEIM, the home of the elves in Norse mythology.

ALGALOA, the Hawaiian sky god.

ALGERIANS, a North African population of mixed Hamitic and Semitic origins, today mostly speaking Arabic and dependent on agriculture and animal husbandry.

ALGONQUIAN-MOSAN LANGUAGES, this large phylum of languages includes the major Algonquian family, comprising Cree, Menomini, Fox-Kickapoo, Shawnee, Ojibwa, Ottawa and Algonquian, Delaware, Micmac, Blackfoot, Cheyenne and Arapaho. The Blackfoot, Cheyenne and Arapaho languages are sometimes classed separately from the Cree, Ottawa, Menomini group. Also included in the Algonquian-Mosan classification are the Kwakiutl, Nootka, Bella Bella and other languages comprising the Wakashan Family, as well as the important Salish family containing 16 different languages, including Bella Coola, Flathead, Spokane and Twana. The Tarascan language isolate is also sometimes grouped in the Algonquian-Mosan family.

ALIMENTARY CANAL, the gut or tube which is primarily concerned with the digestion and absorption of food. The alimentary canal first appeared in Coelenterates (q.v.), in which there is only one opening, but in more advanced animals the canal usually has an opening at one end (the mouth) into which food is taken, and an opening at the other end (the anus) from which the waste material is ejected.

ALISHAR, a tell in Central Anatolia which has yielded remains dating from the Chalcolithic Age (4th millennium B.C.) to the Phrygian (1st millennium B.C.).

ALKATCHO CARRIER, a Northwest Athabascan American Indian people, mainly dependent on fishing but also practicing some hunting and food-gathering.

ALLELES, genes (q.v.) are said to be alleles when they occupy the same relative locus on homologous chromosomes (q.v.), but produce different instead of similar effects in the offspring produced by reproduction (q.v.).

ALLELOMORPH, one of two or more contrasting genetic characters.

ALLEN'S RULE, animals which have evolved in colder climates tend to have shorter limbs, thereby providing a small surface area and reducing the dissipation of body heat.

ALLFATHER, in Indo-European religion, one sky god was widely believed to be the father of all other gods, being known respectively as Dyeus-pater, Dyaus-pater, Zeus-pater, and Jupiter to the Indo-Aryans, Iranians, Greeks and Romans, and as Odin to the Germanic peoples. The Indo-European belief in an 'Allfather' may have inspired the Christian concept of 'Our Father in Heaven'.

ALL FOOL'S DAY, the first day of the month of April, during which, in Western Europe, innocent practical jokes are played upon friends and relatives. The custom appears to reflect an ancient Celtic ritual associated with the Brythonic Celtic goddess Arianrhod, who was renowned for her beauty.

ALLOMETRY, the principle governing the relative sizes of organisms or parts of organisms in different sized animals of the same species.

ALLOPATRIC SPECIES, separate species which occupy different areas of geo-

graphic distribution.
ALLOTROPHS, see AUTOTROPHS.
ALLOY, any mixture of metals producing a harder or more useful amalgam of metal than is provided by the ingredients in pure form. Thus bronze, an alloy of copper, was a far more useful metal than pure copper.
ALORESE, a Malayo-Polynesian speaking people of Alor (Indonesia), largely dependent on horticulture, food-gathering and some animal husbandry.
ALPHABET, any phonetic system of written symbols in which each symbol represents a distinctive sound. The early Semitic alphabet used by the Phoenicians embodied symbols which represented consonants but made no provision for vowels, and it was the Greeks who added symbols for vowels when they adopted this alphabet in the 8th century B.C. By contrast, alphabets which use signs representing ideas rather than sounds require hundreds of different symbols, as did the hieroglyphic (q.v.) and cuneiform (q.v.) scripts of Egypt and the Middle East, while the modern Chinese script, which is still made up of ideograms, contains several thousand different signs. The name alphabet is derived from a corruption of the first two words of the Greek alphabet, i.e. Alpha and Beta.
ALPINE, a branch of the Caucasoid stock, generally characterized as relatively short in stature, dark in eye and hair colouring, and broad in the face. Although the Alpines may at one time have represented a fairly distinct population, the term is best used today to refer to a distinctive combination of characteristics found in a belt running across central Europe from Belgium through northern France and South Germany, to include parts of Switzerland and western Austria.
ALRUNES, the household gods of the Germanic peoples, originally conceived of as ancestral spirits.
ALSEA, a coastal Oregon, Athabascan-speaking American Indian people, mainly dependent on fishing with some hunting and food-gathering.
ALTAIC, the Altaic family of languages represents the eastern wing of the Ural-Altaic phylum; Western and West Central Asia are dominated by the Turko-Tartar group, which includes Turkish, Uzbek, Azerbaijani, Kashgari, Kirghiz, Kazak, Turkoman, Tartar and Uighir, while East Central Asia is dominated by the Mongol group of Mongolia. A third division of the Altaic family is known as the Tungus-Manchu group of Eastern and Northeastern Asia, Manchu being formerly spoken in Manchuria from whence it gave its name to the Manchu dynasty of China. It has also recently been confirmed that Korean, Japanese and Ket belong to separate divisions of the Altaic family, closely related to the Tungus-Manchu group.
ALTAI MOUNTAINS, an important range of mountains, which rise to some 13,000 feet and (together with the Tien Shan) serve to separate western and eastern Asia. However, the grassy slopes of the Altai mountains have traditionally provided extensive summer grazing grounds for pastoralists, and it is in the Altai mountains that the important archeological burial site of Pazyryk (q.v.) is located.
ALTAMIRA CAVES, caves located near Santander in Northern Spain. The Altamira Caves have revealed some of the best examples of Magdalenian, Upper Palaeolithic, Cro-Magnon art, well renowned for the esthetic perfection of the strikingly coloured paintings of animals.
ALTHEIM, a late Neolithic and early Copper Age culture of the Upper Danube, named after an archeological site comprising a large timbered settlement protected by ditches and palisades.
AL'UBAID, a major archeological tell site, close to the ancient city of Ur, which was excavated by Sir Leonard Wooley in 1923-24. The tell comprised numerous layers dating from the late 5th millennium B.C., to late Sumerian times, and is valuable in providing evidence of the evolution of the Mesopotamian culture from the early Neolithic horticultural village culture to the advanced civilization of the Copper Age.
ALUR, a Negroid, Southern Nilotic-speaking people, primarily dependent on horticulture and cattle herding with some hunting and fishing.

AMAHUACA, a South American Indian people who speak a Pano language and live on the upper reaches of the Amazon River, where they are dependent on horticulture, hunting and fishing.

AMALGAMATING LANGUAGE, a language in which a considerable amount of inflection occurs, and affixes become closely linked to the word roots, losing their separate identities.

AMARNA, TELL EL, the site of the city built by the Pharaoh Akhenaton (q.v.) in Upper Egypt as the center for his new monotheistic religion centered on the worship of the Sun. The site comprised a group of palaces, temples, and houses which appear to have been abandoned soon after Akhenaton's death, archeological excavation of which revealed copies of written communications between the Egyptian pharaohs and the kings of the Hittites and Mitanni, as well as the presence of Mycenean artifacts.

AMBA, a Bantu-speaking Negroid peoples (including the Bwamba of Uganda) of the Babwe-Bira group, dependent mainly on horticulture.

AMBER, a fossil formed of pine resin which was greatly valued throughout early Europe up to and including the Roman Age. The main sources were located along the Baltic coast and an extensive trade in amber developed along the Elbe and Vistula rivers, crossing overland to the Danube and so to the Aegean, which reached its peak during the Bronze and Iron Ages.

AMBO, a Southern Bantu, Negroid people, largely dependent on horticulture, herding and some hunting.

AMBONESE, a Malayo-Polynesian speaking people inhabiting the Moluccas in Indonesia.

AMEN, an Egyptian god associated with Upper Egypt, who rose to importance under the Thebean dynasties of the Middle and New Kingdoms. In later times Amen came to be associated with the sun god Ra.

AMERINDIAN, a term sometimes used to distinguish the American Indians from the Indians of Asian provenance. (See INDIANS, AMERICAN).

AMHARA, an Amharic-speaking Semitic people from Ethiopia, dependent on horticulture and animal husbandry.

AMI, an aboriginal, Malayo-Polynesian-speaking people of Formosa. Belonging to the Muong group, the Ami are largely dependent on cultivation with some hunting, fishing and animal husbandry.

AMINO-ACID DATING, the bone tissues of living organisms decay from proteins to peptides and thence to amino-acids, the molecular size of the organic material containing nitrogen becoming smaller as the process continues and thus more likely to diffuse to the bone surface and to be removed by water. The amino-acid analysis of fossil bones can thus be used to establish their age.

AMINO-ACIDS, organic compounds which may be regarded as the fundamental constituents of living matter.

AMNIOTE EGG, the amniote egg represents an important evolutionary development in the mechanism of reproduction. Amniote vertebrates (reptiles, birds, and mammals) produce an embryo in a protective fluid-filled sac. This fluid is necessary for the survival of embryos developing in the dryness of a land environment. In mammals, especially, the fluid also protects the embryo against distortion by the possible pressure of maternal organs against it.

AMOEBA, a classical example of a protozoan (q.v.). A single-celled animal with an irregular and constantly changing shape which is nevertheless capable of movement and of the ingestion of food by a temporary protrusion of parts of the cell to entrap the required material.

AMOK, a term used in Malaya to refer to a pattern of behaviour by which individuals suffering from severe personal tensions 'run amok', killing and wounding as many members of their own society as they can before killing (or being killed) themselves.

AMORITES, a group of Semitic pastoralists who migrated out of the semi-desert land marginal to the Fertile Crescent and conquered the Sumerian city of Ur, eventually achieving domination over a substantial portion of Mesopotamia.

The Amorites absorbed much of the Sumerian culture, and also expanded westwards into Syria and Palestine, in which latter country, they amalgamated, during the Middle Bronze Age, with the Canaanites.

AMPHIBIA, the first class of vertebrates (q.v.) to inhabit the land, probably during the late Devonian period (q.v.) some 370 million years ago.

AMPHORA, a jar equipped with a large broad base, a narrow mouth, and a pair of matching handles.

AMPUTATION, many primitive people, especially in New Guinea and Australia customarily amputate one or more fingers at the joints as a magico-religious mourning ritual. Evidence of similar practices has also been found by archeologists examining the remains of Upper Palaeolithic cultures in Europe and Africa.

AMRI, an archeological site near the Indus River, the excavation of which has revealed a village which probably dates from the early part of the 3rd millennium B.C. A distinctive pottery, painted in black and red geometrical designs, is sometimes named after this site. Houses were constructed from mud bricks, the original culture either evolving into or giving way to that of the Indus Valley civilization.

AMRITA, in Hindu mythology, Amrita is the food of the gods which gives immortality to all who eat it.

AMU, a Sumerian sky god whose temple was situated at Uruk.

AMUD, a relatively complete fossil skeleton, generally regarded as Neanderthal, found by Hisashi Suzuki in 1961 in a cave near Galilee. It is less robust than the Classical Neanderthal and more like the Skhul fossils from Mount Carmel.

AMULET, an object usually worn around the neck or arm believed to possess the magico-religious ability to protect the wearer from the forces of evil. See also CHARMS and TALISMAN).

ANAGENESIS, evolutionary changes arising within a particular phylogenetic continuum, species, or race, resulting in a modification of the continuing lineage without admixture of genes from any other lineage.

ANAGUTA, a Negroid people from the Jos Plateau area, who speak a Niger-Congo language and are largely dependent on horticulture but practice some hunting, food-gathering and animal husbandry.

ANALOGIES, (1) anatomical, physiological, and cultural similarities which arise from parallel environmental needs instead of from descent. (2) historical or ethnographic parallels used in the inference or interpretation of anthropological and archeological data.

ANALYTICAL LANGUAGE, a largely uninflected language comprising an assortment of independent words arranged in sentences with the aid of a series of prepositions and conjunctions rather than in any established word order.

ANAPHASE, that stage in the division or reproduction of a cell in which the chromatids become separated from each other and move to opposite poles of the cell. The two separate sets of chromatids thus created are normally identical to each other.

ANASAZI, a desert culture formerly located in present-day Arizona and Utah, where an early hunting and gathering people evolved a Neolithic pattern of settled life. At first the Anasazi people made no pottery, but the art of basket weaving was highly developed, and the name Basket Maker is frequently given to the early stages of the Anasazi culture. Following the Basket Maker stage, the true Anasazi culture, which included pottery making, emerged circa A.D. 700, this stage being denoted by the term Pueblo, in reference to the established village settlements. After A.D. 1300 there appears to have been a deterioration in the Anasazi culture, which had regressed considerably by the time the Spaniards arrived in the 16th century. The total area occupied by the Anasazi culture also dwindled during this later stage, as a result of pressure from nomadic Apache and Navajo tribes.

ANCESTOR WORSHIP, a sophisticated form of religion which appears to have grown out of animism (q.v.), with which it frequently remained associated. In societies united by strong kinship ties, a belief in the life of the soul after death will lead the living to assume that their loved or respected ancestors still watch over their daily deeds, condemning violations of traditional customs and using their supernatural powers to protect their living descendants from harm. Under these circumstances it is natural that the living should seek to honour and remember the spirits of the dead forebears, frequently supplicating these to intercede on behalf of the living. When ancestor worship is highly developed, as in ancient Greece, Rome, India, China and Japan, it serves as a powerful force in unifying society, since the ancestors would frown upon descendants who show disloyalty to each other, or who fail to treat their kinsmen with respect, honour and fairness.

ANDAMANESE ISLANDERS, a Negrito people found in the Andaman Islands in the Bay of Bengal, who possess a distinctive language which appears to have been separated from all other known languages for a very long period of time. This suggests that they represent the survival of an ancient population which other indications suggest may have formerly been widespread on the mainland of South and Southeast Asia until overrun, annihilated, or in places partially absorbed by immigrant Dravidian and Caucasoid populations in India, or immigrant Mongoloid populations in Southeast Asia. The Andamanese Islanders retain probably the simplest band-type pattern of social organization to persist into modern times. Some few languages in New Guinea have been identified as possibly related to Andamanese (notably Asang, Baru, Bembi and Brivat) implying that the Andamanese Negrito population was once much more widely spread in Southeast Asia than today.

ANDEAN-EQUATORIAL LANGUAGES, a large phylum of South American Indian languages which includes the Andean, the Jivaro, and Macro-Tucanoan languages (all of which q.v.).

ANDEAN LANGUAGES, a suggested grouping of South American languages (within a proposed Andean-Equatorial phylum. q.v.) which would include the Alacauf family, the Quechua-Aymara family (q.v.), the Ona-Chon family (placed by other authorities with Gê, Pano and Carib), and Cahuapanan (Northern Peru).

ANEMIA, SICKLE CELL, a hereditary form of anemia common among Negroes inhabiting malarial areas, in which the red cells acquire a crescent or 'sickle' shape. Although it is usually fatal in the homozygous form the condition affords some protection against malaria in the heterozygous form, and those who possess the trait in this form usually survive long enough to reproduce the trait along Mendelian lines. By contrast those who are free from the sickle-cell trait may die of malaria before reaching the reproductive age. Thus the sickling condition has survived in malarial areas of Africa in what is known as a balanced polymorphism (q.v.), never becoming dominant because it is self-eliminating in the homozygous condition – but never dying out because of its protective value in the heterozygous form.

ANGAKOK, a class of Eskimo shamans who have been accused by some observers of using their alleged supernatural power to exploit the Eskimo laymen unmercifully, even claiming the right to sleep with a man's wife, in return for supposed supernatural favors.

ANGAMI, a Tibeto-Burman (Sinitic) -speaking people largely dependent on horticulture, with some animal husbandry, hunting and fishing.

ANGEL, the concept of winged angels developed in the Persian culture, from which it diffused to Babylon where it was acquired by the Jews while in slavery in that city. In the Judaic beliefs, these messengers of the gods were organized under a hierarchy of archangels. From Judaism the belief in angels passed into Europe, via Christianity, where it remained widespread until the Age of Enlightenment, when it was rejected along with many aspects of Christian doctrine and agnosticism became widespread among the educated upper classes.

ANGKOR, an important archeological site representing the ruins of the former capital city of the Khmer empire, originally founded in the 9th century A.D. under the stimulation of immigration from India. The main city covered a total of nearly two square miles and was protected by a moat, some distance from which stood a most impressive collection of elaborately sculptured temples known as Angkor Wat. The entire site appears to have been abandoned in the

13th century, the ruins having been completely hidden by jungle until rediscovered by European archeologists in the 19th century.

ANGLES, a Northwest German people who formerly lived near the mouth of the Elbe river, but who migrated to England (where their descendants later came to be known as 'English') around the 5th century A.D., settling East Anglia (Norfolk and Suffolk), Mercia and other parts of Central and Eastern England.

ANGLO-SAXONS, a composite term first used in the 5th century A.D. to refer to the Angles who settled England from Denmark and Schleswig-Holstein and the Saxons who originated in the Elbe-Weser lands of the German North Sea coast. Other West German peoples including the Jutes from Jutland and the Frisians from Frisia, an area formerly including the Northern Dutch and West German coastal islands and coastland, also migrated to England and became absorbed into the general Anglo-Saxon amalgam, although the Jute settlements were concentrated largely in Kent and the Isle of Wight, while Frisian settlements were mainly along the general eastern coast of England. The Old English language arose from a combination of Angle, Saxon, Jute and Frisian West German dialects, with some North Germanic (or Scandinavian) elements introduced by the later Viking settlers.

ANGMAGSALIK ESKIMO, an Eskimo people who depend mainly on fishing and hunting.

ANIMAL WORSHIP, the veneration of animals as supernatural beings, frequently involving, for example, the South Indian deification of serpents or, as in Egyptian civilization, the Old European civilization and Mithraism, the deification of bulls.

ANIMATISM, a belief in a supernatural force which may inhabit either organic or inorganic matter, but which does not possess any self-will.

ANIMISM, a belief in the existence of supernatural beings possessing self-will. As souls or spirits these may inhabit either living or nonliving organisms.

ANKH, common symbol used in the Egyptian religion, representing a cross, the upper limb of which divides into a loop. The ankh symbolized the triumph of life over death. This symbol was frequently used to adorn representations of both the gods and the pharaohs, and the term *ankh* was often incorporated in the personal names of pharaohs, as in Tutankhamen, emphasizing the importance the ancient Egyptians placed on the idea of life after death.

ANNAMESE, the major ethnic group in Vietnam, whose Annamese language is related to the Mon Khmer family. Traditionally the means of Annamese subsistence has been agriculture, animal husbandry and fishing, although industry has been introduced recently into the growing urban areas.

ANNAM-MUONG LANGUAGES, a small family of languages related to both Mon-Khmer and Sinitic.

ANTANDRUY, a Malayo-Polynesian Malagasy people of Madagascar, dependent on agriculture, animal husbandry, fishing and some food-gathering.

ANTARIANUNTS, a Southern Paiute (North American) Uto-Aztec (Shoshone) speaking people dependent on food-gathering supplemented by some fishing.

ANTESSAR, a Hamitic-speaking Tuareg people of North Africa, dependent primarily on animal husbandry with some horticulture and hunting.

ANTHROPOCENTRISM, a tendency to regard man as of central importance in the universe, usually to the detriment of other living species.

ANTHROPOGEOGRAPHY, that science which deals with the effect of geographical and climatic environments on the physical and cultural evolution of hominids. In implication, the term tends to stress the ultimate dependence of both the biological and the cultural aspects of man on his environment and the need for ecological adjustments.

ANTHROPOIDEA, a suborder of the order primates which includes monkeys, anthropoid apes and man. The Anthropoidea may be divided into two main groups, the Catarrhine (q.v.), and the Platyrrhine (q.v.) which include the New World monkeys. Anthropoidea are distinguished by the possession of eyes which face forwards, a pronounced ability to use the hands for the manipulation of external objects, and brains which are relatively large, in relation to body size, when compared with those of other mammals.

ANTHROPOLOGY, the term *anthropologia* was first used by Aristotle to refer to a person who held lofty views and who governed his behavior in terms of its significance to man's role and status in the total universe rather than allowing himself to be motivated only by his own narrow, selfish thoughts and goals. In the 16th, 17th and 18th centuries the term 'anthropologie' was usually associated with what we today call 'physical anthropology', and in particular with the study of anatomy and physiology. Such anthropologists became interested in archaeology, however, with the discovery of fossil skeletal remains in Europe during the 19th century, and since these remains were often associated with artifacts similar to those still used by living primitives, they then developed an interest in the reports about the physical type of primitive races and the cultures of primitive societies which were flooding into Europe from explorers and missionaries. Thus anthropology ceased to be concerned only with anatomy and physiology, and instead became a vast synthesizing discipline concerned with all aspects of men and their works. Today, anthropology would be defined in England and America as the study of the origins and evolution of man, society and culture, although on the continent of Europe the term anthropology is still frequently used to refer only to physical anthropology, i.e. the study of the origin and evolution of men including both individual and racial variation.

ANTHROPOLOGY, CULTURAL, the study of those aspects of behaviour which are learned, including such patterns of instinctive behaviour as may become modified by cultural factors.

ANTHROPOLOGY, PHYSICAL, the study of human biology, dealing with the evolution of the human organism, the relation between environment and the human organism, and genetic variations between human individuals and groups.

ANTHROPOMETRY, that branch of physical anthropology which is devoted to the physical measurement and description of individuals and races.

ANTHROPOMORPHISM, the ascription of human qualities to nonhuman objects or phenomena.

ANTHROPOPHAGY, an anthropological term still sometimes used to refer to the practice of cannibalism.

ANTIBODY, antibodies are protective proteins (q.v.) produced in animals when foreign antigens (q.v.) enter into their tissues. The object of the antibody is to combat the existence of the antigen, thus providing a defense mechanism against invasion by parasites, bacteria (q.v.) and viruses (q.v.).

ANTIGEN, any substance capable of creating the formation of protective antibodies (q.v.) when introduced into an alien living organization.

ANTIPATHY, RACIAL, a deep-rooted dislike or distaste for persons displaying alien racial or physical characteristics.

ANUAK, a Nilotic people of the Fung group, primarily dependent on horticulture, but practicing some animal husbandry, hunting and fishing.

ANUBIS, the name of the Egyptian god responsible for guarding the spirits of the dead.

ANWYL, the Celtic world of the dead.

ANYANG, the last capital of the Shang dynasty of China, located in northern Honan. Many of the buildings were extremely large in area, although not more than one story in height. Elaborate ritual burials of nobles, complete with chariots, horses, hunting dogs and servants, have been found under the floors of the buildings, while separate cemeteries have revealed royal tombs equipped not only with chariots and horses but also with the skeletons of large numbers of royal retainers, obviously put to death and buried with the dead king to accompany his soul into the afterlife. West Asian influences have been hypothetical.

AO, a head-hunting Naga people living in the Naga Hills (situated between India and Burma) who subsist on horticulture and animal husbandry, with some hunting and fishing. Their language belongs to the Tibeto-Burman group of Sinitic languages.

APACHE INDIANS, a North American Indian people who originally depended mainly on hunting and food-gathering for their subsistence. However, after learning to tame and ride wild horses (descended from escaped Spanish horses) the Apache became extremely aggressive and gained a reputation for their savage and warlike tendencies.

APAM NAPAT, a somewhat mysterious supernatural being, referred to in Zoroastrian sacred literature as the 'Son of the Waters'.

APES, a variety of large anthropoids, today represented by the gorilla, chimpanzee, orangutan, and gibbon.

APINAYE, a South American Indian people of the Brazilian highlands who speak a form of the Gê language and are dependent on horticulture, hunting, food-gathering and fishing.

APIS, a sacred bull, worshipped in Egypt as a symbol of fertility, whose temple (known as the Apeum) was situated at Memphis.

APOGROPAIC EYE, an artistic representation of the human eye, as for example on the prow of a ship, or even on a vase, the purpose of which is to ward off evil forces.

APOLLO, a Greek god (the son of Zeus) who as patron of archery, music and medicine was frequently symbolically represented by the bow, the lyre and the laurel. Apollo has been described as characterizing the essence of Greek civilization with its emphasis upon beauty, law and order, and an annual festival was celebrated in Athens every May in his honour. Following the Roman conquest of the Greek settlements in southern Italy, the worship of Apollo also spread to Rome, temples being erected in his honour at Actium and on the Palatine Hill.

APOLLONIAN CULTURE, a term invented by Ruth Benedict to refer to cultures which encouraged a sense of dignity, orderliness and restrained behaviour. (See APOLLO, DIONYSIAN CULTURE and PERSONALITY, BASIC).

APPENDIX, an organism situated at the junction of the large and small intestines which still serves a useful function in apes and many other primates, but which no longer appears to have any useful function in man and is therefore classified as a vestigial remnant (q.v.).

ARAB, a term today used loosely to refer to anyone who speaks the Arabic language as his or her mother tongue. However, the term originally and properly applies only to the Mediterranean-Caucasoid, Arabic peoples whose ancestors were indigenous to the Arabian peninsula.

ARABESQUE, an elaborate geometrical decorative design popular among Arabian artists, who were not permitted by Islamic law to portray human or animal forms and consequently concentrated on the use of geometrical figures as the basis of their decorative designs.

ARAMAEANS, a Semitic pastoral people who migrated out of the Syrian semi-desert to conquer Canaan in the 13th century B.C. The Aramaeans used a phonetic script for their language which appears to have provided the basis for the script adopted by the Phoenicians. In fact the Aramaic language eventually succeeded the Akkadian language as the lingua franca (q.v.) of the Near East, and remained in general use until supplanted by Arabic.

ARAMAIC, a Semitic language spoken by the Aramaeans (q.v.).

ARANDA, an Australian aboriginal people of Central Australia, dependent wholly on food-gathering and hunting.

ARAPAHO, Algonquin-speaking North American Indians, of the Southern Plains dependent on hunting with some food-gathering.

ARAPESH, a Papuan people inhabiting North Papua, dependent on horticulture, food-gathering, and hunting and some animal husbandry.

ARAUCANIANS, a people living in Central and Southern Chile, who depend primarily on horticulture and who speak Andean-Equatorial languages. These include the Mapuche.

ARAWAK, a family of American Indian languages spoken in Guyana and the Upper Amazon region of South America as well as in a number of the Caribbean Islands, which the Arawak-speakers appear to have colonized from the South American mainland. The Arawak family of languages includes Goajiro, Taino, Cutipaco, Wapishana, Locono, and Campa.

ARBOREAL, adapted to life in or among trees.
ARCH. an architectural device for supporting a superstructure above an opening without the use of a horizontal beam. The earliest known brick and masonry arches, using a keystone, have been found by archeologists in Mesopotamia around 3500 B.C., but the arch was probably first developed in Europe during the Würm glaciation, the form of the arch having survived to us from this period in the tradition of the Eskimo igloo.
ARCHEOLOGY, the study of past peoples and cultures through the recovery and examination of surviving fossil remains and artifacts. Archeology is not confined to the study of prehistory but has also added much information to the study of historic cultures, not only by providing material evidence concerning the life of historic peoples, but also by uncovering lost documentary records.
ARCHEOMAGNETISM, a method of dating objects made of fired clay by correlating the direction of magnetism with dated positions of the magnetic pole.
ARCHEOMETRY, the application of measurement techniques to the dating and interpretation of archeological materials, artifacts, sites and excavation processes.
ARCHEOPTERYX, the earliest fossil bird, dating around 170 million years ago, closely similar to a reptile (q.v.) but equipped with feathers, the evidence of which is well preserved.
ARCHAIC PERIOD, an expression generally used to refer to the earlier period of any high culture.
ARIANISM, a Christian 'heresy', popular among the early Gothic and Lombard nations, which refused to accept the mystical theory that God could be three different individuals (the father, the son, and the Holy Ghost) at one and the same time.
ARIKARA, Muskogean-Siouan speaking, North American Plains Indians of the Caddoan group. Occupying the Texas Plains, the Arikara were dependent on horticulture (restricted to the river valleys) and hunting and food-gathering.
ARIKI, a caste of Micronesian high-priests.
ARMENIAN, a language spoken in Asia Minor, which is generally classified as Indo-European but which was heavily influenced by an earlier Anatolian language spoken by the indigenous occupants of Armenia who probably fell under the control of a relatively small group of Indo-European warrior families.
ARMENIANS, an ancient Anatolian people, who have given their name to the Armenoid subdivision ofthe Caucasoid race. The characteristic Armenoid physical type represents a survival of an indigenous genetic strain despite the fact that the Armenians acquired an Indo-European aristocracy. Traditionally dependent, in their homeland around Lake Van, on agriculture and animal husbandry, the Armenians are today widely dispersed around the world, many having become prominent in modern commercial and banking activities.
ARMENOID, a Caucasoid local race exemplified by the contemporary Armenian-speaking peoples of Asia Minor, and distinguished physiologically by a convex nose, a high head form, a generally mesocephalic or brachycephalic face, and dark eyes and hair.
ARROW, a form of lightweight spear, projected with the aid of a bow, which was first invented by Cro-Magnons in either the late Paleolithic or Mesolithic period. The subsequent widespread dispersal of the bow and arrow would appear to have occurred mainly with the diffusion of Mesolithic culture.
ARROWHEAD, any small object made of stone, bone or metal which may be fixed to the tip of an arrow to provide greater penetration. The earliest known arrowheads were made by the Cro-Magnons of Europe during the Solutrean period.
ARROW WRENCH, a tool for straightening arrow shafts, comprising a stick or a bone with a circular hook at one end through which the shaft of the arrow is pulled to remove surface irregularities.
ARSENIC, a metal formerly blended with copper to produce an alloy which was stronger than pure copper, the arsenic component being eventually replaced by tin, which produced a superior bronze product.

ARTEMIS, the Greek goddess of hunting, who although the patroness of childbirth, was herself dedicated to chastity. Known to the Romans as Diana.
ARTHARVA VEDA, see VEDIC LITERATURE.
ARTHROPODA, one of the largest phyla in the animal kingdom. Includes centipedes, insects, spiders, and crabs.
ARTHUR, KING, a legendary but seemingly also historical king, reputed to have ruled over parts of Celtic Britain and to have fought against the Saxon invaders of the 5th century A.D.. The Arthurian court, which became a popular subject of medieval legends, mirrors the concept of a heroic king and his band of noble warrior companions or knights. (See BRITONS)
ARTICULATION, ARCHAEOLOGICAL, the process of reconstruction of a culture by the articulation or fitting together of ethnic traits.
ARTIFACT, any structure, tool or object manufactured by man.
ARTIFICIAL INSEMINATION, a practice widely used in animal breeding since the sperm of animals with the desired hereditary qualities can be preserved, conveniently transported over long distances, and used to inseminate a large number of females, thus rapidly changing the direction of evolution in any desired direction.
ARUNTA, an Australian aboriginal people, located in Central Australia, who have been extensively studied, and who consequently figure prominently in many classic works by writers such as Spencer, Durkheim, Freud and Radcliffe-Brown.
ARUSI, a Cushitic people of East Africa, dependent on animal herding and horticulture, supplemented by some hunting.
ARYAN LANGUAGES, a term originally borrowed from the Indo-Iranian group of languages by Max Müller to refer to the entire family of languages now known by the geographical designation 'Indo-European'. Although Max Müller borrowed the term *arya* for linguistic purposes, it was formerly a social or ethnic term, meaning 'noble' (c.f. Iranian and Aryan; Greek *aristos*, Celtic *aire*), and in all cases referred to a ruling aristocracy who are now believed to share descent from an earlier common cultural, linguistic, and ethnic group conveniently termed 'Proto-Indo-European'. (See INDO-EUROPEAN LANGUAGES).
ARYAN RELIGION, the religion of the Aryans who settled India and Iran in pre-Zoroastrian times evolved around a supreme sky god known as Dyeus, who was the Allfather of both gods and men and the consort of the Mother Earth. Fire-worship appears to have been practiced, the hearth fire of every house symbolizing the continuity of the family, and being regarded as directly connected with the ancestral spirits. The sun was worshipped as Svarya, the moon as Mas and the Dawn as Usas. Agni, the god of Fire, was also symbolically the protector of the household. Essentially, the head of each household was responsible for the rituals in honour of the ancestral spirits, and the king of each tribe or group of tribes was responsible for the rituals honoring not only the ancestors of the royal family but also the gods as a whole. However, kings and the heads of noble households appear to have had the assistance of ritual experts or priests. These priests originally belonged to two classes, one being referred to as the 'Lighters of the Fire', while the others, who were known as the 'Callers', were responsible for 'calling' or reciting the ancient ritual prayers and formulae. From a sociological point of view, the Aryan religion of India essentially revolved around ritual sacrifices, ritual prayer and ancestor worship, stressing the sanctity of the family and the individual inheritance of mana-like qualities (q.v.). As a result great emphasis was placed upon the selection of marriage partners from persons of equivalent or similar magico-religious caste status and upon the propagation of the lineage in accordance with the Laws of Manu, the ancestral and eponymous law-giver, from whom all men were descended. Only later did the Brahman ritual experts gain an ascendancy over the kings and heads of households, claiming to constitute the superior caste (q.v.) in Aryan society. The gods of the Aryans and Persians have many cognates throughout Indo-European mythology. The Indo-Iranian *Dyeus* is cognate with the Greek *Zeus* and the Roman *Jupiter*. The *deivo* or gods of light are cognate with the Latin *deus* for 'god'. The Indo-Aryan *Mitra* is cognate with the Iranian *Mithra* of

Mithraism, and Indo-Aryan *Varuna* is cognate with the *Ahura-Mazda* of Zoroastrianism. Indo-Aryan religion taught that men should adhere to the rules and rituals of their ancestors, practising good thoughts, good words and good deeds. Buddhism later adopted this principle as its central moral theme.

ASHANTI, a Kwa-speaking Negroid people of West Africa, of the Akan group, dependent largely on horticulture with some fishing.

ASHURBANIPAL, an Assyrian of the 7th century B.C. whose main contribution to posterity was the collection of a vast library of over 25,000 clay tablets in his palace at Nineveh, which have since been uncovered by archeologists and deciphered.

ASIANIC, a term used for those languages which were formerly spoken in Mesopotamia and Asia Minor, prior to the expansion of Semitic and Indo-European languages into this area. The Caucasian (q.v.) language and the Burushaski (q.v.) language of the Pamirs still survive, but other Asianic languages, which may have included Sumerian, Cappadocian and possibly the language of the ancient Indus Valley civilization (q.v.), are now no longer extant.

ASIANIC LANGUAGES, the possibility of a family of non-Indo-European, non-Semitic Asian languages which may formerly have extended from Anatolia to the Indus Valley is supported by only the flimsiest of evidence. However, the Caucasian languages of the Caucasus mountains, which are divided into a North Caucasian group on the northern slope and a South Caucasian group on the southern slope, seem to be related to a language known as Burushaski (q.v.), still surviving in the high Karakorum Mountains. This suggests that the Caucasian and Burushaski languages might be isolated survivals of an earlier common stock of languages, spoken throughout the intermediate connecting areas prior to the advent of the Indo-European speaking invaders. If such were the case it is possible that the languages of the Indus Valley civilization (q.v.), not yet deciphered, might also have belonged to this hypothetical Asianic group. Other writers have even suggested that the supposed Asianic group of languages may have been ultimately related, via Anatolia, to a hypothetical Early Mediterranean family of languages (q.v.).

ASKELON, the only Philistine city that has so far been excavated. Located near Gaza, on the coast of Palestine, Askelon appears to have been destroyed by the Peoples of the Sea (q.v.) around 1200 B.C., although a new city rose again on the same site during the Roman period.

ASS, the ancient ass of Asia, known as the onager, was widely used by the Sumerians to carry loads and pull carts prior to the introduction of the horse into the Middle East, presumably from north of the Caucasus. However, the modern ass or donkey is descended from a domesticated Ethiopian animal, which was imported into Egypt by the ancient Egyptians, via the Sudan.

ASSELAR, an archeological site near Timbuktu in the modern state of Mali. Asselar was excavated in 1926, and revealed the oldest known skeletal remains of a distinctly Negroid type. These have been dated at 6350 B.P. No artifacts were found in association with Asselar remains, a fact which suggests that the population may have been largely dependent on wood and similar perishable materials for its tools.

ASSEMBLAGE, skeletal or cultural remains which may be regarded as belonging to the same unit because they were found together, as distinct from a 'class' where the identification is based on similarities.

ASSIMILATION, a cultural process by which two diverse cultures become integrated into a single culture system. As sometimes used in physical anthropology, the term 'assimilation' refers to the absorption of an immigrant racial minority into the indigenous population of a given area, resulting in a total genetic admixture of the formerly distinct gene pools.

ASSINIBOIN, Siouan-speaking American Plains Indians, mainly dependent on hunting with some food-gathering and fishing.

ASSOCIATIONS, social groups formed for a specific purpose and possessing their own administrative officials.

ASSORTATIVE MATING, a preference exhibited between the sexes by which mating tends to occur either between males and females sharing a similar genotype (positive assortative mating) or between males and females of a disparate genotype (negative assortative mating).
ASSUR, one of the capitals of Assyria, named after its patron god, Assur, frequently represented as a warrior archer. Following the expansion of Assyrian power in Mesopotamia, attempts were made to impose the worship of Assur on the subjugated cities. (See ASSYRIA).
ASYNJOR, the feminine attendants of Freya, counterparts of the Aesir. (See NORSE RELIGION).
ASSYRIA, a powerful Middle Eastern empire of the 2nd millenium B.C., which originated in the city state of Assur but was later ruled from other capitals at Nineveh and Nimrod. The Assyrians were a Semitic people of originally pastoral and warlike origin, who constantly rivalled the Babylonians for control over Sumeria, creating the resultant empire over which they established themselves as a warrior elite. Assyrian power reached its peak in the 9th and 7th centuries B.C. when its armies, now equipped with iron, controlled an empire extending from the Nile to the Caspian Sea. Infamous for the brutality with which they treated their defeated opponents, the Assyrians attempted to impose a form of monotheism upon the peoples they conquered, largely as a deliberate political measure intended to suppress respect for the local gods and so reduce separatist tendencies.
ASTAR, a sky god widely recognized among the Cushites, Hamites and Semites.
ASTARTE, a Semitic fertility goddess worshipped by the Phoenicians and Canaanites, who may have had parallels in the Babylonian Ishtar, the Egyptian Isis. Known to the Semitic Carthaginians as Tanit.
ASTERION, a small portion of the cranium separated from the remainder by sutures.
ASTRAEA, the goddess of justice in both Greek and Roman mythology, later associated with the constellation Virgo.
ASTROLATRY, a term which differs from the concept of astrology (q.v.) in implying the actual worship of the heavenly bodies as divine beings.
ASTROLOGY, the study of the movements of the heavenly bodies for the purpose of divination – forecasting by mathematical calculations the future fate of individual men and women or even of nations. Astrology, as practiced by the ancient Egyptians, may have grown out of the astrolatry (q.v.) of the Babylonians. Although the early Greeks and the early Republican Romans resisted the pretexts of astrologers, astrology gained widespread acceptance among the Greeks of the later Hellenistic period as a part of the general orientalization of the Hellenic world following the decline of the city-states and the expansion of the brief Macedonian empire. Astrology was also adopted from the Egyptians by the Romans, whose astrologers observed the movements of the entire cosmic system with considerable precision, relating the various constellations of stars to the pantheon of the Roman gods, Thus in the later stages of Imperial Rome, many of the Roman emperors allowed themselves to be guided by astrologers when making the most important and far-reaching decisions concerning the government of the empire – an irrational method of government which would hardly have been acceptable to the Senators of the Republican period.
ASTURIAN. a late Mesolithic culture found in Spain, closely associated with the Azilian (q.v.).
ASURA, the name given in the Vedas to the ruling families of the indigenous Naga civilization which was overrun by the invading Indo-Aryans. The term Naga meant a cobra, and the Asura fought under a cobra or snake banner. It would thus appear to be no accident that images of snakes are today still extremely widespread in the temples of southern Dravidian India, since the pre-Indo-European population of Dravidian India appear to have been snake worshippers.
ASURAS, a collective term applied to the gods and divine spirits of the early Indo-Aryans, but used to refer to evil spirits and demons by the Persians of the

Zoroastrian period, who had rejected the polytheistic traditions of their ancestors in favor of a form of monotheistic dualism.

ASWAN, a town located at the site of the First Cataract on the Nile, where the modern High Dam has been erected. Although the Temple of Abu Simbel (q.v.) has been saved, many ancient Egyptian settlements above the First Cataract have now been submerged beneath the waters of this vast reservoir, and many of the more perishable artifacts are in the process of being destroyed for all time. This is but one example of the high cultural price imposed on mankind by the ongoing world population explosion.

ATACAMA, a South American Indian people occupying the barren lands of northern Chile, and largely dependent on hunting and gathering.

ATACAPA, a Southeastern United States Indian people formerly occupying the marshy flats of southern Louisiana.

ATAVISM, a term used in genetics to refer to a throwback reflecting the characteristics of an ancestral phenotype (q.v.). This is occasionally due to 'reverse' mutations but more often to the survival of recessive genes which reassert themselves when combined in a homozygous condition.

ATAYAL, an aboriginal people of Formosa.

ATERIAN, a Middle Paleolithic industry closely associated with the European Mousterian industry, the remains of which have been located in the Atlas mountains of North Africa, c. 10,000 B.C.

ATHABASCANS, a hunting and trapping people inhabiting the northwestern part of Canada. Linguistically the Athabascans represent a subdivision of the Na-Dene phylum, which is possibly distantly related to the Sinitic languages. The Athabascan languages have been divided into a northern subfamily which includes Dogrib and Chipewyan, a northwest subfamily which includes Hupa, and a southern subfamily which includes Apachean and Navajo.

ATHENS, an ancient Achaean city built around a central acropolis which in Homeric times housed the king, the warrior nobles and the temples of the gods. Athens appears to have been strong enough to have rivalled Knossos in the 15th century B.C. and to have successfully resisted Dorian attacks in the 12th and 11th centuries B.C., to become a major commercial and cultural center from the 7th to the 1st century B.C.

ATJEHENESE, a Malayo-Polynesian people occupying the northern portion of Sumatra.

ATLANTIC NIGER-CONGO LANGUAGES, the Atlantic subfamily of the Niger-Congo (q.v.) languages, spoken in Senegal and Gambia, which includes Wolof, Temne, Conigui, Kisse, and Bijogo.

ATLANTIS, a mythical land reported by the ancient Greeks to have been located somewhere in the Atlantic Ocean beyond the Straits of Gibraltar, and to have been the original homeland of all civilization. The Greeks appear to have acquired their knowledge of Atlantis from the Egyptians, who alleged that the inhabitants of Atlantis were close relatives of the Greeks.

ATLANTO-MEDITERRANEAN, a term used in physical anthropology to refer to a variant of the Mediterranean division of the Caucasoid race. The Atlanto-Mediterraneans are regarded as being similar to the classical Mediterraneans, but of heavier build and more ruddy skin color.

ATLATL, the Aztec name for a spearthrower, a mechanical device first devised by Cro-Magnon man in the Upper Paleolithic.

ATMAN, the life principle or 'universal essence' of Hindu philosophy. The original Sanskrit 'atman' can be interpreted as both 'breath' and 'life' and also as the 'universal self'.

ATON, (also AKHENATON or AKHNATION), the Sun god whom Akhenaton (q.v.) attempted to impose as the central feature of a monotheistic religion on the Egyptians around 1350 B.C.

ATROPHY, the decline in size or effectiveness of a tissue or organ usually as a result of disuse through a number of generations. The natural selection fails to ensure the continued healthiness and efficiency of any tissue or organ which no longer contributes effectively to the survival of the lineage, and with a relaxation of natural selection, deterioration and decay are inevitable.

ATSUGEWI, a Northeastern California, American Indian Hokan-speaking people related to the Shasta Indians, who were traditionally dependent on food-gathering, hunting and fishing.

ATTAWAPISKAT, an Algonquin Cree-speaking North American Indian people, dependent primarily on fishing with some hunting and food-gathering.

AUA, a Malayo-Polynesian-speaking people of the Western Isles of the Bismarck Archipelago, dependent on fishing, horticulture and some hunting.

AUGUR, a member of the priestly college of twelve augurs of ancient Rome, whose duty it was to divine, from the flight of birds and similar auguries, the attitudes of the gods towards proposed courses of action.

AUNJETITZ, an early Bronze Age culture centered on what is today Northern Bohemia, Silesia, Hungary and Lower Austria.

AURIGNACIAN, the earliest of the Upper Paleolithic cultures, separating the Middle Paleolithic Mousterian culture from the more advanced Solutrean (q.v.). Associated with the first appearance of Cro-Magnon man, the name is taken from Aurignac in Southern France, where the first fossils and artifacts were discovered. The Aurignacian culture is distinguished by the sophisticated use of bone artifacts, by a high development of esthetic designs, including animal carvings and cave paintings, as well by the use of beads, necklaces and primitive jewelry. Some authorities believe that the Aurignacian culture evolved in Eastern Europe, being brought into Western Europe by immigrant Cro-Magnons. However this view is disputed by other archeologists, who maintain that Cro-Magnons evolved from Neanderthals and that the Aurignacian culture evolved in Europe from the Middle Paleolithic Mousterian culture.

AURILLAC, an Iron Age site in France which yielded a fine gold Celtic torc, decorated with exuberant imaginative designs.

AUROCHS, an extinct European breed of bison, frequently portrayed in Upper Paleolithic cave paintings.

AUSTRALIAN LANGUAGES, the languages of the Australian aborigines have been grouped into a single phylum, but a fairly sharp division enables a distinction to be drawn between a North Australian group of languages and a South Australian group. Papua/New Guinea still preserves what must have been a universal state of affairs prior to the spread of pastoralists and other colonizing peoples over large areas of the earth's surface, each tribe possessing its own distinctive territory and living to a substantial degree in isolation from its neighbours. As a result, although New Guinea is only a single large island, with a population of as few as two million people, it contains 20 distinct groups of languages, which are subdivided into hundreds of separate local, tribal dialects.

AUSTRALOIDS, one of the major living geographical races, whose members form the aboriginal population of Australia, New Guinea and Tasmania. Traces of Australoid genes are also found among the living populations of parts of Southeast Asia, and, from the evidence of fossil remains, Australoids would appear to have formerly extended across much of India and Southeast Asia, and to include Southern and even Central China, prior to the intrusion of Caucasoids from the northwest into the Indus Valley and the southward movement of Mongoloids from Northern China. The cranial capacity of living Australoids averages 1260 cubic centimeters in the males, and the low forehead, prominent brow ridges and distinctive prognathism led Sir Arthur Keith to regard Australoids as living representatives of one of the earlier types of Homo sapiens. However, contemporary physical anthropologists regard Australoids as a genetic amalgam resulting from the admixture of an immigrant Homo sapiens sapiens population with an aboriginal Neanderthal Wadjak-type population, suggesting a substantial survival of Wadjak genes in this part of the world.

AUSTRALOPITHECINAE, literally, 'Southern Apes'. A term now used generically to refer to a general level of hominid evolution during which manlike creatures are believed to have attempted toolmaking. A subfamily of the family Hominidae, the Australopithecinae included both Australopithecus africanus and Paranthropus robustus, (now usually called Australopithecus robustus) as well as Plesianthropus, Telanthropus and, Zinjanthropus. Generally recognized Australopithecine sites include Taung, Kromdraai, Sterkfontein, Swartkranz, Makapansgat, Olduvai Gorge, Koro (Lake Chad), Omo in Ethiopia, and Lake Rudolf in East Africa. Meganthropus in Java and Hemanthropus from China are also sometimes regarded as Australopithecine remains.

AUSTRO-ASIATIC LANGUAGES, Prior to the entry of Sinitic forms of speech into Southeast Asia, the greater portion of Southeast Asia appears to have been covered by a family of Austro-Asiatic languages, except for small, isolated populations of aboriginal Negritoes, still speaking their own languages. Included in the Austro-Asiatic family is Annamese, spoken by the Vietnamese; the Munda group of languages, still surviving as isolates in India, and the Mon-Khmer sub-family of Southeast Asia. The latter group includes Mon, which survives in Eastern Burma, but is cut off from the other Mon-Khmer languages by the Sinitic language of the Thais; Khmer, the language of Cambodia; Khasi, still spoken on the Indian borders of Burma: and Nicobarese, surviving among the natives of the Nicobar Islands of the Indian Ocean.

AUSTRONESIAN LANGUAGES, see MALAYO-POLYNESIAN languages.

AUTOCHTHONOUS, aboriginal: literally, 'springing from the soil'.

AUTOTROPHS, living organisms that are independent of outside organic sources for the provision of organic constituents. Most plants are autotropic, manufacturing organic materials from inorganic sources. By contrast, most animals are allotrophs, requiring external sources of organic substances and being ultimately dependent upon autotrophs for their existence.

AVESTA, the name used to refer to the entire collection of sacred Zoroastrian texts, including the Yasna, the Vispered, the Vendidad, and the Yashts. (See also VEDIC LITERATURE).

AVOIDANCE, a custom under which certain relatives, usually of the opposite sex, are required to avoid social contact with each other as far as possible. Avoidance would appear to be an extension of the incest principle.

AVUNCULATE, a term used to refer to a close relationship common in matrilineal societies between a man and his maternal uncle. Since the nephew belongs to the same clan as his mother's brother, he may be responsible to his maternal uncle, rather than to his own father, and in some instances may be expected to marry his maternal uncle's daughter.

AVUNCULOCAL, referring to the custom by which a newly-married couple live with the husband's maternal uncle.

AWEIKOMA, a South American Indian people speaking a Gê language. Occupants of the Brazilian uplands, the Aweikoma depend entirely on hunting and food-gathering.

AWL, a tool used to pierce holes, which was invented in the Lower Paleolithic.

AWL, SPLINTER, a piercing tool made from a splinter of animal bone.

AYLLU, a Peruvian patrilineal kinship unit, holding all property communally and inhabiting a single village in the center of the communal lands. Peruvian in origin, it survived into the Inca period.

AZANDE, a Negroid Niger-Congo-speaking people of the Adamawa-Eastern group, dependent largely on horticulture and hunting with some fishing and food-gathering.

AZILIAN, a Mesolithic culture which derives its name from the site excavated at Mas d' Azil in Southern France, renowned for the painted pebbles which are now believed by some authorities to represent the homes of ancestral spirits, in what may have been an ancestor-worshipping society.

AZOIC, an era 'without life' associated with the earliest part of the geological Precambrian period, dating from the formation of the first rocks, over 4.5 billion years ago, until approximately 3.7 billion years ago.

AZTEC, an essentially stone age, high culture, usually described as a civilization, which flourished between the 15th and 16th centuries in Mexico. The Aztecs were a warlike and victorious people who invaded the Valley of Mexico from the north. Speaking a Nahuatl language, they succeeded in building a broad Central American tribute-empire, adopting much of the Toltec and Mayan cultural traditions already long established in that area. The name Aztec is derived from Aztlan, an area located in northwestern Mexico, which may literally be translated as 'White Land'. One justification for the massive numbers of human beings sacrificed annually by the Aztecs was the belief that a normal death led only to perpetual confinement in the underworld whereas death by sacrifice brought the victim into communion with the gods.

AZTEC-TANOAN LANGUAGES, a large phylum of American Indian languages including the Kiowa-Tanoan and Uto-Aztecan families. The Kiowa-Tanoan family comprises Tewa, Tiwa, Towa, and Kiowa, while the Uto-Aztecan family includes 23 languages, notable among which are Paiute, Shoshone, Ute, Hopi, the Huichol, Nahuatl, Pima, Mecayapan, Pipil and Poschtula. The Uto-Aztecan family is sometimes subdivided into 5 major groups, the Utan, Californian, Aztec, Hopi, and Shoshone groups.

AZTLAN, the ancient mythical home of the Aztecs, possibly in northern Mexico, or as some Hispanic Americans claim, in the southwestern USA.

B

BAAL, the Semitic god of fertility, whose rituals (Baalism) emphasized sensuality and orgiastic sexual rites, particularly revered among the Phoenicians, Chaldaeans and Canaanites.

BABOON, a large, predominantly terrestrial monkey of the genus Papio.

BABWA, a Bantu-speaking Negroid people of the Babwe-Bira group, dependent on horticulture with some fishing.

BABYLONIAN CIVILIZATION, Babylonian Mesopotamia combined the cultural traditions of ancient Sumeria with those of the Semitic Akkadians and Assyrians. Although the precise form of worship varied under successive dynasties, attempts were made under Semitic leadership to make Marduk the supreme monotheistic god of the whole Babylonian empire at the expense of the local divinities who had formerly been regarded as dominant, each in his or her own city state.

BABYLONIANS, the former occupants of the ancient Mesopotamian city and empire of Babylon, who originally spoke Sumerian but later acquired Semitic forms of speech under the Assyrians and Chaldeans. Although the old city of Babylon is a ruin, the local population today speaks Arabic and depends on agriculture and animal husbandry.

BACAIRI, a South American people of the Brazilian interior, who speak a Carib language and are dependent on horticulture, fishing and hunting.

BACCHUS, the Roman god of wine who may be equated with Dionysus. Although Bacchus was not recognized in the early days of Republican Rome, the Greek orgiastic and mystical rituals in honour of Bacchus became popular among the masses during the later days of the republic, these orgies being known as Bacchanalia. Since the general debauchery which prevailed at the Bacchanalia offended against the stricter traditions of the Patrician upper class, the Bacchanalia were probihited by decree of the Roman Senate in 186 B.C.

BACHELOR'S HOUSE, a name commonly used to refer to certain large houses in Micronesian villages which are occupied by the young unmarried male members of a totemic society until they become eligible to marry and to establish their own household.

BACK-CROSS, the mating between an individual who is heterozygous for a specific genetic character with one who is homozygous.

BACTERIA, one of the oldest forms of life, these microscopic protozoan organisms first evolved in the Archaeozoic era but have since become diversified (despite their minute unicellular form) into probably tens of thousands of different species.

BADARIAN CULTURE, a Neolithic culture of the 4th millennium B.C., named after an archeological site at El Badari in Middle Egypt. A few early copper artifacts have also been found in association with the later stages of the Badarian culture.

BADEN CULTURE, the final Copper Age stage of the Central European agricultural tradition, employing domesticated horses, wheeled carts and copper axe-hammers. Extending over much of Poland, Czechoslovakia, Austria, Hungary and parts of Germany, the Baden culture succeeded the Lengyel culture around 3500 B.C., and is believed to be connected with an early wave of settlers, a view which is reinforced by the affinities of the Baden culture to the Early Bronze Age Indo-European culture of the Aegean, and by evidence that Baden society was at least mildly stratified.

BAFFINLAND ESKIMO, an Eskimo people who depend mainly on fishing and hunting.

BAFIA, a Bantu-speaking Negroid people from the Middle Cameroons, dependent mainly on horticulture but practicing some river fishing and animal husbandry.

BAGIRMI, a Nilotic-speaking people of the Bagirmi-Sara group, largely dependent on horticulture and animal husbandry.

BAIGA, a proto-Australoid people living in the uplands of India who speak a Munda language and depend on horticulture, hunting, food-gathering, and fishing.

BAJUN, a Bantu-speaking Negroid people of the Swahili group, largely dependent on horticulture and fishing.

BAKHTIARI, a South Iranian people of Indo-European speech who have retained an ancient dependence on animal herding, supplemented by minimal hunting and horticulture.

BAKO, a Western Cushitic-speaking African people, mainly dependent on horticulture and some herding.

BALA, the five objectives of yoga, namely: faith, memory, meditation, wisdom, and energy.

BALDER (also BALDUR), the Norse god of beauty and light, killed by Loki, the latter being the personification of deceit and evil.

BALINESE, a Malayo-Polynesian-speaking people of Bali, largely dependent on agriculture, with some animal husbandry and fishing.

BALINESE RELIGION, although regarded as Hindu, the Balinese religion is more properly called Sivaism, combining Malayan ancestor-worship and animism with the Hinduism brought by Indian rajahs who established themselves as a warrior ruling class above the indigenous peoples. As the descendants of conquered aboriginals, the great majority of the Balinese Hindus belong to the Sudra or 'untouchable' caste. (See CASTE).

BALOMA, that part of the human soul which is believed by the Trobriand Islanders to leave the body at death, but to return annually for the Milamala or festival of ancestral spirits.

BALTIC, a linguistic division of the Indo-European or Aryan group of languages which includes Lettish (or Latvian), Lithuanian, and Old Prussian. The Baltic peoples formerly possessed a distinctive culture and fought bitterly to resist the enforced imposition of Christianity.

BALTIC, EAST, a term used in physical anthropology to refer to a racial variant associated with the East Baltic area. The East Baltic is a Caucasoid racial type characterized in polar form by extreme fairness of skin, light eyes, ash-blond hair and a mesocephalic skull.

BAMBARA, a Negroid West African Mande people, dependent on horticulture and some animal husbandry, fishing and food-gathering.

BAMIKELE, a Bantu-speaking Negroid people of the Cameroon Highlands, dependent mainly on horticulture and some hunting.

BAMUM, a Bantu-speaking Negroid people of the Cameroon Highlands, who subsist mainly on horticulture and some fishing.

BANANA, see BANNA.

BANARO, a Papuan people of North Papua, dependent on horticulture, food-gathering, hunting and some animal husbandry.

BANDA, a Negroid Niger-Congo-speaking people of the Adamawa-Eastern group, dependent largely on horticulture with some hunting.

BANDKERAMIK, a type of Neolithic pottery found in Europe, decorated by bands of lines or dots, often in meander (q.v.) or spiral patterns.

BAND-TYPE SOCIETY, the earliest form of human society, comprising a small group of men, women, and children inhabiting a distinct territory, distinguished from 'troops' of non-human primate societies by the existence of pair-bonding (or family groups) and ties of kinship. Band-type societies are usually 'equalitarian' in that all adult men have equal rights and obligations, being bound to each other by the ties of kinship. Such societies may be exogamous or endogamous. All band societies of this century were found in association with hunting and gathering patterns of subsistence.

BANEN, a Bantu-speaking Negroid people of the Middle Cameroons, dependent mainly on horticulture with some animal husbandry and hunting.

BANNA, an East African, Cushitic-speaking people living north of Lake Rudolph who are mainly dependent on herding and horticulture, but also practice some hunting.

BANNERSTONE, a polished stone shaped in the form of a bird, animal or possibly even a boat, believed to have been used by American Indians for ceremonial purposes.

BANNOCK, an American Indian people of the Eastern Great Basin who speak a Shoshone (Uto-Aztec) language and are dependent on hunting, food-gathering and fishing.

BANTU LANGUAGES (and PEOPLES), the Bantu are a major Negroid pastoral and horticultural peoples of Africa. Believed to have originated in the lands adjacent to the tropical rain forests of Central Africa, they seem first to have expanded into the rain forest areas at the expense of the Pygmies, cutting, burning and clearing the trees to prepare land for horticulture. However, those Bantu peoples adjacent to the grassy uplands acquired the art of cattle-herding – probably from incoming Hamites and Cushites – and embarked upon a vast easterly and southerly expansion, in this case at the expense of the Capoid or Bushman hunters who had previously occupied the African savannah.

The Southeastern Bantu arrived in the area of Zimbabwe and South Africa from Central Africa as late as the sixteenth to nineteenth centuries, supplanting the earlier Hottentot population. This major group of Bantu includes the Zulu, Tswana (Bechuana), Sotho (Basuto), Lozi (Barotse), Venda, and Thonga. The Southwestern Bantu include the Herero or Damara, the Ambo, the Mbundu and the Nyoneka. The Western Central Bantu, who supplanted the Pygmies on the edge of the tropical rain forest, include the Kongo, Kuba, Ndembu, Lele, and Suku. The East Central Bantu (who are matrilineal) include the Bemba, Ila, Yao, Luapula and Nyanja. In Kenya and adjacent areas, the Bantu include the Kikuyu, Chagga, Bajun, Dingo and Hadima. West of Kenya are the Lacustrine Bantu, namely the Ruanda, Nyoro, Amba, Ganda and Kavirondo. The rain forests have been heavily penetrated by Bantu, which include the Fang, Ngomba, Kpe, Banen and Nkundo. There are also some semi-Bantu, speaking languages modified by Niger-Congo forms, which include the Tiv, Katab, Yako and Ibibio.

BANYUN, a West African, Negroid people of Guinea, who combine horticulture with fishing and animal husbandry.

BAPTISM, a concept of purification by ablution appears to have originated in ancient Chaldaea, being perpetuated in the Eleusian mysteries, and adopted into Christianity from late Judaic practices.

BARABRA, a Nubian people largely dependent on horticulture, but practicing some animal husbandry.

BARAKA, a sacred power, analogous to Mana (q.v.). Believed by Moslems to reside in persons descended from Mohammad but also found in Sultans, newly married couples, and children – as well as in certain inanimate objects.

BARAMA RIVER CARIB, South American Indian Carib-speaking people dependent on horticulture and some hunting, fishing and food-gathering.

BARD, a professional Celtic poet-songster. Some bards were responsible for the recounting of heroic legends to the accompaniment of harp music, others for the recitation of genealogies, and still others for the memorizing of the ancient laws. Associated with the earlier Druids (q.v.).

BAREA, a Nilotic people, related to the Kunama and primarily dependent on horticulture and some animal husbandry and food-gathering.

BARI, (1) a Negroid East Sudanese or Nilotic-speaking people of the Bari-Lotuko group, primarily dependent on horticulture and cattle-herding with some hunting. (2) a Brazilian sorcerer who claims to be able to mediate between a human being suffering from sickness and the evil spirits responsible for the sickness.

BARRIO, a Spanish word used to refer to a distinctive neighborhood group found in many Central and South American cities, particularly in Mexico and Peru. The barrio is actually a survival of the older localized descent groups of the Aztecs *(calpulli)* and Peruvians *(ayllu)*, whose members customarily constituted a separate community.

BARTER, the exchange of goods without the aid of monetary symbols of value. Barter appears to have first developed between the members of separate communities, because in close kinship communities men are expected to share what they possess with their kinsmen, and the idea of trading goods for personal gain with a kinsman from one's community would be unthinkable. Thus, the Ituri pygmies of the Congo barter goods with the neighboring Ba-Biri Negroes, but share or lend their possessions freely among the members of their own band.

BASA, a West African Negroid, Middle Niger, Niger-Congo-speaking people, largely dependent on horticulture but also practicing some animal husbandry and fishing.

BASARI, a Negroid, West African Voltaic people, largely dependent on horticulture with some animal husbandry and hunting.

BASHI, a West Lacustrine Bantu people, largely dependent on horticulture and fishing.

BASION, the central point of the anterior edge of the Foramen Magnum (q.v.), used extensively as a base point when determining skull measurements.

BASKETO, a Western Cushitic-speaking African people, mainly dependent on horticulture and some herding.

BASKETRY, one of the earliest techniques developed by men, based upon the ability to connect two pliable lengths of material by interlacing, plaiting or weaving them together. The first baskets were made by interlacing grasses and twigs into simple carrying-baskets, but basketry later became the basis of hut-building in many areas (i.e. Oceania) and of clothing – the principle of weaving grass being replaced in more advanced societies by the weaving of linen, and later of woolen materials. Basketry was also the basis for the invention of pottery, mud being used to close the holes between the basket latticework, until pots made primarily of clay laid over a basketry frame were eventually supplanted by baked clay pottery, using superior clays and dispensing with the basket frame.

BASQUES, a pre-Indo-European Caucasoid people of Atlanto-Mediterranean type, traditionally dependent on agriculture, animal husbandry and fishing and speaking their own distinctive Basque language. Today restricted to northeastern Spain and a part of southwestern France, the Basque language was formerly used over a much wider area including most of the Roman province of Aquitaine, and Basque was still spoken in southern Aquitaine (Gascony) into the Middle Ages – an area which was apparently left largely unsettled by Gauls and Franks alike. The Basques are believed to be responsible for the contemporary incidence of the rare Rh Negative blood category in Western Europe.

BASSARI, a West African Negroid people of the Tenda group who combine horticulture with some animal husbandry, hunting and food-gathering.

BASSERI, a South Iranian people of Indo-European speech who have retained an ancient dependence on animal herding, supplemented by minimal hunting and horticulture.

BATAK, a Malayo-Polynesian speaking people of Indonesia, largely dependent on cultivation with some animal husbandry and fishing.

BATON-DE-COMMAND, a term used to refer to an artifact usually made from antler horn, which was developed in the Upper Paleolithic. Because these artifacts were highly decorated, and vaguely suggestive of a modern Field Marshall's baton, they were interpreted by earlier authorities as having had a magico-religious, symbolic significance, possibly representing primitive wands (q.v.), and to have been ancestral to the modern royal sceptre. Other writers have suggested that they may have served a more prosaic purpose, as arrow straighteners, but this theory would not explain the derivations.

BATTLE-AXE, see INDO-EUROPEANS.

BAULE, a Kwa-speaking Negroid people from West Africa, belonging to the Akan group and largely dependent on horticulture supplemented by some animal husbandry and hunting.

BAYA, a Negroid, Niger-Congo-speaking people of the Adamawa-Eastern group, dependent largely on horticulture and some hunting and fishing.

BEAKER CULTURE, a West-European culture, circa 1500 B.C., characterized by graceful bell-shaped drinking beakers, decorated with geometrical designs. Since the beakers were buried with the cremated remains of the dead, it is possible that they were used in the ceremonial consumption of a sacred beverage.

BEAVER, a Northeastern, Athabascan American Indian people, dependent on hunting, fishing and food-gathering.

BEDOUIN, a term used to refer to Arab nomads still preserving their nomadic and tribal customs.

BEER, an alcoholic beverage made from germinated barley and yeast, formerly regarded as a sacred drink in ancient Europe, but also known in ancient Mesopotamia.

BEER, HONEY, an alcoholic beverage widely manufactured in East and South Africa. (See also MEAD).

BELGAE, a Brythonic Celtic people who held the land immediately to the north of Gaul, from whom present-day Belgium derives its name. (See CELTS).

BELLABELLA, a Northwest American Indian people, primarily dependent on fishing with some hunting and food-gathering, whose language belongs to the Mosan branch of the Algonquin-Mosan phylum.

BELLACOOLA, a Northwest American Indian people, primarily dependent on fishing with some hunting and food-gathering, whose language belongs to the Salish division of the Mosan branch of the Algonquin-Mosan phylum.

BELL MARDUK, see MARDUK.

BELU, a Malayo-Polynesian-speaking people from Timor (Indonesia), dependent on cultivation and animal husbandry.

BEMBA, a Bantu-speaking Negroid people of the Bemba-Lamba group, largely dependent on horticulture.

BENA, a Bantu-speaking Negroid people of the Rufiji group, largely dependent on horticulture and some animal husbandry.

BENDE, a Bantu-speaking Negroid people of the Nyamwezi group, largely dependent on horticulture with some hunting and animal husbandry.

BERBER, a Hamitic-speaking people indigenous to North Africa, whose languages represent a separate subfamily of the Hamitic branch of the Afro-Asiatic linguistic family. The term includes the Tauregs, Siwan, Shluh and Mozabites, all of whom are Caucasoids. (See AFRO-ASIATIC LANGUAGES).

BERDACHE, a homosexual cult, formerly common among certain North American Indian tribes, whose adherents dressed and behaved like members of the opposite sex, male Berdache even attempting to imitate pregnancy.

BERGDAMA, a Khoisan-speaking Hottentot people of South West Africa, largely dependent on cattle-herding and hunting.

BERGMAN'S RULE, the theory that animals which evolved in a colder climate will tend to be larger than those which have become adapted to warmer climates, since large animals have a relatively smaller surface area to permit the dissipation of body heat than smaller animals.

BERINGIA, the name given to the land bridge which is believed to have connected Siberia to Alaska during the last Ice Age.

BETE, a Kwa-speaking West African Negroid people of the Kru group, largely dependent on horticulture with some fishing and animal husbandry.

BETEL, the betel nut is widely chewed in India, Southeast Asia, East Africa, New Guinea and Melanesia. Betel is a stimulant to which the consumer can become addicted and which is believed to preserve the teeth, although it colors the mouth, saliva, and spittle a bright red.

BETROTHAL, the ritual confirmation of a contract of marriage – regarded in some societies as more significant than the actual wedding ceremony.

BHAGAVAD-GITA, a major portion of the Mahabharata (q.v.) one of the major epic poems in India. The Bhagavad-Gita records the dialogue between Krishna and Arjuna, and is believed to be among the most ancient elements of the Indo-Aryan literary traditions.

BHIL, an autochthonous tribal people, who survived Indo-Aryan settlement in the upland regions of western and central India. They originally had their own language, but have since adopted Indo-European speech from the Gujaratis and undergone substantial genetic admixture with the Indian lowland population which they now resemble. Originally horticulturalists and hunters, many now practice agriculture and animal husbandry.

BHUDAS, a genetically isolated population of Hyderabad, in India, whose members constitute a microrace, characterized by hereditary baldness and toothlessness among the males, as a result of a sex-linked recessive genetic defect. Their genetic isolation is culturally rather than physically determined.

BHUT, an evil corpse-devouring creature belonging to the mythology of the Dravidian-descended population of Southern India. The Bhut is also reputed to attack and kill living beings, in order to consume their flesh.

BICUSPID, the submolar teeth situated immediately anterior to the canines.

BIELBOG, a Slavic god, literally translated as 'the White God', who symbolizes the forces of goodness, and can to some extent be equated with the Ahura Mazda of the Zoroastrian Persians.

BIFURCATE, a system of kinship in which groups of relatives on the paternal and maternal sides, respectively, are 'merged' for naming purposes.

BIFURCATE MERGING, a system of bifurcate kinship terminology whereby a clear distinction is made between the mother's and father's families, while groups of relatives on the two respective sides are 'merged' for naming purposes.

BIHARI, an Indo-Aryan language spoken in Bihar, India.

BIJOGO, a West African Negroid people from Guinea, who combine horticulture with fishing and animal husbandry.

BIKINIANS, a Malayo-Polynesian-speaking people of Bikini, in the Gilbert Islands of Polynesia, dependent on horticulture, fishing and some animal husbandry.

BILATERAL SYMMETRY, virtually all animals descended from invertebrate chordates possessed bilateral symmetry, the left half of their body being similar to the right half. This symmetry originally evolved in invertebrate chordates to facilitate ease of locomotion in an aquatic environment.

BILOCAL, the term used to describe societies in which newly married couples may take up residence with or near either the husband's or the wife's relatives.

BILOPHODONT, a dental characteristic found in Old World monkeys, tapirs, and certain ungulates, in which the summits of the opposite cusps of the molar teeth are linked by cross crests.

BINOCULAR VISION, the ability of the eyeballs to direct themselves at an object so that the image falls upon both retinas. This enables animals possessing binocular vision to judge the distance from the object, a facility which is of obvious advantage to the tree-dwelling primates.

BIOCHEMISTRY, the study of the chemical processes of living organisms.

BIOLOGY, the study of living organisms.

BIOMETRY, the application of mathematical and statistical methods to the

study of living organisms, originated by the pioneer statistician, Karl Pearson.
BIOSPHERE, that part of the surface of the earth, including the oceans and the atmosphere, which is capable of supporting life.

BIOTOPE, the plants, animals and total environment of a specific locality considered as an interrelated whole.

BIPEDALISM, the ability to walk erect on the hind limbs, thus freeing the hands for use.

BIRA, a Bantu-speaking Negroid people of the Babwe-Bira group, dependent on horticulture with some fishing.

BIRDSTONE, see BANNERSTONE.

BIRIFOR, a Negroid, West African people, largely dependent on horticulture and hunting and fishing.

BISHARIN, a Cushitic people, heavily dependent on cattle-herding with some horticulture.

BLACK CARIBS, a predominantly Negroid people descended from Negroes who survived from a shipwrecked slave ship, and later massacred the male element of the Carib Indians who had accommodated them, but who had refused to allow them access to the Carib women. However, this massacre occurred only after the Negroes had adopted the language and horticultural arts of the Caribs. The resultant 'Black Carib' population still persists in the Antilles Islands of the Caribbean.

BLACKFELLOW, a term popularly applied by White Australians to the Australian aboriginals in reference to the latter's dark skins.

BLACKFOOT, Algonquin-speaking American Plains Indians, mainly dependent on hunting with some food-gathering.

BLACK MASS, a ritual practiced by a few small groups of educated Europeans at a time when various mystery cults (q.v.) such as Freemasonry were being revived in Europe. Such practices appear to have represented a rebellion against the orthodox teachings of the Christian Church, whose practitioners and adherents sought magico-religious satisfaction in a hodge-podge of cabalistic rituals, combined with information derived from references in classical literature to the ancient, oriental mystery religions.

BLADDER DOT, a device used by Eskimos when hunting seals, comprising an inflated bladder to which is attached an inflated bladder float which serves as a marker, and also slows down the seal in its attempts to escape.

BLADE, a long narrow flake tool, with parallel cutting edges along each side.

BLANK, a term used by archeologists to refer to a partially prepared but unfinished stone tool.

BLASTOGENIC, a term formerly used to refer to hereditarily transmissible characteristics, less frequently used today since heredity is now known to determine the potential of all characteristics possessed by any living organism.

BLESSING, a magico-religious act by which a person skilled in the art of intervention with the gods may attract supernatural powers to aid the beneficiary. In particular the concept of blessing implies the purification of the beneficiary from all sins, blemishes and evil forces.

BLONDISM, a condition characterized by the relative absence of pigmentation in the skin, eyes and hair, resulting in a light coloring. Blondism appears to have originated as a result of genetic adaptation to more northerly latitudes, where heavy pigmentation would have no beneficial survival value and would be harmful to the extent that it retards the manufacture of Vitamin D, for which sunshine is a catalyst. Blondism is thus characteristic of the Nordic and East Baltic varieties of the Caucasoid family of races. The lack of blondism among Eskimos can be explained by the relatively recent nature of their migration into their present Arctic domicile. Blondism should not be confused with albinism (q.v.) a mutant aberration found among all races which manifests itself in a total absence of pigmentation.

BLOOD, a vital fluid which carries oxygen, food materials, unwanted byproducts, etc. throughout the body of animals.

BLOOD, BLUE, the expression 'blue blood in his veins', indicating aristocratic descent, originated in Castile in Spain (Spanish 'Sangré Azul'), where the noble families were formerly of Gothic descent, and because of their Northern racial heritage possessed fairer, more opaque, skin than that of the more darkly tanned Atlanto-Mediterranean population over which they ruled – the opaque texture allowing the blood in the veins to show through their skin with a bluish hue.

BLOOD BROTHERHOOD, an artificial extension of kinship devised to make possible the extension of trust and cooperation in kinship-based societies to persons who are not kinsmen. In a kinship-oriented society, morality does not extend beyond the limits of kinship, and no trust can exist between men who are not kinsmen. Entry into an alien territory, for example, can often be safely attempted only when symbolic ties of blood brotherhood have been established.

BLOOD FEUD, a conflict between distinct descent groups in which the members of one group are obliged to revenge themselves on the second group for an assault, injury, or insult suffered by a kinsman.

BLOOD GROUPS, distinctive patterns of blood polymorphism, resulting from different antigens on the surface of the red blood cells. There are four main blood groups (A, B, AB and O) which are of considerable medical importance for the problem of blood transfusion since agglutination (q.v.) may occur when blood from certain of these groups is mixed. However, there are many other blood group categories present among men and mammals several of which may not result in agglutination when mixed but which nevertheless do set up reactions which can be harmful to the health of patients receiving transfusions. The distribution of the many different blood group systems around the world varies considerably according to lineage and racial descent, but studies beyond the vital A, B, AB and O groups are still poorly developed since these are of less importance medically. Further research into the blood group patterns of the different races of man would, however, be invaluable in the attempt to reconstruct the history of past population movements and admixtures in both historical and pre-historical times.

BLOOD INDIANS, Algonquin-speaking American Plains Indians, mainly dependent on hunting with some food-gathering.

BLOOD VENGEANCE, see BLOOD FEUD.

BLOWPIPE, a relatively sophisticated device comprising a long tube (frequently made from two tubes, one inserted inside the other) which has been carefully bored so as to create a smooth and regular interior through which a lightweight dart may be blown towards a distant target with consistent accuracy. Because of the lightness of the dart, blowpipes are only effective as hunting or war weapons when the dart is tipped with poison.

BOAT BURIAL, a common Viking practice between the 7th and 11th centuries involved the burial of prominent leaders of noble descent in their long-boats, complete with a rich collection of personal armour, weapons and other possessions. One of the richest of these boat burials to avoid the attention of grave robbers in subsequent years has been excavated at Sutton Hoo in Suffolk, England.

BOBO, a Negroid, West African Voltaic people, largely dependent on horticulture with some animal husbandry and hunting.

BODHISATTVA, a devotee to Buddhism who has passed through all ten stages of spiritual attainment, but who has postponed the opportunity to achieve personal Nirvana or oblivion, and has chosen to remain on the earth in order to work for the good of others who have not yet achieved the state of perfection.

BODI, a Negroid Nilotic-speaking people of the Beir-Didinga group, primarily dependent on cattle herding and horticulture with some hunting.

BODROGKERESZTÚR, an important East Hungarian cemetery which contained some fifty inhumation burials. Bodrogkeresztúr has given its name to a Chalcolithic culture occupying East Hungary and Transylvania, which succeeded the earlier Neolithic Starčevo (q.v.) and Tiszapolgár Chalcolithic cultures around 4600 B.C. and survived as a part of the Old European civilization down until around 3500 B.C., when it was overrun by Indo-Europeans with a proto-Baden culture. However, the Bodrogkeresztúr culture does itself reveal Indo-

European type battle-axes, and the precise date of Indo-European penetration may be earlier than 3500 B.C.

BOĞHAZ-KÖY, originally known as Hattusha, Boğhaz-Köy (located on the Halys river in central Turkey) was the capital of the Indo-European Hittites. At the height of the Hittite power, the city covered some 300 acres, all of which was enclosed by a massive city wall of stone and baked mud-bricks. The cemetery reveals a large number of cremation burials, somewhat similar to those of the contemporary Mycenean world. Over 10,000 inscribed clay tablets have been recovered, most of which have been translated, thereby providing us with extensive knowledge of Hittite culture.

BOHOGUE SHOSHONE, an American Indian people inhabiting the Eastern Great Basin, and speaking a Shoshone (Uto-Aztec) language, who depended on hunting and food-gathering and fishing.

BOIAN, a Chalcolithic culture, centered around present-day Bucharest, which was a part of the East Balkan complex of the Old European civilization (q.v.). The Boian culture evolved out of the early Starčevo (q.v.) and Karanovo (q.v.) cultures, to be replaced by the Gumelnita culture (q.v.) around 4300 B.C., and reveals many examples of the Old European linear script.

BOKOR, an expert in Haitian Voodoo, who claims to be able to exercise magico-religious control over the spirits of the dead.

BOLA, a weapon used by certain hunting peoples in South America, comprising a strip of leather divided into three connected lengths, to each of which is tied a round stone ball. When thrown at an animal the balls cause the leather strips to wind around its legs, with the result that the animal falls to the ground where it can be captured or dispatched by other means. There are indications that bola stones were first used in Upper Paleolithic times by Cro-Magnon men.

BOLEWA, a Chad-Sudanese (Hamitic influenced) people related to the Tera, largely dependent on horticulture but practicing some animal husbandry.

BOLLO'S LAW, the principle that evolution is irreversible, and that no organism ever returns to its ancestral form.

BOMBESA, a Bantu-speaking Negroid people of the Ngombe group, dependent primarily on horticulture with some hunting and fishing.

BÖN, an ancient pre-Buddhist animistic religion formerly widespread in Tibet. Although Bön worship was originally rooted in human sacrifice, it appears to have imbibed some of the principles of Chinese Taoism before being suppressed by the rising power of Buddhism.

BONE POINTING, in New Guinea and Australia the belief is widespread that death occurs only as a result of witchcraft and that it is possible to cause sickness and death by pointing a bone (or spear) at a man, while repeating a ritual incantation.

BONE TUBE, a hollow bone used by shamans to cure patients, ostensibly by using the tube to suck the cause of the pain out of their bodies.

BONES, CLASS OF, a variety of individual bones which have common diagnostic attributes (i.e. mandibles).

BONGO, a Nilotic people, primarily dependent on horticulture with some animal husbandry, hunting and fishing.

BONI, an annual Japanese festival celebrating the return of the ancestral souls to the earth.

BOOK OF THE DEAD, in the Old Kingdom of Egypt, only the pharaohs and certain of the nobles could hope to achieve eternal life after death, but in the New Kingdom commoners also sought to achieve eternal life by studying the 'Book of the Dead', which contained the various prayers, rituals and phrases necessary for the guidance of the soul in the afterlife.

BOOK OF THE WORLD, a comprehensive encyclopedia, of over 22,000 volumes, purporting to contain all knowledge, prepared on the directions of Yung-ho, the third emperor of the Chinese Ming dynasty.

BOOMERANG, an Australian throwing stick or 'comeback club', possessing a curved upper surface and a flat lower surface. Some boomerangs will return in the direction of their thrower if they miss their target, but the principle on which they operate is not understood by their makers, so that the behavior of a newly made boomerang cannot be predicted by the aboriginal until it is thrown.

BOREAL PERIOD, a relatively warm period which followed the final termination of the Würm glaciation approximately 10,000 years ago. The warmer Boreal Period dates approximately 7700 to 5500 B.C.

BOREAS, the Greek god of the North wind.

BORER, a stone tool used for carving holes in wood, stone or ivory.

BORORAN, a language belonging to the Gê family, which in turn is today grouped in a Gê-Pano-Carib phylum of languages, which is widely distributed throughout South America and the Caribbean.

BORORO, a South American Indian people of inland Brazil, who speak a language related to Gê, and are dependent on hunting, food-gathering and fishing.

BORORO FULANI, a Niger-Congo-speaking people, possibly revealing Hamitic influences, who are heavily dependent on animal-herding supplemented by some horticulture.

BORREBY, a broad-headed Caucasoid variant found among the otherwise predominantly long-headed Nordic population of Northwestern Europe.

BOSKOP, a site in the Transvaal in South Africa, excavated in 1913 which, together with neighboring sites excavated in 1929, has revealed fossil remains which are dated around 15,000 B.P. and are associated with a crude Middle Stone Age culture (which had already been replaced by the Upper Paleolithic culture as early as 34,000 B.P. in Europe). Boskop Man is regarded as an ancestor of the South African Bushman who had not yet received the benefit of either Upper Paleolithic or Capsian Mesolithic cultural innovations.

BOTOCUDO, a South American Indian people of unidentified linguistic association mainly dependent on food-gathering, hunting and some fishing.

BO TREE, also known as the Pipal Tree, the Bo Tree was regarded as sacred even before Gautama Buddha received Enlightenment while engaged in contemplation under the shade of a Bo Tree.

BOUNDARIES, even simple band-type human societies each possess their own territory, usually clearly defined by traditional boundaries such as specific hills, streams, trees or marshes. In many more advanced societies, the boundaries between different nations, tribes, villages, and even individual fields are sanctified by magico-religious rituals. Such rituals often involve religious ceremonies held at the site of the respective boundary markers, repeated annually so as to renew the sanctity of the territorial boundaries.

BOW, a device for propelling a light-weight spear (i.e. 'arrow') by mechanical means. The bow and arrow were probably invented by Cro-Magnon men in Europe or Western Asia during the late Upper Paleolithic or Mesolithic, and from there spread to many parts of the world with the diffusion of Mesolithic culture. However, the bow never reached Australia, and entered the New World only relatively recently.

BOZO, a Negroid, West African Mande-speaking people of the Marka group who live along the banks of the Niger River and are largely dependent on fishing with some horticulture.

BRACHIAL INDEX, the ratio between the length of the forearm and that of the upper arm, obtained by multiplying the length of the forearm by 100 and dividing it by the length of the upper arm. Apes and other primates generally show a much larger brachial index than hominids, although some considerable difference also exists between the different races of living hominids.

BRACHIATION, a technique by which certain primates are able to move rapidly through an arboreal environment by swinging from their forearms – resulting in substantial anatomical adaptation, especially of the forelimbs.

BRACHIOPODA, a phylum of animals, formerly common in the Paleozoic and Mesozoic times, possessing a two-valved shell somewhat resembling that of the modern mussel.

BRACHYCEPHALIC, broad-headed to the extent of possessing a skull with a width at least 81 percent as great as its length.

BRAGI, the Norse god of poetry who welcomed the heroic dead into Valhalla with a panegyric honouring their achievements during life. It is from the name and function of the god Bragi that we have derived the modern verb 'to brag'.

BRAHMA, one of the triad of major Hindu gods. Together with Vishnu and Shiva, Brahma is the personification of creativity and of the world order who is destined to periodically destroy and recreate the world. Brahma was married to the goddess Saraswati, patron of speech, learning, song and wisdom.

BRAHMAN, a Sanskrit term, associated with the name of the god Brahma, which signifies, in the Upanishads, the ultimate and indescribable reality of the universe, the all-embracing Brahman or world soul with which all the gods are associated, and of which they may be regarded as individual manifestations.

BRAHMIN, a member of the priestly caste of Hindus, devoted to the teaching of the Vedic tradition, the maintenance of temples and shrines, and the performance of religious rituals not only for rajahs (or kings) but also for the heads of the more prominent households.

BRAHUIC, see DRAVIDIAN LANGUAGES.

BRAIN, an enlarged anterior portion of the central nervous system present in most animals from fishes upwards. Among the more advanced animals complex brain centers are capable of coordinating the reactions of the entire body to a remarkable degree of refinement.

BRAIN STEM, that part of the vertebrate brain which excludes the cerebral hemispheres and cerebellum (q.v.).

BRANCHIPODA, a subclass of Crustacea (q.v.) including brine shrimps and water fleas.

BRAZILIANS, a people of mixed American Indian, Negro and Portuguese origins, today speaking Portuguese. Varied sections of the population depend on agriculture, animal husbandry, horticulture, fishing and hunting.

BRECCHIA, a form of rock comprising bones and stones which have become cemented together in the course of time.

BREEDING POPULATION, a group of males and females who customarily reproduce only among themselves.

BREGMA, the point on the cranium where the coronal suture meets the sagittal suture.

BRIBRI, a Central American Indian people speaking a Chibchan language in Panama, largely dependent on horticulture but also practicing hunting, fishing, food-gathering and some animal husbandry.

BRICKS, building blocks made from wet clay or mud, sometimes mixed with straw and sand, which are moulded into shape while wet, then dried to become hard. When baked hard in a kiln bricks are known as terracotta, but when merely left to dry in the sun, they are referred to as 'mud bricks', or (in America) 'adobe'. Sun-dried bricks are not so durable as baked bricks.

BRIDE PRICE, payment of cattle or other wealth made by the groom or his relatives to the family of the intended bride.

BRIDE SERVICE, labor supplied by the groom to the relatives of the bride in lieu of payment of a bride price.

BRIDE WEALTH, see BRIDE PRICE.

BRITONS, prior to the Anglo-Saxon conquest of much of the area presently identified as England, Scotland, Wales and the Isle of Man, these lands were occupied mainly by a Brythonic-speaking Celtic population of *Britannia* from whom the name 'Britain' derives. Ireland, by contrast, was occupied by Goidelic-speaking Celts. Although the Celts were racially Nordic, both territories and populations included substantial Atlanto-Mediterranean components from the earlier Neolithic populations the genetic components of which were presumably strongest in the more remote mountainous and western areas, which are precisely those areas in which Celtic speech has survived to this day. For this reason nineteenth century writers often wrongly depicted the Celts as a short and dark-haired European people, whereas they in fact differed little in appearance from their neighbours, the Germanic people of northern Europe. This we know from the reports of classical authors. Subsequently, Goidelic Celts from Ireland settled in the Isle of Man and in the Highlands of Scotland, planting Manx and Gaelic (both Goidelic languages) firmly in these two areas.

The British Celts were organized in separate tribes, the more prominent among which were the Cantiacii (from whom Canterbury and Kent derive their names), the Icani and Trinovantes (of what was later to become East Anglia), the Belgae of present-day Hampshire (related to the Belgae of Belgium), the Dumnonii (from which Devon derives its name) and the Cornovii (hence 'Cornwall') of the West Country, the Siluri of South Wales and the Ordovices of North Wales, the Brigantes of North Briton, and the Caledonii of Caledonia or the modern Scottish Highlands. The term *Welas* or 'Welsh', meaning 'foreigner', was an Anglo-Saxon epithet not a Celtic name. (See also CELTS and WELSH).

BRNO (BRÜNN), a site in Moravia in Czechoslovakia where Aurignacian tools and Combe Capelle Cro-Magnon type fossil remains have been found.

BROKEN ENGLISH, a term originally developed to refer to a form of English, using many borrowed African words, which was widespread in Liberia and Sierra Leone. Now frequently used to refer to any modified form of English which fails to comply with the prevailing English grammatical usage.

BROKEN HILL, an archeological cave site located in Zambia (formerly known as Northern Rhodesia) where remains of a very primitive Neanderthal skull, classified by some as late Homo erectus, were found in 1921 in association with Pleistocene deposits which have been dated at approximately 40,000 years B.P. This fossil has been named Homo rhodesiensus or Rhodesian Man. Subsequent fossil remains from Fauresmith and Marapansgat, both in South Africa, have since been classified within the same species. The remains of Rhodesian man were found in association with 'proto-Stillbay' tools.

BRONZE, an alloy of copper strengthened by the addition of either arsenic or tin, which had the advantage of being easier to work, since it has a lower melting point, and once fashioned proves to be harder than copper. Because of the relative rarity of deposits of copper and tin, most bronze was used either for shields, helmets and weapons by the military aristocracy, or else for decorative jewelry, drinking vessels or religious equipment.

BRONZE AGE, the use of bronze, an alloy of copper which is harder and consequently more widely useful than pure copper, appears in Europe, Asia Minor and Mesopotamia around 4000 to 3500 B.C. Excavations at Ur in Mesopotamia and in the Danube Valley show primitive bronze to have been in use by c. 3500 B.C., the first bronze alloys combining copper with arsenic before true bronze was discovered. Because copper and tin were rare, bronze was an expensive commodity, the possession of which was largely restricted to the warrior nobility who used weapons and armour and for the manufacture of utensils for religious and ritual purposes as the bronze temple bases of China. In consequence the Bronze Age is usually associated with highly stratified societies dominated by an heroic warrior-like noble caste. The main Bronze Age cultures included the Únětice and Urnfield cultures of Central Europe, the Minoan and Mycenean cultures of the Aegean, and the Wessex culture of England. Bronze was occasionally used in Peru from the 11th century A.D. onwards, and the Aztecs also alloyed copper with tin, but in neither Central nor South America did the use of either copper or bronze reach such significant proportions as in the Old World.

BROTHERHOOD, BLOOD, see BLOOD BROTHERHOOD.

BROW BAND, a band worn by Eskimos as an ornament across the forehead.

BRÜNN, see BRNO.

BRYTHONIC, a division of the Celtic languages and culture including Breton, Welsh, and Cornish. The terms Britain, Brittany, Briton, and Breton are derived from Brythonic.

BUBI, a Bantu-speaking Negroid people of the Biafra coastal region, dependent mainly on horticulture, animal husbandry and some fishing.

BUDDHISM, a religious system with strong philosophical and ethical bases.

Founded by Gautama Buddha (563 B.C.) and propagated by his disciples, Buddhism maintains that all human suffering springs from desire, and that to live merely a normal life is to suffer. The goal of Buddhism is thus the avoidance of suffering by the suppression of all desire. Once desire has been suppressed, the individual may hope to escape from pain and the cycle of rebirth into life, and so achieve *Nirvana* (q.v.) a state of nonexistence. Strict Buddhism thus represents the complete antithesis of the Indo-Aryan heritage, to which Buddha as a man of princely birth was himself an heir, since the Aryan religion more than any other religion asserted the goodness of life on this earth, the subordination of the goals of the individual to those of family and race, and the need to perpetuate the family by leaving heirs who might also continue to live the good life. Although for a time Buddhism gained ascendancy in India under the Maurya dynasty (q.v.), a Hindu revival reasserted most of the old Vedic Aryan values, resulting in the virtual disappearance of Buddhism throughout the Indian subcontinent. Mahayana Buddhism, or the 'broad road' of Buddhism because of its strong missionary orientation permits the use of animistic and indigenous rituals surviving from pre-Buddhist religions. While Hinayana Buddhism has attempted to observe the strict contemplative tradition of original Buddhism, Mahanaya Buddhism has spread widely throughout the Far East as a popular and relatively tolerant missionary religion, permitting coexistence with other religious traditions. Furthermore, in Mahayana Buddhism individuals are exhorted to engage in unselfish acts to assist others to achieve the morally good life, while in Hinayana Buddhism the individual is primarily concerned with his own escape into a state of Nirvana.

BUDJA, a Bantu-speaking Negroid people of the Ngombe group, dependent primarily on horticulture supplemented by some hunting and fishing.

BUDU, a Bantu-speaking Negroid people of the Babwe-Bira group, dependent on horticulture and limited river fishing.

BUDUMA, Chadic (Hamitic-influenced)-speaking people, located adjacent to Lake Chad, where they are largely dependent on fishing and animal husbandry.

BULGARIANS, a Balkan people of Southern Slavic Indo-European speech, representing an amalgam of Slavic Bulgar with earlier Thracian and Gothic peoples.

BULL, the bull appears frequently in Mesopotamian, Indo-European and related mythology, and winged bulls were commonly used in ancient Assyrian architecture, bull-sacrifice playing an important role in the Assyrian religions as it did in later Mithraism (q.v.). Cows, and specifically bulls, were revered in Zoroastrian religion and in modern Hinduism. In Classical Greek mythology the legend of Europa and the Bull may constitute an echo of the bull cult of the Old European civilization (q.v.) of the Balkans and of the Cretan Minotaur.

BULL-FIGHTING, the custom of bull-fighting in Spain and Portugal may represent the survival in sport of former religious rituals, probably common throughout the Mediterranean prior to the advent of Indo-Europeans. The Old European civilization of the Balkans and of the pre-Greek Aegean regarded the bull as possessing mythico-religious symbolism, and a Cretan painting depicts 'gymnasts' engaged in bull-fighting or some similar form of ritual. The Greek saga of the slaying of the bull-like minotaur in its labyrinth at Cnossus, is also suggestive of an ancient ritual of this kind.

BULL ROARER, a piece of wood or bone, fixed to a length of creeper or cord, which is swung rapidly around the head until it emits a roaring sound. Bull roarers were widely used by Australian aboriginals who believed that they could hear ancestral voices in the sound, and it is possible that the instrument may have its origins in the European Upper Paleolithic, which produced similar artifacts.

BUNDA, a Bantu-speaking Negroid people of the Kasai group, largely dependent on horticulture, hunting and fishing.

BUNGI, Algonquin-speaking American Plains Indians, mainly dependent on horticulture with some food-gathering and fishing.

BUNLAP, a Melanesian (Malayo-Polynesian) -people, largely dependent on

horticulture, fishing and animal husbandry.
BUNUN, a Malayo-Polynesian-speaking people of the Muong group, largely dependent on cultivation.
BUREAUCRACY, a method of human cooperation involving an extensive division of labor organized and directed by a hierarchy of coordinators.
BURIAL BUNDLE, a type of burial in which the bones of a decayed corpse are exhumed after the flesh has decomposed, and reburied in a bundle wrapped in cloth or skins.
BURIAL CUSTOMS, the disposal of corpses beneath the ground, either in single or in collective chambers. Cremation differs from burial in that the body is burned, the charred remains and ashes being usually buried in an urn, kept in an urn in a sacred temple or mausoleum, scattered over sacred ground, or actually eaten by the relatives of the deceased. In inhumation (q.v.) the body is placed in the ground in its complete form. In secondary burial, the body is first exposed until the flesh decays or is removed by predators, and the bones are then buried in an ossuary (q.v.).
BURIN, a pointed stone tool, commonly used to engrave objects of antler, ivory, bone or wood. Since the ornamentation of artifacts originated in the Upper Paleolithic, burins are usually found in association with Upper Paleolithic, Mesolithic or Neolithic cultures.
BURJI, a Cushitic people of East Africa, related to the Sidamo, they are dependent on horticulture and hunting.
BURMESE, a Sinitic (Tibeto-Burman)-speaking people, largely dependent on agriculture with some animal husbandry and fishing.
BURUSHASKI (or KHADZUNA), an isolated people inhabiting the mountain valleys of Gilgit in Northwestern Kashmir between the Hindu Kush and Karakorum ranges. It has been suggested that the Burushaski language may be part of a now unreconstructable Asianic phylum which would include the Caucasian languages (q.v.), but this has not been proven.
BUSAMA, a Melanesian-speaking people of Northeastern New Guinea, largely dependent on horticulture with some hunting, fishing, food-gathering and animal husbandry.
BUSHMEN, a Capoid (q.v.) Khoisan-speaking (q.v.) hunting and gathering people who still preserve a band-type social structure in the Kalahari Desert of Southern Africa. As hunters, the Bushmen were formerly widely spread over the uplands of Africa, but were supplanted by the expansion of Negro horticulturalists and herders (mainly Bantu). The best studied Bushmen are the Kung, Hadza and Naron.
BUTMIR, an Adriatic variant of the Old European chalcolithic civilization which succeeded the Impresso culture (q.v.) around 5500 B.C., and was in turn succeeded by the Hvar culture (q.v.) around 4200 B.C. The Butmir culture may be identified by pottery lavishly incised with meander designs.
BUTTONS, small objects which may be used with the aid of a slit to fasten two pieces of cloth together, or as decorations. The first buttons date from the Copper Age and are frequently associated with the Beaker culture. The presence of buttons usually indicates that tailored clothing was worn, whereas the presence of pins or fibulae suggests draped clothing, even where the clothing itself may have decayed.
BUYE, a Bantu-speaking Negroid people of the Bemba-Lamba group, largely dependent on horticulture and some domestication of animals.
BWAKA, a Negroid, Niger-Congo-speaking people of the Adamawa-Eastern group, dependent largely on horticulture with minimal animal husbandry.
BYELORUSSIANS, an East Slavic Caucasoid people (sometimes known as White Russians), traditionally dependent on agriculture and animal husbandry.

C

CAABA (also KA'ABA), the central chamber of the main mosque in Mecca which formerly housed the idols destroyed by Mohammed when he founded the Islamic religion. It contains the sacred Black Stone, kissed by pilgrims, which is of meteoric origin. According to Moslem belief the Caaba stands at the place where Adam took refuge after his expulsion from the Garden of Eden.

CABALA (also KABALA), a collection of occult Jewish writings which accumulated during the last two millennia, and embodied many of the mystical Chaldaean and Egyptian magical traditions. Magical formulae, anagrams, and the names of demons were passed down to chosen initiates, at first only orally, but later as part of a written tradition after the old formulae were committed to paper by medieval rabbis.

CABOCLO, (1) a Negro-American Indian hybrid community living in Brazil; (2) also the name given to their cult, which combines elements of Indian and African religious practices, and worships spirits from both traditions.

CACIQUE, an American Indian term for a clan chieftain, widely used throughout Central America.

CADBURY, the site of a hill-fort complex in Somerset, England, which tradition claims to have been the Camelot of King Arthur. Archeological investigations confirm this possibility.

CADDOAN, see MUSKOGEAN-SIOUAN.

CADUVEO, a South American Indian people who speak speaking a Guaycuri language, and live in Paraguay and adjacent territories, where they are dependent on hunting, fishing and some horticulture.

CAGABA, South American Indians of the Chibchan group.

CACHUILLA, a Shoshone (Utuo-Aztec)-speaking American Indian people of Southeastern California, dependent on food-gathering and hunting.

CAIRN, a pile of stones raised to mark a grave, a boundary point or place sacred to supernatural beings. Cairns were common in the more rugged part of Northern European countries, where there were ample stones but little top-soil from which to contruct earthen barrows for the dead.

CAKE, BRIDE, the custom of baking special cakes to celebrate a wedding or betrothal is found in many diverse cultures, and may possibly be of prehistoric origin.

CALENDAR, any system of measuring the passage of the days and seasons. Many peoples have used the apparent movement of the sun, providing distinct days and years, as a basis for calendrical calculations, while the concept of the month is generally based upon variations of the moon. Successive years were sometimes numbered in relation to the year of the reigning king. The Romans recorded years A.U.C., *Ab Urb Condita*, i.e., 'from the founding of the city', while the ancient Greeks counted years on the basis of successive Olympiads held every fourth year from 776 B.C. onwards. By contrast, the Chinese and many associated eastern peoples numbered the years in successive twelve-year cycles. The present system of numbering years in relation to the year which Christ was born only came into use after the institutionalization of Christianity in Rome during the 4th and 5th centuries A.D.

CALENDRICAL RITES, magico-religious rituals scheduled for routine performance at specified times of the year.

CALLINAGO, a Carib-speaking American Indian people of the Antilles Isles in the Caribbean, dependent primarily on fishing and horticulture, with some hunting.

CALLITHRICIDAE, a division of New World monkeys which includes marmosets.

CALMECAC, an Aztec college in which initiates to the priesthood received training in ritual while being required to participate in severe fasting and self-perpetrated tortures.

CALOTTE, the bones of the skull which together comprise the skull cap.

CALPULLI, an Aztec territorial clan, headed by a Calpullec or clan chieftain. Each Aztec clan possessed its own separate territory.
CAMARACOTO, South American Indian Carib-speaking people, dependent on horticulture and some hunting, fishing and food-gathering.
CAMAYURA, a South American Indian people, who speak a Tupi language and subsist by horticulture, fishing, food-gathering and hunting.
CAMBODIANS, the dominant Khmer-speaking population of Cambodia, traditionally dependent on agriculture with some fishing and limited animal husbandry.
CAMBRIAN, a geological period within the Paleozoic era, associated with the appearance of invertebrate chordates as the highest form of life. Estimated as having occurred between 575 million and 505 million years ago.
CAMEL, the single-humped camel or dromedary appears to have been a native of Arabia and was domesticated probably as early as the 2nd millennium B.C. The Bactrian camel or two-humped camel of Central Asia was probably domesticated during the 2nd millennium B.C., evidence being available from the excavation of archeological sites at Anau and Mohenjo-Daro.
CAMPA, a South American Indian people living in Central South America and speaking an Arawak language, dependent on horticulture, hunting and fishing.
CAMPIGNIAN, a late Mesolithic culture located in Northern France, characterized by oval dwelling houses.
CANAANITES, a Semitic people, possibly related to the Hyksos, who occupied Palestine during the 2nd millennium B.C., but were displaced in the south first by the Philistines and later by the Israelites, while in the north they survived as Phoenicians. Taking advantage of their strategic geographical location on the Mediterranean coast midway between Egypt, Mesopotamia, Minos, Mycenae and Anatolia, they developed commercial activities and played an important role in the development and spread of the alphabet.
CANINE TOOTH, the conical and pointed tooth common to most mammals (sometimes known as the 'dog' or 'eye' tooth) which is located on each side of the upper and lower jaws immediately behind the incisor teeth. The canine tooth is absent in some rodents, but may be found in enlarged form in other mammals as in the tusks of the wild boar and the sabre-toothed tiger.
CANNIBALISM, the term 'cannibalism' is derived from the Canibalis, Carib Indian people, who inhabited the Caribbean at the time of Columbus' arrival in the West Indies. Cannibalism, a cultural complex which centers upon the consumption of human flesh, may have many causes or functions. Thus cannibalism may be: gastronomic, for either pleasure or necessity, other food being non-available; ritual, where the object is magico-religious, rooted in the belief that the act of cannibalism enables the consumer to acquire the fame and skills of the consumed; or simply vengeful, where the flesh of the enemy is eaten out of a spirit of spite and a desire to obtain revenge for old injuries.
CANOE, a primitive boat, usually long and narrow with sharp ends, which is propelled by paddles and lacks both sails and a rudder. Many simpler canoes found in Africa and parts of South America are made from logs of wood hollowed out by fire, but more elaborate canoes can be made from planks of wood, waterproofed at the joints with clay, or from hides drawn tightly over a wooden frame, as in North America.
CANOE INDIANS. a name sometimes used to refer to the Yahgan (q.v.) and Alacaluf (q.v.) of Tierra del Fuego, because of the high proportion of their time spent fishing from canoes.
CANOPIC JARS, jars used by the ancient Egyptians to contain the internal organs removed from the corpse before mummification. These jars were usually placed in a burial chamber alongside the mummified corpse.
CANTONESE, a South Chinese people possessing a distinct form of the Chinese language which is scarcely intelligible to the Mandarin-speaking Chinese of the North.
CAPITALISM, an economic system in which control over the means of production, distribution, and the exchange of wealth is in the hands of private individuals.

CAPOIDS, formerly believed to have occupied very large areas of the sub-Saharan savannah, until overrun by an expansion of the Congoid or Negro peoples, the Capoid population of today is largely restricted to the Bushmen and Hottentot peoples of Southern Africa, where they were protected from Negro expansion by white rule. The Capoids have been described as being in many ways the polar opposite of the Australoids, and may be sharply distinguished also from the Negroes. Skin colouring is light, eyelids reveal the epicanthic fold, though no historical relation to the Mongoloids can be traced and there is a sharp serological contrast between Asian and Capoid blood groups. While possessing broad noses their lips are not as everted as those of the Negroes, and the jaws are less prognathous. Steatopygia is uniquely a Capoid characteristic, although found in less developed form among those Negro populations which are believed to have absorbed Capoid genes.

CAPSIAN, a Mesolithic culture which flourished in North Africa long after the introduction of the Upper Paleolithic culture into Europe and the Middle East, and which appears to have penetrated from North Africa into the Upper Nile as far as Kenya, where it is associated with 'proto-Hamitic' non-Negroid fossil remains. (See GAMBLE'S CAVE and OLDUVAI).

CARAJA, a South American people of the East Brazilian highlands.

CARBON-14, a radioactive substance found in living organisms which disintegrates at a regular rate. By measuring the rate of distintegration of carbon-14 it is possible to estimate the approximate age of organic remains. The technique is reasonably accurate for dating fossils of up to 50,000 years ago.

CARBONIFEROUS, a geological period within the Paleozoic era which lasted from approximately 345 to 280 million years ago.

CARCHEMISH, one of the largest and oldest tell sites to be excavated in the Euphrates valley close to the borders of Turkey and Syria. The site was first occupied in the Chalcolithic Age, but the city of Carchemish reached considerable importance under the Hittites, retaining this prominence until it was annexed by the Assyrians in 716 B.C.

CARCHIQUEL, a Central American people living in Southern Mexico.

CARGO CULT, a cult that developed in New Guinea and Melanesia during the colonial period, the adherents to which believed that the ancestral spirits would return to the earth, bringing with them large ships loaded with cargoes of modern luxury items. The return of the ancestors would also bring about the expulsion of the white men who were accused of appropriating ships containing luxury goods, sent by the ancestral spirits for the use of the natives.

CARIBOU ESKIMO, Eskimos who live in the interior of Northern Canada, dependent mainly on hunting, with considerable fishing and a small amount of food-gathering.

CARIBS, a linguistic and cultural group inhabiting parts of the South American mainland north of the Amazon, and once plentiful in the islands of the Caribbean Sea, which was named after them. The Carib peoples originated in the northern part of South America, but succeeded in annexing the Lesser Antilles from the indigenous Arawak population. An extremely warlike people, they practiced cannibalism, and the English word 'cannibal' is a corruption of the Spanish 'canibalis'. The Northern Carib people include the Callinago, Yupa, 'Black Caribs' (linguistically but not racially), and Carinya. Other Caribs in Venezuela, the Amazon Valley and Guiana include the Panare, Waiwai, Yabarana and Yehuana.

CARIBS, BLACK, see BLACK CARIBS.

CARNAC, a renowned Megalithic site in France, where some 3000 menhirs or standing stones still stand erect in multiple rows of 10 or 13 stones. The site is associated with a large number of burial chambers and cists, which include a rich variety of grave goods (q.v.).

CARNIVORES, an order of placental mammals, largely dependent upon flesh-eating. In order to facilitate this mode of subsistence, most carnivores have highly developed incisor and canine teeth, and many are equipped with powerful claws.

CARNIVOROUS, the tendency to depend upon the consumption of meat for survival.
CAROLINIANS OF SAIPAN, a Malayo-Polynesian-speaking people inhabiting Saipan in Micronesia, and dependent on horticulture, fishing and some animal husbandry.
CARRIER, a North Athabascan American Indian people, dependent on hunting and fishing with some food-gathering.
CARRIER, GENETIC, a term used to refer to a person who is heterozygous for an aberrant or unusual gene (usually harmful), who appears normal in phenotype because of the dominance of a normal allele, but is liable to transmit the aberrant gene to any offspring.
CARTHAGE, a Phoenician city established in North Africa in the 9th century B.C. as a colony of the Phoenician city of Tyre. When the Phoenician territories fell under the domination of Assyria, Carthage emerged as a leader of the various sea-trading Phoenician colonies in the Mediterranean, and established a powerful commercial empire which brought the Carthaginians into conflict with the Greek colonies of Sicily and Southern Italy. The Roman expansion into the same area led to the subjugation of the Greek cities and to the Punic wars, resulting in the final destruction of Carthage in 146 B.C. Although very little Carthaginian literature survived the Roman destruction of that city, archeology has confirmed the Roman claims that the Carthaginians maintained the ancient Semitic custom of sacrificing first-born sons to the goddess Tanit and her consort Baal, as also mentioned in the Old Testament.
CASSAVA, a plant grown in South America from whose roots tapioca, yuca and the intoxicating cashiri drink can be prepared. Cassava juice contains cyanic acid which must be extracted before consumption. (See MANIOC).
CASTE, an endogamous group characterized by a distinctive set of norms and a defined position in the social stratification of the society of which it is a part.
CASTE SYSTEM, HINDU, the Hindu caste system may have had its roots in the culture of the Indus Valley civilization, but received its present form with the arrival of the Indo-Aryans into India as a conquering people around the 15th century B.C. The Indo-Aryans were probably already divided into three castes, namely the royalty and warrior nobility, the priests, and the freemen, below which they recognized a caste of slaves who were not members of the tribal community. The resultant Indo-Aryan caste system comprised Kshatriya (q.v.) or warrior nobles, Brahmans or religious specialists, Vaisya or free commoners, and Dasya, later known as Sudra (q.v.) – the lowest non-Aryan caste who were required to perform all menial tasks and who were not permitted to approach close to or touch an Aryan.
CASTING SEAM, a small protruding ridge or seam, reflecting the joint between two moulds left when clay or metal objects are manufactured by pouring the molten liquids into a mould. Although this seam is sometimes removed by grinding, on other occasions it may remain as a visible blemish.
CASUARINA, possessing graceful limbs and trailing leaves which create a wistful appearance, the Casuarina tree is believed to have played a significant role in West European Megalithic rituals.
CATABOLISM, the process by which living organisms break down complex organic molecules to release energy. An essential part of metabolism (q.v.).
CATACOMBS, underground cemeteries originally established by the Romans for the burial of slaves and members of the lower class, and subsequently used by the early Christians and Jews to conduct their illegal religious ceremonies. The most famous catacombs underlie the city of Rome, although catacomb complexes were also constructed beneath other Roman cities of the same period.
CATAL HÜYÜK, an early urban settlement located in south-central Turkey, the lowest levels of which have been dated circa 6150 B.C. by radiocarbon process. The pottery from the first stages of settlement at Catal Hüyük is primitive, but there is evidence that crops cultivated included einkorn, wheat, barley and peas. The site also reveals numerous shrines, decorated with bulls' heads and wall

frescoes portraying a mother goddess, and many other indications of a close cultural connection with the Old European civilization of the Balkan area.

CATARRHINE, Old World anthropoids, distinguished from the New World anthropoids by a longer and more narrow nasal septum and by a distinctive menstrual cycle. (See also PLATYRRHINE).

CATASTROPHISM, the belief that the world is periodically destroyed and recreated.

CATLINITE, a type of red clay found in the upper Missouri valley and formerly used by American Indians for making tobacco pipes.

CATS, a mammal of the family Felidae, possibly first domesticated in the Nile Valley during Neolithic times as a natural enemy of the rodents which thrived on stored grain and cereals. Cats have frequently enjoyed supernatural status, due in part to their characteristically independent nature, and were regarded as sacred in Egypt, where the city of Bubasti was a centre of cat worship to which the corpses of dead cats to be embalmed and buried were sent. Among the Celts, as among the Indians, ceremonial rituals were held in honor of cats, and the Teutonic peoples also appear to have held cats in special regard, the Norse goddess Freya being usually portrayed as riding in a chariot drawn by two cats. Indeed, their association with pagan religion was so strong that in Christian times witches were invariably portrayed as being accompanied by a black cat, and popular European folklore still regards the sight of a black cat as an omen of bad luck.

CATTLE, cattle are believed to have originated as a wild species inhabiting the woodlands of Eastern and Central Europe, the first evidence of domestic cattle being found in the Danube area around the 7th millennium B.C., from whence cattle-herding and pastoralism diffused to the neighboring Pontic Steppes to become the major element in a steppeland tradition of semi-nomadic pastoralism.

CATTLE COMPLEX, a term used to describe the East African cattle-herding cultures.

CAUCA, a South American people of the Chibcha group.

CAUCASIAN LANGUAGES, a group of over 300 ancient non-Indo-European languages, still spoken in the Caucasus mountains and divided into North Caucasian and South Caucasian sub-groups. (See ASIANIC LANGUAGES).

CAUCASOID, one of the major geographical races of living hominids, otherwise known as Europids and customarily subdivided into Nordic, or Northwestern European, East Baltic or Northeastern European, Mediterranean, Atlanto-Mediterranean, Alpine, Dinaric, Armenoid, Iranic and Indic. Caucasoids are generally characterized by light skin, narrow to medium-broad faces, high bridged noses, and an absence of prognathism. The first Caucasoids are believed to be represented by the Cro-Magnons.

CAULDRON, any large metal cooking bowl, equipped with handles from which it could be suspended over a fire. Early examples are associated with the late European Bronze Age and the earlier civilization of Urartu.

CAUSEWAY CAMP, a term used to refer to a series of concentric ditches and banks which are broken at intervals by solid causeways. These are characteristic of the Early and Middle (Hembury and Windmill Hill) stages of the British Neolithic. No evidence of permanent buildings has been found within these camps, and their purpose remains unclear, since the number of causeways would seem to make them unsuitable for military purposes.

CAVE ART, whereas the Neanderthals revealed little or no aesthetic talent, the Cro-Magnons who occupied Europe and Western Asia in the Upper Paleolithic early demonstrated a high level of aesthetic susceptibility, ornamenting their tools and weapons with carved designs and also painting the walls of their caves, which although abandoned as residences continued to be used as ritual centers.

CAVE DWELLING, although caves have provided archeologists with profuse evidence of prehistoric conditions, this is largely because the dry conditions of many caves have effectively preserved fossil remains, and it must not be assumed that prehistoric men were invariably cave dwellers. Where caves existed they were undoubtedly used, especially in areas with a cold climate, but this does not mean that in many areas Neanderthal and other earlier hominids did not also live in the open.

CAVEMAN, a popular term which generally refers to the European Neanderthals, some of whom undoubtedly lived in caves, although many hominids in other parts of the world have also been cave dwellers, as indeed some primitive living peoples still continue to make their homes in caves in the present century.

CAYAPA, a South American Indian people speaking a Chibchan language. The Cayapa live in Western Columbia and are dependent on horticulture, fishing and some hunting and gathering.

CAYUA, a Central South American people who speak a Tupi-Guarani language, and are dependent on horticulture with some hunting, food-gathering and fishing.

CAYUGA, an Iroquois people of the American Eastern Woodlands.

CEBIDAE, the major division of Platyrrhine (q.v.) or Old World monkeys, which excludes the Callithricadae (q.v.).

CEBOIDEA, a simian superfamily corresponding to the Platyrrhine or New World monkeys.

CELIBACY, the rejection of sexual relations, and consequently – by implication – also of marriage. Required of priests and monks by various religions, including many denominations of the Christian and Buddhist religions, but regarded as a sign of abject poverty in other societies.

CELL, a microscopic living structure comprising a nucleus surrounded by cytoplasm enclosed in a semipermeable membrane.

CELL-DIVISION, the multiplication of cells achieved by a process called mitosis (q.v.).

CELT, a prehistoric stone tool used as an axehead – not to be confused with the term 'Celts' (q.v.) as applied to a people.

CELTIC ART, the Celtic culture was renowned for its exceptional achievements in metalwork, poetry and music and the Celts possess a wide range of musical instruments. Even after the destruction of the central area of the La Tène civilization on the mainland of Europe, as a result of the expansion of the Roman empire, the Celts of the British Isles long preserved their ancient artistic and literary tradition. This art reflects the essentially aristocratic and heroic nature of Celtic society as evidenced by the desire of the Celtic nobility to beautify their weapons, armour and immediate surroundings. Apart from the tradition, it included a variety of graceful if fantastic animal forms, frequently highly stylized, which parallel the Scythian or Indo-European steppeland tradition. Since the Celts built with timber, little of which has survived, the examples of this art comprise mainly jewelry, finely wrought armour and weapons (including the equipment of the war horses), engraved eating and drinking vessels and the monumental stone carvings erected in honour of the dead.

CELTS (or KELTS), classic writers describe the Celts as a tall, fair (red or blond-haired with blue eyes) and extremely warlike people, who were noted for their proud demeanour and flamboyant costume. The nobility customarily wore heavy mustaches and ornamented torcs or neck rings. Linguistically the Celtic languages form an important branch of the western division of the Indo-European or Aryan family of languages, closely related to the Italic group. Celtic possesses two main divisions, the Goidelic or Q-Celtic, which was the language of Gaul and is today still represented by Irish and Gaelic, and P-Celtic or Brythonic, from which the names Britain and Brittany derive. The Brythonic languages were spoken in Northern France and Belgium, as well as on the mainland of Britain, prior to the invasion of the Germanic Anglo-Saxons. They still survive in the Welsh and Breton languages, although the Cornish variant, which was close to Breton, died out in the Nineteenth century.

The Celts appear to have derived from the Hallstatt peoples of the Upper Danube, representing a branch which moved westward to the Upper Rhine, Switzerland and Central France. Their speech probably separated from the related Indo-European Italic languages around 1000 B.C., and their culture, which was characterized by an extremely highly developed sense of artistic ornamentation which reached its peak in the La Tène period around the 6th century B.C., but remained vital until the continental Celts were overrun by the expanding Roman empire, and the Celts in Ireland, who successfully withstood the Roman conquest, fell convert to Christianity. (See also CELTIC ART).

In social structure the Celts appear to typify the Indo-European system and reveal marked parallels with the early Indo-Aryan culture of India. They were an extremely aristocratic horse-riding and chariot-driving people, who in many areas merely established themselves as an Aryan aristocracy (Irish *aire* = noble) over the autochthonous agricultural population. Since the Celts appear to have been the first fair-haired and light-eyed Indo-European peoples to penetrate western Europe, they encountered an indigenous population of predominantly Atlanto-Mediterranean Caucasoid stock, light-skinned with distinguished aquiline features, but with dark brown eyes and dark brown or black hair. Although rigid caste systems probably prevented any immediate blending of the population with the Celtic *aire*, these caste barriers declined after the introduction of Christianity, and as a result the contemporary Celts are frequently portrayed as short dark-haired people.

The Celtic tribes held land on a kinship basis, dividing it amongst families and allocating cattle to the nobles and freemen according to their rank. Kings held court in castles, as in the medieval romances of the legendary King Arthur and his castle of Camelot, which epic lays survived the Anglo-Saxon conquest only among the Britons who migrated to Brittany from Cornwall and Devon. Celtic society thus involved the dual concepts of loyalty to extended family, clan and tribe, on the one hand, and the personal loyalty of a small band of warriors, usually of noble descent, to their divinely-descended sacred warrior-kings. The latter was characteristic of Bronze Age 'heroic society', and closely parallel to Homeric Greece, pre-Zoroastrian Persia, and early Indo-Aryan India.

At one time Celtic power dominated more than one-half of Europe, extending from the Straits of Gibraltar to the British Isles (and even penetrating into Central and Southern Germany for a short period of time) occupying Bohemia (which derives its name from the Boii, a Celtic tribe), dominating the Illyrian, Slavic and Macedonian peoples of the Balkans, and sacking the temple of Delphi in Greece, while one group of Goidelic Celts, the Galatians, penetrated and settled Central Anatolia. However, the Celtic tradition of fierce independence, and their tendency to regard warfare as a series of individual private combats (each chief seeking to engage in single combat with the enemy chieftain, rather than control and direct his army as a strategist) and the softer iron of their weapons, made it impossible for them to resist their more sophisticated kinsmen, the Romans. Despite their epic valour, virtually all the Celtic nations were finally defeated by the Romans and effectively Romanized, their languages giving way to various forms of 'vulgar Latin' which later evolved into the Romance languages of the present day.

CENOTE, natural pools or wells of water which occur frequently and provided an essential supply of water for the Mayan agrarian civilization. Appreciating the importance of these wells, the Mayans threw rich sacrificial offerings into the cenotes; many of such offerings have been recovered from a cenote at Chichén Itzá. The same term has also been applied to artificial wells (cisterns).

CENOZOIC, the geological era in which we live today.

CENTRIST, a tendency in the work of an anthropologist, archeologist, or ethnographer to place undue emphasis on the central or major characteristics of a society at the expense of peripheral phenomena.

CENTUM LANGUAGES, see entry under SATEM LANGUAGES.

CEPHALIC INDEX, the length of the head (measured from the glabella to the occipital) expressed as a percentage of its width.

CERAMIC ANALYSIS, since pottery withstands various climatic and soil conditions, 'potsherds' or crushed fragments of pottery are often one of the few surviving clues to the identity and culture of a people, and the study of ceramics therefore plays an important role in archeological analysis. Most societies have historically tended to be relatively conservative in their technology until such times as they were brought into contact with other cultures, although local internal innovations can also be demonstrated when a series of potsherds from different stages of the same cultural tradition can be assembled. The distinctive pattern of decorative markings, such as incised lines or painted symbols, the colour and the chemical analysis of the basic materials used, and even the mode of manufacture will all serve to provide clues for the classification of potsherds into distinctive cultural traditions associated with particular peoples, areas and ages. In addition, a relatively new dating technique called thermoluminescence (q.v.) permits an 'absolute' age to be assigned to ceramic artifacts, thus providing a significant clue to the age of the stratum in which they were discovered.

CERAMICS, (1) pots made of clay and other mineral constituents. (2) the art of making such objects. Ceramics are of particular importance to archeologists, since unlike flesh, bones, wood, and other organic materials, pottery deteriorates only slowly.

CERCOPITHECOIDEA, that superfamily of primates which corresponds to the Old World monkeys.

CEREBELLUM, a development at the anterior end of the hind brain (q.v.) of vertebrates notable to a conspicuous degree in the brain of birds and mammals. The cerebellum appears to be particularly concerned with the coordination of complex muscular activity at a higher level than more simple nervous reactions controlled by the spinal cord (q.v.).

CEREBRAL CORTEX, the layer of gray matter covering the cerebral hemispheres which is believed to be associated with the process of abstract thought. First found in the record of evolution among reptiles, but well developed only in mammals.

CEREMONY, a traditional pattern of ritual or symbolic behavior attached to important civil or religious actions.

CETACEA, an order of placental mammals which are completely aquatic. These include whales, porpoises and dolphins. Their forelimbs have become adapted to use as paddles; they have no hindlimbs, and only a trace of the pelvic girdle remains.

CHAAMBA, Semitic-speaking Bedouin Arabs of North Africa, mainly dependent on animal herding with some hunting.

CHACOBO, a South American Indian people. Speaking a Pano language and living on the upper reaches of the Amazon River, the Chacobo are dependent on horticulture, hunting and some fishing and food-gathering.

CHAD-NILE LANGUAGES, a suggested phylum, comprising the Nilotic languages, the Central Sudanic, the Nubian and the Kunaman languages of northeastern Africa.

CHAD-SUDANESE LANGUAGES, a large family of languages spoken mainly by those African peoples living in the grasslands situated immediately south of the Sahara desert, but north of the West and Central African rain forests. The Chad-Sudanese family of languages can be divided into nine major groups and one-hundred and twelve individual languages, notable among which are the Hausa, and are so closely related to the Hamitic group of languages (although the speakers are largely Negroid in appearance) that they are sometimes classified as a special subdivision of the Hamitic languages. The term Chado-Hamites has been applied to the people who speak these languages and it is probable that they derive from other Caucasoid immigrant people or conquerors who became submerged in a predominantly Negroid gene pool, but whose languages (and much of whose culture) survive among their predominantly Negroid descendants. The Chadic languages are grouped under East Chadic, including Bata, Bura and Higi; Matam-Mandara, West Chadic, including Afawa, Bolewa, Hausa, Gwandara, Kotoka, Masa, Ngizian, Plateau, and Somrai-Sokoro.

CHAGGA, a Bantu-speaking Negroid people of the Kenyan highlands, largely dependent on horticulture and herding.

CHAKMA, a partially Mongoloid Indian hill people, speaking an Indo-European language related to or influenced by Bengali, who live in the Chittagong

Hill Tracts of Bangla Desh. Horticulture, animal husbandry and some hunting and fishing are practised.

CHALCOLITHIC, a term used to describe metal age cultures which use pure copper, unalloyed with bronze. (See COPPER).

CHALDAEA, a term used to refer to the Babylonian empire during the latter period of its existence, i.e. from 626 to 539 B.C. The title is derived from Kaldu, the name of the ruling Aramaean Semitic dynasty which included Nebuchadnezzar. Although the Chaldaean or later Babylonian empire succeeded in defeating the Assyrians in 612 B.C., it was finally destroyed in 539 B.C. by the Persians under Cyrus the Great.

CHALDAEAN BOOK OF NUMBERS, a collection of magical formulae, originating in the Chaldaean culture, which comprise the major components of the Jewish Cabalistic tradition.

CHALDAEI, the name given by the Romans to the oriental astrologers who introduced Babylonian (Chaldaean) superstitions into the Roman civilization during the Imperial period. The Chaldaei exercised considerable influence among the masses of latter-day Rome, who had largely abandoned the worship of the pantheon of Roman gods and had lost the earlier tradition of ancestor worship (q.v.). Casting horoscopes, the Chaldaei served as popular diviners, and were regarded as exercising such a baneful influence that they were heavily criticized by Juvenal, and were banished from Rome on more than one occasion.

CHAM, a Southeast Asian Malayo-Polynesian people, primarily dependent on horticulture with some animal husbandry and fishing.

CHAMACOCO, a Zamucoan-speaking South American people, dependent on hunting and gathering.

CHAMBER TOMBS, stone burial chambers associated with European Megalithic culture.

CHAMORRO, a Malayo-Polynesian-speaking people of the Mariana Islands in Micronesia, largely dependent on horticulture with some animal husbandry and fishing.

CHANCELADE, an archeological site in France associated with the Magdalenian Upper Paleolithic culture and with skeletal material that closely resembles living Eskimos. The latter suggests that the classic Mongolian racial type may have had ancestral connections with Western Eurasia, during the period when Homo sapiens sapiens proto-Caucasoids were evolving in that area. This is important since it would explain the Upper Paleolithic origin of Mongoloid Eskimo culture and also indicates that other descendants of this population may have subsequently migrated across the Siberian steppes into Eastern Asia, taking the Upper Paleolithic culture eastwards to Northern China, Manchuria, Korea and Japan at a time when Central and Southern China were still populated by Neanderthaloids – possibly closely related in type to Wadjak man (q.v.) and thus to living Australoids – equipped only with a pebble tool culture.

CHANCHAN, the capital city of the Chimu empire, located in modern Peru, which preceded but was later absorbed into the expanding Inca empire. Chanchan covered 11 square miles, and its estimated population of possibly 50,000 people appears to have been subdivided into distinct local communities, each of which is believed to have constituted a separate clan.

CHANE, a South American people of the Upper Amazon.

CHANT, a form of recitation which is monophonic in character and is often used in sacred rituals.

CHARCOAL IDENTIFICATION, the analysis of the charcoal remains of prehistoric hearth fires aimed at the identification of the type of wood and other ecological information relating to the period under investigation.

CHARI-NILE languages, see CHAD-NILE LANGUAGES.

CHARIOT, a light-weight, two-wheeled vehicle, owned by members of the military aristocracies of Europe, Western Asia, India and China during the Copper and Bronze Ages, and thus particularly associated with what are called the 'heroic societies'. Although chariots were in some instances used only as means of rapid transportation, from which the warrior nobility dismounted to engage in combat on foot (to avoid the destruction of their valuable horses), later improvements in the art of producing inexpensive armour led to the design of leather and metal armour for the horses, and chariots were then actually driven into combat for the purpose of throwing enemy ranks into disarray. Although the two-wheeled chariot was probably invented by Indo-Europeans on the Pontic Steppes, it may have had a prototype in the four-wheeled wagons drawn by onagers in Sumeria. Historical records show that the Indo-European Hittites supplied the Egyptians with their first chariots, and it was the Indo-Aryans who introduced the chariot into South Asia (India) and Central Asia, from whence it appears to have been introduced into China as the basic fighting weapon of the Shang nobility; indeed, the early Chinese chariots are closely similar to those of western design. Chariots were widely used by the Homeric or Mycenaean Greeks in the Mediterranean, and were a well-known characteristic of Celtic culture many of whose nobility were buried with their chariots like the Indo-Europeans of the Pontic Steppes and the nobility of the Shang dynasty in China. In combat, the chariot gave way to heavy cavalry only after sufficiently sturdy and powerful horses had been bred to carry the weight of a knight in full armour.

CHARMS, objects believed to contain magical powers. Charms which protect the wearer against harmful forces are called amulets (q.v.), while those which bring good luck or attract beneficial forces are known as talismans (q.v.).

CHARRUA, the language of the indigenous American Indians of Uruguay, now virtually extinct. Charrua belongs to the Gê-Pano-Carib phylum of languages.

CHATELPERRONIAN, the earliest of the Upper Paleolithic industries developed by Cro-Magnon man which reveals some influence from the Mousterian tradition employed by the preceding Neanderthal inhabitants of Europe. Radiocarbon dates of around 34,000 B.P. have been assigned to the earlier finds.

CHATTA, a ceremonial umbrella used in ancient India as a symbol of social status.

CHECHEN, a Checheno-Lesghian people who speak a Caucasian language. The Chechen live in the Caucasus mountains, and are dependent on animal herding and agriculture.

CHECK-STAMPED POTTERY, pottery decorated by a pattern of small impressed squares.

CHELLEAN, a Lower Paleolithic hand axe culture, in which hand-held stone tools are given a cutting edge by striking chips or flakes off both sides of the core, instead of from one side only. Today customarily replaced by the term Acheulian (q.v.).

CHELLEAN MAN, Homo erectus fossil remains revealing a very large brow ridge, found at Olduvai in East Africa in 1961 (dated about 500,000 B.P.), which were formerly called Homo leakeyi after their discoverer, L. S. B. Leakey. Otherwise known as Olduvai Hominid 9, the skull (which is lacking the face) has been associated with Lower Paleolithic tools. The estimated cranial capacity was around 1000 c.c.

CHEMEHUEVI, a Southern Paiute, North American Uto-Aztec (Shoshone) speaking people, dependent on food-gathering, hunting and some animal husbandry.

CHENCHU, a South Indian Dravidian, hill-dwelling, food-gathering and hunting people.

CHENG-CHOU, the earlier site of the capital city of the Shang dynasty, dating between the 15th and 13th century B.C. after which it was replaced by Anyang located in Honan in north China.

CHEOPS, a 4th dynasty Egyptian pharaoh who was responsible for the building of the Great Pyramid of Gizeh, circa 2570 B.C.

CHEPHRAN, the Egyptian pharaoh who erected the second pyramid at Gizeh, some 30 years following the work of Cheops, and who was also responsible for the construction of the famous Sphinx.

CHEREMIS, a Finno-Ugrian (Uralic) people, dependent on cultivation, animal husbandry and fishing.

CHERKESS. a Circassian Caucasoid people, who live adjacent to the Caucasus mountains and speak a Caucasian language containing some Indo-European elements. The Cherkess have been traditionally dependent on agriculture and animal husbandry.

CHEROKEE, North American Woodland Indians who speak an Iroquois (Muskogean-Siouan) language and are largely dependent on horticulture supplemented by some hunting, fishing and food-gathering.

CHERT, an impure form of flint frequently employed in the manufacture of stone implements.

CHEVAUX-DE-FRISE, rows of spikes or sharp upright stones set in the ground for the protection against cavalry charges, in much the same manner as solid cement blocks were erected prior to World War II as a protection against attacks by tanks. Often found as part of the outer defenses of European hill-forts.

CHEWA, a Bantu-speaking Negroid people of the Maravi group, largely dependent on horticulture and hunting.

CHEYENNE, Algonquin-speaking North American Plains Indians, dependent on hunting with some food-gathering.

CHIASMATA, the point at which the exchange of genetic material takes place, during meiosis, between pairs of homologous chromosomes.

CHIBCHA, a group of tribes occupying the Andean portion of Colombia, whose language was closely related to the Páezan languages of Panama, Ecuador and 5 other more isolated languages of the Amazon valley. The Spanish legend of Eldorado, 'the gilded man' seemed to have been inspired by the fact that during their inauguration, the Chibchan chieftains had their bodies totally coated with gold dust, which was then removed by ritual immersion in the sacred lake of Guatavita.

CHIBCHAN-PÁEZAN, a Chibchan-Páezan phylum of languages has been proposed by linguists who seek to link the Chibchan family with the Páezan. The Chibchan family is centered on Colombia, in South America, while Páezan is found in Panama. The Chibchan languages include Cuna, Cagaba, Cayapa, and Tunebo. (See also PÁEZ).

CHICHÉN ITZÁ, the site of a major religious centre established by Mayan Indians in the Yucatan early in the 5th century B.C., which apparently fell into decay before being conquered and renovated by Toltecs under Kukulcan, whose name is equated with the Toltec Quetzalcoatl (q.v.).

CHICHIMECS, a group of barbarian tribes speaking a Nahuatl language some of whom established an independent settlement in the northern part of the Valley of Mexico, following the decline of the Toltec influence around A.D. 1200, and then settled down to a pattern of agricultural life, becoming allies to the Aztecs. However, those Chichimecs who remained behind in the more northerly parts of Mexico which were unsuitable for cultivation, retained their nomadic hunting and food-gathering pattern of life.

CHICKASAW, North American Indians of the Southeastern Woodlands.

CHICMECOHUATL, the Aztec maize goddess, in whose honour a young girl was immolated alive as a part of the annual harvest ceremonies held every September.

CHIEF, a term loosely used to refer to a political or kinship group leader in any relatively simple social system. In more advanced societies the chieftainship is usually, though not always, wholly hereditary in character, but among primitive hunting and gathering peoples, such as the Siriono of Bolivia, a chief may be elected by the band, and enjoy a tenure of only limited duration.

CHIGA, a West Lacustrine Bantu people, largely dependent on horticulture and herding.

CHILAN BALAM, a collection of Mayan records containing mainly magico-religious information.

CHILD SACRIFICE, evidence indicates that the sacrifice of first-born male children was originally widespread among the Semites. Old Testament accounts refer to Abraham's intended sacrifice of his first-born child, which was halted by the god Yahweh, and child sacrifice was customary among the Phoenicians of Tyre and the Carthaginians of Tunisia, who honoured Moloch in a sacrificial ritual which involved the slitting of a child's throat prior to the cremation of its

body in a sacred fire pit.
CHIMARIKO, a Northwestern California Hokan-speaking people, dependent on food-gathering, hunting, and fishing.
CHIMOR, see CHIMU.
CHIMPANZEE, an anthropoid ape whose feral behavior may possibly be equated with that of the Ramapithecine (q.v.) proto-hominids of approximately 12 million years ago. Chimpanzees are more responsive to human beings than other apes, and may possibly be more intelligent than gorillas, orangutans or baboons.
CHIMU, an early Peruvian civilization which extended along the Pacific coast of South America and whose capital was located at Chanchan. The Chimu civilization which developed around A.D. 1000 and reached a peak in the 14th century A.D., was distinguished by elaborate pottery shaped in anthropomorphic or animal figures and by large quantities of ornamented gold and silver products. Extensive irrigation was undertaken, and the major fortified cities were connected by an elaborate road system. The culture of the empire, which was conquered by the Incas around A.D. 1470 appears to have provided the basis for the subsequent Inca civilization.
CHIN, a Mongoloid people who speak a Tibeto-Burman language and live in the forested mountains separating the Indian sub-continent from Burma, where they are dependent on horticulture.
CHINANTEC, a linguistically-isolated, sedentary Central American Indian people, dependent on cultivation, with some fishing and hunting.
CHINESE, a major subfamily of the Sinitic or Sino-Tibetan group of languages. Chinese is divided into a number of major language groups – all deriving from an ancestral form known as Wen Yen – including: Cantonese, Hakka, Hsing, Kan, Mandarin, Min and Wu.
CHINESE LANGUAGES, see SINO-TIBETAN LANGUAGES.
CHINESE RELIGION, while the nobility of the Shang and other early Chinese ruling dynasties appear to have been ancestor-worshippers who recognized a pantheon of nature gods, the peasantry of both Northern and Southern China may have adhered to a more primitive animism involving fertility rites. As Chinese civilization became more highly syncretized, Confucianism developed as a philosophical, quasi-religious ethical system in Northern China, where the Shang tradition of ancestor-worship had been strongest. While Taoism (q.v.) became predominant in Southern China, an area of originally non-Chinese character which was only conquered and settled by the Chinese as late as the second millennium B.C. Taoism comprised a philosophico-religious amalgam of ideas centered to some extent around nature-worship, particularly emphasizing two principles – the 'yang' or male principle and the 'yin' or female principle – which were regarded as prevailing throughout the entire universe. According to the Taoist doctrine, men derived their better qualities from the good spirits known as 'shen' (associated with the 'yang' principle) and their baser qualities from the evil spirits known as 'kwai' (associated with the principle of 'yin'). However, Taoism and Confucianism were never mutually exclusive, for Confucianism stressed a moral order rooted in familistic principles and ancestor-worship, portraying the nation as a family and the emperor as the head of this national family. Confucianism thus stressed the moral and political responsibility of individuals to each other in terms of the familistic obligations of children to their parents and relatives, a principle which was not directly challenged by Taoism. Supplementing both the Confucianist and Taoist intellectual traditions, the worship of the nature spirits abounded throughout China, and after Mahayana Buddhism was introduced from India the new religion was (except for short periods of persecution) permitted to exist alongside Confucianism and Taoism. Only under communist rule have strenuous efforts been made to eliminate all religious activity from the social memory.
CH'ING DYNASTY (1644-1912 A.D.), a Chinese dynasty renowned for its patronage of porcelain making and the arts.
CHINOOK, an Oregon, Penutian-speaking Indian people, mainly dependent on

fishing with some hunting and food-gathering.

CHIPPEWA, Algonquin-speaking North American Indians, related to the Ojibwa, the Chippewa were mainly dependent on fishing, hunting and food-gathering, practicing only a little horticulture.

CHIPPEWAN, a North Eastern, Athabascan American Indian people, dependent on hunting and fishing.

CHIRICAHUA, Athabascan-speaking North American Apache Indians, dependent on food-gathering and hunting.

CHIRIGUANO, Tupi-speaking South American Indian people, residing in Brazil and dependent on horticulture and fishing with some hunting and gathering.

CHIROPTERA, an order of placental mammals which includes bats. The chiroptera are able to fly as a result of a membrane which lines the arms and the legs (and sometimes even the tail), the extremities of which are supported by elongated fingers.

CHISEL, a narrow-bladed cutting tool, first developed in the Mousterian culture of the Middle Paleolithic.

CHLOROPHYLL, a green-colored material found in most members of the plant kingdom. Chlorophyll enables plants to build carbohydrates from carbon dioxide and water through the absorption of energy from sunshine in a process known as photosynthesis.

CHOCO, a Central Mexican people who speak a language related to Mixtec, and are dependent mainly on horticulture with some hunting and fishing.

CHOCTAW, North American Southern Woodland Indians speaking a Muskogean language, largely dependent on horticulture with hunting, fishing and food-gathering.

CHOISEULESE, a Melanesian (Malayo-Polynesian) people, largely dependent on horticulture with some fishing and hunting.

CHOKWE, a Bantu-speaking Negroid people of the Lunda group, largely dependent on horticulture and hunting.

CHOL, a Central American people of Honduras.

CHOLULA, an archeological site in Mexico, first occupied in the pre-Classic period (around 500 B.C.) and subsequently absorbed into the Teotihuacan civilization. Cholula possessed the largest pyramid in Mexico, with a base area covering some 25 acres. Although Cholula came under Mixtec influence in the 9th century A.D., it remained an impressive city, and continued to make polychrome pottery which was highly prized by the Aztecs.

CHONE, a South American people of southern Chile.

CHONTAL, a Central American people located on the Mexican/Guatemalan border.

CHOPPER, an early Lower Paleolithic stone implement, held in the hand and flaked only on one edge, as distinguished from the hand axe (q.v.) which has two edges.

CHORDATA, that phylum of animals which possesses a dorsal nervous chord.

CHOROTI, South American Indians of the Chaco.

CHORTI, a Central American, Mayan people, primarily dependent on agriculture with some animal husbandry, fishing and hunting.

CHOU, probably originating in the steppes, the Chou succeeded in overthrowing the Shang dynasty in 1027 B.C. and ruled northern China until overthrown by the Ch'in in 256 B.C. Although they remained warlike, the Chou were an elegant and highly literate people, whose children underwent regular schooling in the arts of mathematics and writing, architecture, music, charioteering and ceremonial ritual. Politically they maintained a feudal system in which each local nobleman retained a private body of armed companions, usually members of his own clan. Preserving the joint family as their ideal, and using the chariot as their main weapon of war, the Chou dynasty laid the foundation of subsequent Chinese civilization. The Chou emperors claimed to be the 'Sons of Heaven', and established a literate bureaucracy for the effective management of their empire, admission to which was by competitive examination in poetry and other classical subjects.

Although, like the Shang before them, the Bronge Age Chou were ancestor worshippers whose lives were strictly controlled by ancestral custom and ritual, they appear to have introduced a clearly defined penal code to control the behaviour of the subjugated peasant classes who lacked the elaborate ritual which effectively disciplined the Chou aristocracy. Various innovations such as the use of iron swords and the crossbow were made during the period of Chou domination, but this empire finally collapsed as a result of internal conflict between the local warrior nobles, and weakened by intensive strife the Chou were overthrown by the Ch'in (249 B.C.). Once in power, the Ch'in attempted to obliterate the public memory of earlier Chinese dynasties, so as to make themselves appear as culture heroes, but fortunately they kept copies of the earlier records in the Imperial library, while destroying all other documents, so that the earliest literature of China survived the short rule of the Ch'in to be resurrected following their replacement by the Han emperors.

CHOUKOUTIEN, a site 40 miles southwest of Peking, China, where a dozen incomplete fossil skulls and mandibles and 147 teeth, together with some incomplete skeletal fragments were excavated by Franz Weidenreich from what is called the Lower Cave. Those were first known as Sinanthropus pekinensis, but are today labelled Homo erectus. Brown ridges form a single continuous torus, and the neck muscle attachments were very prominent. Evidence regarding the mid-portion of the face is largely lacking. The entire collection excavated by Weidenreich was lost during the Sino-Japanese war. The Upper Cave on the 'Dragon-bone Hill', by contrast, revealed the remains of seven individuals (three skulls in good condition) of a rugged Homo sapiens type, possibly generically related to living Mongoloids.

CHRISTIANITY, a monotheistic missionary religion, experiential and historical in outlook, but rooted in the concepts of revelation and of a God of 'love'. Humanity and all worldly material are classified as inherently sinful, with redemption possible only through the self-sacrifice of Christ. Originally an heretical form of Judaism, influenced by the doctrines of the Essenes (by way of John the Baptist), Christianity was soon to become strongly influenced by Hellenistic thought as converts were sought not only amongst the diaspora Jews but increasingly among non-Hebrew slaves and members of the lower strata of the Roman empire. Eventually the movement grew so strong that Christianity became the official religion of the Roman empire, creating the 'Roman' Catholic church which survived that empire, as well as the Eastern Orthodox Church which survived the Eastern or Byzantine Roman empire. In both cases Christianity became strongly Europeanized and absorbed many pagan myths and concepts, even canonizing mythical pagan figures. Christian churches were deliberately constructed over the remains of pagan shrines and at the site of pagan holy places, the more effectively to supplant and extirpate the older pagan religions. In North Europe, the Protestant Reformation modified the Christian religion even further, undermining the power of the churches and placing emphasis upon the dignity and freedom of the individual in his relationship with the divine and with his own conscience – thus allowing greater freedom for the influence of local mores, but also opening an intellectual door to existentialism. In the present century there has been a strong movement within both the Protestant and Roman Catholic churches for a return to the Judeo-Christian, social-reformist roots of Christianity, with a resultant attempt to purge Christianity of its pagan saints (such as St. George) and to extirpate older European cultural traditions dating from pre-Christian times.

CHRISTMAS, a Christian festival which ostensibly honours the birth of Christ, but as Yuletide represents the survival of an older, pre-Christian pagan winter solstice festival. Thus in Northern Europe, the Christmas tree, Yule-log, Christmas cake, the boar's head, and the general feasting and merry-making all derive from Yule, the Scandinavian and Teutonic winter solstice festival that lasted for a period of 12 days. In southern Europe by contrast the influence of the Roman feast of Saturnalia, also marking the winter solstice, is apparent. Like Yuletide, this festival also involved merry-making and gift-giving. Christ was originally believed to have been born in February and it was not until the 4th century A.D., that the Catholic Church decided to celebrate his birthday on December the 25th, one of the more important days of the pagan winter solstice festivities, as an alternative to suppressing the established and popular Yuletide-Saturnalia-Mithraic traditions.

CHROMATID, a term used to refer to each of the two, usually identical, strands or threads into which a chromosome divides in the process of reproduction.

CHROMATIN, a nucleo-protein found in chromosomes which is easily visible under a microscope when stained with appropriate dyes.

CHROMOSOME, a threadlike chain of DNA molecules which contains the genetic code. Each chromosome comprises a pair of long parallel strands, known as chromatids (q.v.) which are connected at the centromere.

CHRONOLOGY, a sequence of events arranged in order of causal occurrence in time. (See DATING SYSTEMS).

CHRONOLOGY, ABSOLUTE, the application of precise techniques of measurement to the dating of artifacts and fossils, as distinct from methods of 'relative' chronology (q.v.). (See ARCHEOMETRY).

CHRONOLOGY, RELATIVE, dating artifacts, fossils and archeological sites and materials by cross-dating (q.v.) and stratigraphical comparison (q.v.).

CHUGACH ESKIMO, a Western (South Alaskan) Eskimo people who depend on fishing and some hunting.

CHUKCHEE, a Paleo-Asian people, dependent on reindeer-herding, fishing and hunting.

CHUMASH, a North American (California) Hokan-speaking Indian people formerly occupying the Los Angeles, Santa Barbara, and interior areas.

CHURINGA, sacred objects found in most Australian aboriginal cultures, believed to contain a part of the soul of the individual. The churinga of an infant was usually fashioned by a grandfather.

CHYMATRICHOUS, a specific variety of wavy hair, characteristic of the Australoids of both Australia and Asia, such as the Veddahs (q.v.).

CIBONEY, Central American Indians who formerly occupied Cuba.

CICATRIX, a raised scar created for ornamental or ritual purposes by rubbing dirt or some other irritant into an incision in the skin.

CINDERELLA, fossil fragments of the rear end of a skull and upper joints found at Olduvai Gorge in 1963 by L. S. B. Leakey, otherwise known as Olduvai Hominid 13 and classed as Homo habilis. Dated approximately 500,000 B.P.

CINERARY URNS, any urn used to contain the charred bones and ashes remaining from cremation rituals.

CIRCASSIANS, see CHERKESS.

CIRCUMCISION, the total removal of the foreskin of the male in a ritual ceremony, or of the labia minorae and/or clitoris of the female. Circumcision was known in Babylon, where it was probably derived from the Semitic Chaldaeans. It appears to have been widespread among the Semitic and Hamitic-speaking peoples, being preserved to this day as a religious requirement among Hebrews and Muslims, and the ancient Egyptians (a Hamitic people) required all priests and soldiers to be circumcised. Many African peoples who have come under Hamitic or Cushitic influence, such as the Masai, similarly place great importance on this ritual. Circumcision was unknown among European and non-Semitic Asian peoples, except when these came under Judaic or Islamic influence, but has been recorded among the Australian aborigines, who practice a particular variant known as sub-incision (q.v.).

CIRCUMPOLAR CULTURES, the common pattern of Eurasian Circumpolar ecology prevented the penetration of Neolithic agrarian arts into the semi-Arctic regions. As a result the cultures of the circumpolar peoples are restricted to nomadic hunting and gathering practices, supplemented or replaced by some degree of pastoralism where conditions permit this kind of activity. The simpler Circumpolar culture, based upon fishing and hunting, preserves in its artifacts and techniques many of the inventions of the European Upper Paleolithic, which coincided with similar sub-Arctic conditions during the Würm glaciation.

CIRCUS, the name given by the Romans to the arena in which public games and entertainments were held.

CIRE-PERDUE, otherwise known as the 'lost wax' process, cire-perdue represents one of the earlier methods of producing metal objects of detailed or intricate shape. Under the cire-perdue technique, a desired shape, such as a figurine, was modelled in wax and the resultant 'positive' image was then given a thick coat of clay and baked until the clay was hard. However, small holes were left in the baked clay, through which molten metal could be poured into the mould, the heat of the metal melting the wax which escaped through other vents. Once the metal cooled it became solid, and the clay covering could then be broken away to reveal a metal cast which matched the shape of the original carved wax figurine. The first evidence of the use of this technique comes from Sumeria around 3000 B.C., but the cire-perdue technique was also used in Bronze Age China, as well as for casting gold and silver objects in the Meso-American and Peruvian cultures.

CIST, an oblong burial chamber constructed from vertical stone slabs, roofed by horizontal stone slabs. Such cists, constructed above the surface of the land, were usually covered by a protective barrow of earth.

CITHARA, a sophisticated stringed instrument mounted on a heavy wooded sounding chamber and equipped with a device for changing the pitch. Known to the ancient Greeks, the cithara is still used in Eastern Europe.

CITY, an urban community incapable of producing its own food and therefore dependent upon the production of specialized goods and the supply of diversified services in exchange for food. Uruk in Mesopotamia (circa 3500 B.C.) is perhaps the oldest settlement to which the label 'city' may properly be applied.

CITY-STATE, an autonomous state, characteristic of classical Greece and Republican Rome consisting of a single urban center, whose population was organized on a kinship basis.

CIVILIZATION, the term 'civilization' has never been adequately defined, but it is generally agreed that the idea implies a degree of human control over environmental forces as well as a developed system of social control and adequate leisure to permit an advanced level of esthetic appreciation. Most civilizations are characterized by a fairly advanced division of labor, a rather stable system of social stratification and the delegation of social power to a leisured class of aristocrats who play a dominant role in determining the direction of social and economic effort, favoring esthetic activities and interests over the more gross satisfactions of the primitive tribesman.

CLACTONIAN, a Lower Paleolithic industry principally associated with the Mindel-Riss Interglacial period, and named after archeological excavations at Clacton-on-Sea in England. A series of flint flake tools have been found in addition to older type pebble tools, and at the Swanscombe site, such Clactonian flake tools are superseded by Middle Acheulian hand axes. By parallel evidence from continental sites, it seems possible that the Clactonian industry was associated with Homo sapiens steinheimensis variety, although no skeletal remains were found at the Clacton site.

CLADOGENESIS, a term used to refer to the evolutionary process by which diverse distinct life forms evolve from a common ancestor.

CLAN, a unilineal cluster of relatives, part of a larger society, membership of which is determined by descent from a common ancestor, real or imaginary.

CLASS, a social category distinguished by similarities of social and/or economic status. However, members of a social class should not be regarded as a 'social group' unless they share a degree of mutual intercommunication.

CLASS, SOCIAL, a social unit in a hierarchical system of stratification, membership in which is determined by the extent to which different individuals and groups of individuals possess wealth, power, and status. Class systems generally imply some degree of vertical mobility.

CLAVICLE, the collarbone.

CLEAVER, an advanced Lower Paleolithic bifacial stone-cutting tool equipped with a broad cutting or scraping edge and closely related to the coup-de-poing (q.v.) which fell into disuse during the subsequent Mousterian Age.

CLINE, a term generally used in physical anthropology to refer to a progressive change in the frequency of any inherited biological characteristic over a distinctive geographical area, usually as a reflection of changing ecological conditions.

CLITORIDECTOMY, a somewhat crude operation frequently performed on the clitoris in Hamitic and some other cultures, the effect of which is to reduce sexual sensation.

CLONE, the descendant of a single cell, reproduced by a series of mitoses, and therefore possessing the same genetic constitution as the parent.

CLOVIS POINT, an American Indian projectile stone point, distinguished from Old World projectile heads by a longitudinal groove running along much of the length of the tool. Most Clovis points have been found in North America, although a few have been discovered as far south as Panama.

COATLICUE, the Aztec goddess of the earth who is normally represented wearing a robe of serpents.

COCAMA, a South American Indian people speaking the Tupi language who live on the upper reaches of the Amazon River, and are dependent on fishing, horticulture and some hunting.

COCCYX, the vestigial internal tail in man.

COCHISE, a North American Central Pueblo people, who speak a Keresan language, and are primarily dependent upon horticulture. The Cochise culture represents an original adaptation to hunting which was later supplanted by horticulture and a dependence upon maize around 3600 B.C. The later phase of Cochise culture featured settled communities occupying pit dwellings.

COCOPA, a Yuman-speaking people whose language belongs to the Hokan family. Located on the Colorado river, the Cocopa were dependent on horticulture, fishing, hunting, and food-gathering.

CO-DOMINANT, two alleles both of which are fully expressed when they occur together in the heterozygote form, an example being the blood group AB.

COEFFICIENT OF INBREEDING, the degree to which a population is inbred, or in other words the degree of probability that homologous pairs of genes will be present in an individual or in a population.

COELENTERATA, a phylum of metazoa which includes the hydrazoa, and dates from the Proterozoic period. Coelenterata were at first little more than floating mouths, through which food-bearing water passed into a central digestive cavity. Sponges and jellyfish evolved from early coelenterates.

COEUR D'ALENE, a North American Indian people, speaking a Salish (Mosan) language, situated in the Western Rockies and formerly dependent upon hunting, fishing and food-gathering.

COGNATES, (1) a kinship term referring to all who share descent from a common ancestor through either the male or female line. (2) a linguistic term used to describe words which share a close etymological relationship.

COILING, a method of manufacturing pottery without the aid of potter's wheel, using a long rope of clay, which is wound in a spiral formation so that each successive layer builds on the height of the lower layers. Once the required height and shape has been reached, the clay is then smoothed out by hand and baked. A similar process of coiling is sometimes used in basket making, where the weft is wound in a long spiral pattern, starting at the bottom of the basket and finishing at the top, and it is believed that coiling in pottery manufacture is a very ancient technique taken over by early potters from the ancient art of basket making.

COKEET SEEL, an Anasazi cliff-dwelling village containing more than 150 rooms as well as underground kivas.

COLLATERAL RELATIVES, consanguineal relatives linked by common descent from the same ancestor though not related by descent from each other.

COLLECTIVE TOMB, a European Megalithic chamber tomb containing many burials, probably representing a mausoleum for successive generations of the same lineage.

COLONO, a term widely used in Latin America for an agricultural laborer who is paid for his work by the loan of a plot of land which he is allowed to cultivate for his own benefit. The system is believed to have originated in Europe in the later days of the Roman empire, and to have been introduced to America by the Spaniards.

COLORADO, a South American Chibchan-speaking people of Northern Ecuador.

COLOUR BLINDNESS, an inherited inability to distinguish certain colours. Colour blindness is caused by a sex-linked defective recessive gene (q.v.), and is more common in males than in females. The most usual form of colour blindness results in varying degrees of severity in an inability to distinguish between red and green, although other forms of colour blindness do exist. Colour blindness and short sightedness are usually more common among peoples who have been cultivators or have been urbanized over a period of several thousand years than amongst populations who are, or were until recently, hunters. This is possibly due to relaxation of selection among the former.

COLUMBARIUM, a mass burial chamber (also known as a catacomb) used by the Romans to dispose of the remains of slaves, freedmen and other low caste individuals. A columbarium comprised a central underground passage off which rows of niches were hewn, to hold urns containing the remains of the deceased.

COMANCHE, Shoshone (Uto-Aztecan)-speaking North American Plains Indians, dependent on hunting supplemented by food-gathering.

COMBAT, SINGLE, a characteristic custom among Bronze Age Indo-European 'heroic societies', in which a single heroic warrior leader (frequently claiming divine descent) would battle another leader from the enemy camp in full view of the assembled armies, this one struggle deciding the entire combat without any other loss of life. Thus, when the Dorians first invaded the Aegean lands, already occupied by the Achaean Greeks, they withdrew following the death of their king (who claimed to be descended from Hercules), in single combat against the victorious Dorian hero-king.

COMBE-CAPELLE, a shelter site in the Dordogne region of France, excavated in 1909, which revealed fossils which were then known as Homo aurignaciensis and subsequently classified as Combe-Capelle or Brunn. These are now recognized as being Homo sapiens sapiens and part of the Cro-Magnon (q.v.) assemblage, dating from around 36,000 B.P. The excavations also revealed Chatelperronian tools.

COMBED ORNAMENTATION, a form of pottery decoration created by drawing a comb-like instrument over the surface of the wet clay to leave a band of straight or wavy parallel lines.

COMITATUS, a small but permanent band of armed warriors, usually of noble descent, who served an Indo-European king in the relationship of loyal friends and kinsmen.

COMMUNISM, PRIMITIVE, the concept of primitive communism differs from contemporary communist theories in that the characteristic food-sharing and communal 'ownership' of property practiced in simple bands of hunters and gatherers was rooted in the concept of ascribed kinship ties, and totally lacked the repressive bureaucratic structure necessitated by conscious attempts to impose economic equality in a complex society. Primitive familistic communalism is also evidenced in the Slavic zadruga (q.v.) where the obligations of blood and kinship dominate life in sharp contradistinction to the philosophical individualism implied by modern Marxist and existentialist theories. By contrast a form of primitive communism which denied kinship ties was practiced by the Hebraic monastic communities of the Essenes (q.v.), whose membership was essentially male, while a similar community of property was attempted in the earlier Christian monasteries which were more hierarchical in organization.

COMMUNISM, SEXUAL, the concept of complete sexual freedom, in opposition to the traditional hominid pattern of pair-bonding and family-type social organization. Certain early anthropologists, notably Morgan, believed that early man lived in a state of primitive sexual communism before developing the higher level of culture which he associated with the introduction of family life and kinship responsibilities. Marx and Engels inverted the views of Morgan to declare that early men and women lived in a happy and superior state of sexual freedom, and that the family system represented a form of capitalistic exploitation, the male establishing control over one or more females and their offspring, thus converting them into male 'property'. However, the views of Morgan, Maine, Marx, and Engels have all since been shown to be totally without foundation, since although man's non-human primate ancestors may have lived in promiscuous groups like baboons, the principle of male-female pair-bonding on which the family type of society is based appears to have evolved very early in hominid evolution and there is no evidence that sexual communism ever prevailed as a persistent state of affairs in any known human society.

COMMUNITY, a social group or area in which competition and other impersonal relations exist; the smallest unit of society capable of independent existence.

COMPADRAZGO, a system or ritual kinship, or 'godparenthood' practised in Latin America.

COMPARATIVE CULTURE DATING (CROSS-DATING), the comparison of artifacts, such as decorated potsherds (q.v.)' found at one archeological site with those found at another, to establish a relative chronology. (See RELATIVE DATING).

COMPENSATION, a term used in physical anthropology to refer to the tendency for one structure to assume the functions of another inefficiently-operating structure.

COMPETITION, impersonal rivalry for identical goals without the necessary existence of social communication.

CONCH, a marine shell, used as a horn or musical instrument in religious ceremonies. Forms of the conch were common in both India and also among the Aztecs of America.

CONCUBINAGE, a permanent or semi-permanent relationship or a form of pair-bonding between a specific male and a specific female, which, though recognized by society, does not entitle the female to the status and privileges of a married wife. The status of the children born to concubines varies according to the customs of the individual society. Semitic and Turko-Tartar societies usually allowed them the social status of their father, with a right to share in the family inheritance. In the Indo-European tradition, by contrast, the offspring of concubines could seldom achieve the status of the father, although some economic provision might be made for their support. Only in the Middle Ages, under Christianity, did it become acceptable for fathers to grant full status to the children of concubines.

CONDON, the smallest combination of bases in DNA or RNA; hence the ultimate unit of the genetic mechanism.

CONFEDERATION, a league between two or more tribes or nations for social, political or military purposes. Among American Indians, the Iroquois confederation of five tribes proved eminently successful as a military and political combine.

CONFESSION, RELIGIOUS, the cleansing of the soul by the ritual admission of guilt. The practice of confession is common to a number of cultures, but reached particularly significant levels in the Catholic form of the Christian religion.

CONFUCIANISM, an ethical and philosophical religious tradition, based on the original teachings of Confucius, who is believed to have lived in northern China between 551 and 479 B.C. Confucianism represents a philosophical extension of the ancient ancestor-worshipping traditions of the Shang aristocracy, which may well have originated in a common steppeland tradition of ancestor-worship deriving ultimately from the ancestor-rituals of the European Upper Paleolithic Cro-Magnons. Constructed around the concept of familial duty, Confucianism represents the political state as an enlarged family, conceiving of the emperor as a patriarchal head. Since all men should worship their ancestors, the Imperial ancestors were deemed to be sacred to the entire nation. The central moral principle of 'shen' (q.v.) may be defined as familistic love and duty. This principle applies not only to the relations between the members of an individual family as a microcosm, but also as a principle of organization for the entire nation-state, which represented an enlarged family in macrocosm. The principles of Confucianism are contained in four classics composed by Confucius, four classics compiled by his disciples, and various other works, including the Book of Rites (adherence to ritual behaviour being regarded as one of the main sources of character-building and correct moral behaviour). They have also been supplemented by later Confucian philosophers such as Mencius and Hsun-Tzu. Although the Ch'in dynasty attempted to suppress Confucianism, along with all other earlier Chinese traditions, the Han dynasty (which seized power in 206 B.C., after only 14 years of Ch'in rule) reintroduced Confucianism and in 136 B.C. Confucianism was proclaimed the official state religion of China, a national university being established at which all government officials were required to study Confucian and other classical texts. (See CHINESE RELIGION).

CONGO-KORDOFANIAN LANGUAGES, see NIGER-CONGO LANGUAGES.

CONIAGUI, a West African Negroid people of the Tenda group who combine horticulture with some animal husbandry, hunting and food-gathering.

CONIBO, a South American Indian people, who speak a Pano language and live on the upper reaches of the Amazon River, where they are dependent on horticulture, hunting and some fishing and food-gathering.

CONNUBIUM, the term used by the Romans to refer to lawful marriage. All full-born Roman citizens were restricted to specific principles of endogamy, originally being permitted to marry only within the Latin tribes, though the limits of connubium were subsequently extended to include all Italic peoples, while in the later days of Imperial Rome connubium was further extended to include the free residents of all cities which had been given Roman 'citizenship'. With the coming of Christianity, the original concept of connubium was finally destroyed by the total abolition of the principles of endogamy, so that any marriage performed by a church official was regarded as connubium or lawful, no matter how different the national or racial background of the bride and bridegroom might be.

CONSANGUINEAL RELATIONS, persons claiming relationship by common descent from the same ancestor, biological or fictitious, as distinct from persons related by marriage.

CONSONANT, a sound formed by the partial or complete closure of the vocal tract i.e. as in *k* or *b*. The term is used in opposition to that of the vowel, in which no such closure takes place.

CONTAGIOUS MAGIC, magic rooted in the principle that mana (q.v.) may be transmitted by contact.

CONTINENTAL DRIFT, a now more or less established hypothesis that the present continents formerly occupied different positions and were once probably joined together in a single large land mass. This land mass began to break up before 100 million years ago, and the present continents are still shifting at the rate of approximately one inch or more per year. The evidence suggests that North America was formerly joined to Europe and South America to Africa. India broke away from Southeastern Africa, and moved into its present position where it presses against the Asian continent along the line marked by the Himalayas. Australia similarly broke away from the Antarctic mainland to form a separate continent.

CONVERGENCE, the tendency for different living organisms and cultures to develop similar characteristics as a result of independent but parallel or 'convergent' evolution, as distinct from genetic or cultural admixture.

COORG, a Hindu Dravidian people who practice rice cultivation, animal cultivation and some hunting and fishing in the high mountains of the Southern Ghats of Mysore State.

COOS, an Oregon coastal American Indian people, primarily dependent on fishing supplemented by some hunting and food-gathering.

COPE'S LAW, the biological principle that the long term survival of any phylogenetic continuum (q.v.) is dependent upon the degree to which the species develops an ability to respond to environmental changes while avoiding the dead-end of over-specialization.
COPPER, the first metal to be worked extensively by men in the Old World, being found in relatively pure form and requiring no smelting or mineral processing. The earliest copper instruments were manufactured around 4500 B.C. in both the Balkans and the Middle East, and were shaped by hammering. Later the technique of heating the metal until it was molten was developed, and liquid copper was poured into moulds which were broken open after the metal had cooled and hardened in the desired shape. Copper tools, and weapons, were subsequently hardened by alloying the copper with arsenic (and later with tin), to produce bronze. However, as copper and tin were both relatively rare metals, their use was generally restricted to the manufacture of weapons and armour and ornamental jewelry for the warrior nobility, and of ritual utensils for religious purposes. The Neolithic was at first succeeded by a period known as the Chalcolithic or Eneolithic (also written as Aeneolithic), during which stone remained in common use and copper artifacts remained crude and rare, but with improvement in the art of copper smelting, the Chalcolithic emerged as a full Copper Age, which in turn was succeeded by a Bronze Age and an Iron Age. In Europe the Copper Age was closely associated with the Beaker Complex of Western Europe and the Corded Ware culture of Central Europe. The succession from the Chalcolithic to a true Copper Age also appears to be closely associated with the spread of the Indo-European or Aryan peoples throughout Europe.
COPPER ESKIMO, a Canadian Eskimo people who speak an Inuit Eskimo dialect, and who depend mainly on fishing and hunting.
COPTIC, the ritual language of the Coptic Christians of Egypt derives from the Hamitic language of Ancient Egypt. It survived among those Christian Egyptians who kept their own faith following the Islamic conquest of Egypt and who thus avoided Arabization. (See HAMITIC LANGUAGES).
CORACA, the name used to refer to the lower nobility of the Inca empire who were descended not from the Inca clan, but from the ruling families of the various tribes subordinated by the Incas and converted to the worship of the Inca Sun-God. After conversion and re-education, compliant members of the coraca were allocated bureaucratic administrative functions among their own people as agents of the centralized Inca government.
CORACLE, a primitive river craft, made from a circular basketry framework water-proofed with pitch.
CORACORA, a large Tahitian war-canoe.
CORBEL, any protruding block of masonry or wood used in architecture as a support for a roof beam or some other object.
CORBELLED ROOF, a roof somewhat resembling an arch or dome, constructed by successive rows of protruding stones, beams or bricks which finally meet in the middle, thus joining the two walls together in a kind of arch. The best examples of corbelled arches are found in the Mycenean Greek and also in the late Mayan architecture of Central America.
CORDED WARE, a form of pottery ornamented by parallel lines apparently made by binding a length of cord around the clay while the latter was still soft. Corded Ware was commonly found in Central and Eastern Europe in association with battle axes and globular amphorae, and is believed to be associated with the spread of the Indo-European-speaking peoples throughout large areas of Europe.
CORE, the matrix of stone from which flakes may be struck so as to produce a core tool. Alternatively the core is itself sometimes prepared in such a way that a flake struck from the core possesses the desired shape. In such cases the core is usually discarded.
CORE TOOLS, tools manufactured by chipping flakes from a stone core until the core eventually assumes the desired shape.
CORNELIAN, a semi-precious stone of a reddish colour, extensively used for the manufacture of both beads and seals in the Indus Valley civilization.

COROA, a South American Indian people of the Brazilian highlands speaking a Gê language and dependent on horticulture, hunting, food-gathering and fishing.
CORONAL SUTURE, the suture which joins the frontal portion of the cranium to the rear portion.
CORRELATION, COEFFICIENT OF, a measurement indicating the degree of positive or negative correlation measured on a scale of minus 1 to plus 1, with the symbol '0' being used to indicate the absence of any correlation.
CORROBORREE, an Australian social and religious celebration, normally lasting about six weeks. A corroborree is characterized by extensive dancing and other magico-religious rituals, and serves to maintain the bonds of unity between the members of related bands who are separated during the remainder of the year while wandering in pursuit of food.
CORRUGATED POTTERY, coiled pottery common among American Indians of the United States Southwest, the surface of which is not smoothed after finishing. As a result the shape of the coils creates a scalloped effect.
CORTAILLOD, a Neolithic culture named after a site on the edge of Lake Neuchâtel in Switzerland, which revealed evidence of a village constructed on piles above the water of the lake, possibly to provide protection from sudden land attack. Extensive excavations have produced evidence of a rich variety of plants, woods and also of manufactured cloth.
CORVEE, a term of French origin, widely used by anthropologists to refer to any tradition under which the members of a population are required to contribute physically to the construction of roads, fortresses and other public works for a specified number of days each year.
COSMIC TIME, a term used to refer to vast periods of time in which astronomical changes of considerable magnitude may occur, as for example the cooling of the earth, causing it to solidify from an earlier mass of heated gas.
COSMOGONY, the beliefs of any particular society or community concerning the origin and nature of the universe. Thus the Polynesians believed that the world grew out of a cosmic egg, the Egyptians believed that it was created by a master potter, the Babylonians that it originated as a woven fabric, and the Indo-Aryans that it was created through sacrificial rituals. The Babylonian idea is also reflected in Indo-European traditions, as in the Greek Norns who weave the threads of causality. The Hebrews, by contrast, believed that the world was established by a supernatural being with the aid of magical words.
COSSACKS, a term used to refer to the many clans of warlike horsemen of the Russian steppes, who still retained a Scythian-type pastoral life closely associated with early Indo-European social and cultural traditions, as late as the beginning of the present century.
COSSAEAN, one of a supposed Asianic group of languages, formerly spoken in the Zagros mountains between Iraq and Persia.
COSTUME, the first objects worn by men and women on their bodies were probably of purely magico-religious and ornamental significance, taking the form of pubic coverings and necklaces of shells and beads. Clothing as a device for protection against the external climate was a later invention which historically varied according to the climatic conditions and local traditions, the style and quality of clothing also having significance in more complex, stratified societies as a symbol of status. The Cro-Magnon peoples of Upper Paleolithic Europe, and the later steppeland dwellers of central Asia, customarily wore tailored trousers, shirts and shoes cut and stitched from leather. In the warmer climate of the Mediterranean, a straight length of woven cloth, draped around the body, characterized both the Greek and Roman civilizations, while in the still warmer Egyptian and Mesopotamian regions, men and women often wore little more than a skirt tied around the waist. In tropical environments, clothing was seldom made from leather as in the more temperate regions, but from vegetable materials, the grass skirts of the Polynesians being an excellent example of an early type of tropical clothing. Woven clothing evolved as an application of basket making techniques to softer and more flexible vegetable fibers, and only later, in the more temperate climates, was the same technique applied to the weaving of animal fibers, notably wool. Tropical footwear has tended to favour the open sandal made of

wood or leather, held in place by a thong passed between the toes, thus allowing the feet to remain cool, in contrast to the fur-lined and heavy boots worn in Arctic regions.
COTTON, there are two main varieties of cotton in the world, one indigenous to the Americas, the other to the Old World. The cultivation of cotton in the New World appears to have begun in the Tehuacan Valley in Mexico prior to 3000 B.C., while the first evidence for the cultivation of cotton in the Old World is found in the Indus Valley city of Mohenjo-Daro around 2500 B.C.
COUP-DE-POING, a Lower Paleolithic bi-face core tool. Crudely worked, some coup-de-poings were pointed and pear-shaped, others flat and more oval in design.
COUVADE, the practice whereby husbands simulate the birth pains of their wives and/or 'lie in' following the birth of the child. Found among the Amazonian tribes and formerly present among some Mediterranean peoples.
COWICHAN, a coastal Salish Northwest American Indian people, whose language belongs to the Mosan division of the Algonquin-Mosan phylum and who are dependent primarily on fishing with some hunting and food-gathering.
COWRIE, a form of spiral shell widely valued in many societies and imported into Europe in classical times from the area of the Red Sea. Cowrie shells survived as a symbol of value and as a medium of exchange into recent times in East Africa and in the Maldive Isles, south of India.
CRANIAL CAPACITY, the cubic capacity of the cranial cavity – an indication of the size of the brain. While the size of the brain is not itself a direct indicator of mental development (larger animals often having larger brains) and the evolution of the human brain depends mainly upon the increasing size of particular areas such as the frontal lobes and the cerebral cortex, nevertheless the evolution of the hominids – of man's ancestors – reveals a steady increase in cranial capacity from around 500 c.c. in Australopithecus to 1275 c.c. in living Australoid males and an average of 1475 c.c. in living Caucasoid males.
CRANIAL INDEX, the length of the skull, measured from the glabella to the occipital, in relation to its width. The breadth is multiplied by 100 and divided by the length.
CRANNOG, artificial island dwelling in Ireland, constructed from wood, peat and stones, and often protected by a wooden palisade. Each appears to have constituted a single, large homestead, probably inhabited by the members of an extended family.
CRAZY HORSE, a term used by a number of American Plains Indians to refer to any person who failed to follow the traditional customs of community life.
CREE, Canadian Indians of the sub-Arctic Hudson Bay area.
CREEK, North American Southern Woodland Indians, speaking a Muskogean language largely dependent on horticulture with hunting, fishing and food-gathering.
CREMATION, the destruction of a corpse by fire as an alternative to inhumation or burial (q.v.), or exposure (q.v.), in which latter instance birds of prey and wild beasts are allowed to destroy the flesh and pick the bones. In some societies cremation was favoured because it completely destroyed the body and thus prevented the possibility of ghosts haunting the living, while in other cases it was believed that the smoke rising skywards would carry the souls of the beloved departed to a heavenly abode.
CREOLIZATION, Creolization usually takes place, producing a Creole language, under conditions of colonial settlement, when linguistic drift (q.v.) differentiates the colonial form of the language from that of the parent peoples. Considerable hybridization or word-borrowing may also contribute to the further modification of the colonial form. (See PIDGIN ENGLISH).
CRETACEOUS, a geological period within the Mesozoic era which lasted from approximately 136 to 65 million years ago.
CRITICAL RITES, rituals held only at a time of crisis, designed to attract supernatural aid by magical or religious means.
CRO-MAGNON, a shelter site near Les Eyzies in the Dordogne region of south-

Western France excavated in 1868 which revealed some fine skeletons including the 'old man of Cro-Magnon', the name Cro-Magnon having subsequently been used to refer to the wide assemblage of Homo sapiens sapiens who appear to have occupied most of Europe and a large part of Western Asia from approximately 35,000 B.P. onwards, and to represent the ancestors of the modern Caucasoids. The remains were found by Louis Lartet in 1868 in association with Aurignacian tools.

CROMLECH, a term normally used to indicate a Megalithic circle of standing stones or menhirs (q.v.), but also used in Wales to refer to Megalithic chamber tombs.

CROSS, an ancient sun symbol which appears to have originated in the Upper Paleolithic and to have spread widely throughout Asia and India during Mesolithic and subsequent eras. The Christian cross is an imitation of the old European sun symbol, already held in reverence in pagan times. Christ died on a T-shaped structure, commonly used by Romans for the execution of petty thieves and criminals. The later Christian Church merely added an upper arm to the T, so as to be able to claim the ancient and revered sun cross as a Christian emblem.

CROSS-BOW, a type of bow, mounted at right angles on a stock in such a way that when the string is released the arrow or bolt will pass along a groove on the stock and so travel accurately in the direction of its target. The later type of Medieval cross-bow was frequently made of metal, a crank being used to make it possible to pull the string extremely taut, thereby providing sufficient additional power to enable the bolt to penetrate body armour.

CROSS COUSIN, the father's sister's or mother's brother's children.

CROSS-DATING, an attempt to establish the date of a particular geological stratum or site by the comparison of artifacts with those from other sites.

CROSSING OVER, a term used to refer to the exchange of genetic material between two homologous chromosomes by way of the chiasmata (q.v.) during the process of cell division.

CROW, Siouan-speaking North American Plains Indians of the Upper Missouri valley, primarily dependent on hunting with some food-gathering.

CROWD, a temporary gathering of people brought into a collective behavior pattern by identical excitatory stimuli, as distinct from a social group.

CRUCIBLE, a small vessel in which molten metal is smelted before casting.

CRUSTACEA, a class of invertebrates which includes lice and lobsters.

CUBEO, a South American Indian people who speak a Tucanoan language probably related to the Arawak language, and who are dependent on horticulture, fishing and some hunting and gathering.

CUCUTENI, a Chalcolithic variant of the Old European civilization (q.v.) the Cucuteni culture extended from Romania across Bessarabia into the Ukraine as far east as present-day Kiev. Succeeding the earlier Neolithic Dniester-Bug culture around 4800 B.C., the Cucuteni culture lasted until overrun by Indo-Europeans from the neighboring Pontic steppes around 3500 B.C.

CULT, a system of rituals or a group of persons centering upon specific sacred symbols, wherein participation tends to be individualistic or involves only a part of the community. Cults differ from religions in that they do not serve to bind the entire community tighter by the unifying bonds of common veneration and worship.

CULTIVATION, the history of the cultivation of the soil to produce fruit, grain, cereal, root and other crops should be properly divided into distinct though to some extent overlapping categories, horticulture (q.v.) and agriculture (q.v.). The first of these, namely horticulture, implies the absence of any knowledge of the refertilization of the soil or even of crop rotation, and the surface of the ground is usually only broken to a shallow extent with the use of hand tools. Horticulturalists are therefore usually shifting cultivators, obliged to move their fields every two or three years after exhausting the soil. By contrast, agriculture reflects a more sophisticated technology, implying some knowledge of methods of refertilization of the soil by the use of manure or by the rotation of crops, and often includes techniques of irrigation, drainage and the use of an animal-drawn plow, which makes possible the exploitation of heavier but richer alluvial soils. The cultivation of crops may also be accompanied by a pattern of mixed farming employing the domestication of animals. The appearance of horticulture is generally associated with the Neolithic stage of cultural evolution first occurring in an area extending from the Danube Valley in Europe and the valleys of the Zagros Mountains in Western Persia. To what extent the idea of cultivation spread outwards from a common Balkan, Aegean, Anatolian and Zagros area of origin, to reach the Indus Valley, the Nile, Africa and Northern China is still not fully known, and the possibility of the separate invention of cultivation in Southeast Asia, America and Africa remains plausible and is generally accepted in the case of the Americas. Wheat and barley appear to have originated in the Middle East; oats and rye in Europe; millet and rice in Asia; and sorghum in Africa. (See HORTICULTURAL SOCIETIES).

CULTS OF THE DEAD, the term 'cult of the dead' is generally applied in a loose fashion to distinguish practices, probably first evolved among Neanderthal men, which are rooted in fear of the dead or of the malice of the dead, from those more dignified cults which imply reverence rather than fear and which are more properly described as ancestor worship (q.v.). Ancestor worship appears when the ancestral spirits are held in reverence and are believed to assist their living descendants, requiring that the descendants maintain cooperative and loyal relations with each other and obey the ancient customs and ritual prescriptions. In a sense, ancestor worship exemplifies the Durkheimian concept of religion more exactly than any other kind of religious system, whereas cults of the dead are magical systems rather than true religions.

CULTURAL DIFFUSION, the dissemination of the traits of one culture among those who possess a different culture, involving the geographical transmission of culture as distinct from cultural heredity (q.v.).

CULTURAL EVOLUTION, UNILINEAL, a term usually applied to 19th century concepts of cultural evolution, which assumed that all cultures were in effect advancing up a single evolutionary ladder, some simply being at different stages of advancement in comparison to others. The American anthropologist, Morgan in particular popularized the theory that human history could be divided into three essential stages ranging from savagery through barbarism to civilization. The ideas of Morgan heavily influenced those of Marx and Engels, and the British archeologist V. Gordon Childe made extensive use of these three stages, defining savagery as being associated with a pre-Neolithic culture; barbarism with a Neolithic food-producing or herding society which lacked a written language; and civilization with urban communities possessing a written language.

CULTURAL HEREDITY, the dissemination of cultural traits from one generation to another within the same society.

CULTURAL MATERIALISM, the theory that cultural behavior is determined solely by economic forces. Favored by Marxists.

CULTURAL PLURALISM, the existence of a variety of diverse culture and/or ethnic groups within the framework of a large society.

CULTURAL RELATIVISM, the anthropological doctrine that people's values are primarily the product of their social and cultural environment, and that their ideas of right and wrong will therefore reflect the normative systems characteristic of their own culture. According to cultural relativism, culture therefore determines the rightness and wrongness of actions, and there is no external set of values which applies to all societies.

CULTURE, that complex whole which includes knowledge, belief, art, morals, law, custom, and any other capabilities acquired by man as a member of society.

CULTURE AREA, a geographical area in which a distinctive set of cultural traits tend to predominate.

CULTURE COMPLEX, an integrated, functional group of interacting culture traits, commonly found together. Several different societies occupying the same culture area will usually share a basically common culture complex, as in the cattle herding societies of East Africa.

CULTURE CONFLICT, the rivalry of two conflicting cultures or subcultures

within the same society and the tension created by this mental conflict.
CULTURE, IDEAL, the normative patterns of behaviour as described by the members of a society. (See also CULTURE, REAL).
CULTURE PATTERN, a set of cultural traits that tend to be found together.
CULTURE, REAL, patterns of actual behavior as distinct from the ideal culture of the society as defined above. (See CULTURE, IDEAL).
CULTURE SHOCK, the reaction experienced by an individual who finds himself suddenly confronted by an unfamiliar cultural system which differs sharply from that into which he has been enculturated.
CUMANA, South American Carib Indians of the mainland, opposite Trinidad.
CUNA, an American Indian people of Panama, who speak a Chibchan language and are largely dependent on horticulture and fishing supplemented by some hunting.
CUNEIFORM, an early form of writing which developed in Mesopotamia in the 3rd millennium B.C., appearing to have evolved from an earlier pictographic script in which ideas were represented by simplified pictures. The term cuneiform implies something wedge-shaped, and refers to the fact that the writing takes the form of incisions, made with a wooden wedge, on the surface of tablets of smooth damp clay, which were later baked to make them hard and so preserve the written documents permanently.
CUPENO, a Shoshone (Uto-Aztec)-speaking American Indian people of Southeastern California, dependent on food-gathering and hunting.
CUPOLA, a rounded vault or dome forming the roof of a building or part of a building.
CURDLING, a process which takes place when milk is allowed to stand until bacillae have caused the curds to separate from the whey. Many agricultural and pastoral peoples deliberately allow milk to curdle to produce a variety of different milk products.
CURING, even early Paleolithic societies probably made use of animal skins. However, without treatment, animal skins tend to become stiff and useless. Many of the simpler peoples merely chew the skins regularly in order to keep them pliable, but others have learned to apply animal fats to the skin not only to keep them pliable but also to make them water-resistant. (See TANNING).
CURIPACO, a South American Indian people who live in Southern Venezuela and speak an Arawak language, subsisting on horticulture supplemented by some hunting and fishing.
CUSHITIC LANGUAGES, a branch of the Hamitic family (q.v.) of languages, mainly represented today by Somali and Galla, which has also influenced the Southern Nilotic languages spoken by the predominantly Negroid people who are their neighbors to the west and south, and who were probably once dominated by Cushitic elements, or else represent a Cushitic people who were genetically absorbed by the indigenous Negroid population. The Cushites were probably formerly a cattle-herding people of Mediterranean Caucasoid origin, but during the course of the last two millennia they absorbed considerable Negro and aboriginal Bushman-type genetic influences. Other Cushitic languages are Konso, Kafa, and Banna.
CUSP, one of the high points of the crown of a tooth, which plays a leading role in the process of mastication.
CUZCO, the capital city of the Incas situated in the mountains of Peru.
CYBELE, a Phrygian goddess who appears to have reflected the widespread Mediterranean and Middle Eastern tradition of an Earth Mother (q.v.) symbolizing fertility and regarded as the mother of all nature. In later Hellenistic times, rituals in honor of Cybele developed an orgiastic character, some of the devotees castrating themselves in her honour.
CYCLOPEAN MASONRY, masonry walls constructed of extremely large but close-fitting stones of irregular shape. The term derives from the fact that the walls of the Mycenean city of Tiryns were made of such large fitted stones that subsequent Greek myths asserted that they had been erected by the one-eyed but supernaturally powerful Cyclops. Cyclopean masonry is found at other

sites in the Mediterranean and in certain of the South American Inca structures.
CYRUS THE GREAT, an Aryan Persian king who overthrew the Medes in 550 B.C. Locating his fortified palace capital at Pasargarde, Cyrus successfully extended the Persian empire from the Indus to the Aegean and the frontiers of Egypt. As founder of the Achaemenid dynasty, he accepted Zoroastrianism but still worshipped his own Aryan ancestral and household spirits and showed great tolerance towards local cultures and religions, in marked contrast to the despotic attempts by the Semitic Assyrians and Chaldaeans to impose their own monotheistic god upon the peoples they conquered.
CYTOPLASM, that part of the protoplasm which is situated outside the nucleus of a cell. The cytoplasm contains the ribosomes or minute organelles in which protein synthesis occurs.
CZARNOBOG, a Slavic evil spirit, somewhat resembling the Zoroastrian concept of Ahriman.
CZECHS, a West Slavic Caucasoid people, traditionally dependent on agriculture and animal husbandry, who today maintain a heavily industrialized society.

D

DABARKOT, an archeological tell site in Northern Beluchistan, believed to have had importance as a trading post linking the Indus Valley civilization with the highly developed civilizations of Iran.
DAEVA, a term originally used by the pre-Zoroastrians to designate the members of the Aryan Pantheon of gods. Most of these were subsequently demoted under the influence of Zoroastrianism to the level of evil spirits, so that in Zoroastrian literature the term *daeva* is used to signify a malignant spirit rather than a god.
DAHOMEANS, a West African people who established a major conquest empire, managed by a complete bureaucracy and a powerful priesthood, the economic basis of which was slavery and slave-trading. The Dahomean religion was rooted in human sacrifice, and hundreds of slaves and prisoners of war were sacrificed annually in honour of the royal ancestors.
DAHUNI, a Melanesian (Malayo-Polynesian) people largely dependent on horticulture, fishing and some animal husbandry.
DAJMMAPADA, literally translated as 'the Path to Virtue', the Dajmmapada comprises one of the major texts of the Buddhist religion.
DAKOTA, North American Plains Indians. The Dakota were divided into the Yankton, Santee and Tetons.
DALRIADA, a kingdom established by King Fergus, who led an invading army of Scots from Ireland to seize what is today the county of Argyle in Scotland from the aboriginal Picts. The Picts appear to have been a pre-Indo-European Atlanto-Mediterranean people, whereas the Scots who invaded the Pictish lands from Northern Ireland, and subsequently gave their name to the whole of present-day 'Scotland', were Goidelic-speaking Celts.
DAN, West African horticulturalists of the Guinea Coast.
DANAKIL, an East African people (otherwise known as Afar) occupying the Djibuti area.
DANU, the Celtic goddess of knowledge.
DANUBIAN CULTURE, an important farming culture of Central Europe, which had its roots in the Old European civilization (q.v.). During the earliest levels of the Danubian I stage, in the 6th millennium B.C., slash-and-burn techniques of cultivation were applied, and Bandkeramik pottery was common. At this time the Danubian farmers appeared to live in extended families, several nuclear families occupying a large wooden longhouse. During the early 4th millennium, more sophisticated forms of regular agriculture appeared with the Danubian II culture, which is customarily divided into various subcultures, such as the Rössen, Lengyel, and Tisza, and evidence of the existence of a characteristic Indo-European ruling class became apparent circa 3500 B.C.

DARASA, a Cushitic people of East Africa, related to the Sidamo and dependent on horticulture and hunting.

DARDS, an Indo-European-speaking Indic people, dependent on agriculture and animal husbandry.

DARIUS I, (521-486 B.C.), a powerful king of the Achaemenid Persian dynasty, responsible for the rock inscription at Behistan, and for the removal of the royal capital from Pasargardae to Persepolis.

DASYUS, in Vedic mythology the Dasyus were a dark-skinned aboriginal Indian people who were defeated by the invading Indo-Aryans led by Indra. As a result of this conquest, the term Dasyus became synonymous with 'life-long slave', and was adopted as the caste label for the lowest level in the Aryan caste system. (See HINTU CASTE SYSTEM)

DATING, ABSOLUTE, dating of an artifact or fossil by radiocarbon or any other method which establishes an approximate age without reference to stratigraphy or to other objects found with the item.

DATING, RELATIVE, dating by reference to other artifacts or fossils associated with the object by location or similarity of designs, the age of which has been determined.

DATING SYSTEMS, systematic techniques for determining the approximate age of a fossil or artifact. A considerable variety of scientific dating systems have been developed by archeologists. These fall into two main categories: Absolute Dating, where the approximate age of a fossil or artifact is determined by scientific means (as, for example, radiocarbon or uranium dating), and Relative Dating, where dating is attempted by reference to other artifacts or fossils associated with the object by location or similarity of type or design. (See AMINO-ACID DATING, FLUORINE TESTING, GEOCHRONOLOGY, OBSIDIAN HYDRATION DATING, PALYNOLOGY, POTASSIUM-ARGON DATING, RADIOCARBON DATING, STRATIGRAPHY, THERMOLUMINESCENCE, and VARVE COUNTING).

DAUB, a building material comprising a semi-liquid mixture of clay which is smeared onto a framework of interwoven wooden branches, known as wattle. The expression 'wattle-and-daub' is also common.

DEAD LANGUAGE, a language which is no longer spoken in everyday life by the members of a distinct community or society, and which survives only in writing, in ritual, or as a subject of study by scholars.

DEAD SEA SCROLLS, a number of texts recovered from caves near the site of an ancient Essene monastery at Qumran, where they had been hidden to prevent their discovery by the Romans at the time of the Roman suppression of the Hebraic rebellion and the destruction of the Hebrew temple and other symbols of the traditional Hebraic religion. These texts contain much information about the religion of the Essenes, an important monastic sect of Hebrews whose ideas exerted extensive influence upon the origins and development of Christianity.

DECUMANUS MAXIMUS, all Roman military camps and many Roman towns were customarily laid out on a rectangular plan, similar to that which had been used by the Villanovian ancestors of the Latin peoples. This comprised a main meeting place or *Forum* (q.v.) at the center of the main street or *Decumanus Maximus,* surrounded by a regular grid-like pattern of lesser streets, the entire settlement being enclosed within a defensive wall.

DELAWARE, North American Woodland Indians. Living adjacent to the Middle Atlantic Coast, and speaking an Algonquin language, the Delaware were largely dependent on horticulture with hunting, fishing and food-gathering.

DELIM, Semitic-speaking Bedouin Arabs of North Africa, mainly dependent on horticulture and fishing.

DELPHI, a Greek city located in Phocis, Greece, famous for its temple of Apollo. Here the Delphic oracle was consulted by supplicants from all parts of Greece and the Eastern Mediterranean.

DELTA, NILE, an extensive tract of flat alluvial land arising from the continuous deposit of silt from the water of the river Nile. This rich area constituted the centre of Lower Egypt, and to this day reveals a marked contrast in culture and appearance from the more narrow cultivated strips of floodland extending along the upper reaches of the Nile, which formerly constituted the kingdom of Upper Egypt.

DEME, a predominantly inbreeding local population.

DEMETER, known to the Romans as Ceres, Demeter was a Greek corn goddess whose daughter Persephone was carried off by Hades, the god of the underworld (known as Pluto to the Romans). At Demeter's request, Zeus (known to the Romans as Jupiter) ordered Hades to return Persephone to her mother, but because Persephone had been persuaded to eat a small quantity of food in Hades she was subsequently obliged to spend half of each year underground. Her annual return to the earth explained the rebirth of life in Spring and Summer, while her return to the underworld in Autumn and Winter completed the cycle of the seasons.

DEMOGRAPHY, the statistical analysis and description of population aggregates with reference to distribution and vital statistics such as age, sex, race, and social status.

DEMOTIC SCRIPT, a form of cursive writing which developed in ancient Egypt, for primarily commercial and non-religious use, while the original hieroglyphs from which it evolved were retained for sacred purposes. The demotic script first appeared around the 7th century B.C., and was one of the three different scripts used on the famous Rosetta Stone (q.v.).

DENDROCHRONOLOGY, a method of dating wooden artifacts by the analysis of tree rings. With each year of growth an additional layer of wood is added to the circumference of a tree, the thickness of this layer of growth varying according to the climatic conditions of the year. In certain parts of the world, notably the southwestern United States, Alaska and Scandinavia, it has been possible to compile complete records of tree ring growth, which, in the case of the ancient California pines, go back as far as 6500 years, by examining the size of the annual rings and counting the number of successive layers. In such areas, where pieces of wood are recovered from archeological sites, the pattern of rings on such timber can be matched against the master charts, enabling the dendrochronologist to determine the date at which the tree lived.

DENDROGRAM, a term used to refer to a diagramatic 'evolutionary tree' tracing the branching of a phylogenetic continuum into different subspecies and species.

DEOXYRIBONUCLEIC ACID (DNA), an organic substance which has the power to reproduce itself and is therefore fundamental to the survival of life.

DERMATOGLYPHIC MARKINGS, the pattern of ridges which occur on the surface of the skin of the fingers, toes, palms and soles of primates. Certain New World primates, which use the tail for grasping, even possess dermatoglyphic markings on the tip of the tail.

DESCENT, BILATERAL, a descent system which reckons kinship equally through both parents, resulting in the formation of kindreds instead of clans.

DESCENT, BILINEAL (also DUOLINEAL DESCENT), the custom of recognizing a dual system of descent groups in which the individual inherits certain functions and responsibilities through his father's line, and other functions and responsibilities through his mother's line. Each individual is, in fact, a member of two separate clans or lineages: one traced through the male ancestors; the other through the female ancestors.

DESCENT, UNILINEAL, a method of tracing kinship or inheritance through either the father's male ancestry or the mother's female ancestry.

DESCRIPTIVE KINSHIP SYSTEM, ideally, a system of kinship terminology in which there is a distinctive form of address for each individual kinsman.

DESERT CULTURE, a style of nomadic hunting and gathering life, practised by American Indians from Oregon to California and also in parts of Northern Mexico, the first evidence of which dates from around 8000 B.C. Considerable use was made of spear throwers for hunting and of the digging stick for extracting edible roots from the ground. From the 3rd century B.C. onwards, the

Desert Culture tended to be replaced by horticultural techniques and a more sedentary pattern of life, but survived among the Utes and Paiutes until recent times.

DETERMINISM, the belief that chance (and hence free will) does not exist in the universe and that all events result from natural 'laws' or 'sufficient cause'.

DEVA, the term Deva was used by the Indo-Iranian Aryans who invaded India collectively to refer to any of the Aryan gods, but among the Indo-Iranians of Iran, the influence of the Magi caused the old Aryan Deva gods to be portrayed as evil spirits following the rise of the Zoroastrian religion, and converts to Zoroastrianism were required to renounce the *daeva* (q.v.).

DEVIL WORSHIPPERS, a Middle Eastern cult, found among the Yezidis, who claim to be directly descended from Adam rather than from Adam and Eve like the rest of mankind. Deriving their principles from a combination of Zoroastrian, Jewish, Manichean, and Muslim traditions, the Yezidis believe that there is a supreme deity who does not take part in everyday management of the world, having delegated such matters to a number of sub-deities, who may consequently be worshipped instead of the supreme deity. (See also DEVA and DAEVA).

DEVONIAN, a geological period within the Paleozoic which lasted from approximately 395 to 345 million years ago, and was associated with a series of dry periods in which the first amphibians are believed to have appeared on dry land.

DIABETES, a disease caused by the inability of the body to synthesize sufficient quantities of insulin.

DIACRITICAL SYMBOLS, marks or symbols written over or below or across a letter to indicate how the letter should be pronounced or intoned.

DIAGUITA, a South American Indian Monde-speaking people of Central Chile, living immediately north of the Araucanians.

DIALECT, a regular pattern of variations within a language, usually restricted to a particular locality or racial group.

DIALECT GEOGRAPHY, the recording, charting and analysis of local dialects and other minor differentiations within a given speech area.

DIBA, see HAT, CONICAL.

DIBBLE, a digging stick. The dibble may be used by hunting and gathering peoples for digging roots, or by primitive horticulturalists for making holes in the ground into which seeds may be planted.

DIDINGA, a Negroid Niloic-speaking people of the Beir-Didinga group, primarily dependent on cattle-herding and horticulture with some hunting.

DIEGUENO, an American Indian people from Baja California, who speak a Hokan language of the Yuman group and are dependent on food-gathering, hunting and some fishing.

DIERI, an Australian aboriginal people from Central Australia, dependent wholly on food-gathering and hunting.

DIFFUSION, a term used to refer to the spread of cultural traits from one society to another. The diffusion of culture can take place as a result of contact between different peoples through commerce or even war. The 'diffusionist' school of anthropology possibly overemphasized the importance of diffusion, by disregarding the fact that many ideas spread geographically as a result of the migration of entire peoples who carried their culture with them. For example, it would be impossible to explain the transition from the Stone Age to the contemporary advanced agricultural and industrial society of North America by the concept of diffusion, since this transition was accomplished as a result of a vast migration of Europeans who brought their culture with them to the Americas. Although the spread of many cultural traits can be accomplished by diffusion, the spread of cultural traits is more frequently brought about by migration, by conquest, or by the commercial activities of craftsmen and merchants.

DIGGER INDIANS, a term which was used by the earlier white travellers and settlers to describe those American Indians, such as the Paiute, who depended largely upon a diet of root crops extracted from the ground with the aid of digging sticks.

DIGGING STICK, a simple stick, generally sharpened at one end, which is used to break the surface of the ground. Primarily utilized by food-gatherers to uncover roots and small burrowing animals that live underground, the digging stick survived in many simple horticultural communities as a method of planting seeds, except where displaced by the more efficient hoe, which in turn was supplanted in Europe and other agricultural societies by the animal-drawn plow.

DIGO, a Bantu-speaking Negroid people of the Nyika group, largely dependent on horticulture and fishing.

DIKE, the Greek goddess of justice, who represented natural order.

DILLING, a Nubian people who are largely dependent on horticulture, with some animal husbandry and hunting and food-gathering.

DILMUN, the Sumerian land of immortality, described in the epic of Gilgamesh as 'the Garden of the Gods'.

DIMORPHISM, SEXUAL, morphological differences between the sexes. These differences are much more marked among non-human anthropoid and hominoid fossils than among modern hominids.

DINARIC, a term customarily used to refer to a variant of the Caucasoid stock, localized in the Balkan area and parts of the Middle East, and generally characterized by a high degree of brachycephalization and prominent convex nose formation. Used interchangeably with 'Armenoid' by some writers.

DINKA, a Negroid Nilotic-speaking people, primarily dependent on cattle-herding supplemented by some horticulture and hunting.

DIOLA, a West African Negroid people of Guinea, who combine horticulture with fishing and animal husbandry.

DIONYSIAN CULTURE, a term invented by Ruth Benedict to refer to cultures which encouraged the individual to indulge in sensuous self-expression. (See also APOLLONIAN CULTURE).

DIONYSIAN MYSTERIES, an orgiastic cult, originating in Anatolia, which spread throughout the Hellenistic and later Roman world, being particularly popular among the non-Patrician classes of ancient Rome. (See DIONYSUS).

DIONYSUS, the cult of Dionysus probably originated in the Old European civilization as a fertility god worshipped in the form of a bull with orgiastic rites until the invading Indo-European Greeks associated Dionysus with Apollo. Although the Greeks adopted Dionysus into their pantheon during Homeric and Classical times, the orgiastic aspects of Dionysus are little mentioned until, with the declining power of the Indo-European aristocracy, they resurfaced among the artisans and slaves of late Classical and Hellenistic Greece.

DIPLOID, the normal condition of a nucleus in which it possesses a pair of homologous chromosomes (q.v.). The diploid condition is characteristic of all animal cells except the gametes (q.v.) which are haploid (q.v.).

DIPLOID NUMBER, the characteristic chromosome number of the zygote of a species.

DIS, a transcendental Celtic god believed to be the ancestor of all the Gauls.

DISCORDANCE, a term used to refer to distinctive phenotypical traits which distinguish two individuals from each other.

DISES (also DISAR), the 'fates' of the Norse pantheon, major goddesses identified with the Greek Norns. Representing the causal flow of events from the past, through the present, into the future, the Dises are remembered in later folktales as the wise women who foretell the destiny of children shortly after their birth and as the three witches of Macbeth. (See NORNS).

DISTRIBUTION MAP, archeology is not concerned only with the excavation of individual sites, but must also seek to interpret the evidence which such excavations uncover. One of the major aids to the interpretation of archeological data is the distribution map, on which the frequency, occurrence and location of individual traits, such as the occurrence of distinct types of pottery, can be plotted.

DIULA, a Negroid, West African Mande-speaking people of the Marka group, primarily dependent on horticulture with some animal husbandry, hunting and food-gathering.

DIVINATION, any attempt to foretell the future, to discover hidden knowledge, or to discern the wishes of supernatural beings.
DIZYGOTIC TWINS, otherwise known as 'fraternal twins', dizygotic twins are formed from two separately fertilized ova, and although born at the same time are likely to be as genetically different from each other as any other pair of siblings born to the same parents.
DJANGGAWUL, the title given to three ancestral spirits worshipped by the Australian aborigines of Arnhemland in Northern Australia. Believed to be ancestral to all the Australian peoples of Arnhemland, the djanggawul comprised two sisters and their brother, who migrated from a mythical island to the North-east of Arnhemland to which the spirits of their descendants return after death. The djanggawul may reflect the memory of an early Australoid migration from the Indonesian area.
DNA, see DEOXYRIBONUCLEIC ACID.
DNIESTER-BUG, see TRIPOLYE.
DOBUANS, a Melanesian (Malayo-Polynesian) people, largely dependent on horticulture, fishing and some animal husbandry.
DOG, the first member of the animal species to be domesticated, probably from jackals or wolves. The remains of domesticated dogs are found at the Mesolithic settlement at Star Carr in Northern Europe, and are dated from the earlier part of the 8th millennium B.C. The circumstances under which the domestication of the dog took place are unknown, although it is possible that human hunters may have followed packs of wolves and then attempted to seize the quarry after it had been cornered by the wolves, allowing the latter to return to consume the unwanted parts of the corpse. Alternatively, wolves might tend to congregate around human settlements to scavenge for food in the garbage heaps outside the village. In either case, those animals most antagonistic to men were likely to be killed, so that as a result of a process of unintentional selection, a breed of domesticated dogs would evolve, bred from successive generations of those animals which had been least aggressive towards human beings.
DOGON, a Negroid West African Voltaic people, largely dependent on horticulture with some animal husbandry and food-gathering.
DOGRIB, a Northeastern Athabascan American Indian people, dependent on hunting, fishing and food-gathering.
DOLICHOCEPHALIC, a condition in which the breadth of the skull is less than 76 percent of its length.
DOLMEN, Megalithic (q.v.) stone chamber tombs, dating from the Neolithic and early Bronze Ages.
DOLNÍ VESTONICE, a site in Moravia which has produced a variety of Gravettian tools and ornaments made from mammoth ivory (dated from circa 25,000 B.C.). There are a considerable number of baked clay figurines of animals and especially broad-hipped, obese and large-breasted female 'Venus' figurines with stylized heads. These may reflect the ancient origins of the cult of the Great Mother goddess (q.v.), well-established in later Neolithic Europe.
DOMINANCE, a tendency, common in primate societies, in which one animal tends to dominate certain other animals within the same group.
DOMINANCE, GENETIC, the term used in Mendelian genetics to refer to alleles which express themselves in the phenotype of heterozygous (q.v.) individuals, thus masking the effect of the recessive genes (q.v.).
DOMOJOV, the name of the ancestral spirits formerly believed to protect every Slavic household.
DOROBO, a Nilotic African people, primarily dependent on hunting and food-gathering.
DORSET CULTURE, a Canadian and Greenland Eskimo Stone Age culture which persisted from 800 B.C. until A.D. 1300, being progressively replaced by the Thule culture (q.v.) from A.D. 900 onwards.
DOUBLE AXE, an axe with two cutting edges, one on each side of the central shaft hole to which the haft is fixed. Although stone examples are rare, copper and bronze double axes were particularly common among the Minoans, among

whom they appear to have had a religious significance. (See KNOSSOS).

DOUBLE DESCENT, see DESCENT, BILINEAL.

DOWRY, property transferred to the bride or to the groom by the bride's relatives at the time of marriage.

DRAGONS, good-natured creatures, and the bringers of rain and good fortune in the mythology of the Chinese. However, dragons are evil serpents in Indo-European mythology, where they are frequently slain by heroes (c.f. Beowulf, Siegfried, St. George), and the Midgard-dragon takes part in the assault upon the Gods in the last battle of Ragnorak.

DRAVIDIAN LANGUAGES, an important family of languages surviving in Southern India, which appear to have been spoken over much of the Indian subcontinent before the arrival of the Indo-Aryans. The surviving Dravidian languages include Tamil, Telugu, Malayalam and Kannarese, all spoken in the southern portion of the Indian peninsula. Oraon and Gondi spoken to the north of the other Dravidian languages are also identified as Dravidian, while Brahui, spoken in a remote area of Beluchistan to the west of the Indus river offers possible testimony to the former geographical extent of the Dravidian language family. Whether the population of the Indus Valley civilization originally spoke a Dravidian language is unknown, since the script has not yet been deciphered.

DRAVIDIANS, the Dravidians of Southern India are pre-Indo-European in origin and many still practice animistic religions and speak Dravidian languages. Representing the remnants of an earlier Asiatic Australoid population, they still reveal Australoid physical characteristics particularly among the Toda, Gond, Coorg and Chenchu. (See also DRAVIDIAN LANGUAGES).

DREAM INTERPRETATION, a great many societies place considerable importance upon the interpretation of dreams, and the Bantu of South Africa even believe that the dream-life brings the human soul into contact with the supernatural world, and that dreams are more significant than waking experiences, since the supernatural world is more real than the mortal world.

DREAM-TIME, prior to the arrival of the Europeans, the Australian aboriginals lacked any system for counting beyond the number 5, and consequently had no concept of history. All that happened in the distant past was believed to belong to the 'dream time' – that vaguely remembered past, the recall of which seemed analogous to the recall of a dream – during which the heroic ancestors were believed to have achieved great wonders, creating hills, rivers and sacred groves.

DRILL, BOW, a form of drill, operated by the simple method of twisting a bow string around the drilling stick, and then moving the bow backwards and forwards. Bow drilling was used to make holes in bone, ivory, and even stone.

DRUIDS, the organized Celtic priesthood which appears to have been strong among both the Goidelic and the Brythonic Celts. Since the Celts were closely related to the Romans, the Celtic pantheon was parallel to that of the Romans, and like the Roman *flamen* the Druids were responsible for supervision of religious ritual, under the ultimate direction of the divinely-descended Celtic kings. Some Druids specialized in divination, others were lawmen, who memorized the ancient customs, and others, known as the bardi, or bards, memorized the epic deeds of the ancestral heroes. As defenders of the social, legal and religious traditions of the Celtic peoples, the Druids provided the backbone of Celtic opposition to Roman military and cultural expansion, and were therefore deliberately exterminated by the Romans as part of the 'pacification' program introduced into Gaul, Britain, Iberia and other Celtic lands following the victory of the Roman legions. (See also CELTS).

DRUZE, a Semitic sedentary Arabic (Caucasoid) people, localized near Mount Carmel in Israel and dependent almost entirely on cultivation.

DRYADS, the term used in Greek and Roman mythology to refer to the nymphs or spirits of the forest.

DRYOPITHECINAE, an anthropoid subfamily which embraced most varieties of nonhominid Hominoidea living in the Miocene and Pliocene. 'Proconsul' is now regarded as being a Dryopithecine.

DUALA, a Bantu-speaking Negroid people of the Biafra coastal region, dependent mainly on horticulture, animal husbandry and some fishing.
DUN, a Celtic word originally signifying a hillfort, but which survived into later usage in Scotland and Ireland to refer to any fortified household or castle.
DURUMA, a Bantu-speaking Negroid people of the Nyika group, largely dependent on horticulture and fishing.
DUSUN, a Malayo-Polynesian-speaking people from Borneo, largely dependent on cultivation, animal husbandry and fishing.
DUTCH, (cognate with German *Deutsch*) a Nordic Caucasoid people of 'Low' or West German speech, the Dutch and neighboring Frisians are predominantly Nordic, although some remnants of an earlier broad-headed Alpine population survive in the formerly marshy regions at the mouth of the Rhine.
DWARFS, Germanic, Celtic and Slavic mythology portrays dwarfs as a short, round-headed people, skilled in the art of metal-working and magic, especially in the manufacture of jewelry (such as Brisingamen – the necklace of Freya) and weapons (Gungnir – the sword of Odin). It has been suggested that they reflect a memory of the Alpine peoples of Central Europe, who were skilled in the art of working bronze and precious metals from an early date. The relationship between 'black' dwarfs, who lived underground in Swartheim, and elves, who lived aboveground, is unclear. (See SWARTHEIM).
DYAK, a Malayo-Polynesian-speaking horticultural people of Borneo.
DYKE, a form of linear earth work comprising a bank and a ditch. Dykes were often constructed as boundary markers, but also in other cases as defense structures, providing an effective obstacle against the use of chariots and other wheeled vehicles. One of the most famous dykes was constructed by King Offa of Mercia in the 8th century A.D., to serve as a boundary between the Anglian kingdom of Mercia and the British Celtic Welsh provinces.
DYSFUNCTIONAL, a cultural condition arising when certain cultural traits conflict with others, thus preventing the smooth functioning of the culture as an integrated system.
DYSGENIC PROCESS, a decline in the 'long-term' genetic fitness of a phylogenetic continuum, due to the operation of selective forces in opposition to the normally 'eugenic' process of natural selection (q.v.). Dysgenic processes often operate among modern hominids as a result of cultural beliefs and practices that are antithetical to evolutionary principles.
DYSPHORIA, the state of tension which arises when rapid changes in the culture of a society result in the development of sets of contradictory and dysfunctional values, resulting in poorly integrated functional processes.
DZEM, a Bantu-speaking Negroid people of the Fang-Dzem group, largely dependent on horticulture with some hunting and food-gathering.
DZING, a Bantu-speaking Negroid people of the Kasai group, largely dependent on horticulture, hunting and fishing.

E

EAGLE WARRIOR CULT, a ritual cult, of Meso-American (Toltec) origin, in which the members dress as eagles and engage in an eagle war dance. The eagle warrior cult diffused as far as the Great Lakes in North America and Peru in South America. Similar cults in imitation of the jaguar and other animals also arose in Central America and spread widely to many parts of North and South America.
EARLY MEDITERRANEAN LANGUAGES, a purely hypothetical group of languages of which only the Basque language survives today. However, it is

known that the early cultivating people of the Mediterranean and Danube maintained trading relations and shared many physical and cultural attributes, so that the language of the Northwestern Pyrenees, which was formerly spoken over a large part of France and Spain, may have been related to the Pelasgian of the pre-Greek Aegean, to the languages of the Old European civilization of the Balkans, to Cretan Linear A, and even to Etruscan.

EAR SPOOL, a round or spool-shaped ornament worn in the lobe of the ear.

EARTH MOTHER, the heliolithic agricultural civilizations of the Mediterranean revered a female mother goddess as a symbol of fertility and combined this with reverence for the earth as the symbol of fruitfulness. The result was a cult of worship centering on 'mother earth' or the 'earth mother'.

EARTHEN WARE, a form of pottery which has not been glazed or treated in any way to make it impervious to liquids.

EAST BALTIC, (1) a term used in physical anthropology to identify a fair mesocephalic to brachycephalic Caucasoid variant, centred on the eastern shores of the Baltic. (2) a group of Indo-European languages, comprising Old Prussian, Lettish (Lithuanian) and Latvian.

EASTER ISLANDERS, an Eastern Polynesian people, residing in the Easter Islands, who are mainly dependent on horticulture with some fishing and hunting.

EASTERN CREE, an Algonquin-speaking North American Indian people, dependent on hunting and fishing with some food-gathering.

EASTERN MONO (OWENS VALLEY PAIUTE), a Shoshone (Uto-Aztec)-speaking North American Indian people of the Coastal Great Basin, dependent on food-gathering, hunting and some fishing.

ECAD, a physical modification appearing in an individual living organism which is not inheritable.

ECLAT, a flake or splinter made of flint.

ECLIPSES, eclipses of the sun or moon were frequently recorded by the priest-astronomers of early civilizations, and even by primitive peoples, who generally regarded them as bad omens.

ECOCIDE, literally 'the destruction of the environment', generally resulting from man-made changes in the ecological balance which are inimical to the survival of the present forms of life existing in that environment, including man.

ECOLOGICAL COMMUNITY, a community of diverse species occupying the same territory and hence interdependent upon each other.

ECOLOGICAL NICHE, the term used to refer to a pattern of life developed by any living organism which has successfully adjusted to a more or less continuing ecological situation. In the evolutionary process each distinctive form of life must adapt to a specific ecological niche if it is to survive.

ECOLOGY, the study of the relationship between an organism and its environment, especially the spatial-functional patterns which arise as a result of the process of symbiosis. Particular emphasis has to be placed on the wanton disruption of the comparatively stable ecological balance created by nature, as a result of environmental degradation resulting from the hominid population explosion and the deadly problem of massive pollution of the land, air and oceans as a result of the disposal of man-made poisons and waste materials.

ECONOMIC SURPLUS, food and material goods produced in excess of subsistence needs.

ECOLOGY, the study of the relationship between an organism and its environment, and especially of the spatial-functional patterns which arise as a result of the process of symbiosis (q.v.).

ECOSYSTEM, a systematic pattern of balanced relationships which develops between living organisms sharing the same habitat.

ECOTYPE, a race or subspecies which has become specifically adapted to a definite set of environmental conditons.

ECSTASY, a state of intense emotion or rapture, often reaching a stage in which the subject may enter into a trance. In primitive societies, states of ecstasy were associated with magico-religious experiences, and in many cases an attempt might be made to induce ecstasy by the use of intoxicating liquor, drugs, fasting, dancing with powerful, rhythmic movements, or even by self-flagellation and torture.

ECTHLIPSIS, the deletion or suppression of a consonant in either written or spoken form.

ECTOCANTHION, a term used by physical anthropologists to refer to the outer corner of the eye.

ECTODERM, the outer layer of an embryo, from which the skin, nails and external tissues develop.

ECTOGENOUS, an adjective describing a parasitic growth on the body surface of a host.

ECTOMORPH, a person characterized by a thin build as opposed to an endomorph (q.v.).

ECTOPLASM, the outer portion of the cytoplasm of the cell.

ECTOTHERMIC, a term used to describe 'cold-blooded' animals, such as fish and reptiles, whose body temperature varies according to the temperature of the external environment.

ECUMENICALISM, a doctrine aimed at promoting Christian unity throughout the world.

EDDA, a term used to refer to two ancient Icelandic literary works, known respectively as the Elder Edda and the Younger Edda – one representing a collection of mythical and religious sagas, the other a collection of ancient Scandinavian myths, legends and poems compiled by the medieval Icelandic scholar, Snorri Sturluson. Together the Eddas constitute the main surviving source of information regarding the old Scandinavian religion, other records having been deliberately destroyed under the direction of the Christian Church, as also was the case with the deliberate destruction of the library of Teutonic religious doctrines collected by Charlemagne, but destroyed by Louis the Pious at the instigation of the Catholic priests.

EDEN, a paradise in which Adam and Eve were supposed to live before their fall from 'grace'. The term is derived from the Semitic 'Eden', meaning 'delight' or 'pleasure', although the story has Sumerian mythological origins.

EDENTALA, placental mammals with teeth which have been substantially reduced in size or are totally absent. These include the sloth, the armadillo, the American anteater and the renowned aardvark.

EDO, a Kwa-speaking Negroid people belonging to the Ibo-Edo group of West Africa, mainly dependent on horticulture, hunting and food-gathering.

EDUCATION, an institutionalized process by which certain aspects of the culture of the group are deliberately transmitted from generation to generation.

EDUK, the title of a Haida nobleman.

EFFIGY, a three-dimensional representation of a living, dead or supernatural person.

EFFIGY MOUNDS, burial mounds belonging to the North American Indian Late Woodland culture (circa 8th century A.D.) centered in the upper reaches of the Mississippi. These mounds were so-called because their outline was shaped in the image of a totemic bird or animal.

EFIK, a Bantu-speaking Negroid people of Coastal Nigeria, dependent mainly on horticulture and fishing.

EGBA, a Kwa-speaking Negroid people of the Yoruba group of West Africa, largely dependent on horticulture with some animal husbandry and hunting.

EGBO, a secret West African Leopard society.

EGO, a term used in kinship diagrams and charts to refer to the person who is the basic point of reference and from whom the relationship of other persons referred to on the chart is determined.

EGYPTIAN RELIGION, the Egyptian civilization was essentially concerned with two concepts – the cultivation of crops and the problem of life after death. Egyptian religion consequently evolved largely around the worship of the sun, deified as Ra, the flooding of the Nile and the annual vegetation cycle, deified in the myth of Osiris, and the problem of ensuring the well-being of the souls of the dead pharaohs by a variety of magico-religious ritual obligations subsequently incorporated in the 'Book of the Dead' (q.v.). The Egyptian priesthood, which frequently exercised a dominant influence in the affairs of the empire, was divided into two classes of priests: those who maintained the temple rituals, and those who sought to divine the future. Much of the Egyptian ritual revolved around the belief that the name or *ren* of a person was an intimate part of their personality, and had to be guarded and preserved even after their death. It was therefore the duty of all householders to preserve the names of their ancestors for all time. However towards the end of the first millennium B.C., immediately preceding the eventual collapse of Egyptian civilization, the old religion underwent substantial modification, with a trend in the direction of animal worship.

EGYPTIANS, a Hamitic Caucasoid people, dependent on agriculture, animal husbandry and some fishing. The original language of Egypt appears to have been Hamitic in character, part of the Afro-Asiatic family of languages. Although the ancient Egyptian language was replaced by Arabic, following the Arab-Islamic conquest of Egypt, it has been preserved as a ritual language by the Coptic Christians into the present century. (See EGYPTIAN RELIGION).

EHRINGSDORF, a site near Weimar in Germany which revealed an adult jaw and fragments of a child's jaw and cranium dating from the second half of the third interglacial period. These somewhat resembled the Steinheim skull in reflecting certain modern characteristics, although they have generally been loosely classified as Neanderthal. The cranial capacity is estimated at around 1450 c.c. The high forehead and rounded occipital area result in a high cranial vault which Weidenreich identified as reasonably modern, although the lower jaw and brow ridges still revealed primitive characteristics and the fact that the cranial fragments are those of a child may account for the modern appearance.

EIDOLISM, a belief in the existence of disembodied souls, spirits or ghosts.

EINHERJAR, the assembly of dead heroes who lived in Valhalla, the Norse Hall of Valor or Fame, where they formed a military band attendant upon the God-hero Odin.

EINKORN, a type of wheat which appears to have been native to the Balkans and Anatolia, and which was extensively cultivated in both areas as well as in the valley of the Zagreb. (See also EMMER).

EISTEDDFOD, an ancient assembly of Welsh bards at which candidates for the bardship were examined by means of competitive contests.

EJIDO, a term widely used in Latin America to refer to the common lands surrounding a settlement, normally available as pasture for all members of the community.

EKERA, a term used to refer to the souls of the dead among the Cushitic-speaking Galla tribes of Northeastern Africa.

EKITI, a Kwa-speaking Negroid people of the Yoruba group of West Africa, largely dependent on horticulture with some animal husbandry and fishing.

EKOI, see YAKO.

EKONDA, a Bantu-speaking Negroid people of the Mongo group, largely dependent on horticulture with some fishing and hunting.

ELAM, a Mesopotamian kingdom, occupying a broad valley in what is today Southwestern Iran, to the east of Sumer. The Elamite capital was located at Susa, and the Elamites were one of the more powerful peoples of Mesopotamia, until their final absorption into the Persian empire in the 6th century B.C.

ELECTRUM, an alloy of gold and silver found in natural form, possessing a light yellow color.

ELEUSINE, a type of millet cultivated in the Congo.

ELEUSIS, a site in Attica, Greece, which was the centre of worship of the goddess Demeter. In later Greece, Eleusis became the centre of the Eleusian mystery cult, which appears to have comprised a number of pre-Indo-European rituals surviving from the indigenous Pelasgian culture, combined with magico-religious elements borrowed from the Near East.

ELFSTONE, a stone on which offerings might be left to the elves by peoples of Celtic and Teutonic culture.
ELLICE ISLANDERS, a West Polynesian people of the Ellice Isles, dependent on horticulture, fishing and some animal husbandry.
ELLIPSOID, a term used to refer to a skull which appears elliptical when viewed from above.
EL-MEKTA, an archeological site in Tunisia which was excavated in 1952 to reveal Upper Capsian tools, dated around 8500 B.P.
ELYSIUM, the Greek Fields of Paradise, where an eternal spring produced an abundance of flowers, fruits and happiness, a home of the spirits of the heroic dead which contrasted sharply with Hades (q.v.), the cold underworld reserved for the spirits of those who had failed to distinguish themselves in life. The Elysian Fields were supposedly located somewhere along the western edge of the world, that is to say along the Atlantic coast or on an island in the Atlantic Ocean.
EMBRASURE, a loop-hole or opening in a fortified wall, through which missiles may be discharged.
EMBROIDERY, patterns of stitching ornamenting the surface of a fabric.
EMBRYO, an organism in the earlier stages of its development, as in an egg, or (in mammals) prior to the development of the fetus.
EMBRYOLOGY, the biological study of embryos and fetuses, i.e., the development of the individual living organism from the time of conception to the time of birth.
EMERALD, a beryl stone, of green colour, which has been valued among Semitic peoples for several thousands of years. Thus the Moslems believe that the first heaven was made from an emerald, and the Hebrews recorded that the foundation stone of the New Jerusalem was made of emerald. Emeralds were also believed to have magical powers which could be used for curing various sicknesses including dysentery and epilepsy.
EMIR, the title of an Arabian ruler, usually indicating direct descent from Mohammed. The term derives from the Arabic word *Amir* meaning commander.
EMMER, a type of wheat which was first domesticated in Palestine and Syria. (See also EINKORN).
EN-GAI, the supreme deity of the Masai.
ENCAUSTIC PAINTING, a method of painting using pigments mixed with a heated wax base. Encaustic painting was frequently used in Ancient Egypt and in the Classic civilizations of Greece and Rome.
ENCEPHALIZATION, a term used to refer to the evolutionary trend apparent in certain species such as man which leads to a growth in the size and complexity of the brain.
ENCLISIS, the practice of pronouncing two words as a single word, the second word being run together with the first word without any stress being placed upon it.
ENCOMIENDIA, a large tract of land granted to Spanish settlers following the Spanish conquests in America on the understanding that they work to convert the local natives to Christianity and maintain order within the area so granted. In return for these services, the Indians (who were already accustomed to providing annual labor work on bridges, roads, irrigation and other projects prior to the Spanish conquest) were required to work for a specific number of days of the year under the direction of their new Spanish landlords.
ENCULTURATION, the transmission of the culture of a group or society to newcomers (including children).
ENDAMA, a social-sanctioned mating relationship, frequent among the Black Caribs of Honduras, which is regarded as less binding than marriage.
ENDO-CANNIBALISM, a term used to describe that form of cannibalism in which the victim is chosen from among the members of the cannibal tribe, and is consumed by his own kinsmen.
ENDOCANTHION, a term used by physical anthropologists to refer to the

inner corner of the eye.

ENDOCHRONOLOGY, the study of hormones, including the way in which they are produced and their effect upon the behavior of men and other living animals. Anthropologists have in the past paid little attention to the findings of biologists in this respect, but the study of hormone secretions is today playing an increasingly important role in physical anthropology and in certain aspects of sociology such as criminology. The possibility that considerable differences in hormone secretion may distinguish the different subspecies of man also suggests that biological factors may reinforce the existing conception of culturally-determined basic personality differences (q.v.).

ENDOCRANIAL, a term used to refer to the inner surface of the cranium.

ENDODERM, the innermost of the embryonic derm layers from which the digestive tract and many other internal organs evolve.

ENDOGAMY, a social convention confining mating to members of a defined group; the custom of mating only within a specific group.

ENDOGAMY, ROYAL, it was formerly the practice in certain royal families for brothers to marry their own sisters in order to maintain the racial purity of the divinely-descended line. Thus royal endogamy was practiced by several of the Egyptian dynasties, as well as by the Peruvian Incas.

ENDOMORPH, a person characterized by a relatively thick and heavy build, as distinct from an ectomorph (q.v.)

ENDOSKELETON, an internal skeleton, as found in vertebrates.

ENDOTHERMIC, mammals and birds are all to a greater or lesser extent endothermic or 'warm blooded' in so far as their body temperature can be maintained at a level suitable for optimum metabolism, independently of the temperature of the external environment.

END SCRAPER, a stone implement, usually of flint, which has a blunt end that can be used for either planing or scrapping.

ENEOLITHIC, see COPPER.

ENGA, a Papuan people of the East New Guinea highlands, dependent on horticulture with some animal husbandry and hunting.

ENGADJI, the Masai term for a low hut, constructed of cow dung and mud, which constitutes the Masai home.

EN-GAI, the supreme deity of the Masai.

ENGRAVER, a flake tool used in the Upper Paleolithic for engraving ornamental designs on wood, antler, and sometimes even stone.

ENKI, the Sumerian god of wisdom, whose temple was located in the city of Eridu.

ENKIDU, a mythological figure in the Sumerian Gilgamesh epic (q.v.).

ENKOMI, a bronze age settlement in Cyprus, which was seized by Achaeans during the 13th century B.C., and subsequently raided in the 12th century B.C. by the People of the Sea.

ENLIL, the Sumerian storm god, analogous to the Indo-European Thor-Perkun. The subsequent conquest of Sumeria by the Semites led to the identification of Enlil with the Canaanite Baal (q.v.).

ENSI, the Babylonian term for a local government authority.

ENTABLATURE, an architectural term for any wall supported by columns. The entablature in Greek and Roman buildings was usually divided into a cornice, an upper level of mouldings, a frieze, a central area frequently decorated with sculptured scenes, and an architrave, comprising the lower part of the entablature. All of this rested on capitals which surmounted the columns.

ENTREMONT, a Celtic *oppidum* (q.v.) or fortress, located near Aix-en-Provence, which belonged to the La Tène culture. Constructed in the 3rd century B.C., Entremont was systematically reduced to ruins following its capture by the Romans. Excavation of the site has revealed a number of sculptured figures, indicating that it represented an important tribal sanctuary.

ENVIRONMENT, CULTURAL, a term used to refer to the sum total of social, economic, moral, intellectual and all other patterns of learned behavior which influence, together with the genes, the behavior patterns of human beings.

ENVIRONMENT, PHYSICAL, all external physical forces that affect the life of an organism.
ENVIRONMENTALISM, a term used to refer to any theory which stresses the importance of ecological, geographical, climatic and other environmental forces in the shaping of a culture. (See ANTHROPOGEOGRAPHY).
ENZYME, any proteins which serve as essential catalysts in the metabolic process. (See METABOLISM).
EOANTHROPUS DAWSONI, the Latin name given to the fraudulent Piltdown Man (q.v.).
EOCENE, a geological period within the Cenozic era which lasted from approximately 54 to 38 million years ago.
EOLITH, literally 'dawn stone', this term was invented to refer to stones which could have been used as primitive tools by Australopithicenes or other early hominids, but which were so crudely flaked that it is impossible to say whether they were shaped by natural process (and merely picked up for use by the early hominids) or whether they represent the first elementary attempts by the ancestors of man to manufacture cutting stones.
EOLITHIC AGE, a lengthy period in hominid evolution when manlike creatures, notably Australopithecines, were believed to be using eoliths.
EOSTRA, the Teutonic goddess of Spring, who gave her name to the festival of Easter held annually in April to celebrate the rebirth of life after the sleep of winter. Easter was consequently celebrated by the giving of 'Easter eggs' and other symbols of the spring season.
EOZOIC, a term sometimes used to refer to the period in which life first began on earth, now believed to be around 3.7 billion years ago.
EPICANTHIC (or MONGOLIAN) FOLD, a fold of skin on the upper eyelid which is drawn over and obscures the inner corner of the eye. This phenomenon is found only among members of the Mongoloid races.
EPICANTHUS, the inner corner of the eye.
EPIDERMIS, the outer layer of cells covering a plant or animal. In vertebrates the epidermis usually consists of several layers of cells.
EPIGAMIC CHARACTERISTICS, those characteristics of an animal which are concerned with the process of sexual selection. These refer not to the aspects of the immediate biological mechanism of sexual reproduction, such as the gonads, but to the stimuli which promote sexual contacts, as for example the role of bird songs and mating dances.
EPIGONIUM, a harp used in ancient Greece, the epigonium possesses approximately 40 strings.
EPIGRAPHY, the technique of deciphering ancient scripts.
EPILEPSY, an ailment, largely genetic in origin, but sometimes brought on by birth trauma, which results in a periodic loss of consciousness, the recovery from which is often followed by violent behavior. The unusual behavior of persons afflicted with epilepsy gave rise to the belief, common in many animistic societies, that they were periodically 'possessed' by spirits, and epileptics often therefore achieved the status of shamans or oracles.
EPIMESOLITHIC, a term formerly used to refer to what is today described as the Mesolithic.
EPIPHYSES, small bony centers found in children, encased in cartilage, which with increasing maturity fuse with major bones.
EPISTASIS, a genetic term used to refer to the frequent situation in which one gene in a pair of genes is 'dominant' and inhibits or masks the expression of the other 'recessive' gene.
EPOCH, a division of geological time smaller than a Period (q.v.).
EPONYMOUS ANCESTORS, an ancestor whose name is retained by his descendants as a family, clan or tribal name.
EQUATORIAL LANGUAGES, a major group within the Andean family of languages of South and Central America, including Arawakan, Cariri, Guahibo-Pamigua, Mocoa, Salivan, Timonte, Tupi, Yuracanean and Zamucoan.
EQUINE GODS, the Classic Greeks frequently portrayed their gods in riding

positions or standing beside horses, the horse being highly valued thoughout the Indo-European world.

EQUINOX, that time of the year when the midday sun is directly above the Equator and the days and nights are of equal length. March the 21st is known as the Vernal Equinox, while September the 23rd is described as the Autumnal Equinox.

EQUIVALENCE, GENERATION, a term used in kinship classification when all relatives of the same generation are grouped together for classificatory purposes, regardless of consanguineal or affinal ties and genetic relationship, and are assigned the same kinship terms and statuses. Classificatory systems, in which the concept of generation is paramount above all other concepts, may be contrasted with the 'shifting kindred' (q.v.) in which genetic concepts are dominant.

ERH, a Chinese word, of Taoist implications, referring to the combined forces of the active male principle or YANG (q.v.) and the female or passive principle known as YIN (q.v.).

ERIDU, a tell, close to the city of Ur, which represents the remains of the oldest excavated city in Mesopotamia. First occupied in the middle of the 6th millennium B.C., the earliest houses constituted simple rectangular mud brick structures. The site grew in importance during the Early Dynastic period (cir. 2500 B.C.) but declined with the rise of the nearby city of Ur during the 3rd Sumerian dynasty (cir. 2100 B.C.).

ERINYES, the winged maidens of Greek mythology who punished mortals for family disloyalty, the swearing of false oaths, and improper conduct of any kind. Known to the Romans as the Furiae or Avenging Furies.

EROS, the Greek god of passion and of the fertility resulting therefrom. Not mentioned in Homer, Eros is probably of non-Indo-European origin. In later Greece, Eros is often regarded as a child, and consequently is the progenitor of the Cupid so beloved of Renaissance Europe.

ERTEBØLLE, the name used to refer to the last stage of the Mesolithic Baltic culture, characterized by large kitchen middens or dumps of village refuse, the contents of which provide valuable evidence of diet and life style. The Ertebølle culture merged around 5000 B.C., and survived until the Baltic area acquired agriculture (around 3000 B.C.) from the direction of the Rhineland via North German plains.

ERYTHRISM, a condition causing individuals to possess 'carroty' red hair. Erythrism is not peculiar to any particular racial groups and is widely spread throughout the various human sub-species.

ERYTHROCYTE, a red blood corpuscle.

ESKIMO-ALEUT LANGUAGES, a group of languages which includes Eskimo and Aleut and shows an affinity to the Chuckchee-Kamchatka languages of Eastern Asia, which latter are usually grouped with Paleo-Asian languages. The Eskimo languages are usually divided into a Western Eskimo subfamily, which includes Aleut as well as Nunamint, Chugash and Ninuvak Eskimo; and a Central and Eastern group which includes Copper, Caribou, and Polar Eskimo, as well as Angmagsalik and Iglulik.

ESKIMO RELIGION, Eskimo religious beliefs were rooted in animism and shamanism. Animals were believed to have souls like human beings, and these had to be properly propitiated by the hunter at the time of slaying the animal. Magical practices predominated over religious ritual, the purpose of Eskimo ritual being mainly practical and individual, as in the case of shamanistic efforts to cure the sick. (See also SHAMANS).

ESKIMOS, an ancient Arctic people who preserved many of the techniques developed in the European Upper Paleolithic, when much of Europe was covered by the Würm glaciation. The distinctive elements of Eskimo culture can be traced back to the Denbigh flint complex, circa 1000 B.C. The Eskimos, who inhabit Northern Canada, are closely related to the Aleuts of the Aleutian Isles, and appear to have immigrated into the New World in small bands moving slowly from island to island from Northeastern Siberia, sometime between 3000 and 2000 years ago. Although the Eskimos live in small, independent band-type societies, their language has retained a remarkable unity despite the vast distances that separate the Alaskan Eskimos from those of Greenland. However, because of the intermediate progression of linguistic change, the Eskimos of Greenland speak a dialect which is unintelligible to those of Alaska.

ESPRINGLE, the espringle, or Spring Dance, was a round dance of pagan origin associated with the Minnesingers of medieval Germany.

ESSENES, a Hebrew sect which forbade marriage and family life, practicing a communism of property in rebellion against the orthodox traditions of tribal Hebraism. These beliefs seem to reflect Persian Mazdakism (q.v.). The Essenes are believed to have strongly influenced Christianity and Gnosticism and to have been the ultimate source of the inspiration for medieval Christian monasticism. The Jewish Essences obtained the concept of Good versus Evil from Zoroastrian dualism, incorporating this in their Manual of Discipline.

ESTATE SYSTEM, a system of social stratification in which persons holding equivalent ranks in functionally distinct areas of society share equivalent status positions in an integrated hierarchical structure.

ESTONIANS, an East Baltic agricultural people whose language belongs to the Finno-Ugrian group, and who (with the Finns) seem to be the survivors of a pre-Indo-European hunting population that formerly occupied the lands bordering the Baltic Sea.

ESTRUS, the period of greatest sexual responsiveness among mammalian females. This cycle differs according to species.

ESTUFA, an underground chamber, similar to a kiva (q.v.), used as a sweat house in the North American Southwest.

ETA, a class of traders or wandering merchants who were regarded as outcasts in traditional Japanese society.

ETHNIC, a term used to refer to any group distinguished by a self-conscious awareness of common cultural, linguistic or racial characteristics.

ETHNOBIOLOGY, a branch of the study of ethnology which relates to the distinctive physical and racial characteristics of specific ethnic groups or population isolates.

ETHNOCENTRISM, the tendency to judge other societies by the standards or norms dominant in the observer's own society.

ETHNOGENESIS, the evolution of a new ethnic system.

ETHNOGENETIC, referring to the origins of a specific ethnic group.

ETHNOGRAPHIC MODEL, an ethnographic parallel from which inferences can be drawn by comparison with archeological or other data.

ETHNOGRAPHIC PRESENT, an ethnographic convention on the basis of which ethnologists describe cultures as they were immediately prior to contact with Western civilization, thus ignoring modifications arising from subsequent acculturation.

ETHNOGRAPHY, the study or description of individual cultures, communities or societies, as contrasted to ethnology which is essentially concerned with the comparison and interpretation of ethnographic data.

ETHNOHISTORY, a study of the history of specific ethnic groups in history and prehistory.

ETHNOLINGUISTICS, the study of language in relation to ethnology and the history of specific ethnic groups.

ETHNOLOGY, the comparative study of different cultures and societies with a view to interpreting and analyzing the causal circumstances responsible for observable similarities and differences.

ETHNOMUSICOLOGY, comparative study of the musical traditions of different ethnic groups.

ETHNOS, derived from the Greek term meaning 'race', the term 'ethnos' refers to the distinctive, cultural, linguistic or biological heritage of a specific ethnic group. The term 'ethos' is today more customary .

ETHNOSCIENCE, the comparative study of the development of rational thought and scientific knowledge among the diverse peoples and races of man.

ETHNOSOCIOLOGY, a term originally intended to refer to the application ot sociology to the study of simpler societies, and in particular those of early men. However, the term has now been superseded by ethnology (q.v.).

ETHOLOGY, the scientific study of the behavior of animals in their natural environment, as opposed to the study of captive animals in artificial environments.

ETHOS, the distinctive quality of any individual culture or society. Ruth Benedict suggested that the ethos of a society might be classified as either 'Apollonian' or 'Dionysian' (q.v.) but most theorists believe that she over-simplifies the concept of ethos, which is rooted in the complex totality of mores, customs and cultural traits possessed by a society.

ETIQUETTE, that part of the customs and folkways of a society which is accepted as a standard of rules governing behavior between individuals of the same or different rank. Etiquette is generally most highly developed in stratified societies, but some elements of etiquette are to be found in all human societies.

ETRUSCANS, a highly civilized people who occupied the area formerly known as Etruria (present day Tuscany) during the 1st millennium B.C. The Etruscans are first identifiable as a separate people quite distinct from neighboring Villanovians, around the 8th century B.C., and it has been suggested that they represented an immigrant population from the Anatolian region, although this view is disputed, as also is the opinion that their language was non-Indo-European. The Etruscan cities (among which Tarquinia and Veii were pre-eminent) were virtually autonomous city-states, linked in a loose confederation by the kinship bonds which united the ruling families. Etruscan society was highly stratified and completely dominated by its nobility, with the result that their culture placed a heavy emphasis on its impressive architecture and refined art forms. Trading extensively with Greece and Carthage, the Etruscans at one time dominated Rome prior to the rise of Latin power, and their eventual decline may be attributed to the rise of Carthaginian sea power in the Mediterranean, combined with the pressure of invading Celts from the North, with the still nascent Latin nations playing an initially small, if ultimately significant, role in their overthrow.

ETUMO, compensation paid for murder among certain African peoples, (equivalent to wergeld).

ETYMOLOGY, a study of the source derivation of words.

ETYMON, that part of a word which indicates its etymology.

EUGENIC INFANTICIDE, infanticide has been practiced by many peoples, both primitive and highly civilized, in order to prevent infants born with severe physical and/or mental defects from becoming a burden upon the community.

EUGENICS, the deliberate attempt (1) to protect a particular population, or indeed an entire species, against the genetically debilitating effect of a decline in natural selection, or (2) to improve the competitive survival potential of a particular population, or indeed the whole species, either (a) by positive eugenics, e.g., breeding from individuals who are believed to possess the desired characteristics, or (b) by negative eugenics, discouraging the breeding of individuals who are believed to be carriers of defective genes, or who possess a genetic heritage less conducive to the survival of the breeding population.

EUHEMERISM, the theory that a deity originated as a culture hero whose memory was preserved in myth until eventually elevated to the status of a god. Such possibilityies are very real in the case of ancestor-worshipping societies, and the Scandinavian Ynglinga Saga portrays the Norse God Odin as an historical hero-king.

EUHOMINIDS, members of the hominid assemblage which have evolved beyond the level of the Australopithecines.

EUNUCH, a castrated human male. The practice of castrating slaves probably began in ancient Mesopotamia, and it remained customary in the Moslem world to employ eunuchs to guard the 'harem' or women's quarters. In certain Semitic regions, the priests were by tradition required to become eunuchs to ensure celibacy, while other Middle Eastern peoples used eunuchs as male prostitutes. The act of castration always results in the development of certain feminine characteristics, such as rounded hips, a high pitched voice, hypogenitalism, and a general infantile appearance.

EUPATRIDS, literally 'born of good ancestors'. The Greeks were very conscious of the role of heredity in human affairs, and placed great emphasis upon breeding, believing their eupatrid class to be genetically superior to the mass of freemen.

EUPHEMISM, the use of indirect designations to refer to a respected or supernatural being or even to highly prestigious living persons in order to avoid the direct use of their name. Thus the Hebrew deity Yahweh could not be mentioned by name except by the priests at a specific annual ceremony.

EUROPOID (also EUROPID), a term occasionally used as an alternative to Caucasoid (q.v.).

EURYSOME, short stocky person.

EUTHANASIA, popularly known as 'mercy killing', euthanasia refers to the socially-approved killing of individuals who are seriously ill, usually for the humane purpose of freeing them from pain.

EUTHERIAN MAMMALS, a subclass of higher mammals whose offsprings are nourished in the prenatal stage by means of a placenta, thus freeing the fetus from dependency upon the limited food content of an egg yolk.

EVERTED LIPS, lips which protrude outwards and consequently reveal a large surface area. Representing an unusual evolutionary development, the value of which is not understood, everted lips are generally characteristic of the Negroid and Pygmy people of sub-Saharan Africa, but are not found among any other living primates.

EVOLUTION, a process of selective adaptation to environment resulting in a proliferation of diversified species, each specialized to meet the challenge of survival in its particular environment, and frequently resulting in the replacement of simpler life forms by more complex forms capable of producing varying responses to diverse stimuli.

EVOLUTION, CULTURAL, biological evolution demonstrates a tendency for a single species to divide into a variety of subspecies, developing local attributes appropriate to the survival of the lineage under the prevailing local conditions as well as – in some species – an evolution from simple to complex organisms. Similarly the theory of cultural evolution suggests that cultures and societies tend to adapt to the prevailing ecological, social, and political conditions, and that cultures in turn develop separate and diverse patterns when spread over a large area under different conditions. The theory of cultural evolution also assumes that there is a tendency for simpler cultures to evolve into more complex cultures, possessing a more advanced technology, a greater degree of division of labor, and a more extensive system of social stratification.

EVOLUTION, DIVERGENT, a term used to refer to the appearance of diverse populations each adapted to different life styles, as a result of the progressive modification of an originally common form, through a process of natural selection operating on genetically isolated sub-populations.

EVOLUTION, LINEAL, a 19th century theory that all societies tend to follow a similar pattern of evolutionary development. This theory fell into disfavor when it was demonstrated that some societies specialized in cultivation, and others in pastoralism or fishing, and that the latter did not necessarily evolve from the former. It has also been shown that even different groups of pastoralists or cultivators do not necessarily develop identical cultural systems.

EVOLUTION, MULTILINEAL, the contemporary view, widely accepted by many anthropologists, that some degree of evolutionary change occurs in all societies, although not necessarily at a constant rate. The theory of multilineal evolution differs from the 19th century concept of unilineal evolution (q.v.) in recognizing that societies tend to adapt to the problem of survival in the prevailing environmental conditions. Thus some societies have historically specialized in the direction of pastoralism, others have depended on fishing, while yet others developed systems of horticulture or agriculture as their main method of subsistence. In the modern world, societies are attempting to increase their ability to supplement food production by the manufacture of mechanical industrial goods, while others find it more economic to concentrate on the production of food and raw materials. It therefore appears that some degree of multilineal evolution, with its concomitant implication of cultural diversity, will probably continue into the indefinite future.

EVOLUTION, ORGANIC, the evolution of living organisms as superimposed on the evolution of non-living, inorganic material.

EVOLUTION, PARALLEL, a term used to refer to a situation in which two or more groups evolve similar cultural traits by independent invention (q.v.) rather than cultural differences (q.v.), due primarily to similar ecological and environmental conditions.

EVOLUTION, SUPRAORGANIC, a concept first developed by Herbert Spencer who suggested that the evolution of society from simple to more highly complex social systems was parallel to the organic evolution which has taken place among biological species. Spencer claimed that cultural evolution was in fact merely a continuation at a 'superorganic' level of the same processes of diversification, division of labor, and specialization which characterizes biological evolution.

EVOUTEMENT, a form of sympathetic magic in which an image is made of the victim, possibly incorporating a piece of hair, nail-clipping, or even a portion of the victim's foeces. The object is then 'tortured' or destroyed in the manner by which the magician wishes to torture or destroy the living victim.

EWE, a Kwa-speaking Negroid people of the Fon group in West Africa, largely dependent on horticulture, fishing and some animal husbandry and hunting.

EXCAVATION, ARCHEOLOGICAL, most physical evidence of earlier cultures has survived to us by accident through the accumulation of debris, silt or even volcanic lava over the original material, thus preserving it for the archeologist to uncover. Unfortunately it was perhaps natural that early archeological excavation was commonly undertaken by amateur antiquarians for the object of uncovering artifacts. These were usually studied with sincere interest, but such pioneering efforts unavoidably destroyed some of the most valuable sites. Indeed modern archeological techniques for the careful observation and recording of all relevant data had to develop as a result of the trial and error experiences of these early amateurs. Only with time did it become apparent that careful attention should be paid to the relative layers of the various deposits (stratigraphy), and to the physical relationship of one object to another, to facilitate the effective interpretation of their usage. Modern archeology consequently uses a series of techniques such as grid layouts, quadrants, rabotage, and sondage. It is also becoming increasingly apparent that sites should be thoroughly excavated, and that the partial excavation of sites, frequently necessary due to lack of funds or time, fails to provide a complete and accurate picture of the culture under examination.

EXCAVATION UNITS, the sections or units into which an archeological site is divided as an aid to describing its overall plan.

EXCISION, a term used to refer to an operation common among certain Hamito-Semitic peoples particularly of the Dusanic tribes, whereby the clitoris of females is removed before the age of puberty, creating a scar which prevents intercourse until a further operation is undertaken, shortly prior to marriage.

EXCOMMUNICATION, in many religions, such as Roman Catholicism, the priesthood claims the power to partially or totally exclude specific individuals from the religious community, thereby in effect depriving them of all the benefits of communication with, and protection by, the deity. In societies in which the priesthood exercised a dominant influence, as in Medieval Europe, excommunication also in effect deprived the excommunicated from many civil as well as religious rights and privileges, and was frequently used by the Roman Catholic church as a tool to control the actions of the temporal or lay leaders of society. Where the religious indoctrination of the population has been effective, the threat of excommunication represents an extremely effective political and social weapon, giving the priesthood indirect power over the entire community.

EXCREMENT, TALKING, certain North American Indians, including the Ojibwa, believe that a man's foeces can communicate with him, giving advice as to the best course of action that should be adopted in response to his personal problems. Foeces which give such advice are referred to as 'talking excrement'.
EXOGAMY, the custom of mating only with persons chosen from outside the defined social group.
EXORCISM, the expulsion of supposedly evil spirits by magico-religious rituals. Exorcism is frequently used when a spirit is believed to have entered and taken possession of a human body, or to have penetrated the dwelling place of a family. Methods of exorcism vary from one society to another and may be effected with the aid of magico-religious charms, by the repetition of magico-religious formulae, or by sacrifice. Exorcism may be practiced by individual shamans or by members of organized priesthoods. In the Christian religion the mention of the name 'Jesus' was regarded as adequate to expel demons from a 'possessed' body or building, hence the popular expletive still used as a response to bad news.
EX ORIENTE LUX, a concept, rooted in the Christian belief that European culture derived its original inspiration from the Middle East. This idea, which may be literally translated as 'light from the East', was further propagated by the Marxist archeologist V. Gordon Childe. However, improved methods of archeological dating, and continued archeological research in Europe since World War II, have now demonstrated that the cultivation of crops and the domestication of animals evolved in Europe quite as early as in the Middle East, and it would now appear that the Old European Civilization (q.v.) produced the earliest written script that the world has known, predating that of the Middle East by nearly two millennia.
EXOSKELETON, a skeleton covering the outside of the body, as in the case of the Arthropoda (q.v.). It is to be contrasted with the 'endoskeleton' (q.v.) characteristic of mammals.
EXPIATION, the attempt by a person or community, having committed a ritual offense, to propitiate the offended spirit or divinity. In some cases individuals may seek expiation by assuming onerous penalties or tasks, or in other cases the community may attempt to expiate the god by killing or otherwise punishing the offending individual. The ancient Hebrews sacrificed a domestic animal in atonement for their offenses and sprinkled the blood on the sacred ark of the covenant, while the medieval Catholic church sold expiation for cash payments.
EXPOSURE, the disposal of a corpse by exposure to birds and animals of prey, practised amongst others by the Parsees of India, who to this day place their corpses in special 'towers of silence' for this purpose.
EXPOSURE, INFANT, the practice, common in primitive cultures, but also found in many advanced classical civilizations of killing unwanted infants by abandoning them in an unfrequented area where they will die due to exposure to the elements or become the prey of wild animals. (See INFANTICIDE).
EXPRESSIVITY, the degree to which the effect of a specific gene is expressed in the phenotype.
EXUVIA, any part of the body which has been severed or disconnected from the living organism. Exuvia include clippings from the nails, portions of cut hair, that part of the foreskin which is removed in the ritual of circumcision, and even excreta.
EYAK, an American Indian fishing, hunting and food-gathering people, whose language is considered by some authorities to belong to the Na-Dene phylum.
EYE, DOG, a derogatory epithet sometimes used by the Chinese to refer to the typical Caucasoid eye, which lacks the Mongoloid epicanthic fold, and is therefore likened by the Chinese to the eye of a dog.
EYE, EVIL, a superstitious belief, rooted in the principle of contagious magic (q.v.), that certain people have the power to cause injury to others merely by looking upon them. There is evidence that the ancient Egyptians believed in the evil eye, and that the superstition may have entered Europe by cultural diffusion

from Egypt. It is more probable, however, that a belief in the evil eye dates back to the Mesolithic or Upper Paleolithic, since it is known to many peoples throughout the world.

F

FABLE, a short story in which the participants are usually animals who exhibit a combination of both human and animal traits. Such stories are frequently built around a moral. The oldest known collection is Aesop's Fables, which were recorded in Greece around 600 B.C. but fables are common to many societies and may represent a transition of great antiquity in the history of human cultural evolution.

FABRICATOR, a term sometimes used to refer to Paleolithic instruments used for pressure-flaking. These were sometimes made of flint, and on other occasions of bone or antler.

FACE, DISHARMONIC, a term applied to an unusually short face in which the total length of the cranium is smaller than the width measured across the cheek bones.

FACET FLAKE TRADITION, a Lower Paleolithic technique of manufacturing finely shaped stone tools, which are struck as flakes from a carefully prepared core stone.

FACIAL INDEX, the ratio between the total height of the face and its breadth, obtained by multiplying the total height of the face by dividing it by its breadth. The cephalic index is measured from nasion to gnathion and the breadth from zygion to zygion.

FACTORS, MULTIPLE, a genetic term referring to a set of genes which are nonallelic but which have a combined effect upon the same set of morphological characteristics.

FACTORY, essentially a workshop characterized by some degree of specialization of labor. The term need not be restricted to the description of modern industrial societies, but can even be used to refer to Stone Age workshop areas used for the manufacture of stone or other tools.

FAEFEATA, in Celtic Ireland, *faefeata* was the power by which the priests claimed to be able to make themselves invisible. Early Christians also claimed this power for their Saints.

FAIENCE, a type of pottery containing ingredients which, when the finished clay is baked to the appropriate temperature, cause the surface to acquire a blue or green glass-like finish. Originally invented in ancient Egypt around the second millennium B.C., the present term 'faïence' actually derives from the town of Faenza in Northern Italy where medieval pottery was made.

FAIRY, in Celtic mythology, fairies were the gods of an earlier race, skilled in magic, who instead of being down-graded to the level of demons, or incorporated into Celtic mythology as gods, instead survived in diminutive form as the 'little people' of the hills, forests, streams and marshes. Most fairies were customarily well-disposed to mortals, providing they were properly treated, but were notoriously unreliable, and if annoyed by even the most chance happening, were prone to seek revenge through either relatively innocent pranks, or by seriously harmful deeds. Fond of children, they sometimes kidnapped beautiful infants, leaving changelings in their place. Contact with fairies could also be dangerous, although the danger varied according to the kind of fairy. Elves were particularly roguish, sprites, by contrast, were usually innocent, being commonly associated with rivers, streams and other nature places, light and dainty in build, and pleasing in appearance. Brownies stayed close to households, and often undertook useful household tasks at night, in response to kindness and small gifts. Teutonic folklore contained parallel fairy-folk, including the dwarves (q.v.).

FALASHA, a dark, Semitic-speaking people of Ethiopia, who practice Judaic rituals and although they speak no Hebrew, refer to themselves as 'The House of Israel', the term 'falasha' meaning simply 'exiles'. Their origins are unknown.

FAMILIAL, an adjective used to refer to any activity or aspect of family life.
FAMILIAL CHARISMA, a term devised by Max Weber to refer to an hereditary mana-like charisma believed to be inherent in certain families, which endowed royalty with special powers and may have contributed to the formation of the caste system in India.
FAMILIARITY, derived from the term family, the word 'familiarity' refers to the specific freedoms from the normal forms of etiquette which are permitted between members of the same family, but which are sometimes also extended to non-family members.
FAMILIAR SPIRIT, an ancestral spirit, or even bird or animal which protects or assists an individual. The term is also used to refer to a supernatural being which serves as an assistant to a wizard or magician.
FAMILISM, a term used to describe any system of social organization in which the family group constitutes the significant and basic element, and in which family ties and obligations are held in great respect. Familism was particularly strong among the early peoples of Europe, among the great civilizations of Greece, Rome, and Persia, as well as China, Japan, and South East Asia. Indeed, it may be said that the root of all human social organization is to be found in familism. (See FAMILY).
FAMILY, the oldest institution in human society, and one of the four major forms of mammalian social organization. The origin of the human family is to be found in a more or less permanent relationship between specific males and specific females, known as 'pair-bonding', accompanied by a division of labor for the purpose of enhancing the survival chances of the offspring. Found among wolves, the family is universal in one form or another in all known human societies. Most significantly 'pair-bonding' and all subsequent family systems involve food-sharing and collaboration, and the members of a family unit face the problem of survival as a jointly collaborating collective group. Viewed as an evolutionary mechanism it is apparent that 'pair-bonding' arose among certain mammals (and birds) as a means of ensuring the collaboration of the sexes for the protection of their immature offspring, and the perpetuation of the species. In human societies a family may be defined as a socially recognized pair-bond between one or more males and one or more females, whose members share special rights and obligations in respect to each other and to the community to which it belongs. (See FAMILY EXTENDED; MARRIAGE, GROUP; MONOGAMY; POLYANDRY; and POLYGAMY).
FAMILY, COMPOSITE, a term seldom used nowadays which may be regarded as equivalent to the contemporary concept of the Joint Family (q.v.).
FAMILY, CONJUGAL, a term sometimes used in place of the more modern term nuclear family (q.v.).
FAMILY, CONSANGUINEAL, a form of extended family in which the bonds that link the nuclear family (q.v.) are regarded as being of lesser importance than those that link the son to his father in patrilocal societies, and the daughter to her mother in matrilocal societies.
FAMILY, DOMESTIC, a loosely used term generally referring to any family, either nuclear or joint, which occupies a single house.
FAMILY, EXTENDED, a group of related nuclear families linked by either patrilineal or matrilineal ties. Sharing mutual obligations and privileges to each other they are usually also linked by close economic responsibilities under the leadership of a single patriarchal or matriarchal head.
FAMILY, JOINT, a particular kind of extended family in which the constituent related nuclear families not only share economic and other responsibilities but also occupy a common residence or homestead. The joint family also differs from other forms of the extended family in the tendency to pool all productive resources.
FAMILY, LINGUISTIC, a group of languages which can be demonstrated to have been derived from a common ancestral language.
FAMILY, MATRIARCHAL, the concept of a family unit dominated by the wife or mother. While matrilineal (cf.) traditions are common, however, truly

matriarchal societies have seldom been identified.

FAMILY, NUCLEAR, a family unit comprising the parents and their immediate offspring. The term is sometimes restricted to those nuclear families which have established their own households, but is also commonly used to refer to nuclear families comprising parents and their immediate children who live as members of either a joint or an extended family.

FAMILY, PATRIARCHAL, a family led by and legally represented by a senior male progenitor, who is succeeded upon his death by either a brother or a son. Patriarchal families are often joint families (q.v.), although the term may also be used in connection with nuclear families. The patriarchal family is usually associated with patrilineal descent, although not all patrilineal societies are patriarchal, any more than all matrilineal societies are matriarchal.

FAMILY (TAXONOMIC), a classificatory term used by zoologists to refer to groups of related genera. A Family is thus wider than a Genus (q.v.), but smaller than an Order (q.v.). In zoological classification, taxonomic families are usually assigned names with the termination *-idae.*

FANDANGO, a Spanish courtship dance, usually executed to the accompaniment of a guitar.

FANG, a Bantu-speaking Negroid people of the Fang-Dzem group, largely dependent on horticulture, with some hunting, fishing and food-gathering.

FANTI, a Kwa-speaking Negroid people from West Africa of the Akan group, largely dependent on horticulture with some animal husbandry and hunting.

FARANDOULE, a round dance, surviving as a folk dance among the village people of Provence in France, believed to have originated in early pagan religious rituals aimed at encouraging the propagation of the crops.

FARMING, any process of cultivation, whether horticultural or agricultural. (See AGRICULTURE and HORTICULTURAL SOCIETIES).

FARMING, MIXED, a type of farming involving both the care of domesticated farm animals and the cultivation of crops. Mixed farming usually implies a relatively advanced culture and the continuing cultivation of the same land.

FASHION, in simpler societies, customs generally change only slightly from generation to generation, but in times of rapid technological or cultural change, considerable prestige may attach to the introduction of innovations, and the pattern of custom may be disrupted by the rise of fashions. From approximately the 15th century onwards the European upper classes, and to a lesser extent the urbanized merchant classes, began to abandon customary styles of dress in favor of a succession of new styles or fashions, usually in imitation of innovations introduced by some highly respected person, such as a member of the royal family. Considerable social prestige attached to the rapidity with which specific individuals responded to the new fashion. In present day industrial societies, however, fashion changes are deliberately introduced by the manufacturers of clothes, automobiles and similar prestige associated merchandise, to promote sales by out-dating earlier models and so increasing the rate of consumption.

FASTING, the deliberate restriction or total refusal to partake of either food or drink. Fasting is believed to have originated as a purifying ritual or form of expiation. It is frequently resorted to by ascetic individuals who hope to experience hallucinations, which will draw them closer to a supernatural 'reality' when in a semi-starving condition. Thus shamans frequently fast in order to enter into communication with the spirit world, and the Hebrew prophets similarly engaged in fasting while wandering alone in the desert so as to receive (through 'revelations') divine messages from the creator-god they sought to obey.

FATALISM, the belief that all men's actions are predetermined by an all-powerful god, or by some other set of forces working in a preplanned or teleological pattern. The implication of fatalism is that men cannot change the course of their own lives or the course of world history.

FATHERHOOD, social acceptance by the father of all the responsibilities attached to the possession of children. In many societies, such as that of early Rome, the newborn child did not automatically become entitled to family support until he had been accepted by his father as a member of the family. In patrilineal societies fatherhood consequently plays a leading part in the total structure of society.

FAT'JANOVO, a 'singlegrave' culture, named after a cemetery excavated at Yaroslavl on the upper Volga River. Although the graves were not covered by mounds, they contained stone battle-axes and corded, globular amphora, and the Fat'janovo culture is therefore usually classified as belonging to a Copper/Early Bronze Age subdivision of the Indo-European battle-axe peoples.

FAUNA, a general term for the animal population inhabiting a specific area at a particular time.

FAUNAL ANALYSIS, a method of dating artifacts by classification of animal bones found with them on a geological time scale. (See DATING SYSTEMS).

FAURESMITH, the name given to a Paleolithic culture located in South and East Africa, revealing tools reflecting the Acheulian hand axe cultural tradition.

FAYUM, a depression in the desert southwest of Cairo which once contained a lake, and earlier appears to have been part of the delta of the Nile, when the Mediterranean extended further inland than today. Excavations in the Fayum area have revealed many early hominoid fossil remains as well as primitive horticultural settlements from the early Neolithic.

FEAST, a communal meal undertaken to commemorate a special occasion, the table usually being well-supplied with an abundance of food. They may also be arranged to honour individuals at essentially personal ritual celebrations such as births and marriages. Many religions have adopted feasting as a ritual, following the sacrifice of animals, thus in effect placing the worshippers in communion with their deity. Religious feasts are frequently preceded by a period of fasting, in order to purify the members of the congregation before they participate in this communal meal.

FEAST, TOTEMIC, totemic societies frequently practice ritual feasts in which members of the community kill and eat a portion of the totemic animal, which is sacrosanct at any other time of the year.

FEI, small white stones, through which a central hole has been bored, used as coins by the Yap.

FELLAHIN, sometimes abbreviated as 'Fellah', the term is of Turkish origin, referring to peasants, laborers, and persons of impure racial descent. It was under the Ottoman Empire that the term 'fellahin' came to be applied to the Egyptian masses.

FELT, a fabric produced by beating and compressing animal hair. Widely used in the Asian steppelands as early as the Neolithic, felt provides the user with a heavy but flexible fabric, which gives good protection against inclement weather.

FELUCCA, a vessel equipped with oars and lateen sails which can be sailed in either direction. Formerly widely used in the Mediterranean and still in common use on the Nile river.

FEMUR, the thigh bone of a vertebrate animal.

FERAL MAN, a term developed to refer to the idea of a man raised in isolation from other human beings, sometimes in the company of animals. The concept is of considerable interest since it implies the idea of a man raised without the advantages and disadvantages of a cultural heritage, although no truly authenticated cases of feral men have yet been discovered.

FERTILE CRESCENT, one of the major homes of western civilization, the 'fertile crescent' relates to the well-watered lands of the Tigris, Euphrates, and Jordan valleys, bordered by mountains to the north and east, and by desert to the south.

FERTILITY, the actual production of offspring by a population as distinct from the fecundity or potential capacity of a population to produce offspring. In other words, fertility is measured by the birth rate.

FERTILIZATION, a term used in sexual reproduction to refer to the union of special cells known as gametes, drawn from male and female organisms, which results in a single cell known as a zygote. Although the zygote develops into a new living organism there is no actual interruption in the continuing stream of life, for the zygote originates from a combination of two parent cells.

FETISHISM, a word derived from the Portuguese *feitico*, meaning a magical charm, applied by the first Portuguese explorers to the carved objects worshipped by the West African Negroes. Today, the concept of fetishism involves reverence for any material object which is believed to house either a spirit being or any other form of supernatural power. However, strictly speaking, a fetish was originally a material object which housed a soul or spirit that exercised supernatural powers from this material abode. It should therefore be distinguished from an idol, which is a material representation of a god, and from an amulet, which has its own inanimate potency and does not house a spirit being. Most fetishes are of unusual character, such as a human skull, an animal tooth or an animal claw.

FETUS, a term used to refer to the developing offspring of an animal while still in the prenatal state. (See FOETUS).

FEUD, a tradition of mutual hostility persisting between two distinct lineage or kinship groups, each lineage seeking to revenge former injuries against its kinsmen. Feuds could often be avoided by payment of an appropriate penalty by the relatives of the aggressor to the relatives of the aggrieved.

FEUDALISM, a form of social organization more mobile than that of kinship-based tribal loyalties but less complex than that of the bureaucratic state. In feudal societies the king or central chieftain derives his power not from kinship and clan loyalties but from the loyalty of feudal clients, who are rewarded for their military and civil allegiance by an allocation of resources such as land or animals. The feudal distribution of power is usually based on geographical principles. Thus with feudalism the King of the English (a title implying kinship loyalties) became instead the King of England, implying ownership of the land and all who are born on it. The feudal kings of England appointed nobles, who similarly appointed sub-tenants, controlling smaller estates, in return for the obligation to do military service and provide fiscal support to the crown for the administration of the country.

FIBULA, (1) an ornamental pin, similar to a broach, worn on cloaks, togas and other draped garments. The earliest fibulae are found in the Mediterranean area, dating from approximately 1300 B.C. (2) the posterior of the two bones in the lower part of the knee. (See also TIBIA).

FICTIVE KINSHIP, 'honorary' kinship. In kinship-based societies most rights and obligations are rooted in kinship ties, without which there can be little basis for trust or cooperation. In such instances 'blood brotherhood', or similar fictitious kinship ties, may be invented in order to justify social, political, or economic cooperation between nonrelated individuals.

FIELD ARCHEOLOGY, a term used to describe archeological field surveys by which castle mounds, barrows and the evidence of ancient plow fields may be identified and charted without excavation.

FIJIANS, an essentially Melanesian people of the Fiji Islands, on the cultural border between Melanesia, Micronesia and Polynesia.

FINNO-UGRIC, see URAL-ALTAIC LANGUAGES.

FINNS, the Finnish people speak a Finno-Ugric tongue belonging to the Ural-Altaic languages, which are spread widely throughout Asia and portions of Europe. Like the Estonians, the Finns seem to be the relic of a pre-Indo-European population which occupied most of Northern Europe around the Baltic shores in Mesolithic times, and which was largely displaced by incoming Nordics equipped with a Neolithic culture. Today the major part of the Finnish population is largely similar in appearance to the adjacent Nordic peoples, and the inhabitants of Southwestern Finland are of Swedish descent, speaking Swedish. In the interior, however, the population is more distinctive, and is noted for its small highly-inbred communities which have provided geneticists with excellent research material. (See also URAL-ALTAIC LANGUAGES).

FIRE, some Homo erectus populations appear to have known how to make fire, and there is evidence that fire was used in East Africa by early hominids. However, into modern times the Andaman Islanders remained ignorant of any methods of making fire, although they did use fire and in the event of the accidental extinction of a fire, they would acquire new fire from a related band. Fire has frequently played an important role in religion, since the hearth fire has probably from the earliest of times tended to symbolize the group of kinsmen who assembled around it every night. As the older member died, so neonates took their place around the fire, and the hearth came in many cultures to symbolize the continuing family. The Ainu and the Hindus both used fire in their marriage ceremonies, and the Romans led the bride to the bridegroom's home by torch-light. The Parsees, and according to archeological evidence, many other Indo-European peoples, regarded fire as sacred, believing also that it had a purifying effect. One of the reasons why in the Middle Ages Christians burned other Christians, with whose theories they disagreed, is found in the ancient belief that fire would purify the souls of sinners from the sins they had committed during their worldly lives.

FIREARMS, weapons which emit a projectile as a result of an explosion. Gunpowder appears to have been invented by the Chinese in the sixth century A.D., but firearms as we know them date from fourteenth century Europe.

FIRE DRILL, a method of producing fire by friction, in which a drilling stick is twirled rapidly against another piece of wood until the resultant friction produces flames.

FIRE GRATER, a Polynesian fire drill or tool for making fire, comprising a pointed stick of hardwood which is rubbed on a softer piece of wood until the sawdust it creates eventually bursts into flames.

FIRE, GREEK, a Greek invention consisting of a mixture of sulphur, resin, naphtha and oil. Packed in an earthenware pot, complete with a fuse, it was propelled over the walls of besieged cities with the intention of starting destructive fires.

FIRE WALKING, an ordeal whereby a man or woman is required to walk with bare feet through red hot flaming ashes. Fire walking as an initiatory ordeal is particularly associated with certain Hindu cults but it was also used as a test in medieval European church trials to determine guilt or innocence.

FIRE-WORSHIP, since the hearth fire occupies a central place in the life of most households, it frequently plays an important role in ancestor worship. Fire has been treated with reverence by a wide variety of peoples throughout the world, from the Australian aborigines, Ainu and African Bantu, to the South American Incas. But in the case of the Celts, Teutons, Slavs, Romans, Greeks, Persians, Parsees and Indo-Aryans, fire symbolized intergenerational family unity, and this was personified either by the fire on the family hearth or, as in the case of the Romans and Parsees, by a fire on the family altar.

FIRST DEGREE RELATIVES, persons immediately related to each other, i.e. parents, children, brothers and sisters.

FIRST FRUITS, a widespread religious ritual, usually occurring after the collection of the harvest, in which the first agricultural produce is offered to the ancestors, or to the gods, in gratitude for the successful conclusion of the year's agricultural labors. Among the Semites, the ritual obligation to offer the 'First Fruits' to the gods was in some instances even extended to the ritual sacrifice of the first-born son.

FIRST NORTHERN CULTURE (also known as TRB CULTURE), the earliest Neolithic culture of Northern Europe, commencing around 3000 B.C. on the North European plain, and a little later in Southern Scandinavia. The introduction of cultivation into Northern Europe, although early established in the Rhine Valley, was delayed by the need to discover new crops suited to the cooler climate and shorter summers of the north. The First Northern Culture therefore does not reveal any dramatic or substantial advances in technology beyond that of the preceding Mesolithic, except that it is characterized by Funnel Beakers (q.v.) and the evidence of a whole new range of tools such as were needed by horticulturalists. It is a point of unprovable conjecture whether any Indo-European (e.g. proto-German) language was spoken at that time.

FISH HOOK, an invention of Cro-Magnon man, seemingly made during the Magdalenian period, when the fish hooks were carved out of bone.

FITNESS, BIOLOGICAL, the fitness of an invididual or species is measured by the number of offspring who reach reproductive age.
FITNESS, DARWINIAN, the ability to produce offspring who live to reproduce themselves and so continue the lineage.
FLAGELLAE, fine and relatively long protrusions from the cells of certain kinds of Metazoa (q.v.) which assist them in movement, in reproduction, and even in the procurement of food.
FLAKE, any fragment which has been struck off the core or nucleus of a stone. In the course of manufacturing the earlier core tools, flakes were usually discarded, since the object was to shape the core of the stone as a cutting tool. By contrast, in later flake tools, the stone core would be carefully prepared so that when struck at a particular point a flake of the desired shape would result.
FLAKE TOOL, a stone tool comprising a flake which has been struck off a larger core.
FLATHEAD, North American Indians of northern Montana, who speak a Salish language of the Algonquin-Mosan group, and are dependent on fishing, food-gathering and hunting.
FLINT, a type of stone commonly used in the Paleolithic. Hard but brittle, it can be easily worked by percussion or pressure flaking to provide useful cutting tools. Usually found in chalk or limestine areas.
FLOOD, THE GREAT, the Sumerian Gilgamesh epic records the account of a vast flood which destroyed all mankind except for a single family of a man known as Utnapistin. Some archeological evidence from the Mesopotamian research sites confirms the possibility of a major flood having taken place. The story was acquired by the Hebrew people, possibly during their enslavement in Babylon, to become the basis of the Old Testament story of Noah. (See also GILGAMESH EPIC).
FLECTIONAL LANGUAGE, the term 'flectional' refers to the utilization of prefixes and suffixes to reveal the syntactical relationships between words and to modify their meanings. Both agglutinating and amalgamating languages may be said to practice inflection.
FLEMINGS, the Germanic-speaking inhabitants of northern Belgium.
FLESHER, a stone or bone tool used to scrape the flesh from the inner surface of an animal hide.
FLINT, a form of quartz which is eminently suitable for manufacture into stone cutting tools. Although easy to work, flint is actually harder than steel, and this made it a very satisfactory material for Stone Age craftsmen.
FLORA, the plant population of a particular area at any given time.
FLORISBAD, an archeological site in the Orange Free State, excavated in 1932, where parts of a fossil skull suggestive of Homo rhodesiensis have been discovered. These were found in association with Middle Stone Age tools and dated around 33,000 B.P.
FLUORINE TESTING, skeletal material deposited in damp ground tends to be penetrated by ground water. This contains fluorine which slowly replaces the calcium of the bone structure. The rate at which this change takes place depends upon the amount of fluorine in the water, and as a result although fluorine testing cannot provide a reliable estimate of the age of bones excavated from a particular site, it is logical to assume that bones are of the same age as the deposit. Fluorine testing was used to unveil the famous Piltdown hoax (q.v.).
FLUTE, a simple musical instrument which first appeared in the Upper Paleolithic and was probably first used for ceremonial purposes. Musical notes are produced when the musician blows across the end of a long, hollow reed. During the Neolithic Age, additional holes were introduced into the tube at different intervals, which when opened and closed by the application of the fingers resulted in the production of different tones. Some African peoples made flutes out of the longbones of their ancestors, believing that the sounds produced therefrom represented emissions of the ancestral spirit.
FLUTE, AEOLIAN, an early Greek musical instrument comprising a perforated hollow object, which produced musical sounds when hung in the wind.

FLUTE, CROOKED, a musical instrument constructed from bull or ram's horn. Invented by the ancient Egyptians, the crooked flute resembles the Hebrew *shofar* which may be derived from it.
FOETALIZATION, the theory that in the course of the evolution of certain organisms, the development of the individual organism tends to be retarded at a fetal stage. In effect, there is a prolongation of infantilism into adult life. This foetalization process is regarded as being particularly obvious in the case of man, since the more advanced hominid skulls are usually closer in shape to the skulls of infants belonging to the ancestral species. Thus the relatively large size of the cranium in the adult modern Homo sapiens compares with the relatively large size of the head in the fetus of more primitive hominids, even the relative hairlessness of the modern human body has been likened to an infantile retardation. However, the theory is poorly documented and of doubtful validity.
FOETUS, the name given to the mammalian embryo after it has developed most of the more important features of the future animal. Among hominids the term foetus is usually applied to the fertilized embryo at the stage of development reached approximately two months after gestation.
FOLD, EPICANTHIC, see EPICANTHIC FOLD.
FOLD, NORDIC, a fold in the upper eyelid that hangs down to mask the outer epicanthus (q.v.), in contrast with the Mongolian epicanthic fold (q.v.) which covers the inner epicanthus.
FOLIATE, a term used to refer to a willow-leaf stone point, characteristic of the Solutrean Upper Paleolithic cultures of Europe.
FOLK, a term which anciently implied 'the people', but which is frequently used to refer to the mass of common people in any post-tribal society.
FOLKLORE, a collection of orally transmitted traditions comprising a mixture of stories, myths, legends, songs and superstitions surviving from earlier magico-religious traditions.
FOLK SOCIETY, a relatively isolated society operating largely through primary contacts. As originally conceived by Redfield, the 'folk society' was the opposite of the 'urban society'. This clear contrast has been subsequently modified by the concept of territorial zones in contemporary complex societies reflected in the term 'folk-urban continuum'.
FOLKTALE, an oral narrative which may have religious or mythological origins no longer remembered by those who pass the folktale from one generation to another.
FOLKVANG, the palace or home of the Norse goddess Freya, the halls of which were filled with songs of love and beauty.
FOLK-WANDERING, a term used to refer to the extensive migrations, usually involving military conquest, first by the Celtic and later by the Teutonic peoples, in late European prehistory and early European history. This period of folk-wandering is now seen to be but a continuation of an extensive pattern of movement and conquest by Indo-Europeans which appears to have persisted as an accepted way of life over some three or more millennia. In Germany known as 'Volkerwanderung'.
FOLKWAYS, a term invented by Sumner, to refer to the less strongly enforced customs, each of which might be punished informally by means of avoidance, criticism or even ostracism, but contravention of which, unlike the contravention of *mores* (q.v.), does not lead to ejection from the community, death or any other serious punishment.
FOLSOM, an archeological site in New Mexico which revealed the remains of a variety of extinct fauna and channeled or fluted stone projectile points which have been dated from the 9th millennium B.C. The Folsom point, as this type of projectile is called, appears to have developed out of the Clovis tradition (q.v.).
FON, a Kwa-speaking Negroid people from West Africa largely dependent on horticulture, hunting and animal husbandry.
FONTANELLE, the space which separates the bones of the cranium in newborn infants.

FONTECHEVADE, an archeological cave site in Charente, in France, where an important fossil skull cap and small fragment of a frontal bone dating from 200,000 B.P. were discovered by Mlle. G. Henri-Martin in 1947. These were at first regarded as a type of Early Neanderthal man, more modern in type than the Classic Neanderthals of 100,000 to 38,000 B.P., but some authorities today classify the Fontechevade remains as Homo sapiens steinheimensis.
FOOD-GATHERING SOCIETIES, simple band-type societies, each occupying their own territory, which appear to represent the simplest level of hominid subsistence. As appears to have been the case with many of the Lower Paleolithic peoples, simple food-gathering or foraging societies depend upon fruit, berries, roots, nuts, fungus, insects, eggs and any small animals which they can catch, supplemented perhaps by scavenging the meat of dead or dying animals. Some may also supplement food-gathering by scavenging meat left over from the meals of carnivorous animals or by killing animals trapped in such natural obstacles as bogs and swamps. Few purely food-gathering societies have survived into the present age, although the Yahgan of South America and the Andamanese Islanders are largely food-gatherers, who supplement their diet by a conerable amount of fishing and shellfish collecting. Communities depending solely upon food-gathering are invariably small, often not exceeding 20 to 25 people. Each has its own territory and seldom, if ever, moves outside this territory. They invariably lack a pronounced degree of social stratification, except by sex and age, the men being dominant over the women and the adults dominant over the children.
FOOL'S HAT, see HAT, CONICAL.
FORAMEN, any natural perforation or opening in a bone, the usual purpose of which is to permit the passage of a nerve or blood vessel.
FORAMEN MAGNUM, the opening in the base of the skull through which the spinal cord joins the brain.
FORE-BRAIN (PRESENCEPHALON), the anterior of the three divisions of the vertebrate brain. It is within the fore-brain that the cerebral hemispheres and the areas controlling the eyes and the hypothalamus develop.
FORMATIVE PERIOD, a term frequently used to describe simple cultures which later evolved into more complex cultures equivalent to a civilization. The term 'classical period' is usually applied to the more evolved culture which the formative period precedes.
FORMLESS LANGUAGES, languages which do not inflect, and in which, lacking prefixes and suffixes, the exact meaning of the word depends upon the position it assumes in a sentence.
FORMOSA, although primarily populated today by Chinese people, Formosa still contains an aboriginal population of Malayo-Polynesian-speaking tribes, which include the Atayal, Paiwan, Yami, and Ami.
FORUM, the main center of a Roman town, located at the intersection of the major streets, containing the main temples, administrative buildings and market place.
FOSSA, the name used by archeologists to refer to a moat, especially to the moat that usually surrounded a Terramare village (q.v.).
FOSSILS, the remains of prehistoric life forms, sometimes mineralized by the absorption of mineral deposits.
FOSTER PARENTS, in some cultures, including that of the ancient Scandinavian nobility, it was customary to give sons to a close relative or friend to raise. The man adopting such a trust was known as a foster father. The purpose appears to have been rooted in the belief that no father could be expected to train his own son to face death in battle, and among the Celts of Gaul fathers were reputed to avoid the company of their own sons until the latter had come of age and earned the right to bear arms.
FOUNDER EFFECT, the term used in population genetics to refer to the phenomenon, by which, when a single population divides into two separate breeding populations, there is a statistical probability that the two separate populations will not share the genetic components of the original population

in equal or identical proportions. This is particularly true when a new breeding population is formed as a result of the breaking away of a small group from a parent group, which according to the law of averages is unlikely to take with it an exactly proportionate share of all the genes in the parent gene pool. Thus the new breeding isolate starts with a slightly different gene pool.

FOX, Central Algonquin North American Indians, dependent on hunting and horticulture with some fishing and food-gathering.

FRATERNITY, originally a kinship term implying a 'brotherhood' of related kinsmen, the term fraternity has survived in more complex societies as a term which may be applied to any all-male associations.

FRATRICIDE, the killing of a 'brother' or kinsman, widely regarded by kinship-based societies as the most heinous of all crimes.

FRAVISHI, originally used to refer to the ancestral spirits which were worshipped by the early Persians, the *fravishi* were admitted into Zoroastrian monotheism as guardian spirits.

FRENCH CANADIANS, an ethnic group descended from French settlers who occupied Eastern Canada while this territory was still ruled by the French Crown. Some American Indian genetic admixture occurred among them during the colonial period.

FREYJA, the Norse goddess of love, equivalent to the Roman Venus, who gave her name to the day of the week known as Friday.

FRICATIVE, a term of articulation in which the air is expelled through a narrow groove made by the mouth and teeth.

FRIGGA, the wife of the Norse god Odin, and the mother of Thor, who presided over matrimonial relations.

FRONTAL BONE, the large dermal bone which covers the front part of the brain, roughly corresponding to the human forehead.

FRUCTIVORE, an animal that relies primarily upon the consumption of fruit. The adjective 'frugivorous' thus refers to dependence on fruits rather than cereals or meat.

FRUIT, FORBIDDEN, an ancient belief, probably dating back to the Upper Paleolithic, since it was widespread throughout large areas of Europe and Western Asia, concerning a 'Tree of Knowledge,' the fruit of which could provide both gods and men with boundless wisdom and immortality. Among the Greeks, Iduna guarded a tree, the fruit whereof kept the gods immortal. Sumerian mythology also records an ancient story on which the Judeo-Christian and Moslem legend of a creator-god is based, who prohibits Adam and Eve from eating of the 'Tree of Knowledge' and who expells them from Paradise when, tempted by a snake which reveals the secret of the knowledge-giving fruit, they disregarded the creator-god's instructions and tasted the forbidden fruit.

FUKIENESE, a Chinese people of the eastern coastal area of Fukien.

FULANI, a herding and horticultural people of Northwest Nigeria.

FUNCTIONAL THEORY, the anthropological theory, largely popularized by Bronislaw Malinowski, that no cultural trait ever survives unless it fulfills a useful function. Thus even ancient traditional rituals, which seem to have outlived their usefulness, only survive if they still serve some purpose in the living society, even if they serve as symbols which unify the members of the society as a cooperating self-conscious and self-aware group. STRUCTURAL-FUNCTIONAL THEORY.

FUNERAL, a ritual ceremony which probably first appeared with the Neanderthal men of the European and Near-Eastern Middle Palaeolithic, but which still survives as an essential rite of passage (q.v.) in every known society. The English word 'funeral' itself derives from the Latin for 'torch', because the ancient Romans buried their dead kinsmen at night by torchlight. In some societies the funeral rituals may be motivated mainly by the fear of the ghosts of the deceased and by a desire to ensure that such ghosts will not return to haunt or cause trouble for the living. In other societies, however, in which a bond of close sympathy exists between the departed and the surviving, the funeral rituals may be intended purely to assist the spirit of the departed to enter the afterlife without undue difficulty, and also to assist the living psychologically. The attention paid to the performance of the traditional ritual may help to alleviate the grief of the survivors. In some cases funeral feasts may be conducted, in which the spirit of the departed is supposed to participate with the living, and it is usually obligatory upon all kinsmen who attend such feasts to maintain a cheerful and gay demeanour.

FUNNEL BEAKER, a beaker vessel with an extended neck. This type of vessel is closely associated with the First Northern Culture, the earliest Neolithic phase in Northern Europe, hence the term TRB which is sometimes used as a substitute for the First Northern Culture (q.v.) representing an abbreviation of the German word *Trichterbecher.*

FUR, a linguistically unclassified people (otherwise known as Darfur) in north tropical Africa largely dependent on horticulture with some animal husbandry and fishing.

FURIES, the Roman equivalent of the Erinyes (q.v.).

FUT, a Bantu-speaking Negroid people from the Cameroon Highlands dependent mainly on horticulture with some animal husbandry and hunting.

FUTHARK, see RUNES.

FUTAJALONKE, a West African Sedentary Fulani people of mainly Negroid type, dependent on horticulture and pastoralism. Some anthropologists believe they show evidence of Hamitic admixture.

FUTHARK, see RUNES.

FUTUNANS, a West Polynesian people dependent on horticulture and fishing, with some animal husbandry.

FUZZY-WUZZY, a derogatory term first used by British soldiers to refer to the frizzy-haired tribesmen they encountered in the Sudan, but subsequently extended in colloquial Anglo-American to refer to Melanesians, who also possess an ample quantity of frizzy hair.

FYLFOT, a three-armed curvilinear variant of the swastika (q.v.). Common among the Celts, it was originally a sun symbol.

G

GA, a Kwa-speaking Negroid people of West Africa belonging to the Akan group, and largely dependent on horticulture and fishing.

GABRIELINO, a Shoshone-speaking American Indian (Uto-Aztec) people of Southeastern California, dependent on food-gathering, fishing and some hunting.

GAEA, the Greek earth goddess.

GAGU, a Mande-speaking Negroid people of West Africa, largely dependent on horticulture and hunting, with some animal husbandry and food-gathering.

GALATEANS, a Goidelic Celtic people who fought their way through Southeast Europe and eventually settled in Central Anatolia.

GALENA, a blue-grey lead ore, used by American Indians of the Mississippi culture for ornamental purposes.

GALICIANS, a Goidelic Celtic people who settled Northwestern Iberia.

GALLA, a herding people of Southern Ethiopia who speak a Cushite language.

GALLERY GRAVE, a variety of chamber tomb entered by a long passage. The combination of the chamber tomb and the passage entrance creates the impression of a single corridor constructed of stones covered by a mound of earth. Gallery graves were common in Western Europe in the Neolithic and Copper Ages.

GALLEY HILL, an archeological site in England dating from the middle Pleistocene, notable for the discovery of a Cro-Magnon fossil, the cranium of which seems to resemble those of the living Mediterranean Caucasoid stock.

GAMBLE'S CAVE, an archeological site which provides evidence of an African Mesolithic culture dated around 7000 B.P. Since no trace of any native sub-Saharan Upper Paleolithic culture has so far been discovered, Gamble's Cave and the Naivasha site provide substantial evidence that Mesolithic culture was first introduced into sub-Saharan Africa by Caucasoid Hamites.

GAMBLING, a term applied to participation in games of chance and risk. Most such games are believed to have originated as magico-religious attempts to divide the fortunes of the participants, but in more complex societies, games of chance have tended to lose their religious significance and to have been relegated to merely recreational significance. Needless to say, recreational gambling is only found in those societies which have developed some degree of individualization of wealth.

GAME-CHARMING, the attempt to attract hunted animals closer to the hunter by the recitation of magical formulae.

GAMES, most games appear to have originated as magico-religious ritual play-acting, but in more complex societies games have tended to become purely recreational activities in which the players participate in accordance with a customary set of rules. Thus the earlier Roman chariot races and horse races had magico-religious significance, but following urbanization and the rise of Imperial Rome they largely lost their religious significance and became little more than spectacles organized for the amusement of the populace.

GAMETE, a reproductive cell, the nucleus and cytoplasm of which fuse with the same components in another gamete to produce a zygote (q.v.) cell, thus creating a new individual.

GAMEWAY RITUALS, a term sometimes applied to the magico-religious hunting rituals of the Navajo and other North American Indians.

GANDA, an East Lacustrine Bantu-speaking Negroid people mainly dependent on horticulture.

GANDHARA, a satrap of the Persian Achaemenid empire which roughly corresponded to the area of present day Pakistan.

GANESH, the elephant-headed Hindu god of wisdom.

GANGETIC HOARDS, various hoards of valuable copper objects found at different locations in the Ganges valley in India. These vary from antennae swords, axes and harpoons to anthropomorphic symbols. Some of the hoards have been associated with ochre-colored pottery and it is possible, but not provable at the present time, that these sites may be associated with early Indo-European penetration.

GARDEN, a horticultural plantation worked solely by human muscle. Thus a gardener is a man or woman who cultivates the soil using only elementary tools operated by human muscle power.

GARM, the hell-hound of Teutonic mythology, which probably shared a common origin with Cerberus, the Greek guardian dog of the underworld.

GARO, a tribal hill people of Eastern India, who reveal Mongoloid influences and speak a Tibeto-Burman language. The Garo are mainly dependent on horticulture, but practise some animal husbandry and fishing.

GASTROMANCY, a method of divination practised in a number of different societies, in which the diviner peers into a container filled with water or some other liquid. As among the Eskimos, this container may be constructed from animal parts, such as the entrails or stomach.

GATHAS, the oldest of the Zoroastrian *Avesta* (q.v.), or sacred writings, comprising 17 hymns arranged in five different collections or *Gathas*.

GATHERING, FOOD-, food-gathering would appear to be the oldest of the various methods of hominid subsistence. It was possibly dominant at the Australopithecine (q.v.) level of evolution and is still the basic means of subsistence among certain isolated and economically primitive people.

GBANDE, a Mande-speaking West African people, largely dependent on horticulture and animal husbandry, supplemented by some hunting.

GBARI, a West African Negro people of the coastal forests of Nigeria, primarily dependent on horticulture.

GÊ, a South American Indian family of languages, related to Pano and Carib, spoken in the highlands of Brazil. Gê includes Timbiri, Shavante, Sherente, and Apinaye.

GEFION, the German patron-goddess of children and young unmarried women.

GEMEINSCHAFT, a term suggested by the sociologist Tönnies to describe the concept of a small community of persons living in constant face-to-face relationships with each other, who are united by common traditions, learned in childhood, and among whom social contact is governed by informal person-to-person relationships rather than by the necessity of formal legal statutes. (See also GESELLSCHAFT).

GEMEINSCHAFT SOCIETY, a society in which the human relations are predominantly personal and traditional. A good example of the folk society.

GENDER, a system of classification of words, characteristic of Indo-European, Semitic and a number of other languages, by which all nouns are classified as having either masculine, feminine, or possibly even neuter gender. Proto-Indo-European is believed to have had only a neuter and common gender for animate beings which did not distinguish between male and female. Indo-European is the only language family possessing all three forms of gender.

GENE COMPLEX, the total genetic constitution of an individual or of a population isolate (q.v.). The concept is important because the effect of a major gene may be different in one gene complex from its effect in another, e.g., the gene controlling the *G6PD* deficiency may have different effects in different populations.

GENE ECOLOGY, a genetic term used to refer to the study of the genetic basis of phenotypical and behavioral characteristics. All structural and behavioral characteristics have a genetic basis the effects of which are modified during the developmental life history of the organism by environmental conditions and experiences. The former 'nature-versus-nurture' controversy, which conceived of heredity and environment as being mutually exclusive alternates, has been abandoned, and it is now realized that all living organisms depend for all of their qualities on a genetically-defined potential the development of which is constantly subject to modification by the prevailing environmental conditions.

GENE FLOW, the transmission of inherited qualities from one distinct population to another as a result of the acceptance of genes derived from alien individuals into the gene pool of the recipient population.

GENE POOL, the total genetic heritage possessed by a distinct breeding population. The term 'pool' is used since with each successive generation the genes from the common pool are redistributed among the individual members.

GENES, a term used by geneticists to refer to the mechanism by which particular sets of inherited characteristics are transmitted from generation to generation.

GENES, LETHAL, many mutations are so far-reaching in their effect that they create lethal genes which under certain circumstances may make life impossible for the individual inheriting them. However, if the lethal gene is recessive (q.v.) it will only kill individuals when inherited in a homozygous (q.v.) condition. Such recessive genes, though lethal in a homozygous condition may be present in the genotype of heterozygous individuals, thereby avoiding elimination by natural selection and remaining in the gene pool as part of the 'genetic load'.

GENETIC DRIFT, a change in the frequency of specific genes within small and relatively isolated populations arising from 'accidental' factors unrelated to natural selection.

GENETIC LOAD, an accumulation of harmful or undesirable genes in the gene pool of a given population.

GENETICS, the science of heredity, concerned with the inheritance of similarities and the appearance of inherited dissimilarities in related organisms.

GENNA TABOO, a term used by anthropologists to refer to a universal prohibition against certain forms of customary behavior applied to the entire community in specific circumstances such as the death of a divinely-descended chieftain. The word *genna* is borrowed from the Naga language.

GENOTYPE, the entire content of the genetic heritage transmitted from parents to offspring, including not merely the dominant genes responsible for the structure of the organism but also the corresponding recessive genes which may nevertheless contribute to the genetic heritage of subsequent generations.

GENS, a Roman kinship group, the exact nature of which is still disputed. The

Roman 'gens' probably corresponded to a patrilineal clan, except that marriage within the gens appears to have been permitted during the latter part of the Republican era. This development may have occurred as a result of an increase in the number of members of the gens and the desire to strengthen the bonds linking the members, since the gens was an important political, religious and property-owning unit among the patricians.

GENUS, in biological classification a 'genus' is a term used to refer to a group of similar species. Groups of similar genera (pl.) are classified as belonging to a specific family (q.v.).

GEOCHRONOLOGY, the classification of the history of the earth in terms of geological time scales.

GEOLOGICAL DATING, the dating of fossils and artifacts according to the geological classification of the strata in which they are found.

GEOLOGICAL PERIODS, the main geological Periods are listed below, although there is no general agreement on dating:

Approximate Starting Date (million years B.P.)	*Geological Period*
3600	Pre-Cambrian
575	Cambrian
505	Ordovician
430	Silurian
395	Devonian
345	Carboniferous
280	Permian
225	Triassic
190	Jurassic
136	Cretaceous
65	Paleocene
54	Eocene
38	Oligocene
26	Miocene
12	Pliocene
2.3	Pleistocene

Although the earliest forms of unicellular life are associated with Pre-Cambrian rocks, a variety of invertebrates developed in the Cambrian period and primitive land plants appeared in the Silurian period. Amphibians and Arthropoda are found to have lived on land during the Devonian period. It is the enormous accumulation of remains from the deceased plant life of the succeeding Carboniferous period that has provided us with the limited reserves of coal and oil which are being so rapidly exploited today. The Jurassic period was dominated by reptiles, but also saw the birth of the first mammals, which latter achieved pre-eminence during the Cretaceous period. Hominoid fossils survive from the Oligocene, and Hominids first appear in the Pliocene.

GEOLOGIC TIME, all that time which has elapsed since the formation of the earth, customarily divided into separate geological periods.

GEOMANCY, divination by means of an interpretation of lines, shapes and figures. Arab geomancers, for example, study the patterns made in the sand by the action of the wind.

GEOPHAGY, a practice fairly common in many societies, involving the consumption of special types of earth, especially clay, the expressed reasons for which appear to differ considerably, some anthropologists explaining geophagy as an attempt to overcome dietary deficiencies, others attributing it to magico-religious objectives.

GEORGIANS, a Caucasoid people of the Caucasian Mountains, traditionally dependent on agriculture.

GERMANIC SOUND SHIFT, one of the earliest discoveries by nineteenth century linguists was the fact that the German language, which was originally spoken by a single people, experienced two major sound shifts. The first of these, which separated the Proto-Germanic languages from the more closely related Indo-European languages, probably occurred around the 3rd millennium B.C. The 2nd sound shift occurred between the 1st century B.C. and the 8th century A.D. when the West Germanic languages became divided into High German, Middle German, and Low German.

GERMANS, a North European people who speak a Western Indo-European language. Today the term is applied to all German-speaking peoples resident in Central Europe, but the Germans of the time of Tacitus were a remarkably homogeneous Nordic population. The name German is derived from a presumably mythic ancestor named 'Mannus' (q.v.), from whom they 'germinated' or descended. The term 'Germanic' is often used in a collective sense to ininclude the Scandinavian and Anglo-Saxon peoples. (See also TEUTON).

GERONIMO, an Apache medicine man who organized armed American Indian resistance against the spread of European power.

GERONTOCIDE, see SENILICIDE.

GERONTOCRACY, a common form of government in patriarchal cultures in which the older men hold authority over the other members of the community.

GERZEAN, a pre-Dynastic Egyptian culture dated around 3500 B.C., named after an archeological site at El Gerza in the Fayum depression. Many tools were of stone, but some copper axes and daggers were found as well as the earliest known faience work (q.v.). Some Mesopotamian influence is in evidence, particularly in the use of cylinder seals, and in the types of mythical animals represented. Mudbrick constructions resembled those of Mesopotamia and the Gerzean culture generally suggests that the Egyptian civilization, which was to emerge with the commencement of the Dynastic period, cir. 3200 B.C., was probably stimulated by influences from Mesopotamia.

GESELLSCHAFT, the concept of a complex society, as proposed by the sociologist Tönnies, in contradistinction to the idea of 'Gemeinschaft' (q.v.). In a Gesellschaft society, the larger community is held together by reciprocal needs and the division of labour, rather than by personal face-to-face ties. Associations are formed with deliberate purposes, and rules are deliberately conceived for the purpose of achieving the desired goals instead of being handed down as a tradition, to be accepted by all members as in a Gemeinschaft type of society.

GESTA, rectangular slabs, made from stone, ivory or wood, which served as palettes for Egyptian scribes.

GESTATION PERIOD, the period of time during which a newly conceived zygote develops inside the maternal organism prior to birth.

GESTURE, a means of communication involving a movement of parts of the body in a culturally prescribed manner. Symbolic or gesticulatory movements often still play an important role in religious ritual and ceremonial, and are one of the major means by which non-human primates communicate with each other.

GETAE, an Indo-European people closely related to the Thracians, who lived in Romania and Bulgaria in the later Iron Age, around the Fourth Century B.C. Their culture shows strong parallels with both Celtic (La Tène) and Scythian traditions.

GEZER, an archeological tell site near Jerusalem, dating from the late 5th millennium B.C. until the Iron Age. Artifacts discovered include the Gezer calendar (11th century B.C.), which constitutes one of the oldest known inscriptions in the early Hebrew language.

GHAT, a large open staircase in India, usually leading from a temple to a river, to allow the worshippers access to the river waters for ritual bathing.

GHEG, a modern nation occupying a mountainous territory in the European Balkans. The Gheg speak a distinctive Indo-European language and are traditionally dependent on agriculture and animal husbandry.

GHETTO, formerly, in ancient Europe, an area wherein alien communities, usually comprising merchants or craftsmen, were permitted to live in accordance with their own customs. During Medieval and Renaissance times the members of such communities were frequently prohibited from living outside of the ghetto and the term has consequently come to be used to refer to slum areas occupied by socially or economically subordinate ethnic groups.

GHI, a form of butter which has been boiled so as to remain solid in warm climates. Made from cattle, goat, sheep or camel milk, various forms of 'ghi' are found in India, East Africa and Central Asia (where it probably originated).

GHOST, the visible, semi-visible or invisible spirit of a deceased person. Many cultures predicate the idea of a separable soul which survives the death of the body, but which may continue to reside close to the corpse or the place of death if denied the opportunity to find permanent rest.

GHOST DANCE, a relatively short-lived messianic ceremonial, which developed among American Indians as recently as 1889 in a reaction against the incursion of White settlers into the Indian hunting grounds. Believing that the ancestors would soon return to the earth to help the surviving Indians drive the White men out of their homeland, the adherents to the Ghost Dance cult engaged in a ritual dancing ceremonial, which involved self-mutilation and fasting, in an attempt to encourage the return of the ancestral warrior heroes.

GHOST HOLE, a hole sometimes found in cinerary urns, believed to have been made to allow the souls of the deceased to leave and return to the urn at will.

GHOSTS, ROUSING THE, a malicious practical joke played at the expense of the dead and the living relatives of the dead, involving interference with a corpse, usually before burial, with the deliberate intention of disturbing the ghost.

GHOUL, a supernatural monster that consumes corpses and may even attack and eat living people.

GIANTS, many different cultures in all parts of the world possess folklore traditions recounting the former existence of giants, often described as cannibals. This widespread belief in the former existence of giants remains unexplained.

GIBARI, a Kwa-speaking Negroid people of West Africa, largely dependent on horticulture with some animal husbandry, hunting and food-gathering.

GIBE, an East African people of Cushitic origin and speech, who are dependent on horticulture supplemented by some hunting.

GIBRALTAR, Gibraltar possesses two important archeological sites both revealing hominid fossil remains, the earlier of which, found in 1848, was very primitive and has been classified by some authorities as Homo erectus (q.v.). The 1926 fossil discoveries known as Gibraltar II were associated with Levalloisian-Mousterian cultures, and may be dated around 50,000 years B.P., being unquestionably Neanderthal in character.

GIERES, the Lapp name for a sled shaped rather like a boat.

GIFT-GIVING, gift-giving plays an important role in early societies which have not yet developed a market economy, since by the offer of a gift, the giver demonstrates his friendship and goodwill towards the recipient, whether this be a kinsman, or a neighbor. The act of gift-giving may be accompanied by considerable boasting, and substantial friendly rivalry may develop between related social groups, each seeking to out-do the other in munificence.

GIFT, INDIAN, a term common in the United States for any gift which is given on the express understanding that a reciprocal gift or act of beneficence may be expected in return. The expression arose among European settlers in America, who were unaccustomed to the concept of strict reciprocity prevalent among the kinship-based Indian societies with whom they found themselves in contact.

GIFT, MORNING, a Teutonic tradition whereby the bridegroom presents his bride with a gift on the morning of the day after the wedding.

GIGANTOPITHECUS, an extinct fossil hominoid genus evidence of which is found in India (dating from the Pliocene) and in China (dating from the Pleistocene). Discovered by von Koenigswald, the fossil evidence comprised, in both cases, mandibles and teeth. Gigantopithecus was so-named because they were even larger than those of a gorilla.

GILBERT ISLANDERS, a Micronesian people of the South Pacific, dependent on horticulture and fishing.

GILGAMESH EPIC, Gilgamesh, king of Uruk, half god and half man, is the hero of the famous Sumerian epic known by his name. Having annoyed the gods, the latter sent a wild man named Enkidu to harass him, but after the two fought in single combat, they became friends. However, Gilgamesh subsequently rejected the amatory approaches of the goddess Ishtar, who killed his friend Enkidu out of spite. Gilgamesh then sought out the secret of immortality, which he found in the form of an underwater plant, but losing this to a snake, he consequently failed in his search for immortality. The epic contains an account of the Great Flood, of which Utnapishtin was the sole survivor, a legend which inspired the biblical story of the flood.

GILYAK, an East Siberian people dependent on fishing, hunting whales and sea mammals, and somefood-gathering, whose language and culture may be distantly related to that of the Paleo-Asians. Their homeland includes the lower Amur river and the Okhotsk coastal region.

GIPSY, the name given to a widespread people who traditionally call themselves the Romany (a term meaning simply 'men'), the English word Gipsy being derived from 'Egyptian', in accordance with the Medieval European belief that they derived from Egypt. Gipsies appear to have originated in western India, and indeed a study of Gipsy bloodgroup patterns reveals certain similarities to those of the Indus valley today. After wandering westwards through Iran, Armenia and Syria, they first entered Europe in 1417 and, organized in small kinship groups with broader tribal links, remained a migratory people travelling across frontiers whenever permitted. Travelling in groups comprising several families, the Gipsies have traditionally lived as traders, gaining a reputation as horse dealers and frequently, also, as horse thieves, while the women worked as fortune tellers, dancers and entertainers. Historically most European nations have shown great hostility towards the Gipsies, who were even accused of kidnapping children, and local authorities frequently refused to permit them to camp within their territory while by contrast national authorities have sometimes attempted to force them to adopt a sedentary pattern of life and to convert to Christianity. Indeed, efforts to force the migratory Gipsies to adopt a more permanent settled existence have been very strong in the socialist countries of eastern Europe in recent years. Until the present century, however, the Gipsies successfully preserved their own distinctive culture, including their own language and a code of social behaviour known as the *kris*. Migrant bands are known as *vitsas*, and operate under the leadership of a patriarchal chief and a council of family heads. The nuclear family has little economic independence within the vitsa.

GIRIAMA, a Bantu-speaking Negroid people of the Nyika group, largely dependent on horticulture and some animal domestication.

GISU, a Bantu-speaking Negroid people of the East Nyanza area, largely dependent on horticulture with some animal domestication and hunting.

GIYAN, TEPE, an archeological tell site near Hamadan in Western Iran, dating from the first part of the 4th millennium B.C. Evidence of Indo-European occupation appears in the second millennium B.C. in the form of grey monochrome pottery.

GIZA, a site on the west bank of the Nile close to the suburbs of modern Cairo, which is famous for the Great Pyramid, the Sphinx and two smaller pyramids, all erected around 2500 B.C.

GLABELLA, the mid-point between the supra-orbital ridges above the nose, from which many anthropometrical head measurements are taken.

GLABROUSNESS, the term used to refer to the relative absence of hair from the body. Negroids and Mongoloids are generally glabrous, whereas Caucasoids generally possess a considerable amount of body hair. The Pygmy is the most glabrous of living hominids and the Ainu the least glabrous.

GLACIAL TROUGH, a term used to refer to the rounded U-shaped valleys, carved by glaciers which not only carried away all spurs or irregularities from the surface, but also tended to deepen the bottom of the valley into a characteristic U-shape.

GLACIATIONS, during the Pleistocene, and possibly at earlier times, successive cold periods known as glaciations covered northern Europe with heavy layers of ice and snow, resulting especially in substantial glaciation of the Alpine and other mountain valleys. Four European or Alpine glacial ages have been identified, namely Günz, Mindel, Riss and Würm, each named after particular Alpine valleys. These are believed to coincide chronologically with the Illinoian, Kansan, Nebraskan and Wisconsin glaciations which occurred on the North American continent. Although the tropical areas were not directly affected by the major glaciations of the Pleistocene, there is evidence that Central Africa in particular experienced alternating 'pluvial' periods (q.v.) marked by considerable rainfall and interspersed by interpluvial periods of relatively dry weather. An attempt has been made by Grahame Clark to link European glaciations with the Kageran, Kamasian, Kanjeran and Gambian pluvial periods (q.v.) identified in tropical Africa. The four glacial ages named above were preceded by a lengthy Villafranchian period, which is today also frequently included in the Pleistocene, thus extending the Pleistocene back to around 2,300,000 B.P. (See also INTERGLACIAL and INTERSTADIAL).

GLACIER, a solid mass of ice and snow which creeps slowly down a valley, as fresh deposits of snow increase the weight of the upper deposits. Glaciers cut into the surface of the valley, scraping away large quantities of earth, soil and broken rock or rubble and deposit these at lower altitudes in formations known as moraines, as the warmer air melts the glacier.

GLAGOLITHIC, an ancient alphabet comprising essentially geometrical forms, formerly used by the Slavic-speaking peoples and possibly linked to the script of the Old European civilization (q.v.).

GLANDS, organs whose function is the production of specific chemical secretions. Some, such as the sweat glands of mammals, help to maintain body temperature and rid the body of unwanted material, while others located in the intestines serve as digestive glands producing chemicals which help to break down complex organic food materials. Many more complex animals also possess endocrine glands which secrete hormones into the blood stream, as an additional means of stimulating or suppressing organic activity.

GLASS, a transparent material produced by heating silica sand together with an alkali, the knowledge of which was probably discovered by makers of faïence towards the end of the 5th millennium B.C. Glass was at first mainly used for beads, ornaments and other decorative devices.

GLASTONBURY, a site in Somerset, England, in which a lake village dating from the British Iron Age has been extensively excavated. The village was built on large wooden platforms, and contained some 60 round houses constructed from clay, the entire village being encircled by a timber palisade. Artifacts indicate parallels with the La Tène culture, and since the village was occupied in the 3rd and 2nd centuries B.C., it may be assumed to have been Celtic.

GLAZING, a technique by which pottery and other objects may be coated with powdered glass and then heated until the glass powder fuses. The object would seem to be to render pottery vessels impermeable to liquids as well as to improve their appearance.

GLOBULAR AMPHORA, an amphora which is particularly wide in diameter. Globular amphorae are found in association with the First Northern Culture and also with the Corded Ware culture, both of which are also found in association with the large barrows or 'kurgans' dating from the 3rd millennium B.C. in the Kuban and Pontic Steppes.

GLOBULIN, the protein in blood plasma.

GLOGER'S RULE, a principle governing the pigmentation of hominid populations. Gloger's Rule states that natural selection in warm and humid climates favors heavier pigmentation but that there is a selection against the same pigmentation among hominid populations which have evolved in colder and dryer climates. When the temperature and the humidity are high, more eumelanin is found in the skin, whereas when the temperature is high but the humidity is low, pigmentation is mainly due to phaeomelanin.

GLOSSEME, a term sometimes used by linguists to refer to the smallest unit of meaningful sound.

GLOSSOLALIA, a term used to refer to the frenzied babblings of worshippers when in a state of religious ecstacy.

GLOTTAL STOP, the sound produced by the larynx with the closing of the vocal chords.

GLOTTOCHRONOLOGY, the attempt to analyze the history of related languages by comparing their basic vocabulary at different stages in their respective evolution from a common speech. One of the principles of glottochronology is that, assuming a relative state of cultural isolation, the basic vocabulary, sounds and pronunciation of all languages will tend to drift at a fairly constant rate. However, should the speakers of two different languages be brought into close cultural contact with each other, the rate of change is normally accelerated.

GLYPH, any character or figure which is incised or carved in relief.

GNATHION, the middle point of the lower edge of the jaw.

GNOME, in Teutonic mythology, a dwarf who resides in a subterranean home. Gnomes were believed to be capable of manufacturing not only rich and beautiful jewelry but also weapons possessing magical powers.

GNOMON, a rod stuck into the ground so that its shadow indicates the position of the sun. Gnomons are thus primitive sundials which show not only the time of the day but also the season of the year.

GNOSTICISM, despite its strong association with the ideas of the Essenes, Gnosticism incorporated a certain amount of Neo-Platonic philosophical argument, hence its emphasis on the Greek concept of 'Gnosis' or knowledge, implying salvation through knowledge, even though the Gnostic concept of knowledge was early distorted into forms of religious mysticism which ignored Aristotelian logic and the accumulation of Greek mathematical scientific knowledge.

GOAJIRO, a South American Indian people speaking an Arawak language, dependent primarily on animal husbandry with some horticulture, fishing and hunting.

GO-BETWEEN, a person, usually a relative, who acts as a professional matchmaker, negotiating the bride price, dowry and other details when arranging a marriage between the members of two separate kinship groups. The obvious advantage of a go-between is that the two kin groups, who are usually already related and now seek even closer social bonds as a result of the proposed marriage, are spared the embarrassment of the face-to-face haggling over the financial aspects of the transaction.

GOBI, a vast desert area in East Central Asia which formerly enjoyed a milder climate, as evidenced by the number of Mesolithic and Neolithic artifacts that have been found there. The artifacts appear to be associated with West Asian rather than with oriental cultures.

GOBLIN, a house spirit who assists in household chores when treated properly, but may engage in mischievious pranks if affronted by the human occupants of the house.

GODDESS, MOTHER, the worship of a mother goddess or 'Great Mother' who symbolized fertility and procreation, not only of people but also of both crops and herds, and whose worship was formerly widespread throughout those parts of Southern Europe, the Balkans and the Middle East occupied by the Atlanto-Mediterranean peoples.

GOD, FINITE, in most polytheistic systems; the powers of each individual god are believed to be limited, particular functions or particular territories being attributed to individual deities. Such deities are said to have 'finite' powers, as distinct from the presumably 'infinite' powers of a monotheistic god (q.v.).

GOD, HIGH, many polytheistic religions assume a hierarchy of gods which corresponds to the hierarchical social structure practiced by their worshippers on earth. Since most such societies are kinship-based, these gods are frequently also related to each other by marriage or kinship, with one high god being regarded as the patriarchal supreme deity. Thus Zeus was the patriarchal leader of the Greek pantheon, Jupiter filling a similar role among the Romans.

GOD, MONOTHEISTIC, an authoritarian, intolerant god who rejects the claims of all other gods, prohibits the worship of other supernatural beings and claims to dominate the entire universe. Such gods are usually credited with the creation of the universe (i.e. the 'creator gods') and become the subject of missionary religions, their worshippers being required in some cases to use force to persuade other people to accept the 'true' god. Those who regard such a god as the sole 'moving force' in the universe, are by implication obliged to accept his will and his decisions, so that submission to the 'will of God' is an important criterion of all monotheistic religions. Once a people believe that one god is more powerful than the others, myths may develop according to which the more powerful god either subordinates the lesser gods to the role of helpers (e.g. angels) or else enters into combat with the lesser gods, throwing them out of the divine abode, as was the fate of Satan and of the Persian Angra Mainyu.

GOD, any supernatural being of such power that it cannot be controlled by man and must be propitiated by those who live within reach of its powers.

GOD, TRIBAL, a deity who is worshipped by a particular tribe or people. Such tribal gods frequently represent deified ancestral spirits, while others may be nature gods associated with the particular locality in which the worshippers live, or with some natural force which is of supreme importance to the worshippers' style of life.

GOGO, a Bantu-speaking Negroid people of the Rift group largely dependent on horticulture and animal husbandry.

GOIDELIC CELTS, see CELTS.

GOLD, one of the earliest metals to be worked by man, since it could formerly be found in relatively pure form in the beds of streams as gold nuggets or gold dust washed down from natural gold-bearing strata rocks. Although too soft for most practical purposes, gold melts at a low temperature, and in pure form is highly malleable. As a material used for the manufacture of ornaments it is believed to have acquired a magico-religious value at a very early date, gold nuggets and ornaments having been found in Cro-Magnon Upper Paleolithic excavations.

GOLDI, a Tungus Altaic-speaking East Siberian Mongoloid people, dependent primarily on fishing and hunting with some horticulture and animal husbandry.

GONDS, a North Dravidian aboriginal people from the Bastar hills of Southern Central India who depend on animal husbandry, food-gathering and hunting. Three major groups are identified: the Maria, the Muria and the Bisonhorn Gonds. Premarital sex relations are permitted in youth dormitories housing unmarried male and female youths.

GONDWANALAND, a hypothetical sunken continent, today represented only by Sumatra, Java, and Borneo, but supposedly linking Africa, Australia and South Africa. The original theory of Gondwanaland is no longer accepted in its entirety.

GONG, a large metal plate which produces a resonant sound when struck by an instrument resembling a drum stick. The gong appears to have been invented around the 6th century A.D. and was widely used in China and Southeast Asia at religious ceremonies, as also in the Meso-American cultures.

GONIOCRANIOMETRY, the measurement of the various angles of the head.

GONIOMETER, a tool for the measurement of goniocraniometric angles (q.v.).

GOODS, GRAVE, see GRAVE GOODS.

GORDIUM, the capital of the Phrygian empire in Anatolia from which the mythological Gordian Knot derives its name.

GORGE, a double-pointed hook, used with the aid of bait to catch animals and fishes. When the bait is swallowed, the hidden gorge becomes imbedded in the throat of the animal.

GORILLA, a large ape (Pongidae) found in parts of Central Africa. Gorillas have a cranial capacity of around 500 c.c. The cranium of the male is marked by a prominent sagittal crest, to which the jaw muscles, which completely encase the skull, are attached, contributing to the utility of the teeth as offensive weapons.

GOSIUTE, a Shoshone (Uto-Aztec) speaking North American Indian people from the Coastal Great Basin, dependent on food-gathering, hunting and some fishing.

GOUGER, a shovel-shaped cutting tool. Commonly used for carpentry work, or for extracting the marrow from animal bones, stone gougers were first invented in the Paleolithic.

GOURA, a musical instrument found among the Capoids of South-West Africa. The Goura comprises a single string attached to a flexible bamboo rod with a flat quill at one end. The player inserts the quill between the lips and produces music by blowing through the instrument.

GOURD, a fruit somewhat similar to a melon, once widely grown in both the Old and the New World for the sake of its hard rind, which could be used as a storage vessel.

GRADE, AGE, see AGE GRADE.

GRAFFITI, a term applied to inscriptions made on walls or other surfaces which are informal and casual rather than ritual or deliberate. Such graffiti provide a valuable insight into the colloquial forms of speech and less formal aspects of social life.

GRAMMAR, that branch of linguistics which deals with the meaningful arrangement of words in relation to each other.

GRAMMAR, COMPARATIVE, that branch of linguistic science which is concerned with the comparison of the grammatical features of different languages.

GRAPE, a large juicy berry which was probably first domesticated in the Transcaucasus-Turkestan area, and has been used as the basis for the manufacture of alcoholic drinks since at least Homeric times.

GRAPHEMICS (also GRAPHONOMY), the scientific investigation of the various methods of writing and of their relationship to different systems of language.

GRAVE, a cavity in the ground in which the corpses of the dead are deposited by societies which practice inhumation. Many different customs have prevailed regarding burial rites, the body sometimes being laid on its side in a crouched position, sometimes stretched out straight on its back and in other cases sometimes even placed in a sitting position with the knees and arms bent up against the body. In most societies from the Upper Paleolithic until the present day, various items of grave goods (q.v.) have been customarily placed in the grave with the corpse.

GRAVE ESCORTS, persons who accompany the dead into the future world. These may include his wife and other members of his family and very frequently military companions and personal servants or slaves.

GRAVE GOODS, artifacts placed in the grave with the corpse at the time of burial. Sometimes called 'grave furniture'.

GRAVER, a small sharp-pointed cutting tool used for making incisions on the surface of wood; also known as a burin.

GRAVETTE, a slender stone blade, the back edge of which is blunt.

GRAVETTIAN, a European Upper Paleolithic culture.

GREAT BASIN, the name given to the vast internal drainage area in the mountains of the western United States, including much of Nevada, Eastern California Southeastern Oregon, Southern Idaho and Western Utah.

GREAT MOTHER, see GODDESS, MOTHER.

GREAT PLAINS, a term generally used to refer to the vast rolling grasslands lying between the Rocky Mountains and the Mississippi-Missouri river system.

GREEK, a modern nation of ancient Mediterranean (Pelasgian) and Indo-European (Hellenic-Greek) origin, traditionally dependent on agriculture, animal husbandry and some fishing.

GREEK GOD, a term popularly used to refer to someone who is strikingly handsome by Nordic standards. It arises from the custom of Greek pagan sculptors who gave their gods the 'classical' features then regarded as characteristic of the aristocratic 'eupatrids', or persons of 'pure descent'.

GREEK RELIGION, ancient Greek pagan religion appears to have combined the sky gods and ancestor-worshipping traditions of the Indo-Europeans with a number of elements of fertility ritual and ancestor worship from the Old European civilization of the Balkans and the Aegean. Thus the Olympian (Indo-European) sky gods comprise twelve deities, of whom Zeus was the father. However the Indo-Europeans did not regard the gods as the creators of the universe but merely as immortals with supernatural powers who were a part of the universal order just as were men. Ancestor worship played an important role, not only in Homeric but particularly in Classical Greece, but each family also had its own particular nature deities, some 30,000 minor deities having been identified from surviving Greek literature. Towards the end of the Classic period, there was an increase of pre-Hellenic, Anatolian, Middle Eastern and Egyptian influences in Greek religion, as the old Indo-European faith lost its hold with the decline of the aristocracy, and mystery cults (q.v.) developed among the freedmen and the slaves.

GRIFFIN, an imaginary animal with the head of an eagle, the body, legs and tail of a lion, and a pair of wings. The griffin frequently appears on medieval coats-of-arms, but evidence of this fantastic animal is also found in Greek architectural designs.

GRIMALDI, a site just east of Monaco, which has revealed several badly crushed skulls of disputed character. These appear to show a prognathism and general skull shape which is characteristically Negroid, but the pressure to which they have been subjected may have distorted the shape of the skull and jaw. There is also some question as to whether the Grimaldi skeletons are actually to be associated with tools of earlier Mousterian character found at the same site, and although generally classified as belonging to the Cro-Magnon assemblage because of Aurignacian and Upper Paleolithic tools found at various levels, their proper classification remains a subject for dispute.

GRIMM'S GRAVES, a group of Upper Paleolithic mines located in eastern England, which were presumably used for the large-scale mining of flint for purposes of trade.

GRIMM'S LAW, a set of principles tracing the sound changes which occurred when primitive German first evolved out of its earlier Indo-European form. The voiced stops *b*, *d*, and *g* became the voiceless stops *p*, *t* and *k*, while at a later date the latter in turn became the voiceless continuants *f*, hard *th* and *x*. *bh*, *ph*, and *gh*, became *b*, *d*, and *g*.

GRIQUA, a South African community of hybrid Capoid-Caucasoid stock.

GROS VENTRE, Algonquin-speaking American Plains Indians mainly dependent on hunting with some food-gathering.

GROUP, DESCENT, a social group linked by the ties of kinship and common descent.

GROUP, ETHNIC, a group of men and women united by recognition of a common culture, linguistic, national and/or racial heritage.

GROUP, FORMAL, a small group which evolves for a definite purpose.

GROUP, IDENTIFICATION, positive recognition of one's membership in a group and of the responsibilities of such membership.

GROUP, INFORMAL, a social group which evolves without specific intent.

GROUP, PRIMARY, a group with intimate and frequent communications among its members, in which the members have intimate knowledge of each other's social personality.

GROUP, SECONDARY, a social group with impersonal, segmentalized relations among its members, who share a common set of purposes but are seldom aware of each other's behavior outside of this setting.

GROUP, SOCIAL, a number of people who possess distinctive elements of culture in common as a result of shared communication.

GUACA, see HUACA.

GUAHIBO, a South American Indian people who speak a Carib language and are dependent on horticulture, food-gathering and some hunting.

GUAJIRO, a South American Indian people of the Antillean coastal region.

GUAMANIANS, see CHAMORRO.

GUAMONTEY, South American Indians of the Guyana Highlands.

GUANCHE, a Hamitic language of the Berber group, which was spoken in the Canary Islands until around the end of the 17th century when it was replaced by Spanish.

GUANIN, an alloy made from a combination of gold and copper, used for the manufacture of ornamental jewelry by the Arawak Indians of the Caribbean Antilles.

GUAYCURI, The Guaycuran phylum of languages is included within the broad Gê-Pano-Carib grouping. Guaycuri includes Toba, Mataco, Abipon, Choroti, and Caduveo.

GUBO, a primitive stringed instrument common among the Zulu in South Africa, comprising a single string drawn tightly over a narrow strip of wood, at one end of which the husk of a gourd serves as a resonator.

GUDE, a Chad-Sudanese speaking people occupying the Mandara highlands of Africa, dependent on horticulture with some animal husbandry.

GUEST, in most societies in which the family remains the basic social unit and the household constitutes the basic economic unit, important social conventions surround the relationship between the householder and any alien guest who may be permitted to enter the household. Once accepted as a guest, a non-kinsman is invariably treated with courtesy and generosity. Among the Eskimos and certain Siberian peoples, this may even include sexual favours from the mistress or other women of the household. Guests are in turn obligated to their hosts, according to the prevailing conventions which vary from society to society.

GUILLOCHE, a piece of jewelry in which ornamental stones are set in twisted or plaited bands of metal.

GUITAR, a stringed instrument, attached to a round wooden sounding box, used extensively in Mediterranean countries as an accompaniment to folksongs and dancing. The guitar is played with the fingers or with a chip held between the fingers to protect the finger tips from excessive abrasion.

GUJARATI, a North Indian Indo-European language derived from Sanskrit whose speakers subsist by agriculture and animal husbandry.

GUMELNITA, a Chalcolithic culture centered around present-day Bucharest which succeeded the Boian culture (q.v.) around 4,300 B.C. and reveals many examples of the Old European linear script inscribed on pottery. The Gumelnita culture was overrun by Indo-Europeans around 3,500 B.C.

GUNYOL, an Australian name for an aboriginal lean-to shelter.

GUNZ, the first of the four major Alpine glaciations of the Pleistocene. See also GLACIATIONS.

GURAGE, an Ethiopic or African Semitic people of East Africa, connected with the Cushitic Sidamo, who are dependent upon horticulture and herding.

GURANI, see TUPI-GURANI LANGUAGES.

GUR LANGUAGES, see VOLTAIC LANGUAGES.

GURO, a Mande-speaking Negroid people from West Africa, largely dependent on horticulture with considerable hunting and some animal husbandry and food-gathering.

GUSII, a Bantu-speaking Negroid people of the East Nyanza area, largely dependent on horticulture and animal husbandry.

GUTTUS, a pottery vessel used by the Romans and distinguished by a narrow neck.

GYNEOCRACY, a term devised to describe a form of society which according to Bachofen and Briffault formerly constituted a more or less universal social system, but which had been preceded by an even earlier stage of primitive promiscuity, against which the women finally rebelled, forcing the men to marry them and help support their children. This 19th century 'unilineal' theory of marital evolution from promiscuity, through gyneocracy to patriarchal polygyny and thence to an eventually patriarchal monogamy has now been totally rejected. Although the term matriarchal is still used to refer to a family system in which women exercise dominant influence, few examples of matriarchal societies can be substantiated. Even in a matrilineal society – such as that of the Hopi in which the name and property is inherited through the females – the males usually retain substantial status and occupy many influential offices.

GYPSY, see GIPSY.

H

HA, a West Lacustrine Bantu people, largely dependent on horticulture and herding.

HABITAT, the physical environment to which an organism has become adapted in the course of phylogenetic evolution.

HACHIMAN, the Shinto god of war. (See SHINTOISM).

HADES, the Greek god of the nether world, the abode of the shades of ghosts of the dead, who, as Pluto, was also regarded as the giver of all material wealth and earthly blessings.

HADIUM, a Bantu-speaking Negroid people of the Swahili group, largely dependent on horticulture and some animal domestication.

HADRIAN'S WALL, a 76-mile long stone wall, between 8′ to 10′ thick and 12′ to 16′ high, protected on the outside by a 9′ deep ditch. Constructed by the Roman emperor Hadrian (circa A.D. 122 to 133) to protect the Roman empire in Britain from attacks by the Picts from north of the Tyne and Solway, it was overrun on several occasions, before being finally abandoned around A.D. 400, when the Romans evacuated Britain as the empire came under pressure from the expanding Germanic nations.

HADZA, a small pocket of Khoisan-speakers still surviving as an isolate among the surrounding Bantus of Tanzania.

HAIR FORM, the texture shape, and density of hair differs dramatically between races. Caucasoids generally have straight or wavy, fine hair, of light-colour among the North European peoples, which is oval in cross-section. Mongoloids have straight, stiff black hair, which is round in cross-section; while the Negroids have stiff black hair which is oblong in cross-section, and spirals in tight coils.

HAKO, a Pawnee ritual dance, embodying prayers for longevity and fertility.

HALAK, the name given by the Semang of Malaya to their shamans.

HALAM, a West African musical instrument. The halam comprises an oblong piece of wood, hollowed out on one side and covered by parchment or stretched skin. The box amplifies the vibrations produced by strings made from animal gut.

HALBERD, a weapon which originated in the early Bronze Age in Europe and was probably of Celtic origin. The halberd comprised a pointed blade, attached at right angles to a long shaft, which was wielded in a chopping motion.

HALLSTATT, an important late Bronze Age and Iron Age archeological site situated in a picturesque setting beside a lake in the Austrian Salzkammergut Mountains, east of Salzburg. Excavation has revealed a prosperous Bronze and Iron Age settlement, dependent largely on salt mining, and a cemetery containing several thousand graves. The latter have yielded a wealth of information regarding the culture of Central Europe during the Bronze and Iron Ages, and the term Hallstatt has consequently been adopted to refer to what was a characteristic and relatively enduring form of Central European culture which is believed to have been ancestral to both the Celtic and Italic cultures. Hallstatt A, which flourished in the 12th and 11th centuries B.C., and Hallstatt B, covering the 10th, 9th and 8th centuries B.C, reflect a late Bronze Age level of development and are associated with cremation rituals and urnfield cemeteries. Hallstatt C, corresponding to the 7th century B.C., reveals the appearance of iron artifacts and is marked by the construction of a large number of hill-forts throughout Bohemia, Bavaria and Austria, occupied by a new nobility whose members were buried in lavish four-wheeled wagons, each in a separate mortuary house beneath a barrow. The later Hallstatt nobles wore beautifully decorated bronze armour, but used iron swords. During the Hallstatt D period, corresponding roughly to the 6th century B.C., wagon burials and other customs continued, and an expansion of Hallstatt influence brought the culture as far west as Burgundy and the Rhineland, the westward migrants being generally identified as the ancestors of the Celts (q.v.).

HAMITIC LANGUAGES, a major subdivison of the Afro-Asian group of languages, mainly spoken North of the Sahara and in the Horn of Africa. The ancient Egyptian language has been demonstrated to have been Hamitic, and the Hamitic Coptic language, still used for ritual purposes by the Coptic Christians, is a contemporary survival of the ancient Egyptian tongue. Further west are spoken the Libyan language of Libya, the Berber language which is still widespread in the mountains of North Africa and large areas of the Sahara desert, and the Tuareg language of the camel-riding nomads of the Sahara, all of which belong to the Hamitic family. The Cushitic group of languages is generally regarded as a subdivision of the Hamitic family. Concentrated in Northeastern Africa, these languages are primarily represented today by Somali, spoken in Somaliland and by the Galla language of Ethiopia. Some authorities classify the Chad-Sudanese family of languages as Hamitic. These are spoken by a predominantly Negroid people living immediately South of the Sahara, but in view of the strong Niger-Congo influence in these languages it is probably better to regard the Chad-Sudanese languages as today constituting a separate family. However, the Nilotic languages also reveal some Hamitic (Cushitic) influence.

HAMITO-SEMITIC LANGUAGES, see AFRO-ASIATIC LANGUAGES.

HAMMERSTONE, a round stone used by Palaeolithic man as a hammer, frequently employed in the manufacture of other stone implements.

HAMMURABI (1792-1750 B.C.), the 6th king of the Semitic Amorite dynasty of the Babylonian empire. Under Hammurabi's rule the Amorites were able to extend Babylonian power over most of Sumeria, although the ancient Sumerian culture remained largely intact, and the famous Code of Hammurabi (q.v.) would appear to reflect a collection of essentially Sumerian customs and laws, possibly modified by the Semitic tradition. The Amorite-controlled Babylonian empire was finally destroyed by a combination of Indo-European Hittites and Kassites, circa 1595 B.C.

HAMMURABI, CODE OF, largely based on earlier Sumerian customs the code contained some 300 paragraphs dealing with all aspects of social behavior and appears to have heavily influenced the social and moral thoughts of the Hebrews as expressed in the Old Testament. Our knowledge of the code is derived from 51 stelae, made of black diorice, each about 6 feet in height, found by Morgan at Susa, on which the code had been inscribed in cuneiform characters which were subsequently deciphered.

HAMSTRING, a number of primitive foot-herding and horticultural societies 'hamstring' domesticated animals so that they cannot wander away from the settlement grazing land. The main tendons of the rear leg are cut in such a way that the animal retains the ability to drag its rear legs slowly and laboriously over short distances to enable it to graze, but is sufficiently crippled to be unable to roam any distance.

HAN, (1) an early Chinese dynasty. (2) an Athabascan people of the North American sub-Arctic.

HAND AXE, a term broadly used to refer to any bifacial stone core tool which can be held in the hand and used for chopping or scraping purposes. The earliest hand axes probably evolved out of the earlier pebble tools, which were customarily flaked on one side only to produce a crude cutting edge. Hand axes, by contrast, were flaked on both sides to produce a better cutting edge, and were usually oval or pear-shaped possessing a smooth, round end which could be conveniently held in the palm of the hand. They were most commonly associated with Abbevillian and Acheulian industries, but continued to be used as late as the Mousterian or Middle Paleolithic.

HANDCRAFTS, manufacturing techniques which do not involve the use of elaborate machinery.

HANDS, LAYING ON OF, a magico-religious ritual by which a person of superior status lays one or both hands on the head or body of an inferior, in order to improve the latter by transmitting some of his mana (q.v.). The principle appears to have derived from the installation rituals of Babylonian and Egyptian kings, who touched the image of a deity as one of the inauguration rites. Among the Hebrews, new members of the Sanhedrin were installed in their office by the laying on of hands, and the early Christians passed the custom on to the Roman Catholics who install bishops by the same process, thus continuing a tradition of Babylonian or Egyptian origin.

HANDSTONE, see MANO.

HANJA, a musical instrument, found mainly in North Central Africa, comprising a series of hollow gourds arranged in a progression according to size, across which wooden strips are fastened. The result is a primitive xylophone.

HANO, an Aztec-Tanoan-speaking North American Western Pueblo people related to the Tewa, dependent on horticulture and (in post-Columbian times) animal husbandry.

HANUMAN, the god of monkeys, who, according to the Vedic Indo-Aryan legend of the Ramayana, assisted Rama in the conquest of Ceylon in order to recover Rama's abducted wife, Sita.

HANUNOO, a Malayo-Polynesian-speaking people of the Southern Philippines, largely dependent on cultivation with some animal husbandry and fishing.

HAOMA, a ritual drink, comprising a mixture of the haoma plant with milk and sugar, which was believed by Persians of the Zoroastrian period to convey immortality.

HAPLOID, a condition occurring in sexual reproduction wherein each daughter nucleus possesses only a single set of unpaired chromosomes.

HAPPU, a Chinese drum, filled with rice powder so as to produce a distinctive sound when struck.

HARA-KIRI, a Japanese ritual sacrifice, practiced by noblemen of the Samurai warrior caste, who were required by custom to disembowel themselves with ceremonial swords after suffering a disgrace or a defeat.

HARAPPA, one of the two largest cities of the Indus Valley civilization. Situated on the banks of the river Ravi, a tributary of the Indus, in the middle of the rich Punjab plain, Harappa appears to have arisen on the site of a more primitive pre-Indus Valley settlement. As a major center of the Indus Valley civilization, however, Harappa grew into a substantial city, protected by massive forty-foot thick mud brick walls which enclosed a total area of some 80,000 square yards. Several cemeteries have been excavated, the largest of which reveals inhumation rites. The city was eventually destroyed by invaders, presumed to be Indo-Aryans. (See INDUS VALLEY CIVILIZATION).

HARDY-WEINBERG RULE, the principle that under conditions of random mating and in the absence of natural selection (q.v.), genetic drift (q.v.), or mutation (q.v.), the proportion of the various genotypes in any population may be expected to remain constant through successive generations.

HARE, an Athabascan hunting and gathering people of the Northern sub-Arctic area of Canada.

HARP, an instrument popular among the Celts of Europe, comprising a large number of strings of different length, drawn tightly between a resonator and a supporting neck. These are plucked by the fingers. The more sophisticated harps permit the adjustment of the strings for more efficient tuning.

HARP, JEW'S, a simple musical instrument, comprising a frame which is held in the mouth and a protruding tongue which can be plucked with the finger. Since the mouth serves as a resonance chamber, different notes are produced by changing the shape of the hollow in the mouth.

HARPOON, a spear tipped by barbed shafts in such a way that it is impossible for a harpooned animal to pull free once the point has entered its body. In case the shaft should break, the barbed head is often attached to a long line of rope fibre, so as to prevent the harpooned animal from escaping before the hunter can approach and kill it with other weapons. As an innovative device, the harpoon appears to have originated in the European Upper Paleolithic, at which time the barbed point was usually made from carved bone or antler.

HARUSPICES, the name given to Roman priests who divined the future and foretold the auspices by examining the entrails of sacrificed animals, or by observing the flight of certain birds. Many authorities believe that this practice was acquired from the Etruscans.

HASANIA, a Semitic-speaking people in East Africa, dependent on herding and horticulture.

HASHISH, a narcotic derived from hemp, widely used from India to Africa. Certain of the Moslem warriors who fought against the crusaders were known as 'assassins', a name derived from 'hashish', because they consumed hashish before entering battle in order to render themselves impervious to danger.

HASINA, a term used among the Malayo-Polynesians of the Malagasy Republic (Madagascar) to refer to a supernatural force roughly equivalent to the concept of mana (q.v.).

HASINAI, the Muskogean-Siouan-speaking North American Indians of the Caddoan group. The Hasinai occupied the Texas Plains and were dependent on horticulture, carried out in the river valleys, hunting and food-gathering.

HAT, CONICAL, a conical hat, sometimes called a 'cloud hat,' appears in a variety of cultures around the world, generally in association with the occult. In New Guinea, for example, the conical hat takes the form of the 'diba', while in various 11th century European lands, Jews were required to wear conical hats because of their alleged dealing with the infernal powers. For the same reason, persons condemned to death by the Spanish Inquisition for involvement in Black Magic had to wear a conical hat while en route to their place of execution, as also had those condemned for heresy. In later centuries the hat lost its association with infernal knowledge and heresy and instead became associated with ignorance, becoming known as a 'fool's cap', school children who failed to achieve an adequate grade being required to wear such a hat in order to shame them into studying harder.

HATSA, a Khoisan-speaking Capoid people previously known as the Kindiga, largely dependent on hunting and food-gathering.

HATTUSHA, the original name of the Anatolian city which after conquest by the Hittites was renamed Boghaz Koy and became the capital of the Hittite empire.

HAUSA, a warlike herding people of Northern Nigeria, who speak a Chad-Sudanese (q.v.) language, and are probably part-Caucasoid in origin. The Hausa were the only non-Caucasoid African people to possess a written language prior to the introduction of modern schooling by the European colonial powers.

HAUSTAFEL, a German word which refers to the ancient unwritten code of correct household and family behavior, defining the proper moral relations which cover the behavior of the individual members of the house, and in pre-Christian times, their ritual obligations to the ancestral spirits and household gods.

HAVASUPAI, a Hokan-speaking, Plateau Yuman American Indian people, dependent on animal husbandry, food-gathering and hunting.

HAWAIIANS, an Eastern Polynesian people, wholly dependent on fishing and horticulture with some food-gathering.

HAWAIKI, the ancient mythological homeland of the Polynesians, supposedly located far beyond the western horizon, and sometimes associated with India.

HAYA, an East Lacustrine Bantu-speaking Negroid people, mainly dependent on horticulture with some animal husbandry and hunting.

HAZARA, an Iranic (Indo-European)-speaking people who occupy the northern part of the Northwest Province of Pakistan, and were traditionally dependent on agriculture and animal husbandry.

HEAD-HUNTING, desultory warfare between neighbouring horticultural villages, the object of which is to kill enemy tribesmen and obtain their decapitated heads. In some cases, the victim's brain may be extracted and eaten, in order to acquire its magical powers through a form of ritual cannibalism. In other cases the severed head may be sought as a symbol of manly courage by a young adult male who seeks the right to marry. In both cases, the severed head may be permanently preserved as a magico-religious trophy. Head-hunting was formerly common in the East Indies, New Guinea, South America, West Africa, and Nagaland in India.

HEADMAN, a term often used loosely by European colonial officials to refer to any tribal or village head, or even to the leader of a band of migrant hunters and gatherers.

HEADREST, an ornamented, carved log or bench, used to support the head during sleep. Widely used in Africa, where it serves the purpose of the European pillow.

HEART, there is a widespread belief in many societies that the heart symbolized the basic seat of life and the center of emotions. This idea may have emerged as early as the Paleolithic, being suggested by the fact that the rhythmic beating of the heart ceases with the death of the individual. The Aztecs placed great importance on the supernatural qualities of the heart, believing that their supreme god required a diet of living human hearts. They accordingly sacrificed large numbers of prisoners of war every year. Holding their victims spreadeagled across an altar as the priest slit open their chest they extracted the living heart while it was still beating.

HEARTH, the place in which the household fire is normally situated. In many cultures (including traditional European society,) the fire on the hearth was associated with the concept of the continuity of the family through the generations, and hearth-worship is a frequent concomitant of ancestor-worship.

HEAVEN, the ancient Indo-Europeans widely believed that the heavens (PIE **Haekmon*) were the home of a body of heroic gods, and that after death the souls of the divinely-descended warrior nobility joined these gods in their heavenly abode, while the souls of lesser persons were relegated to a gloomy and cold underworld. Although certain other cultures also envisaged a heavenly afterworld, most placed the home of the dead beneath the surface of the soil.

HEBREW, the Northwest Semitic language in which most of the Old Testament was written. Hebrew subsequently experienced a number of modifications under the Rabbinical scholars of the Middle Ages, but has recently been revitalized as a result of the Zionist movement and the founding of the modern state of Israel.

HEDONISM, a philosophical school of thought, founded by Epicurus, who taught that men should seek pleasure (intellectual as well as physical) and avoid pain. Epicurus, himself, lived an austere life, and advocated peace of mind as the highest good. Some psychologists have sought to explain human behavior along the same lines, but it is now known that pain and pleasure are not causal forces.

HEHE, a Bantu-speaking Negroid people of the Rufiji group, largely dependent on horticulture and some animal husbandry.

HEIDELBERG, an archeological site near Heidelberg in Germany, in which the jaw of what may have been a Homo erectus (q.v.) type of hominid was found in strata which also revealed mammoth bones. 'Heidelberg man', as this fossil is labelled, is now estimated to have lived in the Günz-Mindel interglacial period, circa 900,000, or in an interstadial of the Mindel glaciation.

HEIDIKI, small figurines worn by Maoris around the neck. Carved in jade or bone, the 'heidiki' are believed to contain the spirits of ancestors and are revered as valued heirlooms.

HEIGHT, BODY, as with other physiological elements, the potential range of height for individuals, populations and races seems to be genetically controlled, but not by any simple mechanism, and within the limits of the genetic potential vast differences may arise in the achieved potential of the individual as a result of dietary and other environmental conditions. Thus, Icelandic graves reveal that the average stature of a male in Viking times was around six feet, but that without any migratory change in the gene pool, the average height of Icelandic males fell by four inches in the later Middle Ages as a result of disease and malnutrition, but in recent centuries has again increased nearer to six feet.

HEKE, the name given by the Maoris to the great migration which took their ancestors from Rarotonga to New Zealand around the 14th century A.D.

HELA, the Norse goddess of death. The modern word 'Hell' derives from the Norse 'Helheim' or 'home of Hela'.

HELIOLITHIC, the term formerly used to refer to the advanced horticultural and agricultural civilizations which arose in the warm temperate climates of the Mediterranean and Middle East. The term was particularly common among anthropological diffusionists (q.v.), who believed that all civilization had originated from these heliolithic farming settlements.

HELIOPOLIS, the central city of the Egyptian cult of the sun god Ra. Marked by pyramids and obelisks, the remains of Heliopolis are located some five miles east of the present-day city of Cairo.

HELLADIC, a general term used to refer to the Greek peoples of the Cycladic and Mycenaean Bronze Age. While the Mycenaean era belongs to the late Helladic, the Cycladic culture, associated with Minyan ware, is divided into Early and Middle Helladic stages. The Early Helladic period commenced around the 20th or 19th century B.C. and is generally associated with the arrival of the first Indo-European peoples into the Aegean.

HELMET, a form of protective armour worn over the head. There is ample evidence that the Sumerians wore leather helmets, and the crowns of the Pharaohs of Egypt were probably evolved from helmets. The Mycenaean Greeks wore metal helmets, often adorned with boar's tusks – similar to the Viking helmets adorned with bull's horns. At the beginning of the first millennium B.C., the Villanovans of Italy frequently covered the urns, which contained the remains of their dead, with the helmets of the deceased, and elaborate helmets were also worn by the Greek and Roman war leaders of the Classical period as well as by the Celtic nobility. Elaborate ceremonial helmets were devised in Medieval Europe, and the royal crowns of Europe likewise derived from early ceremonial war helmets.

HEMANTHROPUS, a possible Australopithecine species, the sole evidence for which is based on incomplete fossil remains found in southern China.

HEMATILE, see OCHRE.

HEMNURY, an archeological site near Honiton in Devon, England, which gave its name to the earliest phase of the Neolithic in Britain (3500-3000 B.C.). The Hembury site represents a causeway camp.

HEMOGLOBIN, the iron-containing protein which enables the red blood cells to transport oxygen to the parts of the body.

HEMOPHILIA, a sickness resulting from the inability of blood to clot and form a protective scar when exposed to the air. Persons suffering from hemophilia can bleed to death when they suffer a sufficiently serious abrasion of the skin. Hemophilia results from a recessive gene which is sex-linked, being carried by females but revealing itself phenotypically only among males.

HEMP, a plant, first cultivated in the Far East, which produces fiber, oil, and hallucinogenic drugs.

HENGE, the name for a type of ritual site, which was common in Britain during the latter part of the 3rd century B.C., but also persisted into the Early Bronze Age. Henges were usually circular in shape, but varied considerably in size, some occupying several acres. In most cases the external circumference was marked by a ditch inside a bank, which would imply that the bank was a boundary marker rather than a military defense. Some henges, such as Stonehenge and Avebury, contained circles of upright stones, while others, such as Woodhenge, contained arrangements of timber posts and burial pits.

HEPALIDAE, a family of New World monkeys corresponding to the marmosets.

HERALDRY, a medieval European practice, whereby families of noble descent distinguished themselves and their retainers by sets of 'armorial' symbols, the design and constituent elements of which reflected the family genealogy. Such heraldic emblems served not only to distinguish their wearers in battle but also served as a source of family pride because of the deeds associated with their bearers which made them important symbols of family continuity and loyalty.

HERB LORE, many cultures prescribe the use of specific herbs as magico-religious remedies for sickness, some prescriptions possessing genuine medical qualities.
HERBIVORE, an animal which depends exclusively upon a vegetable diet.
HERBIVOROUS, plant-eating, as distinct from carnivorous or meat-eating.
HERCULES, the Greek hero-god, son of Zeus, the father of the Greek gods, Hercules was renowned for the performance of twelve impossible 'labors', including the acquisition of the golden apples of the Hesperides which conveyed immortality. Regarded as the ancestor of the royal houses of the Dorian Greeks, Hercules was also known to the Romans as Heracles, son of Jupiter (the Roman equivalent of Zeus).
HERD, a group of female mammals and their offspring, sometimes accompanied by one or more males.
HERDING SOCIETIES, otherwise known as pastoral societies, herding societies depend primarily upon the care of the larger domesticated animals such as sheep, goats, and cattle.
HEREDITABILITY, the extent to which specific characteristics are likely to be inherited.
HEREDITY, the transmission of physiological characteristics from parents to their offspring by means of the genetic mechanism.
HERERO, a Southwestern Bantu Negroid people, dependent on cattle-herding supplemented by hunting.
HERO, CULTURE, a person remembered in myth as a major benefactor to the community. Although such persons may in some cases have been purely mythical, the possibility of an original historical figure having been associated with the introduction of some of the qualities attributed to the culture hero cannot be discounted.
HEROIC AGE, a period of proto-feudal social organization frequently associated with Bronze Age and early Iron Age societies when centralized chieftains, attended by bands of knights, warriors, or 'companions', were the dominant power in society.
HERO WORSHIP, literally the worship of the spirits of dead heroes. In those societies in which the members of the warrior nobility were believed to be descended from gods, heroic leaders who had accomplished much for their people during their lives were customarily deified after their death. Occasionally the belief developed that these great heroes might return to the world to save their people in times of future crisis, a concept known as Messianism (q.v.).
HESTIA, the Greek goddess of the hearth and protectress of domestic and family life. Known to the Romans as Vesta.
HETAERAE, cultured and accomplished courtesans, popular in Classical Athens, but prohibited in Sparta.
HETERODONT, a term used to describe species which possess various forms of teeth specialized for different purposes. Most mammals, for example, possess incisors, canines, premolars and molars, while most reptiles, on the other hand, are homodont, being equipped with a set of teeth which are unspecialized and essentially similar to each other.
HETEROGAMETIC, referring to the possession of one X and one Y sex chromosome in the male genotype.
HETEROGAMY, the mating of relatively dissimilar individuals within a genetically disparate population.
HETEROGRAFT, a term used by geneticists to refer to a genetic graft made between members of different species of animals.
HETEROSIS, sometimes described as 'hybrid vigor', heterosis has been observed in certain first generation hybrid crosses between distinct subspecies of plants. The phenomenon is characterized by increased size and improved resistance to disease, and is apparently due to the suppression of less advantageous recessive genes by healthier dominant genes. However, under the principles of Mendelian genetics, hybrid vigor is seldom projected into second or subsequent generations, since the deleterious recessive genes are not eliminated and there-

fore recombine in subsequent generations. Hybrids do not acquire any genes that are not already present in the parent lines, and therefore no permanent improvement in the genetic heritage can result from hybridization in the absence of selection. The principle of heterosis has proved particularly valuable to corn-growers, who are only interested in the first generation product, but since the desired genetic combination does not persist beyond the first generation, each hybrid generation has to be reproduced anew from the selected pure lines. Although the principle of heterosis is well established in the case of plants, which have relatively simple genetic formulae, it has not been demonstrated in the case of genetically more advanced organisms, such as mammals, where the variety of potential genetic combinations in hybrids, even of the first generation is more considerable.

HETEROZYGOUS, a condition in which an organism possesses two different allelomorphs on the corresponding loci of a pair of chromosomes, as opposed to a homozygous condition in which the allelomorphs are similar. Homozygous organisms reproduce themselves exactly when crossed with a similarly homozygous member of the same subspecies, whereas heterozygous organisms are unlikely to produce offspring which will resemble the parents phenotypically.

HETMAN, the headman of a Cossack village or community.

HEUNEBURG, a major Iron Age hill-fort, associated with an Indo-European Hallstatt people, located on the Upper Danube in Würtemberg. The Heuneburg fortress possessed massive ramparts constructed of mud-bricks erected on a stone foundation, and resembles the Greek fortresses of the same or slightly earlier periods. A number of princely burials have been excavated close to the site, mostly belonging to the 7th and 6th century B.C.

HEX, a Germanic word for witchcraft.

HEXADACTYLISM, an aberrant condition, genetically determined, whereby the affected individuals are born with 6 toes or fingers on each foot or hand.

HIBERNATION, a biological response during winter when the temperature falls sufficiently to affect the rate of metabolism. The organism then enters a period of sleep or hibernation until the external temperature rises again in spring.

HIDATSA, Siouan-speaking North American Indians living on the Upper Missouri river, largely dependent on horticulture with some hunting, fishing and food-gathering.

HIDE, a commonly recognized unit of land in Anglo-Saxon England, which was regarded as being equivalent to the area necessary to support one family, or more precisely the amount of land that could be ploughed annually by the members of one family.

HIERATIC, a form of cursive hieroglyphic writing which developed in early Egypt during the latter part of the Old Kingdom. Hieratic writing originated from the earlier hieroglyphic symbols, tending to become more cursive when the older method of laborious engraving on stone came to be supplemented by the transcription of symbols on papyrus with the aid of brush pens.

HIEROGLYPHS, Egyptian hieroglyphs first appeared around 3000 B.C., and may have been stimulated by the older pictograms or ideograms (each representing a complete word or meaning) which were already in use in Uruk in Mesopotamia. The Egyptian hieroglyphs, a word which means literally 'sacred carvings', totalled some 500 characters, normally read from left to right, which were primarily used for inscriptions on funerary monuments and equipment, although they were later adopted for commercial purposes in the modified cursive forms known as hieratic (q.v.) and demotic (q.v.). The Egyptian hieroglyphs were first deciphered in 1822 as a result of the discovery of the Rosetta Stone, on which a single proclamation was inscribed in three different scripts, one of which was already known – thus making possible the decipherment of the others.

HILL BHUIYA, a proto-Australoid people of the Central Indian uplands, who speak a Munda language and subsist on horticulture with some hunting, fishing and animal husbandry.

HILL-FIGURE, an ancient monumental form, widely found among the Chalk Downs of Southern England. Many of these take the form of horses carved out of the green turf to lay bare the underlying white chalk in the desired shape. The oldest hill-figure in England is a white horse which dates from the late Celtic Iron Age, while other anthropomorphic forms date from Anglo-Saxon times.

HILL-FORT, the ancient European practice of building fortified hill-top residences for nobles and their attendant warrior bands appears to be associated with the spread of an Indo-European aristocracy as early as the Hallstatt and Urnfield cultures. In some cases the smaller hill-forts housed only a noble or royal family and their immediate retainers, but in other cases larger forts known as oppida (pl.) housing entire urban populations, developed around the royal residences, as was the case with the Celtic oppidum of Trisov in Czechoslovakia. In some places earthen and timber hill-forts were constructed as places of temporary refuge for villagers and their animals in times of war.

HILL SUK, a Negroid Nilotic-speaking people of the Nandi group, primarily dependent on horticulture, cattle-herding, and some hunting.

HINAYANA BUDDHISM, literally the 'narrow path' to salvation, Hinayana Buddhism retains the conservative monastic tradition of early Buddhism in which the individual seeks his own personal salvation rejecting the imagery and ritual of other religions in favor of an ascetic philosophy. (See BUDDHISM).

HINDU, correctly speaking the term 'Hindu' refers to a member of the Hindu religion, but since the Hindu castes practice strict endogamy the term is often also used to refer to the Indic local race which is a branch of the Caucasoid geographical race. (See also HINDUISM).

HINDUISM, the dominant religion of India which originally derived from the Indo-Aryan Vedic beliefs, but with the passing of time absorbed many indigenous Dravidian animistic beliefs, as well as ideas believed to have originated in the Indus Valley civilization. Thus the original Aryan complex combining ancestor worship with a pantheon of sky-gods and the maintenance of a strict social caste system constructed around the Laws of Manu (q.v.) steadily gave way to a confused complex of polymorphic deities and primitive animistic traditions, giving rise to widely disparate cults ranging from the frenzied orgiastic worship of Kali to Yoga and asceticism, and to a philosophical tradition rooted originally in the Vedic belief in causality and the survival of the soul after death, but later acquiring many novel concepts which are distinctly non-Vedic in character. (See also CASTE SYSTEMS).

HINDUSTANI, a language descended from Sanskrit, which is widely spoken as a lingua franca throughout India. Hindustani was also parent to Urdu, the official language of Pakistan, which differs from Hindi only in the possession of a number of Arabic and Persian loan words, and the fact that it is customarily written in the Arabic script.

HINTERLAND, the land lying behind a seaport or major coastal region. Literally, 'the backland'.

HIPPOCAMPUS, a creature from Mediterranean mythology, comprising the head, body, and forelegs of a horse, plus the twisted tail of a dolphin.

HIPPOMANCY, a form of divination, common to the ancient Indo-European and certain Uralic pastoral peoples, based on the interpretation of the movements of sacred horses.

HISSARLIK, a large mound overlooking the Dardanelles which proved to be the site of the ancient city of Troy. Hissarlik was first excavated by the German archeologist Heinrich Schliemann, between 1870 and 1873. Schliemann took great pains to identify the site from Homeric literature, and although his discovery was at first disputed, further excavation proved beyond doubt that Schliemann was right, and that Hissarlik was in fact the true site of Troy (q.v.).

HISSAR TEPE, an archeological tell site situated near Damgan in Northern Iran, dating from the 4th millennium B.C., at which time it appears to have shared in the common agricultural traditions of Iran, Beluchistan and India. However, there is evidence of an Indo-Iranian conquest around 2500 B.C. and of various cultural changes including the introduction of grey monochrome ware, although the town appears to have been destroyed somewhere around

1800 B.C., possibly by a new wave of Iranian war-bands.

HITTITES, an Indo-European people who invaded Anatolia, probably from the region of the Caucasus to impose themselves on the indigenous Hatti. Retaining their own Nasila language, the Hittites made extensive use of chariots, and established a powerful empire which lasted from around 1750 B.C. unti 1200 B.C. The discovery of written Hittite records reveals the essentially Indo-European character of the upper classes, even though the indigenous peasantry retained their Hurrian language and customs. Practicing an essentially proto-feudal system, the Hittite kings granted large estates to members of the warrior nobility, who participated in the government of the empire by the way of a council of nobles. As with other Indo-European societies, there was also a third political group which among the Hittites was known as the Pankus. This represented an assembly of the able-bodied heads of households of true Hittite descent. The subject Hurrians, who continued to live in their Zadruga-type collective villages, appear to have been without political representation. The technique of smelting was developed in the Hittite empire around 1800 B.C., and because of the superior value of iron weapons, the Hittites deliberately protected the secret of iron smelting for several centuries, until their empire was destroyed circa 1200 B.C.

HOABINH, a Mesolithic or early Neolithic culture which developed in Southeast Asia in the area of present-day Vietnam, close to the higher culture of Southern China. It is possible that considerable information regarding rice-growing and agriculture may have reached Indonesia via the Hoabinh culture.

HOARD, a collection of valuable articles, usually hidden by their owners for fear of theft or pillage with the intention of recovering them at a later date, although some hoards, generally dating from the Bronze Age, have been interpreted as hoards of loot hidden by victorious raiders, who failed to return to recover their hidden spoils.

HOE, a hand-operated digging tool comprising a blade set at right angles to a haft, the hoe is most commonly associated with the Mesolithic period as an improvement upon the primitive digging stick. Extensively used by horticulturalists of both the Old and the New World, the hand hoe was steadily replaced by the animal-drawn plow in those parts of the Old World in which agriculture replaced horticulture.

HOGAN, a beehive-shaped Navaho hut, constructed from pieces of wood or stone held together by mud.

HOHOKAM, based upon a horticultural life style, which developed out of the Chochise culture of Southern Arizona around 100 B.C., the Hohokam culture was roughly parallel to the Anasazi (q.v.) at its more advanced level (A.D. 500 to A.D. 900), when the introduction of irrigation techniques was accompanied by the appearance of large villages of mud-bricked houses. The main crop was maize, although cotton was introduced at a later date. The early Hohokam Indians lived in pit-houses, but later built surface huts, and developed a distinctive tradition of pottery, decorated with figures of animals, birds and humans beings. Considerable influence can be traced from the Meso-American culture, platform mounds and ball-courts being constructed during the latter part of the first millennium A.D., and pueblos appearing after A.D. 1100 as a result of Anasazi influence. However, the Hohokam culture deteriorated in the 15th century A.D. and was eventually replaced by the more primitive Pima and Papago cultures.

HOKAN, a large phylum of American Indian languages which includes the Yuman, Pomo, Palaihnihan, Shastan, Yanan, Salinan, Chumashan, Comecrudan, Tlapanecan and Tequistlatcean families, together with various isolates, including Jicaque, Washo, Karok and Chimariko.

HOLIDAY, today widely regarded as a day of rest and recreation, holidays were originally holy days on which sacrificial feasts were held, the normal routine of work being suspended as a sign of respect for the supernatural being in whose honor the feast was scheduled.

HOLISM (Adj. HOLISTIC), the theory that to a greater or lesser extent all parts of an operative culture must be interrelated.

HOLLOW-WAY, tracks or roads lying well below the level of the surrounding land are frequently found in parts of Western Europe. In most cases the deep cuttings in which these roads lie are believed to be due to erosion by water, since heavy rains would tend to wash away soil already broken by wheeled vehicles. There is no reason to suppose that they were deliberately excavated for any purpose, except for a few hollow-ways dating from the Celtic period when Celtic fields were separated from each other by trenches which would conceivably have been used as roads and so became progressively deepened by erosion with the passage of traffic and the action of rainfall.

HOLLY, an evergreen bush whose branches were frequently used for religious ritual purposes in pagan, pre-Christian Europe. Together with ivy and mistletoe, holly is still used on the anniversary of the pagan festival of Yuletide, commemorating the winter solstice, despite the fact that under Christianity this festival has acquired a superficial Christian interpretation.

HOLOCAUST, a substantial sacrifice involving the mass slaughter of animals or even human beings by burning.

HOLOCENE, the most recent period dating from approximately 10,000 B.P. (i.e., from the end of the Würm glacial period.) to 1200 B.P. The Holocene and Pleistocene together comprise the Quaternary.

HOLSTEIN INTERGLACIAL, the name sometimes given to the North European equivalent of the Alpine Mindel-Riss interglacial (q.v.).

HOMEOSTASIS, a term borrowed by anthropologists from physiology to refer to the tendency of a society to make internal adjustments to adapt its culture functionally to changing ecological, technological and other conditions.

HOMEOSTASIS, GENETIC, the propensity of a population to equilibriate its genetic composition and to resist sudden changes in the hereditary component.

HOMESTEAD, any dwelling or group of dwellings whose members together represent a household, i.e. a single economic unit oriented around the concept of a central family or kinship group. (See HOUSEHOLD).

HOMINIDAE, any creatures whose anatomical structure approximates to our current concept of Homo sapiens rather than to that of the Pongidae (q.v.). Technically they are distinguished by an adaption of the lower limbs to permit habitual bipedal locomotion and by the absence of the heavy canines of the apes. A subdivision of the super-family Hominoidea, the Hominidae generally comprise Homo sapiens (q.v.), the Neanderthals (q.v.), Pithecanthropines (q.v.) and Homo habilis (q.v.).

HOMINOIDEA, a primate super-family comprising Pongidae (apes) and Hominidae (q.v.).

HOMINY, a form of coarse hulled maize, cultivated, boiled and eaten by American Indians.

HOMO, the term used to apply to the genus which includes all manlike creatures, including all hominid fossil species which resemble the surviving hominids of today. However, the term is generally restricted to those hominid fossil remains that reveal a cranial capacity commonly found among sane adult living hominids. Where living hominids reveal brain cases of less than 1000 c.c. capacity they are invariably of such low intelligence as to be moronic, hence the basis of this arbitrary restriction of the term.

HOMODONT, a term used to describe animals all of whose teeth are similar in kind, as is the case with most reptiles.

HOMO ERECTUS, a term now used collectively to refer to a general level of hominid evolution at which the entire skeletal framework from the neck down had evolved to a form comparable to that of modern men, although the skull remained somewhat primitive. Homo erectus fossils date from around 900,000 to 250,000 years B.P. Originally regarded as a distinct genus of the family Hominidae (q.v.), and recognized as a member of the genus Homo, the brain size of Homo erectus (800 cc to 1100 cc) was intermediate between that of Homo habilis (q.v.) and the modern races of man (which vary substantially in this respect). Most Homo erectus adults stood to a height of not more than 5 feet and their skulls differed substantially from that of Homo sapiens (q.v.), not only in the smaller brain case, but also in the receding forehead, the absence of a chin, and the prominence of the brow ridges. The first discovery of Homo erectus was made in the 19th century in Java, subsequent discoveries being made at a variety of locations including Choukoutien near Peking in Northern China, Bed 11 at Olduvai in East Africa, and Ternifine in North Africa. There is some question whether the Mauer jaw found in Germany can be classified as Homo erectus, and in fact whether Homo erectus ever entered the geographical area corresponding to present-day Europe, especially as it is no longer customary to classify the Vertesszöllöz remains as those of Homo erectus, but to recognize them as early Homo sapiens. Generally speaking Homo erectus remains are associated with pebble tools, choppers and in some cases hand-axes.

HOMO FABER, a term sometimes applied to Neanderthal man.

HOMOGAMETIC, referring to the possession of a matching pair of X chromosomes in the genotype, the bearer of which will be a female.

HOMOGAMY, the mating of genetically similar individuals.

HOMOGRAFT, a graft of tissue obtained from a member of the same species (other than from an identical twin).

HOMO HABILIS, an early form of man, found at Olduvai by Dr. Louis Leakey and reliably dated at around 1.8 million years ago. The Homo habilis skull reveals a larger brain size than that of the Australopithecinae, (q.v.) a distinctly opposable thumb, and a more modern shape of skull, all of which in the opinion of Dr. Leakey distinguish them clearly from the Australopithecus hominids with which they were contemporary. In consequence, it is becoming increasingly accepted that Homo habilis may be ancestral to Homo sapiens (q.v.), and may have been responsible for the use of the eoliths and early pebble tools found in East African archeological sites of this age, whereas the Australopithecines may represent a less advanced relative of Homo habilis whose members were finally driven into extinction, possibly due to their inability to compete with this more sophisticated hominid variant.

HOMO HEIDELBERGENSIS, see HEIDELBERG.

HOMOIOTHERMIC, a term used to describe warm-blooded animals which are able to maintain a more or less constant body temperature which facilitates maximum body metabolism despite changes in external temperature. Both birds and mammals are homoiothermic, the body temperature being controlled by a thermostatic device located in the hypothalamus.

HOMOLOGOUS, the organs of different animals are said to be homologous when they share a fundamental similarity of structure or function, usually especially marked during the period of embryonic development. The possession of homologous organs is generally an indication of a generic relationship, differences in the character or use of the respective organs having risen as a result of subsequential evolutionary change under diversified environmental conditions.

HOMOLOGOUS CHROMOSOMES, the pair of chromosomes which participate in the crossing-over process during meiosis.

HOMO MODERNUS, a term formerly used to refer to a group of fossil remains found in Europe, including Swanscombe man. These reveal certain 'modern' features and are believed by some to have been directly ancestral to Cro-Magnon man. Also known as Homo sapiens steinheimensis (q.v.).

HOMONYM, a word which is similar in sound to another word but which has a different meaning, normally revealed by the context.

HOMO RHODESIENSIS, see RHODESIAN MAN.

HOMO SAPIENS, or 'intelligent man'. This term was formerly applied to all the living races of men and to Cro-Magnons. However, since virtually all characteristics of Neanderthals have since been found to fall within the range of certain of the living races of man, the term is now used to include Neanderthals and all post-Homo erectus sub-species.

HOMO SAPIENS NEANDERTHALENSIS, see NEANDERTHAL.

HOMO SAPIENS SAPIENS, a term first used to distinguish Cro-Magnons from Neanderthals, but now loosely applied to include all Upper Paleolithic sub-species and their extant survivors. Homo s. s. was distinguished from Neanderthals being characterized by a high forehead, virtually non-existent brow ridges, reduced prognathism and the frequent absence of the third molar.

HOMO SAPIENS STEINHEIMENSIS, a fossil species whose remains have been found in association with Acheulian tools, dated at around 400,000 B.P. Now regarded by some authorities as being potentially ancestral to Cro-Magnon man. (See also STEINHEIM and HOMO MODERNUS).

HOMO S. INDENT, a term used by some to identify the advanced Homo habilis (q.v.) near-erectus, hominid subspecies exemplified by Skull 1470 (q.v.) and Skull 1590. Found by Richard Leakey in the area of Lake Turkana, this fossil species was already in existence 1.8 million years ago. The term implies an undetermined species of intelligent men. Described as Homo habilis because of evidence of tool-using abilities (an attribute no longer attributed with certainty to the Australopithecines), the skull shape is surprisingly modern and is in advance of that of most H. erectus fossils. The cranial capacity is 800 to 900 c.c. It would seem possible that the old hypothesis tracing the evolution of Cro-Magnon Homo sapiens sapiens (q.v.) via Neanderthal from Homo erectus and the Australopithecines may be completely wrong, and that the ancestry of Cro-Magnons may be directly from some kind of Skull 1470 type sub-species, by way of Homo sapiens steinheimensis (e.g. Swanscomb and Fontechevade).

HOMOSEXUAL, a term used to refer to any individual who engages in sexual activities with persons of the same sex. Many primitive societies have institutionalized homosexuality, the Siwans of Africa taking it for granted that young men and boys will practice sodomy. Male homosexuality is also common in the New Hebrides and New Guinea. Other societies, however, have rigidly prohibited homosexual activities. Among free-ranging primates living under natural conditions, homosexual activity has not been observed, but its incidence increases rapidly in the case of animals whose natural patterns of behavior have been inhibited by overcrowding or by restriction of movement, as in the case of zoo animals.

HOMOSTADIAL, cultures are sometimes defined as homostadial if the artifacts produced represent a roughly similar level of technological advance, even though dating processes may indicate that they existed at quite separate times.

HOMO WADJAKENSIS, see WADJAK.

HOMOZYGOTIC TWINS, twins derived from a single ovum fertilized by the same sperm and therefore genetically identical.

HOMOZYGOUS, a term used to refer to a situation in which there is relative uniformity of genes within a particular gene pool, thus ensuring that members of the group mating with each other will 'breed true', i.e. produce offspring that closely resemble the parents in phenotype.

HOOKAH, a type of pipe, still popular in the Middle East, comprising a bowl filled with scented liquid, and a long flexible pipe stem. The object is to permit the smoker to draw the tobacco fumes through the scented or aromatic liquid, which not only cools the tobacco smoke, but also adds a distinctive flavor.

HOPEWELL, a distinctive culture, formerly centered in the area of present-day Ohio and Illinois, which represented the Woodland culture at the peak of its cultural achievement. Hopewell Indians practiced an advanced form of horticulture and produced fine pottery ornamented with corded or stamped decorative designs. Elaborately carved tobacco pipes, ceremonial knives made from obsidian, and ornaments simply cut out of sheet copper were also characteristic. The dead were buried under conical burial mounds. The Hopewell culture had its origins around the first century B.C. but began to decline around the beginning of the fifth century A.D., when the quality of manufactured artifacts began to decay.

HOPS, the name given to a type of climbing herb, commonly grown in western Europe, which was used not only as an ingredient for making beer, but also as a herbal cure for many types of sickness.

HORDE, any cooperating group of peoples who normally lack consistent political cohesion but who become cohesive in times of war or crisis. Thus among the Ural-Altaic peoples, the member tribes do not necessarily admit to any kinship obligation to other tribes in the horde, and may on occasion remove their allegiance from one horde to another, the efficiency of the horde being largely dependent upon the abilities of a temporary leader, chosen from among the leaders of the various member groups. At a lower level of social organization, a group of socially cooperating Australian Aboriginal bands is sometimes known as a 'horde'.

HORDE, GOLDEN, the name of one of the major Uralic pastoralist hordes (q.v.) which made extensive conquests throughout large areas of Central Asia, and invaded both Europe and Southwest Asia with eminent success.

HORGEN, an early European culture, characterized by agriculture and pottery vessels decorated with applique designs. One of the major Horgen sites is situated on the coast of Lake Neuchatel, the Horgen culture being recognized as belonging to the Middle Neolithic or post-Cortaillod period.

HORIZON, CULTURAL, hypothetical boundaries marking the areas in which specific artifacts have been found by archeologists.

HORIZONTAL STRATIGRAPHY, while the term 'stratigraphy' normally refers to the fact that older deposits of artifacts are usually found at a lower level of excavation than more recent deposits, 'horizontal stratigraphy' applies to sites such as cemeteries which have been in use over periods of time, where the oldest graves are likely to be those situated nearest to the settlement and the more recent graves are likely to be situated farther away. However, the principle of horizontal stratigraphy must be applied with discretion, as many factors can invalidate inferences of this type.

HORNS OF CONSECRATION, a Minoan religious symbol, which has been interpreted as a highly stylized and symbolic representation of the horns of the bull. Frequently found in Cretan shrines, as well as in the ruins of the palace at Knossos, this symbol may well have derived from the horned bull's head symbols of the Old European civilization (q.v.).

HORNS, MUSICAL, during the late Bronze Age, both the Teutonic and especially the Celtic people in Northern Europe made great use of bronze horns, frequently applying these in military operations to communicate commands and at the same time purposefully to strike fear into the hearts of the enemy by their almost unearthly blare. Such bronze horns would appear to have been evolved from earlier horns made literally from the horns of cattle.

HORSE, two varieties of wild horses appear to have existed prior to the human domestication of the horse and the resultant creation of domesticated breeds. These were a heavier variety of horse, which inhabited the woodlands of Europe, and a lighter but faster horse which was adapted by natural selection to the conditions of the East European and Asian steppelands. The horse was probably domesticated in the Pontic Steppes as early as the 7th millennium B.C., and the Indo-Europeans who accomplished this feat and brought the domesticated horse to so many parts of the world, had adapted it for use as a chariot-drawing animal by the 3rd millennium B.C. even though chariots, being wheeled vehicles, are only suitable for relatively open country — or for use on roads. The medieval horses of Europe, used both for riding and for agricultural and transportation purposes, may be primarily evolved from the heavier wild European horse, rather than from the lighter steppeland horses, which although faster, were incapable of carrying a knight in full medieval armor or for the heavy work required by the European agriculturalists. Wild horses also ranged over wide areas of the American continent in pre-Columbian times, but appeared to have been exterminated by American Indians who hunted them for food but never learned to ride them until horses were brought from Europe by the Spanish in the sixteenth and seventeenth centuries. Those of the Plains Indians who adopted horse-riding experienced a rapid socio-cultural transmutation from relatively peaceful and equalitarian hunting communities to new, rank-conscious, warlike and aggressive patterns of behaviour.

HORSE SHOE, a metal device, invented in the Iron Age to protect the horse's hooves from the excessive wear to which they were exposed under domestication, and in particular to the wear resulting from work on hard road surfaces. The iron horse shoe acquired magical connotations in most of the societies in which it is found, probably due to the ancient respect in which iron was held and the unusual shape of the manufactured shoe.

HORTICULTURAL SOCIETIES, Neolithic societies which depend primarily upon the cultivation of plants, using hand tools rather than plows, with little knowledge of soil fertilization or other advanced agricultural techniques.
HORTICULTURE, in an anthropological context, the term is used to describe less sophisticated methods of cultivation which often result in the exhaustion of the soil and the need to clear fresh virgin land for planting every few years (a practice which is known as 'shifting agriculture' among some writers). Horticulture differs from the more advanced methods of cultivation known as agriculture by the use of primitive hand tools and the lack of knowledge regarding soil refertilization.
HORUS, The falcon God of ancient Egypt, symbol of the son of Isis and Osiris. Each reigning pharaoh was regarded as the reincarnation of Horus.
HOSPITALITY, see GUEST.
HOTTENTOT, a Southern African herding people who belong to the Capoid race and speak a Khoisan language. The best studied are the Nama Hottentots of Southwest Africa, since the Cape Hottentots early lost their traditional culture and even genetic identity under the influence of European contacts. The Hottentots appear to derive from a Bushman-Negro (Bantu) admixture, and are believed to have learned cattle-herding from the Bantu.
HOTTENTOT APRON, a genetic or racial characteristic of Capoid women, among whom the labia minora is so large that it hangs like a small apron.
HOTTING, a late Bronze Age archeological site belonging to the Urnfield culture, the economic basis of which appears to have been the substantial copper mines worked in the immediate vicinity.
HOURGLASS, an early device for measuring the passage of time, comprising two glass vessels, one surmounting the other, connected by a narrow neck. The upper glass is filled with a quantity of sand or similar substance which takes an exact period of time – usually one hour – to pass from the upper section into the lower section. At the end of the hour, or other appropriate period of time, the hourglass is simply turned upside down, so that the process may repeat itself.
HOUSE COMMUNITY, a community comprising the members of a single extended family in which all property, work and produce is organized and distributed on a communal basis. While the house community may represent a single joint family (q.v.) living under the same roof, it is more common for individual nuclear families to have their own separate apartments or separate buildings, so that a large house community will outwardly resemble a small village.
HOUSEHOLD, a social, economic, and sometimes political group comprising one or more nuclear families sharing a common area of residence and a common set of resources.
HOUSE INSCRIPTION, any magico-religious dedication or other inscription, inscribed on a dwelling-house. Such inscriptions are frequently placed close to the main entrance.
HOXNIAN INTERGLACIAL, the name sometimes given to the British equivalent of the Alpine Mindel-Riss interglacial.
HSIA, the name by which the legendary first dynasty of Chinese emperors was known. While the Hsia may well have been a pastoral warlike people coming from the western steppes, and are described as being grey-eyed and red-haired, it has been difficult to identify their remains archeologically, although their existence is undoubted. The Hsia dynasty was superseded by the Shang dynasty, whose ancestors were also a warlike pastoral people with a culture resembling that of the Indo-Europeans of Western Eurasia.
HUACA, the Peruvian term for an ancient grave, derived from *quaquero*, which refers to the act of searching for graves in order to rob them.
HUACA PRIETA, a North Peruvian coastal site, which appears to have been established around 2500 B.C. before the introduction of pottery – gourds being used as containers in place of pottery. The population lived mainly on seafood but cultivated some beans and squashes. Maize was later introduced, and cotton textiles were manufactured without the aid of a loom.
HUARI, a city located in the central Peruvian mountains which played an im-

portant part in the development of pre-Inca Peruvian culture. Reflecting considerable Tiahuanaco (q.v.) influence, the people of Huari appear to have expanded their influence by military conquest during the 7th century, but the Huari empire was short-lived, soon giving way to the Chimu (q.v.) empire, which absorbed much of the Huari culture.

HUARPE, a South American people of the Patagonian area.

HUASTEC, a Central American cultivating people – adjacent to the Gulf of Mexico.

HUEHUITL, a drum made from a long hollow log, mounted on a tripod and covered with dried skin. Customarily struck with the hands, the huehuitl was used at Aztec religious festivals.

HUICHOL, a West Coast Mexican Indian people, speaking a Uto-Aztecan language, and dependent on horticulture, animal husbandry and some hunting, food-gathering, and fishing.

HUITZILOPOCHTLI, the chief deity of the Aztecs, particularly associated with the sun, warfare, and hunting.

HUKUNKIKA SHOSHONE, a Shoshone (Uto-Aztec)-speaking North American Indian people of the Coastal Great Basin, dependent on food-gathering, hunting and some fishing.

HULA, a Hawaiian dance, which was formerly part of the pre-Christian Hawaiian religious rituals, but today survives only as an entertainment.

HULDA, the Germanic goddess of domestic life.

HUMERUS, the bone comprising the upper arm of man.

HUNDE, a West Lacustrine Bantu people, largely dependent on horticulture and herding.

HUNGARIANS, a Ugric (Uralic)-speaking people whose language is known as Magyar. The modern Hungarian is of Caucasoid type, sometimes revealing elements of Central Asian ancestry. Some Magyar minorities are also to be found in Transylvania.

HUNS, a Turkic (Ural-Altaic)-speaking people of Western Asia, of nomadic herding origins, who conquered large parts of Europe and Asia in historic times. They are related to the Altai, Kirghiz and Uighar people.

HUNTING AND GATHERING SOCIETIES, societies which have not yet developed pastoral, advanced fishing, or horticultural arts.

HUNTING SOCIETIES, ADVANCED, band or tribal societies, each occupying their own distinctive territory, which differ from simple hunting societies in the possession of more sophisticated weapons. The instruments employed may include spear-throwers, bows and arrows, harpoons, and blow-pipe darts, to stupefy or kill animals too large to be incapacitated by the impact of the projectile itself.

HUNTING SOCIETIES, SIMPLE, small band-type societies, each occupying their own distinctive territories, which depend for existence upon elementary hunting techniques, using only primitive weapons, supplemented by food-gathering and scavenging.

HUNTING WITH FIRE, many prairie hunters set fire to the grass, in order to drive animals towards prepared ambushes, or alternatively create a complete circle of fire around a herd of animals in order to scare them by the smoke to permit an easy killing.

HUPA, a Northwestern California Athabascan-speaking people, dependent on fishing and food-gathering with some hunting.

HURON (or WYANDOT), Muskogean-Siouan-speaking North American Indians, dependent upon horticulture, fishing, and food-gathering.

HURRIANS, a people who inhabited the area immediately southwest of the Caspian Sea, around 2300 B.C. Under the leadership of an immigrant warrior class of Indo-Europeans, they may have contributed to the establishment of the kingdom of the Mitanni in Syria around 1500 B.C. Their own language is known from certain texts which have survived, but is not related to any of the Indo-European, Sumerian or Semitic languages. The Hurrians succeeded in preserving their independence in Urartu for considerable periods of time, despite pressure from the Syrians and Hittites.

HUT CIRCLE, a term used to refer to an archeological site revealing evidence, such as the foundations of a wall or of a ring of boulders or post holes, or even a simple circular depression of the former presence of a hut or building.

HUYUK, a Turkish word equivalent to 'tell' or 'tepe' (q.v.).

HVAR, an Adriatic variant of the Old European Chalcolithic civilization (q.v.) which succeeded the Butmir culture around 4,200 B.C., and continued until around 3,000 B.C., when it was overrun by Indo-Europeans, the area subsequently being occupied by Illyrians (q.v.).

HYBRID, an individual produced by a cross between the members of distinct gene pools possessing disparate genetic qualities. Although some attempt has been made to draw a parallel between the hybridization of human stocks or races with the concept of heterosis in plants (q.v.), there is a very serious possibility that even in the first generation the hybridization of organisms possessing highly complex genetic patterns may create disharmonies by breaking up the 'supergenes' (q.v.) which are responsible for the proper balance of genetic factors necessary to ensure a functional harmony in complex living organisms.

HYBRIDIZATION, a process of genetic admixture between two disparate populations, resulting in heterozygosity replacing homozygosity.

HYBRID SWARM, an extensive variety of forms resulting from the crossing and backcrossing of hybrids over a number of generations. The individuals thus created often reveal considerable variability due to the tendency of genes and supergenes to resegregate themselves into new patterns.

HYBRID VIGOR, see HETEROSIS.

HYDROCEPHALY, an abnormal condition resulting from an excess of cerebrospinal fluid in the ventricles of the brain. This often results in an enlarged head and a general condition of mental and physical debility.

HYGEIA, the Greek goddess of health and hygiene.

HYKSOS, the name given to an originally nomadic pastoral people who made extensive use of the horse-drawn chariot and succeeded in conquering Egypt around the end of the so-called Middle Kingdom, and who established a dynasty subsequently known as the Shepherd Kings. The Hyksos may also have introduced the upright loom into Egypt, as well as a number of other cultural innovations which stimulated the already ancient Egyptian culture to a new period of achievement between 1640-1570 B.C. It is unknown, although they have been traced to Bronze Age Palestine, whether they were Semitic or Indo-European in origin.

HYLOBATES, members of the anthropoid family Hylobatidae, of which the main surviving representatives are the gibbons and the siamangs.

HYMEN, the Greek god of marriage, son of Apollo.

HYPERBOREAN, a people who according to Greek accounts lived in a far northern land, bathed in perpetual sunshine. Since it is recorded that the Hyperboreans sent offerings to the temple of Apollo at Delos, it is probable that this term may have referred to a real people who lived close to the Arctic Circle, where they would enjoy perpetual sunshine during the summer months.

HYPERGAMY, a marriage between a socially inferior female and a socially superior male.

HYPNOS, the Greek god of sleep whose brother was Death.

HYPOCAUST, a heating system used by the Romans whereby a supply of hot air, originating from a furnace, circulated through passages beneath the floor and within the walls to provide an efficient form of central heating.

HYPOGAMY, a marriage between a socially superior female and a socially inferior male.

HYPOGEUM, that part of an ancient building which lies underground.

HYPOTHALAMUS, the lower side of the brain of a vertebrate situated immediately beneath the attachment of the cerebral hemispheres. The hypothalamus is actually a part of the forebrain, and in mammals it is known to be concerned with the direction of many activities ranging from the control of the body temperature to manifestations of rage and anger. It may also be related to the gland which controls endocrine glands, located immediately beneath the former.

I

IATMUL, an Arapesh people of New Guinea, dependent on horticulture.

IBAN, a Malayo-Polynesian people of Borneo, largely dependent on cultivation, animal husbandry and fishing.

IBERIANS, a pre-Indo-European, Caucasoid, Atlanto-Mediterranean people who appear to have been conquered by the Celts, and then overrun by the Romans, from whom they acquired the Latin language. Unlike the Basque of the Northern Pyrenees, who kept their old language, the Iberians thereafter spoke a form of Vulgar Latin, which eventually evolved into Spanish.

IBIBIO, a Bantu-speaking Negroid people living in Coastal Nigeria, the Ibibio are mainly dependent on horticulture, fishing and animal husbandry.

IBO, a Kwa-speaking Negroid people of West Africa, who belong to the Ibo-Edo group and are mainly dependent on horticulture.

ICELANDERS, a Nordic population of primarily Norwegian and possibly some Irish origin, who speak a modified form of Old Norse, and were traditionally dependent on fishing and some cultivation and animal husbandry.

ICON, a three-dimensional representation of a saint, usually made of wood or plaster. The Russian Orthodox Church is well known for its extensive use of icons in religious symbolism.

ICONOCLASM, the destruction of idol worship, first attempted by the Egyptian pharaoh Akhenaton during the 14th century B.C. Akhenaton's attempt to replace the worship of the old gods by a monotheistic concept of a single sun god influenced subsequent Hebrew prophets to adopt monotheism and condemn the worship of images. (See also TUTANKHAMEN).

ICONOCLAST, a term used to describe a person who is opposed to the worship of idols or to the keeping of images of the gods.

IDENTICAL TWINS (MONOZYGOTIC TWINS), twins which are genetically identical due to a division of the embryo of a single fertilized egg. Being identical, such twins must always be of the same sex.

IDENTIFICATION, ARCHEOLOGICAL, a procedure the object of which is to identify sets or classes of artifacts, characterized by specific traits.

IDEOGRAM, any written symbol which portrays the meaning of a complete word or idea. Ideograms are distinguished from pictograms by the less obviously pictorial nature of the representations involved.

IDEOGRAPH, a written symbol which represents a complete word or idea instead of a sound. Modern Chinese is still written in ideographs, the only handicap involved in such a system of writing being the large number of symbols that must be learned before a child can become literate.

IDIOM, a word or phrase commonly used by a sub-group within a larger society which has acquired distinctive meaning as a result of historical-cultural influences which cannot be explained by reference to the conventional meanings and/or syntactical rules.

IDOL, any three-dimensional object, frequently but not necessarily carved and painted, which purports to represent or house a supernatural being, and therefore serves as a central focus of worship. Although the Old Testament prophets condemned idolatry, they nevertheless permitted the worship of the 'Ark of the Covenant', since the Ark merely contained the scrolls on which the sacred revelations were written, instead of constituting a 'graven image' of Yahweh. Nevertheless, the Israelites regarded any attempt to touch the Ark as sacrilege.

IDOLATRY, evidence of the worship of idols first appears in Europe among the Cro-Magnon population of the Aurignacian period and further evidence has been found throughout the Balkans, Anatolia and in the Middle East dating from the Mesolithic and Neolithic eras. The concept of idolatry actually represents a quite sophisticated form of religious activity, and despite Judeo-Christian condemnation, there has been a substantial transfer of idolatrous practices into

Christianity, ranging from Catholic images of Saints to more abstract symbols symbolizing the deity – such as the Star of David and the Christian crucifix.
IDOL, DOLMEN, a particular type of idol, represented by a stone roughly shaped to resemble a standing human figure. Dolmen idols are found in various sites along the North African coast, as well as in the Middle East and Anatolia, and are believed to have been associated with the earliest cultivators of these areas.
IFALUK, a Malayo-Polynesian-speaking people from the Central Caroline Islands of Micronesia, dependent on horticulture, fishing and some animal husbandry.
IFE, a Kwa-speaking Negroid people of the Yoruba group in West Africa, largely dependent on horticulture with some animal husbandry and hunting.
IFUGAO, a Malayo-Polynesian-speaking people of the Luzon highlands, largely dependent on cultivation and hunting with some fishing and animal husbandry.
IGBIRA, a Kwa-speaking Negroid people from West Africa, largely dependent on horticulture with some fishing and animal husbandry.
IGLOO, a dome-shaped hut constructed by the Eskimoes for hunting quarters. An igloo is quickly constructed from blocks of ice, and is usually entered by way of a small, semi-subterranean passage, also constructed of ice blocks. The design appears to resemble certain types of pit houses constructed by Cro-Magnon men during the cold Würm glacial period in Europe, many thousands of years earlier.
IGLULIK, an Eskimo people who depend mainly on fishing and hunting.
IGOROT, a horticultural people of the northern Philippines.
IGUVINE TABLETS, a set of seven bronze tablets found at Eugubium in Italy, inscribed in Umbrian, Etruscan and Latin. Believed to have been written between 400 and 300 B.C., the contents describe ritual procedures for the worship of the ancestral spirits.
ILA, a Bantu-speaking Negroid people of the Ila-Tonga group, primarily dependent on horticulture and herding.
ILI-MANDIRI, a Malayo-Polynesian-speaking people inhabiting the Flores Isles (Indonesia), largely dependent on cultivation and fishing, with some hunting and animal husbandry.
ILIUM, the dorsal part of the hip-girdle, which provides a stable base for the attachment of the hind limbs.
ILLA, the local name given to amulets and other ornaments worn for their magico-religious significance by members of the Inca civilization.
ILLINOIAN GLACIATION, the name given to the first North American glaciation which probably corresponded to the Alpine Riss glaciation (q.v.).
ILLINOIS, a North American Indian people of the Eastern Woodlands.
ILOKANO, a cultivating people of the Northern Philippines.
IMAGE, any object intended to represent another object or person. (See also ICON, IDOL, and MAGIC, IMITATIVE).
IMAM, a term widely used throughout the Islamic world for the chief authority governing a mosque.
IMMORTAL, a person gifted with supernatural qualities who never dies. To the Greeks and other Indo-Europeans, the prime difference between the gods and men rested in the immortality of the gods and the mortality of men. The concept of immortality involves eternal life for both soul and body and should be distinguished from the idea of reincarnation.
IMMUNITY, the ability of a living organism to resist infection by alien or parasitic organisms. Since all living organisms are subject to attack by bacteria, viruses and parasitic animals, the ability to develop an impervious skin covering, an antiseptic stomach, or chemical defense by antibodies, plays an important role in the process of natural selection. In some cases survival from a first attack by parasitical organisms may result in immunity against subsequent attacks. Mammalian mothers are able to transmit limited immunity to their offspring during the prenatal state and also, to a lesser extent, during breast-feeding.
IMPALING, a form of capital punishment in which a stake is driven through the body of a victim as he lies prostrate on the ground, or alternatively in which

the living victim is hurled into a pit containing upturned, pointed stakes.

IMPRESSED DECORATION, the name given to all kinds of pottery decoration achieved by pressing a stick, a bone, a piece of cord or even a carved object into the surface of the clay.

IMPRESSED WARE, a specific term applying to Neolithic pottery found in the Western Mediterranean, the Adriatic coast of Italy and the Balkans. Impressed Ware pottery is so called because of the impressed decorations on the surface, which take a variety of forms.

IMPRESSO CULTURE, the first Neolithic culture, originating in the Adriatic circa 6000 B.C., and subsequently spreading to the Western Mediterranean.

INBREEDING, mating between close relatives. Despite popular belief, no genetic deterioration results from inbreeding. Indeed man's ancestors, and those of most mammals, have customarily inbred within relatively small groups over millions of years. Inbreeding combined with severe natural selection, effectively ensures the reduction of harmful recessive genes to a minimal level, and many incestuous royal families, such as those of the Greek Ptolemies, rulers of Egypt, the Inca royal family, and the kings of Hawaii, retained their superior genetic qualities through many generations of close inbreeding, as is evidenced by their political success. Only when inbreeding is accompanied by a reduction in the purifying effect of natural selection can the effects be harmful.

INCAS, the Incas originated as a clan situated at Cuzco around A.D. 1200, and subsequently succeeded in creating a vast centralized military empire extending over the entire coastal regions from Northern Ecuador into Central Chile, including much of the Andean mountains. Claiming divine descent from the Sun God, the ruling Inca kings invariably married their own sisters in order to maintain the puritv of the lineage, and apparently must have been remarkablv healthy from a genetic point of view since not only was there no evidence of genetic deterioration, but the Inca Empire reached its peak under the efficient management of the 9th and 10th generation of inbred Incas. Since the Inca emperors took a number of secondary wives or concubines, and since other members of the royal Inca clan were also permitted plural wives and the possession of concubines, they produced a sufficiently prolific number of offspring to occupy the key administrative positions in the vast bureaucracy which controlled the constantly expanding empire. All conquered peoples were converted to the worship of the Sun God, and hence to the acceptance of the divinity of the ruling Inca family. This empire was held together by an impressive and efficient system of military roads, and in the absence of riding animals or wheeled vehicles, chains of state-employed runners carried official messages to and from the capital at Cuzco at the rate of 150 miles per day. A central college or 'university' was established at Cuzco, in which members of the Inca ruling class received an education in administrative and military duties and in the ritual of the Inca religion to ensure their efficiency and loyalty as future officers of the state, and sons of chieftains of conquered tribes were also reeducated in this central university, after which (provided they accepted the Inca religion and culture) they were returned to their people to serve as minor bureaucrats helping to control the newly subjugated tribes and to keep them loyal to Inca domination. Each village within the Inca empire represented a specific clan or kinship grouping, no villages being allowed to grow too large. In the event of a famine, food was transferred from the royal granaries, and in the event of overpopulation, the surplus young men and women were removed, either to serve the Inca ruling class as craftsmen, servants or concubines, as laborers to work the Inca estates, or else as colonists newly conquered territories. The Inca empire was brought to an abrupt end by the victory of the Spanish conquistadores under 1532.

INCARNATION, the physical appearance on earth of a supernatural being in animal or human form. The Greeks frequently believed that their gods appeared to humans in human form (see ANTHROPOMORPHISM). Christianity similarly regarded Jesus as the incarnation of the deity, in that it denied the Arian view which regarded the members of the 'Holy Trinity' (God the Father, God the

Son, and God the Holy Spirit) as three separate beings and insisted instead on the principle of a somewhat contradictory monotheism.

INCENSE, a sweet-smelling aromatic substance derived from trees or herbs, frequently used in association with religious rituals.

INCEST, a social invention prohibiting sexual relations between certain persons regarded by their society as being close kinfolk. The conventions which control incest do not necessarily match those which control marital relations, although obviously, persons prohibited from incestuous sexual relations with each other must also be prohibited from enjoying marital relations. Although Westermarck, who incorrectly believed that close inbreeding was genetically harmful, suggested that biological reasons were the basis for the widespread incest prohibitions common to almost all human societies, further ethnographic study has revealed that incest prohibitions have existed in societies which were totally ignorant of genetics and even of the fact of paternity. Incest prohibitions are, in fact, merely social conventions which seldom have any direct relationship to genetic kinship, and the purpose of incest prohibitions might well be to prevent rivalry and the possibility of conflict between members of the same household. Excluding persons of divine, royal or noble descent (see INCEST, DYNASTIC), most societies prohibit incestuous relations within the nuclear family and also with a variety of other kinsmen, depending on the social, economic and kinship structure of the society in question.

INCEST, DYNASTIC, royal and noble families claiming descent from divinities, and believed to inherit familial charisma (q.v.) or mana (q.v.) may frequently practice extremely close inbreeding in order to preserve the purity of their lineage. Thus the Ptolemies of Egypt, the Incas of Peru, and the Hawaiian kings frequently married their own sister: the Greek Aeolus married his six sons to his daughters; and the Teutonic hero Siegfried was a product of the genetic and ritual purity of the mating of a divinely-descended brother and sister.

INCISION, a widespread ritual mutilation involving a longitudinal slit in the rear portion of the foreskin of the male penis. (See also CIRCUMCISION and SUB-INCISION).

INCISORS, chisel-shaped front teeth, common among primates and many other mammals.

INCISORS, SHOVEL-SHAPED, a racial condition in which the upper central incisors are characterized by a pronounced hollow on the rear side. Very common among Mongoloids, the incidence of shovel-shaped incisors decreases with distance from the epicenter of the Mongoloids in Northern China and Mongolia, yet is still found amongst Eskimos and American Indians. Since Sinanthropus pekinensis remains reveal the same feature, it provides evidence of a phylogenetic link between living Mongoloids and Peking Man.

INDEPENDENT INVENTION, an indigenous innovation.

INDEX, the ratio between two specific anatomical measurements.

INDIANS, AMERICAN, although some authorities claim the possibility that Neanderthal men may have arrived in the New World prior to the last glacial period, it is generally agreed that the present American Indian stock is descended from successive movements of immigrants (mainly comprising relatively small bands) from Siberia across the Bering straits to Alaska (probably via the Aleutian Isles) at various intervals from between 20,000 B.P., and 2000 B.P., the last migrants being the Eskimos. Although American Indians are generally classified as Mongoloids in racial type, it would appear that considerable Paleo-Asian elements may have been present in certain immigrant bands. This fact, together with genetic drift (q.v.) and local selection following their arrival in North America has caused them to be viewed as a new racial stock by some writers.

INDIC (INDO-ARYAN) LANGUAGES, an extremely large group of languages, comprising the major part of the Indo-Iranian division of Indo-European, which derive from Sanskrit and Pali. The main sub-divisions are Dardic, which includes Kashmiri and Kohistani and is also close to Iranian, and various Indian 'zones', namely: a Central Indic zone of languages, which includes Gujerati and Bhil, Hindi and Urdu, Punjabi, and Rasthani; an Eastern Indic zone, which includes

Bengali, Assamese, Bihari, Orija, and Marathi; a Northern Himalaya zone, which includes Nepali, Garhwali and Pahari; a Northwest zone, which includes Sindhi and Romany or Gipsy; and Singhalese-Maldivian (the language of Ceylon and the Maldives) and Vedda.

INDO-CHINA, that area of Southeast Asia occupied by the Thais, Vietnamese, Cambodians, Laotians, and related peoples, so-called because of the dual cultural influences which reached the area from India to the west and China to the north.

INDO-EUROPEAN LANGUAGES (and PEOPLES), formerly known as the Aryan languages. The term Indo-European (IE) expresses the limits of the geographical expansion of this family of languages in the prehistoric period. The original home of the Proto-Indo-Europeans (PIE) is now generally held to have been Eastern Europe, and it is believed from various linguistic evidence that during the Neolithic the Proto-Indo-European language was spoken by a relatively small and compact people – perhaps one or several tribes – who possessed horses and wheeled vehicles. If they may be associated with the kurgan burials of Southern Russia, they would have been a cattle-raising people, who nevertheless practised, or were familiar with, agricultural techniques and procedures.

After the development of metalurgy, the IE appear to have spread outwards in successive waves of migration, conquest, and settlement, establishing themselves as an 'Arya' or ruling class over many different peoples throughout Europe, Asia Minor, Anatolia, and India, retaining, however, the essential structure of their language, social system, customs and mythico-religious beliefs. Their possession of and dexterity with horses, chariots, and swords facilitated their success in this respect, but their ability to impose their language and hierarchical social structure upon the diverse peoples they conquered over such a wide area is probably due to their highly developed oral literary tradition, and their belief in the inherited nature of human qualities. These convictions served to preserve their ethnic identity as a ruling class by favoring purity of descent in both the mother's and the father's lineages. Indo-European incursions into the old European civilization (q.v.) began around 5000 B.C., with the first ancestors of the Greeks reaching the Aegean in the second millennium B.C. The forebears of the Slavs, Germans and Celts spread throughout Europe, and the Italic family of languages separated from the Celtic, around 1000 B.C., when the Villanovians moved southwards into central Italy. Celtic divided into Brythonic (Welsh, Breton and Cornish), Gaelic (still represented by Irish, Scottish Gaelic and Manx); and Gaulish, a language which died out following the Roman conquest of Gaul.

The Italic languages diversified into Oscan, Umbrian and Latin. Because the Latin languages and customs were close to those of the Celts, the Gauls of Gaul (France), Iberia (Spain) and North Italy (Cisalpine Gaul) easily assimilated the Roman language and culture. Italian, French, Spanish, Portuguese and Romanian (the Romance languages) all derive from Latin. Germanic language and culture was also parallel to that of early Latium, but less so than Celtic. Thus the Germans tended to keep their vigorous individuality – eventually overthrowing Rome. North German dialects slowly evolved into the modern languages of Scandinavia, but the East Germanic 'Gothic' language was lost when the Goths spread themselves too thinly throughout Europe in continuous sequences of conquest, war and migration. West German survives today in the form of English, Frisian, Dutch, Flemish, Plattdeutsch and High German.

The Slavic branch of the Indo-Europeans became divided geographically and linguistically into the West Slavic (Polish, Sorbian, Czech and Slovak), the South Slavic (Bulgarian, Slovene and Serbo-Croat), and the East Slavic (Russian and Ukrainian). Meanwhile another division, the Baltic, developed into Lithuanian and Lettish (Latvia) and Old Prussian, which language, however, did not survive conquest by the Teutonic Knights. In the Balkans, Albanian, which is an IE language distantly related to Greek, still flourishes. Thracian, by contrast, became extinct long ago.

During the second millennium B.C. or earlier, Indo-Europeans also entered Asia Minor, giving rise to the Anatolian group of IE languages. These included Phrygian, Armenian, Luwian, Lycian, Lydian, Palaic, and Hittite, few of which survived. Entering Persia around 1900 B.C., the Iranian branch of the Indo-Iranian IE-speakers established themselves as Medes, Persians and Kurds, others moving on into Afghanistan, where they gave rise to the Nuristani and Dardic groups of languages. The Indo-Aryans entered and conquered India, where Sanskrit gave rise to the Indic (q.v.) group of modern languages ranging from Hindi to Bengali and from Scindi to Singhalese. For some centuries Indo-European speech flourished in Indonesia under Indian rajahs. A quite separate IE group of languages, known as Tokharian, was spoken in Sinkiang some two millenia ago, until this Indo-European outpost eventually succumbed first to Turkic and subsequently to Sinitic control.

INDO-IRANIAN LANGUAGES, the Eastern branch of the Indo-European family of languages. (See INDIC, IRANIAN and NURISTANI).

INDONESIANS, a Malayo-Polynesian-speaking people, whose language belongs to the Malayo-Polynesian or Austro-Asiatic family of language, the Indonesians today inhabit the islands of Sumatra, Java, the Philippines, the Celebes and a multitude of smaller islands. The physical type appears to constitute a Mongoloid, Australoid (q.v.) and Negrito (q.v.) admixture, although small groups of true Negritoes still survive in the forested interior of the Philippines and in a few other inland areas. The Malayo-Indonesian group of languages includes Malay, Javanese, Balinese, Batak, Bicol, Bisaya, Bontok, Buginese, Dayak, Formosan (the language of the aboriginal peoples of Taiwan), Ilocano, Macassar, Maduran, Malagasy, Sundanese, and Tagalog.

INDRA, the Indo-Aryan god of thunder and lightning, somewhat equivalent to the Germanic Thor. Just as Thor rivaled Odin in popularity in the Germanic religion, Indra also rivaled Dyaus among the Indo-Aryans.

INDUSTRIAL SOCIETY, a society which is characterized by mass production and which depends primarily for its energy supply upon inanimate resources rather than upon human or animal muscle.

INDUSTRY, an archeological term which refers to a collection of artifacts of roughly the same age uncovered at the same site or from a series of related sites, which share a set of common distinctive traits.

INDUS VALLEY CIVILIZATION, an extensive agricultural civilization which formerly flourished in the Indus Valley and in the area drained by the major tributaries to the Indus, now known as the Punjab. The main cities of Harappa and Mohenjo-daro were separated by many hundreds of miles, and only extensive river communications could explain the extent to which this widely dispersed civilization, covering a total of some 1500 square miles, retained its remarkable uniformity of culture. There is some evidence that horticulture was first introduced into the Indus Valley from the direction of Persia and Afghanistan, subsequently evolving in the fertile lands of the Indus Valley and the Punjab into an advanced system of agriculture and irrigation. Trading connections were maintained with the Sumerian civilization by coastal traffic along the Indian Ocean and the Persian coast as well as by overland routes through Persia. However, the Indus Valley civilization developed its own distinctive characteristics, which included large walled cities with well laid-out planned streets, and buildings constructed of baked bricks. Each of these cities appears to have had a monumental 'Great Bath' (the purpose of which is believed to have been religious), a central assembly hall, and other monumental buildings. The possibility that Indus Valley society was heavily stratified is indicated by the disparity in the quality and size of buildings in the distinctively separate quarters of the cities. Indeed although the later Indian caste system acquired its contemporary character from Indo-Aryans (q.v.), it is possible that a caste-like social system was already in existence at the time of the Indus Valley civilization. The economy of the Indus civilization was based very largely upon the growth of rice, wheat, barley, vegetables and cotton. Crops were hauled in wheeled vehicles, and the domesticated animals included the camel and the brahman cow. A hieroglyphic script was used, although this has not yet been deciphered, and in addition to a system of weights and measures, beautifully designed seals (mostly carved from steatite) were utilized to confirm written contracts and other documents. Although there is clear evidence that many of the major Indus Valley cities were finally destroyed and left uninhabited following a series of military attacks, the Indus Valley civilization fell into decay some centuries before the first Indo-Aryans arrived on the Indian subcontinent. The exact reason for this decay is unknown, although various reasons have been suggested, such as over-exploitation of the soil, a change in the level of the water table, and even social or genetic decay. The original inhabitants appear to have been of typical Mediterranean Caucasoid type, not dissimilar from those who occupied Iràn, the Middle East and the Mediterranean, although some evidence of aboriginal Australoid (or Veddoid) and even Negrito types may be found, the latter most notably represented by a bronze statuette of a dancing girl.

INDUSTRY, an archeological term which refers to a collection of artifacts of roughly the same age uncovered at the same site or from a series of related sites.

INFANTICIDE, an anthropological term referring to the practice of killing infants shortly after birth. There are many causes of infanticide, economic reasons being common among many peoples. Thus at one time Polynesians were reported to have killed two-thirds of their children to avoid overpopulation. Similarly, Australian aboriginal women who have to migrate long distances every day, and can only carry one young infant at a time, frequently killed children born too soon after the birth of an older sibling, burying them alive in the sand. Alternatively, infanticide may result from ritual cannibalism, while female infanticide among the Todas, who killed a high proportion of newborn female offspring, was due to the practice of polyandry which rendered it unnecessary to rear more than a few females. Eugenic infanticide (q.v.) has also been common among the more advanced civilizations such as ancient Greece, Rome and Japan.

INFIBULATION, an operation on the female genitals, intended to prevent sexual intercourse prior to marriage, probably once universal amongst Hamitic and Semitic-speaking peoples.

INFORMANT, a term used by ethnographers to refer to persons who provide the ethnographer with information about their culture and society.

INFRAORBITAL FORAMEN, an aperture in the skull below the eye socket orbit.

INGADA, an Arunta 'headman' or band 'leader'.

INGALIK, a North Athabascan American Indian people of the Lower Yukon dependent on hunting and fishing with some food-gathering.

INGIET, a secret society among the Melanesians of New Britain, membership of which is restricted to males.

INGOT, a piece of metal cast into a specific shape. Most ingots were of a standard weight, shape and purity, varying according to the requirements of the society which produced them and were used both as a convenient method of storing wealth and also as an early form of money.

INHERITANCE, customs concerning the inheritance of property vary from one society to another. Kinship-based societies frequently regard property as belonging to the family, to be passed on to successive generations following the deaths of individual family heads, and the current idea prevalent in western society that an individual may 'will' his property to persons outside the family arose only after Christianity destroyed the older traditions of ancestor-worship and familism, and persuaded dying heads of families to donate a substantial portion of the wealth of their family to the church in order to purchase immunity from the dangers of hell-fire for their own individual souls.

INHERITANCE, COLLATERAL, the custom whereby property is inherited by the brothers, sisters or other collateral relatives instead of by the children of the deceased.

INHERITANCE, LINEAL, the passage of property to the sons or daughters of the deceased, rather than to collateral relatives.

INHIBITION, NERVOUS, the prevention of any otherwise automatic or semi-automatic activation of an effector. The ability to inhibit reflex actions is essential if the central nervous system of an organism is to effectively control the activities and prevent reflex actions which might be dangerous in unsuitable

circumstances.
INHIBITIONS, SOCIAL, to some extent social inhibitions parallel nervous inhibitions (q.v.) by preventing the individual from creating disturbing or potentially dangerous social situations through reactions which might have been beneficial in a less complex social environment. Thus civilization is largely dependent upon social inhibitions.
INHUMATION (also INTERMENT), the burial of the dead in contrast to (a) 'cremation', the destruction of the remains by fire, or (b) the 'exposure' of a corpse to birds and animals of prey.
INION, the point at which two muscle attachment ridges meet on the base of the external occipital protuberance of the skull.
INITIATION RITES, rituals held at the time of initiation of an individual into a new status in his society, or possibly into a secret society (q.v.). Such initiation rituals frequently involve ordeals. (See also RITES OF PASSAGE).
INNOVATION, the introduction of a new norm, artifact or tradition into a culture, either by independent invention or by borrowing (cultural diffusion).
INSECTA, a class of arthropoda which contains ants, bees, butterflies, lice, termites, flies, and fleas, etc.
INSECTIVORA, an order of placental mammals primarily dependent upon insect-eating as a means of subsistence. Common in the Cretaceous period, they are today represented by the mole, hedgehog and spiny anteater.
INSTINCT, an elaborate pattern of animal reactions which occur in response to certain stimuli and which have evolved as a result of natural selection over innumerable generations because of their inherent survival value to the species, if not to all individuals at all times. Notable among the instincts would be the tendency of the mammalian mother to protect her offspring. Nevertheless, a disruption of the traditional environment such as the confinement of zoo animals under strict or unnatural conditions, may severely affect the normal pattern of responses. Thus caged animals have been known to attack and kill their infants instead of providing them with instinctive care and protection. A similarly unnatural reaction may occur as a result of the over-crowding of an animal population far above the optimum density to which the species has become adapted by natural selection. Thus homosexuality among animals appears to be at least partly related to overpopulation.
INSTITUTION, a relatively enduring set of socially approved practices, usually of a kind which serve to meet the basic needs of the individual and his society.
INTELLIGENCE QUOTIENT (I.Q.), a figure indicating the intelligence of an individual relative to other persons of the same age, the average IQ for the group under study being taken as 100. While the exact nature of intelligence is still debated, as also the efficiency of IQ tests, it is not to be denied that IQ test results have proved to be remarkably accurate indicators of the tested individual's ability to achieve in intellectual activities. Some have protested IQ testing on the grounds that the tests are discriminatory, while others have demonstrated that 'culture-free' tests are possible, but the prime objections seem to center on the fact that IQ test results reveal wide differences between individuals and smaller, but consistent, statistical differences between races. The degree of heritability of IQ is also disputed, although tests of identical twins have indicated that this is possibly as high as 85 - 90%. It has been further argued that scientific progress is dependent upon the achievements of persons in the top 2.5% of IQ grades, and that the 15% of persons with an IQ of below 85 are becoming increasingly unemployable in this scientific age. Statistically, it would appear that few of the 85% of the American population whose IQ is below 115 ever read serious books unrelated to their livelihood, and therefore depend for their opinions on the other 15%. Furthermore, it has been claimed that lasting intellectual relationships are unlikely between individuals whose IQs differ by more than 20 to 25 points.
INTERGLACIAL, a warmer interlude between any two glaciations of the Pleistocene period. (See also INTERSTADIAL).
INTERGRADE, see RACIAL CLINE.
INTERMENT, an alternative term for inhumation.

INTERPHASE, the normal or 'resting stage' of a nucleus when neither meiosis (q.v.) nor mitosis (q.v.) is taking place.
INTER-SOCIETAL SELECTION, a process of selection which eliminates some societies and cultures while permitting the survival of others more suited to meet the environmental challenges.
INTERSTADIAL, a temporary period of relative warmth and mildness of climate intervening between periods of extreme coldness. An interstadial is to be distinguished from an interglacial period – a more enduring period of greater warmth which separates two major glacial periods within the same glaciation.
INTESTINES, that portion of the alimentary canal which links the stomach and the anus. In vertebrates the intestines are concerned primarily with the absorption of the products of digestion occurring within the intestines. The material to be digested is moved through the intestines by movement of the muscular walls known as peristalsis. The small intestine is primarily concerned with digestion, while the large intestine is responsible for the preparation of feces and the removal of water.
INTROCISION, see CIRCUMCISION.
INTROGRESSIVE HYBRIDIZATION, a term used to refer to the steady infiltration of genes from one subspecies into the gene pool of another subspecies. When two species are brought into contact, hybrids inevitably tend to backcross with the more favored of the subspecies, resulting in the ultimate elimination of the pure forms of both the less and the more favored species, and their replacement by a hybrid and modified form. This principle may have played an important part in the creation of the present races of man, as more successful subspecies repeatedly expanded over the globe, only to absorb genetic elements from older, less successful subspecies in the areas of colonization. The progressive hybridization of the various races or subspecies of man appears to be proceeding with increasing rapidity at the present time.
INTRUSIVE CULTURE, any culture which intrudes into an area formerly dominated by a different culture, without becoming substantially modified by the indigenous culture.
INUIT, the name by which the Eskimos know themselves. As is so often the case, the term is best translated simply as 'men'.
INVALIDICIDE, the custom of killing chronic invalids, a practice regarded as morally correct in many societies.
INVENTION, an innovation arising from a new combination of information or concepts.
INVENTION, CULTURAL, the introduction of a new or modified pattern of thought or behaviour.
INVERSION, a term used by geneticists to refer to the situation which arises when, due to aberrant crossing over within chromosomes, a segment becomes inverted and the genes appear in the wrong order.
INVERTEBRATE, a general term for all animals which lack vertebrates, i.e. amoeba, sponges, worms, snails, starfishes, etc.
IOWA, Muskogean-Siouan-speaking North American Plains Indians of the Siouan group. The Iowa are dependent on horticulture, practised in the river valleys, supplemented by hunting and food-gathering.
IPIUDAK, the largest Eskimo settlement site yet discovered by archeologists. Located in Alaska it is dated around A.D. 300. Ipiudak contained the evidence of some 600 separate homes, as well as a fine collection of carved ivory and bone objects which reveal the Siberian background of the Eskimo culture.
IPSWICHIAN INTERGLACIAL, the name sometimes given to the British equivalent of the Alpine Riss-Würm interglacial.
IRANIAN LANGUAGES, a major division of the Indo-Iranian branch of the Indo-European family of languages. The Iranian languages include Avestan (the extinct language of the Zoroastrians), and an Eastern group which includes Alanic, Ossetic, Sarmatian, Sogdian, and Scythian; a Pamir group which includes Pushto, Wakhi (Afghanistan), Afghan, Parachi (Afghanistan), and Sarikholi

(Soviet Union); a Western group which includes Baluchi and Bakhtiari (Southern Iran); and Kurdish, which is closely associated with the Luri of Luristan and with Persian.

IRANIANS, the Iranians are generally regarded as a local sub-race of the major Caucasoid geographical race, the designation including not only the Iranians of Iran but also the population of most of Afghanistan and West Pakistan. Linguistically the Iranian language is one of the major Indo-European languages, being closely related to Sanskrit and to the living Indic language of Northern and Eastern India.

IRAQI, (1) a southern Cushitic people of East Africa, dependent on animal herding and agriculture, and (2) the Arabic-speaking majority population of modern Iraq. The Iraqis are genetically diverse in their origins, with probably relatively little genetic affinity to the ancient Sumerians who formerly inhabited this region.

IRIS, the colored part of the human eye which is responsible for controlling the amount of light admitted. It comprises a thin sheet of tissue which is dark brown in color when heavily pigmented, and blue in color when lightly pigmented. Controlling muscles cause the iris to enlarge or reduce the pupil, thus regulating the amount of light permitted to stimulate the retina and optic nerve.

IRISH, a Celtic Indo-European people of mixed Atlanto-Mediterranean and Nordic descent. The Irish language is of Goidelic-Celtic origin, derived from Indo-European invaders who appeared to superimpose themselves upon an older indigenous population. The name 'Irish' derives from *Eire*, believed by some authorities to be synonymous with *Aryan*, as also the term *aire* which they applied to cattle-owning noblemen. Traditional Irish society was strongly Indo-European in character, and has been shown to reveal close parallels with that of the early Indo-Aryans who – in contrast to the Irish who settled the extreme western fringes of the Indo-European world – penetrated the subcontinent of India, and established the most eastern of Indo-European settlements (excepting only the Tokharians in central Asia, and the Indonesian Hindu settlements of later centuries).

IRMINSUL, the Saxon 'Tree of Life'. There is a widespread mythological tradition, common to both the Indo-Europeans and Sumerians, of a sacred 'Tree of Life'. Not only was this reflected in the Yggdrasil of Norse mythology, the Irminsul of the Saxons and the Maypole of later European folklore, but we also find evidence of a belief in sacred trees whose fruit gave knowledge or immortality to the gods among the Greeks, Romans, Slavs, and Balts. The presence of parallel myths among the Sumerians is further evidence of possible common early roots, or at least contacts, between the proto-Indo-Europeans and the forebears of the Sumerians – possibly as far back as the Mesolithic.

IRON, techniques for smelting and working iron were not developed until around 1800 B.C. when Anatolian craftsmen under Hittite rule learned how to smelt and use this hard and plentiful metal. Crude iron is stronger than bronze. It can also be hardened by hammering it in heated form, and can be made even stronger by heating it for long periods before plunging the red hot metal into cold water. Realizing that properly-worked iron weapons were much stronger than bronze weapons, the Hittites succeeded in preserving the secret of iron metallurgy until their eventual defeat by a combination of Phrygians and Assyrians, after which the use of iron spread rapidly because iron was more widely available than copper and tin. At first, wide differences in the ability to work iron effectively continued to persist, so that it is reported by the Romans that their victory over the Celts at the strategic battle of Apulia resulted primarily from the superior quality of iron used to make the short Roman swords, in contrast to the long Celtic swords which due to the poorly-tempered iron bent after use – and became useless unless the owner had time to straighten the blade under his foot. Because iron ore was more widely available than copper and tin, the introduction of iron-working also brought about a significant social and economic revolution. From the military point of view it became possible for nations to equip large numbers of lower class infantrymen with effective iron weapons and even iron armour, whereas the use of bronze weapons and armour had been confined to the nobility on account of the scarcity of the metals involved. This fact weakened the authority of the nobility, by raising the military effectiveness of the lower classes. In addition iron was cheap enough to be used for agricultural and other industrial purposes, iron plowshares soon replacing the older stone plowshares. The use of iron, either by forging or by casting, spread rapidly throughout Europe, the Middle East, India, and even into Africa and China. In fact although iron was undoubtedly introduced into China from Europe, it is possible that the technique of casting iron, as opposed to forging it, may have been developed by the Chinese earlier than in any other part of the Old World. No iron was used in the New World until introduced by the Spaniards. Among the Indo-Europeans iron early developed magico-religious significance as a protective charm against the supernatural forces of evil, but other peoples, such as the Semites, insisted upon retaining their traditional stone knives for religious rituals, such as circumcision, and excluded iron from all religious usages. The earliest known iron may have been meteoric iron, and this explains the ancient belief that iron swords came from heaven. Indeed both the Babylonian and Egyptian characters for iron indicate a heavenly origin.

IROQUOIS, Muskogean-Siouan-speaking Northern American Indians, dependent on horticulture, hunting, fishing and food-gathering. The Iroquoian family of languages includes Huron, Cherokee, and Delaware.

IRRIGATION, a means of supplying water by artificial canals to agricultural land which receives irregular rainfall. The Sumerians developed elaborate irrigation systems in the flat alluvial plains of Mesopotamia.

IRRITABILITY, a response to a change in environment which in normal circumstances would serve to promote adaptive activity but which may result in nervous debilitation in social situations in which the individual is obliged to suppress his normal adaptive response to environmental change.

ISHTAR, the Sumerian goddess of love and procreation, who was associated by the priest-astrologers with the planet Venus. Her consort was the god Tammuz, with whom she participated annually in the reprocreation of life, being responsible for the coming of Spring and the cyclical rebirth of vegetation on earth. Ishtar appears to have been worshipped throughout Mesopotamia and to have been adopted by the Semites of the Levant under the name of Astarte.

ISIS, the wife of the Egyptian god Osiris, and the mother of Horus, Isis is regarded as a moon goddess (usually portrayed with a moon disc inscribed on her brow) who succeeded in collecting the disembodied remains of her murdered brother-husband, Osiris, and in conceiving Horus from the reconstituted corpse.

ISLAM, the religion of the Islamic, Moslem or Mohammedan peoples. Of Semitic origin, the Islamic religion developed in Arabia from the teachings of Mohammed, regarded as the major prophet of a monotheistic god known as Allah. Borrowing much from the Hebrew and Christian religions, as well as from ancient Egyptian and Babylonian sources, the Islamic religion, like the Christian religion, believes in an all-powerful creator god whose revealed desires must be accepted by all men as the source of human law. However, the Islamic religion places even greater emphasis than does the Christian religion upon the concept of Allah as a God of History who is responsible for every event, thus implying a much stronger fatalism and accepting all suffering, as well as all success, as 'the will of Allah'. Like Christianity, the Islamic religion has shown powerful missionary interests, and shortly after its appearance 'holy wars' of Arab conquest carried the Islamic religion over extensive areas of North Africa and the Middle East into Turkestan, Pakistan and even as far East as the East Indies, to which it was carried by Arab merchant-raiders. As an effective missionary religion, Islam promises the equality of all men – at least in the afterlife – but since all earthly events occur only as planned by Allah, the wealthy and successful are not required to devoid themselves of their wealth, rank and power, but merely to donate a prescribed portion of this income to charity. Thus Islam is in many ways more favorably disposed to capitalism than is modern Christianity.

ISLANDS OF THE BLESSED, a legendary group of islands representing an earthly 'Paradise', references to which may be found in both Celtic and Greek mythology.

ISLAND, SPEECH, a relatively small geographical area, the residents of which speak a language unrelated to those of the neighboring communities. Thus the Mon-Khmer languages, formerly spoken over a large contiguous area, today survive as speech islands surrounded by larger Sinitic-speaking populations.

ISLETA, a Uto-Aztec, Tanoan-speaking North American Indian, Eastern Pueblo people, dependent on horticulture with a small amount of hunting and, in post-Columbian times, animal husbandry.

ISOGENE, a line drawn on a population map indicating similar frequencies of a specific gene.

ISOGLOSS, the name given to a line on a dialect map which is supposed to represent a division between different dialects. Unless an abrupt break in the continuity of languages has arisen as a result of the movements of peoples due to political or physical barriers, dialects tend to merge into each other, and are seldom as sharply defined as isoglosses would tend to suggest.

ISOKO, a Kwa-speaking Negroid people from West Africa, belonging to the Ibo-Edo group, and mainly dependent on horticulture and fishing.

ISOLATE, POPULATION, a population which is genetically isolated from contact with other populations. This isolation may arise due to geographical or cultural reasons, and over a sufficiently long period of time will inevitably result in an emergence of a new sub-species as a result of 'genetic drift' (q.v.) if not of 'natural selection' (q.v.).

ISOLATING MECHANISM, that causal factor or combination of causes, frequently geographical but sometimes sociological, which tends to isolate the members of a single population into separate breeding populations, enabling these to evolve into different subspecies.

ISOLEXIC LINE, a line drawn on a linguistic map to delineate areas possessing a more or less common lexicon (or vocabulary).

ISOPHONIC LINE, a line drawn on a linguistic map delineating areas in which similar phonetic features are dominant.

ISOSTASY, a term used to refer to changes in the relative height of the land and sea, particularly in association with glacial and interglacial periods. Not only does the melting of the ice during the warmer interglacial periods lead to a rise in the level of the sea, but it is suggested that the weight of the glaciers or certain land masses actually forces these landmasses downwards during glacial periods, thus effecting further changes in the pattern of world geography.

ISOSYNTAGMIC LINE, a line drawn on a linguistic map to indicate areas in which a similarity of syntax can be demonstrated.

ISRAEL, the name given to the land originally occupied by Canaanites, following its seizure by the Hebrews after their escape from captivity in Egypt. For a time there were two Hebrew kingdoms, one of which was known as Israel and the other as Judea, but the term Israel was later extended to include all the Hebrew peoples. In 721 B.C. Israel was overrun by the Assyrians under King Sargon, and according to tradition ten of the twelve tribes of Israel were taken off into captivity by the Assyrian or Babylonian victors. Although the Israelites who were held captive in Babylon were subsequently given their freedom by the Aryan Persians, following the Persian conquest of Babylon, and permitted to return to Israel, the myth of the lost tribes of Israel persisted in the minds of the people of Judeo-Christian religion, so that as late as the 19th century many travelers, explorers and amateur anthropologists claimed to have found remnants of the lost tribes in the most unlikely corners of the world.

ITALIC LANGUAGES, a large group of Indo-European languages, most of which are now extinct. The main sub-groups were Pre-Italic, including Ligurian, Illyrian, Paetic, Sicil (of Sicily), and Venetic (of Venice); Latino-Faliscan, including Latin, Faliscan, Praenestinian, and Lanuvian; and Umbro-Sabellian, including various Umbro-Sabellian dialects spoken from Calabria to the Arno. The Italian-speakers appear to have been closely related to the Celts, from whom they probably separated about 1200-1000 B.C., and Ligurian in particular seems to be intermediate between Italic and Celtic.

ITANAME, a sweet potato which plays an important role in the diet of the New Caledonian peoples.

ITHYPHALLIC, a term used to refer to phallic symbols, of magico-religious source, comprising exaggerated representations of sexual organs.

ITSEKIRI, a Kwa-speaking Negroid people of coastal Nigeria, dependent mainly on fishing with some animal husbandry and hunting.

ITZAMNA, a Mayan sky god represented as an aged toothless male figure.

ITZCOUATL, the first of the Aztec kings.

ITZPAPALOTL, the Aztec goddess of the stars.

IVORY, any form of animal tusk, ranging from the mammoth tusks of Upper Paleolithic Europe to those of the contemporary elephant and the walrus. Ivory is easily carved and has been used extensively for decorative work.

IVY, a plant widely regarded as sacred in ancient Europe and believed to possess magico-religious healing properties. Not only was ivy sacred to the Egyptians, but crowns of ivy were used by the Greeks to honor athletes in the Olympics, and also played a part in the Druidic rituals of the Celts.

IWA, a Bantu-speaking Negroid people of the Rukwa group, largely dependent on horticulture.

IXCHEL, a Mayan goddess of childbirth, medicine and weaving, customarily associated also with the moon and the rainbow.

IXTAB, the Mayan goddess of suicide who seduces men into taking their own lives.

IXTLILTON, the Aztec god of health and song.

IZAPA, a ceremonial center in Chiapas, Mexico, important for its art which reveals a transition from the Olmec to the early Mayan tradition.

J

JADE, a form of nephrite stone which was highly valued in many Neolithic cultures because of the ease with which it could be polished and the beauty of the resultant object. Jade objects were frequently used in religious ceremonies especially in Chinese and Oriental cultures.

JAGUAR WARRIOR CULTS, (See EAGLE WARRIOR CULT).

JAINISM, a Hindu cult, which originated in 6th century B.C., and rejects the Brahman rituals, stressing asceticism as a means towards individual salvation. The Jain symbol is a swastika.

JAKUN, a forest-dwelling tribe of hunting and gathering peoples of Malaya.

JANJEIRO, a Western Cushitic-speaking African people, mainly dependent on horticulture and some herding.

JANUS, the two-faced but single-headed god of the Romans, capable of seeing in both directions and regarded as the god who presided over doorways. Since Janus presided over all 'beginnings' (which, with the traditional emphasis upon causality in Indo-European religion, were regarded as representing simply doorways between the past and the future) it was appropriate that he should face towards the past as well as to the future. Janus was also patron of the month of January (named in his honor), the 'beginning' month of the year.

JAPANESE, the modern Japanese people represent a combination of an aboriginal Neolithic (Jōmon) population in the Southwest, aboriginal Paleolithic, (Ainu) elements in the North, and invading Japanese Bronze Age invaders who arrived from Korea around 400 B.C., and imposed themselves on the two foregoing groups as a ruling aristocracy. These invaders brought with them the Japanese language which is now identified as being Altaic in origin, and especially related to Korean and Ket. The Japanese were traditionally agriculturalists and sea fishermen, and have become one of the leading industrial powers of the world.

JAPHETIC, a term originally used by von Leibnitz (1646-1716) to refer to the non-Semitic languages of the Western world. The term is no longer used, except by a few writers who have attempted to apply it to the mostly dead and not necessarily related early Mediterranean-Asianic languages which supposedly included Basque, Etruscan, Sumerian and the living languages of the Caucasus mountains.

JAR BURIAL, a form of inhumation (q.v.) in which the body is deposited in a large pottery vessel. Jar burials should not be confused with urn burials, which utilize a small jar as a container for the cremated remains of the body. Jar burial was formerly common in the East Mediterranean and Anatolian areas.

JARGON, a term sometimes used to refer to a specialized terminology, as for example in the expression 'sociological jargon', but more commonly applied to an emergent dialect, used by a specific sub-section of society. Thus the members of a criminal subculture may possess their own distinct criminal jargon. Jargon may also arise as a result of the borrowing of words where two or more ethnic groups live in close contact with each other.

JARLSHOF, an archeological site on the southern tip of the Shetland Islands which originated as a late Neolithic settlement, survived through the late Bronze Age, and was finally supplanted by an Iron Age *broch* or fortified Viking farm complex.

JARMO, an archeological site in the Zagros mountains of Northern Iraq which has been dated at approximately 6500 B.C. Jarmo is important as one of the earliest sites of horticulture, revealing evidence of the cultivation of wheat and barley as well as of the domestication of the goat. No evidence of pottery is found at the earliest levels.

JASPER, a semi-opaque stone frequently used for the manufacture of gems, vases and statuettes and often believed to have magical powers.

JATI, an Indian subcaste. The major Hindu castes (q.v.), which seem to have been of Aryan origin, are subdivided into largely endogamous jati or subcastes of an occupational and to some extent regional nature. The subcastes may owe their origin to an earlier Dravidian system of castes, based on occupational specialization by specific families. However, the jati do not represent totally exclusive gene pools, since a male member of a jati is usually permitted to take a wife from the jati immediately beneath his own.

JAVA MAN, a term originally used to refer to a variety of Pithecanthropus erectus remains which were found in Java by Eugene Dubois in 1891. Also known as 'Trinil Man', these remains – comprising a skull cap, femur, three teeth and jaw fragments – have been dated at 5000,000 B.P.

JAVANESE, a Malayo-Polynesian-speaking people of Java, largely dependent on agriculture with some animal husbandry and fishing. Although like other Indonesians, the Javanese trace their ancestry to Mongoloid peoples who brought a Neolithic culture into the islands, mixed with autochthonous Australoids, and some pockets of Negritos, their culture (like that of neighboring Bali) has been heavily influenced by India, both islands having been the seat of a number of Hindu principalities during past centuries.

JAVELIN, a light spear, designed to be thrown as distinct from a spear used for thrusting.

JEBEL IRHOUD (also JEBEL IGHOUD), two crania, one with a face, were found in a mine near Marrakesh by Emile Ennouchi in 1961. Identified as Neanderthaloid, the fossils belong to the early Würm glaciation and were the first clearly Neanderthal remains to be located in Northern Africa.

JEMEZ (TOWA), an Uto-Aztec Tanoan-speaking North American, Central Pueblo people, dependent on horticulture with some hunting and food-gathering.

JERICHO, first excavated by German archeologists in 1907, Jericho reveals evidence of continuous occupation from the late 8th millennium B.C., a prepottery Neolithic settlement having been established around 7,000 B.C. The site was occupied by a succession of walled towns from the 3rd millennium onward, one of these representing an important Hyksos settlement. The town was later seized by the Israelites under Joshua, but was finally abandoned during the Iron Age.

JERUSALEM, the city of Jerusalem appears to have been founded by Canaanites in the late Bronze Age, but was captured by the Israelites under King David around 1000 B.C., the renowned Israelite temple being constructed by King Solomon shortly thereafter. Seized by Babylonians in 587 B.C., Jerusalem was rebuilt by Israelites with the approval and encouragement of the Persian

Achaemenid king following their release from Babylonian captivity after the Persian conquest of Babylon, but was again subsequently destroyed by the Romans, following an Israelite revolt, only to be rebuilt under the Roman emperor Hadrian.

JET, a form of very soft black lignite stone, commonly found in Yorkshire, which was frequently used for decorative and ornamental purposes during the British Bronze Age.

JEWS, Jews describe themselves as adherents to Judaism, involving the worship of Israel's covenanted Saviour-God, Yahweh, in accordance with the teaching of the Torah. Their religion derived from tribal Semitic religious concepts modified by Moses and later prophets. Originally, the term Jew was regarded as synonymous with the tribes of Judaea, and therefore represented a distinctive racial group, probably of Mediterranean Caucasoid type. As a result of the diaspora or dispersal of the Jews throughout the Mediterranean, North Africa and the Middle East, both prior to and following the destruction of Jerusalem by the Romans, a varying degree of racial admixture occurred between Jews and the local populations of the lands in which they settled. Ethnically European Jews are customarily divided into two groups: those of Central and East European origin, known as Ashkenazim Jews, who sometimes reveal blond hair and blue eyes due to intermarriage with Northern Europeans (although Armenoid traits are more common); and secondly, those of North African origin, known as Sephardic Jews, who were expelled from Spain to North African and West European countries. Large numbers of Jews still live in various Middle Eastern countries, and there is even a small community in India, who claim descent from one of the 'lost tribes'. In Africa, the Falasha of Ethiopia are recognized as being of at least part Jewish origin. However, the conversion of non-Jews to the Jewish religion is discouraged by Orthodox Jewish sects, and the Jewish people have tended to comprise a number of related microraces. (See ISRAELITES).

JIE, a Negroid, Nilotic-speaking people of the Karamojong group, primarily dependent on horticulture and cattle-herding.

JIHAD (also JEHAD), an Arabic word referring to a holy war fought for the purpose of forcibly converting non-Moslems to the Islamic faith.

JIMMA, a Cushitic people from East Africa, dependent on horticulture and some animal herding.

JINGU, a Shinto shrine.

JINN, in Islamic folklore a supernatural being, who, though normally invisible, can assume any desired visible shape at will. Jinns are seldom helpful, and frequently bring misfortune upon humans.

JIVARO, a warlike South American Indian people of the Upper Amazon who speak an unclassified language and who are dependent on horticulture, fishing and some hunting and gathering.

JOKING RELATIONSHIP, insulation techniques designed to reduce the possibility of friction and to reinforce social bonds between specific individuals.

JŌMON, Neolithic Japanese pottery-making culture which flourished in the Japanese islands as early as 7000 B.C. Large shell mounds indicate that seafood formed an important part in the general diet, but later Jōmon settlements reveal evidence of the cultivation of millet, buckwheat and vegetables by the 4th millennium. The Jōmon people constructed small huts, and used stone and bone as the main materials for their tools until they were conquered by invading Japanese warriors, from Korea circa 600/400 B.C., equipped with a complete Bronze and Iron Age technology. (See also YAYOI).

JORD, the Norse goddess of the Earth, who was the mother of Thor by Odin.

JÖTUNN, in Scandinavian mythology, the Jötunn are a race of giants who generally behave as the enemies of both gods and men.

JÖTUNNHEIM, a Norwegian mountain range, the home of the Jötunn (q.v.).

JUDGMENT DAY, according to Egyptian religion the discarnate soul was required after death to enter into the Judgment Hall of Osiris, where it was weighed against an ostrich feather to determine its degree of virtue or guilt.

JU-JU, a term originating in West Africa and referring to a specific fetish or to

magical forces in general.
JUKUN, a Negroid people of the Tiv-Jukan group, who speak a Niger-Congo language and are dependent on horticulture and some hunting and fishing.
JUNO, the wife of the supreme Roman god Jupiter, and protectress of all Roman matrons.
JUOITEN, a form of prayer-like communication with the ancestors, used by the Lapps of Lappland in northern Scandinavia.
JUR, a Negroid, Northern Nilotic-speaking people, primarily dependent on horticulture with some cattle-herding and fishing.
JURASSIC, period within the Mesozoic era dating from 190,000,000 to 136,000,000 B.P. which was largely dominated by reptile life, but also noted for the appearance of the first modern types of fishes and also of the earliest birds.
JUTES, a branch of the West Germanic-speaking people who were formerly settled in Jutland in Northern Denmark, but also colonized Kent, the Isle of Wight and parts of the neighboring mainland, around the present city of Southhampton, during the 5th century A.D. Although Kent retained its independence as a separate kingdom – under kings descended from two brothers who led the invasion, Hengist and Horsa (reputed to be great-great grandsons of Woden) – for a considerable time, the Jutish settlement around Southampton was early absorbed into the Anglo-Saxon Kingdom of Wessex.

K

KA, the ancient Egyptians believed that Ka was one of the seven parts of man, representing a supernatural force, which came into existence at birth as an advantageous force throughout life and also after death.
KA'ABA, see CAABA.
KABABUSH, a branch of the Baggara (q.v.) people of Africa.
KABAKA, the title of the Baganda chieftain.
KABALA, see CABALA.
KABRE, a Negroid West African Voltaic people, who are largely dependent on horticulture but also practice some animal husbandry and hunting.
KABTA, the Sumerians were the first people of the world to build extensively with the use of mud bricks named Kabta, after the god who presided over the brick manufacturing process.
KABYLE, an Algerian Berber, Caucasoid people, dependent on agriculture and animal husbandry.
KACHIN, a Tibeto-Burman (Sinitic)-speaking people, largely dependent on horticulture, with some animal husbandry, hunting and food-gathering.
KACHINA, the name given by the Hopi and other Pueblo Indians to the ancestral spirit-gods who visit the earth every winter. The term may also correctly be used to refer to the masks worn by the men who enact the role of the kachinas at religious ceremonies.
KADARA, a Negroid people from the Jos Plateau area, who speak a Niger-Congo language and are largely dependent on horticulture with some hunting, food-gathering and animal husbandry.
KAFA, a Western Cushitic-speaking African people, mainly dependent on horticulture and some herding.
KAFFIR, (1) the Sotho Kaffir speak a Bantu language, containing a series of click sounds which were probably acquired by contact with, or absorbtion of, a Khoisan-speaking peoples during the outward migration which resulted in the Bantu displacement of most Khoisan speakers. (2) the Kaffirs of Afghanistan are an Indo-European-speaking tribal peoples, of warlike reputation, dependent upon agriculture.
KAFTAN, a term formerly referring to a padded or quilted coat, made from wool and worn by the Kazaks and other peoples of Turkestan, but now also applied to a loose cotton coat worn widely throughout the Middle East.
KAGGEN, the name by which the Bushmen of South-West Africa refer to the deadly praying mantis, which they identify with their supreme god.

KAGORO, a Negroid people from the Jos Plateau area, who speak a Niger-Congo language, and are largely dependent on horticulture with some hunting, food-gathering and animal husbandry.
KAIBAB, a Southern Paiute, North American Uto-Aztec-(Shoshone) speaking people, dependent on food-gathering and hunting.
KAIGA'U, a powerful form of magic believed by Trobriand Islanders to protect them from evil forces.
KAINGANG, a South American Indian people of the East Brazilian highlands.
KAKKO, a small drum which probably originated in Central Siberia and appears to have been brought to Japan at the time of the Bronze Age settlements of Japan from Korea, circa 600-400 B.C.
KAKOLI, a Papuan people, inhabiting the Eastern New Guinea highlands, who are dependent on horticulture, supplemented by hunting, food-gathering and animal husbandry.
KALAMATH, a North American Indian people, living in Southern Oregon and Northern California, who speak a language generally classified as a Penutian dialect of the Sahaptin group, and are dependent on fishing, food-gathering and hunting.
KALAMBO FALLS, a site southwest of Lake Tanganyika which provides one of the most continuous of archeological sequences yet excavated in sub-Saharan Africa. The oldest deposits, dating from approximately 60,000 B.C., reveal the remains of a wooden club and digging sticks, and also evidence that the inhabitants used fire. Later artifacts correspond to the Sangoan culture, and the subsequent microlith-using Wilton type, Stone Age culture gave way around the 4th century A.D. to a horticultural, iron-using people. These are assumed to be the ancestors of the present-day Negroid population which supplanted the earlier Capoid and pre-Capoid populations.
KALDEBEKEL, an association of young unmarried men of the Mariana and Carolina islands, who live in a communal clubhouse, or Bai, where they are allowed free sexual relations with the unmarried girls of their community.
KALEVALA, the national epic poem of the Finns. The Kalevala resembles the national heroic epic of the related Estonian peoples, but also – particularly in connection with the story of the creation of the world – corresponds to certain of the Norse epics. It is probable that some of the wars of the Finnish heroes were actually fought against the Norse, so that the Finnish heroes could possibly be the frost-giants of Norse mythology – the traditional enemies of the Norse Aesir (q.v.).
KALI, a many-armed Hindu goddess, the wife of Shiva, who personifies both creation (life) and death. Kali is customarily represented wearing a necklace of human heads and carrying a bloody sword, a severed head, and similar objects symbolizing death. Philosophically, Kali is believed to reflect the close links between death and rebirth, death being as vital as birth to the Hindu theory of reincarnation.
KALIBANGAN, an important Indus Valley site overlaying an earlier Chalcolithic settlement. The fortified Indus civilization town dates from approximately 1950 B.C. and is unusual in containing a separate walled citadel inside the walled town, although in other respects the grid pattern of the streets and the type of artifacts uncovered coincide with the typical Indus Valley civilization tradition. After 1750 B.C., the town began to show signs of decay, as do the remains of other excavated Indus Valley cities.
KALINGA, a Malayo-Polynesian-speaking people of the Luzon highlands, largely dependent on cultivation, hunting and some fishing and animal husbandry.
KALKI AVATAR, the last reincarnation of Vishnu, during which he will once again ride the earth, mounted on a white horse with drawn sword, to search out and destroy the forces of evil and restore purity.
KALLOFALLING, an undersea monster, reputed in Eskimo mythology to drag hunters to their death beneath the water.
KALMUK, a Mongol people of the east central Asian steppes who speak a

Mongolian-Altaic language and are almost totally dependent on pastoralism, supplemented by some hunting and only minimal horticulture.
KALOA, a primitive log raft used by the Australian aboriginals of Northern Australia. These are believed to be little changed from the first rafts which brought the ancestors of the Australian aboriginals to the Australian continent during the period of the Würm glaciation, when the sea level was much lower than it is today and only a small channel of water divided Australia from the mainland of Asia.
KALU, the term used among the inhabitants of Fiji to refer to any supernatural person or thing.
KAMBA, a Bantu-speaking Negroid people of the Kenya highlands, largely dependent on horticulture and animal husbandry.
KAMCHATKAN LANGUAGES, a group of Siberian languages which includes Kamchadal, Alutor, Chukchee and Koryak, spoken in the Kamchatka peninsula and northeastern Siberia.
KAMI, the name used by the Japanese to refer to the ancestral spirits and gods of the Shinto religion.
KAMIA, a Yuman-speaking people located on the Colorado river, whose language belongs to the Hokan family and who are dependent on horticulture, fishing, hunting and food-gathering.
KAMILAROI, an Australian aboriginal hunting and gathering people.
KAMINALJUYU, an excavated Central American settlement close to Guatemala City. Originating around 1500 B.C., in association with the Mayan culture, the town became part of the Teotihuacan civilization when it was occupied by a new people arriving from Mexico circa A.D. 400.
KAMITOK, the name used by the Chukchee to refer to the ritual killing (senilicide) of aging members of the community.
KAMPONG, a Malayan term for a house or settlement.
KAMUAI, a term used by the Ainu to refer to objects believed to possess supernatural qualities.
KAMUKU, a West African, Negroid, Middle Niger, Niger-Congo speaking people, largely dependent on horticulture with some animal husbandry and fishing.
KANARESE, one of the major languages of the Dravidian family of languages, spoken by some 20 million persons in southern India, mostly around Mysore.
KANAWA, a Chad-speaking (Hamitic influenced) Hausa people, largely dependent on horticulture with some animal husbandry and food-gathering.
KANEMBU, a people living South of the Sahara who speak a Sudanic or Nilo-Saharan language and are largely dependent on horticulture, with some animal husbandry and fishing.
KANJERA, an archeological site in Kenya, first excavated in 1932, which revealed Neanderthaloid remains associated with an Acheulian stone industry dated around 60,000 years B.P.
KANOON, a Turkish stringed musical instrument.
KANSA, a North American Indian people of the Great Plains.
KANSAN GLACIATION, the name given to the first North American glaciation which probably corresponded to the Alpine Mindel glaciation (q.v.).
KANTELE, a Finnish musical instrument reputed by tradition to be of supernatural origin.
KANUNA, an elaborate stringed instrument used in India, the strings of which are struck with small hammers.
KANURI, a people who live South of the Sahara and speak a Sudanic or Nilo-Saharan language, largely dependent on horticulture with some animal husbandry and fishing.
KANURIC (or CENTRAL SAHARAN) LANGUAGES, a group of Nilotic languages which includes Teda, Kanuri and Kanembu.
KAOLIN, a form of feldspar rock, popularly known as China clay, which is essential to the manufacture of porcelain. First used by the Chinese for the manufacture of fine porcelain ware, porcelain could not be made in Europe until

European merchants imported Kaolin from the Far East.

KAONDE, a Bantu-speaking Negroid people of the Bemba-Lamba group, largely dependent on horticulture and some domestication of animals.

KAPAUKU, a Papuan people of the West New Guinea highlands, dependent on horticulture, but also practicing some animal husbandry, hunting and fishing.

KAPINGAMARANGI, a Polynesian people of Micronesia, dependent on horticulture and fishing with some animal husbandry.

KAPSIKI, a Chad-Sudanese-speaking people occupying the Mandara highlands of Africa, dependent on horticulture and some animal husbandry.

KARA, a Bantu-speaking Negroid people of the East Nyanza area, largely dependent on horticulture and animal husbandry.

KARANKAWA, North American Texas Coastal Indians whose language is unclassified, and who are dependent on fishing, hunting and food-gathering.

KARANOVO, an archeological tell site in eastern Bulgaria which has given its name to a distinctive local culture. Essentially a part of the Old European civilization, occupation of the site appears to have begun in the middle of the 7th millennium B.C., having its origin in the early European Neolithic (q.v.) Starčevo culture. The original settlement which comprised some 50 or 60 scattered square huts, constructed of wattle and daub, was subsequently replaced by large, rectangular, plastered and painted buildings. The site has given its name to a continuing East Balkan cultivating tradition which lasted into the 4th millennium B.C., when it was overrun and occupied by Thracian Indo-Europeans circa 3500 B.C.

KAREN, a Sinitic (Tibeto-Burman)-speaking people, largely dependent on agriculture with some animal husbandry, fishing and hunting.

KARIERA, an Australian aboriginal people from Central Australia, dependent wholly on food-gathering, hunting and some fishing.

KARMA, a Hindu concept of fate, which can only be understood when interpreted in terms of the ancient Indo-European emphasis upon the principle of cause and effect as a basic law governing the universe. The Hindu karma does not imply the same fatalistic resignation associated with the Moslem kismet. Hinduism preaches that behavior in this life will affect the status of the soul in future reincarnations, and that the status of the individual in the present life reflects the conduct of the soul in previous incarnations. Thus the actions of the individual do play some part in determining the future.

KARNAK, a modern town adjoining Luxor and Thebes, the ancient capital of Upper Egypt, wherein was located the great temple of Amen.

KARNAL, an ancient Persian trumpet equipped with a cupped mouthpiece and a wide bell-like opening.

KAROK, a Northwestern California Hokan-speaking people, dependent on food-gathering with some hunting.

KARYOTYPE, the character of the chromosomal constituents in the nucleus of a cell.

KASENA, a Negroid West African Voltaic people, largely dependent on horticulture and some food-gathering.

KASHMIRI, a Caucasoid Indic Indo-European-speaking people who occupy the mountain valleys of Kashmir and depend largely on animal husbandry, with some agriculture, and food-gathering.

KASKA, a North Athabascan American Indian people, dependent on hunting and fishing and some food-gathering.

KASSITES, a chariot-riding warlike people who appear to have had an Indo-European aristocracy. Occupying Babylon from the direction of the Zagros mountains of western Persia, the Kassite dynasty ruled Babylon for several centuries until their eventual defeat by the combined forces of the Assyrians and Elamites in the 13th century B.C. Recovered inscriptions indicate that the Kassite nobility worshipped Indo-European gods closely related to those of the Indo-Aryans who invaded India. Thus the name of the Kassite god Shuriash is cognate with that of the Indo-Aryan god Suryu.

KASSO, a West African stringed instrument made from a hollowed-out gourd covered with a parchment membrane and pierced by a protruding wooden stick.

KATAB, a Negroid people from the Jos Plateau area, who speak a Niger-Congo language and are dependent on horticulture, with some hunting, food-gathering and animal husbandry.

KATAKANA, a system of writing used in Japan, derived from Chinese ideograms adapted to represent syllables.

KATIKITEGON, Algonquin-speaking North American Indians related to the Ojibwa, dependent mainly on fishing, hunting and food-gathering.

KATIKORO, the title of a Baganda who served as the chief officer of the divinely-descended monarch.

KATTA, the Australian aboriginal name for a digging stick.

KAUWA, the Hawaiian name for a slave.

KAVA, a non-alcoholic drink made from the roots of a pepper plant, widely used throughout Oceania.

KAYAK, a canoe, made from a whalebone frame covered with skins, containing a small cockpit. The single occupant wears a waterproof leather cape which is attached to the cockpit cover to keep him dry and insulated against the icy waters of the Arctic. Should the canoe turn upside down in rough seas, the water is unable to enter it, and a deft stroke of the double-ended paddle will quickly right the canoe, bringing the occupant out of the water.

KAZAK, a Turkic-Altaic-speaking people of the Central Asian steppes, almost totally dependent on pastoralism, with some hunting and minimal horticulture.

KEBAREH, MUGHARET EL, a cave located on Mount Carmel in Palestine, first excavated in 1931, when it revealed Upper Paleolithic artifacts.

KEI ISLANDERS, a Malayo-Polynesian-speaking people inhabiting the Kei Islands in Indonesia, who are largely dependent on horticulture, fishing and some hunting and animal husbandry.

KEILOR, a skull found in Southern Australia, claimed to be around 100,000 years in age. Although it resembles that of Wadjak man in shape, the Keilor skull is very large, with a total cranial capacity of nearly 1600 c.c., in dramatic contrast to the 1290 c.c. of contemporary Australoid skulls.

KELA, a Bantu-speaking Negroid people of the Mongo group, largely dependent on horticulture but also practicing some fishing and hunting.

KELANTAN, a Malayo-Polynesian people living in Central Sarawak.

KELLEK, a very ancient type of raft still used in Iraq and Armenia, which is supported by a large number of inflated sheep or goat skins, stitched together so as to be air-tight.

KELOID, a name sometimes used to refer to a raised scar or ritual mutilation resulting from the introduction of particles of earth or other foreign matter into a wound, after the skin has been cut in the desired pattern.

KELTS, see CELTS.

KENNIFF CAVE, one of the oldest archeological sites yet discovered in Australia. Located in Queensland, the earliest indications of hominid occupation date from 13,000 B.P. and are associated with simple stone tools.

KENT'S CAVERN, a cave located close to Torquay in Devon, England, which reveals Mousterian and Aurignacian occupation.

KERAKI, a Papuan people from the Gulf of Papua who depend mainly on horticulture, supplemented by some hunting, fishing and animal husbandry.

KERALA, a Dravidian, Hindu people who occupy the Southwest Indian State of Kerala, practicing agriculture, animal husbandry and some sea fishing.

KEREWE, an East Lacustrine Bantu-speaking Negroid people, mainly dependent on horticulture and some animal husbandry.

KERO, a Quechua (South American) term for a cup made from either pottery or wood.

KERRES, an open sleigh made by the Lapps from canoe-shaped planks of wood.

KET, a Central Siberian people who speak a branch of the Altaic languages sharply different from those of their neighbors. This has now been shown to share a genetic relationship to the Japanese and Korean languages, both of which may have originated in Central Asia. The Ket depend mainly on fishing, but also practice some hunting and reindeer herding.

KEWEYIPAYA (SOUTHEASTERN YAVAPAI), a Hokan-speaking, Plateau Yuman American Indian people, dependent on food-gathering and hunting.

KEY, in archeology, the scheme of diagnostic qualities prepared by an archeologist as a guide to the taxonomic classification of fossils and artifacts.

KHA, an aboriginal hill people inhabiting the Vietnamese-Laotian mountain border. Reputed to have formerly practiced cannibalism, the Kha have rejected Buddhism and other major Southeast Asian religions, in favor of their own traditional animism.

KHABUR BASIN, a broad valley formed by a tributary to the Euphrates in eastern Syria which contains many sites of archeological importance because of their strategic position abreast the communication routes linking Mesopotamia, Syria and Anatolia.

KHADZUNA, see BURUSHASKI.

KHALKA, a Mongol people speaking a Mongolian-Altaic language of the east central Asian steppes, almost totally dependent on pastoralism with some hunting and minimal horticulture.

KHAMSIN, a hot, dry wind which blows over Egypt in springtime.

KHAN, a title used by various Ural-Altaic pastoralists to designate a chieftain, born into an eminent family, who has been elected head of a horde (q.v.) or combination of tribes.

KHARIBU, a Semitic foot-herding pastoral people who are generally recognized as being ancestral to the Hebrews (q.v.). The Kharibu were known to Egyptians by the name 'Apiru'.

KHAROSS, an African robe, made from skins, which is worn over the shoulders, the ends being tied across the chest by a leather thong.

KHASI, a tribal hill people, living in eastern India who reveal Mongoloid influences and speak a Mon-Khmer language. The Khasi depend mainly on horticulture but practice some animal husbandry and fishing as well as hunting and gathering.

KHETAM, a 6th Dynasty Egyptian roller seal, deeply carved in ivory, wood, copper or porcelain, so that the design stood out in relief. After wetting the roller with a coloured dye, the seal could then be rolled on papyrus to leave the desired imprint.

KHEVSUR, a Caucasoid Georgian people, speaking a Georgian variant of the Caucasian languages and dependent primarily on horticulture and animal husbandry, with some hunting and fishing.

KHMER, the national term by which the Cambodians refer to themselves.

KHOISAN (KHOIN), a small language family today represented by only four surviving Hottentot (or Nama) dialects and two surviving Bushman dialects. (See also BUSHMEN and HOTTENTOT).

KIAMA, an age-grade among the Kikuyu of East Africa.

KIAOTSU, a Chinese form of the European palanquin, used for the carriage of dignitaries and ladies of noble birth.

KIBITKA, a Mongolian mobile home, comprising a permanent yurt (q.v.) mounted on a wagon drawn by oxen.

KIDUTOKADO (SURPRISE VALLEY PAIUTE), a Shoshone-(Uto-Aztec) speaking North American Indian people of the Coastal Great Basin, dependent on food-gathering, hunting and some fishing.

KIKUYU, a Bantu-speaking Negroid people of the Kenya highlands, largely dependent on horticulture and herding.

KILIWA, an American Indian people from Baja California, speaking a Hokan language of the Yuman group and dependent on food-gathering, hunting and some fishing.

KILLING, SECOND, the custom, common in some societies, of driving posts into the body of a corpse to fix it to the ground so that the soul cannot escape from the body to haunt the living. The principle of the second killing is exemplified by the European folk belief that the spirit of a vampire could be controlled by a stake driven through the heart through the host corpse.

KILN, a chamber deliberately designed for the baking of pottery or the manufacture of baked bricks.

KIMBUGWE, the Baganda priest-official who supervises the royal tombs – literally the 'Keeper of the Royal Umbilical Cord'.

KIN, persons who are linked to each other by mutual responsibilities, due to a common recognition of the rights and duties implicit in either real or fictive kinship or marital relationship.

KIN, AFFINAL, persons related by marriage, i.e. relatives of the spouse.

KIN, CONSANGUINEAL, persons related by blood or genetics.

KINDRED, SHIFTING, the system of kinship used by Germanic peoples, based on the concept of actual genetic affinity. Blood relatives on the mother's side are deemed as important as those traced through the father, and brothers and sisters are more important than cousins, uncles and aunts. The kindred 'shifts' with each generation, as children recognize the relatives of both parents as members of their own kindred. The possibility of clan systems is excluded.

KING, a term derived from Anglo-Saxon *Cyninga* or 'descendant of the kin'. Although the term 'king' has been loosely applied to refer to almost any person exercising supreme political authority, the term is historically valid only for Indo-European societies in which the king, roi, rex, or rajah was regarded as the chief ritual, administrative and judicial officer, as well as being divinely-descended and the 'purest of the pure' by blood. In such kinship-based ancestor-worshipping societies, kings were often selected from among the sons of the royal family by merit, but reigned by virtue of the inherited magico-religious powers believed to be responsible for this merit, exercising these for the benefit of their kinsmen in accordance with the limits set by custom and tradition rather than ruling arbitrarily. Only with feudalism (q.v.) did kings acquire a degree of arbitrary authority, when they came to be regarded as the owners of the land, and consequently of the people who dwelt on the land, who were then treated as their 'subjects' rather than as their kinsmen.

KINSHIP, a socially defined relationship regulating the various aspects of social order on the basis of actual or assumed genetic relationship.

KINSHIP, AGNATIC, kinship that is traced through the male line.

KINSHIP, BILATERAL, kinship traced through two parents, recognizing both paternal and maternal relatives, but distinct from double descent kinship systems (q.v.) in that bilateral kinship systems are organized into kindreds (q.v.) instead of into unilineal clans (q.v.).

KINSHIP, CLASSIFICATORY, any system of kinship which tends to ignore precise genetic relationships and aggregates selected kinsfolk of the same generation into the same kinship status. (See also EQUIVALENCE, GENERATION).

KINSHIP, MERGING, a system of kinship nomenclature which classifies and designates both consanguineal and affinal relatives by the same kinship term. Thus the term 'aunt' may be assigned to a wide variety of female kin.

KINSHIP SYSTEM, a pattern of basic social organization whereby the rights and responsibilities of the individual members of the society are determined by the order of birth. In societies organized along kinship lines, all aspects of human behaviour – such as economic, political and social – are primarily dependent on kinship obligations, the society being held together by a complex network of kinship and familistic relations.

KINSHIP, TOTEMIC, a group of persons, usually related consanguineally, who share the same totem or believe themselves to be descended from a common mythological totemic animal.

KIOWA-APACHE, Athabascan-speaking North American Plains Indians, dependent on hunting with some food-gathering.

KIPSIGI, a Negroid Nilotic-speaking people of the Nadi group, primarily dependent on horticulture, cattle-herding and some hunting.

KISAMA, a Bantu-speaking Negroid people of Western Angola, largely dependent on horticulture with some herding of animals and hunting.

KISH, an early Sumerian city state which occupied a leading position in the Mesopotamia of the Early Dynastic period until supplanted by the city of Ur around 2600 B.C.

KISSAR, an African musical instrument, equipped with a resonance chamber made from a gourd, a tortoise shell, or possibly a human skull, across which strings are attached.

KISSI, a Mande-speaking Negroid people from West Africa, largely dependent on horticulture with some animal husbandry.

KITCHEN MIDDEN, a heap or dump situated outside a village upon which domestic refuse, chiefly the remains of food, was thrown. Commonly applied to the settled Mesolithic fishing villages of the Baltic coast, kitchen middens are characteristic not only of the Ertebølle culture in the Baltic, but also of the Jōmon in Japan and of various American Indian coastal sites along the Gulf of Mexico.

KITE FISHING, a form of fishing which appears to have originated in China, spreading thence to Melanesia. Kite fishing permits the kite flyer to fish deep or rough waters without venturing from the safety of the shore. Standing on the nearby land, the fisherman is able to fly a large kite well out over the water, to support a long fishing line, the end of which (equipped with hooks and bait) dangles in the water.

KIVA, an American Indian underground chamber, associated with the Anasazi (q.v.) culture. Entered through a hole in the roof, by means of a notched pole, which served as a ladder and could be removed at will, the kiva originated in the underground chambers formerly used as dwelling places, but survived into the Pueblo period as ritual and ceremonial clubhouses for the villagers' secret societies.

KIVIK, an archeological site in Southern Sweden containing a group of burial mounds, the largest of which, constructed around the 10th century B.C., is around 200 feet in diameter. Inside the barrow the central cist is constructed of stones, the faces of which are carved with religious processional scenes, as well as chariots, ships, horses, sunwheels, battle axes and other characteristic Bronze Age North European culture traits. Unfortunately the contents (probably including valuable gold and silver artifacts) which would have been of the greatest archeological value had already been plundered when the barrow was first opened by antiquarians in the 18th century.

KIWAI, a Papuan people of the Gulf of Papua, who depend mainly on horticulture with fishing, hunting and some food-gathering.

KLALLAM, a Coastal Salish Northwest American Indian people, whose language belongs to the Mosan division of the Algonquin-Mosan phylum, and who are dependent primarily on fishing with some hunting and food-gathering.

KLAMATH, a North American Indian people localized in the Rocky Mountains.

KLONGKGK, a Siamese drum, comprising a hollow cylinder with both ends covered by stretched parchment.

KNIFE, a relatively short cutting instrument possessing a longitudinal cutting edge. Knives originated in the Stone Age, becoming diversified in the Bronze Age into shorter knives used as hand tools and longer daggers designed for use as cutting or stabbing weapons. These daggers were in turn developed among the Indo-Europeans into still longer weapons, known as swords.

KNITTING, a form of netting, in which the meshes are drawn tightly together to produce a solid fabric lacking the holes which characterize regular netting.

KNOBKERRIE, a knobbed or weighted throwing stick used extensively among the Bantu peoples of Africa.

KNOSSOS, the palace of a Minoan dynasty of kings which was first excavated by Sir Arthur Evans (q.v.), to reveal an enormous rambling palace, covering a ground area of over 160,000 square feet and rising to three stories in some areas. Although the major buildings were grouped around a large central court, there appears to have been little plan to the layout of the palace, some areas of which were obviously devoted to ceremonial and religious purposes (as for example the Throne Room and various shrines). Other rooms were reserved for living quarters, and yet other areas were used for the storage of commercial merchandise, thus giving the impression that the priest-kings of Knossos controlled a large part of the thriving Cretan maritime commerce. Nevertheless, the palace reveals a luxurious interior equipped with paved floors, walls decorated with beautiful frescoes, water closets, and an elaborate system of drains. The town and palace of Knossos are, in fact, the first example of planned city sanitation in the world, rain water being used to flush out an underground system of sewage culverts.

KNOTS, MAGICAL, knots have played an important role in the magico-religious symbolism of many different societies. Thus, in Hindu wedding rituals the clothes of the bride and bridegroom are knotted together as a symbol of the binding nature of the marriage ceremony, and many societies untie knots as a magical act intended to frustrate threatening forces of evil.

KNUCKLE-WALKING, a term first used by Sherwood L. Washburn to refer to the manner in which chimpanzees and gorillas clinch their hands in the form of a fist and put their weight on their knuckles when walking on all four limbs. Washburn believes that this represents an important evolutionary advance designed to protect the interior surfaces of the fingers which are already being extensively used for grasping objects at their level of primate evolution.

KO, the New Caledonian name for that part of the spirit which leaves the body during sleep.

KOHAU, a form of pictograph writing carved on tablets by the former, now extinct, occupants of Easter Island.

KOHISTANI, an Indo-European-speaking Indic people, primarily dependent on cultivation and animal husbandry with some hunting and gathering.

KOHL, a cosmetic of black or green colour, used in ancient Egypt and in many contemporary Middle Eastern and North African countries, to paint the eyelids as a cosmetic and as a protection against infection by flies.

KOIARI, a Papuan people inhabiting Southeast New Guinea, who supplement horticulture with hunting, food-gathering and some animal husbandry.

KOINE, a form of universal and popular Greek speech which developed during the Hellenistic Age as a result of the amalgamation of several distinct Greek dialects. Koine was adopted for general usage during the period of Macedonian domination.

KOITA, a Papuan people of Southeast New Guinea, who supplement horticulture by hunting, food-gathering and some animal husbandry.

KOJIKI, a Japanese document, compiled early in the 8th century A.D., which outlines the early forms of Shinto belief.

KOL, a proto-Australoid people, living in the hills of Maharashtra state in India, who speak a Munda language and depend on horticulture, hunting and food-gathering.

KOLN-LINDENTHAL, an archeological site close to the modern city of Cologne in Germany, which revealed wooden long-houses, and is now regarded as being an outpost of the Danubian I and Danubian II cultures.

KOLOTL, an Aztec god with a human figure and the face of a dog.

KOMA, an East African people of the Koman group, primarily dependent on horticulture supplemented by some animal husbandry, hunting and fishing.

KONDO, the main hall of worship in a Buddhist temple.

KONGO, a Bantu-speaking Negroid people living in the lower Congo, largely dependent on horticulture, some domestication of animals and hunting.

KONJO, a West Lacustrine Bantu people, largely dependent on horticulture and fishing.

KONKOMBA, a Negroid West African Voltaic people, dependent on horticulture and some animal husbandry, fishing and food-gathering.

KONSO, an East African Cushitic-speaking people, dependent on horticulture and herding.

KORAN, the sacred book of the Muslims, containing a biography of the life of

the prophet Mohammed and a complete inventory of the moral code of Islam.
KORDOFANIAN LANGUAGES, see NIGER-CONGO-LANGUAGES.
KOREANS, a Mongoloid people whose language, related to Japanese, has now been demonstrated to be of Altaic origin. Traditionally dependent on agriculture, animal husbandry and sea fishing, the Koreans have become substantially urbanized and industrialized in recent years.
KORONGO, a Kordofanian-speaking (Niger-Congo) people of the Nuba group, largely dependent on horticulture, animal husbandry and some hunting.
KÖRÖS, the Hungarian equivalent of the Starčevo culture (q.v.), distinguished from the Starčevo by the relative lack of painted pottery and the possession of footed vessels.
KORYAK, a Paleo-Asian people dependent on reindeer herding, fishing, and hunting.
KOSI, the name used by the Trobriand Islanders to describe the basic substance of the soul.
KOTA, a Bantu-speaking Negroid people of the Fang-Dzem group, largely dependent on horticulture with some hunting and food-gathering.
KOT DIJI, an early tell site located close to the site of Mohenjo-daro in West Pakistan, revealing evidence of an early pre-Indus Valley culture represented by a mud brick, fortified horticulturalist settlement, which was supplanted around 2100 B.C. by a more fully-evolved Indus Valley type settlement.
KOUITARA, a Moroccan musical instrument comprising four pairs of strings and a pear-shaped resonance chamber.
KOWTOW, a traditional Chinese gesture conveying respect, in which a socially subordinate person kneels and touches his head on the ground repeatedly as a form of greeting for an important superior.
KPE, a Bantu-speaking Negroid people of the Biafra coastal region, dependent mainly on horticulture, animal husbandry and some hunting and fishing.
KPELLE, a Mande-speaking Negroid people from West Africa, largely dependent on horticulture, animal husbandry and some hunting.
KRAAL, a term used in Eastern and Southern Africa to refer to an enclosed village, housing both people and domestic animals at night. The term is sometimes also used to refer to an enclosure which contains only animals.
KRAPINA, an assemblage of fossil fragments including a large array of teeth, representing the remains of some 15 individual men, women, and children, found by Gorjanovic-Kramberger in northern Croatia in 1899. Considerable variation in physical type characterizes the remains, which are classified as Neanderthal and are associated with Mousterian tools. The fossils appear to have belonged to an early Würm Interstadial.
KRIS, a dagger with a curved, wavy blade, common in Malaya and Indonesia.
KRISHNA, the most popular of Hindu deities, Krishna is generally portrayed as a warrior-hero and slayer of dragons, although he also plays practical jokes on human beings and was renowned as a lover. Krishna is also regarded as one of the incarnations of Vishnu, the supreme deity.
KROMDRAAI, a site in the Transvaal, in Southern Africa, where Paranthropus robustus fossil remains were found in 1938.
KSHATRIYA, an ancient Hindu caste comprising nobles and warriors, believed originally to have been higher than the Brahman or priestly class in early Aryan times, but subordinate in rank to that class for the past three thousand years.
KUANGSI, a province in Northern China in which excavations carried out in 1930 in the Upper Cave at Choukoutien revealed Upper Paleolithic burial sites containing Homo sapiens sapiens fossil remains which varied considerably in individual type, one appearing to be of proto-Mongoloid, another of Eskimoid and a third of Melanesian type. Since it is doubtful whether these variable types occupied the Choukoutien Upper Cave at the same time, the evidence appears to indicate substantial prehistoric migrations.
KUBA, a Bantu-speaking Negroid people of the Kasai group, largely dependent on horticulture, hunting and fishing.
KUBAN CULTURE, a distinctive Copper Age culture, located on the Northern

slopes and adjacent steppes of the Caucasus Mountains, marked by rich barrow or 'kurgan' graves, as at the site at Maikop (q.v.). Evidence such as copper battle-axes and hammer-headed pins point to an Indo-European identity.

KUBU, a Malayo-Polynesian-speaking people of Indonesia, largely dependent on hunting and gathering with some fishing and horticulture.

K'UEI, a Bronze bowl equipped with a handle, commonly manufactured in China during the Chu Dynasty and believed to have been used as an eating utensil.

KUKU, a Negroid East Sudanese or Nilotic-speaking people of the Bari-Lotuko group, primarily dependent on horticulture and cattle herding with some hunting.

KUKULCAN, the Mayan culture hero who was regarded as a civilizing deity. Kukulcan appears to have been the Quetzalcoatl (q.v.) of the Aztecs and Toltecs. A bearded white god who arrived in the Americas in a large boat from across the ocean, Quetzalcoatl brought civilization with him, but being subsequently driven out of the Toltec empire, he was supposed to have established himself among the Mayans, who knew him as Kukulcan.

KULA RING, an institutionalized pattern of reciprocal gift-giving, involving substantial sea voyages by the inhabitants of the Trobriand and other islands off the coast of New Guinea, for the purpose of the ritual exchange of symbolic necklaces and armbands.

KULLI, a Chalcolithic culture, dating from around the first part of the 3rd millennium B.C., which was located in Beluchistan. Excavation reveals small tell sites of mudbrick houses, occupied by cultivators, and cremation burials, which provide strong evidence of cultural influence from Early Dynastic Mesopotamia, both in the pottery and in the carved stone vessels. On the other hand, other Kulli material reveals links with the Indus Valley Civilization, such as painted pottery illustrated with humped bulls which resemble the Brahman bulls so characteristic of the Indus Valley Civilization and of contemporary India.

KÜLTEPE (or KANESH), an archeological tell site in Cappadocia, Central Anatolia, comprising a Bronze Age citadel built on a mound which dominates an older Assyrian settlement, dating from the 19th century B.C., situated on lower ground. Kültepe appears to have been an important trading station for caravans passing between Anatolia and Mesopotamia. The cuneiform Assyrian records found on clay tablets in the lower settlement throw considerable light on the customs and culture of the population, before the town was engulfed by the expanding Hittite empire, and confirm the arrival of Indo-Europeans (who were probably responsible for the Bronze Age citadel) prior to the Hittite conquest.

KULTURKREIS, a modification of the unilineal theories of cultural diffusion expressed by Elliot Smith which combined the concept of mutilineal evolution with diffusion, and suggests that successive high civilizations have been responsible for most innovations and for 'radiating' most new ideas outwards to neighboring societies. This school is strongly identified with the names of W. Schmidt, W. Koppers and F. Graebner.

KUMARA, the Polynesian name for the sweet potato, which may have been introduced into Polynesia from Peru, where it was cultivated (for some centuries prior to the settlement of Polynesia), under the Peruvian name of *kumar.*

KUMISS, an alcoholic drink manufactured by the peoples of Turkestan and other Ural-Altaic pastoralists, made from fermented camel or donkey's milk.

KUMU, a Bantu-speaking Negroid people of the Babwe-Bira group, dependent on horticulture and some fishing.

KUMYK, a Turkic, Altaic-speaking people of southwest Asia, primarily dependent upon agriculture and some animal husbandry.

KUNAMA, a Nilotic people related to the Barea and primarily dependent on horticulture supported by some animal husbandry, hunting and food-gathering.

KUNDA, a Bantu-speaking Negroid people of the Maravi group, largely dependent on horticulture and fishing.

KUNDU, a Bantu-speaking Negroid people of the Biafra coastal region, dependent mainly on horticulture, animal husbandry and some fishing.

KUNG, a Khoisan-speaking Bushman people of South West Africa, primarily dependent on food-gathering and some hunting.

KUPE, the legendary Polynesian chieftain who reputedly led the expedition from Tahiti that colonized New Zealand around the 10th century A.D.

KURDAITJA, the Arunta name for a sorcerer who possesses the ability to bring death to his victims.

KURDS, an ancient nation, speaking an Indo-European language related to Persian, today surviving as a minority within the borders of Iraq and Iran. Traditionally dependent upon animal herding and agriculture, with some fishing, they were reputed for their military proclivities and the most famous leader of the Saracens at the time of the Crusades, namely Saladin, was a Kurd.

KURGAN, the term 'kurgan' is derived from the Russian word for a 'barrow' or burial mound, and has been popularized by Professor Marija Gimbutas whose theory that the Proto-Indo-European peoples were identical with the kurgan-constructing semi-pastoral population of the Pontic steppes (who can be traced back as far as the 7th century B.C.) now receives wide acceptance among archeologists, although still disputed by archeologists and linguists who favor either a Central European or a Caucasian home for the Indo-Europeans (q.v.). It has been argued that the kurgan-building Indo-Europeans of the Pontic steppes were not the only Indo-Europeans, but were only one section of a larger array of Indo-European-speaking peoples already more widely spread throughout Europe. Kurgan burials often contain the skeletons of horses, wives and numerous armed retainers of the deceased prince. The Neolithic and Chalcolithic kurgan graves reveal the globular amphorae, corded ware pottery, and battle axes commonly associated with recognized Indo-European settlements throughout Europe, and the later kurgans of the Kuban Copper Age were elaborately equipped with a wealth of distinctively Indo-European grave furniture.

KURNAI, an Australian aboriginal food-gathering people of South Australia.

KURTAR, a musical instrument traditional to India, comprising clappers with ringed handles which can be fitted onto the fingers. These clappers are usually also adorned by small bells which jingle with every movement of the fingers.

KURTATCHI, a Melanesian Malayo-Polynesian people from the Louisiade Archipelago, largely dependent on horticulture, fishing, food-gathering, hunting and some animal husbandry.

KURUMBA, a cultivating people of southern India.

KUSAIANS, a Malayo-Polynesian-speaking people, inhabiting the Eastern Caroline Islands of Micronesia and dependent on horticulture, fishing and some animal husbandry.

KUSASI, a Negroid West African Voltaic people, largely dependent on horticulture and animal husbandry.

KUSSIR, a Turkish musical instrument similar to a kettledrum, but with five strings stretched across the top of the drum, so that it can produce both string and percussion music.

KUTCHIN, a North Athabascan American Indian people of the Upper Yukon, dependent on hunting and fishing with some food-gathering.

KUTENAI, a North American Indian people, speaking a language not yet classified, situated on the border of the Canadian and United States Rockies.

KUTSHU, a Bantu-speaking Negroid people of the Mongo group, largely dependent on horticulture with some fishing and hunting.

KUTTURU, an Australian aboriginal fighting stick.

KUTUBU, a Papuan people of the East New Guinea highlands, dependent on horticulture and food-gathering, with some hunting and animal husbandry.

KUYUIDOKADO (PYRAMID LAKE PAIUTE), a Shoshone (Uto-Aztec)-speaking North American Indian people of the Coastal Great Basin, dependent on food-gathering, hunting and some fishing.

KWA LANGUAGES, a subfamily of the Niger-Congo group of languages. Eastern Kwa (Guinea Coast) includes Fon (Dahomean), Ibo, Yoruba, Nupe and Ewe. Western Kwa includes Ashanti, Bete, Baule, Sapo and Fanti.

KWAI, a Chinese term which represents the ethical principle of wrong behaviour in Confucianism (q.v.), but which is also applied to the evil spirits that comprise the female principle of yin (q.v.) in Taoism.
KWAKIUTL, a Northwest American Indian people, primarily dependent on fishing with some hunting and food-gathering, whose language belongs to the Mosan branch of the Algonquin-Mosan phylum.
KWANGA, a form of manioc cake made in Africa.
KWAT, a secret society of the Banks Islanders.
KWI-IRU, a secret society existing among the Karu of West Africa.
KWOMA, a Papuan people of North Papua, dependent on horticulture, food-gathering, hunting and some animal husbandry.
KWOTH, a prominent sky god of the Nilotic Nuer of East Africa.
KYLWER STONE, a large standing stone, raised in 5th century Scandinavia as a memorial to the dead. The Kylwer stone was heavily ornamented with both linear designs and runic inscriptions, which latter have been successfully deciphered.

L

LA CHAPELLE-AUX-SAINTS, an important archeological site in Correze, Southwestern France, where the abbés A. and J. Bouyssonie and L. Bardon discovered a complete skeleton of a Classic Neanderthal, in association with Mousterian artifacts. The slouching posture indicated by the skeleton is probably due to old age and arthritis of the spine, and may not be characteristic of all Neanderthals as formerly believed.
LA FERASSIE, an archeological site in the Dordogne region of France where D. Peyrony found remains of adult male and female and infant Neanderthal skeletons in 1909 which are believed to date from the early Würm.
LA QUINA, an archeological site in Charente, France, where Dr. Henri Martin found Classic Neanderthal fossil remains and Mousterian artifacts in 1911. The Neanderthal bun-shaped occiput is very pronounced in the La Quina finds.
LA TÈNE, a major archeological site at the east end of Lake Neuchatel in Switzerland, dating from the beginning of the 5th century B.C. until the Roman conquest of Gaul. The site appears to have also served as a centre for votive offerings, which were thrown into the shallow waters of the lake from two timber causeways, and archeologists have been able to recover a massive collection of bronze, iron and even well-preserved wooden weapons and artifacts, among which weapons, armour and ceremonial objects predominate. The richness and artistic quality of this collection of archeological material subsequently led archeologists to apply the term 'La Tène' to most of the Celtic Iron Age cultures which formerly flourished throughout most Western Europe. The Indo-European nature of the decorative tradition is stongly evidenced by similarities between the art of the La Tène Celtic culture and that of the Scythians and Myceneans. Similar patterns of ornamentation on Celtic chariot burials at Arras and on other Celtic work recovered from Glastonbury confirm the coherence of the Celtic tradition. (See CELTS).
LA VENTA, La Venta represents one of the earliest of the Olmec ceremonial centers – comprising a large pyramid constructed of clay and a number of subsidiary structures, which appears to have been constructed as early as 1000 B.C., spreading over a fairly extensive area. La Venta is situated on a small island, surrounded by extensive swamps which contain no stone, and the earliest and most important buildings are ornamented by sculptured stones which must have been brought from sites 100 miles or more distant.
LABRADOR ESKIMO, an Eskimo people who depend mainly on fishing and hunting.
LABRET, a long wooden lip plug worn by Aleut and Eskimo women.
LABRYS, a double-headed Cretan axe of apparent religious significance, many representations of which have been found in the excavation of Minoan ruins.
LACTATION, the production of milk by the mammary glands. Most mam-

malian females are infertile during the period of lactation.
LACUSTRINE, referring to the Negroid population inhabiting the regions adjacent to Lake Victoria and the neighbouring East African lakes close to the headwaters of the Nile.
LADDER, INDIAN, a ladder made from a single notched tree trunk, widely used among North American Indians.
LADINO, (1) a language used by the Sephardic Jews of western Europe and North Africa. (2) a term used in Central America to refer to a modified form of Spanish spoken by persons of Mestizo origin. (3) the Ladino-speaking Mestizo population of Central America in contradistinction to the Indian rural population.
LADINOIZATION, a term used to refer to the absorption of Central American Indians into the Mestizo, Spanish-type culture of the Ladino speakers.
LADOGAN, a term derived from Lake Ladoga, situated between Finland and Russia, formerly used to refer to a supposedly distinct local race inhabiting the general East Baltic (q.v.) area.
LAGASH, a Sumerian city which achieved considerable importance in the 3rd millennium B.C. The excavation of Lagash has revealed many cuneiform tablets which have been extremely valuable in providing detailed historical evidence of the cultural and social life of the Sumerians of the Early Dynastic period.
LAG, CULTURAL, a state of cultural lag is said to exist when innovations in a culture have not yet brought about corresponding and necessary changes in related cultural characteristics. The result is a lack of general integration of all parts of the cultural system with consequent dysfunctional effects.
LAGOZZA, a western Neolithic lake village situated near Milan in Northern Italy. Spindle whorls provide evidence of the manufacture of textiles, and a radio-carbon date of 2850 B.C. has been determined. The Lagozza culture was influenced by the Neolithic Chassey and Cortaillod, and may have contributed to the later Bronze Age Apennine Culture.
LAGUNA, a North American Indian people of the United States Southwest.
LAKALAI, a Melanesian (Malayo-Polynesian) people from New Britain, mainly dependent on horticulture and fishing with some animal husbandry, hunting and food-gathering.
LAKALAKA, a ritual Fijian dance which probably originated among the people of the Tonga Islands.
LAKE VILLAGES, a fairly widespread Neolithic form of settlement comprising a group of huts constructed on piles driven into the mud of the edge of a lake. The resultant location possibly provided a degree of security against attack by enemies. (See GLASTONBURY).
LAKHER, a Mongoloid people, speaking a Tibeto-Burman language, who inhabit the heavily forested mountains which separate the Indian subcontinent from Burma. The Lakher are dependent on horticulture, hunting and some animal husbandry.
LAKSHMI, the Hindu goddess of beauty and consort of Vishnu, the supreme Hindu deity. Like the Greek Aphrodite, who was also a goddess of beauty, Lakshmi arose from out of the waters of the ocean. Also like Aphrodite, who was the mother of Eros, the Greek god of love, Lakshmi was the mother of Kama, the Vedic god of love, and the parallel functions of Lakshmi and Aphrodite may well indicate a common Indo-European mythological tradition.
LALA, a Bantu-speaking Negroid people of the Bemba-Lamba group, largely dependent on horticulture and fishing.
LALIA, a Bantu-speaking Negroid people of the Mongo group, largely dependent on horticulture with some fishing and hunting.
LAMA, a term meaning 'teacher', used to refer to a Buddhist monk in Tibet and Mongolia.
LAMARCKISM, the false theory, first expounded by Lamarck (1744-1829), that physiological modifications acquired during the life of an individual organism could be transmitted genetically to its offspring. Contrary to Lamarckian beliefs, only those influences that directly affect the gametes can modify the

genetic heritage of the next generation.

LAMBA, a Bantu-speaking Negroid people of the Bemba-Lamba group, largely dependent on horticulture with some hunting and fishing.

LAMET, a Mon-Khmer (Khasi-Nicobarese)-speaking people, largely dependent on horticulture, some hunting and animal husbandry.

LAMP, any vessel designed to contain a fluid which will burn slowly and steadily with the aid of a wick. Used invariably as a source of light, the earliest lamps made from saucer-shaped stones can be identified in Cro-Magnon settlements of the Upper Paleolithic, evidence of their use of lamps being found in the burn marks where the wick lay against the rim.

LANCE, a light spear, otherwise known as a javelin.

LAND DYAK, see DYAK.

LANGO, a Negroid Western Nilotic-speaking people, primarily dependent on horticulture and cattle herding who nevertheless still practice some hunting.

LANGUAGE, a system of verbal symbols by which a relatively sophisticated degree of communication can be attained. Some writers use the term language only when a written form is present and employ the term speech for strictly verbal forms of communication.

LANGUAGE, CLASSIFICATION OF, languages may be classed either generically, referring to their ancestry, or typologically, according to structure and form. In reality, however, a typological classification of language frequently leads to the realization of some earlier genetic relationship, especially when typological changes are analyzed on a historical basis. The genetic classification of languages is particularly useful as an aid to the reconstruction of cultural history. (See PALEONTOLOGY, LINGUISTIC).

LANGUAGE, INFLECTIVE, a language which largely depends on prefixes and suffixes to modify the meaning of words and show their relationship to the remaining words in the sentence.

LANGUAGE, ISOLATING, a language in which each word represents a number of different ideas, the identification of which depends upon its position in the sentence.

LANGUAGE, JUXTAPOSING, a language which uses classifiers in front of words to indicate their syntactical relationship to each other. The Bantu languages are examples of juxtaposing languages.

LANGUAGE, LIVING, a language still regularly used as a day-to-day means of communication by a living community of people.

LANGUAGE, POLYSYNTHETIC, a language which uses words comprising several morphemes, each of which conveys a separate idea and would be a separate word in another language. The Eskimo language and many American Indian languages are polysynthetic.

LANGUAGE, RITUAL, a language employed for ritual purposes, rather than for everyday use. Such languages are usually archaic survivals of an earlier language, formerly spoken by the entire society or by a ritually dominant caste within that society.

LANGUAGE, SIGN, communication by signs or stylized movements. These are frequently made with the hands, but any part of the body may be involved and even external objects may be utilized – as for example smoke signals. Sign languages have usually developed where a variety of different peoples, each with their own different spoken language, have been brought into frequent contact with each other. Thus the Plains Indians of North America developed an elaborate sign language, and sign language has similarly been used in Asiatic India as an aid to communication between members of different linguistic groups.

LANGUAGES, SYNTHETIC, see LANGUAGE, INFLECTIVE.

LANGUAGES, TONE, languages, such as those of the Mon-Khmer group, in which the same sound element may convey a different meaning when spoken in a different tone.

LANUGO, a name given to the fine hairy covering which envelops the human fetus between the 6th and 8th month of development. Although the lanugo is usually lost before birth, its occurrence constitutes evidence that the ancestors of the living hominids once resembled other mammals in the possession of a much more dense covering of hair than is found on living hominids.

LAO, the people of Laos who speak a language of Thai origin.

LAO TZU, the 6th century B.C. Chinese founder of Taoism, who lived in Southern China, an area which retained a strong tradition of vegetation myths and agricultural traditions in contrast to Northern China, where the tradition of ancestor worship took root as early as the Shang dynasty. The philosophy of Lao Tzu was particularly popular during the Ch'in and Han dynasties, and reveals aspects which have been superficially likened to the metaphysical doctrines of Plato.

LAPIS LAZULI, a semi-precious stone, notable for its rich blue color extensively used in the Near East for decorative work and jewelry. Although most lapis lazuli came from the northern mountains of Afghanistan, ornaments made from this material appear to have been traded as far west as ancient Egypt.

LAPPS, a nomadic reindeer-herding pastoral people, occupying parts of Northern Scandinavia, who reveal certain characteristically Mongoloid hereditary traits in combination with obviously Caucasoid genes. Generally brachycephalic, and equipped with broad protruding cheekbones, Lapps are usually short in stature with black hair and brown eyes, and speak a language which is a branch of the Uralic (q.v.) speech family. References in the early Norse legends to Scritlings are believed to indicate early Caucasoid contact with Lapps.

LARES, the Roman *Lare* are originally believed to have been nature spirits responsible for the protection of the farmlands and farm boundaries. With the increasing urbanization of Roman society, however, the *Lare* came to be regarded as household gods, and as protective guardians of the family and later of the family state. Not to be confused with the *Penates* (q.v.) or protective ancestral spirits.

LASCAUX, a cave in the Dordogne region of France, which was discovered as recently as 1940 and contains an excellent variety of Upper Paleolithic polychrome paintings and engravings.

LASSO, a rope with a sliding noose at one end which is thrown in such a way that the noose encircles the neck of a running animal, thereby enabling the thrower to pull the animal to the ground.

LATIFUNDIA, large agricultural estates, which were established following the expansion of Roman power, and which were generally owned by absentee landlords and supervised by professional managers. The 'latifundia' became an important element in the economy of the Roman Empire during the Imperial era, supplanting the simpler tribal economies of the conquered regions by what was in effect a colonial plantation system.

LATINS, an Iron Age people who inhabited Latium, an area lying to the south of the site of present-day Rome, and whose remains have been uncovered from various cemeteries. The Latins spoke an Italic language related to Oscan and Umbrian, and probably derived from the Villanovan (q.v.) and Terramare (q.v.) peoples. A branch of the Latins may be regarded as the ancestors of the Patrician class of Romans, constructing a small settlement on the Palatine Hill around the 9th century B.C., from which the city of Rome was to evolve.

LATVIANS, an East Baltic people, of Indo-European speech, who are today, with the Lithuanians, the sole survivors of the original Baltic group, following the elimination of the Prussian language and peoples. The Baltic nations were the last Indo-Europeans to retain their pagan religious beliefs, and fought strenuously against the Christian Order of the Teutonic Knights, who had been commissioned by the Pope to enforce their conversion.

LAU FIJIANS, a Melanesian (Malayo-Polynesian) people from the Fiji Islands, largely dependent on horticulture, fishing, food-gathering, hunting and some animal husbandry.

LAUGERIE-HAUTE, an archeological site, close to Les Eyzies in the Dordogne region of France, which has provided a continuous sequence of Upper Paleolithic artifacts commencing with the Perigordian and followed by Aurignacian, Solutrean and finally Magdalenian artifacts.

LAUSITZ CULTURE, an important branch of the widespread Urnfield culture (q.v.), which occupied East and Central Germany, Northern Czechoslovakia and parts of Poland around 1200 B.C. The earlier stages belong to the Bronze Age, and reveal evidence of an Indo-European people who lived in timber houses with thatch roofs, grouped in villages which were protected by timber stockades and elaborate gate towers, these defenses usually being reinforced by a moat. During the later stages of the Lausitz culture iron tools appear, presumably derived from the adjacent Hallstatt culture.
LAVA, a form of stone, usually comprising an admixture of several minerals, which erupts in heated liquid form from a volcano and may flow for a considerable distance before hardening.
LAW, whereas custom is obeyed as a result of training in childhood, and usually represents a collection of very ancient traditions, laws are required patterns of social behavior which have been specifically formulated by authorized officials and which are enforced by a specific system of penalties. Laws tend to replace custom in the same way centralized political institutions replace kinship systems as the basis of political organization.
LAW, PRIVATE, a system in which disputes arising from breaches of custom or law are regarded as constituting disputes between separate kinship units within the community, rather than as challenges to any centralized authority representative of the total community.
LAW, PUBLIC, a term used by anthropologists to refer to a situation in which any dispute arising between individuals or any breach of established law is regarded as a challenge to the authoritative structure of the community or society as a whole, and corrective action is instigated by individuals authorized to apprehend and punish the offender.
LAWS, norms of behavior which have been codified by a society, the contravention of which attracts specific penalties.
LEAN-TO, any primitive shelter comprising a loose structure of branches and leaves erected as a protection against the sun, wind or rain.
LEBANESE, a Semitic-speaking people, descended primarily from the Mediterranean Caucasoid Phoenicians, who were traditionally dependent on agriculture and some animal husbandry combined with a measure of international commerce.
LEGENDS, narrative accounts of real or fictitious events of unusual significance in the past history of the group, often involving supernatural beings or forces.
LEGIONS, although the Sumerians were perhaps the first people to train their infantry to fight in disciplined phalanxes, it was the Romans who developed military drill and the use of the organized phalanx to the highest degree. Although the Roman armies did use cavalry, the main backbone of the Roman legion comprised heavily armed and rigidly disciplined infantry organized in groups of approximately 6000 men.
LEISURE, any time available to man after laboring to produce the material wealth considered necessary for the maintenance of the desired standard of living.
LELE, a Bantu-speaking Negroid people of the Kasai group, largely dependent on horticulture, hunting and fishing.
LE MOUSTIER, an archeological site comprising a cave shelter on the banks of the Vezēre river in the Dordogne region of France, where a complete but fragmented skeleton of Classic Neanderthal Man was discovered by Otto Hauser in 1908, in association with 'Mousterian' tools (q.v.) which reflect an Acheulian tradition. These have been dated at around 80,000-90,000 years B.P.
LEMUROIDEA, a primate superfamily within the suborder Prosimii represented mainly by the lemurs of Madagascar.
LENCA, a Central American Indian people of Northern Nicaragua, who speak a Chibchan language and are dependent on horticulture with some hunting, fishing, and food-gathering.
LENDU, a Nilotic-speaking people of the Moru-Madi group, largely dependent

on horticulture with some hunting and animal husbandry.

LENGE, a Bantu-speaking Negroid people of the Shona-Thonga group primarily dependent on horticulture with some herding, hunting and food-gathering.

LENGUA, a South American Indian people speaking a Mascoian language possibly related to Guaycuri and dependent on hunting, fishing and some horticulture.

LENGYEL, a later Chalcolithic form of the earlier Neolithic Danubian or Old European culture, which developed in the western parts of Hungary, and included Czechoslovakia, Austria, and Southern Poland. The Lengyel culture was closely related to the Tisza culture of the Hungarian plains, and evolved out of the linear culture around 4800 B.C. It survived until replaced by the Indo-European Baden culture around 3500 B.C.

LEOPARD SOCIETY, a secret society, which formerly existed among several West African peoples, whose members claim to be able to turn into leopards at nighttime, attacking and killing their enemies, and mutilating the bodies with iron claws to make the deaths look like the work of leopards.

LEPCHA, a Tibeto-Burman-speaking largely Mongoloid people who inhabit Sikkim, but whose culture and genetic constitution have been affected by proximity to India. They are dependent on agriculture and animal husbandry, with some hunting.

LEPENSKI VIR, an important site located on the banks of the Danube just above the famous Iron Gates. First occupied in the 7th millennium B.C., by a Mesolithic fishing community building trapezoidal houses, the early settlers were later replaced by a Starčevo population of village cultivators.

LEPRECHAUN, properly known as a 'cluricaune', the leprechaun is an Irish elf, which resembles a miniature wrinkled old man. Although the main duty of leprechauns is to make shoes for the fairies, tradition represents them as authorities on the location of buried treasures who have a mischievous nature and love to play tricks on human beings.

LEPTOPROSCOPIC, possessing a relatively narrow face, i.e. one on which the facial index (q.v.) is above 80.

LEPTORRHINE, referring to a narrow nose, or one in which the nasal index (q.v.) is less than 70.

LEPTOSOME, a constitutional type reflecting a tall and slender physique.

LERNA, an ancient coastal settlement near Argos in the Peloponnese which reveals a continuous sequence from the old Aegean Neolithic, through fortified Indo-European Helladic settlements associated with Minyan Ware, to Achaean (Mycenaean) strata revealing important royal burials. Excavation of the Lerna cemetery by Lawrence Angel has also revealed skeletal evidence of the original Mediterranean Pelasgian population, as well as of the incoming Greek Indo-Europeans, whom he identifies as essentially Nordic in type.

LESE, a Nilotic people primarily dependent on horticulture, some animal husbandry and fishing.

LESU, a Melanesian (Malayo-Polynesian) people from New Ireland, mainly dependent on horticulture and fishing, with some animal husbandry and hunting.

LETTS, see LATVIANS.

LEVALLOISIAN, a highly developed Lower Paleolithic tool-making technique by which a stone core was pre-shaped so that when struck in the correct manner the resulting flake would possess the desired form. This technique was particularly useful for the manufacture of small cutting implements. The earliest Levalloisian finds are dated at approximately 300,000 years ago, and may have evolved from the Clactonian tradition now dated at 500,000 years ago. The subsequent Mousterian Middle-Paleolithic tradition also made use of Levalloisian as well as Acheulian techniques. The core, which is usually discarded after a flake has been obtained by the Levalloisian technique, reveals a crude resemblance to the shape of a tortoise, and is often called a Levalloisian 'tortoise core'.

LEVALLOISO-MOUSTERIAN, a local variation of the Mousterian culture reflecting a strong survival of the Levalloisian tradition.

LEVANA, the Roman goddess who presided over the initiation ritual of newborn infants, who were accepted by the *pater familias* as members of the family, in a ceremony in which the father lifted the young child from the floor of the house in full view of the assembled household. Once accepted in this manner, the child was a recognized member of the family, with all the privileges and obligations that this involved.

LEVIRATE, the custom whereby a woman marries the brother of her deceased husband.

LEVIRATE, ANTICIPATORY, a custom whereby a husband may permit his younger brother to take sexual privileges with his wife, on the assumption that after his death the younger brother will in any case inherit his wife. Anticipatory levirate is sometimes regarded as a special form of polyandry.

LEXICOGRAPHY, a study of words as distinct entities, without regard to grammatical considerations.

LEXICOLOGY, a scientific study of the semantics or morphology of a group of languages.

LEXICON, the total variety of morphemes used in a language.

LEX TALIONIS, the ancient principle of retaliation in kind for injuries received. Although the principle of lex talionis originated in kinship-dominated societies and was the basis of the blood feud, it sometimes survived into public law (q.v.), as was the case in the Code of Hammurabi, whereby the public authorities enforced the same basic retaliatory principle of 'an eye for an eye' as a state punishment, instead of leaving the responsibility of retaliation to the kinsmen of the victim.

LEY, an area of land subject to crop rotation, being cultivated for one or more years and then allowed to revert to pasture in ensuing years, so as to preserve its fertility. The word is of Germanic origin and usually refers to the richer low-lying land found in river valleys.

LHOTA, a Sinitic-speaking people of the Tibeto-Burman group who are largely dependent on horticulture, but also practice some animal husbandry, hunting and fishing.

LI, (1) a Sinitic-speaking people of the Tibeto-Burman group who are largely dependent on horticulture, but also practice some animal husbandry, hunting and fishing. (2) a ceremonial or ritual vessel used in China during the Bronze Age, sometimes made of pottery but more frequently constructed of Bronze. Li vessels are distinctive in that their vases are divided into three hollow compartments which taper off into tripod legs. The remarkable parallel between the Bronze Age and Late Neolithic Chinese use of the tripod in ritual ancestor-worshipping ceremonies with the use of tripod vessels in similar ancestor-worshipping ceremonies in western Eurasia may be regarded as further evidence of early West-East cultural diffusion.

LIANA, a tropical climbing plant which when stripped of its leaves can be conveniently used as a rope.

LIBATION, an offering of a liquid drink to a deceased ancestor or god. Among the Bantu, a small quantity of beer is habitually poured on the ground, at meal times, as an offering to the ancestors. The ancient Romans offered libations at the family altar in honour of their ancestors and the spirits of the household. A libation may even be drunk by the supplicant after first being dedicated to the deity, this latter procedure being the origin of the practice of 'toasting' in Europe prior to imbibing an alcoholic beverage, when a chosen individual or planned venture is commended to the gods before the libation is drunk.

LIBYANS, Egyptian paintings reveal that the Libyans were originally blue-eyed and blond-haired Caucasoids, in sharp contrast to the population of Egypt, which is mainly represented as a dark-haired and brown-eyed Caucasoid stock with some Negroid admixture among the more southern Nubians. Customarily wearing long leather clothes, the Libyans attacked Egypt on several occasions and succeeded in establishing two Egyptian dynasties, the 22nd and 23rd, respectively known as the Bubastite and Tanite.

LICHENS, a plant which actually constitutes a dual organism, combining a symbiotic association between a fungus and an algae. Lichens are ecologically important in the primary colonization of bare land.

LICHGATE, a small roofed building, normally found at the entrance to a churchyard. The word *lich* is Anglo-Saxon for 'corpse', and lichgates were constructed as a resting place for the corpse during the religious ritual prior to burial, since corpses were not permitted into the sacred precincts of the 'house of god' for fear of ritual pollution. Even after the corpses of royalty and noble men and women were buried in the church the corpses of commoners were denied admittance to the sacred building.

LIFE, a metabolic process involving growth, reproduction, and evolution. (See METABOLISM).

LIFE CYCLE, a term given to the progressive series of physiological changes through which an organism passes from the time of fertilization of the initial zygote until death. From the evolutionary point of view it is only necessary that the individual organism should survive long enough to reproduce to ensure the survival of the lineage, although in the case of more complex organisms living in groups, the survival of the individual organism after the period of reproduction may have an evolutionary value in so far as it is able to contribute to the survival chances of members of the ensuing generation.

LIFU, a Melanesian (Malayo-Polynesian) people from the Loyalty Isles, largely dependent on horticulture and fishing with some animal husbandry.

LIGHTNING, a discharge of atmospheric electricity from a cloud to the earth, regarded by most cultures as being of divine or supernatural significance.

LILLOOET, a North American Indian people who speak a Salish (Mosan) language, and inhabit the Northern Plateau area of British Columbia. They are dependent on hunting, fishing and food-gathering.

LILY, a plant, representing 'purity', which plays a significant role in Indo-European symbolism. Held in reverence in India, the lily or 'fleur-de-lis' was also the heraldic symbol of the kings of France.

LIMBO, (1) an acrobatic dance, during which the dancer must pass his body under a low stick, without touching the ground other than with the soles of his feet. (2) in Christian mythology, that place to which innocent souls that are not qualified for admission to heaven are consigned.

LINEAGE, a unilateral kinship group (smaller than a clan) tracing descent from a known ancestor.

LINEAR A & B, forms of linear writing inscribed on clay tablets surviving from Bronze Age Crete. It is suggested that there may be a relationship between the undeciphered Linear A (used from the late 3rd to the middle of the 2nd millennium B.C.) and the early forms of writing found in the Old European Civilization (q.v.) of the Balkans. Linear B, which was introduced in the 15th century B.C., has been deciphered and is described as syllabaric, since each symbol represents a different syllable. The language employed represented a form of Mycenean Greek and its introduction followed the conquest of Crete by Mycenean Greeks.

LINEAR POTTERY, see BANDKERAMIK.

LINGAM, a simple phallic stone symbol found in temples dedicated to the Hindu god Shiva. The lingam appears to be pre-Aryan in origin, since it is quite unknown in other Indo-European societies, whereas examples have been found in excavations of the early Indus Valley sites. In many cases the lingam is used for the ritual defloration of girls prior to their marriages, in the belief that defloration by the symbol of Shiva will promote their subsequent fertility.

LINGUA FRANCA, any language which is commonly used as a medium of communication between members of societies possessing separate and mutually unintelligible languages. Examples of linguae franca are Hausa (q.v.), Swahili (q.v.), and Pidgin English (q.v.).

LINGUISTIC DRIFT, all languages tend to change with time, and unwritten languages change more quickly than written languages. This 'linguistic drift' tends to be a steady phenomenon, the rate of which can be measured with some accuracy – although change can be accelerated by contact with the speakers of other languages.

LINGUISTIC PALEONTOLOGY, the analysis of the vocabulary of an earlier form of a language in order to obtain information concerning the culture and life style of its speakers, as indicated by the presence of absence of specific terms.

LINGUISTICS, COMPARATIVE, the analysis and description of a language at a particular point in time. However, since languages are constantly changing, the study of comparative linguistics often contributes greatly to the development of historical linguistics (q.v.).

LINGUISTICS, DIACHRONIC, the study of diachronic linguistics emphasizes an historical approach to linguistic change, in contradistinction to synchronic linguistics (q.v.). (See also LINGUISTICS, HISTORICAL).

(See also LINGUISTICS, HISTORICAL).

LINGUISTICS, GEOGRAPHICAL, the study of the worldwide distribution of languages and dialects viewed in historical perspective.

LINGUISTICS, HISTORICAL, the study of the changes that occur in a language or a group of languages through time, with particular emphasis upon the relationship between those which are generically related by common descent from a single original language.

LINGUISTICS, STRUCTURAL, the study of languages as coherent homogeneous entities. (See also LINGUISTICS, SYNCHRONIC).

LINGUISTICS, SYNCHRONIC, this term is used to emphasize the analysis of language at a particular time in the history of its development, in contradistinction to the concept of 'diachronic linguistics' (q.v.).

LINKAGE, a genetic term referring to the tendency for a number of non-allelomorphic genes to be associated together and passed on from parental to filial generations as coherent units instead of breaking down into independent assortments. The term 'supergene' has sometimes been used to refer to such gene linkages. Gene linkage is important in the successful replication of finely balanced complex biological organisms.

LINKAGE, GENETIC, genes situated at the same position on the same chromosome will be inherited together when 'crossing over' (q.v.) occurs.

LINKED GENES, two or more genes, appearing on the same chromosome, which tend to be inherited together. The complex physiological structure of the advanced multicellular animals, and in particular of complex animals such as reptiles, birds and mammals, can only be achieved as a result of substantial gene linkage.

LINTEL, a horizontal stone or timber used to span the space over a doorway or window so as to carry the weight of the superstructure above it.

LION, an animal which formerly ranged widely throughout Africa, India, the Near East and parts of Europe. In Europe and Western Asia the lion was early adopted as an emblem of royalty and imperial power.

LIPAN, Athabascan-speaking North American Apache Indians, dependent on food-gathering and hunting.

LIP PLUG, a form of female decoration, carrying a certain status with it, by which a stick of wood, bone or some other valuable object is inserted through a hole made in either the upper or the lower lip. Common among African Negroes, Pygmies and also among certain North American peoples, a lip plug may protrude as far as two or three inches beyond the normal skin contour.

LIRA, a primitive wind instrument used in Africa, comprising a bamboo tube, the lower end of which is split so as to vibrate when air is blown down the tube.

LITHOSPHERE, the solid portion of the earth, not including the surrounding liquids and gases.

LITHUANIANS, a Caucasoid people, whose language belongs to the East Baltic branch of Indo-European and who were traditionally dependent on agriculture, animal husbandry and some fishing. Also known as Letts.

LITTER, a hammock or chair, supported on a pair of long poles, in which a passenger may conveniently be carried by two or more porters.

LLAMA, one of the few indigenous animals to be domesticated in the Americas, the llama was used as a pack animal in the Peruvian and related Andean civilizations. However, it was not strong enough to support the weight of a man, and therefore could not be used as a riding animal.

LO, a large Chinese gong, stuck with a padded mallet to indicate the arrival of guests. The number of strokes usually indicates the rank of the individual.

LOBI, a Negroid, West African, Voltaic people, largely dependent on horticulture and food-gathering with some hunting and animal husbandry.

LOBOLO, the Bantu term for a bride price, usually paid in the form of cattle.

LOCONO, a South American Indian people of the Arawak linguistic stock. Residing on the Guyana Coast, the Locono are dependent on horticulture, fishing and some hunting and gathering.

LOCUS, (in genetics) the site occupied by a gene on a chromosome.

LODGE, EARTH, a subterranean or semi-subterranean chamber, used as a dwelling-place by the Pawnee Indians, and as a ritual cult center in certain other American Indian cultures.

LOGGIA, a roofed passageway open on one or both sides.

LOIN CLOTH, a short piece of cloth wrapped around the loins and tucked in at the waist.

LOKELE, a Bantu-speaking Negroid people of the Riverain Congo, primarily dependent on fishing with some horticulture and hunting.

LOLO, a Tibeto-Burman-speaking people occupying the Tien Shan mountains who are dependent on cultivation and animal husbandry with some hunting

LONGEVITY, the average expectation of life may vary considerably according to environmental, dietary, and cultural conditions. Attempts at determining the longevity of prehistoric populations have been handicapped mainly due to the inadequacy of skeletal material.

LONGUDA, a Negroid Niger-Congo-speaking people of the Adamawa-Eastern group, mainly dependent on horticulture and animal husbandry.

LOOM, a mechanical device invented for the purpose of weaving cloth. Looms were in early use in Neolithic Mesopotamia, Europe, Egypt, and South Asia, the Far East and Central America.

LORIS, a member of the Lemur family (Lemuridae), found in India, South-East Asia and Africa.

LOST WAX PROCESS, see CIRE-PERDUE.

LOTHAL, an important archeological site in the southern portion of the Indus Valley, representing the remains of a city which (formerly situated on the sea) appears to have a major port. Equipped with brick-faced docks, and the usual Indus Valley ceremonial bath, grid-plan streets, and city walls, Lothal clearly played an important role in sea trade between the Indus Valley, the Persian Gulf and Mesopotamia, and may also have maintained trading contacts with the Chalcolithic cultures of southern India. The city appears to have been constructed early in the 2nd millennium B.C.

LOTUKO, a Negroid East Sudanese or Nilotic-speaking people of the Bari-Lotuko group, primarily dependent on horticulture and cattle-herding with some hunting.

LOTUS FLOWER, the lotus flower was widely used as a symbolic motif in both ancient Egypt and Buddhist Asia, but no relationship between these two traditions has so far been established.

LOVEDU, a Bantu-speaking Negroid people of the Shona-Thonga group, primarily dependent on horticulture and animal herding.

LOVE PHILTER, a magical drink intended to cause the drinker to fall in love. Love philters usually contain some form of drug, as well as a portion of the exuvia (q.v.) of the person with whom the drinker is intended to become enamoured.

LOWESTOFT GLACIATION, the name sometimes given to a period of glaciation affecting Britain, which corresponds to the Alpine Mindel glaciation (q.v.).

LOYALTY ISLANDERS, a Melanesian people inhabiting the Loyalty Isles, dependent on horticulture and fishing.

LOYANG, a city situated in Honan province, close to the banks of the Hwang-Ho, which served as the capital of the Chou empire from 771 B.C. until its seizure by the Ch'ins in 256 B.C.

LOZI, a Bantu-speaking Negroid people of Barotseland, primarily dependent on horticulture with some herding and food-gathering.

LUAPULA, a Bantu-speaking Negroid people of the Bemba-Lamba group largely dependent on horticulture and fishing.

LUBA, a Bantu-speaking Negroid people of the Luba group, largely dependent on horticulture with some hunting and fishing.

LUCHAZI, a Bantu-speaking Negroid people of the Lunda group, largely dependent on fishing, hunting and some horticulture.

LUGBARA, a Nilotic people primarily dependent on horticulture and animal husbandry, with some food-gathering.

LUIMBE, a Bantu-speaking Negroid people of the Lunda group, largely dependent on fishing, hunting and some horticulture.

LUISENO, a Shoshone (Uto-Aztec)-speaking American Indian people of South-eastern California, dependent on food-gathering supplemented by some hunting and fishing.

LULUA, a Bantu-speaking Negroid people of the Luba group, largely dependent on horticulture supplemented by some hunting and fishing.

LUMMI, a coastal Salish (Northwest American Indian) people whose language belongs to the Mosan division of the Algonquin-Mosan phylum, dependent primarily on fishing with some hunting and food-gathering.

LUNDA EMPIRE, a despotic conquest state formerly dominant in the Southern Congo.

LUNG SHAN, a Neolithic culture which flourished on the rich soil of the alluvial Hwang-Ho river basin of Northern China. Characterized by the use of polished stone, by bone arrowheads, and black burnished pottery made on potter's wheels, the Lung Shan culture also included Honan, overlaying the indigenous Yang Shao culture where these two overlapped. Both the Yang Shao and the Lung Shan cultures later came under Shang domination.

LUNULA, crescent-shaped gold chest decorations, often as large as eight inches in diameter, which were worn as ornaments during the early Bronze Age by the peoples of Northern Europe.

LUO, a Negroid, Southern Nilotic-speaking people, primarily dependent on horticulture and cattle-herding with some hunting and fishing.

LUR, a particularly long bronze musical horn shaped in a double curve, found primarily in Denmark. Since 'lur' have almost always been found in pairs it is believed that they may have had ritual significance, being deposited in lakes as votive offerings.

LURISTAN, an area in the Central Zagros mountains of Western Iran, notable for the extensive manufacture of a wide variety of decorative bronze ornaments in both animal and human forms, as well as decorated bronze weapons and horsebits. The people of Luristan porbably migrated southwards from the Caucasus and may have been associated with the Cassites (who represented an indigenous people, governed by an Indo-European aristocracy.). Certainly the people of Luristan themselves came under Indo-European domination not later than the beginning of the 2nd millennium B.C.

LUSTRATION RITES, ceremonial purification rites, intended to cleanse peoples or places from ritual defilement, as in the ritual cleansing of a polluted temple or even the cleansing of a people or town threatened by sudden danger, to allay the anger of the gods for past offenses and to free the occupants from the handicap of magico-religious penalties for their misdeeds.

LUTE, a stringed musical instrument which may have originated in ancient Egypt.

LUVALE, a Bantu-speaking Negroid people of the Lunda group, largely dependent on horticulture and fishing.

LUWA, a Bantu-speaking Negroid people of the Lunda group, largely dependent on horticulture and fishing.

LYNCHET, a ridge of topsoil which may accumulate along the uncultivated lower end of a sloping field, as a result of erosion by rain-water after the surface vegetation has been removed to permit cultivation. The identification of ancient lynchets provides evidence of former cultivation.

LYRE, a musical instrument resembling a harp, the strings of which are stretched between a hollow framework, which serves as a resonator, and a transverse bar. Evidence of the existence of the lyre has been discovered by archeologists as early as 5000 B.P., and the instrument was particularly popular in ancient Greece.

M

MAAT, the ancient Egyptian Goddess of Truth and Order, usually symbolized by an ostrich feather, since the Egyptians believed that on the day of judgment the souls of the dead were weighed against an ostrich feather.

MACAQUE, a widely diversified Old World monkey, today represented by some fifty different species.

MACASSARESE, a Malayo-Polynesian-speaking people of Macassar (Indonesia), largely dependent on cultivation, fishing and animal husbandry.

MACE, any weapon designed from a heavy weight affixed by means of a shaft hole to a haft or handle.

MACEDONIANS, an Indo-European-speaking people, closely related to the Greeks and the Albanians, who formerly lived in the area still known as Macedonia, and who retained an essentially tribal monarchical structure long after Greece had developed urban, republican institutions. Preserving their cultural and genetic homogeneity, they were able to subordinate Greece to their control, and subsequently create a brief empire under the leadership of Alexander the Great.

MACHA, a Cushitic people of East Africa, dependent on horticulture and hunting.

MACHISMO, a custom widely prevalent among the Ladino peoples of Central and South America requiring a strong display of male assertiveness.

MACHU PICCHU, a mountain city situated high on a saddle of the Andean mountains, with deep drops of 1500 feet on either side. After Cuzco fell to the Conquistadores, the Incas of Machu Picchu managed to maintain for several generations their national traditions and religion in this mountain retreat.

MACROPHAGUS, a term used to refer to animals which feed on pieces of food so large that they require a lengthy time for digestion. All land animals are macrophagus and consequently tend to feed at intervals.

MACRO-TUCANOAN LANGUAGES, a major group within the Andean-Equatorial class of languages of South America, which includes the Catukina, Macu-Puinave, and Tucanoan families.

MACUBA, a ritual drink comprising a mixture of blood and rum, used in the initiation ceremonies of the Nanigo in Cuba. Initiates are required to prepare their own drink, by biting the head off a rooster, and allowing the blood to pour into a cup of rum.

MACUSI, a South American Indian Carib-speaking people, dependent on horticulture, and some hunting, fishing and food-gathering.

MADAN, 'Marsh Arabs' who speak Arabic (a Semitic language) and depend largely on fishing, horticulture, food-gathering and some animal husbandry.

MADI, a Nilotic people primarily dependent on horticulture, animal husbandry, and fishing supplemented by some hunting.

MAFULU, a Papuan people from East Papua, dependent on horticulture, hunting, fishing and animal husbandry.

MAGADIS, an ancient Egyptian musical instrument comprising a set of strings drawn over a sounding board.

MAGDALENIAN, the last stage of the Upper Paleolithic culture in Western Europe, named after an archeological site at La Madeleine in the Dordogne region of France. Magdalenian tools show an adaptation to the particularly cold conditions of the last stages of the Würm glaciation, when the hunting of reindeer and fishing were the main means of subsistence. A large number of barbed weapons made from bone ivory and antler reveal exquisite decorations, including carved representations of birds and animals. Magdalenian cave art, such as that found in the Spanish Altamira caves, ranks among the most accomplished products of Cro-Magnon man.

MAGHREB, the Western Mediterranean coastal region of Africa, occupied by a mixed population of Hamito-Semitic origin.

MAGI, a clan, whose members appear to have been well-versed in the ancient Chaldaean magical arts practiced in Persia prior to the arrival of the Indo-Iranians. Darius I initially opposed the influence of the Magi, who may have been of pre-Aryan origin (the 'Wise Men of the East' mentioned in the Bible), but as the old Aryan polytheism of the Indo-European invaders was transformed into a Zoroastrian monotheistic (or more correctly dualistic) religion, the Magi came to occupy a position in Persian society somewhat analogous to that of the priestly clan of the Levites among the Hebrews. Most of the old Indo-Aryan gods were disclaimed as devils, or reduced to the status of mere retainers of Ahura Mazda (q.v.), and ritual worship passed under the control of the Magi, who alone were permitted to prepare the sacred *haoma* drink. (See also MAGICIAN).

MAGIC, any technique or formula aimed at achieving control over the forces of the supernatural, in contrast to religion (q.v.), which involves attempts to placate such forces. Magic is also significant in that it appears to represent a pre-scientific attempt to apply the concept of causality to the control of the environment. Magic used for anti-social purposes was traditionally known as 'black magic' in Europe, while magic used for the benefit of society or of the community has been labelled 'white magic'.

MAGIC, CONTAGIOUS, an attempt to manipulate the supernatural on the principle that supernatural power can be transferred by touch or physical proximity.

MAGIC, IMITATIVE, the belief that the construction of images or symbols will give the possessor power over the subject so represented.

MAGICIAN, any expert in the control of magical forces whose services are for hire. The term derives from the name of the Persian clan of the Magi, who were magico-religious experts inheriting much of the older Chaldaean magical tradition.

MAGLEMOSIAN, the earliest Mesolithic culture of the North European plain, revealing a pattern of hunting, fishing and food-gathering well adapted to forest, river and lakeside conditions. Considerable numbers of stone microliths were manufactured for the purpose of carving bone and antler harpoons and spearheads, as well as for general carpentry use. Bows and arrows, dugout canoes and paddles were made, together with a wide range of fishing equipment. The domestication of the dog was certainly achieved by the beginning of the Maglemosian Mesolithic (circa 8000 B.C.) if not earlier.

MAGNETOMETER, a device designed to measure the intensity of the earth's magnetic field, the magnetometer is used by archeologists to plot magnetic irregularities over particular areas of land believed to conceal archeological sites. Thus the presence of buried hearths and weapons, or even of ancient pits and ditches, can be detected without any need to disturb the ground. Only when the magnetometer indicates positive irregularities need exploratory excavations be attempted.

MAGYAR, the Uralic language of Hungary. (See also HUNGARIANS).

MAHABHARATA, the longest of the epic Vedic poems, comprising nearly a quarter of a million lines, which nevertheless comprised only a small part of the total oral literature of the Indo-Aryans who settled India shortly after the 15th century B.C. The Mahabharata was first written down between 800 and 500 B.C., by which time it had been considerably modified by the influence of the Brahman priests who had gained supremacy in all religious and literary matters. Its subject-matter deals with the conquest of large parts of India by Aryan kings and princes, the Bhagavad-Gita, especially, comprising an imaginative, but mythologically important account of the Aryan conquest of Ceylon (Sri Lanka). (See also VEDIC LITERATURE).

MAHADEVA, a Sanskrit word, literally meaning 'Great God', popularly applied to Shiva as the supreme deity of the original Indo-Aryan pantheon.

MAHORI, a term sometimes used to refer to all the various dialects and forms of the Polynesian group of languages.

MAIDEN CASTLE, a large hill-fort near Dorchester in Britain. Excavation has revealed an early Neolithic camp, on the site of which a large long barrow was subsequently erected. A later fortress, covering a total of 45 acres, was constructed by Celts during the Iron Age, containing a permanent settlement of both stone and wooden houses. Additional earthworks were added until there were four concentric ramparts, and piles of slingshot stones were accumulated at various strategic points for the defense of these walls. At the time of the Roman conquest, Maiden Castle was the ritual capital of a tribe of Belgic Brythonic Celts, who unsuccessfully attempted to defend the fortress against the victorious Roman legions of Vespasian.

MAIDU, a California Penutian-speaking people, dependent on food-gathering, hunting and fishing.

MAIKOP, one of the most famous of the Kurgan burial sites, containing a mortuary house constructed of timber and divided into three sections, the whole being covered by an earthen barrow. The burial house appears to have contained the remains of a prominent king, whose corpse had been sprinkled with ochre and laid to rest beneath a canopy supported by gold and silver ornamented poles. A profusion of weapons and of copper, gold ornaments and gold and silver vases and drinking vessels, engraved mainly with animal figures, had also been placed in the mound. The burial is dated around the middle or later part of the 3rd millennium B.C., and reflects what has been described as the Early Kuban culture (q.v.).

MAILU, a Papuan people of Southeast New Guinea who supplement horticulture with hunting, food-gathering and some animal husbandry.

MAIMING, the cutting off or deformation of a part of the body as a punishment for a crime or as a sacrifice to appease supernatural beings.

MAIZE, wild maize probably originated in the high Mexican uplands, but the first evidence of cultivation is found in the Tehuacan valley around the 5th millennium or early 4th millennium B.C. There is no certainty as to whether the cultivation of maize was invented independently in different parts of central and southern America, or whether the maize cultivated in the southwestern United States by the Cochise people around 2500 B.C., and maize cultivated in Peru during the first part of the 3rd millennium B.C. represents a cultural diffusion from the Tehuacan valley. Certainly an improved quality of maize was introduced into Peru from Mexico around 1000 B.C.

MAJURO, a Malayo-Polynesian-speaking people occupying the Marshall Islands of Micronesia, who depend for subsistence on horticulture, fishing and some animal husbandry.

MAKAH, a Northwest American Indian people, primarily dependent on fishing with some hunting and food-gathering, the Makah speak a language which belongs to the Mosan branch of the Algonquin-Mosan phylum.

MAKAPANSGAT, a cave site in the Transvaal, South Africa, excavated by J. S. and B. Kitching and A. R. Hughes, in 1947, which revealed a fossil skull, jaw fragments and teeth of Homo rhodesiensis type, which were dated around 55,000 B.P. Tools of Acheulian type were found in association with these remains. Professor Dart at one time believed that evidence of fire was present, and the name Australopithecus prometheus was used for a time. Other authorities have preferred to class the remains as Australopithecus africanus, rather than with the more Neanderthaloid Homo rhodesiensis.

MAKIN, a Malayo-Polynesian-speaking people from Bikini in the Gilbert Islands of Polynesia, dependent on horticulture, fishing and some animal husbandry.

MAKITARE, a South American Carib-speaking Indian people, who subsist by horticulture, hunting, fishing and some food-gathering.

MAKONDE, a Bantu-speaking Negroid people of the Yao-Makonde group, largely dependent on horticulture and fishing.

MAKUA, a Bantu-speaking Negroid people of the Yao-Makonde group, largely dependent on horticulture and fishing.

MALACHITE, a form of copper carbonate which was applied to the eyelids of children in Egypt and the Middle East partly as a cosmetic and partly to discourage flies.
MALAGAN, carved memorial stones raised in commemoration of the dead in New Ireland.
MALAGASY, the Malayo-Polynesian people of Madagascar. The ancestors of the Malagasy travelled by sea from Southeast Asia, and after establishing some settlements on the east coast of Africa (presumably later eliminated by the Bantu) settled Madagascar which was then unpopulated. They called Madagascar 'the land without death', since for some time after their arrival it remained relatively free from diseases that affected human organisms.
MALAR, scientific term for the cheekbone.
MALARIA PARASITE, a protozoan organism which, commonly carried by mosquitoes, causes malarial sickness in humans.
MALAY, DEUTERO, a supposed second wave of Malay immigrants who are believed to have entered Malaysia and Indonesia subsequent to an earlier wave of settlement by 'Protero-Malays' (q.v.).
MALAYO-POLYNESIAN (or AUSTRONESIAN) LANGUAGES, a phylum of languages comprising four major families. The Malayo-Indonesian family of languages are still spoken in the original homeland (roughly corresponding to Indonesia) but this family also includes the language of the Philippines, who are relatively recent immigrants to the Philippine Islands, and Malagasy, the language of the Malayo-Polynesians who sailed westwards to colonize Madagascar off the distant east coast of Africa. To the east of the main Malayo-Indonesian area, Melanesian languages are spoken in the islands around New Guinea by a population which appears to be partly Negrito in character, the major islands in the Melanesian speech area being the Solomon Islands, the New Hebrides, New Caledonia and the Fiji Islands. Micronesian languages are spoken in the small islands north of Melanesia , notably in the Marianas, Guam, the Carolines, and the Marshalls, as well as Yap and Wake. But it is the fourth family of the Malayo-Polynesian phylum, namely Polynesian, which is most widely dispersed. This family includes not only the language of the Hawaiian Islands, but also those of the Gilberts, the Marquesas, the Samoas, the Tongas and the Society Islands. The most remote outlyers of this family are found as far as Easter Island and as far south as New Zealand, where Polynesian is represented by the Maori languages.
MALAY, PROTERO, according to the theory that the ancestors of the Malays arrived in Malaysia and Indonesia in two successive waves, the term Protero-Malay has been used to refer to the descendants of the earlier invaders, who mixed genetically with the aboriginal Negrito (q.v.) population. Protero-Malays consequently reveal relatively broad noses, short stature, and wavy to kinky hair. (See also MALAYO-POLYNESIAN).
MALAYS, a Malayo-Indonesian people today inhabiting Malaya, but whose ancestors settled Malaysia and Indonesia in two successive waves, known as Protero-Malays and Deutero-Malays, becoming assimilated with the indigenous Negritoes and Australoids.
MALDIVIANS, the inhabitants of the Maldive and Laccadive islands in the Indian Ocean speak an Indo-European language related to Singhalese.
MALEKULANS, an Australian aboriginal hunting and gathering people.
MALIM, an Arab holy man.
MALINKE, a Negroid, West African, Mande people, dependent on horticulture and some animal husbandry, fishing and food-gathering.
MALLIA, an archeological site on the north coast of Crete which has revealed the ruins of a palace as well as other buildings.
MALOCCLUSION, the faulty positioning of the teeth preventing them from functioning with full efficiency. The condition is more common among Europeans and other races with small, non-prognathous jaws than among the more prognathous races.
MALTA, Malta was already settled by an advanced people producing im-

pressed ware pottery as early as 4000 B.C. These constructed a remarkable series of somewhat unique megalithic temples throughout the 3rd millennium. The prime subject of worship appears to have been an obese fertility goddess. Malta was later settled by Greeks, who lost control of the island to the Carthaginians, who in turn yielded it to the Romans in 216 B.C.

MAM, a Central American, upland Mayan people (of the Penutian language family) dependent on agriculture and limited animal husbandry.

MAMA COCHA, the Inca goddess who was regarded as the mother of all mankind.

MAMAIA, a nativist or messianic movement which arose in 19th century Polynesia, seeking to combine Christianity with many elements of the older indigenous traditions. Its leader claimed to be the resurrected Jesus Christ, and during its brief life the movement swept rapidly through those islands which had been Christianized.

MAMALOI, a Haitian Voodoo priestess.

MAMBILA, a Negroid people of the Tiv-Jukan group, speaking a Niger-Congo language and dependent on horticulture and some animal husbandry.

MAMBWE, a Bantu-speaking Negroid people of the Rukwa group, largely dependent on horticulture and some animal husbandry.

MAMMALIA, a class of 'tetrapods' or four-footed vertebrates, divided into monotremata, marsupialia, and placentalia (q.v.). The former two classes are sometimes known as protomammals. All mammals are distinguished by the possession of a thermostatic heat control mechanism, a lower jaw made of a single pair of bones and three auditory ossicles in each middle ear, some form of hair, and the ability of females to lactate. Monotremata are today represented by the duckbilled platypus and the spiny anteater of Australia and New Guinea, possess a type of body hair and secrete milk from mammary glands dispersed over the chest, instead of being concentrated in teats as in placentalia. They are equipped with reptilian features such as reproduction by the laying of eggs. The marsupialia of the Americas and Australia include the opossum, the kangaroo and the koala 'bear'. The young are nourished by a yolk sac contained in the egg, and are born at a very early state of development, after which they are sheltered in a pouch containing mammalian teats which secrete milk. The Placentalia nourish their young through a much longer pregnancy by means of a placenta.

MAMVU, a Nilotic people primarily dependent on horticulture with some animal husbandry, hunting, and food-gathering.

MAN, a term which appears to have originally had an eponymous tribal origin among the Aryan or Indo-European peoples. Not only did the Romans worship the Manes (q.v.) or ancestral spirits, but Tacitus reports that the German people believed themselves to be descended from a common eponymous ancestor Mannus (q.v.), and the Indo-Aryans recognized an original ancestral law-giver by the name Manu. The root **man* is to be found in a number of other Indo-European cultures, e.g, the Greek name 'Menelaos'. However, among English-speaking peoples in historic times the honorific term 'man' has come to be extended by courtesy to all living hominids. 'Woman' derives from Anglo-Saxon *Wifman*, or 'wife of man'. (See also MANNUS, MANES, MANU).

MAN, FALL OF, an ancient Sumerian myth, later adopted by the Hebrews into the Old Testament and passed from thence into Christianity, which records a story of temptation and disobedience by the first man and woman and of their consequent expulsion from the Garden of Eden. The concept of 'original sin' as an hereditary defect resulting from this ancestral transgression is a facet added by Christian theologians.

MANA, a term borrowed by anthropologists from the Melanesian language and applied generally to the idea of a vague and diffused supernatural power that may pervade inorganic as well as organic matter. The concept of mana should be distinguished from that of a spirit or soul which possesses a will of its own, as implied by animism. The concept of mana is reflected in the Algonquin 'manitou', the 'hasina' of Madagascar, the 'hamingja' of Scandinavia, the 'baraka' of Morocco, and the 'manngur' of Queensland, Australia.

MANAM, a Melanesian-speaking people from Northwest New Guinea, largely dependent on horticulture and fishing, with some animal husbandry.
MANCHU, one of the major Altaic-speaking Mongoloid peoples who gave their name to Manchuria and to the Manchu dynasty of China. Traditionally dependent on agriculture and some animal husbandry, Manchuria has long been under Chinese influence and considerable industrialization has taken place in recent years. (See also ALTAIC).
MANCO CAPAC, the founder of the royal Inca clan, descended from the sun and the moon, who married his sister Mama Oulla Huaca, and founded the Inca dynasty, establishing its capital city at Cuzco. Their son and daughter followed the custom of the Inca brother-sister marriage to keep the lineage pure, as did each successive generation of Inca (q.v.) rulers.
MANDAN, a Siouan-speaking North American Indian people who lived on the Upper Missouri river, and were largely dependent on horticulture with some hunting, fishing and food-gathering.
MANDE LANGUAGES, a subfamily of the Niger-Congo group of languages, associated with the slave-based empires of protohistoric Ghana and Mali. The subfamily includes Bambera, Mande, Kpelle, Malinka and Ngere.
MANDERIN LANGUAGE, see CHINESE LANGUAGES.
MANDIBLE, the lower jaw-bone.
MANDINGO, an African people of the West Sudanese area.
MANDRAKE, a poisonous plant which grows in various Mediterranean countries. Taken in small quantities the mandrake produces drowsiness and sleep, but larger quantities can be fatal. Owing to the crude resemblance between the shape of the root of a mandrake and the human body, folklore frequently attributes supernatural qualities to the mandrake plant.
MANES, the Roman ancestral spirits of the dead, otherwise known as Di Parentum, who were honoured at three annual festivals namely the Feralia, the Lemuria and the Parentalia. The Latin term *Manes* is cognate with the Germanic *Mannus,* the eponymous legendary ancestor of all the Germanic peoples, and the Indo-Aryan 'Manu' or ancestral lawgiver. (See also MAN).
MANES (also MEN), a Phrygian god who embraced both heaven and earth and was generally represented with a crescent moon above his shoulders. Probably equivalent to the Norse Mani (q.v.).
MANGAIANS, an Eastern Polynesian people, wholly dependent on fishing and horticulture.
MANGBETU, a Nilotic-speaking people of the Mangbetu group, primarily dependent on horticulture and hunting but also practicing some fishing and animal husbandry.
MANGKE, a secret age grade (q.v.) society of the New Hebrides.
MANGO, a large and juicy fruit which appears to have originated in East Asia, but is now grown widely in many tropical countries.
MANI, the Norse moon god, known to the Lithuanians as *Menu* and to the Celts as *Mane.*
MANIC-DEPRESSIVE, a form of psychosis causing sufferers to experience alternate moods of elation and melancholia.
MANICHAEISM, a religion founded by a certain Mani, reputed by some to be a member of the Magi and by others to have been a Semitic Aramaian. Born in Persia during the 3rd century A.D., Mani preached a pacifist religion derived from a synthesis of the Sermon on the Mount and ideas taken from the Old Testament, Gnosticism, Mazdaism and Buddhism. Although Mani was opposed by the more orthodox Persian Magi priests and finally executed, his ideas spread rapidly to Egypt and North Africa, and eventually penetrated as far west as Central Europe and as far East as China, where they were held only by secret cult-groups because of the opposition of the prevailing tradition of Confucian ancestor-worship. However, since Manichaeism preached celibacy, it failed to prevail against other religions since their converts left no children who could be reared in its traditions.
MANIHIKIANS, an Eastern Polynesian people wholly dependent on fishing

and horticulture.

MANIOC (or YUCA), manioc, known by various names among the different American peoples, appear to be native to tropical South America, where the regular cultivation of manioc may have begun as early as 2000 B.C. in Venezuela. Certain varieties of manioc are poisonous unless first soaked in water and then squeezed to extract the prussic acid.

MANISM, a term coined by Herbert Spencer (q.v.) to refer to the worship of the spirits of the dead. Borrowing the Roman term *manes*, meaning the ancestral spirits, and observing that ancestor worship was quite widespread throughout the world, Herbert Spencer advanced the idea that modern monotheistic religions had in fact evolved out of more primitive religions involving manism or the worship of ancestral spirits and ghosts. This idea has since been substantially challenged, and it has been demonstrated that ancestor-worship has flourished in many of the world's leading civilizations, while the concept of monotheism frequently dominates the supernatural beliefs of many of the most primitive peoples, such as the Bushmen of South Africa, whose 'supreme being' takes the earthly form of a praying mantis.

MANITOU, a North American Indian belief in vaguely diffused supernatural powers operating throughout the universe. (See also MANA).

MANNHEIM, that part of Midgard (q.v.) which was inhabited by man, as distinct from Jotunnheim (q.v.) and Alfheim (q.v.).

MANNUS, according to Tacitus, *Mannus* was the eponymous ancestor of all the Germans, and may well have been the ancestral forebear of the Indo-European peoples, being recognized as such by the Indo-Aryans under the name of *Manu* (q.v.).

MANO, a term used by anthropologists studying American Indian cultures to refer to the upper stone used against a bowl-shaped 'metate' (q.v.). (2) the Gnostic Lord of Light, possibly derived from 'Manu' (q.v.).

MANOR, an early European community comprising a manor house, occupied by a family of noble descent, and a village community made up of craftsmen and farmers who are frequently tied to the land as serfs. Although the manorial system was typical of feudal Europe, it had many more ancient roots than has commonly been realized, and a quasi-feudal system appears to have existed in early Celtic, Teutonic, Homeric Greek and other Indo-European societies from one to two thousand years or more before the emergence of the Medieval feudal system.

MANTHRA, an Avestan term, cognate with the Indo-European *mantra* (q.v.). In the Zoroastrian religion *manthra* was the magical or sacred word by which the creation of the earth was accomplished.

MANTIC, a term used to refer to a form of magic which involved the manipulation of a supernatural being, as for example an attempt to secure the assistance of the devil by magical means. Such mantic activities may consequently be regarded as transitional between magic, representing techniques for the control of the supernatural, and religion, conceived of as the propitiation of supernatural beings whose powers are greater than those of men and who therefore cannot be controlled by magic.

MANTIS, PRAYING, the South African bushmen recognize the praying mantis as the earthly personification of their supreme deity, believing that it was a chthonic god sprung from the African soil that devoured its mate following the procreation of its offspring.

MANTRA, the Vedic (Indo-Aryan) term for any traditional hymn or prayer addressed to the gods.

MANTUS, the ancient Etruscan god of the dead.

MANU, (1) the mountain of the sunset from behind which the Egyptians believed that the sun god Ra rose daily at dawn. (2) the Indo-Aryan progenitor of the Aryan race, and author of the Laws of Manu. (See ARYAN RELIGION, MAN, MANNUS and VEDIC LITERATURE).

MANU, THE LAWS OF, an ancient Vedic text which purported to order the social, political and religious behavior of all Indo-Aryans. Regarded as the forefather of all the Aryan peoples, Manu (cognate with the Latin *mannus* and Germanic *man*) left strict instructions for the behavior of his descendants, obedience to which was implicit in Aryan ancestor-worship. The Code specifically called for the maintenance of ancestor-worshipping rituals and for a strict racial consciousness in the selection of wives and the perpetuation of the lineage. Because the Aryans who settled India found themselves in a land already thickly populated by diverse races, the Code of Manu expressly prohibited intermarriage with any of the Dasya or indigenous population, imposing severe punishments including self-castration and even death upon any non-Aryan who should attempt sexual relations with a caste Aryan.

MANUMISSION, a term derived from the Latin language and the Roman culture to refer to the act of freeing a slave. In Indo-European society, freed slaves did not immediately acquire the full tribal rights of freemen, but became members of a subordinate class known as freedmen, who retained certain obligations to their former masters.

MANUS, (1) the Roman term for the authority of a husband over his wife. Manus was strongly protective in nature, and by no means as complete as the *potestas* or power which the *pater familias* exercised over his children, slaves and other members of his household over all of whom he had the right of life and death. (2) a Melanesian (Malayo-Polynesian) people inhabiting the Admiralty Isles, mostly dependent on fishing but also rearing a few pigs.

MANYARG, a Mongolian people of Eastern Siberia.

MAO, an East African people of the Koman group, primarily dependent on horticulture but practicing some animal husbandry, hunting and fishing.

MAORI, a Southern Polynesian people who were the first men to settle New Zealand, primarily dependent on horticulture, hunting, food-gathering and fishing.

MAPA, a limestone cave north of Canton in China where a Neanderthal skull cap complete with one eye socket was found in 1958. The date is estimated vaguely at Middle or early Upper Pleistocene.

MAPUCHE, a South American Indian Araucanian-speaking people living in central Chile, dependent on agriculture, animal husbandry and some fishing and food-gathering.

MARABOUT, a Moslem hermit or saint.

MARACA, a West Indian musical instrument made from a gourd containing pebbles.

MARAE, a Polynesian ceremonial site, surrounded by a low wall. Only those of noble birth were allowed inside this wall, and although commoners were required to attend most of the ritual ceremonies, they were obliged to congregate outside the wall.

MÄRCHEN, a German diminutive of *mär* meaning legend, used to refer to fairy tales and folk stories.

MARDUK, the Babylonian deity whose worship was imposed upon all peoples within the Semitic-Chaldean Babylonian empire.

MARIANA ISLANDERS, a Micronesian people dependent on horticulture and fishing.

MARICOPA, a Yuman-speaking people whose language belongs to the Hokan family. Located on the Colorado river, the Maricopa were dependent on horticulture, fishing, hunting, and food-gathering.

MARIGOLD, a scented garden flower regarded as sacred by the Aztecs.

MARIMBA, a primitive wooden xylophone, found in both Southern Africa and Central America.

MARINDANIM, a Papuan people from the Gulf of Papua who depend mainly on horticulture, hunting, fishing and food-gathering.

MARKET ECONOMY, an economic system in which the problems of production, distribution, and consumption are decided by the free operation of the price mechanism.

MARMOSET, a small New World monkey, possessing claws instead of nails and a long non-prehensile tail. Marmosets do not live in groups, but instead mate with a single partner and raise their offspring jointly. The distinction between the marmoset 'family' and the true mammalian family lies in the absence of food-sharing between adult marmoset males and females, and consequently of any true division of labour.

MAROVANE, an ancient Egyptian instrument constructed from bamboo tubes using a resonator made of palm leaf.

MARQUESANS, an Eastern Polynesian people residing in the Marquesas Isles, mainly dependent on fishing and horticulture with some animal husbandry.

MARRIAGE, a socially recognized pair-bond between one or more males and one or more females.

MARRIAGE, COUSIN, possibly the most common mating practice known to mankind in pre-industrial societies is that of marriages between cross cousins, that is with the child of the father's sister or the mother's brother or parallel cousins, with the child of the father's brother or the mother's sister.

MARRIAGE, GROUP, based on the supposed evidence of baboon and certain other simian animal societies in which a group of males and a group of females (accompanied by their offspring) appeared to live promiscuously, some early social philosophers assumed that man's early ancestors (at a fully sapiens level) practised 'group marriage'. It is now known, by contrast, that the roots of the human family predate the evolution of man to sapiens status, and no true instances of human 'group marriage' have ever been authenticated, except in the case of experimental communes, where the practice invariably failed to persist for more than a short time. (See FAMILY).

MARRIAGE, PREFERENTIAL, marriage within a traditionally preferred category.

MARSHALL ISLANDERS, a Micronesian people dependent on horticulture and fishing.

MARSUPIALIA, a subclass of mammals found in North and South America and Australia, which includes the opossum, the kangaroo and the koala 'bear'. The young are nourished by a yolk sac contained in the egg, and are born at a very early state of development, after which they are sheltered in a pouch containing mammalian teats which secrete milk.

MASA, a Negroid, Niger-Congo-speaking people of the Adamawa-Eastern group, dependent mainly on horticulture and fishing, with some hunting and animal husbandry.

MASAI, a warlike East African Nilotic people, almost wholly dependent on cattle herding supplemented by a limited amount of hunting.

MAS D'AZIL, an archeological cave site located in the Ariege area of France. Excavated in 1959 the site revealed Magdalenian tools and a now famous set of Cro-Magnon cave paintings.

MASK, any cover made to be worn on the human face. Frequently executed with considerable artistic talent, masks are generally constructed for use in magico-religious rituals, during which the wearer assumes the symbolic role of a specific deity or supernatural spirit. They may also be worn as symbols of authority and prestige. Not only has the wearing of masks been common in Africa, Asia and America, but masks were also worn in religious rituals associated with the Old European civilization (q.v.). Romans used ancestral death masks, made from facial impressions taken at the time of death. These were worn by the living on solemn ceremonial occasions such as the burial of a newly deceased member of a family, the implication clearly being that the ancestral spirits were participating in the rituals.

MASQUERADE, any function in which the participants conceal their identities by masks and costumes.

MASSIM, a Melanesian people dependent on horticulture and fishing.

MASTABA, simple structures made from mudbrick, raised over the tombs of the early Egyptian Pharaohs of the First Dynasty. These became progressively larger, until they were eventually replaced by stone pyramids directly ancestral to the large pyramids of the 4th Dynasty (See PYRAMID).

MASTOID PROCESS, a bony projection appearing on the base of the skull the early Egyptian pharaohs of the First Dynasty. These became progressively larger, until they were eventually replaced by stone pyramids directly ancestral to the large pyramids of the 4th Dynasty. (See PYRAMID).

MATAKAM, a Chad-Sudanese-speaking people, occupying the Mandara highlands of Africa, who are dependent on horticulture with some animal husbandry.

MATAMBALA, a secret society in the Solomon Islands.

MATERNAL EFFECTS, the effects of the physiological condition of the mother on the developing fetus, independent of genetic factors.

MATHA, an ancient Sanskrit term used to refer to the stick with which the Brahmans created a new sacred fire by friction. The word may be cognate with the root of the Greek 'Prometheus', the name of the Greek hero who stole fire from the gods on Mount Olympus. The linguistic evidence is reinforced by the fact that the Greek prefix *pra-* implies the act of stealing by force.

MATRIARCHAL SOCIETY, theoretically a society in which power is vested in the matriarchs or senior women. In reality, it is difficult to find examples of such societies, even amongst matrilineal societies, in which names and property are inherited through the female line. Polyandrous societies are never matriarchal, women having a low social status in such societies, as among the Toda.

MATRILINEAL DESCENT, descent traced through the female line.

MATRILOCAL, a term used to describe the custom whereby a newly-married couple take up residence with the family of the wife's mother or kinship group. (See also AVUNCULOCAL, NEOLOCAL, and PATRILOCAL RESIDENCE).

MATRIONALIA, the Roman festival held in honour of Juno, the wife of Jupiter and the protectress of all married women.

MATTING, a sophisticated form of weaving in which more flexible materials are used than in basketry-making. Essentially matting may be regarded as an intermediate state in the evolution of cloth-weaving from basketry.

MAUE, a South American Indian people of Tupi speech, who live in Brazil, where they are dependent on horticulture, hunting, fishing and food-gathering.

MAUER, a site near Heidelberg in Germany where a jaw-bone, representing a hominid species known as Homo heidelbergensis was found. Although Homo heidelbergensis has frequently been classified as Homo erectus, it is now questionable whether true Homo erectus men ever lived in Europe. The jawbone is identified with the Günz-Mindel interglacial because of elephant bones and other fossil finds which were present in Europe at that time, and is now assigned an age of around 900,000 years B.P. (See also STEINHEIM).

MAUI, a Polynesian culture hero who was reputed to have introduced the use of fire to the earth, and to have raised islands from underneath the waters of the Pacific Ocean. An interesting parallel with Matha (q.v.).

MAU-MAU, a secret terrorist society, recruited from amongst the Kikiyu tribe of colonial Kenya, whose members were sworn by magical oaths to drive out the European settlers by killing and maiming Africans who worked for the Europeans and farm animals owned by the Europeans.

MAUPUK, the Eskimo name for the technique of killing seals by sitting in ambush for them beside breathing holes cut in the ice.

MAURYAN EMPIRE, a powerful and extensive empire founded by Chandragupta, a Bihari Aryan king, who succeeded in expelling the Greeks from India following the death of Alexander the Great towards the end of the 4th century B.C. From his capital near modern Patna, Chandragupta and his descendants were able to expand their power over a large part of India, excluding the mountains and forests and swamp regions where the more aboriginal peoples mostly retained their freedom. Chandragupta's grandson, Ashoka, became a convert to Buddhism (q.v.) and attempted to introduce Buddhism as the official religion of the Mauryan empire, but both Buddhism and the Mauryan dynasty eventually declined as a result of a reaction by the ancient Aryan Brahman caste against Buddhist influences.

MAUSOLEUM, any above-ground structure intended to serve as the last resting place of a corpse. The term derives from the tomb of Mausolus, built in 350 B.C. in Asia Minor.

MAXILLA, the upper jawbone.

MAYAHUEL, Axtec goddess of *pulque,* the intoxicating drink, and of drunkenness.
MAYAN LANGUAGES, the Mayan linguistic family is a member of the Penutian phylum and includes Yucatec Mayan, Huastec, Quiche, Pokomam, and Cholan.
MAYANS, a Neolithic cultivating people, who achieved a degree of civilization in the lowland jungles of Yucatan and neighboring Honduras. The Mayan language belongs to the Penutian family which includes a group of Californian languages and also Tsimshian. The foundations of the Mayan culture were laid in what is called the Pre-Classic period and appear to have been stimulated by contact with the Olmecs, so that by 200 B.C. ceremonial pyramids were being built throughout the Mayan area. The famous ceremonial site at Tikal dates from approximately 298 B.C., and from then onwards it is customary to speak of the Classic Mayan civilization. The Mayan civilization was exceptional, however, in its almost total absence of urban centers, since the Neolithic peasantry continued to reside in small clan-centered villages, whose members cultivated small clearings in the forest with hand hoes. Nevertheless their nobility lived an elegant life, and a sophisticated priesthood managed elaborate ceremonies in the temples constructed on the tops of stone pyramids. Religion governed the entire routine of the daily and seasonal life of the people, a primitive form of hieroglyphic writing was developed and an elaborate calendar was devised, the activities of one class of priests being devoted to the astronomical observations of the heavenly bodies. Blood sacrifice played an important role in Mayan religion, but the greatest achievement which has survived until today is the massive religious architecture and the flamboyant, deeply-carved sculptures which decorated all ceremonial buildings. The highest level of esthetic development was reached in the Late Classic period, cir. A.D. 600-900. It was during this period that Chichén Itzá and Uxmal were constructed. Following A.D. 900, however, the Mayan civilization suffered a steady decay in what is known as the Post-Classic Period. The power of the Toltecs in the nearby Mexican highlands increased, and much of Yucatan fell under Toltec (q.v.) and subsequent Aztec (q.v.) control before the Spaniards arrived in 1541.
MAYATAN, one of the few cities to develop in the Mayan civilization, rising in importance during the Post-Classic Period. Although the quality of construction was generally poor, Mayatan contained some 3000 houses. Following the fall of Chichén Itzá to the Toltecs around A.D. 200, it assumed the leadership of the Mayan culture, until it was destroyed around A.D. 415.
MAZDAISM, see ZOROASTRIAN RELIGION.
MAZDAKISM, a politico-religious cult which appeared in Persia in the 5th century B.C. at a time when the Persian empire was in a state of decadence. Following the example of Manicheism, Mazdak, the founder of Mazdakism, carried the revolt against Zoroastrianism still further, and preached a philosophy of complete economic and sexual communism. An intellectual precursor of Karl Marx, via the Jewish literary, Philosophical and scholastic traditions which kept alive so much of the ancient cultures of the Middle East, Mazdak converted the ideas of Manicheism into an effective political, social and revolutionary movement. Claiming that all pain, strife and animosity arose from selfish desires for wealth and pleasure, he condemned private property as well as family and marriage ties. Since his teachings not only offended the mores of Zoroastrian religion, which were strongly rooted in the concept of familism, and also threatened to challenge the entire social and political structure of the Persian state Mazdakism was suppressed and Mazdak himself was eventually murdered by one of his followers.
MBALA, a Bantu-speaking Negroid people living in the lower Congo, largely dependent on horticulture, some domestication of animals and hunting.
MBANJE, a plant smoked by certain Bantu peoples as a protection against the forces of evil.
MBORI, the name of the Azande supreme deity.
MBUGWE, a Bantu-speaking Negroid people of the Rift group, largely de-

pendent on horticulture and animal husbandry.

MBUM, a Negroid Niger-Congo-speaking people from Western Angola, largely dependent on horticulture with some herding of animals and hunting.

MBUTI, a pygmy people living in the Congo forests, largely dependent on hunting and gathering.

MDOKI, an evil spirit whose existence is recognized by several Congo tribes.

MEAD, an intoxicating liquor produced by the fermentation of honey diluted with water. Mead was used as a ritual drink by the Teutonic peoples and was reported to be the customary beverage of the gods.

MEAL, SACRAMENTAL, a ritual meal in which those who participate are believed to consume (at least symbolically) a portion of the god whom they worship. The sacramental meal appears to derive from early totemic cults, in which the participants consumed the flesh of the totemic animal in a sacramental feast. Christianity continued the tradition of the sacramental meal in the ritual of 'holy communion', at which the worshippers symbolically partake of the body and blood of the sacrificed god-king.

MEANDER, a decorative design comprising one or more continuously twisting lines, following a curving, spiral, or sometimes a rectangular fashion.

MECHTA EL ARBI, a site in Algeria, excavated 1907-27, which revealed artifacts belonging to the Upper Capsian industry, dating around 8000 B.C.

MEDES, the Medes were, with the Persians, one of two major groups of Indo-European speaking Iranians who probably entered Iran during the 10th century B.C. While the Persians occupied southwestern Iran, the Medes settled the northwest and achieved considerable power between the 8th and 6th centuries B.C. After successfully challenging and destroying the power of Assyria in 612 B.C., they subsequently became subordinate to the Persian Achaemenid Dynasty, but preserved their independent identity by continuing in their old endogamous ways, until the ultimate Arab conquest of Iran and the enforced Islamization of all who survived this conquest.

MEDICINE, the art of curing diseases, healing wounds and alleviating pain. In most simpler societies medical techniques depend upon magical formulae and the utilization of herbs, a few of which may be scientifically efficacious, but most of which often have no practical value. Although an Egyptian papyrus dating from around 2000 B.C., describes early Egyptian medical techniques and reveals a considerable knowledge not only of the working of the human body, but also of techniques such as surgical stitching to close wounds, possibly the earliest known evidence of medical surgery dates from the Neanderthal age, when stone knives were used to remove bone fragments of the scalp, after fractures had occurred in combat or by accident. Although the fossil evidence suggests that most patients died during or shortly after this operation, a few fossils reveal a considerable growth of new bone, indicating that the patient lived for a number of years following the completion of the operation.

MEDICINE MAN, a term used to refer to experts in the supernatural who use their powers to benefit other members of their society, frequently for personal reward. In particular the term has been applied to a class of shamans (q.v.) in North American Indian societies, who underwent a degree of professional training as members of a secret society. Recruits were usually selected from families traditionally believed to possess inherited magico-religious powers.

MEDITERRANEAN LOCAL RACE, a division of the Caucasoid geographical race characterized by dolichocephalic heads, narrow noses, dark wavy hair, dark eyes and relatively light body build. Some physical anthropologists have attempted to trace the ancestors of the Atlanto-Mediterranean peoples back to the Galley Hill and Combe Capelle Cro-Magnons of the Upper Paleolithic, but the present evidence is inadequate to substantiate these claims. Some evidence of the old Atlanto-Mediterranean local race is still apparent in the genetic composition of the present-day population of Ireland, Scotland and Wales, but the classic Mediterranean population is today best represented by the Spaniards, Italians, Arabs, Berbers and Egyptians, although many of these people, especially the Arabs, Berbers and Egyptians are substantially admixed with Negroid and/or other elements. The ancient Semites, like the early Sumerians and the major part of the Indus Valley population were also Mediterranean in type, but influences from an Armenoid subrace, characterized by large, hooked noses, are apparent in later Sumeria and in many parts of the modern Near East, as well as among the East European Jews.

MEGALITHIC CULTURE, a term used to refer to a variety of West European cultivating societies of the late Neolithic, whose members constructed monuments comprising large standing stones. These include menhirs, stone chambers and alignments, circles, and a variety of henge (q.v.) ceremonial centers as well as chamber tombs.

MEGANTHROPUS PALAEOJAVANICUS, the name given to fragments of a fossil mandible found in Java by von Koenigswald in 1941, which reveal some similarities to those of the pre-Zinjanthropus mandible found at Olduvai Gorge. Sufficient evidence is not available to permit classification of the fossil as either Australopithecus or Homo erectus. Meganthropus is otherwise known as the ancient 'Java ape man'.

MEGARON, a classical Greek architectural design comprising a large rectangular hall entered by way of a covered frontal porch, the roof of which was generally supported by pillars. In domestic buildings the main hall usually contained a central hearth, sacred to the occupants as a symbol of the ancestral spirits, or in religious temples the central position might be occupied by an anthropomorphic image of a deity. The earliest Megaron style buildings are found in the Greek Sesklo culture, a part of the Old European Civilization (q.v.) of the Helladic and Homeric Greek period. These formed a nucleus for the palaces of the Achaean nobility, who surrounded the central hall by a range of private rooms which were allocated to the married sons of the head of the family. Honoured guests slept in the main hall, less distinguished visitors being accommodated on the entrance porch.

MEIOSIS, cellular reproduction by 'reduction division', involving duplication of chromosomes which differs from mitosis (q.v.) in that each daughter cell receives only a single set of unpaired chromosomes (see Haploid). This is the essential process in sexual reproduction which permits a new independent assortment of genes to arise.

MEKE, a Fijian dance in which both sexes participate.

MEKEO, a Papuan people from Southeast New Guinea, who augment horticulture with hunting, food-gathering and some animal husbandry.

MELANESIA, the islands surrounding New Guinea, notably New Britain, New Ireland, the Solomons, the New Hebrides, New Caledonia, Fiji, the Santa Cruz and the Admiralty Islands.

MELANESIANS, a distinctive people, who appear to represent a combination of Australoid, Negrito and Malayo-Polynesian genetic elements. In appearance they are generally dolichocephalic, but reveal a considerable prognathism, with broad noses. Their skin and eyes are dark brown in colour and their hair is black. In general, the Melanesians speak languages which have been classified as Malayo-Polynesian. The Massim region contains the Trobrianders and Dobuans; Western Melanesia contains the Manus, Lasu and Lakalai of the Bismarck archipelago; the Solomon Isles contain the Buka, Kaoka, Ulawans and Choiseulese; the Santa Cruz Islands include the Mota and Seniang; while Eastern Melanesia includes the Fijians and Rotumans.

MELANIN, an element of pigment present in the lower layers of the epidermis as well as in the eyes and the hair, which provides protection against certain components of the sun's rays. Although the ability to manufacture melanin is inherited and consequently varies substantially from race to race, all individuals of all races (except in albinism q.v.) can usually manufacture some additional pigmentation when exposed to heavy sunshine over protracted periods of time.

MELON, the melon was probably first cultivated in the Indus Valley region, since it appears to be native to southern Asia, but it is today also widely cultivated in Africa.

MEMPHIS, one of the major cities of ancient Lower Egypt, situated at the head of the Nile delta. During certain dynasties it served as the seat of the Pharaoh and consequently was the capital of the whole of Egypt. As a result Memphis became the site of a number of palaces, temples, and cemeteries, including the famous Pyramids and the Sphinx of Giza.
MENANGKABAU, a Malayo-Polynesian Batak people of Sumatra.
MENARCHE, the commencement of menstrual periods in human females.
MENDE, a Mande-speaking Negroid people of West Africa, largely dependent on horticulture with some hunting.
MENDELIAN GENETICS, the basis of modern genetic theory was developed by Gregor Mendel, a German monk in the monastery at Brünn (now Brno in Moravia) who carried out a series of experiments with the cultivation of peas and discovered that the specific characteristics of any organism tended to be inherited in pairs, and that individuals were not necessarily homozygous (possessing similar genes) for the same characteristics. When an individual organism inherits heterozygous (unlike) genes, one gene is frequently 'dominant', the other being 'recessive', in which case the characteristic or trait implied by the dominant gene will be that which reveals itself in the 'genotype' – that is to say in the individual's own physical makeup. However in sexual reproduction each parent organism gives only one of each pair of its genes to any particular offspring, and the offspring might inherit either the dominant or the recessive gene from a heterozygous parent, and may therefore in fact inherit two recessive genes from heterozygous parents, one from each parent. If homozygous for the recessive gene this gene must necessarily shape the genotype or outward characteristics of the offspring which may be different from both the heterozygous parents. Parents which are both homozygous for the same characteristics will therefore necessarily 'breed true', i.e. their offspring will resemble them in their features. However, if two organisms manifesting the same dominant and recessive traits are heterozygous for both traits, then by a random assortment 50% of their offspring are likely to be heterozygous, carrying both the dominant and the recessive genes (and will themselves be shaped genotypically by the dominant gene), 25% are likely to be homozygous for the dominant trait (and will therefore also be shaped genotypically by the dominant gene) and 25% are likely to be homozygous for the recessive trait (thus being shaped genotypically by the recessive trait). Remarkably, despite violent reaction against Darwin's revelation of evolution, Mendel's discovery, so significant to the proper understanding of evolutionary development, passed unnoticed in 1866. It was not until the turn of the century that three other scientists, one English, another Dutch and a third Austrian, each independently announced the same genetic principles already determined by Mendel, quite unaware of his prior discovery, that his research gained the attention it deserved.
MENDELIAN POPULATION, a population which customarily inbreeds among its own members and only occasionally outbreeds with neighboring populations.
MENEHUNE, a legendary people of short stature, traditionally believed to have occupied Polynesia before the arrival of the Polynesians. The legend of the Menehune probably refers to the Negrito peoples who occupied Indonesia and much of Melanesia before the arrival of the Malayo-Polynesians, but who are unlikely to have reached the Polynesian islands.
MENES, according to Greek tradition, Menes was the name of the Pharaoh who united Egypt and founded the first dynasty in 3200 B.C. The correct Egyptian name was more probably *Narner,* the Greeks confusing this name with *Menes* in view of the widespread Indo-European belief in an eponymous culture hero of this name, as reflected in the Germanic *Mannus,* Hindu *Manu,* and the Greek Menelaos.
MENHIR, a large solitary standing stone belonging to the Megalithic period, commonly found in Ireland and southwestern England and Brittany. Although most Megalithic monuments date from the Neolithic, many Menhirs have been found to be associated with the Beaker people of the Middle or Late Bronze Age.

MENOMINI, Central Algonquin North American Indians dependent on hunting and horticulture with some fishing and food-gathering.
MENSTRUAL CYCLE, a modification of the oestrous cycle peculiar to catarrhine primates, by which sudden destruction of the mucosa of the uterus produces bleeding.
MENSTRUATION, the periodic discharge from the human female of an unfertilized ovum together with accompanying material. Since this discharge usually occurs monthly and is accompanied by a certain amount of blood, many primitive peoples have attached considerable significance to the event, regarding women as ritually unclean at such times, and prohibiting sexual intercourse or participation in religious rituals during this period. Many American Indians actually isolated their womenfolk at the time of menstruation.
MENTAL PROMINENCE, a biological term referring to the protrusion of the chin or frontal portion of the lower jawbone which is particularly marked in certain races of man. This term should not be confused with the idea of intellectual prominence.
MENTAWEIANS, a Malayo-Polynesian-speaking people inhabiting the offshore Sumatra Islands, the Mentaweians are largely dependent on cultivation with some animal husbandry and fishing.
MEO, see MIAO.
MERBOK, an extensive system involving the exchange of ritual gifts between related bands of Australian aboriginals, which, like the gifts presented by those participating in the 'kula ring' (q.v.), may travel in a circular fashion over hundreds of miles ultimately returning to the original owners. As with the ceremonial gifts involved in the kula ring, such ritual objects are given as a proof of friendship.
MERCIA, an Anglican kingdom located in Central England which rose to considerable prominence during the 7th and 8th centuries A.D., but subsequently succumbed to pressures from the Saxon Kingdom of Wessex and invading Danish Vikings from across the North Sea.
MERE, a Maori club or sword, equipped with a cutting edge made from sharp stones inserted into a wooden haft. The Aztec warriors of Central America carried similar Stone Age weapons, except that the Maori 'mere' was primarily used for thrusting, while the Aztec weapon was designed for both cutting and thrusting.
MERI, an ancient god of Punt, later introduced into the Egyptian pantheon.
MERINA, a Malayo-Polynesian people of Madagascar, dependent on agriculture, animal husbandry and fishing.
MERISSA, a form of beer made from fermented grain, widely manufactured and consumed in Sub-Saharan Africa.
MERLIADTA, a ritual fire-walking ceremony, required as a rite of passage (q.v.) by adolescent boys.
MERMAID, a mythological female creature who inhabits the sea, possessing human form above the waist, but the form of a fish from the waist downwards. The existence of Mermen has also been cited.
MERU, (1) a Bantu-speaking Negroid people of the Kenya highlands, largely dependent on horticulture, hunting and fishing. (2) the Vedic designation for the Land of Bliss or Paradise.
MESA, a flat-topped hill with a horizontally stratified rock formation which stands out sharply above lower lying land.
MESAKIN, a Kordofanian-speaking (Niger-Congo) people of the Nuba group, largely dependent on horticulture, animal husbandry and some hunting.
MESA VERDE, a cliff-dwelling site in Arizona, where a large number of houses have been carved into the cliffs on the face of the mesa by Indians of the Anasazi culture. Many of the rooms possessed floors and roofs of timber, and walls faced with adobe.
MESCALERO, Athabascan-speaking North American Apache Indians, dependent on food-gathering and hunting with some horticulture and fishing.
MESCALINE, an intoxicating drug extracted from the Peyote cactus (q.v.).

MESOCEPHALIC, possessing a skull of medium width, that is, in which the width is 76 to 80.9 percent of the length;

MESOLITHIC, a term referring to the transitional period between the Upper Paleolithic and the Neolithic. Today it is customary to regard the Mesolithic as merely a later stage of the Upper Paleolithic involving certain changes in the style of life in Europe following the withdrawal of the Würm Glaciation as the subarctic conditions gave way to a more temperate climate with resultant changes in the flora and fauna. Thus the effects of the Mesolithic are more obvious in Northern Europe than in Southern Europe or the Middle East, where the transition from the Upper Paleolithic to the Neolithic is more abrupt. In particular the North European Mesolithic is associated with a decline in big game hunting and increase in the number of settled communities dependent on fishing as a style of life.

MESOMORPH, a person lacking either ectomorphic or endomorphic characteristics, that is to say a person who is neither thin nor plump in body build.

MESOZOIC, the era of 'middle life' characterized by large reptiles and the appearance of flowering plants and mammals, circa 225 and 65 million years B.P. ago, respectively.

MESSIANISM (also MILLENARIANISM), a cultic religious movement built around the belief that some mythical ethnic hero will return to earth to 'save' the people from current misfortunes.

MESTIZO, a word of Spanish origin indicating a person of mixed Caucasian and American Indian descent.

METABOLISM, the chemical life processes that occur within a living organism, by which autotrophs build up organic compounds from external non-organic sources such as sunlight, and allotrophs break down complex organic substances to secure energy.

METAPHASE, that stage in the process of cell-division in which the equators of the chromosomes arrange themselves on separate spindles. The metaphase succeeds the prophase (q.v.) and precedes the anaphase (q.v.).

METATE, the term used by American archeologists to refer to the stone slab on which maize was ground. In effect a metate was the equivalent of the European quern stone. (See also MANO).

METATHERIA, a mammalian sub-class represented by the kangaroo, wombat, wallaby, and koala 'bear' of Australia and the more widely distributed opossum. The females produce eggs with small yolks, but retain these in their own bodies for a brief period of 'pregnancy'. The offspring are still immature at birth, following which they are carried in an abdominal pouch and fed from teats.

METAZOA, multicellular life forms in which some specialization or division of labor has developed between the member cells. Porifera, or sponges, are not usually regarded as Metazoa, but are described instead as Colonial Protozoa.

METEMPSYCHOSIS, the belief that the human soul will be reborn after death in the body of another person or even in an animal. The doctrine of metempsychosis was widespread among the ancient Egyptians and is still adhered to by orthodox Hindus in India; but interestingly enough is also reflected in the teachings of Pythagoras and Plato.

MIAMI, Central Algonquin North American Indians, dependent on hunting and horticulture with some fishing and food-gathering.

MIAO, a non-Chinese aboriginal people, calling themselves the Hmao Yünnan in the Kweichow province in China, and Meo in Thailand and Laos. Their language appears to be affiliated to the Mon-Khmer languages, and they survive in isolated groups surrounded by immigrant Sinitic speakers.

MICHELSBERG CULTURE, a Neolithic agricultural complex extending from Belgium across Northern France and the Rhineland, to include Northwestern Switzerland. To some extent it represented a combination of culture traits reflecting both the Danubian Culture and the First Northern Culture, as well as aspects of the Western Neolithic traditions as reflected in the British Windmill Hill culture. Some elements of class stratification have been detected, with village chieftains receiving slightly more impressive burials.

MICMAC, a maritime Algonquin people of the Cree group, primarily dependent on fishing and hunting with some food-gathering.
MICROEVOLUTION, a term sometimes used to refer to the small changes in gene frequency which occur within a Mendelian Population (q.v.) from generation to generation. When subject to natural selection (q.v.) continued microevolution may result in major evolutionary changes.
MICROLITHS, extremely small stone tools usually comprising either blades or flakes. Many microliths occur in geometrical shapes being set into shafts of wood, bone or possibly antler to serve as barbs or as tips for the arrows. Microliths are particularly characteristic of the European Mesolithic.
MICRONESIANS, a Malayo-Polynesian people, with some Negrito admixture, who are sometimes divided into the Western Micronesians of the West Carolines and the Marianas, including the Yapese, the Palauans, and Chamorro; the Central Micronesians of the Eastern Caroline Islands, including the Trukese, the Ponapeans, Kusaians, Woleaians and Lamotrek; and the Eastern Micronesians of the Gilbert and Marshall Islands, including the Makin, Naurans, and Majuro.
MICROPHAGOUS, a term given to animals, such as barnacles, which live on very minute particles of food and are consequently obliged to feed continuously.
MID-BRAIN, otherwise known as the mesencephalon, the mid-brain is the central section of the three main divisions of the vertebrate brain. It is particularly concerned with the functions of sight and hearing.
MILK TEETH, see TEETH DECIDUOUS.
MILLENARIANISM, see MESSIANISM.
MILLET, the first cultivated millet is recorded in Mesopotamia, from whence its cultivation spread to Neolithic Europe and possibly also to Africa, India and China. A distinctive variety of millet also formed an important part of the diet of the people of Mexico as early as 6500 B.C. being at that time collected from wild plants, becoming deliberately cultivated only at a later date.
MILPA, a term used in American archeology to refer to a maize field which was cultivated for several years until the soil was exhausted, when it was abandoned and fresh land was cleared and planted.
MIMETIC, the practice of mimicking other species, as for example when a bird copies the cries of other birds, or even of human beings and mammals.
MIMETIC MAGIC, see MAGIC, CONTAGIOUS.
MIMICRY, the tendency for one species to develop a protective resemblance to another more dangerous or more poisonous species. Organisms which acquire the distinctive markings or behavior of a more dangerous species thereby improve their own survival chances, predators being less likely to attack them because of the similarity of their appearance with that of the more dangerous species.
MIMIR, the Norse God of wisdom, who drank from the waters of the sacred well located at the foot of the world ash, Yggdrasil (q.v.) or 'tree of life', and thereby gained complete knowledge.
MIMKA, a Papuan-speaking people of West Papua who depend mainly on horticulture, hunting, fishing and food-gathering.
MIN, an ancient South Chinese people, dependent on agriculture and animal husbandry – originally immigrants from Northern China who mingled to some extent with the aboriginal occupants, leaving isolated aboriginal groups in control of many of the more remote mountain valleys.
MINAHASA, a Malayo-Polynesian people of Celebes.
MINANGKABAU, a Malayo-Polynesian-speaking people of Sumatra, largely dependent on cultivation with some animal husbandry and fishing.
MINCHIA, otherwise known as the Pai in their own language, the Minchia are a non-Chinese people indigenous to Yünnan province who depend mainly on rice-cultivation, some animal husbandry and a little fishing. Their language however, belongs to the Tibeto-Burman division of the Sinitic family of languages.
MINDEL, the second of four major Alpine glaciations of the Pleistocene.
MINDEL GLACIATION, the second of the major Alpine glaciations of the Pleistocene, dated around 800,000 to 700,000 B.P.

MINERVA, the Latin goddess who presided over all craftsmen and was worshipped by the members of the craftsmen's guilds.
MINIANKA, a Negroid West African Voltaic people, largely dependent on horticulture with some food-gathering and animal husbandry.
MINISCULE, a form of writing which developed in Europe around the 9th century B.C., involving the use of lower scale letters which came to be known as miniscule writing.
MINOANS, a term coined by the archeologist Sir Arthur Evans (who derived it from the name of King Minos, the legendary ruler of Knossos), to refer to the people of Bronze Age Crete. The roots of the Cretan or Minoan culture are to be found in the Old European civilization (q.v.) which flourished in the Balkans and Aegean isles, Crete being marginal to that area. However, early in the 3rd century B.C., the cultural horizons of the Minoans began to extend rapidly, largely as a result of the establishment of trading connections with other Eastern Mediterranean centers. At that time, known as the Middle Minoan period, a number of substantial but politically independent towns appeared, each with its own priest-king and palace. An examination of the three major palaces in Crete, Knossos, Phaistos, and Mallia reveals that the kings were not only political and religious leaders, but were also merchant princes, their palaces containing chambers for the storage of large quantitities of merchandise. Crete acquired a large fleet of trading ships, all of which had to be armed as a defense against piracy, and these provided the island of Crete with considerable security. In addition to merchandising the produce of other Mediterranean cities, the Minoans exported Cretan olive oil in large quantities, packaged in attractively painted jars. In return for exporting olive oil, raw materials such as copper, tin, silver and gold were imported, and Cretan craftsmen manufactured a wide variety of ornaments and equipment from these valuable products. Both men and women adorned themselves with lavish quantities of exquisite jewelry, and while the younger Minoans and persons of lower class wore only a brief loincloth, attached to the waist by a belt, the men of the upper classes attired themselves in a loose gown similar to the Roman toga, their womenfolk wearing highheeled shoes, blouses, skirts and stylish hats. (See KNOSSOS and PHAISTOS).
MINYAN WARE, a high-quality, yellowish-grey form of pottery, made on a potter's wheel, which first appears in Greece and in the ruins of Troy IV at the beginning of the Helladic period, around the 19th and 20th century B.C. Minyan Ware appears to be associated with the arrival of the first Greeks in the Aegean area, and is directly ancestral to the pottery of the Mycenean civilization which evolved out of the Helladic at the end of the 2nd millennium B.C.
MIOCENE, a period in the Cenozoic, extending from 26 to 12 million years ago, during which substantial hominid evolution took place.
MIR, a traditional pattern of village government in Russia, under which all property and all wealth produced was deemed to belong to the villagers as a whole. This late survival of the collective kin-group, sharing the means of subsistence, was destroyed following the introduction of the communist 'çollective farm', which, though superficially parallel in concept, ignored kinship ties – moving families from one collective to another to suit production needs – and deprived the villagers of effective ownership rights by placing their operations under the control of distant urban bureaucrats.
MIRIAM, a Papuan people, inhabiting the Gulf of Papua, who depend mainly on horticulture with fishing and some animal husbandry.
MISCEGENATION, cross-breeding between the members of two normally distinctively separate breeding populations.
MISKITO, a Central American Indian people, speaking a Chibchan language of the Misumalpan group in Eastern Nicaragua, dependent on food-gathering, hunting, fishing and some horticulture and animal husbandry. (Also known as Moskito and Mosquito.)
MISSING LINK, after Darwin first drew attention to the evolutionary origin of the living hominids from earlier primitive forms of life, and in particular showed them to have shared ancestors common to living apes, fierce opposition

from Christian theologians sought to emphasize the absence of fossil evidence for the existence of any species intermediate between the apes and man. This presumed gap in the fossil evidence linking man to apes was popularly referred to as the 'Missing Link', and used as an argument to confound the supporters of Darwinian evolution. However, since the mid-19th century, a profuse supply of 'Missing Links' or fossil evidence of life forms intermediate between the living apes and men has been uncovered.

MISSISSIPPI CULTURE, an American Indian culture which emerged around A.D. 700 and lasted until the arrival of Europeans. The influence of Mexican and Woodland cultural traditions is apparent, although the Mississippi culture has its own distinctive elaborate pottery, and distinctive fortified villages with ceremonial centers, usually erected on raised platforms.

MITANNI, a people who established a kingdom in Northern Mesopotamia, in the foothills which divide the Tigris and Euphrates rivers. Arriving from the north in the 16th century B.C., they appear to have comprised a mainly Hurrian population, led by a ruling Aryan aristocracy. It has been established that the gods worshipped by the Mitanni nobility were analogous to those of the Aryans who settled India. However, the Mitannian kingdom was short-lived, being absorbed into the Hittite empire around 1370 B.C.

MITGARD, the home of man in Norse mythology, literally 'the middle garden'.

MITHRA, an ancient Indo-Iranian deity, mentioned in the Vedic hymns as one of the sons of Vishnu and Aditya, who was regarded as one of the guardian gods of the different months of the year. Among the Iranians he became the symbol of the Heavenly Light, and eventually emerged as the chief god, or Ahura, in the Zend culture. Following the Zoroastrian revolution, Mithra was supplanted by Ahura Mazda, his status being reduced to one of Ahura Mazda's aides, whose duty it was to assist in saving men from the forces of evil. During the Hellenistic and Roman period, however, a new cult of Mithraism developed which portrayed Mithra as a warrior god who led the forces of goodness in the perpetual war against Ahriman, the spirit of evil. Admitting only male initiates, Mithraism spread rapidly among the Roman legions in the 2nd century A.D. following the decline of Roman patrician power and the traditional Roman religion. Preserving the Zoroastrian reverence for cattle, but under the influence of prevailing Middle Eastern mystery cults, initiation into the Mithraic cult involved purification by flagellation, followed by baptism in the blood of a sacrificed bull. For a time the Mithraic religion rivalled Christianity for the control of the Mediterranean world, but was suppressed throughout the empire when the later Roman emperors accepted Christianity as their official religion.

MITLA, an archeological site 25 miles southwest of Oaxaca in Mexico. Originally a part of the Monte Alban civilization, its foundation appears around 600 B.C., but the site was later abandoned until the 8th century A.D., after which a new fortified town was constructed by the Zapotecs complete with pyramids. Considerable Mixtec influence is apparent, but the Spanish conquistadores reported that Mitla was the major ceremonial site of the Zapotec people, and the town presumably escaped Mixtec domination.

MITOSIS, the normal process by which the nucleus of a cell divides into two parts as a necessary preliminary to the separation of the cell into two independent cells. In mitosis each chromosome duplicates itself so that the daughter nuclei normally inherit an identical complement of chromosomes and consequently share matching genes. However, the process does not always take place without complications, and on rare occasions the resultant nuclei may contain an imbalance of genetic components. The process of mitosis is divided into a series of successive stages known as the 'interphase', 'prophase', 'metaphase', 'anaphase', and 'teleophase' (q.v.).

MIWOK, a North American, Californian Indian people.

MIXCOATL, an Aztec god of the stars and lightning, sometimes referred to as 'the cloud serpent' and also regarded as the originator of fire.

MIXE, a Central American people speaking a Mixteco-Zapotecan language,

primarily dependent on agriculture and some hunting.
MIXED FARMING, a pattern of subsistence combining the cultivation of crops and production of food from domesticated animals.
MIXTEC, the Mixtec appear towards the end of the 7th century A.D. as immigrants infiltrating into Zapotec territory, occupying much of the Valley of Oaxaca and the city of Monte Alban (q.v.). Well known for their craftsmanship in stone carving, painting and metal work, the Mixtec produced art which had an important influence in the development of Aztec art, and in fact Mixtec craftsmen may have been responsible for much of the Aztec artwork and architecture after they were conquered by the Aztecs. Only a small number of Mixtecs remained independent of the Aztecs at the time of arrival of the Spanish conquistadores. The Mixtec language was related to Zapotec.
MJOLLNIR, the name of the sacred hammer or axe of the Norse god Thor.
MNONG GAR, a Cambodian Mon-Khmer-speaking people, traditionally dependent on agriculture, animal husbandry and fishing with some food-gathering.
MOBILITY, SOCIAL, the ability of the individual to change his situs in the social matrix, usually implying vertical social mobility, that is, the ability to move up or down the class structure. (See also CLASS, SOCIAL).
MOCHICA (also MOCHE), one of the early Peruvian cultures, distinguished by large temple platforms made from mud bricks and by the distinctive painted pottery often shaped in the form of human heads. Mochica culture existed as an independent but a distinctive entity from around the first century A.D. until the 7th century A.D., when it was absorbed into the Huari (q.v.) culture.
MODIFYING GENES, minor genes which serve to modify the expression of major genes in the phenotype.
MODOC, a North American Indian people, of Southern Oregon and Northern California, who speak a language classified as Penutian, within the Sahaptin group, and are dependent upon food-gathering, hunting and fishing.
MOGH, a Horticultural Mongoloid people who speak a Tibeto-Burman language and live in the Chittagong hill tracts of Bangla Desh.
MOGOLLON, a Cochise version of the desert culture which first appeared in Southeastern Arizona and Southwestern New Mexico around 100 B.C., and survived until the 14th century A.D. The Mogollons were horticulturalists who lived in pit-houses until around A.D. 1000, when under the influence of the Anasazi (q.v.) they began to construct pueblo villages and to produce high quality pottery decorated with stylized animals in black on white backgrounds.
MOGHULS, a former branch of the Altaic-speaking Mongol peoples of Central Asia, who invaded Afghanistan and India and established themselves as the ruling dynasty of the Moghul Empire.
MOHAMMEDANISM, one of the major 'missionary' religions of the world, which first arose amongst the Semitic peoples of Arabia. Strongly monotheistic in character, the peoples of Mohammedan, Moslem, Muslim, or Islamic faith derive their beliefs from the teachings of Mohammed, whom they regard as the most recent of god's prophets and therefore the most accurate. Their religion owes much to Christianity and Judaism, and something to the old pagan Arabic beliefs, though most of the latter were strongly condemned. Mohammedanism teaches that Allah, the one god, is all powerful, and determines all events, and that his word is law.
MOHAVE, a Yuman-speaking people whose language belongs to the Hokan family. Located on the Colorado river, they are dependent upon horticulture.
MOHAWK, a North American, Iroquois Indian, East Woodlands people.
MOHENJO-DARO, one of the major cities of the Indus Valley civilization (q.v.), situated some 400 miles down the Indus river from Harappa, another major Indus Valley city. The lowest levels have not been excavated, because of the relatively high water table, so that the origin of the city and early development have not been traced. However, the levels that have been excavated date from between 2300 to about 1750 B.C. A marked pattern of social stratification is obvious from the fact that substantial areas of the city were occupied by small and poorly contructed residences. To the west side of the city a citadel

stood on raised ground, protected by baked mud brick walls. This contained the usual Great Bath, a granary, an assembly hall, and rows of single rooms suggestive of a college or monastic type of institution. Unfortunately the Indus Valley script has not been deciphered and the only evidence that we have of the culture of the Mohenjo-daro and the Indus Valley civilization is that which can be derived from the interpretation of the archeological evidence. One statue has been interpreted as being that of a 'priest-king' but this is only a relatively uninformed guess. The upper levels of excavation indicate very distinctive evidence of substantial cultural decay before the final collapse of the city, poorly constructed huts being raised over the foundations of what had previously been much more elaborate, larger, better-constructed buildings. The end of Mohenjo-daro came with a military defeat, evidenced by large numbers of unburied skeletons found lying in the streets and houses, the skeletons showing clear indications of a violent death, with an occasional broken weapon as additional evidence. It is possible, but not yet generally accepted, that Mohenjo-daro, like many other Indus Valley cities, finally fell victim to the onslaught of the invading Indo-Aryan peoples. Certainly, ample military references in the Vedic literature of the Indo-Aryans refer to the storming of walled cities, and no other walled cities have been identified in India, prior to the arrival of the Indo-Aryans, other than those of the Indus Valley civilization.

MOI, an isolated aboriginal people of Southeast Asia.

MOIETY, a major kinship grouping, usually exogamous, which arises when a tribe is divided into two parts.

MOIRAE, the Greek sisters of fate. The Indo-Europeans believed in a form of destiny or fate which was more closely equivalent to the idea of causality than was the Islamic and Judeo-Christian concept of a preconceived teleological Will of God. Among both the Greeks, Romans, and Germanic peoples, fate was represented by a fabric woven by three sisters, known to the Greeks as the Moirae and to the Romans as the Parcae. Norse mythology similarly denotes these sisters as: Urda, the Past; Verdandi, the Present; and Skuld, the Future.

MOLARS, the large posterior mammalian teeth used for grinding.

MOLLUSCA, a phylum of animals which includes snails, mussels, and octopuses. Most are aquatic, although some possess hard shells.

MOLOCH, the Phoenician solar deity, symbolized by two pillars and a bull, to whom children were regularly sacrificed. Moloch was also known to various other Semitic peoples, such as the Canaanites and Israelites.

MON, a Southeast Asian people native to southern Burma, whose language is related to that of the Khmer. (See AUSTRO-ASIATIC LANGUAGES).

MONDARI, a Negroid East Sudanese or Nilotic-speaking people of the Bari-Lotuko group, primarily dependent on horticulture and cattle-herding with some hunting.

MONDSEE, a Copper Age site in upper Austria, revealing the remains of a village of pile dwellings, inhabited by a people who were primarily engaged in the smelting of local copper ore.

MONGO, a Bantu-speaking Negroid people, largely dependent on horticulture with some fishing and hunting.

MONGOLIAN FOLD, see EPICANTHIC FOLD.

MONGOLIAN SPOT, a dark patch of skin located on the back, at the lower end of the spine, the Mongolian Spot is common amongst persons of Mongoloid race, especially those of Mongolian and North Chinese origin. The frequency decreases amongst populations of partial Mongolian ancestry located at greater distances from this racial epicenter.

MONGOLOIDS, characteristically brachycephalic, with straight, black hair, little facial or body hair, low prognathism, but eyes characterized by the epicanthic fold. Four thousand years ago, Mongoloids appeared to have been restricted to Northern China and parts of Eastern Siberia, but have expanded dramatically during the past four millenia, become admixed in Siberia with paleo-Siberians, and in Indonesia and Oceanic with Negrito and possibly Caucasoid strains (from India). The Japanese and Koreans represent an intrusion of more dolichocephalic central Asian peoples into the Mongoloid territories, with resultant hybridization, the Japanese and Korean languages being related to the Uralic group.

MONGOLS, a pastoral, Mongoloid people inhabiting Mongolia.

MONGUOR, a Mongol Altaic-speaking people, largely dependent on cultivation of some animal husbandry and fishing.

MON-KHMER LANGUAGES, see AUSTRO-ASIATIC LANGUAGES.

MONOGAMY, marriage of one man to one woman.

MONOGENY, the phylogenetic descent of a species or of a group of organisms directly from an earlier source, without any differentiation into divergent evolutionary forms.

MONOPHYLETIC, the members of a taxonomic group who are descended from a common ancestor and who consequently share substantial phylogenetic characteristics.

MONOTHEISM, a belief that a single god created and guides the world.

MONOTREMATA, a subclass of mammals, today represented by the duck-billed platypus and the spiny anteater of Australia and New Guinea, which possess a type of body hair and secrete milk from mammary glands dispersed over the chest, instead of being concentrated in teats as in placentalia. They are equipped with limited means of heat control, but nevertheless possess certain reptilian features such as reproduction by the laying of eggs. (See also PROTOTHERIA).

MONOZYGOTIC TWINS, identical twins which are descended from a single fertilized ovum, and therefore share an identical genetic heritage.

MONOTHEISM, the belief that a single god created and guides the world.

MONTAGNAIS, an Algonquin Cree-speaking North American Indian people, dependent primarily on hunting, with some fishing and food-gathering.

MONTE ALBAN, a major Zapotec ceremonial center in the Oaxaca valley of southern Mexico. The earliest buildings were constructed around 600 B.C., by which time a form of hieroglyphic writing was already in use, accompanied by a round calendar, which was based on a 52 year cycle. After 300 B.C., some pre-Classic Mayan influence is identified, as well as evidence of influence from Teotihuacan after A.D. 50. Between A.D. 300 to 700, Monte Alban achieved the zenith of Zapotec cultural progress. Most surviving ceremonial buildings date from this time, which is known as Period III. Thereafter a period of decadence set in, and the site was actually abandoned from A.D. 800 until early in the 14th century, when it was again occupied by the Mixtec tribes who used the Zapotec tombs for their own burials, contributing more gold and silver ornaments to the total archeological remains.

MONTE CIRCEO, an early archeological site south of Rome, Italy, where A. C. Blanc found a complete adult male Neanderthal skull in 1939.

MONTMOURIAN CAVE, an archeological site in the Haute Garonne, in France, where in 1945 fossil remains classified as Homo sapiens steinheimensis were found, dating from the Riss Interstadial around 30,000 B.P.

MOORS, (BLACKAMOORS), a popular term applied in Elizabethan England (cf. Shakespeare) and later to refer to the Moslem Hamito-Semitic peoples of Northern Africa. The prefix 'Blacka-' suggests that already at that time the population of North Africa had been genetically influenced by the large Negro slave population drawn from sub-Saharan Africa.

MORO, a Kordofanian-speaking (Niger-Congo) people of the Nuba group, largely dependent on horticulture, animal husbandry and some hunting.

MORPHEME, the smallest units of speech that may possess a distinct meaning.

MORPHOGENESIS, the tendency of a life form during its ontogeny or life history to recapitulate the entire genetic history of its taxon.

MORPHOLOGY, the study of biological forms.

MORTUARY ENCLOSURE, a structure which appears to have been erected as a charnel house in which bodies may be stored before a collective burial. Mortuary enclosures like mortuary houses are often enclosed under barrows or large earthen mounds.

MORTUARY HOUSE, a house, constructed of either wood or stone, depending on the prevailing architectural style, which was used as a tomb for the burial of a member of the upper class. Such mortuary houses were usually covered by a protective barrow or mound of earth.
MOSAIC, a method of decorating walls and floors in which small pieces of coloured stone, glass or other material are cemented together in ornamental patterns. Mosaics were particularly popular in cities of the Roman Empire.
MOSSI, a Negroid, West African Voltaic people, largely dependent on horticulture and some food-gathering.
MOTA, a Melanesian (Malayo-Polynesian) people inhabiting the Banks Islands, largely dependent on horticulture and fishing with some animal husbandry.
MOTHER-IN-LAW TABOO, a social custom requiring a man to avoid or severely restrict social contact with his wife's mother.
MOTOR HABITS, routine patterns of body movement which have socially determined origins.
MOTU, a Malayo-Polynesian-speaking people of Southeast New Guinea, who combine cultivation with fishing and some food-gathering.
MOULD, a material containing a carefully shaped cavity, into which melted metals may be poured, in order that they will retain the shape of the mould after solidification. Most moulds were constructed of baked clay, pottery, or stone. Simple moulds might be cut out of a single piece of material, but two-piece and even three-piece mouldings were subsequently invented to permit the casting of more elaborate shapes. (See also CIRE-PERDUE).
MOUNT CARMEL, a group of caves, located on the side of the Palestinian Mount Carmel, which have provided archeologists with a sequence of archeological data covering much of the Paleolithic period. The lower levels reveal coarse flaked tools, above which Acheulian hand axes are found, and above which, in turn, Levalloiso-Mousterian tools. Remains found at this level, particularly in the caves at Tabun (q.v.), and Skhūl (q.v.) have raised considerable controversy. Though some of these are distinctively Neanderthal, others show a marked resemblance to Cro-Magnons, and it has been suggested that the latter represent an intermediate type midway between Neanderthal and Cro-Magnon, which could reflect the evolution of Cro-Magnons from Neanderthals or could have resulted from hybridization. It is of particular interest that the skulls from the Tabun cave are all undoubtedly Neanderthaloid, while those from Skhūl, which reflect characteristics intermediate between Neanderthal and Cro-Magnon, could be possibly 10,000 years later than those belonging to the Tabun cave. This evidence has been used to support the argument that the available fossil evidence indicates a process of rapid evolution from Neanderthal to Cro-Magnon, as against the alternative theory of hybridization. However, the differences which separate the Classic Neanderthals from the Cro-Magnon are so substantial that it would seem impossible that the one could evolve from the other within such a short period of time, and the possibility that the Skhul remains may represent hybrid Cro-Magnon-Neanderthal types cannot be rejected. The higher levels reveal Cro-Magnon type Aurignacian tools, but no Perigordian or earlier tools have been found – as would have been expected if the Mount Carmel site were in fact an area in which Neanderthals evolved into Cro-Magnons. The presence of the more advanced Aurignacian tools, without the evidence of intermediate tools, therefore supports the theory that this area was possibly penetrated by Cro-Magons with an advanced culture, who appeared on the scene as immigrants and mixed genetically with the pre-existing Neanderthals. The final and upper levels at Mount Carmel reveal a Natufian (q.v.) technology. (See KEBAREH, MUGHARET EL; SKHUL; and TABUN, MUGHARET EL).
MOUSTERIAN, named after the archeological site at Le Moustier (q.v.) in France, the Mousterian industry dominated the period known as the Middle Paleolithic, and is generally associated with Classic Neanderthals. The tradition seems to represent a combination of flake and core traditions, including side scrapers, disc cores, hammerstones and bifacial and oval flake tools. The first Mousterian artifacts date from the Riss glaciation, and continue into the earlier

part of the Würm glaciation. Mousterian technology is definitely associated with Neanderthal skeletal remains (q.v.).

MPONGWE, a Bantu-speaking Negroid people of the Biafra coastal region, dependent mainly on horticulture, animal husbandry and some fishing.

MR. PLES, the name jokingly applied by Robert Brown to a fossil type of Australopithecus africanus (also called Plesianthropus transvaalensis) identified by fossil remains which he discovered at Sterkfontein near Johannesburg in 1947.

MU, the mythological ancestors of the first Hawaiian settlers of the Hawaiian islands.

MUD BRICK, a brick which has been dried in the sun instead of baked in a kiln. Common in societies with less sophisticated technology or which lack fuel for brick-kilns. Such bricks have a more limited life, depending upon the climate, than bricks baked in a kiln. In the Americas, mud brick is known as adobe.

MUJU, a Papuan people of the West New Guinea highlands, dependent on horticulture, with some animal husbandry, hunting and fishing.

MULATTO, a word of Spanish origin indicating a person of combined Caucasian and Negro descent: literally, 'little mule'.

MULTILOCAL HOUSEHOLD, an extended family which may formerly have shared a single roof but has since become diversified into separate households.

MUMMY, the body of a man, woman or animal which has been preserved by ritual embalmment. In particular the term usually refers to Egyptian Pharaohs, their queens and other royal personages whose remains were preserved in this fashion. Among the Egyptians the internal organs were first removed, and placed in separate jars, then the remainder of the body was treated with natron (q.v.) to completely dry the flesh. Following the completion of this process the body was wrapped in long strips of linen cloth, various magico-religious amulets being enclosed within the wrappings to help preserve the vitality of the body for the future use of the soul. The bandaged corpse was then placed in a wooden, stone or gold container of approximate human shape, which was also painted with ritual symbols. However, the practice of mummification was by no means restricted to Egypt, mummified bodies, wrapped in textiles, having also been found in Peru among other places.

MUMMY LABEL, the ancient Egyptians customarily identified their mummies by attaching an inscribed piece of wood to the wrappings of the corpse with a string of papyrus.

MUMUYE, a Negroid Niger-Congo-speaking people of the Adamawa-Eastern group, mainly dependent on horticulture with some animal husbandry and hunting.

MUNDA LANGUAGES, a group of relatively isolated languages found in the central hills of India, where they survive among tribal peoples who appear to be aboriginal to the sub-continent. Some Mon-Khmer characteristics have been identified in the Munda language, and to a lesser extent in the related Kolarian, Santal, Ho, Bhuiga and Baiga.

MUNDANG, a Negroid Niger-Congo-speaking people of the Adamawa-Eastern group, dependent mainly on horticulture and animal husbandry.

MUNDUGUMOR, an Arapesh, horticultural people of Papua-New Guinea.

MUNDURUCU, a South American Indian people of Tupi speech in Brazil, dependent on horticulture, hunting and some fishing and food-gathering.

MUNSELL COLOUR CHARTS, accurate colour descriptions of human skin, pottery, earth or other objects may be obtained by matching these against a colour chart devised by A. Munsell, which takes account of differences in hue, chroma, and shade.

MUONG, an Annam-Muong (Mon-Khmer related) people largely dependent on horticulture with some hunting, food-gathering and animal husbandry.

MURA, a South American Indian people of the Central Amazon.

MUREX, a Mediterranean shellfish used by the Phoenicians as a source of purple dye. Purple was widely recognized in the ancient world, particularly among the Phoenicians and Romans, as a symbol of imperial dignity.

MURNGIN, an Australian aboriginal people of Northwestern Australia, primarily dependent on food-gathering, hunting and fishing.

MUSES, in Greek (and subsequently Roman religion), the Muses were the nine daughters of Zeus (Jupiter), each of whom presided over a specific area of the arts, sciences or literature.

MUSICOLOGY, the study of the anthropological history of music. The earliest musical instruments are traced to the Cro-Magnon cultures of Europe. Rhythm was probably the first dominant component, produced by primitive percussion instruments, and has remained dominant in African and Black American music. Only with the development of stringed and wind instruments in the Neolithic was it possible to augment rhythm by melody, which became the salient feature of the music of medieval and renaissance Europe. Interestingly the commercialization of art and music in recent times has led to a fresh emphasis upon rhythm, following the rediscovery of the 'primitive appeal' of 'beat'.

MUSKOGEAN-SIOUAN, a phylum of languages which has been proposed to include the Muskogean and Macro-Siouan sub-phyla. The Muskogean family, sometimes also associated with the Algonquin family, can be subdivided into a Southeastern group, which includes Creek and Seminole; a Choctaw group, with which would be associated the Alabama and Muskogean; and a number of isolates, such as the Natchez language, the Tunica, and Tonkawa. The Macro-Siouan sub-phylum contains the Siouan family proper, which includes Crow, Hidatsa, Winnebago, Mandan, Iowa, Omaha, Kansa, and Dakota; the Iroquoian family, comprising the Seneca-Onondaga group, Mohawk, Oneida, Huron, Tuscarora, and Cherokee, and the Caddoan family, comprising Caddo, Wichita and Pawnee. The Yuki language isolate is also regarded as Macro-Siouan.

MUTAGENS, mutation-inducing agents. These can include unduly high or low temperatives, ionizing radiation, and various chemical substances such as mustard gas, formaldehyde, and even caffeine.

MUTAIR, Semitic-speaking Bedouin Arabs of North Africa, mainly dependent on animal herding with some hunting.

MUTATION, a sudden and permanent change in the number or structure of the genes or chromosomes which is genetically transferable to subsequent offspring. Mutations appear to be random, and do not arise from any internally motivated directive forces. Thus the direction of evolution depends primarily upon the influence and efficacy of natural selection (q.v.).

MUTATION RATE, the rate at which mutations occur at any specific locus on a chromosome, usually expressed in terms of mutations per gamete per generation.

MUTATION, SOMATIC, a mutation occurring in any cell other than a germ cell.

MYCENAE, a major city of Bronze Age Greece, located on a spur overlooking the plain of Argos in the Peloponnese, from which the entire Achaean or Homeric culture derives its archeological name, 'Mycenean'. The outer city of Mycenae was protected by massive encircling walls of cyclopean masonry, the main entrance to which, known as the lion gate, being ornamented by two monumental figures of standing lions. Within the city there was a separate walled acropolis comprising the palace of the royal family and certain temples of worship, but archeologically the most important discoveries have been in the excavation of several royal 'shaft graves'. These and later 'tholos' tombs have revealed a rich collection of metal weapons, drinking and ritual vessels, jewelry, death masks, and pottery decorated with pictorial evidence illustrating the high sophistication of the Mycenean culture, and corroborating the historical accuracy of the sociological content of the Homeric legends.

MYCENEANS, a term which has been popularly used by archeologists and historians to refer to all the members of the late Bronze Age civilization which covered the Greek mainland and Aegean Islands. According to literary sources, such as the Homeric epics, these people called themselves the Achaeans. The Achaean aristocracy and freeman class appear to have been descended from Indo-European invaders who entered Greece from the Danubian area, bringing in Minyan pottery, early in the 2nd millennium B.C. The Mycenean civilization has an early Helladic phase, which was partly rooted in the Old European civilization (q.v.) of the aboriginal Pelasgian inhabitants of the Aegean, as well as in the culture of the invading Indo-European aristocracy. The influence of the Cretan Minoans, who maintained a high civilization of their own until conquered by Myceneans around 1450 B.C., is also apparent at this stage. In later times the Myceneans maintained extensive commercial connections not only in the East and Central Mediterranean, but also with the Upper Danubian cultures, trading as far north as the Baltic for amber. However, the Mycenean or Achaean civilization, which was characterized by constantly disturbing internecine warfare between the small princely city-states, was completely disrupted by a new invasion of Greek-speaking peoples from the North around 1000 B.C., the invaders being Dorian Indo Europeans (q.v.).

MYSTERY CULT, a cult whose members constitute a secret society, initiation into which involves the use of mystical and cabalistic rites.

MYSTERY RELIGIONS, a name used to describe religious cults whose adherents are organized into associations possessing secret ritual knowledge which is divulged only to properly initiated members. Most of the mystery religions of post-classical Europe originated from ancient Mediterranean beliefs which had survived among the lower classes throughout the period of aristocratic Indo-European domination or else were imported from Anatolia, Egypt and the Middle East during Hellenistic and later Roman times. Such mystery religions became particularly popular among the slaves and freedmen of Greek and Roman society, who relished the sense of personal identity, status and the hope of individual salvation conveyed by initiation into such cults. The leading mystery cults were the Dionysian, which included orgiastic rites involving the consumption of living flesh, the Eleusian, centered on the worship of Demeter (q.v.), the Phrygian, honoring Cybele (q.v.), and the Egyptian, worshipping Isis and Osiris, which became especially popular after the Roman conquest of Egypt.

MYSTIC PARTICIPATION, the tendency for men in primitive societies to ascribe to external objects qualities which they believe themselves to possess. According to Levy-Brühl, primitive men tend to see the world through a 'pre-logical' mystical haze, attributing to animals, trees, and even non-living objects the same emotional qualities which they feel characterize their own existence.

MYTH, legends which explain the origin of the customs, rituals, and magico-religious beliefs.

MZAB, a Hamitic-speaking 'Oasis Berber' people of North Africa, dependent primarily on horticulture with some animal herding.

N

NABESNA, a North Athabascan, American Indian people of South Central Alaska, dependent on hunting and fishing with some food-gathering.

NACOM, the military head of a Mayan city state.

NA-DENÉ, a phylum of North American Indian languages, divided into Haida and Tlingit on the one hand and the Athabascan family on the other. Some linguistic authorities have suggested the existence of generic ties between the Na-Dené languages and the Sinitic languages of Eastern Asia.

NAGA. (1) an archeological site located in East Africa, comprising many well-preserved ruins from the ancient Cushite civilization, including an engraving of a lion god possessing four forelegs and three heads. (2) Mongoloid horticulturalists of Southern Assam, whose language is closely related to Thai, Shan, and Laotian. The Naga were headhunters until early in this century.

NAGARA, a sacred drum used in Indian temples, beaten by two curved drum-sticks.

NAGGAREH, a double drum, made from brass covered with parchment and commonly used in ancient Arabia and Syria.

NAGUAL, a part of a person's soul which according to a widespread Central and South American belief inhabits an animal. Should this animal suffer injury or death, then the human owner of the Nagual soul will likewise suffer a similar fate.

NAIAD, nature spirits believed by the Greeks and Romans to inhabit streams, rivers, water-falls and lakes. Naiads were similar to the nymphs of Slavonic mythology, with whom they probably shared a common origin.

NAKA, a New Zealand Maori war dance.

NAKATOMI, priests of the Japanese Shinto (q.v.) religion.

NAMA, a Khoisan-speaking Hottentot people of South West Africa, largely dependent on cattle-herding and hunting.

NAMBE, a North American Indian people of the Southwestern United States.

NAME, many people believe that a name contains an intrinsic part of the owner's personality, and in such societies the real name of a person may be a closely guarded secret known only to a limited number of privileged kinsmen. In societies which believe in reincarnation, such as the Masai of Africa and the Haida of North America, an attempt may be made to determine the correct name of the soul which is being reincarnated in the newborn child. However, many societies regard it as undignified to address a god or even a mortal person of superior rank by his or her personal name.

NAME-CHANGING, although many societies do not permit their member to change personal names that are given to them at or after birth, other societies may require a change of name in the event of a change of status, because of the close relationship between name and status. Thus, a man who achieves distinction by some memorable achievement may acquire a new name to commemorate that event. Similarly, a woman who marries may assume the name of her husband, while among the Tikopia, both the bride and bridegroom take new names after marriage.

NANAK GURU, the 15th century founder of the Indian Sikh religion, who (having been born a Muslim in a Hindu country) combined elements of the Hindu and Muslim religions to create the Granth or sacred book of the Sikhs.

NANDI, Negroid Nilotic-speaking people of the Nandi group, primarily dependent on cattle herding and horticulture.

NANISM, a term for arrested growth, usually caused by defective pituitary or thyroid glands.

NANKANSE, Negroid, West African, Voltaic people, largely dependent on horticulture with some animal husbandry, hunting and fishing.

NANNAR, the Sumerian moon god whose temple was located on a ziggurat at Ur. Nannar is generally regarded as equivalent to the Semitic god Sin.

NAORW, Khoisan-speaking Bushman people of Southwest Africa, largely dependent on food-gathering and hunting.

NAOS, in ancient Egypt, a small shrine which housed the spirit of a deity.

NAPIWA, a Blackfoot god reported to have been white-skinned.

NARES, a term used to refer to the nostrils of vertebrates.

NARNER, the pharoah who founded the Egyptian First Dynasty, cir. 3200 B.C., and united the White Crown of Lower Egypt with the Red Crown of Upper Egypt.

NARRINYERI, an Australian aboriginal hunting and gathering people.

NASAL INDEX, the ratio between the length and width of the nose as determined by multiplying the maximum width of the nasal aperture by 100 and dividing this figure by the length of the nose from the nasion to the naso-spinale.

NASAL SEPTUM, the membrane of cartilage which separates the two passages of the nose. Among the peoples of New Guinea, Australia and Oceania, the nasal septum is frequently pierced in order to permit the insertion of ornaments, such as boars' tusks, for both decorative and ritual purposes.

NASAMONIAN, an aboriginal custom requiring brides to submit to the male relatives of the bridegroom before cohabiting with their new husbands.

NASION, the central portion of the nasal suture from which the length of the head is measured when taking cranial measurements.

NASKAPI, an Algonquin Cree-speaking North American Indian people, dependent primarily on hunting with some fishing and food-gathering.

NASSA, the shells of a small sea snail, used by Melanesians as a form of currency.
NATAL KINSHIP, kinship traced by brith, that it, consanguineal kindred.
NATCHEZ INDIANS, a North American Indian people, formerly occupying the Lower Mississippi, who possessed a highly stratified society which reflected strong Central American cultural influences. Their language is usually classed as Muskogean-Siouan, although it forms a separate isolate within this phylum. The Natchez were dependent on horticulture, hunting and fishing.
NATION, the nation is distinguished from the concept of a political 'state' in that a nation comprises a grouping of people who proudly cherish a common racial and cultural heritage, whereas a state is merely a geographically-defined body of people under the rule of a common government. Only in the case of the 'nation state' are the two concepts complimentary.
NATIONAL CHARACTER, a distinctive system of norms, values, attitudes and behavior associated with the members of a particular national group.
NATIVE METALS, a term used to refer to metals which are found in a more or less pure state and which can be worked to produce crude spears, arrowheads and other objects without prior smelting or metallurgical process to extract impurities.
NATIVISM, a Messianic movement among peoples subject to cultural contact with technologically more advanced societies, often heralding the return to a precontact way of life. Also known as millenarianism or messianism.
NATRON, a form of sodium carbonate obtained by the Ancient Egyptians through the evaporation of lake water. Natron was an essential ingredient used in the process of the mummification of corpses.
NATUFIAN, a late Mesolithic culture centered upon Palestine. Archeological evidence indicates that many Natufian communities had adopted a settled way of life even though hunting and gathering appears to have been the main basis of subsistence, since tools such as sickles, pestles and mortars imply that they systematically collected cereals and that advanced food-gathering played an important role in their lives. Later Natufians may even be regarded as having adopted elementary horticulture, following which Natufian influence became apparent in the Nile delta around the 6th millennium B.C.
NATURAL AREA, a distinctive geographical area set apart by physical or climatic conditions which tends to influence the cultural pattern of any community or society domiciled within its limits.
NATURAL SELECTION, the selective elimination over a period of generations of physical characteristics which are not conducive or are less conducive to the survival of the sub-species.
NATURE AND NURTURE, during the 19th century, and even in the earlier part of the 20th century, furious debates raged concerning the respective importance of 'nature' and 'nurture' – the genetic heritage 'versus' the environment – in the shaping of the individual. To some extent these outdated concepts are still reflected in debates concerning the educability of children with different I.Q.s. However, it is now realized that the potential limit of ability of all living organisms is precisely determined by heredity, but that the actual development of an organism within the limits defined by heredity depends upon environmental influences operating throughout the entire pre-natal and post-natal history of the organism. (See also I.Q.).
NATURE WORSHIP, the worship of natural forces, such as the sun, wind, water, earth, sometimes, but not always, represented as anthropomorphic gods. Nature worship probably evolved out of animism (q.v.) and frequently flourishes alongside ancestor-worship (q.v.).
NAU, a recognized stage in the life of the young Hottentot male, midway between childhood and adulthood.
NAUALIA, ritual body markings worn by Australian aboriginals.
NAURUANS, a Malayo-Polynesian-speaking people inhabiting the Eastern Caroline Islands of Micronesia who are dependent on horticulture and fishing.
NAVAHO, an American Indian people found in Arizona, New Mexico and

Utah, whose language is closely related to Apache and belongs to the southern sub-group of the Athabascan family of languages.

NAVICELLA, a fibula or brooch shaped in the form of a small boat, characteristic of the European Hallstatt culture.

NAYAR, a southwest Indian people of the Coromandel Coast.

NDAKA, a Bantu-speaking Negroid people of the Babwe-Bira group, dependent on horticulture with some fishing.

NDAU, a Bantu-speaking Negroid people of the Shona-Thonga group, primarily dependent on horticulture with some herding, hunting and food-gathering.

NDEBELE, a Bantu-speaking Negroid people of Southern Africa, largely dependent on horticulture and cattle-herding.

NDEMBU, a Bantu-speaking Negroid people of the Ngombe group, dependent primarily on horticulture with some hunting and fishing.

NDENGEI, the supreme god of the Fijians.

NDONI, small wooden shields, commonly carried on the shoulder by various Kenyan tribal warriors.

NEANDERTHAL, otherwise known as Homo sapiens neanderthalenis, Homo primogenicus or Homo mousteriensis. The first Neanderthal fossil, comprising a nearly complete skeleton, was found in a cave in the Neandr Valley in Germany and identified by J.K. Fuhlrott in 1856. Characterized by a low sloping forehead and heavy brow ridges, the European Neanderthal has given its name to a wide assemblage of fossils representing a primitive Homo sapiens level of evolution. The Classic Neanderthal probably occupied Europe until around 35,000 B.P., when they were supplanted by Homo sapiens sapiens, the first Cro-Magnons or modern Europeans. Some writers have suggested that Neanderthals evolved into Cro-Magnons, but there is no positive archeological evidence of this, and the dramatic physical differences could hardly have occurred as a result of the evolutionary process in the very brief time and limited number of generations available. It is more likely that Cro-Magnons supplanted the Neanderthals, possibly interbreeding with individuals and small groups in certain areas. (See also NEANDERTHALOIDS).

NEANDERTHALOIDS, while the term Neanderthal is properly applied only to certain specific European and West Asian fossil remains, many other early sapiens sub-species which inhabited other parts of the Old World represent a roughly equivalent level of human evolution. These are called Neanderthaloids. Virtually all Neanderthaloid characteristics can be matched among the diverse living races surviving today (one reason why Neanderthaloids are now classified as sapiens) and it would seem that most of the living hominid subspecies were created by the admixture of immigrant Homo sapiens sapiens stock with locally specialized Homo sapiens (Neanderthaloid) populations. This would explain the persistence of slow-evolving and presumably long established local adaptations, such as skin color, hair form, etc. among many living populations. Australian aboriginals, for example, closely resemble the Neanderthaloid Wadjak.

NEANTHROPIC, referring to those various hominid varieties of man which present a modern appearance.

NEARCTICA, that part of the Arctic area (Holarctica) which falls within the New World.

NEAPOLITANS, a South Italian population of composite Italic, Greek and general Mediterranean origins, traditionally dependent on horticulture with some fishing and animal husbandry, who speak Italian, an Indo-European language.

NEBRASKAN GLACIATION, the name given to the first North American glaciation, which probably corresponded to the Alpine Günz glaciation (q.v.).

NEBUCHADNEZZAR, (circa 605-562 B.C.), a Babylonian king, son of Nabopolassar, who secured the independence of Babylon from Assyria, and established a Chaldaean or neo-Babylonian empire. Nebuchadnezzar successfully expanded this empire as far as the Mediterranean, capturing and sacking Jerusalem, and deporting the majority of its population into exile in Babylonia.

NECKLACES, the first necklaces worn by hominids appear in association with Cro-Magnon remains in Europe. Normally comprising circular strings of stones, beads, seeds or shells worn around the neck, the early necklaces are believed to have had magico-religious rather than purely ornamental value, although primitive societies do not always distinguish sharply between the religious and the esthetic. More complex societies often regard the possession of necklaces and other ornamental jewelry as a status symbol.

NECKLET, any necklace which circles the neck closely. Necklets are particularly popular in sub-Saharan Africa.

NECROMANCY, foretelling the future by magical means through communication with the spirits of the dead. It is believed that those who have already passed from the world of the living into the world of the dead will have greater knowledge of the future as well as of what is happening in the present. They are therefore able to give valuable advice to the living if approached in the proper manner.

NECROPOLIS, a word derived from Greek, meaning 'the city of the dead'. Today used to refer to any ancient (and usually large) cemetery, usually situated near a major settlement.

NEEDLE, the first needles appear to have been made by Cro-Magnons of the Magdalenian Age from fine pieces of bone, ground into a long narrow shape, eyeholes being bored with the aid of a flint awl.

NEEDLE, CLEOPATRA'S, a term used to refer to each of two obelisks dating from the reign of the Pharaoh Thothmes III which originally stood in front of the temple at Heliopolis, but were removed to Alexandria by the Romans following the Roman conquest of Egypt. Although they are not connected with Cleopatra in any way, they received this name when 19th century Egyptologists removed them from Egypt to their present positions – one on the embankment of the Thames River in London and the other in Central Park in New York City.

NEEMBO, an initiation society found among eastern Congolese tribes.

NEFER, an Egyptian pendant, usually dating from the 12th and 13th dynasties, comprising beads of gold, silver, emerald or porcelain. These beads were usually inscribed with anthropomorphic representations of the gods, for the protection of the wearers, both living and dead, against the forces of evil.

NEGATIVE PAINTING, a process of pottery decoration, employed in several parts of the Americas, by which portions of the surface of the vessel were covered with wax or clay prior to exposing the vessel to heavy smoke, the carbon from which penetrated the porous surface of the exposed areas of the pottery, so that when the protective wax or clay covering was removed from the remaining areas, the design stood out sharply against a black background.

NEGRILLO, a term formerly used to refer to the Pygmies (q.v.) of Africa, and sometimes to the diminutive Negritoes (q.v.) of tropical Southeast Asia.

NEGRITO, a term used to define a relatively prognathous, dark-skinned, curly-haired pygmy strain found in Southeast Asia, the Philippines, New Guinea and parts of India. Negritoes seem to be physiologically parallel to the Negroes of Africa, but no evidence of migration has been found. It is therefore believed that the two racial types represent parallel survivals from an older widely spread form of hominid, adapted to the tropical rain forests.

NEGROIDS (or CONGOIDS), a heavily pigmented people with spiral to peppercorn black hair, narrow pelves, long forearms and legs, dolichocephalic headform, and generally short faces with rounded foreheads, low bridged noses, flaring nostrils and marked prognathism. The clinal center of the Negro population of Africa appears to be the forests of the Congo and West Africa, but 30,000 year old fossil remains from Kangira in East Africa closely resemble living Negroids. Many living Negro populations adjacent to the Sahara probably represent a Caucasoid-Negroid admixture of (Hamitic origin) and present physical and facial features which are intermediate between the true Negroes and the Caucasoids of North Africa. Even the true Negroes of sub-Saharan Africa seem to derive from admixture between earlier Rhodesian (q.v.) type hominids and successive groups of immigrants from Eurasia, who brought with them Upper Paleolithic, Mesolithic and subsequent innovative technologies, and admixed with, rather than extirpated, the indigenous populations of sub-Saharan Africa.

NEGUS, the title of a chieftain in the Semitic-speaking areas of the Horn of Africa, and the official title of the Emperor of Ethiopia, the term may be regarded as the Amharic equivalent of 'king'.
NEOASIATIC, a Central East Asian subdivision of the Mongoloid race, characterized by the pronounced character of the epicanthic fold (q.v.).
NEO-DARWINISM, a term used to refer to more sophisticated modern conceptions of the evolutionary process which have resulted from the application of Mendelian genetics (about which Charles Darwin was ignorant) to the theory of natural selection first advanced by Darwin in 1859.
NEOLITHIC, a term originally invented to refer to that late period of Stone Age culture in which polished stone tools were employed, but now customarily used to refer to any Stone Age society which is primarily dependent upon the cultivation of crops or the domestication of animals as its means of subsistence. Most Neolithic cultures, particularly those dependent upon the cultivation of crops, enjoy a relatively settled pattern of life, and are therefore able to develop a much larger range of heavy utensils for eating, ritual or other purposes than nomadic hunters and gatherers could hope to carry with them in their periodic migrations.
NEOLOCAL RESIDENCE, the custom by which newlyweds establish their own households in a new locality, separate from that of the parental families.
NEONATES, a term referring to newly born children.
NEOPALLIUM, an area roughly corresponding to the cerebral cortex of man the function of which appears to be related to the intelligent coordination of behavior.
NEOTECHNIC, a term sometimes used to refer to the recent decades of the present century characterized by rapid technological advances.
NEOTENY, the persistence into adulthood of certain characteristics which were formerly found only among the juvenile members of an ancestral species.
NERVOUS SYSTEM, a complex biological mechanism which enables animals to coordinate their activities to meet survival requirements in the external world. Found in all multicellular animals above the level of sponges, it comprises a threadlike series of nerve cells which pass messages from the sense organs via the spinal cord to the brain, from which area an appropriate message is likewise conveyed to the effector organs enabling them to produce an appropriate response.
NETS, net-making appears to be one of the most ancient techniques developed by Paleolithic man. Early nets were made from vegetable fibers, carefully selected for their suitability and durability. Thus the Pygmies of Africa use nets to snare game, while the peoples of New Guinea and Melanesia still commonly use carrying bags made of net, closely similar to the net shopping bags common in modern western society. The art of plaiting vegetable fibers to make nets also inspired the construction of primitive shelters, made from interlaced branches or long leaves, and may have constituted the origin of woven clothing.
NETS, FISHING, nets can be used for fishing by fixing weights to the edges so that when the net is cast into the water, the weights will carry it down to entrap any fish caught within the enclosed area. Alternatively, dipping nets are made by attaching nets to a wooden frame, equipped with a long handle. Other fishing nets include gill nets, with a wide mesh appropriately spaced to entangle fish behind the gills when they try to swim through the net. Trawling nets are designed to be pulled behind vessels.
NEUROCRANIUM, that portion of the skull containing the brain.
NEUROSIS, a form of illness characterized by substantial mental strain, usually caused by the inability of the individual to achieve his desired objectives.
NEUTRAL TERRITORY, although man, like most mammals, has historically been a territorial animal, traditionally band and tribal hunting and food-gathering areas may sometimes overlap. Such overlapping areas are generally described by anthropologists as 'neutral territories'.
NEW FIRE CEREMONIES, the custom of periodically extinguishing and then relighting sacred fires is remarkably widespread, and may have ancient Paleolithic origins. Thus the Aztec priests extinguished the sacred altar fires every 52

years, to kindle a new fire symbolic of new life. Flaming torches lit from the new fire were carried by runners to relight the extinguished fires on the altars of temples in neighboring towns, while the individual householders likewise took flames from this fire to relight their own hearth fires. In many Indo-European cultures, there is evidence that the semi-sacred hearth fires were ritually extinguished once a year, and then relit from the ashes of the last year's fires. Similar rituals have been recorded in Africa, implying that the practice may be extremely ancient.

NEZ PERCÉ, a French term for certain American Indian peoples who inhabited parts of Washington and Oregon. This name was given to them by French trappers because of their habit of piercing the nose in order to insert shells which were highly valued as a form of money. The Nez Percé Indians speak a Penutian language of the Sahaptin-Nez Percé group, and were traditionally dependent on fishing, food-gathering and hunting.

NGALA, a Bantu-speaking Negroid people of the Riverain Congo, primarily dependent on fishing and horticulture.

NGANDON, the Javanese site in which Homo soloensis was found, near the Solo River, by W. W. F. Oppenoorth in 1931.

NGANGA, a Bantu witch doctor who specializes in divination.

NGARAWAPUM, a Papuan people from East Papua, dependent on horticulture and hunting, with some food-gathering and animal husbandry.

NGBANDI, a Negroid Niger-Congo-speaking people of the Adamawa-Eastern group, dependent largely on horticulture with some hunting and fishing.

NGERE, a Mande-speaking Negroid people of West Africa, largely dependent on horticulture with some animal husbandry and fishing.

NGOMA, an African kettledrum, covered with cowhide and normally beaten with the hands.

NGOMBE, a Bantu-speaking Negroid people, dependent primarily on horticulture with some hunting and fishing.

NGONDE, a Bantu-speaking Negroid people of the Ngonde group, largely dependent on horticulture and some animal husbandry.

NGONGE, a wooden bell frequently worn in sub-Saharan Africa by mourners attending a funeral.

NGUMBA, a Bantu-speaking Negroid people of the Fang-Dzem group, largely dependent on horticulture with some hunting and food-gathering.

NGUMBI, a Southwestern Bantu, Negroid people, largely dependent on horticulture and herding and some hunting.

NIAH CAVE, an archeological site in Borneo, excavated by Tom Harrison, which was found to contain the cranium of a boy, which closely resembled an advanced Neanderthal. Unreliably dated at approximately 38,000 B.P., some claim has been made that the Niah cave boy represents the earliest fossil Homo s. sapiens. However, the skull survived in a badly crushed condition, and although it does resemble the crania of the living Australoids of New Guinea, it was not as highly evolved as the skulls of the Cro-Magnons of Upper Paleolithic Europe, and cannot properly be classified as Homo s. sapiens.

NIASSANS, a Malayo-Polynesian people of Western Sumatra.

NIBELUNGENLIED, a Teutonic, Anglo-Saxon, and Norse legend recounting the events following the seizure of the ill-fated treasure of the dragon Fafnir by the hero Siegfried and the subsequent adventures of Siegfried and his sister Brunhilde (also known as Sigurd and Brunnhilde in the Scandinavian version, known as the Volsung Saga). Germanic pagan literature was destroyed following the conversion of the Germans to Christianity, and a collection of folklore compiled under Charlemagne was destroyed on the orders of the Frankish king, Louis the Pious, on the advice of his bishops. However, the massive Nibelungenlied legend was Christianized, and combines elements relating to the old Germanic gods and their mythology with those relating to the wars against the Huns in Christian times.

NICKNAMES, nicknames (Anglo-Saxon *ek-name*) are sometimes given to ridicule and sometimes to honor an individual for a specific event in his life. In other cases, as among various Melanesian peoples, a child is not regarded as a true member of the community until he has reached puberty, and he is therefore identified by a nickname until he is entitled to be referred to by his proper name.

NICOBARESE, a people of largely Negrito origin, speaking six different but related languages, who are still found in the Andaman and Nicobar Isles, as well as in parts of Northwest Sumatra. The Nicabarese languages are identified as belonging to a formerly widespread Mon-Khmer phylum (q.v.).

NIFLHEIM, a Norse name for one of the four inhabited regions of the universe, which according to Norse mythology, were the Kingdoms of Hela (q.v.), Niflheim, Mitgard, (q.v.) and Asgard (q.v.); Niflheim, one of the homes of the dead, was reputed to be cold, damp and misty.

NIGER-CONGO LANGUAGES, a large phylum of African languages spoken mainly in the sub-Saharan region, the Niger-Congo languages are also sometimes known by the alternative appellation, Congo-Kordofanian, since the Kordofanian language, located on the eastern edges of the Sahara, has also been identified as belonging to this group. The Niger-Congo phylum contains some six major groups of languages, totaling in all some two-hundred and three different languages. The largest of these are the Western or Atlantic group (which includes Yoruba and Ibo) and Bantu, the latter being today the most widely spoken because of the vast expansion eastwards and southwards of the warlike Bantu peoples during the last millennium. The Niger-Congo languages are essentially linked to the Negro peoples, originating in the forest areas of the Niger-Congo region, but spreading – as with Bantu – into the eastern and southern uplands formerly inhabited by small bands of Capoid hunters and gatherers. The Niger-Congo family of languages also includes the Kwa, Fulani, Manda, Voltaic, Eastern Niger-Congo, and Atlantic subfamilies (q.v.).

NIGER-KORDOFANIAN LANGUAGES, see NIGER-CONGO LANGUAGES.

NILE RIVER, the Nile river was sacred to the Egyptians, who honored a river god known as Hapy. Although regarded as a male deity, Hapy was customarily represented as possessing a pair of female breasts, symbolic of fertility, because the annual flooding of the Nile made possible the cultivation of the adjacent land.

NILI-AN-CAN, a white-skinned Arapaho god.

NILO-SAHARAN LANGUAGES, see NILOTIC LANGUAGES.

NILOTE, a name given to the tall, dark inhabitants of Ethiopia and the Sudan who speak languages heavily influenced by Cushitic speech.

NILOTENSTELLUNG, a term invented by German anthropologists for the habit of Nilotic tribesmen, who spend long hours watching their flocks, of standing on one leg, the second leg being rested in a bent position with the foot supported against the knee of the first leg.

NILOTIC LANGUAGES, a large class of languages, sometimes referred to as Nilo-Saharan, which is divided into 6 main groups of 63 different languages. Among these, the Dinka and Masai are perhaps the best known. The Southern Nilotic languages reveal considerable Cushitic influence, thus supporting the theory that the culture of the cattle-herding Nilotics is largely derived from an original immigration of Cushitic cattle-herding clans and the subsequent absorption of these peoples into the indigenous Negroid population. The Southern Nilotic languages (often known as Nilo-Hamitic) include Masai, Nandi, Turkhana, Doroba and Baro. The Northern Nilotes are relatively uninfluenced by Cushitic traditions, and include the Shilluk, Nuer, Alur, Dinka and Luo.

NIMBUS, a term used to refer to the halo of divine light which in Christian iconography usually appears above the head of Christ, the Virgin Mary and other saintly beings. The idea of the nimbus appears to have been inspired by the Persian concept of *xvarenah*, which may have a widespread Indo-European root as similar representations of a light which hovers above the head of a divine being are also to be found in India and among the early Greeks and Romans.

NIMROD, the 'mighty hunter' referred to in the Book of Genesis is believed to have been the Sumerian-Babylonian mythical hero Gilgamesh.
NIMRUD, one of the three cities which served as capitals for Assyria, the others being Assur and Nineveh. The earliest city of Nimrud was founded around 1274 B.C., but a new city was built in 883 B.C., complete with a ziggurat or temple platform and palaces enclosed within a fortified citadel. Although this city was apparently burned by the Medes after their victory in 612 B.C., many ivory and stone carvings survived the fire, and provide us with valuable evidence of the art, mythology and general cultural history of the Assyrians.
NINEVEH, one of the three capital cities of Assyria, the other two being Assur and Nimrud. The site of Nineveh appears to have been occupied from early Sumerian times, but did not become important until it became a joint capital of Assyria early in the 1st millennium B.C. The site has revealed many impressive architectural monuments, together with valuable collections of clay tablets found in the palaces of Sennacherib and Ashurbanipal.
NIPIGON, Algonquin-speaking North American Indians, related to the Ojibwa, who are dependent on hunting, fishing and food-gathering.
NIPPUR, the city and ritual cult centre of Enlil, the supreme deity and 'Lord of the Storms'. Because of the extreme respect in which Enlil was held by all Sumerians, Nippur was regarded as a sacred and neutral city, and thus avoided involvement in the constant warfare which was customary between Sumerian city-states. As a result, much of what we know of ancient Sumeria comes from the decipherment of tablets which have survived to us in excellent condition in the ruins of Nippur.
NIRVANA, the goal of Buddhism is escape from the cycle of rebirth or reincarnation – a process in which both Buddhists and Hindus believe. But Buddhists differ from Hindus in believing that life on earth is essentially a matter of pain and suffering, rather than a joyful experience, and that it is desirable for the individual soul to seek escape from the constant rebirth and pain implied by life. Since pain and suffering are supposed to arise from desire, hatred and delusion, Buddhists seek to overcome these three 'fires' and achieve a state of *nirvana,* or non-being, thus securing freedom from the otherwise eternal cycle of rebirth or *sansara.* Nirvana, implying literally 'to be blown out' like a flame, means only the extinction of the worldly self, comprising evil passions and false views, the elimination of which brings bliss. There are two types of Nirvana. The first of these represents the bliss that is obtainable during life, but the second – which means total freedom from life – comes only with the death of the successful *arhat* or disciple.
NISENAN, a Californian Penutian-speaking people traditionally dependent on food-gathering, hunting and fishing.
NISIR, in Sumerian Mythology Nisir was the name of the mountain on which Utnapishtim's ark first came to rest as the waters of the Great Flood began to subside.
NITROGEN CYCLE, a symbiotic process by which autotrophic plants absorb inorganic nitrogen compounds from the soil or from the sea and process these into organic compounds. Those organic compounds which do not decay are consumed by animals and then returned to the soil or the sea as excreta or by the death and subsequent decay of the animal. The resultant organic compounds are then reconverted into inorganic nitrogen compounds by the activity of bacteria.
NIUEANS, a West Polynesian people dependent on horticulture and fishing.
NIYOGA, a term used in India to refer to the right of a childless man to select a substitute male, invariably a close relative, to cohabit with his wife in order that she might provide him with an heir to inherit his name and property.
NIXIE, in Teutonic mythology, the nixie is a potentially malevolent water spirit, customarily half-human and half-fish in form, but capable of appearing in totally human guise.
NKASA, a poison used in Congo poison oracles (q.v.).
NKUMBA, a Congo secret society.
NKUNDO, a Bantu-speaking Negroid people of the Mongo group, largely

dependent on horticulture with some fishing and hunting.

NOA, a term used among Polynesians to designate an object which is devoid of supernatural forces and is consequently free from taboos.

NOMADS, a community of hunters, food-gatherers or pastoralists which moves its location at fairly regular intervals in pursuit of subsistence.

NOMLAKI, a California Penutian-speaking people, traditionally dependent on food-gathering, hunting and fishing.

NOOTKA, a Northwest American Indian people, primarily dependent upon fishing with some hunting and food-gathering, whose language belongs to the Mosan branch of the Algonquin-Mosan phylum.

NORDIC LOCAL RACE, a major variant of the Caucasoid stock, centered in historical times in Northwest Europe, notably Germany, Holland, Scandinavia, and the British Isles, but admixed in certain of these areas with various earlier Caucasoid peoples from pre-Germanic and pre-Celtic populations. Essentially characterized by relatively long heads, medium to long faces, somewhat fragile, delicate features, narrow prominent noses, and light coloured hair and eyes, with light pigmentation generally, their hair form is either straight or wavy, and their stature is above the Caucasoid average.

NORMS, the patterns of learned behavior by which a group judges its members.

NORNS, the three 'fates' of Scandinavian mythology. Closely associated with the concept of causality and the three Greek Moirae (q.v.), their names were appropriately, 'Was', 'Is', and 'Will Be', reflecting the inevitability of events.

NORMALIZING SELECTION, when any species or subspecies has become well adjusted to the problem of survival in its prevailing environment, further mutations are unlikely to contribute towards the survival of the lineage and all deviants are thus likely to be eliminated by natural selection. Under such circumstances natural selection (q.v.) works to preserve the species in a substantially unchanged form, and the resultant elimination of deviants is sometimes known as 'normalizing selection'.

NORSE RELIGION, there were twelve principal deities in the Norse polytheistic religion of which Odin was regarded as the Allfather or supreme god. These twelve were known as the Aesir (q.v.). In addition the North Germans recognized a group of goddesses known as the Asynjor (q.v.), attendants to the supreme goddess Freya, and also a group of hero-warriors known as the Einherjar (q.v.) who lived with Odin in Valhalla. Opposed to the gods and the Einherjar were the forces of evil comprising dragons, serpents and monsters.

NORTHERN SAULTEAUX, Algonquin-speaking North American Indians related to the Ojibwa.

NORTHUMBRIA, an Anglo-Saxon kingdom in Northeastern England which had its capital at York. Northumbria was subsequently subjected to substantial Viking invasions and settlement.

NOTOCHORD, a firm quasi-skeletal rod running lengthwise from front to rear in all simple chordates. In vertebrate chordates the notochord appears only in the embryo stage, being later replaced by the vertebrae.

NSAW, a Bantu-speaking Negroid people from the Cameroon Highlands, dependent mainly on horticulture with some animal husbandry and hunting.

NUBIA, the name used by the ancient Egyptians to refer to that portion of the Nile which lies above the First Cataract. Largely Caucasoid in early times, it appears to have become increasingly Negroid with the passing of centuries, but in earlier times provided Egypt with good soldiers, large numbers being hired as mercenaries. Less civilized than Egypt, Nubia was Egypt's gateway to Central Africa, through which passed gold, ivory, Negro and even Pygmy slaves. Nubia was annexed to Egypt at an early date, but gained a degree of autonomy under the New Kingdom. The name is still used to refer to the East Sudanic Nubians.

NUCHAL LINE, a protrusion above a recessed line on the rear of the cranium, to which the neck muscles are attached.

NUCHAL CREST, a marked protrusion on the rear of the skull of many non-human primates to which the neck muscles are attached.

NUCLEOTIDE, the monomer composing the DNA chain.

NUCLEUS, the central portion of a cell which contains the chromosomes.
NUER, a Negroid, Northern Nilotic-speaking people, primarily dependent on cattle-herding with some horticulture and fishing.
NUMEN, a divine force or power which was believed by the Romans to be present in certain rivers, fields, mountains, trees, and even people. The concept of Numen has sometimes been likened to mana (q.v.), but was historically personified in spirit form.
NUNAMIUT, Eskimos who live in the interior of Northern Canada, dependent mainly on hunting, supplemented by fishing and food-gathering.
NUNIVAK ESKIMOS, Western Eskimos who depend on fishing, supplemented by hunting and some minimal food-gathering.
NUPE, a Kwa-speaking Negroid people of West Africa, largely dependent on horticulture and some animal husbandry.
NURI, an Indo-European-speaking Indic people, primarily dependent on cultivation and animal herding with some hunting. Often known as Kafiri, the Nuri occupy parts of eastern Afghanistan. Nuristani is one of the main branches of the Indo-Iranian group of languages.
NURISTANI LANGUAGES, a division of the Iranian group of Indo-European languages, which includes the various Kafiri languages of Afghanistan and the northwest of Pakistan.
NUTCRACKER MAN, see ZINJANTHROPUS.
NYANKOLE, a West Lacustrine Bantu people, largely dependent on horticulture and herding.
NYAKYUSA, a Bantu-speaking Negroid people of the Ngonde group, largely dependent on horticulture with some animal husbandry.
NYAMWEZI, a Bantu-speaking Negroid people of the Nyamwezi group, largely dependent on horticulture, with some hunting and animal husbandry.
NYANEKA, a Southwestern Bantu Negroid people, largely dependent on horticulture and herding.
NYANJA, a Bantu-speaking Negroid people of the Maravi group, largely dependent on horticulture and hunting.
NYDAM, a peat bog in Schleswig-Holstein which appears to have been used as a ceremonial site for votive offerings during the later Iron Age. The peat has preserved both woodwork and ironwork in excellent condition, and has yielded up a 70 ft. Viking boat, in addition to a large number of highly ornamented iron swords and other valuable artwork.
NYIMA, a Nubian people largely dependent on horticulture with some animal husbandry and hunting.
NYMPH, Indo-European nature divinities of a lesser order, usually represented as beautiful young female spirits. Nymphs were usually protective towards human beings, some inhabiting the woodlands (Dryads), others the mountains (Oreades), the rivers and seaports (Nereides) and even the oceans (Oceanids).
NYORO, an East Lucustrine, Bantu-speaking Negroid people, mainly dependent on horticulture with some animal husbandry.
NZAMBI, a Bantu sky god of the Congo.

O

OBEAH, a cult which uses corpses for Satanic sorcery. Prevalent among the Negroes of Jamaica, Obeah is somewhat similar to the Voodoo of Haiti.
OBELISK, a monumental stone pillar, square in cross-section but tapering towards the top which terminates in a pyramidal form. Obelisks originated in the predynastic period of ancient Egypt as upright stones on which the sun was believed to rest after rising. Frequently bearing hieroglyphic inscriptions, obelisks become very common during the New Kingdom, being erected in pairs at the entrance to temples.
OBERKASSEL, an archeological site in Germany which was first excavated in 1914 and revealed Cro-Magnon fossil remains associated with Magdalenian artifacts, dated around 17,000 B.P.

OBIO EKPU, the Nigerian 'Ghost Land' or 'Place of the Afterlife'. The wives and many close relatives of Nigerian chiefs were ritually slain at the time of his death in order that their souls could accompany him to the Obio Ekpu. The mass slaughter of the chief's relatives and retainers also served to ensure the chief's successor against possible rivalry by close relatives. Similar practices were common in other African empires, such as that of the Baganda of Uganda.
OBONGO, a Negroid horticultural people of the Congo coastlands.
OB OSTYAK, a Ugrian, Uralic-speaking people who live on the river Ob in what is largely tundra country. The Ob Ostyak depend primarily upon reindeer herding, fishing and hunting.
OBSIDIAN, a form of natural glass associated with earlier volcanic activity. Generally regarded as superior to flint, obsidian was frequently flaked to make cutting tools or ground into vessels and figurines. Its use was distributed throughout the Mediterranean, the Balkans, Anatolia, and Mexico. The approximate age of objects manufactured from obsidian can be measured from the slow chemical changes which commence when a fresh surface of obsidian is exposed to the atmosphere as a result of flaking or grinding.
OBSIDIAN-HYDRATION DATING, a method of absolute dating (q.v.) of stone artifacts made from obsidian based on measurement of the degree of hydration that has occurred on the face of the chipped obsidian, due to the absorption of water from the atmosphere since the flaked surface was first exposed.
OCCIPITAL BONE, that part of the skull which covers the back of the head and the lower part of the brain case.
OCCIPITAL BUN, a ringlike protuberance circling the rear or occipital area of the skull.
OCCULTISM, a general term used to refer to any attempt to manipulate the supernatural by semi-magical pseudo-scientific means, such as astrology, palmistry and alchemy.
OCHRE, an oxide of iron, varying from yellow to red in colour. Since it occurs naturally, ochre was commonly used in the Upper Paleolithic as a colouring pigment for cave paintings and other decorative purposes during the Neolithic. Because of its resemblance to the colour of blood, red ochre was believed to have life-giving properties and was sprinked on corpses in many European Mesolithic, Neolithic and Chalcolithic cultures.
OCHRE GRAVE, a grave in which a corpse has been covered with a thick layer of red ochre, which after the decay of the body usually stains the skeleton. This mode of burial was common on the Pontic Steppes of southern Russia during the period of Indo-European occupation, from whence it spread with the Indo-Europeans to a number of neighbouring countries.
ODONTOLOGY, the study of the origin and evolution of teeth among different forms of life.
OEDIPUS COMPLEX, a hypothetical emotional conflict, invented by Sigmund Freud, who believed that every human child developed a suppressed form of antagonism against its parent of the same sex and a repressed sexual attraction for the parent of the opposite sex. Although this hypothesis may have been appropriate to the small East European Jewish communities in which Sigmund Freud spent his life, Malinowski disproved the universality of Freud's Oedipus complex, and of many other of Freud's psychoanalytical theories, in his studies of the Trobriand Islanders. Being organized around matrilineal systems of kinship, the children of Trobriand Islanders do not display any signs of Freud's supposedly innate and universal Oedipus complex; in fact among the Trobriand Islanders a reverse Oedipus complex applies indicating that where such feelings do exist they are culturally rather than biologically motivated. Abram Kardiner has also demonstrated that the Oedipus complex, where it exists, is essentially a cultural phenomenon, and is by no means universal.
OESTROUS CYCLE, a brief period in the reproductive cycle of mature mammalian females during which ovulation occurs and the female is willing to mate with a male. The length of the cycle will vary according to the species with the result that different species have different breeding seasons. Oestrous does not

OGHAM, a written script comprising groups of parallel or crossing lines, usually carved along the edge of a stone or wooden slab. The origin of the Ogham script is not known. It was used among the Celts of Ireland and Wales as a religious script during the 2nd century A.D., but was also found among the Picts (q.v.), who continued to use it until the 9th century A.D.
OJIBWA, Algonquin-speaking North American Indians, dependent on hunting, fishing and food-gathering.
OKINAWANS, inhabitants of the Ryukyu Islands who speak a form of Japanese and depend primarily on agriculture with some sea fishing and animal husbandry.
OLD BERING SEA CULTURE, a culture which persisted in Northeastern Siberia and parts of Alaska during the first five centuries A.D., and which is particularly noted for ivory carvings. The Old Bering Sea Culture was undoubtedly associated with the Eskimo peoples.
OLD COPPER CULTURE, the term used by American archeologists to refer to metal work produced by American Indians in the Great Lakes region between approximately 3600 and 1500 B.C. Native copper, which was found in relatively pure form around Lake Superior, was simply heated and hammered into the desired shape. Smelting and casting techniques were not invented, and in general the Indians who worked these copper ornaments were simple hunters and gatherers who were ignorant of both pottery-making and the cultivation of crops.
OLD CORDILLERAN CULTURE, a primitive North American hunting and gathering culture which flourished between 9000 and 5000 B.C., and was characterized by stone tools with leaf-shaped points.
OLD EUROPEAN CIVILIZATION, the earliest European pottery-making and food-cultivating civilization flourished in the Balkano-Danubian area between 5000-1500 B.C. Animals were domesticated, crops raised, and pottery manufactured by the seventh century B.C., and the oldest writing known to archeologists was in use prior to 5000 B.C., comprising a system of hieroglyphic symbols (suggestive of the Linear A of the late Minoan civilization of Crete) which have not been deciphered. This high culture, involving elaborate masked religious rituals, and the veneration of the bull and of a fertility goddess figure, had as its social basis a settled village-population, each probably comprising Zadruga-type clans, with organized trading practices and regional centers which in some cases grew to one or two thousand inhabitants in size. Ships with sails traveled the Mediterranean and Aegean, but the incursion of the more warlike Indo-Europeans from 3500 B.C. onwards led to the Indo-Europeanization of the area and the establishment of the classical Indo-European Mycenean culture. The Cretan civilization of Knossos was possibly a last surviving remnant of the Old European civilization, although this also fell under Indo-European (Dorian-Greek) control when the Linear B script supplanted Linear A. The pre-Greek Pelasgian population of the Aegean was similarly a survivor of the Old European civilization, customs relating to which eventually resurfaced in the classical period of Athenian and Greek civilization as the enslaved pre-Greek population was increasingly granted citizen status. This permitted cultic remnants of the old cultural tradition to resurface and gain admission to the mainstream of popular 'Greek' culture.
OLDOWAN, a term used to refer to the simple pebble tool industries of Eastern and Southern Africa, samples of which have been found at Olduvai.
OLDUVAI (also OLDOWAY), an archeological site in North Tanzania which has revealed an extensive sequence of various levels of hominid evolution and of Stone Age tool-making. Clearly stratified deposits reflect the entire Lower Paleolithic period, revealing pebble tools, choppers and later flake artifacts. These are dated from approximately 1.9 million years until 1.7 million years ago. Corresponding layers have revealed the bones of Zinjanthropus bosei (q.v.) recognized as Australopithecine, and of Homo habilis (q.v.), to whom Louis Leakey, who supervised much of the excavation work, attributes the manufacture of stone tools. Crude hand axes, which may be classified as Abbevillian and Chellean appear in strata which have been dated between 1.2 and .5 million years

ago, and are associated with fossil remains which have been definitely identified as Homo erectus (q.v.). The higher strata, notably Bed 4, reveals Acheulian tools and are found in association with hominid fossil remains closely similar to those of Rhodesian Man (q.v.) found at Broken Hill (q.v.) in Zambia, which is classified by some authorities as Neanderthaloid but by other authorities as a late advanced Homo erectus fossil. The uppermost stratum reveals the penetration of a Capsian (q.v.) industry – derived from the penetration of North African peoples into the Kenya and Tanzania region, fossil remains of which were first found in 1913 and at that time labelled as 'Olduvai Man'. At the present time a reassessment of the relationship between the earlier levels excavated at Olduvai and of the earlier hominid varieties has been necessitated by the discovery of Skull 1470 remains east of Lake Rudolph. Although dated some 600,000 years earlier than the Homo habilis (q.v.) remains, these reveal a number of more modern characteristics, and place the whole relationship between Australopithecines, Homo habilis and the Skull 1470 remains in an entirely new light.

OLFACTORY, an adjective describing the sense of smell.

OLIGARCHY, the concentration of authoritative power in the hands of a small segment of society.

OLIGOCENE, a division of the geologic Tertiary period lasting from 38 to 26 million years ago.

OLMEC, a people who inhabited the more hot and humid plains of the Mexican Gulf Coast. The Olmecs were responsible for the erection of a group of three ceremonial centers in South Vera Cruz, between 1500 and 1250 B.C., which places them in the pre-Classic phase of Meso-American cultural evolution. They were particularly noted as stone carvers, not only of small jade figurines, but also of massive heads varying from 9-10 feet in height, carved from basalt rock. Generally speaking the Olmec civilization made a major contribution to the development of Central or Meso-American civilization. Since the soil of the coastal plains which they occupied was rich, they were able to construct imposing ceremonial centers such as that found at La Venta. The Olmecs also possessed a form of hieroglyphic writing which has not yet been deciphered but which may have provided the stimulus from which later Mayan hieroglyphs developed. The Olmec civilization achieved its peak at the beginning of the first millennium B.C. but disappeared somewhere around the sixth century B.C., probably as a result of fresh invasions of tribal peoples from the north.

OLYMPIC GAMES, the ancient Greeks exhibited their national unity every four years by celebrating the Olympic Games, from 776 B.C. until A.D. 394, when these were finally discontinued under Christian edict. In contrast to the modern Olympics, only members of the Greek aristocracy were permitted to compete.

OLYMPUS, a high mountain in Thessaly, rising to 10,000 feet above sea level, popularly regarded as the Home of the Gods. Hidden in clouds, which were perceived as the gates to heaven, the summit was described by Homer as being ever-radiant in cloudless sunshine, and unruffled by either wind or rain.

OM, a mystical term revered and used by both Hindus and Buddhists, which may have originally simply denoted assent, and was traditionally placed at the commencement of any sacred utterance, whether a prayer or a recitation of the scriptures. The correct form is 'aum', denoting Agni (fire), Varuna (water) and Maruts (air).

OMAHA, Muskogean-speaking North American Plains Indians of the Siouan group, who originally lived in the Ohio river valley before migrating to Nebraska. The Omaha were dependent upon horticulture, practised in the river valleys, supplemented by some hunting and food-gathering.

OMNIVOROUS, a term used to refer to animals which are both herbivorous and carnivorous.

ONA, an American Indian people occupying inland areas of Tierra del Fuego, and adjacent parts of the mainland of South America, whose language was related to that of the Yahgan and Alakaluf, but who practised hunting as well as fishing and food-gathering.

ONEIDA, a North American Iroquois people of the Eastern Woodlands.

ONONDAGA, a North American Iroquois people of the Eastern Woodlands.

ONOTOA, a Malayo-Polynesian-speaking people of Bikini in the Gilbert Islands of Polynesia, dependent on fishing, horticulture and some food-gathering.

ONTOGENY, the life history of an individual organism.

ONTONG-JAVANESE, a Polynesian people isolated in Central Melanesia, dependent on fishing and horticulture.

OPATA, an American Indian people of Northwestern Mexico.

OPHIDIA, a limbless order of Reptilia (q.v.) or snakes, the Ophidia possess exceptionally wide jaws and immovable eyelids but lack eardrums.

OPPIDUM, a term which has been used in various senses. Oppida (plural) were correctly the administrative capitals of separate territories of the Roman Empire, but Julius Caesar also used the term to refer to the Celtic hill fortresses (q.v.) of Gaul, and in recent years the term oppidum has been widely used to refer to any Indo-European fortified capital dating from the Chalcolithic, Bronze or Iron Ages.

OPPOSABLE THUMB, primates are distinguished, among other features, by the ability to oppose the thumb to the finger in a prehensile grip, a biological trait which facilitated the use of tools among early hominids.

ORACLE, a person (or object) serving as a medium for communication with the spirit world.

ORACLE BONE, animal bones used for consultation with supernatural beings for the purpose of divining answers to specific questions. A common West Eurasian practice involved the use of the shoulder blade of an ox, which was heated over a fire, the answer to the required questions being determined by the pattern of the resultant cracks. It is thus of considerable significance that animal shoulder blades were also used as oracle bones in China under the Shang dynasty of China, which appears to have had steppeland origins. In China the shoulder blades were frequently inscribed with the question to which an answer was sought, and the decipherment of these inscriptions has added considerably to our knowledge of Shang history and culture.

ORACLE, POISON, a technique for consulting supernatural beings for the purpose of determining the guilt or innocence of particular individuals. In extreme cases the poison can be fed to those who are suspected of guilt, but in many cases, as for example among the Azande, the poison can be administered to a series of chickens, each of which represents a suspected offender. It is believed that the chicken which represents the guilty person will be the first to die.

ORACLES, a form of divination by which divine forces are consulted by an expert in the supernatural. The reply, which may take the form, for example, of the rustling of oak leaves, is usually interpreted in deliberately ambiguous and obscure fashion.

ORAL LITERATURE, the total collection of legends, epics, myths, folklore and songs which are usually preserved from generation to generation with surprising accuracy in pre-literate societies. Even after the adoption of writing, the reduction of sacred literature to written form may be proscribed in favor of oral retention.

ORANG LAUT, a people of Southern Borneo.

ORANIAN, an Upper Paleolithic North African culture, restricted to the coastal regions between Morocco and Cyrenaica, the excavated remains of which include a wide variety of microliths. The Oranian culture is dated between 12,000 and 8000 B.C.

ORAON, a North Dravidian people who practise agriculture, animal husbandry and some fishing.

ORBIT, that portion of the skull which surrounds the eye socket.

ORBITAL INDEX, the orbital height expressed as a percentage of the length.

ORDA, the Uralic word from which the term 'horde' (q.v.) is derived.

ORDER, a taxonomic group of related organisms comprising a number of related families, but smaller than a class.

ORDOS DESERT, a large desert lying north of the Hwang Ho river of Northern China, which formerly enjoyed a more fertile climate. One Upper Paleolithic archeological site in the Ordos desert reinforces the evidence for an expansion of the European Upper Paleolithic across the grassy steppes of Central Asia to Northern China, Manchuria and Japan.

ORDOVICIAN, a geological period within the Paleozoic era, which lasted from approximately 575 to 395 millions years ago.

OREOPITHECUS, a fossil hominid (q.v.), the remains of which have been found in Italy. Believed to have dwelt in a swampy environment, some authorities consider that Oreopithecus was possibly ancestral to the hominids (q.v.) but this opinion is disputed.

ORGAN, any part of a plant or animal which operates as a functional unit.

ORGANELLES, small structures within a cell (q.v.) which have specific functions. The ribosomes (q.v.) which are responsible for the synthesizing of proteins (q.v.) are organelles.

ORGANISM, any individual living thing.

ORMUZD, see AHURA MAZDA.

OROCHI, a Siberian people of the East Manchurian area.

OROKAIVA, a Papuan people of East Papua, dependent on horticulture with some fishing, food-gathering, hunting and animal husbandry.

ORTHOGENESIS, a former theory that specific species may reveal an evolutionary trend in a consistent direction over an extended period of time as a result of an innate driving or guiding force. The theory of orthogenesis is no longer accepted, since natural selection alone directs the course of evolution. Evolutionary change therefore reflects the disparate ability of individual life forms and of different species to survive and reproduce in the prevailing environmental conditions.

ORTHOGRADE, vertical stance, as found in Australopithecines and their descendants.

ORTHOSELECTION, a relatively direct and uninterrupted process of adaptive evolution.

OSAGE, a North American Indian people of the Great Plains.

OSIRIS, the Egyptian God of Death, who was slain by his brother Seth but whose dismembered body was collected by his wife Isis and reassembled, thus enabling her to conceive a posthumous son, Horus (symbolizing the Spring) from the body of her dead husband. The myth of Osiris and Horus became the basis of an earth and vegetation cult, reflecting the annual agricultural cycle on which Egyptian prosperity rested.

OSSETES, an Indo-European-speaking people, whose language is related to Persian. The Ossetes depend primarily on animal herding, supplemented by agriculture and some hunting.

OSSUARY, any container used for the burial of human bones, including not only small articles such as urns, but also especially constructed burial chambers intended to house the remains of many generations of the same family.

OSTEODONTOKERATIC, a hypothetical stage in the evolution of hominid technology in which extensive use would have been made of bones, teeth and horn tools, before stoneworking techniques were developed.

OSTYAK, a North Siberian people.

OTO, Muskogean-Siouan-speaking, North American Plains Indians of the Siouan group. The Oto occupied the Great Plains and were dependent on horticulture, in the river valleys, supplemented by hunting and food-gathering.

OTOMANI, a Bronze Age culture of Eastern Hungary and Northwestern Rumania, dating from approximately 1600 to 1300 B.C., which was closely related to the Únetiče culture.

OTOMI, a Central American people located in the highlands of North-central Mexico.

OTORO, Kordofanian-speaking (Niger-Congo) people of the Nuba group largely dependent on horticulture, animal husbandry and some hunting.

OVAMBO, see AMBO.

OVIMBUNDU, a Bantu cultivating people of the southern Congo.
OYO YORUBA, Kwa-speaking Negroid people of the Yoruba group in West Africa, largely dependent on horticulture with some animal husbandry and fishing.

P

PAEZ, a South American Indian people of Western Ecuador, who speak a language related to Chibchan and are dependent on horticulture, some animal husbandry and hunting and gathering.
PAGODA, a mound, building or tower constructed by Buddhists to house any sacred relic associated with Gautama Buddha. Such relics might comprise anything from a bone to a piece of the Bo Tree under which Gautama Buddha was supposed to have received enlightenment.
PAHARI, North Indian Indo-European language, derived from Sanskrit, whose speakers subsist by agriculture and animal husbandry.
PAIR-BONDING, the tendency in family-type mammalian societies for a permanent or semi-permanent bond to form between a particular male and a particular female (or females). This bond involves sexual prerogatives, cooperation in the rearing of the offspring, food-sharing, and an elementary division of labor, the evolutionary purpose of which is the protection and rearing of the offspring.
PAIWAN, Malayo-Polynesian-speaking people of the Muong group, largely dependent on cultivation with some hunting, fishing and animal husbandry.
PALATAL LAW, a law of phonetics which traces certain basic relationships between Sanskrit, Greek and Latin.
PALAUANS, Malayo-Polynesian-speaking people from Palau, largely dependent on horticulture and fishing supplemented by some animal husbandry.
PALAUNG, a Mon Khmer-speaking people, largely dependent on cultivation and some animal husbandry.
PALAWAN BATAK, a branch of the Malayo-Polynesian Batak people inhabiting the island of Palawa located between Borneo and the Philippines.
PALENQUE, an important ceremonial centre of the Classic Mayan civilization, located at Chiapas in Mexico. The most notable building is the Temple of the Sun, which stands on a relatively low pyramid but contains important hieroglyphic inscriptions.
PALEO-ASIAN LANGUAGES, no true family of Paleo-Asian languages can be demonstrated since the East Siberian area is occupied by small hunting and gathering bands which reveal an enormous variety of languages that cannot be effectively related to each other. The term 'Paleo-Asian' therefore refers more to a geographical agglomeration of languages than to a generically related 'family' of languages. The Ainu language of Hokkaido and the Sakhalin Islands is often included in the Paleo-Asian group, as also is Gilyak, spoken in the Kamchatka peninsula, which reveals definite affiliations with the languages of the Eskimo and the Aleuts.
PALEOBOTANY, the study of botanical remains surviving from earlier periods. Most organic material tends to decay, but considerable evidence of past forms of plant life comes into existence with improvements in archeological techniques. Needless to say, any evidence obtained regarding the flora prevailing in specific regions at specific times is of immense importance in the archeologist's attempts to reconstruct the human culture history. See also PALYNOLOGY.
PALEOCENE, a geological period, within the Cenozoic era, which lasted from approximately 65 to 54 million years ago.
PALEOLITHIC AGE, the Old Stone Age, during which hominids were dependent entirely upon hunting and food-gathering subsistence techniques. Commonly divided into a Lower, a Lower Evolved, a Middle, and an Upper Paleolithic level of technological evolution, each was based upon particular improvements in stoneworking techniques.
PALEOLITHIC CULTS OF THE DEAD, there is clear archeological evidence that the Neanderthals who inhabited Europe and the Middle East during the

Middle Paleolithic believed in the existence of a soul which survived the death of the body. It has been suggested, however, that Neolithic attitudes towards corpses may have been inspired more by fear of the deceased spirit than by any reverence implied in the concept of ancestor worship (q.v.). By contrast, the Cro-Magnons of the Upper Paleolithic have left evidence which suggests that ancestor worship had already begun to evolve by the Magdalenian period.

PALEOMAGNETIC DATING, the dating of rocks according to their context in the changing magnetic field of the earth, possible where the magnetic polarization has been preserved by an accumulation of sediments. The dating of such rocks permits the establishment of an approximate age for any fossils or artifacts found in the same sedimentary strata. (See DATING SYSTEMS).

PALEOPATHOLOGY, it is now realized that skeletal remains may frequently reveal the evidence of disease, dental decay, malnutrition, and even of fractures and other trauma-induced lesions indicative of a particular lifestyle.

PALEOSEROLOGY, because desiccated and frozen human remains frequently contain evidence of the serological characteristics of the original living organism, paleoserology, although only lightly developed at the present time, may eventually produce important evidence regarding the blood groups of ancient hominid populations with the resultant implications concerning their relationship to living peoples and to each other.

PALEO-SIBERIANS, see SIBERIANS.

PALEONTOLOGY, the study of the fossil remains of extinct life forms.

PALEONTOLOGY, LINGUISTIC, the use of the historical analysis of language to contribute to our understanding of cultural history. If it can be demonstrated that any people living at a specific time or place had a word for a particular object, then it follows that they must have been acquainted with that object even though archeological evidence to this effect may be lacking. Similarly an observable similarity between different languages indicates that the speakers of the two languages must have shared a degree of culture relationship at some former time.

PALEOZOIC, a major geological era dating from 575 to 225 million years ago in which the first chordates and vertebrates appeared.

PALIKUR, a South American Indian people of Arawak speech, dependent on horticulture, fishing and hunting.

PALLAS ATHENE, the Greek goddess of wisdom, whose main temple was situated at Athens.

PALM WINE, a wine made from the sap of the palm tree, in South and Southeast Asia. Palm wine is otherwise known as 'toddee'.

PALYNOLOGY, the study of pollen. Certain types of pollen possess a protective outer skin which is resistant to decay, and as a result, a number of archeological sites have yielded pollen samples which have been identified by palynologists. In many cases radiocarbon dates have been obtained for these samples of pollen, thus making it possible to compile definite chronologies of the flora occupying specific areas at specific periods of time.

PAN (or FAUNUS), a supernatural being regarded by the Greeks as the protector of herdsmen, Pan was generally represented as possessing a human head, shoulders and torso, but goatlike lower limbs.

PANAMINT, a Shoshone-(Uto-Aztec)-speaking North American Indian people, inhabiting the Coastal Great Basin and dependent on food-gathering and hunting.

PANARE, a South American, Carib-speaking Indian people, dependent on horticulture, with considerable hunting, fishing and some food-gathering.

PANO, a South American Indian family of languages, belonging to the Gê, Pano and Carib Group. Panoan includes Amahuaca (Peru and Brazil), Chacobo (Bolivia), and Aruau (Peru). A Macro-Panoan phylum has been suggested, which would include Guaycuri, Mataco, and Tacana.

PAPAGO, a North American Indian people of the United States Southwest, related to the Pima (q.v.).

PAPUANS, the collective name for the many diverse tribal peoples of aboriginal origin occupying the central and northern parts of New Guinea (e.g. Arapesh, Kwoma, Orokaiwa, etc). The Papuans are of Australoid racial stock, and due to their extreme localization and division into numerous socially isolated groups, they speak literally hundreds of quite different languages, although these have been grouped by scholars, for convenience, into a single Papuan linguistic phylum. The highland Papuans are more Australoid than those of the lowlands.
PAPYRUS, a reed which grew widely in the delta of the Nile and was used by the ancient Egyptians as a writing material, as well as for other purposes such as boat-building. The method of manufacture of papyrus 'paper' was simple, involving the splitting of the stem and the pasting of the separate layers together to make a long role. The term *papyrus*, which is the Latin not the Greek name for this particular reed, is the root from which the modern term 'paper' is derived. Large bundles of papyrus reeds were used for the construction of lighter than water boats, for both river and open sea navigation.
PARADISE, the concept of Paradise appears first in the Sumerian religion, where it was regarded as a home for the gods, to which no mortal being could gain entry. In Indo-European religion, by contrast, mortals who had distinguished themselves by heroic deeds might be admitted to the company of the gods after death, becoming semi-deities, while the souls of lesser folk passed into a cold underworld, where they survived in a state of suspended animation. Slaves, not being recognized as members of the community, were not regarded as having souls and therefore could not look forward to any afterlife. The Semites appear to have borrowed the Sumerian idea of Paradise, but opened Paradise to the souls of all mortals who had lived a virtuous life.
PARALLEL COUSINS, cousins who are descended from two brothers or from two sisters. In many societies in which kinship is based upon a lineal clan system, such cousins would find themselves in the same clan, and thus be prohibited from marrying. In other societies, as among most Moslems, such marriages may actually be favored.
PARAMORPH, a taxonomic variant existing within a species which does not vary with sufficient consistency to warrant classification as a distinct species. In the contemporary world, many hybrid human populations may be regarded as paramorphs rather than as distinct subspecies.
PARANG, a long knife used by Malays.
PARANTHROPUS ROBUSTUS, an African hominid today regarded by most anthropologists as a species of Australopithecinae, and now known as Australopithecus robustus. (See AUSTRALOPITHECINAE).
PARASITE, in biology a parasite is an organism which lives in or upon a host organism, from which it obtains food without any symbiotic relationship existing between the two organisms. Certain human groups and communities have been defined as parasitic in their ability to obtain subsistence from a host society, without contributing to the welfare of the host society through any type of symbiotic relationship.
PARAUJANO, a South American Indian people who speak an Arawak language and are dependent on horticulture and food-gathering supplemented by some hunting.
PARCHMENT, a form of writing material made from the hide of a sheep after soaking the skin in lime water, scraping off the outer flesh and hair, stretching and drying it and finally rubbing it with a pumice stone. Parchment was invented by the Greeks as an alternative form of paper, since the papyrus grown in the Nile delta could not be cultivated in the Aegean.
PARE, a Bantu-speaking Negroid people of the Kenya highlands, largely dependent on horticulture and animal husbandry.
PARESSI, an Arawak-speaking South American people of Northern Argentina, dependent on horticulture with some hunting , fishing and food-gathering.
PARTHENOGENESIS, a biological process by which an unfertilized ovum is inserted into and develops in the body of a different individual. In the future

it may prove possible to develop a zygote from a human ovum without fertilization from a male sperm cell. However, this would circumvent the element of genetic recombination which is implicit in sexual reproduction and an essential part of the evolutionary process, so that only females could be reproduced by this method.

PARTHIANS, an Indo-European people of steppeland origin, closely related to the Medes and Persians, who entered Northeastern Persia around 250 B.C., and established a kingdom which embraced much of the older Seleucid and Bactrian empire. This Parthian empire survived until about A.D. 100, when it was overthrown by a renaissance of Persian vitality under the Sassanid dynasty.

PARTICULARISM, HISTORICAL, the theory that each culture should be studied independently as a separate organic unit. Originated by Franz Boas (q.v.).

PASSAGE-GRAVE, a common type of Megalithic chamber tomb, in which the main burial chamber was approached by a narrow covered entrance-passage. Passage graves were common throughout Western Europe from Scandinavia to Iberia, surviving into the late Copper Age in the Iberian peninsula.

PASTORALISM, a pattern of culture based upon the herding of domesticated animals commonly involving some degree of nomadism.

PATAGONIANS, American Indians, probably descended from the earliest human settlers of the Americas, who inhabit the plains of Southern Patagonia in Argentina. These include the Ona and the Tehuelche.

PATELLA, a Pushtu-speaking (Iranic, Indo-European) people, inhabiting much of Northwestern Pakistan and parts of East Afghanistan. They were traditionally dependent upon agriculture with some animal husbandry.

PATHOLOGY, the study of diseased tissues.

PATRIARCHAL SOCIETY, a society in which power is primarily vested in the senior males.

PATRILINEAL DESCENT, descent traced through the male line.

PATRILOCAL, residence in or near the hone of the husband's parents.

PATRIMONY, property which properly belongs to the family in a patrilineal society, and cannot be alienated at the will of any individual member. It passes to the trusteeship of the eldest son or to the children generally, according to custom, following the death of the family head.

PATWIN, a Penutian-speaking California people, dependent on food-gathering, hunting and fishing.

PAVILAND CAVE, an archeological site near Swansea in England, where in 1823 a fairly complete Cro-Magnon fossil skeleton, then known as the 'Red Lady', was discovered. This has been dated to sometime in the Würm glacial period and has been associated with Aurignacian tools. The term 'Red Lady' was applied because the bones were stained red as a result of the Cro-Magnon custom of sprinkling corpses with red ochre.

PAWNEE, Muskogean-Siouan-speaking North American Indians belonging to the Caddoan group. The Pawnee practiced horticulture in the river valleys of the Great Plains, supplemented by hunting and food-gathering.

PAZYRYK, the site of a group of tombs located in the high Altai mountains of Central Asia, several of which have been excavated. Dating from between the 5th and 3rd century B.C., these tombs comprised burial chambers covered by low barrows – or more correctly by cairns. Due to the high altitude and cold climate, water that seeped into the graves froze in the winter, and remained frozen, thereby preserving the undecayed corpses and rich grave furnishings in a protective covering of ice. Although some of the tombs had been broken into, sufficient evidence remained to indicate that they belonged to Scythian or other Indo-European nobles who had penetrated into Central Asia, bringing their characteristic Indo-European culture with them, before becoming genetically admixed with indigenous Mongoloid peoples. Thus, although the artifacts are clearly western, one of the three complete corpses preserved in the ice was that of a chieftain of Caucasoid physical type, one was that of a chieftain revealing certain Mongoloid racial characteristics, and the third was that of a female, believed to be the wife of the second male, who was of blond Caucasoid type. Both the men were heavily tattooed – a mark of nobility – and had been buried with horses, horse equipment, four-wheeled wagons, and a rich collection of clothing, sumptuously embroidered felt hangings and jewelry.

PEASANT SOCIETY, an agricultural society producing crops for personal subsistence rather than for an organized market economy.

PEAT, an accumulation of deceased plant material which has only partially decomposed principally due to a lack of oxygen. Peat bogs are common in poorly drained and consequently waterlogged areas. Being comprised of organic material, lumps of peat may be cut and dried and burned like coal.

PEBBLE TOOLS, the earliest stone tools which (unlike eoliths) reveal clear indications of hominid manufacture were pebble tools. These were manufactured by a standard process in which a few flakes were struck from one side of the pebble to produce an irregular cutting edge. More refined pebble tools have been called 'handaxes' in Africa, and 'chopping tools' in the Far East.

PECTORAL, a piece of jewelry or ornamentation worn on the breast.

PECTORAL GIRDLE, a system of bones which provides support for the front limbs of vertebrate animals, found in Tetrapoda (q.v.).

PEDI, a Bantu-speaking Negroid people, related to the Sotho and largely dependent on horticulture and cattle herding.

PEDIGREE, a record of an individual's ancestors. In genetics (q.v.) the term is used to refer to a record compiled to trace the frequency with which a specific genetic characteristic reveals itself phenotypically among individuals of a particular lineage.

PEDOLOGY, the chemical and organic analysis of soil. Pedology can be of value to an archeologist as an aid to the identification of the content of filled pits for traces of decayed timber or other material in the earth that he is excavating. Furthermore, the nature of the topsoil will be affected by the prevailing climate, vegetation and other conditions, and the surface soil may therefore differ from the subsoil, with the result that any earlier human interference with the natural layering of the soil (as occurs in the construction of a house) can readily be identified with the assistance of pedology.

PEKANGEKUM, Algonquin-speaking North American Indians, related to the Ojibwa and dependent on hunting, fishing and food-gathering.

PEKING MAN, otherwise known as Sinanthropus pekinensis, is the name first given to Homo erectus remains found by W. C. Pei in 1929 at Choukoutien, near Peking. (See CHOUKOUTIEN).

PELASGIANS, the pre-Greek inhabitants of the Aegean, who were a part of the Old European (q.v.) civilization.

PELVIS, a bone structure occurring in land vertebrates, which appears to have evolved for the purpose of providing a firm base for the hind limbs.

PENATES, the household gods of the Romans, to whom the hearth and table were sacred. Although the term Penates was often used to include the Lares (q.v.), each household had only one Lar or protective household spirit, but many Penates or ancestral spirits. Since the Roman state was still regarded as nothing more than a large household made up of a number of related member families, the spirits of the more famous leaders of past generations were regarded as the Penates of the nation-state.

PENDE, a Bantu-speaking Negroid people, living in the lower Congo, the Pende are largely dependent on horticulture and some domestication of animals.

PENETRANCE, a term used by geneticists to refer to the frequency with which any gene expresses itself in the phenotype of a population.

PENIS, because of the magico-religious implications of reproduction in primitive societies, the penis has been subjected to a variety of ritual mutilations among many people of diverse pre-scientific cultures, and has also been artistically represented as a symbol of fertility worship in many religions. (See also CIRCUMCISION and PHALLIC WORSHIP).

PENOBSCOT, a Northeastern Woodland Indian people formerly occupying South Maine.

PENUTIAN LANGUAGES, this phylum of American Indian languages includes many small families of North American Indian languages, including Yokuts, Maidu, Witun, Miwok, Costanoan, Nez-Percé, Coos, Yakonan, Kalapuyan, and Chinook, as well as the Tsimshian and Zuni isolates and the Central American Mixe-Zoque and Mayan language families.

PEOPLE OF THE SEA, the name given in Egyptian records to a warlike seagoing people whose attempt to conquer Egypt in the 13th or early 12th century B.C., was defeated largely as a result of a storm which dispersed their fleet and placed them at the mercy of the Egyptians. Today they are customarily identified as either Myceneans or – more likely – as a closely related Indo-European people who had settled on the Dalmatian coast of the Adriatic and become sea-raiders like the Vikings who settled the Scandinavian coast. Following the failure of the attack upon Egypt, some settled on the Palestine coast as Philistines, whereas others returned to their homeland or possibly colonized local areas in the Central or Western Mediterranean. Some authorities have even suggested that the Etruscans were derived from the People of the Sea (q.v.), but this view is not generally accepted.

PERCUSSION FLAKING, a Stone Age technique for shaping stone, bone or even wooden tools by striking them with a hammer stone or a sharpened blade.

PERCUSSION INSTRUMENT, a musical instrument which is struck either by the hand or by some more elaborate striking device. Percussion instruments may have been among the earliest musical instruments known to man, dating from at least the Upper Paleolithic.

PERICUE, a Baja California American Indian people related to the Cochima.

PERIGLACIAL, see INTERGLACIAL.

PERIGORDIAN, named after a site in France, it is generally believed that the Perigordian industry represents an initial stage of the Upper Paleolithic. The Perigordian has itself been divided into a series of stages: notably Early Perigordian, corresponding to the Chatelperronian artifacts, which possibly developed into an Upper Perigordian industry represented by Gravettian. This in turn finally evolved into a form known as Proto-Magdalenian, which was abruptly terminated by the appearance of Solutrean technology, possibly reflecting the influence of a new Cro-Magnon Upper Paleolithic people who penetrated Central and Western Europe from the Eastern steppeland. The above-proposed sequence is based entirely upon typological analysis, and not upon the concrete evidence of stratigraphy, since there is no archeological site which reveals a comprehensive series of Upper Paleolithic strata. Furthermore, the above proposed sequence assumes that the peoples of the Aurignacian culture occupied Europe simultaneously with those of the Perigordian culture, without overlapping or even influencing each other's cultural traditions, a view which is also regarded as questionable.

PERIOD, one of the major subdivisions of the Cenozoic, Mesozoic, and Paleozoic eras.

PERMAFROST, a term used to describe the condition of the permanently frozen subsoil in tundra and arctic regions.

PERMANENT TEETH, the second set of teeth which replace the deciduous teeth in most mammals.

PERMIAN, a geological period within the Paleozoic era which lasted from approximately 280 to 225 million years ago.

PERSEPOLIS, a city founded by the Persian King Darius I at the end of the 6th century B.C., from which time it served as the capital city of the Achaemenid empire, until captured and destroyed by Alexander the Great in A.D. 331.

PERSIANS, closely related to the Indo-Aryans of India and also to the Scythians of the Pontic steppes, the Persians were an Indo-European or Aryan people who invaded Northwestern Iran early in the 2nd millennium B.C., probably by way of the Caucasus. Under the leadership of the Achaemenid dynasty, they built a vast empire which survived from 558 to 331 B.C. Following the brief conquest by Alexander the Great, Persian power re-emerged under the Sassanid dynasty, and a more durable empire was re-established in 224 B.C. which lasted until it was overrun by Arabs in A.D. 617. Under the Achaemenids, the original Aryan or Iranian religion was modified into a monotheistic religion, known as Zoroastrianism, in which the god of Truth and Light, namely Ahura Mazda, was worshipped, in opposition to the spirit of the Lie, Angra Mainya.

PERSONALITY, BASIC, personality traits which are implanted by the prevailing culture pattern of the group.

PETROLOGICAL IDENTIFICATION, the use of mineralogical analysis to identify the geographical source of the materials used in the manufacture of stone tools and megaliths.

PEUL, see FULANI.

PEYOTE CULT, the peyote is a cactus which grows in Central America and the Southwestern parts of North America, from which a liquid known as Mescaline (or mescal) is extracted. This drug serves as a stimulant and also an intoxicant, and if taken in adequate quantities will induce visionary experiences. As a result a peyote cult spread widely to many American Indian tribes, even those as far north as the Crow and the Sioux, in which the cactus was regarded as the incarnation of a deity and consumption of mescaline (either in liquid form, or by eating part of the cactus, or even smoking the dried plant) became a recognized ceremony accompanied by ritual prayers, songs and dances. Far from being purely individualist in its nature, the peyote cult encouraged loyalty to the family and to the tribe, and emphasized the importance of ritual prayers, songs and contemplation.

PHAISTOS, a Minoan palance located in the southern part of Central Crete. Phaistos was constructed around 1900 B.C., and resembles a smaller version of Knossos, complete with a court which is believed to have been used for the same bull-baiting rituals. The Phaistos disc is a small six-inch diameter clay disc, decorated with a large number of stamped inscriptions arranged in a spiral pattern, the origin and meaning of which have not been determined.

PHALLIC WORSHIP, a form of fertility ritual, in which the generative principle of nature is represented by the male genital or phallus. Phallic worship appears to have been particularly widespread among the Semites, and was also known to the ancient Egyptians and to the pre-Indo-European inhabitants of India, from whom it was carried over into the subsequent Hindu religion.

PHARAOH, the title of the god-kings of ancient Egypt. The living pharaohs were regarded as being earthly reincarnations of the god Horus, and a substantial portion of the resources of Egypt was directed towards ensuring that their souls would be properly cared for after death. In all, 31 dynasties of pharaohs ruled Egypt, the longest living of all the various civilizations of the world.

PHENOTYPE, the manifest genetic makeup of an individual as distinct from the genotype (q.v.). Each individual possesses a pair of genes for each specific genetic quality, but only one of these manifests itself in his or her physical development. Thus the term phenotype is used to refer to the genetically determined character of the individual organism, as distinct from the genotype or total genetic material inherited by the individual.

PHILIPPINES, the modern Philippine population is predominantly of Malayo-Polynesian origin, having been settled by possibly two waves of immigrant horticulturalists. However, there are numerous minority racial groups, largely of Negrito type, which include the Ifugao, Kalinga, and Iagarot of the Northern Philippines, and the Hanunvo, Subanun, Sugnuhanon and Tagbanua of the Southern Philippines.

PHILISTINES, known to the Egyptians as the Pulesati, the Philistines appear to have been descended from a portion of the Peoples of the Sea (q.v.) who failed in their attack upon Egypt around 1200 B.C. but succeeded in seizing the adjacent coastal region – still known as Palestine in their memory – from the Semitic Canaanites. The Aegean character of the culture of the Philistines, clearly revealed by archeological excavations at Askalon, indicates an Indo-European origin. The Philistines appear to have been a cultured, elegant people until they were defeated and extirpated by the less urbanized Israelites, in whose records their memory is vilified.

PHOENICIANS, a branch of the Semitic Canaanite people who occupied the Levantine coast during the 1st millennium B.C., their major cities being Tyre, Sidon and Biblos. Although these cities were conquered by the Babylonians in 574 B.C., the Phoenicians remained a powerful Eastern Mediterranean sea-going merchant people, and were able to establish a large and subsequently powerful colony at Carthage in modern Tunisia. Phoenician traders ventured to the Atlantic coast of Europe and North Africa, and may have circumnavigated the African continent. However, as the Carthaginian power increased they came into conflict with the Greek colonies in Sicily and Southern Italy, and subsequently with the expanding Romans, who finally destroyed Carthage completely. As Semites, they worshipped a supreme god, Moloch, to molify whom they sacrificed their first born children at times of crisis.
PHOENIX, a mythological bird, which is reborn from the flames, derived from the *bennu* or sacred bird of Osiris and was in some way linked to the Sumerian legend of the Great Flood. Its hieroglyphic symbol was three wavy lines, believed to refer to the legend of the flood which had reached Egypt from the Fertile Crescent.
PHONEME, the smallest units of sound that may be identified in any form of human speech.
PHONETIC LAWS, generalized statements about any changes which may have taken place within the history of a language, or a family of languages, in the method of articulation.
PHONOLOGY, the study of sounds in a language.
PHOSPHATE ANALYSIS, decayed animal bodies leave behind a residue of phosphates which remain in the soil or grave even after the organic material has decayed, being only slowly dissipated by the percolation of water. The chemical analysis of earth gathered from caves and other areas believed to have been occupied by early men can therefore sometimes provide evidence of the former existence of animal remains, even though the human corpses, including even the skeletons, may have completely disappeared.
PHOTOSYNTHESIS, the process by which green plants synthesize organic compounds from water and carbon dioxide, with the aid of energy absorbed from sunshine.
PHOTOTROPHIC, the ability of certain simple organisms to move in response to light, usually towards light, to permit photosynthesis.
PHRATRY, an exogamous unilineal subdivision of a tribe comprising two or more sibs or clans. The term phratry is borrowed from the Greek, membership or citizenship in the Greek city states of classical times being dependent on birth into a phratry. The term is congnate to the Slavic *bratsvo* and to the modern English *brother.*
PHRYGIANS, at one time known as the Muski, the Phrygians were an Indo-European or Aryan people closely related to the Thracians, who are believed to have migrated from the area of Thrace into Western Turkey and established their own kingdom, following the downfall of the Hittite empire, to whose overthrow they probably contributed. Under the legendary King Midas, the Phrygians established their capital at Gordion, and although this city was destroyed by the Cimmerians from the Pontic Steppes in 80 B.C., they succeeded in maintaining a substantial degree of cultural and national unity under the Lydians.
PHYLOGENETIC CONTINUUM, species and subspecies do not possess characteristics which are fixed invariably for all time, instead they change and evolve through the generations. Thus the evolutionary reality is the evolving intergenerational racial unit, which is best conceived as a distinctive gene pool persisting and evolving through the generations. Successful evolution depends substantially upon a fairly high degree of genetic isolation for such gene pools, without which speciation and specialization, hence evolutionary progress, is impossible. For this reason rapid evolution occurs only in relatively small genetic isolates.
PHYLOGENY, the evolutionary history of any taxonomic group.
PHYLUM, (1) (biological) a classificatory term for a group of similar or related

classes of animals. (2) (linguistic) A group of distantly-related languages and language families.

PHYSIOLOGY, the study of the life processes in living organisms.

PIAPOCO, a South American Indian people, living in Southern Venezuela, who speak an Arawak language and are dependent on horticulture and some hunting and fishing.

PIAROA, a South American Indian people living around the Middle Orinoco River in Venezuela, language unidentified, dependent on hunting, fishing, food-gathering and some horticulture.

PICTOGRAPH, a picture intended to symbolize a particular concept or event; an early form of written communication.

PICTS, known to the Romans as the *Pictae,* or 'painted peoples', the true name of the Picts seems to have been *Cruithni.* Although their origin remains unclear, and there is some evidence that they possessed matrilineal traditions, the decipherment of Pictish and Ogham inscriptions reveals no less than three different Pictish languages, one of which appears to have been pre-Indo-European, indicating an Atlanto-Mediterranean population, the other two languages being forms of Celtic, with the implication that the Picts were originally an indigenous people who later came under Celtic domination. Constantly threatening Roman Britain, and several times succeeding in breaking through Hadrian's Wall, the Picts maintained their independence from the Romans, but were eventually absorbed by the Celtic Dalriada in the 9th century as a part of the new kingdom in Scotland.

PICURIS, an Uto-Aztec, Tanoan-speaking North American Indian, Eastern Pueblo people, dependent on horticulture supplemented by a small amount of hunting and (in post-Columbian times) animal husbandry.

PIDGIN ENGLISH, a term used to refer to an imperfect form of English, originally employed for communication between Chinese and Europeans. However, the term is now widely used for various forms of 'broken' English spoken anywhere in the world. See also CREOLIZATION.

PIEGAN, Algonquin-speaking North American Plains Indians, mainly dependent on hunting with some food-gathering.

PIGS, the native pig of Western Asia appears to have been domesticated in the Balkans as early as the 7th century B.C. However in the 18th century A.D. a different variety of pig was introduced into Europe from Southeast Asia. This latter variety appears to have originated in Neolithic China, and the pigs domesticated by modern western farmers derive from the imported oriental variety, rather than from the ancient and medieval European pigs, which resembled a wild boar in appearance.

PILAGA, a South American Indian people living in northern Paraguay and southern Brazil.

PILE-DWELLINGS, the European Neolithic reveals a number of 'lake villages', containing 'pile dwellings' built on wooden platforms supported by wooden piles driven into the mud of the lake-bed. In some cases it seems possible that these villages were built over the water for protection, but in other cases the evidence indicates that the pile dwellings were not actually built over the lake, but were constructed on marshy ground so close to the water's edge that it flooded periodically. Many such lake villages were located in the valleys of the Jura mountains, Southern Germany, Northern Italy and Switzerland, in the 3rd millennium onwards, some still surviving in the Iron Age. (See LAKE VILLAGES).

PILLAR CULT, in Mycenean Greece, columns and pillars were believed to possess a supernatural significance which may have originated from an earlier age, when house and temple pillars were made from timber posts which were carved with religious symbols, and the traditional sanctity of such carved poles may well have survived even after these were functionally replaced by stone pillars of stylized shape and form.

PILTDOWN, the site of a gravel quarry in Sussex, England, in which early excavations revealed a variety of Paleolithic tools and a number of relatively recent hominid and animal remains. However, the reported discovery of a cranium of distinctly modern type in association with a definitely ape-like jawbone from the quarry led to the hypothesis that a new hominid variant, dubbed Piltdown Man, had been discovered. Since the modern shape of the forehead and cranium contrasted so sharply with the distinctly ape-like nature of the jaws, the supposed Piltdown Man failed to fit in with any rational concept of hominid evolution, and the hoax was eventually demonstrated by fluorine testing, which showed that the skull was that of a Homo sapiens of only slight antiquity but that the jaw belonged to an entirely modern orangutan, which had been artificially treated to give the bone and teeth the appearance of age to match the skull. The very low fluorine content of the jawbone proved beyond doubt that it was not, in fact, as old as the cranial remains.

PIMA-PAPAGO, a North American Indian people of Southern Arizona who speak a Uto-Aztecan language and are traditionally dependent on horticulture, food-gathering and hunting.

PIMBEWE, a Bantu-speaking Negroid people of the Rukwa group, largely dependent on horticulture and fishing.

PIN, any narrow shaft, shaped to a point at one end and equipped with a broad head at the other, which might be used to secure garments. Pins differ from fibulae in that the latter are normally equipped with some form of a clip, making them equivalent to the modern safety pin. The heads of pins found in association with the graves of nobility or of wealthy members of society are usually ornamented with attractive designs.

PIPESTONE, see CATLINITE.

PIRO, a South American Indian people of the Upper Amazon.

PISE, a technique of building in which wet mud or clay is placed directly in position without any previous treatment such as is involved in brick-making, and allowed to dry *in situ.* Successive layers are then added until the desired wall has been created. Pise was commonly used in the older cities of the Near East, although the resultant walls were not as durable as those made from baked or even from sun-dried mud brick. Houses contructed of *pise* were therefore frequently levelled off and replaced with new structures.

PIT, any hollow in the ground used for storage, for the disposal of rubbish, as a silo, or even as a trap for wild animals.

PIT-COMB WARE, a coarse type of pottery decorated with pit-comb impressions, commonly made by the Mesolithic hunting and fishing peoples of the Baltic. Pit-comb ware and associated cultural traits remained common components of the circumpolar culture which survives into the present century in subartic areas.

PIT-DWELLINGS, an early type of dwelling first constructed in the Upper Paleolithic. The dwellings are so-named because a portion of ground was first hollowed out and the excavated earth was raised around the edges of the excavated area to form low walls. In advanced pit-dwellings these walls were raised higher by panels of wattle and daub, before being surmounted by a skin-covered or thatched roof. The advantage of pit-dwellings was that they provided warmth in the winter, and coolness in the summer.

PITHECANTHROPINE, a term sometimes used to refer to any fossil, found anywhere in the Old World, which equates roughly with the Homo erectus or Pithecanthropus erectus level of hominid evolution.

PITHECANTHROPUS ERECTUS (or JAVA MAN), now customarily placed in the general category of Homo erectus, Java Man was the first fossil to be found which represented this level of hominid evolution, and at the time was believed to represent the first hominid accustomed to walking fully erect. It has been said that Pithecanthropus erectus was human up to the neck, but still largely apelike above the neck, being similar to living men in general carriage, but possessing a brain which was only two thirds the size of that of the average living Caucasoid. While it follows, by definition, that all sapiens stocks must have passed through a pithecanthropine (q.v.) stage of evolution it seems possible that the ancestry of Homo s. sapiens might be by way of Homo steinheimensis not Homo erectus. (See STEINHEIM).

PITHOS, any large pottery jar which might be used for storage purposes.
PLACENTA, that outgrowth from the embryo (q.v.), found among certain mammals, which enables the embryo to obtain food and oxygen direct from the maternal organism, as well as to allow for the dissipation of waste products.
PLACENTALIA, a class of mammalia which includes most living mammals. Placental mammals are distinguished by the fact that the embryo develops within the mother's uterus and is actually attached to the maternal tissues by a placenta, thus enabling oxygen and food substances to reach the embryo from the mother, and waste products to leave the embryo. This process permits a longer period of pregnancy so that the more complex ontological developments required by the offspring of mammals are able to take place within the protection of the maternal body prior to birth.
PLAINS CREE, Algonquin-speaking American Plains Indians, mainly dependent on hunting with some food-gathering and fishing.
PLAINS SUK, a Negroid Nilotic-speaking people of the Karamojong group, primarily dependent on cattle-herding with some horticulture.
PLANKTON, minute forms of life which float in the water and are of great ecological importance as producers of oxygen and also as food for fishes.
PLASTICITY, the ability of individual organisms to respond or adapt to their environment within the limits of their genetically-determined potential.
PLATYRRHINE, New World monkeys characterized by a broad nasal septum and frequently equipped with prehensile tails. Platyrrhine monkeys are particularly distinguished from the Catarrhine or Old World monkeys by a different dental formula. (See also PREMOLAR).
PLAYA, a term used in America to refer to a shallow inland basin which collects water and becomes a temporary lake during the rainy season, but which normally dries out by evaporation or absorption during periods of dry weather.
PLEBIANS, the term applied to that class of commoners in ancient Rome who were of free but not aristocratic status and lineage.
PLEIOTROPY, a term used in traditional genetics to refer to the multiple effects of a single gene.
PLEISTOCENE, a geological period which is now assumed to have commenced around 2.3 million years ago with the Villafranchian period (q.v.) and which includes the four subsequent major Alpine glacial periods, the Günz, Mindel, Riss, and Würm (q.v.). The exact dates of these glacial periods are still undetermined, due to the inability of radiocarbon dating to provide effective dates for the older glacial periods, while potassium-argon dating is unreliable for objects less than two or three million years in age.
PLESIOSAURIA, an extinct order of reptiles which were common during the Jurassic and Cretaceous geological periods. Being primarily marine creatures they swam with the aid of paddle-like limbs, their long necks giving them a total body length sometimes exceeding 50 feet.
PLIOCENE, a geological period within the Cenozoic era which lasted from approximately 12 to 2.3 million years ago.
PLOUGH, a tool designed in the Neolithic, the purpose of which was to break the surface of the earth with the aid of animal power thus relieving cultivators of dependance on the more primitive hand hoe. Early ploughs were usually constructed of wood, further reinforced with sharp cutting stones, but iron plough shares were introduced in the Iron Age, when a heavier type of plough equipped with wheels was invented. This latter was particularly useful in the rich and heavy soils of the European valleys. The plough appears to have been invented in Europe, and to have spread from thence to the Middle East, Egypt and Southern Asia, reaching China relatively late. It was never used in the New World until introduced by the Spaniards.
PLUMBATE WARE, a particularly fine pottery made from high quality clay and finished with a glazed surface, frequently adorned with animal shapes. Plumbate ware first appears on the Pacific coast of Mexico in Post-Classic times, and was widely traded during the Toltec period.
PLUTO, the Roman equivalent of the Greek Hades, the god of the dead.

Not surprisingly the name Pluto is cognate with the Greek *plutos*, meaning wealth, since Pluto was believed to control the vast treasure hidden beneath the earth.

PLUVIAL, several major glacial periods of the Pleistocene are believed to have affected the climate of the entire world, even though the tropical, subtropical and warmer tropical areas were never covered by ice-sheets. Attempts have therefore been made to identify pluvial periods in which there was a considerably higher rainfall in the tropical regions, and to correlate these with the Pleistocene glaciations. No conclusive correlation has yet been established. However, the pluvial periods were nevertheless of great significance, and substantial changes of flora and fauna are recorded at these times.

PODCORN, a variety of American Indian corn.

PODOKWO, a Chad-Sudanese-speaking people occupying the Mandara highlands of Africa, where they are dependent on horticulture with some animal husbandry.

POKOMO, a Bantu-speaking Negroid people of the Nykia group, traditionally dependent on horticulture and fishing.

POLAR ESKIMO, an Eskimo people who depend mainly on fishing and hunting.

POLIPOD BOWLS, bowls standing on several feet, a pottery tradition which was common among the Beaker Folk of Western Europe.

POLITICAL SYSTEM, that part of the social structure related to the attainment of public goals through which social order is enforced.

POLLEN ANALYSIS, see PALYNOLOGY.

POLYANDRY, a marriage system in which the female customarily takes more than one husband at the same time, as is the practice amongst the Todas of Southern India. More objectively, the practice should be perceived of as several men (usually brothers) sharing a common property, namely a wife, for reasons of economy.

POLYGAMY, a marriage system in which a member of either sex customarily takes more than one spouse at the same time.

POLYGENY, the interaction of a variety of genetic tendencies resulting in a complex hereditary trait.

POLYGYNY, a marriage system in which the male may take more than one wife simultaneously, as is permitted in Islamic societies.

POLYMORPHISM, a term employed to indicate the survival of a wide variety of genetic qualities within a freely interbreeding population. Thus the term may be used to refer to the existence of a marked degree of dimorphism between the two sexes, to the variety of human blood groups which may exist within a single subspecies, or to any other such instance of polymorphic variation within a single Mendelian population.

POLYMORPHISM, BALANCED, a static condition in which an allelic gene remains at a fairly constant level through the generations, due to its advantageous selective utility being balanced by correspondingly disadvantageous survival qualities.

POLYNESIANS, the main body of Malayo-Polynesians who settled the South Pacific probably comprised a substantial Indian or non-oriental component, which was less mixed with indigeneous Negrito and Australoid elements in the case of the Polynesians than were the Micronesians (who reveal Negrito admixture) and the Melanesians (who show strong Australoid admixture). The Western Polynesians include the Samoans, the Tongans and Ellice Islanders; the Eastern Polynesians include the Marquesans, Tahitians, and Easter Islanders; the Southern Polynesians include the Maories of New Zealand; and the Northern Polynesians who settled Hawaii. Other Polynesians include the Tikopians (actually located geographically in Melanesia) and the Ontong-Javanese.

POLYPEPTIDE, a chain of amino-acids, united by peptide bonds, one or more of which chains comprises a protein molecule (q.v.).

POLYPHYLETIC, a taxonomic term used to refer to a group of species or subspecies which are generally classified together because of a marked correspondence of characteristics, but do not share a common biogenic history, and are therefore not related to each other by common descent.

POLYSOME, a ribosome (q.v.) which (together with the RNA (q.v.) which directs its activities) determines the nature of the protein that will be synthesized within the cell.

POLYTHEISM, the worship of more than one god.

POLYTYPIC SPECIES, any species which is divided into a number of different subspecies or races (q.v.).

POMO, a Northern California people speaking a Hokan language of the Pomo-Yuki group, dependent on food-gathering, hunting and fishing.

PONAPEANS, a Malayo-Polynesian-speaking people from the Eastern Caroline Islands of Micronesia, dependent on horticulture, fishing and some animal husbandry.

PONCA, Muskogean-Siouan-speaking North American Plains Indians of the Siouan group, dependent on horticulture in the river valleys and hunting and food-gathering.

PONDO, a Bantu-speaking Negroid people of Southern Africa, largely dependent on horticulture and cattle-herding.

PONGIDAE, that taxonomic family of primates which includes the gorilla, chimpanzee and orangutan.

POPOI, a Nilotic-speaking people of the Mangbetu group, dependent on horticulture with some hunting and animal husbandry.

POPOLUCA, a Central American people who speak a Mixteco-Zapatecan language and are primarily dependent upon agriculture and some hunting.

POPULATION CYCLE, although most living organisms tend to have an optimum population density as members of an ecological community (q.v.), local conditions usually permit a moderate, cyclical increase or decrease in the total population around this optimum, an extreme example of such a population cycle being found in the ten year population cycle of the snowshoe rabbit in North America.

POPULATION DENSITY, the recognition of ecological adaptation as a meaningful area of anthropological enquiry (involving a two-way relationship between population and environment) has led to an interest in the relative density of human populations as a factor related to climate, prevailing flora and fauna, human technology, and means of subsistence. In addition, experimentation with animal populations has revealed that density of population, and in particular overcrowding, can result in substantial modification of behavior patterns, even to a pathological extent in extreme conditions. The recent Third World population explosion, made possible by western innovations in medicine and agricultural pesticides and fertilizers, is also a force calling for urgent enquiry, and one which is not only changing the pattern of human life everywhere (as a result of increasing migratory pressures), but which threatens the very ecological balance of life throughout the entire world.

POPULATION GENETICS, the study of racial or genetic changes in Mendelian populations.

PORIFERA, the term for certain non-mobile animals which comprise a number of cells but which cannot properly be classified as metazoa (q.v.) because these cells lack any true division of labor. Most Porifera are classed as sponges (q.v.).

PORTUGUESE, a nation originally of mixed Celtic-Iberian descent, with a Visigothic nobility, who pioneered the development of modern sailing ships nad navigation, and who were the first sea-going Europeans to extensively explore the oceans of the world. Being Catholic Christians, however, the Portuguese interbred freely with the colored races with which they came into contact, regarding them all as children of God and eventually permitted massive non-European immigration into Portugal.

POST-CLASSIC PERIOD, a term used by archeologists to refer to that stage of Meso-American civilization which immediately followed the rich Classic period during which an obvious decay was apparent. This Post-Classic period of progressive degeneracy commenced in the 10th century A.D. and continued until America was conquered by the Spaniards in the 16th century A.D.

POST-GLACIAL PERIOD, see HOLOCENE.

POSTHOLE, a term used by archeologists to refer to a hole or socket which formerly supported an upright post. Although the wooden post may have decayed, evidence of the posthole is usually apparent in the discoloration of the earth and the disparate chemical content of the material filing the hole, when contrasted with that of the surrounding earth or building material.

POTASSIUM-ARGON DATING, a dating technique based upon the knowledge that living organisms absorb potassium 40, a radioactive substance which breaks down into argon 40 at a regular rate. By measuring the rate of conversion it is possible to determine the approximate age of fossil remains or even of carbon deposits derived from extinct life forms, as far back as the beginning of life although this technique is not suitable for use in the case of fossil remains less than one million years of age, since the margin of error is too large.

POTATO, the potato first appears to have been cultivated in the area between Cuzco and Lake Titicaca, in the western Andes of South America. From thence it spread over a large portion of the Inca empire and was imported into Europe and other parts of the world following the Spanish conquest of the Inca empire.

POTAWATOMI, Central Algonquin, North American Indians, dependent on hunting and horticulture with some fishing and food-gathering.

POTO, a Bantu-speaking Negroid people of the Riverain Congo, primarily dependent on fishing with some horticulture.

POTLATCH, a North American, Northwest Coastal Indian ceremony in which property is given away or destroyed to enhance the owner's social status. Particularly practised among the Kwakutl and Tlingt, families vie with each other to host the most splendid banquets and to give the most generous gifts to their guests, or to compete in the destruction of valued property including slaves.

POTO, a Bantu-speaking Negroid people of the Riverain Congo, primarily dependent on fishing with some horticulture.

POTSHARDS (also POTSHERDS), see SHERD.

POTTERS'S WHEEL, see WHEEL, POTTERS.

POTTERY, a utensil made from clay, molded to the desired shape while still wet, and then dried by baking to a high temperature which also converts the molecules of the clay in such a manner that water cannot be reabsorbed.

PRAYER WALL, a long low mud wall, several hundred yards or more in length, set with flat pieces of stone bearing sacred inscriptions. Devoted Buddhists walk the length of the wall (keeping it on their right side) so as to obtain magico-religious benefits from close proximity to the inscriptions.

PRE-CAMBRIAN, the earliest geological period, which includes both the Archeozoic and the Proterozoic eras, extending from approximately 3600 million to 575 million years ago.

PRE-CLASSICAL PERIOD, otherwise known as the Formative Period, this term refers to that period in Meso-American cultural history characterized by Neolithic pottery-making techniques, but prior to the appearance of the architectural and artistic achievements of the subsequent Classic period.

PREDMOST, an important late Upper Pleistocene site in Czechoslovakia, dated around 30,000 B.P., comprising a collective grave revealing skulls intermediate between Neanderthals and Cro-Magnons.

PRE-DYNASTIC, a term usually used by Egyptologists to cover the 6th, 5th, and 4th millennia B.C., prior to the emergence of a unified Egyptian kingdom ruled by historically identified pharaohs. The pre-Dynastic period may be divided into the Natufian, Fayum, Badarian, Amratian and Gerzean traditions.

PREHENSILE, the ability to grasp objects with hands, feet, or even tail.

PREHISTORY, a loosely defined term which is generally used to refer to the entire time span of human activity prior to the development of historical or written accounts or records. Archeological research provides evidence of prehistoric life and culture. Since archeologists sometime uncover early written records when excavating what were previously believed to be prehistoric cultures, the term 'proto-history' (q.v.) has sometimes been used to refer to those periods from which some scanty written records are available, but concerning which most of our knowledge still derives from the analysis of artifacts and fossils and the interpretation of verbal legends (mythology).

PRELOGICAL MENTALITY, a term popularized by the French psychologist-anthropologist Levy-Bruhl which suggested that primitive man had not developed the habit of thinking rationally, and tended to think irrationally, being more dominated by his emotions than by rational thought. While it is true that the principles of logic were only developed in Classical Greece, and further restated and clarified with the Renaissance, Levy-Brühl's theory has been subject to substantial criticism by other anthropologists who point out that the Cro-Magnon men probably possessed mental equipment in no way inferior to that of living hominids, but merely lacked the accumulated data which we possess today. Although Levy-Brühl's theories are not fashionable at the present time, some support can be found for his views in the fact that Homo erectus, for example, must necessarily have been mentally inferior to living hominids. It must also be admitted that his concept of a 'prelogical mentality' does not depend upon genetic incompetence, since we can demonstrate that there has been a decline in reliance upon magical beliefs in western societies during the last two or three thousand years without any evidence for an increase in the intelligence of man during this period.

PREMAXILLA, the dermal bone which comprises the front part of the upper jaw in vertebrates and supports the incisor teeth in mammals. The premaxilla forms the upper beak in birds.

PREMOLAR, the small grinding tooth located between the canine and the molars. New World monkeys customarily possess three premolars on each side of their upper and lower jaws while Old World monkeys have only two premolars.

PRESSURE FLAKING, an advanced Lower Paleolithic technique for the production of stone tools, in which thin flakes of stone are removed by pressure applied with the aid of subsidiary implements of stone, bone or wood. Although laborious, pressure flaking allows for the production of much more finely finished stone tools than is possible with percussion techniques, this being particularly useful in the preparation of daggers and arrow-heads.

PRIEST, a functionary who specializes in the propitiation of the god or gods of a society.

PRIMATE, a taxonomic order of placental mammals which includes the Anthropoidea (monkeys, apes, and men) and Prosimii (Lemuroidea and Tarsioidea). Characterized by stereoscopic vision, nails (rather than claws) a large cerebrum, and prehensile feet and/or hands.

PRIMATOLOGY, the study of primates, usually with particular reference to the nonhuman primates.

PRIMITIVE, (1) a term used by biologists to refer to an early stage in the evolutionary history of a distinct genetic continuum. (2) a term used by cultural anthropologists to refer to cultures which have not developed any substantial division of labor, any elaborate oral or written literature, any distinctive degree of social stratification, or any elaborate pattern of economic or socio-political organization.

PRIMOGENITURE, the custom whereby the eldest son inherits all family titles, distinctions, and landed property.

PROBE, a rod which may be pushed into unexcavated deposits in a somewhat crude attempt to determine the existence of solid features lying beneath the surface. Obviously a probe can only be used in certain types of soil, sand or silt which are relatively free of stone.

PROCONSUL, a Miocene hominid fossil found in East Africa and now classified as Dryopithecus.

PROGNATHISM, ALVEOLAR (and FACIAL), a protrusion of the jaws, associated with a receding chin. Facial prognathism has declined in the course of hominid evolution, although Australian aboriginals, Andamanese, and most Negro and Negrito peoples still reveal substantial prognathism. While alveolar prognathism implies only a protrusion of the area immediately adjacent to the teeth, facial prognathism involves a much larger area of the jaws and face, implying a relative primitivism from the evolutionary standpoint.

PROMETHEUS, the Greek mythological figure who was reputed to have stolen the secret of fire from the gods, for the benefit of man. This theft led Zeus to avenge himself on Prometheus, by a form of eternal punishment, and on mankind, by sending Pandora to earth, with her jar full of evil spirits.

PROPHASE, the initial stage in mitosis (q.v.) and meiosis (q.v.) during the course of which the chromosomes become visible. In the case of meiosis the nucleus undergoes pairing.

PROPOSITUS, the term used by geneticists to refer to the individual through whom the investigation of a pedigree is begun.

PROSIMIAN, any fossil or living primate which has not evolved to the level of the Anthropoidea (q.v.), such as the living lemurs and tarsiers.

PROSTHION, an alveolar point on the inter-dental bone from which anthropomorphic measurements are taken.

PROSTITUTION, SACRED, in Sumerian, Anatolian and certain Middle Eastern religions, many temples were attended by a body of female priestesses who were regarded as concubines to the god, and who practiced temple prostitution to enable the male worshippers to gain a heightened religious thrill. Among the Semitic peoples temple eunuchs also existed, these being known as 'male prostitutes'.

PROTEIN, a highly complex organic compound, each protein molecule comprises hundreds of thousands of amino-acid molecules strung together in chains, with the result that most protein molecules are unusually large. Some twenty different kinds of amino-acids are commonly found in proteins, which form the essential basis of life.

PROTEROZOIC, the era of 'former life' from 1.2 billion to 575 million years ago, characterized by the appearance of complex multicellular life forms.

PROTISTA, unicellular plants and animals.

PROTO, used as a prefix, the term 'proto-' implies an early form of either a biological or cultural organism, out of which later (usually more complex) varieties can be demonstrated to have evolved.

PROTO-HISTORY, any period characterized by the presence of inadequate historical records, for information about which we must therefore rely largely upon evidence derived from archeological sources.

PROTOMAMMALS, see MARSUPIALIA and MONOTREMATA.

PROTOPLASM, organic living matter which constitutes the basic material in living cells.

PROTOTHERIA, a subclass of mammals which today survive only in Australia, where they are represented by the duckbilled platypus and the spiny anteater (echidna). Prototheria have a furry or spiny covering, are warm-blooded, and the females have breastlike glands. Unlike other mammals, however, the females reproduce by laying eggs and the adults are toothless.

PROTOZOA, a phylum which includes all unicellular animals.

PRUSSIANS, an earlier people of Baltic speech (q.v.), who as pagans strongly resisted the Christianity forced on them by the Teutonic Knights.

PTAH, the Egyptian patron deity of the crafts, whose main center of worship was located at Memphis.

PTC (PHENYL-THIO-CARBAMIDE), a white powder, which can be tasted by some individuals and not by others. The ability to taste PTC is genetically controlled, and the frequency of tasters and non-tasters varies substantially from one racial group to another.

PTERODACTYLA, an extinct order of flying reptiles which lived during the Jurassic and Cretaceous geological periods. Although Pterodactyls did not survive, they exhibited many structures analogous to those of birds and probably evolved simultaneously with birds from a common species of nonflying reptilian ancestors.

PUBIS, one of the pair of front pelvic bones.

PUCARA, an urban site dated between the 2nd and 1st centuries B.C., notable for its carved stone statues and polychrome pottery. Pucara was located close to the shores of Lake Titicaca, and may have contributed to the later Tiahuanaco culture.

PUJA, a name given to the daily rites of worship in orthodox Hindu households and temples. The house worship in honour of the ancestral spirits and household deities is usually supervised by the head of the household, or by a brahman priest in the more wealthy families. The temple puja is performed by the temple priest.

PUKAPUKANS, a West Polynesian people of Pukapuka, dependent on horticulture, fishing and some animal husbandry.

PUKU, a Bantu-speaking Negroid people in the Biafra coastal region, dependent mainly on horticulture, animal husbandry and some fishing.

PUNT, a land frequently referred to in Egyptian records, from which Egyptians appear to have derived gold, ivory, and myrrh. Since it was reported to be located on the mouth of the Red Sea, Punt probably corresponded to the modern Somaliland and Ethiopia.

PURANAS, a collection of eighteen Sanskrit texts which contain the basic sources of the popular Hindu religious beliefs, as distinct from the original Vedic literature.

PURARI, a Papuan people of the Gulf of Papua, dependent mainly on food-gathering with some hunting, horticulture, fishing and animal husbandry.

PURDAH, a cloak or heavy veil, used in many Moslem societies to conceal women from the jealous gaze of non-kinsmen, and in some countries, even of kinsmen. The practice is probably of Babylonian origin.

PURE LINE, a genetic term used to refer to a succession of generations in a single phylogenetic continuum in which all organisms are homozygous for all or most genes. Such pure lines result from intensive inbreeding combined with constant selection over long periods of time, most genetic variations that arise from time to time due to mutation being eliminated by natural selection providing the environmental circumstances remain unchanged.

PURIFICATION RITUALS, magico-religious ritual procedures for cleansing places and people, sacred and non-sacred, from ritual contamination.

PURUM, a Mongoloid people, speaking a Tibeto-Burman language, who live in the forested mountains separating the Indian sub-continent from Burma. The Purum are dependent on horticulture, hunting and some animal husbandry.

PYGMIES, a diminutive hunting and gathering people who live in the rain forests of the Congo. The two best known Pygmy people are the Twa or Batwa and the Mbuti. The Pygmies probably once occupied the entire tropical rain forests of Africa, from the Atlantic to the Great Lakes, but equipped only with a Sangoan culture, they have been largely expropriated by Negro horticulturalists over the course of the past two thousand years, and have even lost their own languages, today speaking the language of whichever Negro people live adjacent to them.

PYLON, an impressive, monumental gateway normally constructed at the entrance to Egyptian palaces and temples. Pylons were usually heavily ornamented with carved representations of human and animal figures as well as with hieroglyphics.

PYLOS, the capital city of King Nestor, on the west coast of the Peloponnese. Constructed in the usual Mycenean fashion, it comprised a walled town and an inner acropolis containing a palace. Excavation has revealed a very large number of tablets, written in the Linear B script, some of which record preparations to resist an enemy attack (probably by Dorians) which subsequently destroyed the city. The archeological evidence largely confirms the description of Nestor's capital as contained in the Odyssey.

PYRAMID, a monumental tomb constructed in ancient Egypt to house the mummified remains of a Pharaoh or his consort. In geometrical terms, a pyramid is essentially a pentahedron.

PYTHAGORAS, an early Greek mathematician and philosopher of the 6th century B.C. whose teachings reflected the ancient Indo-European belief in the eternity of the human soul, but who adopted metempsychosis (q.v.). Pythagoreanism particularly reflected the Indo-European belief in mechanical causality, as suggested by the Greek concept of the Moirae (q.v.) and developed this into the supposition that the secrets of the universe could be resolved into mathematical symbols. As a result Pythagoras laid the foundations of many of the basic principles of mathematics.

Q

QUARTERNARY, the latter part of the Cenozoic, customarily divided into the Pleistocene and the Holocene.
QUECHUA-AYMARA LANGUAGES, a South American Indian family of languages embracing Inca and Aymara, and constitutes a major division of the Andean Group (q.v.) within the Andean-Equatorial phylum.
QUERN, a hard stone used for grinding corn.
QUETZALCOATL, a prominent Aztec god, credited with the invention of agriculture and the calendar. Evidence of the worship of Quetzalcoatl can be found amongst the Toltecs, and there is evidence of his worship at pre-Aztec Teotihuacan, as well as at the late Mayan religious center at Chichén Itzá. Aztec legends portray Quetzalcoatl as a White god who arrived in Central America by sea, and later left by sea, promising to return. In consequence of this legend, the Aztecs believed that the invading Spanish conquistadors represented Quetzalcoatl and his followers, returning in compliance with his promise.
QUICHE, a Central American upland Mayan people who speak a Penutian language, and are dependent on agriculture and limited animal husbandry.
QUILEUTE, a Northwest American Indian people whose language belongs to the Mosan division of the Algonquin-Mosan phylum and who are dependent primarily on fishing with some hunting and food-gathering.
QUIPU, a device used in ancient Peru, comprising a number of knotted cords of different thicknesses and colours. The quipu was used for record-keeping by the Incas. A similar device was also known and used in ancient Mesopotamia.
QUMRAM, see DEAD SEA SCROLLS.

R

RA, an ancient Egyptian sun god who was head of the Egyptian pantheon before being displaced by Amen. His main temple was located at Heliopolis.
RABOTAGE, an important archeological technique, involving the careful scraping of an excavated surface to identify soils of different colours or textures — evidence of decayed organic material such as pit-posts or even decomposed corpses. This technique is particularly effective in sandy soil and gravel.
RACE, a genetically distinct inbreeding division within a species. The term 'race' is often used interchangeably with 'subspecies'. Successive hominid races have arisen throughout the course of hominid evolution due to anagenesis, or phyletic evolution (taking place in different directions and at different rates within different populations), and kladogenesis, or 'branching', due to geographical or even cultural isolation. While many animal subspecies may be regarded as incipient species, hominid behavior has been modified by cultural accretions, some of which (e.g. 'race prejudice') have served to facilitate speciation while others, such as those which have reduced the significance of geographical barriers, have tended to reduce genetic isolation, by enabling more successful subspecies to expand into other territories, where they have customarily mixed their genes with those of the autochthonous populations. The living hominids have been conceptually classified into various major geographic races, such as Australoids, Caucasoids, Mongoloids, Negroids and Negritoids, subdivided into innumerable local races. These in turn tend to be made up of clusters of microraces, which are closer to the genetic reality of Mendelian or near-Mendelian populations, and are the essential basis of all race differences. (See SPECIES).

RACE-CONSCIOUSNESS, the conscious recognition by an individual of his or her membership of a distinct racial group, characterized by either a real or an ideal phenotype, as distinct from religious, political or cultural identification.
RACIAL CLINE, racial clines fall into two categories: intra-racial clines and inter-racial clines. Intra-racial clines result from the expansion of a single population over a widespread area and its division into a number of relatively separate breeding populations. Because of the different environments under which these populations find themselves living, natural selection will tend to favor certain genetic combinations in some areas and other combinations in other areas. The result will be an intergrade or steady pattern of genetic change which expresses itself as a clinal gradient extending from the original area of occupation into the various colonial territories. Inter-racial clines arise from the admixture of the genes of two already separate races, brought into contact with each other as a result of the migration of members of one or both races into the same territory.
RACIAL HYGIENE, a term formerly in popular use among eugenicists implying a deliberate attempt to prevent the multiplication of deleterious genes within a specific gene pool, including attempts to prevent the admission of such genes to the gene pool by crossbreeding with less favoured groups or subspecies.
RACIAL LIKENESS, COEFFICIENT OF, a statistical formula developed by the founder of biometry, Karl Pearson, to express the degree of likeness or dissimilarity between the genetically determined characteristics of different races.
RADIOCARBON DATING, carbon 14 is a radioactive isotope produced by cosmic radiation which is absorbed by living tissues. However, when a plant or animal dies, the absorbed carbon 14 tends to diminish at a constant rate. The half life of carbon 15 is 5740 ± 30 years, and the remains of organic material of not more than 50,000 years of age can therefore be dated with reasonable accuracy by measuring the rate of breakdown of the accumulated carbon 14 contained in the remains.
RAMAPITHECUS, the earliest hominoid fossil species yet discovered. Ramapithecus fossils were first identified in Western India, and subsequently also in Kenya, being dated between 12 and 15 millions years B.P.
RAMCOCAMECRA, a South American Indian people of the Brazilian highlands who speak a Gê language and are dependent on horticulture and hunting.
RAN, the Teutonic goddess of the sea, who cared for drowned men in her underwater palace.
RANGI, (1) a Bantu-speaking Negroid people of the Rift group, dependent on horticulture and animal husbandry. (2) The name of the Maori great Sky father.
RAROIANS, an Eastern Polynesian people, wholly dependent on fishing and horticulture with some food-gathering.
RAYMI, an Inca festival celebrating the summer equinox.
RAZOR, the use of a sharpened blade for shaving may have originated in the European Bronze Age, and ornamented bronze razors designed in a variety of pleasing shapes testify to the widespread practice of shaving in Bronze Age Europe.
RECAPITULATION, EMBRYONIC, many organisms reveal a tendency in the embryonic or ontological history of the individual to repeat successive earlier stages in the history of the phylogenetic continuum (q.v.). This fact is reflected in the phrase 'ontogeny recapitulates phylogeny'. For example, young lion cubs are born with spots and this suggests that lions were once spotted like leopards.
RECEPTORS, those parts of an animal which detect changes in the external environment and transmit these to the nervous system, enabling the organism to respond to facilitate its own survival.
RECESSIVE GENE, a term used in Mendelian genetics to refer to an allele which only expresses itself in the phenotype when homozygous in the genotype.
RECIPROCITY, see GIFT EXCHANGE.
RECOMBINATION, a rearrangement of gene linkages (q.v.) which occurs at the time of reproduction, as a result of a crossing over (q.v.) between loci. This serves the evolutionary function of providing variation.

REDUCTION DIVISION, see MEIOSIS.
REFLEX, the simplest and most immediate kind of response to external stimuli operating in animals which possess a nervous system. Most reflex responses are controlled from the spinal cord rather than from the brain.
REGA, a Bantu-speaking Negroid people of the Luba group, largely dependent on horticulture supplemented by some hunting and fishing.
REGEIBAT, Semitic-speaking Bedouin Arabs of North Africa, mainly dependent on animal herding and some hunting.
RELATIVE DATING, dating processes used by archeologists to order artifacts and fossils in relative time sequences. (See DATING SYSTEMS).
RELATIVES, COLLATERAL, relatives, such as nephews, cousins, uncles, who are not in the direct line of descent.
RELATIVES, LINEAL relatives who are in the direct line of descent, such as grandfather, father, son and daughter.
RELIGION, no final or conclusive opinion has yet been reached regarding the origin of a belief in gods (polytheism) or in a single god (monotheism). Although all human societies appear to have expressed a belief in the existence of supernatural beings at some time in their cultural history, the simplest and probably most appropriate explanation for this phenomenon may be that human beings, aware of a sense of 'consciousness' which appears in some way to be distinct from their material body, presuppose the existence of an ethereal 'soul' which is not attached to the body, is capable of leaving the body in dreams, and does not die with the body when the latter ceases to function. This concept of an animate soul is frequently extended to animals, and even to inanimate objects. Early man may have attempted to control the souls or spirits of the dead. Such human attempts to control supernatural forces are generally defined as 'magic'(q.v.). However, at certain points in time, the members of some societies came to the conclusion that these spirits possessed a mind of their own and came to the conclusion that those supernatural beings which could not be controlled by magic should be flattered and propitiated, so as to remain friendly to those mortals who sought to propitiate them in this fashion. Religion was consequently born when men, believing in the existence of supernatural beings who possessed a will of their own, attempted to propitiate these beings by prayer, sacrifice, fasting, feasting, and magico-religious ritual ceremonies – such supernatural spirits being known as 'gods'. Once it was considered desirable to propitiate a particular divinity, it would logically follow that the wishes of that divinity would also be followed carefully, being equated with the mores of society. Many shamans (q.v.), or experts in the manipulation of supernatural powers became priests concentrating on the propitiation of the gods. (See also DIVINATION).
RELIGION, COMPARATIVE, the comparative study of religion, placing emphasis on the historical development of religious thought in its variety of diverse forms.
RELIGION, ETHNIC, a set of religious attitudes which is closely tied to the culture of a particular society. Ethnic religions usually serve to reinforce the sense of group identity and seldom seek or admit converts from other societies.
RELIGION, MISSIONARY, a religion which does not restrict its appeal to any one nation or society, and whose supporters actively seek converts from among members of other nations and societies.
REPRODUCTION, a process by which new living organisms are generated. Evolution (q.v.) has only been possible because living organisms enjoy limited life spans, and survive by reproducing successive generations of their own kind. Asexual reproduction permits only occasional genetic change, but sexual reproduction, involving a selection of genes from two different individuals of the same species, enhances the possibility of phenotypical variation and hence of evolution as a result of selection.
REPTILIA, a class of vertebrates which include turtles, lizards, snakes, crocodiles, as well as extinct fauna such as dinosaurs and Therapsida (q.v.), the early ancestors of mammals. Reptiles were probably the dominant land animal in the

Mesozoic, and are generally distinguished by the production of an amniote egg, and by the possession of relatively small brains in proportion to their total body size, and by the lack of body covering such as feathers or hair. No sharp dividing line can be drawn between reptiles and mammals in the fossil record since mammals evolved from reptiles.

RESHE, a West African Negroid, Middle Niger, Niger-Congo-speaking people, largely dependent on horticulture supplemented by some animal husbandry and fishing.

RESURRECTION OF THE DEAD, the ancient Sumerians believed that the spirits of the dead could be resurrected by magico-religious rituals, a belief which was to influence subsequent Christian doctrines. It is possible that this belief was in fact common to most of the Mediterranean and Middle Eastern regions, and parallel notions were basic to the religious belief of Ancient Egypt.

RETOUCHING, a form of secondary flaking used in the preparation of stone implements for the purpose of refining the finished tool. Retouching is normally associated with the more advanced Stone Age techniques and is usually effected by pressure flaking (q.v.).

REVITALISM, a movement which attempts to revive a former religious system by promising political, economic or supernatural rewards.

RHADE, a Southeast Asian, Malayo-Polynesian people, primarily dependent on horticulture and some animal husbandry.

RHODESIAN MAN, a complete fossil skull and fragments from the skull of a second individual, found at Broken Hill, in Northern Rhodesia, in 1921 by T. Zeviglaar. The dating is uncertain, but seems to be not more than 60,000 years old, and possibly as late as 40,000 B.P. Generally classified as Homo erectus (q.v.) the brain size of what is believed to be a female specimen is approximately 1280 c.c. Rhodesian man is seemingly ancestral, in part at least, to living African peoples though whether by subsequent direct evolution, or through admixture with more advanced immigrant Homo sapiens sapiens sub-species, is not known.

RHYTON, a ritual vessel, usually of considerable depth, equipped with a single handle. Rhytons were used by the Greeks and the Persians to pour libations to gods and ancestors alike. Being of ritual significance they were commonly manufactured from valuable metals, and were often elaborately ornamented.

RIBONUCLEIC ACID (RNA), a substance formed by nucleotides containing sugar ribose which transmits 'coded' instructions from the nucleus of the cell to the surrounding cytoplasm.

RIBOSOMES, small organelles, contained within cells, the purpose of which is to synthesize proteins.

RIDGEWAY, a road or path constructed along the summit of a range of hills, usually by Neolithic peoples. Such ridgeways have the advantage of a clear view, and consequently of freedom from ambush, and seldom pass close to an occupied settlement so that traders travelling along a ridgeway do not constitute a threat to the local population.

RIFFS, Moroccan Berbers, primarily dependent on agriculture and animal husbandry.

RIGVEDA, a part of the originally oral literature of the Indo-Aryans containing thousands of poems of great historical and mythological value. Probably created during the second half of the 2nd millennium B.C., it is believed that the Rigveda was probably written down around the 11th century B.C. in an early form of Sanskrit, prior to which it was transmitted orally. (See VEDIC).

RINYO-CLACTON, a distinctive style of pottery characteristic of the Late Neolithic period in Britain.

RIPPLED DECORATION, burnished pottery the surface of which has been rippled to create the appearance of light fluting.

RISHI, a Hindu term for any divinely-inspired authority on the Vedic literature (q.v.).

RISS, the third of the four major Alpine glaciations of the Pleistocene.

RITA, the basic Indo-European concept of cosmic order which was revealed in the Vedic literature (q.v.) of the Indo-Aryans, with the implications that human moral behaviour is an integral part of the natural order. Indo-European Greek philosophers such as Pythagoras also conceived of a natural law rooted in this same concept of 'cosmic order', of which Varuna was the guardian in the Aryan Rigveda.

RITES OF PASSAGE, a term applied to ritual ceremonies associated with birth, puberty, marriage, death, and similar crucial occasions when the individual passes from one status of life into another.

RITUALS, prescribed patterns of magico-religious or social behaviour the constant repetition of which tends to reinforce the ideological concepts associated with the rituals in the minds and behaviour of the participants. As Confucius indicated, ritual ceremonies are in fact the bonds that hold a society together, and once these bonds are removed, any society is likely to disintegrate. In most traditional societies both the temporal and the religious authorities play important roles in the performance of public rituals, thus reinforcing the sense of political and religious solidarity within the society.

RNA, see RIBONUCLEIC ACID.

ROCK-CUT TOMB, a form of chamber tomb cut into solid rock. Commonly located on cliff faces.

ROCK SHELTER, a shelter used by Paleolithic hunters and gatherers comprising an overhanging cliff.

ROCKER-STAMP POTTERY, a zig-zag decorative design produced on pottery by the simple method of rocking a sharp implement backwards and forwards across the surface of the damp clay.

ROMAN RELIGION, Roman religion combined ancestor and nature worship with a variety of antique animistic traditions, such as the worship of the Numen (q.v.). The strong Roman conviction that the individual was but a chain in the link of the ideally eternal family, combined with a strict emphasis on genetic quality among the Patrician class, made the family the basis of Republican Roman religious, social and political organization. Even the Roman state was seen essentially as an enlarged family to the degree that the state possessed its own state 'hearth fire' tended by the Vestal virgins. Ritual dominated every aspect of Roman religious, political and social life, and the strict adherence to the mores or customs of the ancestors, obligatory as an aspect of ancestor-worship, provided Romans with a strong sense of loyalty, order and self-sacrifice that facilitated the conquest and maintenance of a powerful empire. Since Rome was ideally conceived of as a large extended family, the Romans personified and worshipped the city as *Dea Roma* in the same way that they revered their own individual families as ultimately real and distinctly personal entities. As among the Hindus, the roots of religious worship were to be found in the individual household, where a central atrium or room of the atta or ancestors contained an altar, on which burned the symbolic hearth fire, and also the marriage bed on which successive generations of newly-wed heirs to the family name consummated their marriages in a sacred act of procreation which would ensure the continuation of the family into the future. The walls of this atrium were at first hung with death masks, and later with three-dimensional sculptured busts of the ancestors. Only during the later days of the Republic and during the Imperial period, when the Patrician families were heavily outnumbered by the freedmen and by multiple citizens and slaves of heterogeneous origin, did the old Roman religion begin to lose its hold, and political power shifted to dictatorial emperors who were able to manipulate the masses against the small minority of conservative Patrician families. Under these circumstances various philosophies and mystery religions (q.v.) from all parts of the Mediterranean and the Middle East seeped into the life of the lower class Romans, and the former unity and loyalty of Romans to the ideal of the family and the family state decayed in the face of individualism and increasing heterogeneity, each individual seeking personal salvation through a variety of diverse and conflicting religious cults. Thus the ancient religion of Rome was already virtually dead when Christianity appeared on the scene, and the pagan cults which competed with the Christians for the allegiance of the Romans of the later Imperial Age were mostly of alien origin.

ROMANCE LANGUAGES, a term derived from 'Roman', used to refer to those European languages which are of Latin origin. These are numerous, and have been divided into Eastern or Balkan, including Dalmatian and Rumanian; Gallo-Romance, including French, Provencal, and overseas French creole languages; Ibero-Romance, including Catalan, Portuguese, and Spanish (Castilian), various pidgin-Spanish languages including Ladino (Jewish Spanish), and Italian; and Rhaeto-Romance, including Freulian, Ladin (South Tyrol) and Romansch (Engadine).

ROMANIANS (also RUMANIANS), the people of Romania who are distinguished from their Slavic neighbors by speaking a Romance (q.v.) language derived from Latin.

ROSETTA STONE, a large slab of basalt rock inscribed by order of Ptolemy V (cir. 196 B.C.) with a royal decree in three different scripts: Greek, Demotic, and Hieroglyphic. Discovered on the western edge of the Nile delta during Napoleon's brief occupation of Egypt, the discovery of the Rosetta stone made possible the translation of the ancient Egyptian demotic and hieroglyphic scripts (the ability to read which had died out around the 4th century A.D.) by comparing these with the inscription in Greek.

ROSSEL ISLANDERS, a Melanesian (Malayo-Polynesian) people inhabiting Louisiade Archipelago, the Rossel Islanders are largely dependent on horticulture, fishing, food-gathering and hunting.

RÖSSEN, a version of the late Danubian culture, which extended from Bohemia to the Rhine (including modern Bavaria and Switzerland). The name Rössen is taken from the site of a cemetery located near Merseburg in Central Germany.

ROTUMANS, a Melanesian (Malayo-Polynesian) people from the Fiji Islands largely dependent on horticulture, fishing, food-gathering, hunting and some animal husbandry.

RUANDA, a West Lacustrine people, largely dependent on horticulture and herding.

RUMBI, a Bantu-speaking Negroid people of the Babwe-Bira group, dependent on horticulture with some fishing.

RUMINANT, a herbivorous mammal, lacking incisor teeth on the upper jaw, but possessing a complex stomach into which unchewed food may be passed and from which it is subsequently returned to the mouth for chewing. Ruminants include deer, sheep, goats, oxen, cattle, and antelopes, and are frequently herded by members of pastoral societies.

RUNDI, a West Lacustrine Bantu people, largely dependent on horticulture and herding.

RUNES, a script mainly comprising angular lines, normally carved in wood or stone. The oldest extant examples of the Runic script date from the 3rd century A.D., and are located in Denmark, but the script was used widely throughout Northern Europe and was later carried by Vikings to Russia and Greenland. Traditional views suggested that the Runic script was modified from the Greek and Latin alphabet, but there are many problems involved in such a hypothesis, and the Runic alphabet may have older roots than are presently recognized. (See also OGHAM).

RUTILISM, the occurrence of red-headed individuals in a population whose normal hair color is other than red.

R'WALA (also RUWALLA), Semitic-speaking Bedouin Arabs of North Africa, mainly dependent upon animal herding and some hunting.

RYUKYUAN ISLANDERS, a Mongoloid people occupying the Ryukyu Islands immediately South of Japan. The main group is that of the Okinawans.

S

SAALE GLACIATION, the name given to the first North American glaciation which probably corresponded to the Alpine-Riss glaciation (q.v.).

SACAE, see SCYTHIANS.

SACRA PRIVATA, the sacred rituals of the Roman household, in which the *pater familias,* or house father, acted as priest, and the children as acolytes, in rituals honouring the ancestors and the household gods.
SACRAL VERTEBRAE, the articulated vertebrae of tetrapods of four-legged animals.
SACRED GROVES, early Teutonic, Celtic and pre-Zoroastrian Iranian religious ceremonies appear to have been held in outdoor settings rather than in temple buildings. Woodland groves, in particular, were frequently chosen as ritual centres sacred to the honour of specific deities.
SACRO-CANNIBALISM, in some cultures it was regarded as the duty of the living to consume the flesh of the deceased ancestors in order to benefit from and perpetuate the magical or religious properties of the deceased. Thus the aboriginal inhabitants of New Guinea consumed the flesh of the deceased members of their own society and many South American Indians consumed the ashes of their cremated ancestors mixed with flour.
SADANG, a Malayo-Polynesian people of Celebes.
SAGA, the Norse goddess of history, equivalent to the Greek Clio.
SAGADA IGOROT, a Malayo-Polynesian speaking people of the Luzon highlands, largely dependent on cultivation and animal husbandry.
SAGITTAL CREST, the raised crest or ridge running along the top of the skull of the living apes. The sagittal crest is found among many fossil hominids, and at least one early hominid, Australopithecus robustus possessed a sagittal crest. (See AUSTRALOPITHECINAE).
SAGO, a starch product prepared from the juice of the palm tree, which constitutes a staple part of the Indonesian diet. The Asmao of New Guinea carefully extract the brains from the decapitated heads of their enemies and mix these with sago, to make the cake which is then consumed in a ritual ceremony, presumably for the purpose of acquiring the mana of the victim.
SAKAI, an aboriginal people living in the interior of Malaya, who speak a language related to Semang, and associated with the Mon-Khmer linguistic family (q.v.).
SAKALAVA, a Malayo-Polynesian Malagasy people of Madagascar, dependent on animal husbandry, agriculture and some fishing.
SAKATA, a Bantu-speaking Negroid people of the Kasai group, largely dependent on horticulture, hunting and fishing.
SAKKARA, a cemetery close to Memphis in Egypt, containing a number of mastaba tombs from the earlier part of the Archaic period of the Old Kingdom, as well as a step pyramid dating from the 3rd dynasty B.C.
SALADERO, an archeological site in Venezuela located in the Orinoco delta, which has revealed the existence of pottery-making horticulturalists as early as the 10th century B.C. This tradition survived until approximately A.D. 1000 and there is some evidence that it was the work of Arawak Indians who carried the culture with them when they conquered Trinidad and the lesser Antilles.
SALDANHA BAY, an archeological site at Hopefield near Saldanha Bay in Cape Province, South Africa. Excavated in 1953 by Ronald Singer and Keith Jolly, the site revealed a skull cap and mandible which closely resemble the Rhodesian man fossils classed as Homo rhodesiensis. Saldanha man can be dated around 55,000 B.P., and has been found in association with Acheulian tools.
SALISH LANGUAGES, a family of North American Coastal Indian languages which includes Twana, Bellacoola, Puyallup, Stalo and Quinalt.
SALTATION, an abrupt evolutionary modification of the contents of a specific gene pool.
SAMA VEDA, see VEDIC LITERATURE.
SAMOANS, a West Polynesian people occupying the Samoan Isles, dependent on horticulture, fishing and some animal husbandry.
SAMOYED, a Mongolian people located in the far north of central Siberia.
SAMSARA, the Hindu wheel of life, sometimes implying the transmigration of the soul into animal form in cases where the behavior of its owner has been unsatisfactory during his lifetime.

SANDAWE, a Khoisan-speaking Capoid people isolated in the Rift Valley of Africa, largely dependent on horticulture and some animal husbandry.
SANDIA, an American Indian people of the Southwestern United States.
SANDIA CAVE, an archeological site situated in New Mexico where a variety of early projectile points (equivocally dated between 12,000 to 20,000 B.C.) have been found. These resemble the Old World traditions and lack the distinctive fluting characteristic of the later Folsom projectiles which are uniquely American in design.
SANEMA, a South American Indian people of unidentified linguistic affiliation, dependent on hunting, food-gathering and some horticulture.
SANGA, a Bantu-speaking Negroid people of the Fang-Dzem group, largely dependent on horticulture with some hunting and food-gathering.
SANGAMON INTERGLACIAL, the name given to the North American interglacial period which probably corresponded to the Alpine Riss-Würm interglacial.
SANGIRAN, the site in Java where the remains of Meganthropus paleojavanicus were found by von Koenigswald. These fossils have not as yet been satisfactorily dated, but some authorities regard Sangiran man as a form of Australopithecus robustus. By 1939, Pithecanthropus (homo erectus) remains had already been found at the same site, and these have been dated at around 700,000 B.P. They represent, however, a very primitive form of Homo erectus, implying lagging evolution in the Southeast Asian area.
SANGOAN, a Central African Acheulian-type Lower Paleolithic industry, contemporary with Middle Paleolithic Mousterian industry of Europe.
SANGU, a Bantu-speaking Negroid people of the Rufiji group, largely dependent on horticulture and some animal husbandry.
SAN JUAN PAIUTE, a North American Uto-Aztec (Shoshone)-speaking people, dependent on food-gathering supplemented by some fishing and animal husbandry.
SAN LORENZO TENOCHTITLAN, an archeological site in Southern Veracruz in Mexico. Tenochtitlan is important in providing evidence of a long pre-Classical sequence, which casts light on the problem of the origins of the Olmec civilization. The earliest phase of occupation is dated 1500 B.C., although no architectural monuments were constructed until around 1200 B.C. when an artificial platform was built, foreshadowing later Central American pyramid construction.
SANPOIL, North American Indians who speak a Salish language of the Algonquin-Mosan group, and are dependent on fishing, food-gathering and hunting.
SANSKRIT, a classical Indo-European language spoken by the descendants of the Indo-Aryan invaders of India. The earlier form is known as Vedic Sanskrit (the language in which the earliest Vedas were written down) and the later form is called Classical Sanskrit. Most of the living languages of India, excluding those of Dravidian and pre-Aryan origin, are derived ultimately from Sanskrit, which was closely related to the Iranian group of languages, and more distantly to the major languages of Europe. (See INDO-EUROPEAN LANGUAGES).
SANTA ANA, a North American Indian Central Pueblo people who speak a Keresan language. The Santa Ana subsisted on horticulture and animal hunting, but adopted some animal husbandry following the introduction of domestic animals to the Americas by the Spaniards.
SANTA CRUZ ISLANDERS, a Melanesian (Malayo-Polynesian) people inhabiting the Santa Cruz Islands, largely dependent on horticulture and fishing supplemented by some animal husbandry.
SANTAL, a proto-Australoid people of the Eastern Indian uplands who speak a Munda language and rely upon horticulture supplemented by some hunting, fishing and animal husbandry.
SANT'ANA, an American Indian people of the Southwestern United States.
SANTEE, Siouan-speaking American Dakota Plains Indians, mainly dependent on horticulture in the river valleys.
SAPIR-WHORF HYPOTHESIS, the theory, now generally accepted in broad form, that the traditional meanings attached to the words in any one language exert a powerful force in the intergenerational transmission of culture, shaping

the mind and personality of each succeeding generation.

SAPO, a Kwa-speaking Negroid people from West Africa of the Kru group largely dependent on horticulture with some fishing and animal husbandry.

SARA, a Nilotic-speaking people of the Bagirma-Sara group, largely dependent on horticulture and animal husbandry.

SARAMACCA, a South American population of 'Bush Negroes' who speak a form of pidgin Portuguese. The Saramaccas are traditionally dependent on horticulture, fishing and hunting.

SARASVATI, the Hindu goddess of speech and the arts, who was the wife of Brahma.

SARCOPHAGUS, a container (usually made from stone or terra cotta) used as a repository for human corpses. The Etruscans made extensive use of the sarcophagus usually ornamenting it with mythological scenes, religious inscriptions, and sculptured images of the deceased persons, portrayed in a semi-reclining position.

SARGON, the Semitic founder of the Empire of Akkad in Northern Mesopotamia, cir. 2370 B.C. The same name was also held by two later Sargons, who ruled Assyria in the 19th and 8th centuries respectively.

SARSI, Algonquin-speaking North American Plains Indians, mainly dependent on hunting and food-gathering.

SASSANID, the clan name of the Persian dynasty which overthrew the Parthians in A.D. 224, and reestablished a Persian Zoroastrian empire which they ruled until defeated by the Moslem Arabs in A.D. 651.

SATEM LANGUAGES, those Indo-European languages, particularly of Avestan-Iranian and Sanskrit derivation, which have replaced the presumed proto-Indo-European cultural K sound by an S. The word *satem* is an East Indo-European form for 'hundred' represented in Western Indo-European languages by word forms similar to the Latin *centum* (q.v.).

SATRAP, a quasi-feudal administrative unit which formed the basis of the organization of the Achaemenid empire.

SATUDENE, a Northeastern Athabascan American Indian people, dependent on hunting, fishing and food-gathering.

SATWA, a Bantu-speaking Negroid people of the Rukwa group, largely dependent on horticulture and some animal husbandry.

SATYRS, mythological creatures, half-human and half-goat, reputed by the ancient Greeks to live in the forests and hills where they were devotees of the god Dionysus. Devoted to sensual pleasures, the satyrs sometimes fought with and were greatly feared by mortal beings.

SAXONS, a West Germanic people whose original homeland was located on the shores of the North Sea, north of the River Elbe. The Saxons were formerly devoted pagans until finally forced to accept Christianity by the armies of Charlemagne the Great, after continued resistance which lasted for some 40 years. Following their final defeat, their conversion was effected by the cold-blooded murder of virtually the entire aristocracy (who, by virtue of their birth, were the only persons qualified to supervise the rituals to Saxon gods and ancestors) and by the imposition of a fine equivalent to the penalty for killing a slave on every man who failed to baptize his children into the Christian Church. Many Saxons migrated to England in the 5th and 6th centuries A.D., where they settled to the south of the Germanic Angles, while on the continent other bands migrated overland in a southeasterly direction to occupy the area of present-day Saxony. Those Saxons who settled England initially established a number of separate kingdoms, namely Wessex, Sussex, Essex, and Middlesex, under kings who claimed descent from Odin. Of these, Wessex emerged as the more powerful, eventually unifying most of England under the royal house of Wessex at the kingdoms, namely Wessex, Sussex, Essex, and Middlesex, under kings who claimed descent from Odin. Of these, Wessex emerged as the more powerful, eventually unifying most of England under the royal house of Wessex at the beginning of the 10th century A.D.

SCAPULA, the shoulder blade, which plays an important role among primates in facilitating the free movement of the forelimbs.
SCARAB, a beetle, regarded by the ancient Egyptians as a sacred symbol of the power of the sun. Scarabs made from faïence or semi-precious stones became common as magico-religious ornaments, being worn around the neck or mounted on rings to be worn on the fingers.
SCARLET WARE, a form of pottery associated with the Sumerian Early Dynastic period of the earlier part of the 3rd millennium B.C. The earliest scarlet ware was decorated by geometrical designs accented in black paint against a scarlet background, but later forms included animals and human figures appearing in scarlet against a black background.
SCEATTA, a silver coin minted in Anglo-Saxon England during the 7th century A.D. by King Penda of Mercia, who also gave his name to the English 'penny'.
SCOTS, Scotland was formerly occupied by the Picts to the south of the Forth and Clyde rivers, and by the Caledonii to the north. The former seem to have been a matriarchal Atlanto-Mediterranean people who spoke a non-Indo-European language, but may have had some Celtic influences, while the latter were a Brythonic-Celtic speaking tribe, who may have absorbed some Atlanto-Mediterranean elements. However, Goidelic Celts from Ulster in neighboring northern Ireland, first raided and later settled the area now known as Argyll, and established the Gaelic-speaking 'Kingdom of Dal' or Dalriada (*ri-athe*, 'kingdom'). These *Scoti* or 'raiders' subsequently extended their influence over most of the Highlands as well as the valley of Strathclyde, until eventually the whole of what is now called Scotland came to be known by this epithet. (See CELTS).
SCRAMASAX, a long ornamented knife with a single cutting edge, customarily found with the bodies of noblemen in pagan (and later) Saxon burials.
SCRAPER, a Paleolithic tool, made from chipped stone or flint, distinguished by a convex cutting edge which may have been used either for carpentry or for scraping animal skins.
SCYTHIANS, a largely pastoral, but partly horticultural, semi-nomadic horse-riding people who appear to have remained behind in the Pontic steppes following the departure of other Indo-European peoples. They subsequently displaced the related Cimmerians from the area immediately north of the Black Sea, causing the Cimmerians to cross the Caucasus and to invade Anatolia. Distinguished by a highly stratified society, centered around kings attended by a band of noble warrior companions, Scythian society appears to represent a survival of early Indo-European culture. Some Scythians carried their culture into the steppes of Central Asia, as evidenced by the Pazyryk tombs. Others penetrated south of the Caucasus, but were prevented from further penetration by the Achaemenid Persian empire. Those of the Scythians who remained in the Pontic steppes were eventually absorbed by the related Sarmatians after suffering a final defeat at the hands of the Goths who invaded the area north of the Black Sea during the 3rd century A.D.
SEAL, a carved device used for making an impression on soft clay or wax. Often elaborately carved with heraldic designs, seals may be classified into two main types: the simple stamp seal which leaves its impression when merely stamped onto soft clay or wax, and the cylinder seal which, as its name indicates, is cylindrical in shape so that it may be rolled over a soft surface to make repeating designs like a long frieze. Seals were widely used in the ancient Sumerian, Egyptian, Indus Valley and Mycenean civilizations as well as throughout Medieval and Renaissance Europe.
SEAL KILLER, an Eskimo implement used to club seals to death, comprising a heavy stone enclosed within a net or leather thong.
SECONDARY FLAKING, the final trimming of a stone tool to improve its form after primary flaking has produced the approximate desired shape. Secondary flaking was frequently achieved by 'pressure flaking' devices (q.v.).
SECRET SOCIETY, in anthropology this term is applied to any society whose

members share closely guarded (usually ritual) secrets, whether or not membership of such societies is a secret matter.
SEKANE, a Northeastern Athabascan American Indian people, dependent on hunting, fishing and food-gathering.
SELECTION PRESSURE, the relative effectiveness of natural selection in affecting an alternation in the gene pool of a population of plants or animals occupying a given environment.
SELEUCID, the name of the Greek dynasty which ruled Persia following the conquests of Alexander the Great.
S'ELKNAM, see ONA.
SEMA, a Tibeto-Burman (Sinitic) speaking people, largely dependent on horticulture, with some animal husbandry, hunting and fishing.
SEMANG, an aboriginal people of Mon Khmer speech, still occupying inland forest areas of the Malay peninsula, dependent on food-gathering, hunting and fishing.
SEMANTICS, the study of the relative meaning of words as separate units.
SEMINOLE, American Indians from Southern Florida.
SEMITES, a term which originally referred to a large variety of essentially Mediterranean Caucasoid peoples, all of whom spoke languages belonging to the Semitic branch of the Afro-Asian family of languages. These included Akkadian, Aramaic and Assyrian, Caananite, Carthaginian, and Phoenician (now dead) language. The living Semitic languages are primarily represented by Arabic, Hebrew, Tigré, and Amharic, the last two languages being localized in the Horn of Africa. Originally a pastoral people, the Semites spread outwards from the grassy steppelands between the Arabian desert and the Fertile Crescent to occupy a large portion of the Middle East, and may even have been ancestral to the Hamitic-speaking peoples who today occupy portions of North Africa, whose ancestors appear to have migrated into Northern Africa from the Middle East.
SENA, a Bantu-speaking Negroid people of the Maravi group, largely dependent on horticulture and fishing.
SENECA, North American Indians of the Iroquois group.
SENIANG, a Melanesian (Malay-Polynesian) people of Malekula, largely dependent on horticulture and fishing with some animal husbandry.
SENILICIDE (also GERONTOCIDE), in some societies, the practice of killing the older members either as an act of mercy, or to ensure the survival of the younger members. The elderly might request their own children to kill them in times of famine, so that they should not be an unnecessary drain upon the resources of the family group.
SENNACHERIB, an Assyrian king (704-681 B.C.) whose capital was located at Nineveh, and who succeeded in conquering and destroying Babylon.
SENOI, a partly aboriginal peoples of Mon Khmer speech, still occupying inland forest areas of the Malay peninsula. The Senoi are dependent on horticulture, fishing and some hunting and gathering.
SENUFO, a Negroid, West African people, largely dependent on horticulture supplemented by some food-gathering and animal husbandry.
SENUSSI, a pastoral Hamitic people of Libya.
SEPHARDIC, the North African and Middle Eastern Jews of the diaspora were known as Sephardic Jews, as distinct from the Ashkenazim Jews of Eastern Europe. (See also JEWS).
SEQUENCE DATING, an archeological technique for dating the various strata at an excavation site by a comparison of the artifacts with artifacts found at different levels at other sites, thus making the construction of relative chronologies possible. Although sequence dating still plays an important role in modern archeology, absolute dating (q.v.) with the aid of scientific methods such as radiocarbon dating, has made it possible to translate many hitherto relative chronologies into more precise sequence-based scientifically demonstrable dates.
SERBS, a Southern Slavic (Indo-European) speaking Caucasoid people. The Serbs comprise the dominant ethnic group in the population of present-day Yugoslavia.

SERER, a Negroid West African Senegalese people, dependent primarily upon horticulture, animal husbandry and food-gathering.
SERI, a Northeast Mexico Indian coastal people, who speak a Hokan language and are dependent on sea fishing supplemented by some hunting and gathering.
SERIES, a term broadly used to refer to a related sequence of cultural traits which belong in a continuous and demonstrable series, each stage developing from a known preceding stage as a result of the continuing modification of a single tradition.
SEROLOGY, a science dealing with the properties of blood serum, useful in identifying genetic relationships between different species of animals.
SERRA D'ALTO, a Chalcolithic culture which flourished on the Adriatic coast of Italy circa 5300–3500 B.C., evolving out of the older Neolithic Impresso culture (q.v.).
SERRANO, a Shoshone (Uto-Aztec) speaking American Indian people of Southeastern California, dependent on food-gathering and hunting.
SESKLO, an important archeological site located near Volvos, in Thessaly, belonging to the old European Neolithic civilization of the Aegean area. Sesklo pottery has a distinctive pattern of fine white slip covered with red geometrical designs. The Sesklo culture, which covered a considerable portion of mainland Greece in the late 6th and early 5th millennium B.C., appears to have evolved out of a proto-Sesklo culture – essentially a branch of the Starčevo (q.v.) culture – around 5800 B.C., evolving in turn into a Late Neolithic Aegean culture around 4500 B.C.
SETH, the Egyptian god of evil, who killed his own father, Osiris, but was later killed by his brother Horus. Seth is frequently represented by a human figure wearing an animal head.
SEX CHROMOSOMES, those chromosomes which are responsible for the determination of sex. There are two kinds of sex chromosomes, identified as X and Y. Among vertebrate animals, the genotype XX results in a female phenotype, whereas the genotype XY gives rise to a male phenotype.
SEX LINKAGE, a genetic process by which particular qualities reveal themselves phenotypically only in males or else only in females. Sex linkage is more usually associated with the X chromosome.
SEXUAL DICHOTOMY, any differences of structure or function distinguishing males and females of the same species.
SEXUAL DIMORPHISM (also SEXUAL DICHOTOMY), anatomical differences distinguishing males from females of the same species, as in size, hair, etc.
SEXUAL SELECTION, a debated area of study concerning the extent to which secondary sexual characteristics affect the course of evolution by influencing the number of offspring produced by different members of subspecies.
SHAFT AND CHAMBER TOMBS , a distinctive method of burial in which the body is laid in a side chamber, opening off the bottom of a narrow shaft.
SHAFT GRAVE, a method of burial in which the body is deposited at the bottom of a deep narrow shaft.
SHAMAN, a term borrowed from certain Ural-Altaic peoples and used by anthropologists in a generic sense to refer to any specialist in supernatural affairs who is not a member of a regular religious association or priestly hierarchy. Shamans are generally more concerned with magical than religious activities, but not all magico-religious practitioners can be readily classed as either shamans or priests.
SHAN, a Mongoloid people of Eastern Burma.
SHANG, sometimes known as Yin, the Shang are the first Chinese dynasty to be identified archeologically, although Chinese histories refer to a 'Hsia' (q.v.) dynasty which reputably preceded the Shang. A warlike chariot-riding people of original semi-nomadic pastoral background who entered China from the direction of the east Asian steppelands, the Shang introduced advanced Bronze Age techniques and established themselves as an aristocracy over the Lung Shan Neolithic peasantry. The Shang were undoubtedly ancestor worshippers who buried their divinely descended nobility in pit graves, complete with horses, dogs, re-

tainers and chariots. Indeed the Shang Bronze Age culture closely resembles that of the Indo-European semi-pastoral societies of Eastern Europe, and especially that of the Homeric Greeks. Undoubtedly many of the cultural traits which the Shang introduced into China, such as the ritual tripods and battle axes (which are reminiscent of those of the Scythians) indicate an ultimate diffusion of the West Eurasian equestrian tradition across the steppelands into Northern China, where the Shang established themselves as a quasi-feudal aristocracy in much the same way as the Indo-European chariot-riding warriors established themselves as a quasi-feudal aristocracy in Europe, Asia Minor, Iran and India.

SHANG-TI, the supreme deity of Chinese Taoism. (See CHINESE RELIGION).

SHANIDAR, a cave site in Iraq, first excavated in 1953 by Ralph Solecki, which revealed the complete skeleton of a Classic Neanderthal adult in association with Mousterian artifacts. This individual had been born with a defective right arm, which had been amputated later in life. Other excavations in later years have revealed a variety of Mousterian tools and Neanderthal fossils, none later than 45,000 years B.P.

SHANTUNG CHINESE, a North Chinese people occupying the rich agricultural land between the Yellow Sea and Honan, the site of China's earliest Neolithic culture in the alluvial valley of the Yellow River. Traditionally dependent on agriculture supplemented by some animal husbandry and fishing.

SHASTA, a Northwestern California, Hokan-speaking people, dependent on food-gathering, fishing and hunting.

SHAWABTI, a small statuette which the Egyptians buried with the dead to provide a servant for the dead man's soul in the afterlife.

SHAWIA, a Berber people of Eastern Algeria.

SHAWNEE, Central Algonquin North American Indians, dependent on hunting and horticulture with some fishing and food-gathering.

SHEEP, the first sheep to be domesticated belonged to a wild breed known as mouflon, which lived in the mountains of Asia Minor and Zagros, and was domesticated around 9000 B.C. A second and different variety, known as the urial, was domesticated in the mountains of Turkestan, the earliest evidence of which was found at Anau and dates from around 4000 B.C. It is this second breed that appears to be ancestral to most modern breeds. A third variety of wild sheep, known as the argali, lived in Central Asia, but although domesticated there, was not adopted by other societies. (See URIAL).

SHELL GOUGE, an adze with a cutting edge made from a heavy sea shell.

SHELLS, shells are frequently used in primitive societies for decorative purposes or as symbols of value. In other societies large shells have been used as tools, while the Conch shell is still used in modern India as a ceremonial horn.

SHEN, a Chinese concept representing the ethical principle of wrong behaviour in Confucian philosophy (q.v.) and the good spirit associated with the male principle of yang (q.v.) in Taoism. (See CHINESE RELIGION).

SHERBO, a West African, Negroid people largely dependent on horticulture with some fishing and animal husbandry.

SHERD, more correctly known as a 'potsherd', the term sherd refers to any broken fragment of pottery. Much of the pottery found in archeological sites is uncovered in a broken condition, due to the pressure of overlaying deposits of earth, but such sherds can nevertheless provide valuable information as to the age and nature of the culture under excavation.

SHERENTE, a South American Indian people inhabiting the Brazilian highlands, the Sherente speak a Gê language and are dependent on horticulture, hunting, food-gathering and fishing.

SHERPA, a Tibeto-Burman-speaking Mongoloid people who inhabit the Himalayan valleys of Eastern Nepal where they practise agriculture and animal husbandry.

SHEVENTA, a South American people of the Eastern Brazilian highlands.

SHIELDS, although copper, bronze and iron shields are well known in classical antiquity, shields are believed to have been invented in the Upper Paleolithic, when they were probably made from leather stretched over a wicker-frame.

SHIFT HOLES, holes penetrating the surface of large pieces of stone masonry, which appear to serve no functional purpose, but are believed to have been made by the builders to assist in moving the stone into position.

SHIFTING CULTIVATORS, horticulturalists who are periodically obliged to transfer their operations to new land to escape the effects of soil exhaustion.

SHILA, a Bantu-speaking Negroid people of the Bemba-Lamba group, largely dependent on horticulture and fishing.

SHILLUK, a Nilotic people of the Fung group, primarily dependent on horticulture, but practicing some animal husbandry, hunting and fishing.

SHINTOISM, the national religion of the Japanese, which developed out of the ancestor and nature-worshipping traditions of the original Bronze Age Japanese invaders. Following the 5th century A.D., Shintoism became increasingly sophisticated, and sacred books written in the 8th century A.D. trace the ancestry of the Mikado and the Japanese people back to divine ancestors, known as Kami (q.v.), who lived at the time of the original creation of the world. Because Shintoism is essentially an ancestor-worshipping religion, it results in a highly stratified pattern of social organization and encourages hero-worship, binding all members of the Japanese nation together by strong familistic bonds and by a common loyalty to the divinely-descended emperor. Because dramatic and beautiful objects of nature are believed to house the spirits of supernatural beings, Shinto temples and shrines commonly tend to be located in situations of great natural beauty. The Japanese brought much of the culture of Western Eurasia with them when they invaded Japan, and there are strong parallels between Shintoism and the ancient religion of Greece and Rome.

SHIRIANA, a South American Indian people of unidentified linguistic affiliation, dependent on hunting, fishing and food-gathering.

SHIVWITS, a Southern Paiute, North American Uto-Aztec (Shoshone)-speaking people, dependent on hunting, food-gathering, and some animal husbandry.

SHLUH, Moroccan Berbers primarily dependent on agriculture and animal husbandry.

SHOGO, a Bantu-speaking Negroid people of the Shona-Thonga group, primarily dependent on horticulture with some cattle herding and hunting.

SHOGUN, a Japanese feudal ruler with extensive military power.

SHONA, a Bantu-speaking Negroid people of the Shona-Thonga group, primarily dependent on horticulture with some cattle herding and hunting.

SHOSHONES, a North American Indian people of the Great Basin of the Rocky Mountains. Linguistically the Shoshone belong to the Uto-Aztecan group, and include Ute, Comanche, Kaibab, Luiseno, and Paiute.

SHRADHA, memorial rituals performed by the relatives of a deceased Hindu until such time as the deceased spirit has had the opportunity to be born in a new body.

SHUSWAP, a North American Indian people, speaking a Salish (Mosan) language and situated on the Northern Plateau area of British Columbia, where they are dependent upon hunting, fishing and food-gathering.

SIA, a North American Indian Central Pueblo people, speaking a Keresan language and primarily dependent on horticulture and minimal hunting. Some animal husbandry has been practiced since the time of the Spaniards.

SIALK, TEPE, one of the most important of Iranian archeological tell sites, excavated to date. The earliest settlement dates to the 6th millennium B.C., and comprised the home of a small group of Neolithic farmers using painted pottery and metals. By the 6th millennium, Sialk had developed sophisticated copper age culture heavily influenced by Mesopotamia, and the wealth of jewelry found in the graves indicates a high degree of prosperity. However, early in the 2nd millennium B.C., Sialk appears to have been conquered by an Indo-European warrior aristocracy, whose remains are found in a site known as Cemetery A, and the excavation of Cemetery B dating from the early 1st millennium B. C. reveals the prosperity of a well-established and prosperous Indo-European aristocracy.

SIAMESE, a Sinitic (Thai-Kadai) speaking people (also known as Thai), largely dependent on agriculture augmented by some animal husbandry and fishing.

SIANE, Papuan people of the East New Guinea highlands, dependent on horticulture supplemented by some hunting, food-gathering and animal husbandry.
SIB, an extended kinship group larger than a family but fulfilling many functions of a family.
SIBERIANS, much of Siberia appears to have been occupied from the Upper Paleolithic onwards, with some areas being settled by Neanderthaloid peoples with Middle Paleolithic cultures. In proto-historic and historic times, the area has been occupied by a variety of peoples. The oldest of these are the diverse Paleo-Asian groups, which include the Chukchee and the Koryak, and may earlier have included Ainu-type populations. The Tungus appear to have originally resided in western Siberia, and Ugric, Samoyed and Ostyak (Uralic-speaking) peoples are indigeneous to much of western Siberia and the adjacent parts of eastern Europe. Central Arctic Siberia contains the Turkic-speaking Yakut, Yukaghir and Yenesei Ostyak (Ket).
SIBLINGS (SIBS), two or more offspring of the same parents, i.e., brothers and sisters.
SIBYL, the title awarded to women who were believed to be able to foretell future events and to intercede with the gods on behalf of men. The Sibyls played an important role in Greek and Roman societies, and it is interesting to note that the Celtic, Persian, Lybian, Phrygian and Teutonic peoples also believed that some women were capable of foreseeing the future.
SICKLE, a curved cutting tool designed for reaping corn. The first flint sickles were manufactured by the Natufian advanced food-gatherers of Palestine. These frequently comprised a series of small stone blades set into a wooden shaft. In the Bronze Age occasional bronze sickles are found in Sumeria, with a more distinct crescent shape, but metal sickles are not common until the coming of the Iron Age, after which sickles were customarily made of iron or steel in the sickle shape still standard in 20th century Europe.
SICKLE CELL TRAIT, an inherited disease, most common among persons of Negro and Pygmy descent, but also found occasionally in other populations which have undergone natural selection (q.v.) in malarial environments or which have absorbed the sickle cell trait by hybridization with carrier races. The effect of the disease is to cause numbers of the red blood cells to adopt various shapes some of which resemble a sickle. In this condition they are less capable of transporting oxygen. On the other hand, persons who carry the trait in a recessive condition appear to have a higher degree of resistance to malaria, so that in a recessive condition the sickle trait is advantageous in malarial areas. However, when the sickle cell trait is inherited in a homozygous condition it will result in serious anemia, which may lead to premature death. The sickle cell trait is a prime example of Balanced Polymorphism (q.v.).
SIKHS, a militaristic sect of Hindus, residing in the Punjab, who have become genetically distinct from other Indian populations.
SILURIAN, a geological period in the Paleozoic era which lasted from approximately 430 to 395 million years ago.
SIN, the concept of sin appears to have originated in the Sumerian religion. Men who 'sinned' or offended against the gods were deprived of divine protection, in which condition a demon could then enter and take possession of their bodies. Such persons could only be saved by an exorcist ceremony conducted by the priests. This concept of sin, alien to Indo-European and many other religions, was adopted into Judeo-Christian beliefs via Babylonian influences on Judaism, and to this day both Jews and Christians place great stress on the concepts of sin, guilt, atonement, punishment and salvation.
SINAI, the peninsula which separates the Gulf of Suez from the Gulf of Akaba and acts as a land bridge between Africa and Asia. The Sinai mountains, which extend along the center of this land bridge, were at one time an important source of copper as well as of turquoise and malachite.
SINANTHROPUS PEKINESIS, see PEKING MAN.
SINDHI, the name given to the contemporary inhabitants of the Indus Valley, who belong to the Iranic sub-division of the Caucasoid race but who speak an

Indo-European language derived from the Sanskrit of the ancient Indo-Aryan invaders of India. The Sindhi were traditionally dependent on agriculture, animal husbandry, fishing and commerce.

SINGLE GRAVE CULTURE, a term used to refer to a cultural tradition in which bodies were inhumed in single corpse graves, either under a barrow or occasionally within a mortuary house covered by a barrow. The Single Grave Culture appears in North Germany and Scandinavia towards the end of the First Northern Culture (the later part of the Neolithic, circa 2500–2000 B.C.). These sites usually contain stone battle-axes and corded-pottery, and may represent the immigration of corded-ware, battle-axe Indo-European-speaking peoples into the area if, indeed, these people were not indigenous to North Europe as may be the case.

SINHALESE, a predominantly Buddhist, Indo-European-speaking people, who acquired their language from the Indo-Aryans of the 6th century B.C. who invaded the island of Ceylon off the southern tip of India. However, the Sinhalese are separated from the Indo-European speakers of India by the large Dravidian-speaking population of Southern India. Agriculture, animal husbandry and sea fishing are the main occupations.

SINKAIETK, North American Indians who speak a Salish language of the Algonquin-Mosan group, and are dependent on fishing, food-gathering and hunting.

SINKYONE, a Northwestern Californian Athabascan-speaking people, dependent on food-gathering, hunting, and fishing.

SINO-TIBETAN LANGUAGES, the Sino-Tibetan group of languages includes the languages of China, such as Mandarin, Cantonese, Wu and Hainanese, and those of the Tibeto-Burman division, which include Chin and Karen (spoken by hill tribes living on the border between the Indian subcontinent and Burma). Faro, a language spoken in Annam, also belongs to the general Tibeto-Burman group. In addition, there may be a relationship with the non-Austro-Asiatic languages of Southeast Asia, including Laotian, Thai and various lesser languages, such as Naga, spoken in India, and Shan, spoken in parts of Eastern Burma.

SIPAPU, the name for the small circular pit found in the floor of the ancient pit houses and kivas of the Anasazi culture, through which the American Indians believed that the spirits of their ancestors re-entered the world every winter.

SIRIONO, a South American Indian people of Tupi speech located in present day Brazil, the Siriono are dependent on horticulture, hunting, and some fishing and food-gathering.

SIUAI, a Melanesian (Malayo-Polynesian) people inhabiting Bougainville, largely dependent on horticulture, food-gathering and animal husbandry.

SIVOKAKMEIT, Western Eskimos who depend on fishing and some hunting.

SIWANS, a Hamitic-speaking 'Oasis Berber' people of North Africa, dependent primarily on horticulture with some animal herding.

SKARA BRAE, a Neolithic village in the Orkney Isles. Since the islands were devoid of timber, all house furnishings were made of stone. As a protection against the cold winter climate, the passages or lanes between the houses were roofed over, so that it was possible to pass from one house to another without facing inclement weather.

SKELETAL ANALYSIS, considerable evidence concerning the racial origins, migrations and history of people can be derived from an examination of their skeletal remains. The anatomical measurement of the skull and of the proportions of the skeleton is commonly known as anthropometry. However, the identification of certain blood groups is sometimes possible by way of 'paleolithic serology' (q.v.) and age at death can be calculated by an examination of the skull sutures and the state of the teeth. Paleopathology (q.v.) provides information regarding prevailing diseases as well as of the type of injuries to which a population was susceptible because of its life style. The sex of individual skeletons can be determined from the shape of the pelvis.

SKHUL MUGHARET, ES, a cave on Mt. Carmel in Palestine where important fossil remains were discovered by T.D. McCrown in 1931. These comprise fragments of some ten individuals, intermediate between Neanderthal and Cro-Magnons. Dating around 35,000 B.P., there has been substantial debate as to whether they represent a stage in the evolution of Homo sapiens sapiens (q.v.) from Homo sapiens neanderthalensis (q.v.), or whether they represent instead hybrid forms resulting from crossbreeding between Cro-Magnons and local Neanderthals. Although Neanderthaloid in form, the skulls generally fall within the range of the more primitive living hominids in individual characteristics, most of which seem to have resulted from Homo sapiens sapiens admixture with older, localized Neanderthaloid populations.

SKULL WORSHIP, there is considerable evidence from various parts of the world that Neanderthal men collected skulls and arranged these in some kind of ritual order which implies an early form of skull worship. Skull worship was subsequently extremely widespread in Old World societies, both in the preservation of ancestral skulls, as among the Polynesians, or in the preservation of the skulls of victims of cannibals, as in Papua.

SLASH-AND-BURN CULTIVATION, a primitive form of horticulture, involving the chopping down of small trees and bushes and the killing of larger trees, usually by the cutting of rings in the bark and the burning of all remaining ground vegetation. Since this technique is usually practiced by people who do not know how to re-fertilize the soil by manuring or crop rotation, the cleared plot is normally cultivated for one or two years, after which the old plot may be abandoned as crop yields decline, and a new stretch of virgin land will be brought under cultivation.

SLAV LANGUAGES, the Slavic branch of the major Indo-European family of languages is divided into West Slavic, which includes Czech, Lusatian (Wend) or Sorbian, Polish, Kashubian and Slovak; South Slavic, including Serbian, Bulgarian, Macedonian, Croat and Slovene; and East Slavic, which includes Bielorussian (White Russian), Russian (Great Russian), and Ukrainian.

SLAVE, (1) a person who has no legal existence except as the possession of a 'free' person. Slavery has been common at one time or another in the history of virtually all complex societies, generally being acquired by conquest or, in the case of ancient Sumeria, by legal submission of debtors to creditors, when unable to pay off their debts by any measure other then their own forced labor. (2) a Northeastern Athabascan American Indian people, dependent on hunting and fishing.

SLAVE KILLER, a special club used by the Haida and other Northwest Coastal Indians to kill slaves when engaged in property-destroying potlatches.

SLED, a vehicle equipped with two runners which may be drawn over the snow. The sled appears to date from at least as early as the Mesolithic.

SLEDGE, a flat-bottomed vehicle without wheels or runners, used for dragging heavy objects over ice or snow.

SLING, an instrument used for both warfare and hunting, comprising a pouch attached to two thongs. A stone of suitable size is inserted in the pouch, and then whirled around the head of the slinger until the required velocity has been obtained, after which the release of one of the thongs results in the stone being projected with considerable velocity towards its destination. The sling probably dates from the early Upper Paleolithic, but was subsequently replaced in most cultures by the bow and arrow.

SLIP, a layer of fine clay applied to the face of pottery by dipping the vessel into a mixture of clay and water prior to firing. The process serves to make the pottery more resistant to permeation by liquids, and also improves the appearance by forming a fine coating over the coarser clay from which the major part of the pot is made.

SLOVENES, a Southern Slavic peoples who today live as a minority in Yugoslavia.

SNAKE GODDESS, a Minoan divinity who is represented as a female figure adorned with snakes, who was a goddess of fertility as well as a house goddess who protected the family. Snakes were widely associated with fertility in pre-Indo-European Europe, and were kept as house pets in ancient Egypt.

SNAKE-WOMAN, the title of one of the chief political officers of the Aztec empire, who, despite the peculiar nomenclature, was always a male.
SOAN, a culture formerly located in the Punjab and Northwestern Pakistan in which pebble tools and choppers predominate. At a high level, the Soan tools give way to flake tools, some of which reflect the western Levalloisan technique.
SOCIAL ANTHROPOLOGY, a term, more widely used in Britain than America, which differs from the concept of cultural anthropology in that the emphasis is placed upon patterns of social organization rather than on material culture and methods of subsistence.
SOCIAL DISTANCE, a feeling of separation existing between individuals due to the recognition of cultural differences, sometimes but not always as a consequence of status or caste distinction.
SOCIAL HEREDITY, the transmission of culture to successive generations by a process of successful enculturation.
SOCIALIZATION, the process of communicating the culture of a group to newcomers.
SOCIAL SANCTIONS, the enforcement power of a society aimed at obtaining conformity to its content or function.
SOCIAL STRUCTURE, the forms and modes of social relationship as distinguished from their content or function.
SOCIETY, the sum total of people occupying a specific territory who have fairly consistent intercommunication with each other and who share significant sections of culture in common.
SOCIETY ISLANDERS, a Polynesian people of the South Pacific, dependent on horticulture and fishing.
SOCIOLOGY, the controlled observation and interpretation of differing patterns of human relationships, their sources, and consequences. Properly a branch of anthropology, some see sociology as concentrating on the description and analysis of complex contemporary societies, while others see it as the study of group behavior. The term was invented by Auguste Comte, a disciple of the Comte de Saint Simon (one of the mentors of Napoleon) who envisaged the creation of a scientifically organized society. Since the days of Comte many sociologists have sought to be social engineers rather than detached scientists.
SOCKET, a hole made in any object to enable it to be fitted onto a haft. Sockets are distinguished from shaft-holes in that shaft-holes penetrate the object completely, having two openings, whereas a socket hole has only one opening.
SODALITY, a term widely used amongst anthropologists to refer to male or female associations formed with limited goals, such as a religious order.
SOGA, an East Lacustrine, Bantu-speaking Negroid people, mainly dependent on horticulture and some animal husbandry.
SOIL ANALYSIS, see PEDOLOGY.
SOLAR RADIATION HYPOTHESIS, the suggestion that the successive Ice Ages of the Pleistocene resulted from variations in the intensity of solar radiation. Also known as the Milankovich Radiation Theory.
SOLO MAN, a fossil hominid transitional between Homo erectus and Neanderthaloids, whose fossil remains were discovered in an archeological site at Ngandong in the Solo Valley in Java. Technically known as Homo soloensis, the age of these remains have not been determined, except to the extent that they are Pleistocene. It is possible that Solo Man may have been part of a phylogenetic continuum which later included Wadjak Man (q.v.).
SOLOMAN ISLANDERS, a Melanesian horticultural and fishing people.
SOLUTREAN, an Upper Paleolithic culture. Named after the archeological site at Le Solutré near Macon in France, the Solutrean culture preceded the Magdalenian and may represent an incursion of a distinctive group of Upper Paleolithic people from Eastern Europe. The Solutrean industry places great emphasis upon leaf-shaped projectile points, as well as barbed arrow heads, and may reflect a more warlike culture than is suggested by the earlier Upper Paleolithic artifacts, implying increased combatant activities.
SOMA, the sacred drink of the Vedic Indian literature, and the name of the

Vedic god associated with this drink. Soma may have been an alcoholic drink, prepared from a plant the identity of which is unknown.

SOMALI, a Cushitic people inhabiting the Horn of Africa, almost wholly dependent on animal herding supplemented by minimal horticulture.

SOMATIC CELL, a body cell as distinct from a reproductive 'gamete'.

SOMATOLOGY, the study of constitutional variations in man.

SONDAGE, an archeological term for a deep trench cut by archeologists across a site under excavation in order to reveal the stratigraphy.

SONGALA, a Bantu-speaking Negroid people of the Riverain Congo, primarily dependent on fishing with some horticulture and hunting.

SONGE, a Bantu-speaking Negroid people of the Luba group, largely dependent on horticulture with some fishing and hunting.

SONGHAI, a Nilo-Saharan or Nilotic language, spoken by a West African people living on the Upper Niger river who are dependent on horticulture, animal husbandry and fishing.

SONGO, a Bantu-speaking people of the Kasai group, largely dependent on horticulture, hunting and fishing.

SONINKE, a Negroid West African Mande-speaking people, dependent on horticulture and some animal husbandry, fishing, and food-gathering.

SONJO, a Bantu-speaking Negroid people of the East Nyanza area, largely dependent on horticulture and some animal husbandry.

SORCERER, an expert in black magic (q.v.).

SORORATE, the custom whereby a widower is expected to marry one of his deceased wife's sisters.

SOTHO, a Bantu-speaking Negroid people, largely dependent on horticulture and cattle herding.

SOUL, primitively believed to constitute the vital element of life, the soul of a man or woman is often believed to possess its own independent consciousness and even will. Thus it was believed by some peoples to be able to leave the body during sleep, and to depart permanently at the time of death. Often the soul is held to possess two parts, one of which may reside permanently outside the body. The idea of ghostly hauntings at the scene of violent death can often be traced to a belief in an abruptly disembodied soul which cannot find rest.

SOUTHERN UTE, a North American Indian people from the Eastern Great Basin, who speak a Uto-Aztecan language.

SPANIARDS, a modern nation of composite Atlanto-Mediterranean, Celtic and Gothic origins, with some Berber admixture and Arabic influence in the South. Traditionally dependent on agriculture, animal husbandry and some sea fishing, the Spanish speak a language which is of Romance (Latin) origin.

SPATULA, a bone tool, with a broad but usually thin blade, which was probably used for a variety of purposes, including the burnishing of pottery, the working of animal pelts, and as a cooking utensil.

SPEARHEAD, a blade designed primarily for thrusting, which was mounted on the end of a long shaft for use either as a hunting or war weapon. The first evidence of spearheads designed to be fixed to shafts appears in the Mousterian culture (q.v.).

SPEAR-THROWER, a tool invented by Cro-Magnon man in the latter part of the Upper Paleolithic which in effect lengthens the arm and in consequence increases the velocity of a spear. It essentially consists of a stick, some 18 to 24 inches in length, with a hook or knob at one end designed to hold the butt of the spear. Spear-throwers or atlatls were still used in America when the Spanish conquistadors arrived in the sixteenth century.

SPECIALIZATION, EVOLUTIONARY, the acquisition of special characteristics, as a result of natural selection, which promote the survival of the species.

SPECIATION, the process of evolutionary divergence whereby two new species evolve from common stock as a result of genetic segregation, prolonged genetic isolation, and differential selection.

SPECIATION, ALLOPATRIC, the process by which new species evolve rapidly by the splitting of a single population or subspecies into two or more separate lineages or races, either by selective breeding or more likely by geographical isolation and subsequent rapid selection under different survival conditons.

SPECIES, a group of living organisms that share a marked degree of genetic homogeneity and consequently resemble each other closely. No comprehensive and universally satisfactory definition of a species exists, but geneticists frequently use the term to refer to distinct populations that are unable to reproduce except with their own kind. Subspecies would thus be defined as subdivisions of species, whose members resemble each other in the possession of distinctive genetically-controlled characteristics which set them apart from other members of the species with whom they seldom interbreed for psychic, geographical, or other reasons, even though they still retain the potential for fertile cross-breeding within the species. From the evolutionary point of view, subspecies that preserve their genetic isolation eventually become separate species. The hominid races may be regarded as subspecies.

SPECTOGRAPHIC ANALYSIS, a scientific method for the analysis of a metal, pottery, glass and certain other materials, which provides archeologists with information concerning the possible source of the materials available to the original manufacturers, as well as the method of manufacture employed.

SPEECH, MONOGENESIS OF, a theory that all languages are ultimately derived from a single tongue. In view of the enormous antiquity of speech, which appears to have been evolving for at least as long as hominids have existed, the possibility of the monogenesis of speech may to some extent be tied to the question of the degree of relative monogenesis or separate evolution of the major racial divisions of mankind.

SPHINX, a mythological creature with the body of a lion and the head of a man, believed by the Egyptians to guard the Gates of Sunset. Statues of Sphinxes were frequently erected to guard temples and tombs against unauthorized intruders. Human-headed lions are also sometimes portrayed by the Greeks and Hittites.

SPINAL CORD, a portion of the vertebrate central nervous system which is located within the backbone from which the complex nervous system of fishes or more advanced animals appears to have evolved.

SPINDLE WHORL, a circular object made from stone, pottery, or bone which serves as a fly-wheel for a spindle to help make the spindle rotate at a regular speed. Identifiable by a central shaft-hole, the archeological discovery of spindle whorls provides evidence of the existence of spindles and the art of spinning thread, long after the decay of the woven cloth and the wooden parts of the spindle.

SPONGES, are descended from 'porifera', and as such represent a survival of one of the oldest life forms, or 'colonial protozoa', dating from the Archeozoic.

SPY, a cave site in Namas, Belgium, where two adult skeletons were found in association with Mousterian tools. Spy I is Classic Neanderthal but Spy II, which is also believed to date from early Würm, is more modern in type, though still within the Neanderthal range. The disparity has not been accounted for, unless some admixture with descendants of Steinheim is suggested.

SQUAMISH, a coastal Salish Northwest American Indian people whose language belongs to the Mosan family of the Algonquin-Mosan phylum. The Squamish were traditionally dependent on fishing with some hunting and food-gathering.

STADIAL, since the major glacial periods of the Pleistocene were generally extensive in length, and subject to considerable climatic fluctuations, the shorter periods of cold within each glaciation are known by the distinctive term stadials, the warmer periods between stadials being termed as interstadials.

STALO, a coastal Salish Northwest American Indian people, whose language belongs to the Mosan division of the Algonquin-Mosan phylum. The Stalo are dependent primarily on fishing with some hunting and food-gathering.

STARČEVO, the name given to the major component of the early Neolithic phase of the Old European civilization of the Balkans. The Starčevo culture emerged around 6500 B.C. in the Central Balkan region and was contemporary to the closely similar Karanovo culture of the East Balkans, the proto-Sesklo culture of the Aegean and the Impresso culture of the Adriatic. Characterized by towns of up to 1000 inhabitants, with hard-baked, burnished pottery, the Starčevo culture is known as Körös in Hungary and Cris in Romania. It continued until around 5300 B.C. when it evolved into a variety of distinct local subcultures notably Vinča, Tisza, Petresti, Lengyel and Butmir, each possessing a Linear type of script inscribed on pottery.

STATUS, the relative rank of an individual or group of individuals in the social hierarchy, based upon the possession of characteristics highly valued in that culture.

STEATITE, otherwise known as soapstone, steatite is a green or sometimes gray colored stone which is easily carved into figurines, utensils and even finely engraved objects such as seals. Steatite has also been used for making moulds because of its resistance to high temperature and the ease with which it can be carved to the desired shape.

STEATOPYGIA, a genetically-based condition, characteristic of the Capoids but also found among Negro populations believed to have acquired Capoid genes, resulting in the accretion of large deposits of fat on the buttocks.

STEINHEIM, a gravel pit near Stuttgart, Germany, in which the important but incomplete remains of a fossil skull and part of a face known as Homo sapiens steinheimensis were found by Berckheimer in the year 1933. These remains date from approximately 450,000 B.C., and correspond to the Late Hoxnian strata of the Mindel-Riss interglacial. The cranial capacity of 1100 c.c. is somewhat larger than that of Homo erectus, and the developed forehead and less pronounced muscle markings are more modern in appearance than those of many Neanderthals. While some authorities have suggested that the Steinheim man was an early Neanderthal, others prefer to place him (or her) in a separate category, and even to hypothecate a separate line of evolution from Steinheim man to Cro-Magnon man (modern Caucasoids), excluding the Neanderthals.

STELA, an upright stone column or slab, usually bearing carved inscriptions or pictorial symbols.

STEPPELANDS, Europe and Western Asia are linked to Eastern Asia by a broad belt of rolling, grass-covered land which separates the mountain ranges of Northern Persia and Tibet from the forest belts of Siberia. The continued existence of a steppeland belt, sometimes further north and sometimes further south, depending on the prevailing climatic conditions, linking Western Eurasia with Eastern Eurasia, appears to have been a more or less permament feature throughout the Pleistocene and Holocene. Prior to the recent introduction of mechanical cultivation equipment, artificial fertilizers, and sophisticated methods of irrigation which have facilitated the cultivation of large areas of the Eurasian steppelands, the steppes were occupied first by foot-herding primitive hunters and gatherers, and later by advanced horse-riding pastoralists. Because pastoralists are by nature nomadic, the steppes have served as an important cultural link between Western and Eastern Eurasia from the days of the Upper Paleolithic hunters down to more recent times when the riding animals possessed by advanced pastoralists facilitated rapid travel over vast distances. It was probably along the steppes that the Upper Paleolithic first expanded from Western Eurasia into Manchuria, North China and Japan, and many Neolithic culture traits certainly passed into Northern China by this route. Many of the secrets of metallurgy undoubtedly entered China via the steppes, as did various ceramic techniques. Since the steppes cover such a large area, however, there are substantial genetic or racial differences between the peoples of the western steppes and those of the east, with the occupants of the central steppes reflecting intermediate stages between the extremes of the east and the west. In the European and West Asian steppes, Indo-European-speaking Caucasoids have historically predominated; in the central steppes Ural-Altaic speech has traditionally been dominant, while in the eastern steppes Ural-Altaic speech appears to be autochthonous. Archeological excavations in the central steppes reveal the evidence of considerable Caucasoid Indo-European penetration, the Tokharians being an Indo-European-speaking people who survived in Chinese Turkestan (Sinkiang) until they were replaced by Altaic speakers around the 10th century A.D. However subsequent westward movements of Mongoloid and partly Mongoloid peoples brought Ural-Altaic languages into use over the entire extent of the Asian steppes by the early 19th century, a movement which has since been reversed by the establishment of industrial and agricultural settlements of Russian-speaking Caucasoids under Czarist and Communist Russian political domination.

STERILIZATION, a physiological alteration of either the male or female with the purpose of rendering that individual incapable of procreation. Sterilization can be employed for eugenic purposes, where the individual is known to be the carrier of deleterious genes (for the altruistic purpose of protecting future generations therefrom) or, as in modern India, to prevent an excessive increase of population. Sterilization has also been utilized in other societies for diverse purposes, as with the castration of eunuchs, in Moslem societies, to provide guards for harem women.

STERKFONTEIN, a site in the Transvaal where Australopithecus africanus remains were uncovered by Robert Broom in 1936, dating from the Vallafranchian period. The nearly complete vertebrate column, pelvis and rib cage are distinctively human rather than apelike.

STETTEN CAVE, a site in Germany excavated in 1931, dated between 25,000 and 30,000 B.C., to reveal Aurignacian tools.

STILUS, a wooden, bone, ivory, bronze of iron instrument, with one sharp end and one flat end (for erasing errors) used for writing upon wax tablets.

STIPENDIUM, a Latin term for the pay allocated to Roman soldiers, and also for the tax levied upon conquered provinces, from which our modern term 'stipend' derives.

STOICISM, a philosophy which gained widespread popularity among the educated leaders of the later Roman Empire. Its exponents advocated stern self-control, a sentiment in harmony with older Roman traditions, but broke with those traditions in advocating a universalist ethic, in contrast to the earlier Roman traditions of ancestor worship and nationalism.(See ROMAN RELIGION).

STONE AGE, a term which has long been used to refer to the earlier levels of human technological evolution prior to the invention of metallurgy. The Stone Age is customarily divided into the Lower, Middle, and Upper Paleolithic, the Mesolithic, and the Neolithic. (See separate entries under each of these headings).

STONE BOILING, a method of heating water or cooking food employed by societies unable to produce pottery capable of withstanding the direct heat from a fire. The technique of stone boiling involved the heating of stones or clay balls which were then dropped into containers of water or food).

STONE CIRCLES, prehistoric European ritual monuments comprising standing stones arranged in circles. (See CAIRN, HENGE, and MENHIR).

STONEHENGE, the most impressive of the British Megalithic 'henges' (q.v.). Stonehenge is situated on Salisbury Plain, near Avebury in Wiltshire. Surrounded by many barrows and lesser ritual sites, the entire henge is contained within a circular earthwork nearly 400' in diameter, within which a considerable number of cremation burials had taken place around the end of the 3rd millennium B.C. Two parallel banks of ditches connect the henge with the river Avon, a distance of 2 miles away. The standing stones which visitors see today mostly belong to the period known as Stonehenge III, when Sarsen stones, weighing as much as 50 tons each, were brought from a site some 25 miles away from the henge. These were worked into regular shape and then erected in a standing circle, the upright stones being linked to each other by curving lintel stones in a continuous circle within the original cursus. Inside this stone circle, five trilithons were arranged in a circle, and radiocarbon evidence from a tool made of antler, which was found in association with one of the standing Sarsen stones, indicates that the erection of those stones was the work of people of the Wessex culture. A series of 82 bluestones, which had earlier stood within the cursus and which appear to have been brought from Pembrokeshire in Wales, were re-erected about this time within the main Sarsen circle. The purpose of Stonehenge was clearly religious, and the arrangement of the stones, particularly the placing of the so-called central 'altar stone' suggests that some form of sun-worship was involved.

STRATIFICATION, SOCIAL, the process or condition whereby society is conceptually divided into several classes on the basis of wealth, power, influence, prestige, and any other determinants of status.

STRATIGRAPHICAL COMPARISON, the comparison of geological strata and archeological deposits with each other and their interpretation in terms of the deposit or stratum or era or period at which a coincidence in terms of content or time can be established.

STRATIGRAPHY, a major technique of archeological interpretation which is based upon the principle that where one deposit overlies a lower deposit, the lower deposit may generally be regarded as being the more ancient of the two. In cases where any disruption of the strata may have occurred, this can usually be detected by the experienced archeologist. Such disruption frequently arises as a result of subsidence or movement of the ground, the burrowing of animals, or simply excavations to permit the erection of new structures by later occupants of the site.

STRIKING PLATFORM, a term used to refer to that portion of a prepared core which is struck in order to detach the desired flake or blade. Striking platforms are consequently associated with flake industries.

STRINGED INSTRUMENT, a device designed to produce musical sounds by the vibration of taut strings. Often made of animal gut, such strings are usually attached to a resonator which amplifies the sound. It is probable that the first stringed instruments were developed in the early Mesolithic, at roughly the same time as the invention of the bow and arrow.

STRUCTURAL-FUNCTIONAL THEORY, the theory advanced by the French sociologist Emile Durkheim and the British anthropologist A. Radcliffe-Brown which in effect draws an analogy between the working of a culture and a machine. The structural-functional theory claims that all the component parts of a culture tend to become integrated into a holistic and inter-related complex, which functions smoothly, somewhat in the same way that a machine functions, provided the balance is not interrupted by the diffusion of unassimilated alien traits or by rapid invention of new traits. (See also FUNCTIONAL THEORY).

SUBANUN, a Malayo-Polynesian-speaking people living in the southern Philippines, largely dependent on cultivation supplemented by some animal husbandry.

SUBBUHANON, a Malayo-Polynesian-speaking people of the Central Filipino group, largely dependent on agriculture and fishing, and some animal husbandry.

SUBCULTURE, the distinctive meanings and values held by a subgroup in a society which distinguishes them from other members of the same society.

SUB-INCISION, a ritual incision imposed upon many Australian aboriginal males, involving a slit in the rear of the uretha extending to an inch or more in length. Among the Australian aboriginals sub-incision is usually accompanied by circumcision.

SUBSPECIES, a group within a species whose members share a common gene pool and therefore resemble each other in a variety of characteristics, but differ observably from other members of the species. Although there can generally be only limited cross-breeding between species if they are to remain separate, reproductive isolation is not always complete and many subspecies may grade imperceptibly into each other where they have a common territorial frontier. Subspecies constitute new species in the making whenever they remain genetically isolated from other subspecies over long periods of time, the rate of evolutionary change being particularly rapid whenever the selective process is particularly severe. Human races are generally regarded as subspecies, although genetic isolation has seldom been complete and is now tending to break down in areas characterized by substantial mobility of populations.

SUCKING TUBE, a tube made from a reed or a hollow bone, used by Hottentots and Bushmen to suck water from the damp earth underlying a dried-up water hole. Sucking tubes are also used by Shamans in a number of societies when drinking magical potions

SUDANIC LANGUAGES, a major family of languages in sub-Saharan Africa comprising a Central Sudanic subfamily, an Eastern Sudanic subfamily, and the Nilotic group of languages (q.v.). The Central Sudanic subfamily includes the Mangbetu, Mamva, Bagirma, and Madi languages. The Eastern Sudanic subfamily includes Fur, Nuba (Nubian), Mao and Korongo. The Eastern subfamily is linguistically diverse, however, and Furian, Koman, Kordofanian and Makan are substantially disparate and relatively independent languages.

SUDRA, the lowest of the four major castes of the Hindu caste system, the Sudras, originally known as the Dasya, are the descendants of the aboriginal occupants of the Indian subcontinent, relegated to their present low caste following the invasion of the Indo-Aryans, whose descendants constitute the three upper castes. (See CASTE SYSTEM, HINDU).

SUKU, a Bantu-speaking Negroid people living in the lower Congo, largely dependent on horticulture and some hunting.

SUKUMA, a Bantu-speaking Negroid people of the Nyamwezi group, largely dependent on horticulture and animal husbandry.

SUMBANESE, a Malayo-Polynesian-speaking people of Sumba (Indonesia), largely dependent on agriculture with some animal husbandry.

SUMER (SUMERIA), a collection of independent city-states formerly occupying the lower part of Mesopotamia between Babylon and the Persian Gulf, the latter of which formerly reached further inland than it does today. Sumer was, until recently, regarded as the sire of the world's earliest known civilization, although the claim may now possibly be challenged by what is called the Old European Civilization of the Balkans. This was contemporary to Sumer, but (due to the rich supply of available timber) most construction was of timber and wattle-and-daub, and therefore did not leave the imposing tell sites which the mud-brick and later baked-brick cities of Sumer left behind them. Adjacent to Sumer was the important state of Elam, whose history was parallel to that of Sumer, but whose language and culture reveals important differences. Each city-state in Sumer had its own god, who was regarded as the owner of the entire land, and who was believed to reside in an anthropomorphic image housed within a temple mounted on a raised platform or 'ziggurat' (q.v.). Sumerian society was highly stratified under the direction of divine kings and a highly educated priesthood. Each Sumerian city-state maintained its own army of professional soldiers, controlling a surrounding group of farming villages. The peak of Sumerian civilization coincided with the copper and bronze ages, although all metals had to be brought from the mountains of Anatolia and Persia. Long after the Sumerian cities had advanced into the metal ages, the rural areas remained essentially Neolithic in character. A written script was developed based first upon pictographic and then a cuneiform style of writing. This was used not only by the priests, but also by merchants, lawyers and bankers in the complex economic life of the city-state. There are important parallels between the early social structure of the Sumerian society and that of the early Indo-Europeans, and since the Sumerian language has been deciphered we have detailed historical records of the daily life of the residents of the Sumerian city and a fairly complete history of the many wars and diplomatic relations between the different city-states. The early inhabitants of Neolithic Sumeria were typical Mediterranean Caucasoids, although there appears to have been an infusion of a broader-headed racial type (somewhat corresponding to the modern Armenoid race), into Sumeria at a later date, probably from the region of Anatolia. The Sumerian language has not been successfully related to any other known family of languages. Despite cultural parallels with the Indo-European-speaking peoples, attempts to relate the Sumerian language to Indo-European, or to the Semitic, the Basque, Etruscan or any other non-Indo-European languages of the Caucasoid world have proved inconclusive.

SUMERIAN RELIGION, the Sumerians conceived of men as being dominated by the wishes of the gods. These they divided into superior gods, associated with the natural functions of the universe, and minor gods, concerned with the welfare of individual families or places. Each Sumerian had his personal god, and each Sumerian city had a personal deity who was regarded as owning the land and all that was on it. Priests served as stewards to the gods, being responsible for the care of the god's earthly possession. Each deity was believed to reside in the anthopomorphic statue which stood in the centre of the temple erected in his honor, usually on a stepped pyramid known as a ziggurat (q.v.) and possessed a harem of human concubines, who also served as temple prostitutes. The wishes of the god were interpreted by a corps of temple priests under the direction of a high priest, through the interpretation of omens and dreams. The female attendants were similarly organized under a high priestess who was frequently a sister of the king. Once a year, at the annual vegetation fertility rite, the king assumed the identity of the god of vegetation, commonly known as Tammuz, and cohabited with one of the high priestesses, who became the incarnation of the goddess Inanna or Ishtar.

SUMO-MOSQUITO, a Central American Indian people of Nicaragua.

SUMPTUARY LAWS, societies which reveal a considerable degree of social stratification frequently possess sumptuary laws regulating the style of clothing and/or behaviour of the different classes or castes. The object of sumptuary laws is to preserve class or caste, seriously prohibiting members of the lower classes or castes from imitating the distinguishing symbols or distinctive lifestyle of the superior members of society. Ancient Rome, Medieval Europe and feudal Japan, as well as Inca Peru and many other societies, all enforced sumptuary laws which reserved the more ostentatious lifestyles as a privilege of the upper classes.

SUN DANCE, an eight day ceremony, widely recognized among the Plains Indians of North America, during which the performance of secret rituals was accompanied by fasting and ritual smoking. Essentially the Sun Dance was a form of ritual penance or purification.

SUNDI, a Bantu-speaking Negroid people living in the lower Congo, largely dependent on horticulture, some domestication of animals and hunting.

SUN-DISK, a bronze or gold disk, usually highly decorated, believed to symbolize the sun, which played an important role in religious rituals throughout Bronze Age Europe.

SUNG MING-HSU, the mythological Chinese Tree of Life and Knowledge, which reveals distinct parallels with the corresponding mythological traditions of a Tree of Life and Knowledge found in Western Asia and Europe, indicating a common Upper Paleolithic origin.

SUN WORSHIP, the worship of the sun, frequently personified as an anthropomorphic sun god, has been widespread in many societies around the world, and is probably of Paleolithic origin. Needless to say it forms an integral part of nature worship, and is frequently associated with ancestor worship – both the Inca emperors and the Japanese emperors having claimed descent from the sun as an anthropomorphic deity.

SUPERGENE, a pattern of gene linkage, whereby constellations of linked or coordinated genes tend to be inherited as a coherent unit, thereby ensuring the efficient functioning of the more complex life forms from generation to generation.

SUPERNATURAL, that which cannot be explained by the laws of the natural world.

SURI, a Negroid, Nilotic-speaking people of the Beir-Didinga group, primarily dependent on cattle herding and horticulture with some hunting and fishing.

SURVIVAL VALUE, the effectiveness of any particular characteristic, physiological or cultural, in promoting the ability of the possessing organism, group or society to propagate itself into the future.

SURYA, the Vedic Sun god, usually represented as riding in a chariot drawn by seven horses.

SUSA, an ancient city in southwestern Iran, today surviving only as a ruined tell. Excavations confirm that it was formerly the capital of Elam in the 2nd millennium B.C., and that it was subsequently also one of the capitals of the Persian Achaemenid empire.
SUSU, a Negroid, West African Mande people, dependent on horticulture and some animal husbandry, fishing and hunting.
SUTTON HOO, an archeological site in Suffolk, England, which revealed the funeral remains and grave furniture of a 7th century East Anglian king. The contents of the largest group of royal burial mounds included a Saxon longboat, the form of which had been preserved in the surrounding sand despite the decay of the timbers, and a rich variety of weapons, armour, jewelry and other artifacts. An iron standard and a gilt bronze represented symbols of royal status. No body was found in the mound, which appears to have served simply as a cenotaph, possibly commemorating King Redwald.
SUTURES, hairline seams which join the separate bones comprising the cranium. The complexity of the sutures seems to be linked to the growth of the brain. Among Caucasoids the coronal suture (which runs across the top of the skull) is the most complex, among Mongoloids the sagittal suture (which links the parietal bones) is the most complex, while among Negroes it is the lambdoidal suture. These differences imply different rates of maturation.
SWAHILI, an East African people of the Tanzanian coastal plain, comprising several tribes, the most prominent of which are the Bajun and the Hadice.
SWANSCOMBE, a gravel pit situated on a terrace of the river Thames in Kent, where important remains, comprising an occipital bone and parietal bones, dating from the Mindel-Riss Interglacial period, were discovered by A. T. Marston and J. Wyner in 1935 and 1955 respectively. Tools from the lower levels are of Clactonian type, while the upper levels reveal Acheulian handaxes. Parts of a skull recovered from an upper level have been regarded as remarkably modern in type, and since they pre-date the appearance of Neanderthal skulls, the Swanscombe skull has been grouped with that of Steinheim in the sapiens category as Homo sapiens steinheimensis. This classification has been disputed, but is becoming increasingly accepted. (See also STEINHEIM).
SWARTKRANS, a site in the Transvaal of South Africa, where a variety of early hominid fossil remains were found by Robert Broom and J. T. Robinson in 1949 and subsequent years. Those which were first called Paranthropus robustus are now classified as Australopithecus robustus, and those that were initially labelled Paranthropus crassidens are now classified as Australopithecus africanus.
SWASTIKA, a cross or sun symbol the tips of which are bent at right angles in either a clockwise or anti-clockwise direction, The Brahmin priests of India create new fire from a wooden device shaped in the form of a swastika, containing a small hollow at the point of intersection, in which fire is created by friction. The swastika was found not only throughout the Indo-European world, embracing Europe, Persia, and India, but also in China and Japan, as well as among North American Indian tribes, namely the Kickapoos and Potawatomis, who also use it as a sun symbol. The evidence would therefore suggest that the swastika may date from the Upper Paleolithic, and that the symbol became widely diffused with the expansion of Mesolithic culture. Another form of sun symbol closely related to the swastika, and popular among the Celts, was the fylfot (q.v.) comprising either three or four curving arms joining at the center.
SWAZI, a Bantu-speaking Negroid people of Southern Africa, largely dependent on horticulture and cattle herding.
SWEAT LODGE, a virtually airtight hut, commonly employed by both the Navaho and Iroquois, as well as certain other North American Indians, as a kind of sauna bath, water being poured on heated stones creating the desired steam. Sweat lodges were used in ritual purification.
SWEDES, a Nordic Scandinavian people who have occupied their present territory since at least the Bronze Age. Swedish is a variant of the Scandinavian or North Germanic group of Indo-European languages.

SWISS, the residents of modern Switzerland are of Germanic descent and speech in the north, of French origin and speech in the west, and of Italian origin and speech in the south. The mountainous habitat encouraged the different peoples of neighboring cantons to cooperate in defense, while avoiding internal strife by encouraging autonomy each within their own valleys.
SWORD, a weapon which was first developed in the Bronze Age, and is distinguished from the dagger, from which it was derived, by the relative length of its blade. Technically swords are also differentiated from the later rapiers by their broader blades, intended for cutting as well as for thrusting. Widely revered among Indo-Europeans, the sword originated in the Danubian area and spread outwards from this centre to reach the Aegean by 1650 B.C. The Homeric warriors used relatively short swords, and those of the Roman legions were only slightly longer. However, among the Celtic and Teutonic peoples in particular, a much longer and heavier variety of sword developed, which tended to be restricted in use to members of the aristocracy. In particular, the medieval Franks developed a two-handed sword whose blade sometimes exceeded six feet in length. This was swung around the head and appears to have been carried by a select group of warriors who spear-headed an attacking force, with the object of 'softening-up' the ranks of the defenders immediately prior to the onslaught of the main part of the attacking army.
SYLLABARY, a form of writing in which each symbol represents a distinct syllable, i.e., a consonant and a vowel. Modern Japanese, like the Linear B Script of ancient Greece, uses a syllabaric alphabet.
SYLLABLE, a group of phonemes comprising a vowel and a continuant or sonorant articulated as a complete unit in the formation of a word.
SYMBIONT, a term sometimes used to refer to an organism which enjoys a close symbiotic relationship with another organism.
SYMBIOSIS, a relationship between dissimilar organisms which is beneficial to the survival of the two organisms, although each may benefit in a different manner. In point of fact, all members of an ecological community (q.v.) are to a greater or lesser extent linked in a symbiotic relationship with each other.
SYMPATRIC, a term used when two or more different species, subspecies or races occupy the same geographical territory. In point of fact, the coexistence of two rival species and races in the same territory over long periods of time is very rare, because of their inherent tendency to compete with each other for the same resources. Separate species which do not compete with each other for the same resources may, however, successfully occupy the same territory without difficulty. (See also ALLOPATRIC SPECIES).
SYMPATRIC SPECIES, separate species which occupy overlapping geographic areas.
SYNTAX, the study of the structure of sentences and of meaning as affected by the order of words in a phrase or sentence.
SYRIANS, a Semitic-speaking (Arabic) population of Mediterranean Caucasoid type, traditionally dependent on agriculture and animal husbandry.

T

TABU (TABOO), a Polynesian and Melanesian term used to refer to any prohibition, the violation of which attracts magico-religious penalties. Further study of the concept of tabu suggests that it is related to the idea of mana (q.v.) as a supernatural power force, contact with which can be dangerous to unauthorized persons or those who are inept at its management. The term 'taboo' is generally applied by anthropologists to refer to prohibitions existing in any society against the defilement of sacred objects or persons.
TABU, NAME, a prohibition against use of the personal names of specific gods, sacred objects, or even of individual persons, which may only be pronounced aloud under authorized ceremonial conditions.
TABUN, MUGHARET EL, an archeological site on Mt. Carmel, excavated in

1932 by T.D. McCown, which has revealed a complete female Neanderthal skeleton and other fossil fragments. These were associated with both Mousterian and late Acheulian tools.

TAGALOG, a Malayo-Polynesian people living on Luzon, in the Philippines.

TAGBANUA, a Malayo-Polynesian-speaking people of the Southern Philippines, largely dependent on hunting and fishing.

TAHITI, the name of an island in Polynesia. The Polynesian Tahunas or high priests claimed that the ancestors of the Polynesian nobility were descended from ancient gods who lived in a heavenly abode named 'Tahiti'. This was supposedly somewhere to the west of Polynesia, and certain Polynesian legends imply that the ancestral home was India.

TAHITIANS, an Eastern Polynesian people residing in the Society Islands, mainly Tahiti, dependent on horticulture, fishing and some animal husbandry.

TAHLTAN, a North Athabascan American Indian people, dependent on hunting and fishing with some food-gathering.

TAHUNA, a Hawaiian priest, whose duty it was to preserve the ancient legends associated with the origins and deeds of the ancestors of the aristocracy.

TAHUNAISM, the ancient religion of Hawaii. Built around the central concept of the inherited sacred power of the divine royal family, participation in the Tahuna religion was restricted to the nobility and royalty, commoners being denied admission to the shrines, or access to the priesthood. Although protected by the powers of the royalty and priesthood, the commoners were therefore largely dependent on animism and the guidance of shamans in their personal relations with the supernatural.

TAIAHA, a wooden sword club used by Polynesians for martial exercises.

T'AI CHǏN, the Chinese Taoist symbol of 'The Great Absolute', comprising a curved line bisecting a circle, one side of which is portrayed in red to represent the 'yang' or male principle, associated with light, life and warmth, while the other side represents the 'yin' or female principle, and is portrayed in black to indicate darkness, cold and death. It is believed that these two components together make up the universe.

TAIGA, the frequently swampy coniferous forest belt extending across Siberia, north of the grassy steppelands and south of the tundra.

TAINO, an Arawak-speaking American Indian people of the Antilles Isles in the Caribbean, dependent primarily upon horticulture, but also on fishing and some hunting and food-gathering.

TALISMAN, an object believed to have the power of attracting beneficial forces to the aid of the wearer. (See also AMULET and CHARM).

TALKING CHIEF, a Polynesian official who speaks to the commoners on behalf of the king, since the latter is prohibited by taboo from addressing the commoners personally. The Talking Chief may also speak to foreign visitors on behalf of both the king and the people.

TALLENSI, a Negroid, West African Voltaic people, largely dependent on horticulture with some animal husbandry and food-gathering.

TALUD-TABLERO, a distinctive principle of Meso-American architecture, characteristic of the stepped pyramids such as those of Teotihuacan. Instead of a smoothly sloping pyramid, such as is characteristic of ancient Egypt, the talud-tablero pyramids of Mexico comprise in effect a series of terraces, superimposed upon each other, each terrace being smaller than that on which it stands, the small uppermost terrace serving as a platform for the performance of the desired religious rituals.

TALUS, the ankle bone or *astralagus*.

TAMATE, the name of a New Hebrides secret society intimately associated with the propitiation of the spirits of the dead. Indeed, the word *tamate* is also a general term used throughout Melanesia for a spirit.

TAMBERAN, a New Guinea cult involving the use of bull roarers (q.v.).

TAMBOURINE, a shallow cylinder covered with parchment or skin, with bells or pieces of metal attached to the rim. The instrument may be either rattled or struck with the hand like a small drum.

TAMIL, a major Dravidian language and Hindu ethnic group practicing agriculture and animal husbandry in the densely populated valleys and plains of Southeast India.
TAMMUZ, the Babylonian god of vegetation and consort of Ishtar.
TAMOUANEHAN, the name given by devotees of the Aztec religion to the home for unborn souls.
TAMPU, a staging house of a type constructed at regular intervals along the Inca imperial roads to accommodate the *chagi* or relay runners. These runners carried messages for the Inca government from one tampu to the other.
TANAINA, a North Athabascan American Indian people of South Central Alaska, dependent on hunting and fishing with some food-gathering.
TANALA, a Malayo-Polynesian Malagasy people of Madagascar, dependent on agriculture, animal husbandry and fishing.
TANE, a Polynesian creator god, responsible for the beauty of the world.
T'ANG, the Chinese dynasty (A.D. 618 to 906) during whose reign porcelain was first made. The period is also notable for its glazed pottery.
TANGA, a small triangular apron made from the bark of trees, or more recently from beads, worn as pubic coverings by many South American Indians and West Indian women.
TANGENA, a form of trial by ordeal in Madagascar, by which those who are on trial are required to swallow pieces of chicken, after which they are given an emetic. If the emetic causes them to vomit what they have eaten, they are regarded as guilty; conversely those who do not vomit are regarded as innocent.
TANGI, a Maori mourning ceremony for the dead.
TANIMBARESE, a Malayo-Polynesian-speaking people of Tanimbar in Indonesia, largely dependent on horticulture, fishing and some animal husbandry.
TANIT, the Carthaginian goddess equivalent to Astarte (q.v.).
TANNESE, a Melanesian (Malayo-Polynesian) people from the Southern New Hebrides, largely dependent on horticulture and fishing with some animal husbandry.
TANNING, a process which replaced primitive methods of curing skins in many advanced cultures. Tanning involves the use of tannic acid, obtained from oak or willow bark or from other sources. (See also CURING).
TANOAN, a Pueblo North American Indian language family which may be related to the Uto-Aztecan languages of Central America, as well as with Kiowa, Tiwa and Tewa (Hopi).
TANTRAS, see VEDIC LITERATURE.
TAOMATE, a knotted cord used in Polynesia as a mnemonic aid to the recitation of the genealogies of noble families, many of which extended over several score of generations.
TAOS (TIWA), an Uto-Aztec, Tanoan-speaking North American Indian, Eastern Pueblo people, dependent on horticulture with a small amount of hunting and (in post-Columbian times) animal husbandry.
TAPA, a form of fabric formerly used throughout Oceania. Tapa is manufactured from the inner bark of the mulberry tree which is pounded until it becomes soft and pliable, after which it is dried in the sun and customarily decorated with vegetable dyes.
TAPIA, a building material comprising a mixture of clay and lime, widely used throughout Spain and Latin America. The mixture is usually poured into a prepared frame and allowed to solidify before the framework is removed.
TAPIRAGE, (1) a South Amazon technique whereby bright red feathers are produced for personal body adornment. The process involves plucking the feathers from a bird, and then dyeing its skin with the blood of a local species of frog. The next growth of feathers are then more brightly colored than they would otherwise have been. (2) a South American Indian people of Tupi speech, occupying the lower Amazon and dependent on horticulture, fishing and some hunting and gathering.
TARA, an archeological site 20 miles north-west of Dublin, where the residence of the High Kings of Ireland was situated from the 3rd to the 6th centuries A.D.

Older passage-graves and burial mounds have also been found on the site, some dating from the 3rd century B.C.

TARAHUMARE, a North Mexican Indian people, speaking an Uto-Aztecan language and dependent on horticulture, animal husbandry, and some hunting and food-gathering.

TARASCO, a linguistically isolated sedentary Central American Indian people, dependent on cultivation and some fishing and hunting.

TARDENOISIAN, a Mesolithic culture centered on southwestern France. Tardenoisian sites are characterized by trapeze-shaped arrowheads and small stone blades. The influence of the Tardenoisian culture extended from Spain through France into Central Europe from the 7th millennium B.C. until the close of the Mesolithic when it was replaced by the Neolithic culture.

TAREMIUT, an Eskimo people who depend mainly on fishing and hunting.

TARNHUT, a cap reported in the Germanic mythology to have the power of making its wearer invisible.

TAROT CARDS, a set of playing cards, decorated with a wide variety of traditional pictures, used widely throughout Europe during the Middle Ages, not only in card games but also for fortune-telling.

TARPAN, a wild horse, indigenous to the East European steppelands, which may have been ancestral to the domestic riding horse.

TARSIER, a primitive primate today found only in Indonesia and Southeast Asia, approximately the size of a rat. Adapted to arboreal life, the tarsier resembles the ancestors of the Oligocene monkeys, and formerly inhabited much more widespread areas of the Old World.

TARSIUS, a primitive prosimian, largely intermediate between lemurs and monkeys, which still survives in the East Indies.

TARSUS, the group of foot bones which includes the ankle and heel bones and the five small instep bones.

TARTARIA, a local Transylvanian version of the Vinča Middle Neolithic culture. Notable among Tartarian artifacts are clay tablets bearing pictographic symbols closely resembling those used at Uruk in Mesopotamia in later centuries.

TASIAN CULTURE, the name given to the culture associated with the archeological site of Deir Tasa in Upper Egypt. The Tasian culture is represented by a number of primitive horticultural settlements which probably originated as an extension of the Badarian culture.

TASMANIANS, an ancient population still found in Tasmania in the 19th century which represented the most primitive form of living hominids to survive into recent times. The average cranial capacity of an adult male Tasmanian was approximately 1250 c.c. and their crania revealed considerable prognathism. Unfortunately for anthropological science, the Tasmanians have not survived in a pure form, although their genes survive among contemporary European-Tasmanian hybrids.

TATTLER, in North American Indian folklore, a tattler is an animal which befriends a man and warns him of the infidelity of his wife or of other plots against him by his enemies, but usually dies as a result of providing this information.

TATTOO, a colored pattern ingrained in the skin by a process involving the insertion of pigments beneath the surface of the skin, usually as a symbol of social status. The ancient Scythian chieftains were extensively tattooed, and the custom was widespread among the nobility of Polynesia, being practised among the Maoris of New Zealand into this century. Tattooing can be accomplished by puncturing the skin in a pattern of dots by cutting making continuous incisions in the skin. or by drawing a thread impregnated with soot or some other coloring material through the skin.

TAU, red feathers used as a form of money or as a token of value in the Santa Cruz Islands.

TAUARI, a form of cloth made from thick beaten bark in the Amazon basin of South America.

TAULIPANG, a South American Indian, Carib-speaking people, dependent on horticulture and some hunting and food-gathering.

TAUNG, a quarry in the Transvaal, in which Australopithecus africanus remains were identified in 1924 by D. A. Dart in strata associated with the Villafranchian era. These comprise the face, jaws and endocranial cast of an infant — sometimes described as 'Dart's baby'. (See AUSTRALOPITHECINAE).

TAUREPAN, see TAULIPANG.

TAUROBOLIUM, baptism in the blood of a sacrificed bull. Taurobolium appears to have originated in rituals associated with the worship of the Mediterranean Mother Goddess, particularly as represented by the Mother Goddess Cybele, but was later adopted into the Mithraic cult (widespread in Anatolia and the Mediterranean area) during the later stages of the Roman empire, as a ceremony in which a male initiate prayed in a pit or subterranean room, while the animal was sacrificed on an overhead platform so that the fresh blood poured down to engulf his face, head, and body.

TAURODONTISM, a characteristic of Homo erectus and Neanderthal man. present in certain of the large-toothed and more prognathous of the living races of man, in which a large pulp cavity exists in the molar teeth. Taurodontism was not present in Homo sapiens steinheimensis or in Cro-Magnon man, a fact which suggests a largely separate evolution of Cro-Magnons and modern Caucasoids from Homo sapiens steinheimensis, and of Neanderthal man from Homo erectus, with the possibility of the later admixture of Neanderthal genes with those of Cro-Magnon descendants in various parts of the world.

TAXILA, a site in northern Pakistan which has revealed a succession of city settlements mostly associated with the Persian Achaemenid empire between the 5th and 2nd centuries B.C., and later with the Indo-Greek culture of the 1st century B.C. and the 1st century A.D., introduced to India by Alexander the Great.

TAXON, a term used to refer to any taxonomic group, no matter what its rank in the system of biological classification.

TEETH, the original mammalian dental formula was 3 incisor, 1 canine, 4 submolars and 3 molars on each side of the upper and lower jaws. Old World monkeys did not evolve beyond this point, but New World monkeys, apes and hominids have a dental formula of 2-1-2-3, Among the less prognathous of the living races of man there is a tendency towards modification of this formula to 2-1-2-2, with one out of every six Caucasoids never growing 'wisdom' teeth, even as adults.

TEHUACAN VALLEY, a high valley in Mexico where desert conditions have tended to preserve a wealth of archeological remains from Central American cultures between the 9th millennium B.C. and the arrival of the Spanish conquistadors. The earliest evidence is of nomadic hunting and food-gathering bands, but by the 7th millennium B.C. evidence suggests that squash and pepper may have been cultivated. Maize may have been cultivated in the Tehuacan Valley by the 5th millennium B.C., and pottery appears around 2300 B.C. Since there is no evidence of settled villages prior to the 3rd millennium B.C., some authorities claim that the evidence for the use of squashes, peppers and maize in earlier times should more correctly be interpreted as advanced food-gathering rather than the actual cultivation of those plants. Indeed, the existence of village settlements is not definitely attested to until around 1500 B.C., after which life in the valley appears to have been increasingly influenced by the developing pre-Classic and subsequent Classic cultures which developed in the more fertile regions of Mexico.

TEHUELCHE, a South Andean people who speak a language belonging to the Ona-Chon division of the Andean groups of languages. They are closely related to the Puelche of the Argentinian pampas.

TEITA, a Bantu-speaking Negroid people of the Kenya highlands, largely dependent on horticulture and animal husbandry.

TEKE, (1) the earliest human settlers to reach the Marquesas Isles. (2) a Bantu-speaking Negroid people living in the lower Congo, largely dependent on horticulture, some domestication of animals and hunting.

TEKNONYMY, a fairly widespread custom by which the parent of a child is referred to as a parent of such-and-such, rather than by his own name. This practice is only found among societies which possess a strong sense of family lineage and continuity, and who therefore regard the production of children as one of the major achievements in life.

TELANTHROPUS CAPENSIS, the name first given to fossil remains found at Swartkrans, in South Africa, now generally classified as Australopithecus.

TELEOLITHS, a term formerly used to refer to any stones which had been deliberately shaped by man, in constrast to eoliths, which may have been used by man but cannot be demonstrated to have been deliberately manufactured or shaped for use by any recognizable technique.

TELEOLOGY, the belief common among primitive people that all events must be 'willed' or preplanned and are therefore directed toward some preconceived end.

TELL, the Arabic name for a mound which rises above the level of the surrounding countryside as a result of the accumulation of debris from a series of successive settlements. The existence of tells as evidence of continuous village or city life is normally restricted to those areas which used mud bricks. Since the life of mud brick buildings is short it is customary to level the older buildings as they deteriorate and build new mud brick structures on the debris of the older buildings. By contrast, timber buildings decay and are replaced by new wood, while baked brick and stone materials are more permanent than mud brick and consequently tend to be reused when new buildings are constructed. As a result tell sites are common throughout the Middle East, but are absent in heavily forested areas and even in the Middle East, dating only from the period prior to the replacement of sun-dried mud bricks by kiln-baked bricks.

TELOPHASE, the name given to that stage in the process of cell division which commences after the daughter chromosomes have taken up opposite positons at the poles of the dividing cell, and which continues until the daughter cells enter the 'interphase' or resting stage, after the process of reproduction has been completed.

TELPUCEHCALLI, Aztec 'schools' maintained by each clan for the purpose of educating children, from the age of 15, in the arts of war and in the traditions, customs, and religious beliefs of the clan.

TELUGU, a Hindu people of South India who speak a Dravidian language and practice agriculture and animal husbandry in the densely populated valleys and plains of Southeast India.

TEMBETA, a long lip plug, inserted into the lower lip, commonly worn by the Tupi and Guarani women of South America.

TEMNE, a West African, Negroid people, largely dependent on horticulture with some fishing and animal husbandry.

TEMPLE, a term broadly used to refer to any place or building used for the worship of one or more gods. Early evidence of cave 'temples' is found in excavations of European Upper Paleolithic cave sites, and wooden temples were constructed in the European Balkans in the 6th millennium B.C. Both the Sumerians and the Egyptians developed elaborate stone or brick temple structures. Sumerian temples were erected on the top of a raised stepped mound known as a 'ziggurat' (q.v.). Most Greek and Roman temples, erected of stone, tended to follow the architectural style of the earlier timber constructions of the Upper Danube, from whence the Greeks and Romans originated, although the basic floor plan followed the traditional Aegean megaron plan. Most Mesopotamian, Egyptian, Greek, Roman and Indian temples housed an image of the deity to whom they were dedicated. However, this was not always the case in the Far East, where Confucian and Shinto temples in China, Korea, and Japan generally lacked images of the gods.

TENDON, a band of connective tissue which attaches a muscle to a bone.

TENETEHARA, a South American Indian people of Tupi speech, situated in the lower Amazon where they are dependent on horticulture, fishing and some hunting and gathering.

TENINO, North American Indians, speaking a Penutian language of the Sahaptin-Nez-Percé group and dependent on fishing, food-gathering and hunting.

TENOCHTITLAN, the name of the Aztec capital city which was built on a series of largely artificial islands in the shallow waters of the large lake which formerly existed in the centre of the Valley of Mexico. The modern Mexico City stands on the site of the Aztec capital, and owes its origin to the Spanish colonial city which replaced Tenochtitlan.
TENT, a folding portable shelter, which originated among nomadic peoples. Possibly the most primitive shelter was a wind-break, constructed of brushwood, which was usually abandoned when moving camp. By contrast, tents comprise a portable framework usually covered by skins, bark or felt, which can be transported with the migrant peoples. Evidence of the earliest known tents has been discovered in the European Upper Paleolithic.
TEOTIHUACAN, a major archeological site approximately 25 miles north of Mexico City. Although pottery fragments have been found at Teotihuacan which can be traced back to the 2nd or 1st century B.C., the major pyramids of the 'Sun' and 'Moon', together with the various temple shrines built along the so-called 'Avenue of the Dead', were constructed during the 2nd century A.D. During the Classic period a large city covering around 7 or 8 square miles grew up adjacent to the temple complex, and by A.D. 600 the rulers of Teotihuacan controlled most of the highlands of Central Mexico, and maintained political and commercial relations with the Mayan and Oaxacan civilizations. However, a period of cultural decline appears to have set in around A.D. 650, and the city of Teotihuacan was finally destroyed by enemy forces around A.D. 750.
TEPEXPAN, a site in the main Valley of Mexico in which a Homo sapiens skeleton, dated at approximately 10,000 B.C., has been found in association with a number of flake tools. This constitutes one of the earliest authenticated hominid fossil remains discovered in the Americas.
TEPIDARIUM, the heated room in a Greek or Roman bathing house.
TERA, a Chad-Sudanese (Hamitic-influenced) people related to the Bolewa. The Tera are largely dependent on horticulture with some animal husbandry.
TERENA, an Arawak-speaking South American people living in northern Argentina, and dependent on fishing, horticulture and food-gathering supplemented by hunting and animal husbandry.
TERNIFINE, an archeological site in Algeria, North Africa, where Atlantothropus mauritanicus fossils were uncovered by C. Aramgourg in 1954. These date from the early Mindel glaciation around 800,000 years ago, and are today generally classified as Homo erectus (q.v.).
TERP, an artificial mound built by the Germanic peoples who settled Frisia and other parts of the North German and Dutch plains, to raise the foundations of their village settlements above the level of periodic sea water floodings. The oldest *terpen* (plural) have been dated around the 3rd century B.C.
TERRACOTTA, any form of baked clay (literally 'cooked earth') may be described as terracotta. In addition to its use as a material for pottery, terracotta has been widely used for the making of figurines, children's toys and small functional objects, such as spindle whorls and weights to sink fishing nets.
TERRAMARE, a mound marking the site of a North Italian Bronze Age village, which has also been used to refer to a complete 'Terramare' culture complex reflected by similar Bronze Age fortified village sites. Terramare villages were characterized by streets laid out on a regular grid pattern and appear to have been constructed by an Indo-European people who migrated into Italy from the Upper Danubian region during the middle of the 2nd millennium B.C. (bringing with them Urnfield burial sites and cremation practices) to become the ancestors of the Italic-speaking peoples who settled Central Italy.
TERRITORIALITY, in the zoological sense territoriality refers to the existence of separate territories occupied by individual birds or animals or groups of birds or animals of the same subspecies, beyond which the 'proprietors' will seldom trespass. Any invasion of the territory by other animals dependent upon the same natural resources is likely to be opposed, even to the extent of physical combat, especially in the case of carnivores. Breeding behavior is also frequently associated with territorial limitations, the females of certain species of birds and

animals refusing to mate with males which do not possess territories of their own and who therefore lack a reliable source of food.

TERTIARY, a geological period which lasted from approximately 70 million until 2.3 million years ago.

TESHIK-TASH, a cave site in Uzbekistan containing remains dating from between 100,000 to 30,000 B.P. In particular, Neanderthal remains were found in association with Mousterian tools.

TESO, a Negroid Nilotic-speaking people of the Karamojong group, primarily dependent upon horticulture, cattle-herding and some hunting.

TETON, Siouan-speaking North American Plains Dakota Indians, mainly dependent on hunting with minimal good-gathering.

TETRAPODA, four-footed mammals, reptiles and amphibia. Birds are also usually included within this classification, their forelimbs having evolved into wings to facilitate flight.

TEUTONS, a term which originally meant 'men of the nation' (Old German *teuta*, Old Gothic *thiuda*, 'nation', cognate with Irish *tuath*), customarily used to refer to members of the West German branch of the German-speaking peoples of Northwestern and North-Central Europe. Historically the Teutons originated to the north and east of the Celts, and to the west of the Slavs. Most Teutons succeeded in maintaining freedom from Roman rule, after inflicting a severe defeat upon Varus, exterminating three complete Roman legions, at a renowned battle fought in the Teutoburger Wald, but for which victory English and the other Germanic languages probably would not exist today. (See GERMANS).

TEWA, a Uto-Aztec, Tanoan-speaking, North American Indian, Eastern Pueblo people, dependent on horticulture supplemented by a small amount of hunting and (in post-Columbian times) animal husbandry.

TEXTILE, any fabric produced by a process of spinning and weaving fibers of either a vegetable or animal origin.

THAI, see SIAMESE.

THAI-KADAI LANGUAGES, the speakers of the Thai-Kadai languages are found mainly in Thailand, Laos and Southern China, and probably originated amongst the descendants of early migrants from China.They may be related to the Miao-Yao group, but the latter has Mon-Khmer affinities indicating an older, more aboriginal, Australoid-type survival.

THALAMUS, that part of the vertebrate forebrain which is responsible for the coordination of the major sensory activities.

THANATOMANIA, a term used to refer to the reliably authenticated fact that in certain cultures a person who becomes aware of the fact that he has been doomed to death by magical means may fall sick and actually die. The incidence of thanatomania is particularly high among Australian aboriginals.

THAUMATURGY, the use of magic to bring about otherwise impossible events.

THEBES, the capital of Upper Egypt during the greater part of the Middle and New Kingdoms, and the seat of the god Amen. In addition to the temples of Karnak and Luxor, Thebes possessed a wealth of other tombs and temples including a number situated in the famed Valley of the Kings. The Thebes of Egypt should not be confused with the Thebes of Boeotia in Central Greece. As the capital city of the Thebans, the Greek Thebes was first established by Achaean Greeks during the Bronze Age, and has remained in continuous occupation from that time.

THEOCRACY, a form of government in which political power is assumed by officials who purport to act on behalf of a god who claims supreme authority over the lives of men.

THEOLATRY, a belief in and the worship of an invisible deity.

THEOLOGY, an elaborate system of arguments arising from the application of philosophical techniques to the discussion of prevailing fashions of magical and religious belief.

THEOMACHY, actions directed in opposition to the wishes of a god.

THEOMANCY, the use of oracles (believed to be inspired by one or more gods) for the purposes of divination. Theomancy forms an important part of the Jewish Cabala. The Greeks also consulted oracles who were believed to be capable of forecasting future events by consultation with the gods. In medieval Europe the church courts practised 'trial by ordeal' (q.v.) in the form of theomancy, believing that the god would indicate the guilt or innocence of an accused individual.

THEOPHAGY, a form of divine communion in which food or drink, symbolising a portion of the flesh or blood of a god, is consumed by the worshippers. The idea of eating the flesh and drinking the blood of a sacrificed god may arise from the ritual of eating portions of a totemic animal on appropriate ceremonial occasions.

THEOPHANY, the physical manifestation of a divine being to one or more human beings. Thus the Greek gods sometimes appeared before the heroes of the Iliad, and references to theophany also occur in the Hebrew Book of Genesis.

THERAPSIDA, an extinct group of reptiles which revealed many mammalian tendencies, and flourished during the Permian and Jurassic period. The fossil evidence clearly reveals that all living mammals evolved from therapsida.

THERMOLUMINESCENCE, a technique used by archeologists for dating mineral crystals. A number of variable factors are involved and the technique has not been perfected, but it is already possible to obtain approximate dates on pottery and other artifacts by an examination of the period of time that has elapsed since the crystals were heated at the time the pottery was baked.

THOMPSON INDIANS, a North American Indian people speaking a Salish (Mosan) language. Situated on the Northern Plateau area of British Columbia the Thompson Indians were traditionally dependent on hunting, fishing and food-gathering.

THONGA, a Bantu-speaking Negroid people of the Shona-Thonga group, primarily dependent on horticulture with some cattle-herding and hunting.

THOR, the Norse god of thunder and patron of farmers, known as Donar among the Germans. The Hammer (or war-axe) of Thor became a widespread religious symbol among the Germanic and Scandinavian peoples, marriages, burials and oaths being hallowed over its image. Our modern day of the week, Thursday, is named in honor of this god.

THORACIC INDEX, the breadth of the chest expressed as a percentage of its depth.

THORAX, that region of the body which contains the heart and lungs, and which in mammals is clearly separated from the abdomen by a diaphragm.

THRACIANS, an Indo-European people, closely related to the Phrygians (and possibly also to the Cimmerians), who migrated from the Pontic Steppes into that part of modern Bulgaria, European Turkey, and Eastern Greece, which is still known as Thrace.

THROWING BOARD, see ATLATL.

THULE CULTURE, an Eskimo culture which spread from Siberia to Alaska, around A.D. 600, and to Greenland by A.D. 1300.

THYROID GLAND, an endocrine producing gland. common to most verte-

TIAHUANACO, an archeological site representing the remains of a former city with ceremonial temples, located close to Lake Titicaca in the Bolivian Andes. The first signs of occupation appear around the 2nd and 3rd centuries A.D., when most of the temple platforms were built. From then until the rise of the Aztecs, the Classic Tiahuanaco style of pottery and stone-carving, frequently decorated with puma and eagle heads as well as various geometrical designs, occurs widely throughout the Western Andes.

TIBETANS, the Tibetans are a predominately Mongoloid people who show considerable genetic diversity because of the relative isolation of so many small populations in different and often distant mountain valleys. Their speech is Sinitic, belonging to the Tibeto-Burman subfamily. Subsistence is by agriculture and animal husbandry. The Tibetan subfamily of the Tibeto-Burman languages include Lepcha, Sherpa, Lolo and Abor.

TIBETO-BURMAN LANGUAGES, a family of languages, related to Sinitic, which includes Tibetan (q.v.) and Burman. In Burma the Burman subfamily includes Lakher, Karen, Purum and Akha. In Assam it includes Garo, Kachin, and Naga.

TIBIA, the frontal bone of the lower part of the leg.

TIGRÉ, a Semitic language, closely related to Amharic, spoken in Abyssinia.

TIGRINYA, a Tigré-speaking Semitic people from Ethiopia, dependent on horticulture and animal husbandry.

TIKAL, a major Mayan ceremonial centre, Tikal may have been inhabited as early as 600 B.C., although the construction of the surviving temples did not commence until around 200 B.C.

TIKOPIA, a Polynesian people living in Eastern Melanesia, dependent on fishing and horticulture.

TILL, GLACIAL, the deposits of unstratified rock and earth left behind when glaciers disappear as a result of a change in the climatic conditions.

TIMBER LACING, a technique which first appears to have been used in Troy II, but also found in later Minoan and Mycenean archeological sites, by which an earthen rampart was reinforced with a pre-constructed timber framework. Timber-lacing is also found in the Urnfield, Hallstatt and La Tène cultures.

TIMUCUA, North American, Southern Woodland Indians, speaking a Muskogean language and largely dependent on horticulture with hunting, fishing and food-gathering.

TIN, an important component of bronze, an alloy comprising approximately 90% copper and 10% tin. Supplies of tin in ancient Europe were largely restricted to Spain, Bohemia and Cornwall, with some minor deposits in Eastern Anatolia and Italy. Although the peoples of the New World never discovered how to produce bronze alloys, tin was nevertheless readily available in Mexico, where it was widely used in virtually pure form for the manufacture of ornaments.

TING-TS'UN, an archeological site in Shansi (China) where a Neanderthal fossil known as "Ting-ts'un man" was uncovered. Its age is uncertain, but an approximate date of 50,000 B.P. has been assumed.

TINKER, an itinerant metal worker or blacksmith.

TIPI, a portable conical tent constructed of skins and supported by sloping poles tied together at the top. Frequently used among North American Plains Indians, the tipi is closely similar to the early tents used by Cro-Magnon men in the European Upper Paleolithic.

TIRA, a Kordofanian-speaking (Niger-Congo) people of the Nuba group, largely dependent on horticulture, animal husbandry and some hunting.

TIRIKI, a Bantu-speaking Negroid people of the East Nyanza area, largely dependent on horticulture and animal husbandry.

TIRYNS, a fortified Mycenean citadel, situated some 10 miles south of Mycenae, which was famous for the 'Cyclopean Stones' used in the construction of the city walls. The palace of the king was constructed in the usual megaron style, but was extensively decorated with frescoes which reflect a Minoan influence.

TISSUE, a group of cells of similar character, all performing the same function, held together (in animals) by intercellular material.

TISZA, a branch of the Danubian culture which was located along the banks of the river Tisza, and dates from the early part of the 4th millennium B.C. Early copper artifacts are found in company with a selection of anthropomorphic pottery. The Tisza culture was closely related to the Lengyel cultures which lay to the north and west of the river, and the term Tisza is sometimes used to include the Lengyel cultures.

TISZAPOLGÁR, the earliest stage of the Hungarian Copper Age dating from approximately the middle of the 4th millennium B.C., which in turn gave way to the Bodrogkeresztur culture.

TITHE, a levy imposed by the Christian church upon the income of all households, traditionally equivalent to one-tenth of the total household income.

TIV, a Negroid people of the Tiv-Jukun group, who speak a Niger-Congo language, and are dependent on horticulture with some hunting, fishing, food-gathering and animal husbandry.

TIWI, an Australian aboriginal people from the North Australian offshore isles, largely dependent on food-gathering, hunting and fishing.

TLACATECUHTLI, the title of an Aztec monarch, literally 'the chief of men'.

TLALOC, the Aztec rain god who appears to have been borrowed from the Teotihuacan culture, and may probably be traced back to the Olmec culture.

TLAXCALANS, a Central American Pueblo Nahuatl (Uto-Aztecan)-speaking people, dependent on agriculture and animal husbandry.

TLINGIT, a North West American Indian fishing people, who practice some hunting and whose language belongs to the Na-Dené phylum.

TOBA, a South American Indian people speaking a Guaycuru language who live in Paraguay and adjacent territories, and are dependent on hunting, food-gathering, horticulture and fishing.

TOBACCO, a perennial plant bearing broad leaves that are dried and chewed or else smoked and inhaled. The plant, correctly known as *nicotina tabacum*, contains the drug nicotine, and probably originated in South America. Tobacco smoking was common among American Indians, before being introduced to Europe following the European settlement of the Americas.

TOBACCO, INDIAN, a variant form of tobacco probably derived from the original South American tobacco plant, known as *nicotina rustica.*

TOBELORESE, a Papuan-speaking people of the New Guinea group, largely dependent on horticulture with some fishing, hunting and food-gathering.

TOBIAS' NIGHT, many early Christian sects opposed sexual relations as sinful, and even advocated that sexual activity should be avoided or at least severely restricted even between married persons. Whereas in pagan Indo-European Europe the consummation of the marriage was the crucial phase of a total religious ritual, in the early Catholic religion the consummation was frequently postponed for several nights, so that the 'immorality' of the act should not follow too closely after (and thereby contaminate) the sanctity of the church wedding service. The term Tobias' night refers to the Biblical Tobias, whose wife did not conceive until long after her marriage.

TODA, an aboriginal proto-Australoid polyandrous people of India's southern Nilgiri hills, almost totally dependent on the herding of buffalo. The Toda adopted a Dravidian form of speech but never accepted the Hindu religion, although many have since adopted Christianity in place of their traditional religion.

TOHUNGA, a Polynesian term for a skilled craftsman, usually a carpenter.

TOKELAU, a West Polynesian people, dependent on horticulture and fishing.

TOKHARIAN, a dead language of Indo-European origin, known in two dialects commonly referred to as A and B (West Tokharian and East Tokharian) but also properly known as Kuchean and Agnean respectively. First discovered when manuscripts bearing inscriptions were found by Sir Aurel Stein during his explorations in Chinese Turkestan in the 19th century. Although there are some similarities between Tokharian and the Germanic language, it is believed that the Tokharians were the descendants of a pastoral quasi-nomadic Indo-European people who moved eastwards over the Siberian steppes, instead of entering the more populous regions of Europe and Southwestern Asia. The Tokharian culture and language were abruptly terminated during the 10th century A.D., when the whole of Chinese Turkestan fell under Turko-Uralic control.

TOLDO, a Patagonian skin tent.

TOLKEPAYA (WESTERN YAVAPAI), a Hokan-speaking, Plateau Yuman, American Indian people, dependent on food-gathering and hunting.

TOLLUND MAN, an excellently preserved corpse of an Iron Age Dane recovered from a peat bog in Central Jutland. The body was so well preserved that it was possible to analyze even the contents of the stomach, and the clothes, namely a cap, cloak and belt, were also in excellent condition. The fact that Tollund Man had died by hanging, as testified by the leather rope still around his neck, indicates that he may have been a person of royal blood, sacrificed to Odin.

TOLOACHE, a drug extracted from jimson weed, which became the object of a mystical cult among the Indians of Southern California, Arizona, Colombia and Ecuador. Sometimes the jimson flower is chewed, and sometimes the toloache drug is extracted and drunk as an intoxicant.

TOLOWA, a Coastal Oregon, Athabascan-speaking American Indian people, dependent on fishing, food-gathering and hunting.

TOLTECS, a people descended from the Chichimec tribes of North Mexico who dominated central Mexico from the 10th until the 12th century A.D. Under Toltec rule, primitive metallurgy developed in Mexico, and a number of architectural innovations are to be found in the remains of their capital city of Tula. The second of the Toltec kings, Topiltzin, who was later worshipped as the god Quetzaltcoatl, appears to have been driven from Tula after an internal conflict, and to have taken refuge by boat on the Gulf of Mexico, promising to return at a later date. Mayan records confirm an invasion in the 10th century by a group of Toltecs led by a certain Kukulcan (which is the Mayan equivalent of Quetzacoatl) and archeological evidence indicates that around this time invading Toltecs seized the Mayan city of Chichén Itzá, and dominated Yucatan for the next two centuries.

TOMA, a Mande-speaking Negroid people, largely dependent on horticulture and fishing.

TOMAHAWK, an American Indian war-axe of Stone Age antiquity, comprising a spherical stone head attached to a wooden shaft by thongs.

TOMB, BEEHIVE, a vaulted masonry tomb resembling a beehive in shape, common in the Bronze Age Aegean and particularly in Crete.

TOMB, CORBELED, a tomb with a vaulted roof (instead of a flat horizontal slab roof), in which the vault is constructed of layers of stones, each of which project beyond the supporting course below.

TOMBE, a ritual drum used by American Indians in the southwestern parts of North America.

TOMTOM, a small drum, beaten with the hands.

TONATIUH, the Aztec sun god, who demanded to be fed on the fresh blood and living hearts of newly-killed, sacrificial human victims.

TONG, a secret Chinese society, membership of which is usually restricted to individuals from related families. Such 'tongs' provide social and economic protection to their members, but frequently become involved in politics and even crime, so that feuds between rival tongs are by no means uncommon.

TONGA, LAKESHORE, a Bantu-speaking Negroid people of the Maravi group, largely dependent on horticulture and fishing.

TONGA, PLATEAU, a Bantu-speaking people of the Ila-Tonga group, primarily dependent on horticulture and herding with some hunting and food-gathering.

TONGANS, a West Polynesian people from the Tonga Isles, dependent on horticulture, fishing and some animal husbandry.

TOOLS, any instrument designed to be used in the hand. The ability to manufacture primitive tools was at one time regarded as a criterion by which the first hominids might be distinguished from their 'non-human' relatives. However, it has now been demonstrated that even primates, such as chimpanzees, are capable of manufacturing primitive tools from pieces of stick and of using a handful of leaves as a sponge to absorb water. There can be no sharp dividing line between the later hominids or members of the family of 'man' and their earlier hominid ancestors, since any distinction drawn is purely arbitrary. So far as the use of tools is concerned, living men differ from earlier hominids in having become totally dependent on the use of tools. Early hominids probably used wooden tools before they developed regular techniques of stone-working. The earliest tool-making period is known as the Lower Paleolithic (q.v.) and this is generally associated with hominids up to the level of Homo erectus (q.v.). Neanderthals were responsible for the improved methods of stone working associated with Middle Paleolithic (q.v.) stone, bone, and antler industries. Large numbers of microliths, useful for the manufacture of a variety of equipment, appear in the Mesolithic Age (q.v.) which gave way to the Neolithic (q.v.) when men ceased to be hunters and began to construct tools appropriate to a more sedentary cultivating or pastoral pattern of existence. The Neolithic was in turn succeeded by the Copper, Bronze, and Iron Ages, when metals were used to supplement stone in the manufacture of a variety of tools.

TOOTH, a tooth essentially comprises a crown, or hard cutting or grinding substance, a neck and a root which holds it in place. Most vertebrate animals possess teeth, although the earlier more primitive forms of teeth, found in some fishes and many reptiles, are unspecialized (see 'homodont'). At the mammalian level, most animals possess 'heterodont' or specialized teeth, namely incisors and canine teeth used for cutting, and molars and pre-molars used for chewing and grinding. Since teeth, like bone, do not decay as rapidly as other tissues, they frequently survive to provide evidence which has contributed greatly to the reconstruction of the paleontological record; paleoanthropologists can learn much regarding the evolution of man from the study of a single jaw bone if this still possesses a number of teeth. Earlier hominids generally had larger jaw bones and teeth than more recent sapiens varieties, although several living races still possess relatively large teeth, set in heavy prognathous jaws, characteristics generally found among the thicker-skulled races of man.

TOOTH EVULSION, the deliberate removal of teeth for magico-religious purposes. Tooth evulsion is particularly common among Australian aboriginals, who practise it as one of a variety of initiation rites involving physical mutilation.

TOPOKE, a Bantu-speaking Negroid people of the Mongo group, largely dependent on horticulture with some fishing and hunting.

TOPONYMY, the study of place names. Toponymy can play an important part in the reconstruction of prehistory; thus many rivers and mountains in Europe are still known by names which were originally Celtic, even though the areas around them are now occupied by non-Celtic speaking-peoples. Such evidence reinforces archeological evidence indicating that the Celts once occupied a much more extensive area than is associated with the surviving Celtic languages of today.

TOPOTHA, a Negroid, Nilotic-speaking people of the Karamojong group, primarily dependent on cattle-herding, horticulture and some hunting and food-gathering.

TORADJA, a Malayo-Polynesian-speaking people inhabiting the Celebes, and largely dependent on cultivation with some hunting and animal husbandry.

TORC, a spiral neck ring or chain made from twisted strands of bronze, gold or other metal. Torcs had a socio-religious significance among the Celts of the Bronze Age, indicating either divine or noble status.

TORCH, a flame used as a source of light. The earliest, simpler torches comprised a burning stick or bundle of brushwood. Oil and tallow are burned, with the aid of an absorbant wick, to provide light in more sophisticated societies. In both simple and advanced cultures, however, burning torches are often used in magico-religious rituals.

TORO, a West Lacustrine Bantu people, largely dependent on horticulture and some animal husbandry.

TORQUE, see TORC.

TORTOISE CORE, the core of stone which remains after the flake or blade tool has been struck from it. Since the core stone must be carefully prepared to ensure that the resultant flake will possess the desired shape, the residual core, which is usually discarded, tends to resemble the shape of a tortoise, hence the distinctive name.

TORUS, SUPRAORBITAL, the heavy, raised or protruding browridge which extends over both eye sockets.

TOTEMISM, the worship of a totemic plant or animal from which a particular kinship group believes itself to be descended. In most cases members of the kinship unit identified with the totemic plant or animal are prohibited from killing or eating the totemic animal on any occasion except specific totemic feasts, when the flesh of the animal is consumed in a form of ritual communion.

TOTENSCHUHE, literally 'shoes of the dead'. A term given by German anthropologists to shoes presented to the dead to assist them in the long journey to the nether world.

TOTONAC, a linguistically isolated, sedentary Central American Indian people, dependent on cultivation, supplemented by some fishing and hunting.

TOURNETTE, a pivoted disc or potter's wheel.

TOVODUN, the ancestral gods of the Dahomeyans from which name the West Indian Negro word *vodun* (q.v.) is derived. Many of the slaves brought to the West Indies and the Americas were of Dahomeyan origin.

TRACHEA, a tubular structure which plays an important role in the breathing apparatus of land vertebrates. In mammals the trachea or 'windpipe' constitutes a single tube which passes from the throat to the lungs, but in insects the trachea are spread throughout the body and open directly through the body tissues.

TRADITION, in the archeological sense, a tradition comprises a series (q.v.) of cultural traits (q.v.) which evolve out of each other, and which possess a distinctive continuity through time.

TRAIT, CULTURAL, a general term used to refer to any identifiable cultural element, either material or non-material.

TRANCHET, a stone tool with a chisel-shaped end which appears to have developed out of earlier scraper tools, but which was more probably used for chopping, like the blade of an axe or an adze. Blunted tranchets were resharpened by simply removing additional flakes. Tranchets were common in the Mesolithic period.

TRANSFERRIN, a serum protein which combines with iron and is an essential ingredient in hemoglobin.

TRANSFORMATION, (1) the process by which certain bacteria are able to acquire the DNA or genetic characteristics of the cells upon which they have become parasitic. (2) The ability of certain supernatural beings and some magicians to change themselves into animate or inanimate objects.

TRANSHUMANCE, a seasonal migration of a community which is sedentary for part of the year, but which migrates annually to allow grazing animals to take advantage of upland pastures. Transhumance is thus common among people who are partly cultivators and partly herders. In such cases the migration is arranged at appropriate times of the year to permit the sowing and reaping of crops while still meeting the needs of the animals.

TRANSLITERATION, the substitution of the letters of one alphabet by those of another.

TRANSMIGRATION, a term which is roughly equivalent to 'metempsychosis'. Transmigration implies the ability of the soul of a deceased person to be reborn into another body. This body need not necessarily be human or animal, and in many cultures the soul can be reborn in a plant, or even in the form of a demon or a divinity. In Hinduism, the rebirth of the soul in the body of a lower form of life is regarded as a punishment for failure to adhere to the moral codes of society in the present life.

TRANSVESTITE, a man or woman who behaves as though he or she were a member of the opposite sex. This phenomenon was common in many North American Indian societies.

TRAP, a device intended to entrap an animal or even a human enemy.

TRB CULTURE, see FIRST NORTHERN CULTURE.

TREE RING DATING, see DENDROCHRONOLOGY.

TREES, SACRED, trees have been worshipped in many different societies, including those of ancient Europe and contemporary Hindu India.

TREPANNING, a practice otherwise known as trephining, which involves the cutting of a large-sized hole in the skull of a patient, using only stone cutting tools. In Paleolithic Europe and in the Pre-Columbian Inca empire, the purpose of trepanning may have been to remove splinters from a fractured skull, but it is more likely that the objective was purely magico-religious, as primitive peoples who practiced trepanning into historical times did so in the belief that it was a cure for insanity, the purpose of the hole being nothing more than to allow troublesome spirits to escape from the head. Even in Paleolithic times many patients may have survived this primitive form of surgery, since several crania which had been subjected to this operation indicate a growth of the surrounding bone over the hole to an extent which shows that the patient must have lived for several years after the operation.

TRIAD, HOLY, Indo-European religion frequently grouped deities in a sacred trinity. Thus Krishna, Vishnu and Shiva are commonly associated in Hinduism. Jupiter, Juno and Minerva are similarly grouped in the Roman religion, and three Furies were recognized, of the earth, the air and heaven, respectively. This traditional grouping of deities into triads influenced Christian thought and resulted in the Christian concept of 'the Holy Trinity'.

TRIAL BY ORDEAL, a practice based upon sympathetic magic (q.v.).

TRIASSIC, a geological period within the Mesozoic era which lasted from approximately 225 to 190 million years ago.

TRIBAL INITIATION, rituals which are performed to commemorate the admission of individuals into full membership of the tribe.

TRIBE, a poorly defined term used by different anthropologists in a variety of different ways. In the broadest sense, the term tribe has been frequently applied to groups of exogamous bands whose members share a common genetic, cultural, and linguistic heritage. More strictly, however, the term tribe should be reserved for those inbreeding social groups which not only preserve a common cultural, genetic, and linguistic heritage but are united also by the possession of a coordinating political system, such as a tribal council and/or chieftain.

TRIBES, THE FIVE CIVILIZED, during the 19th century it became customary to refer to the Cherokee, Chickasaw, Choctaw, Creek and Seminole as the five 'civilized' tribes because their customs were regarded by the Europeans at that time as being substantially in advance of the other North American Indians.

TRIBUTE, a payment of regular gifts, services or pecuniary contributions by subordinate communities to dominant communities. Pastoralists who regularly raided agricultural settlements might agree to receive tributes in place of exacting plunder. Such was the case among many semi-nomadic Semitic tribes, living on the borders of Sumeria, as also with the Scythian pastoralists in Eastern Europe and the Mongols on the borders of China. The later Vikings of Scandinavia similarly collected 'Danegeld' or tribute from the settled Anglo-Saxons of the coastal regions of England. Established empires have also customarily drawn tribute from subordinate tribal peoples, as did the Assyrians, the Hittites, the Persians, and the Aztecs. The Homeric Greeks exacted tribute from defeated enemy peoples, and the ancient Romans required the many different peoples they ruled to pay a regular *stipendium*. Ironically, after the conversion of the Romans to Christianity the weakened Roman empire was itself forced to pay tribute to the Goths and other Teutonic tribes before the latter finally broke up the western half of the empire and established a multitude of separate political states which eventually evolved into the nations of modern Europe.

TRICKSTER, the figure of a trickster is common in North American folklore, but is also found in other parts of the world. Tricksters are usually human beings but may be animals or may have an animal companion. Although they tend to exploit the people with whom they come into contact, they are frequently the heroes of the stories told about them.

TRIDENT, a spear with three barbed points, usually associated with the Greek god Poseidon and his Roman equivalent, Neptune.

TRILITHON, a Megalithic structure comprising two upright standing stones, with a third stone placed like a lintel across the intervening space.

TRILOBITES, members of the class Trilobita of the phylum Arthropoda, now extinct, but formerly abundant in the Cambrian and Silurian periods.

TRINIL, a site in Java at which the fossil remains of Pithecanthropus erectus (q.v.), now classified as Homo erectus, were found in 1891. These were associated with the Middle Pleistocene and are dated around 500,000 B.C.

TRIPLET, a term used in molecular genetics which may be regarded as equivalent to a codon.

TRIPOLYE, a West Ukrainian and Bessarabian culture which emerged around 6300 B.C. and extended from the Neolithic to the Copper Age. Named after a site near Kiev, the earlier phases of the Tripolye culture are sometimes referred to as Dniester-Bug, and the later phases, commencing around 4700 B.C., as Cucuteni (q.v.). The evidence indicates a settled cultivating people who lived in large villages, comprising as many as 100 longhouses (each presumably housing an extended family), and who produced polychrome pottery ornamented with geometric and curvilinear designs. The Tripolye culture was the first of the Old European cultures to be overrun by the expanding Indo-European peoples from the Pontic Steppes.

TRISKELE, an ancient European symbol comprising three human legs, bent at right angles at the knee, and joined at the point of the thigh. The triskele appears to be a modified form of fylfot (q.v.), and serves as the heraldic emblem of the Isle of Man, formerly the Kingdom of Man.

TRISTAN DA CUNHA ISLANDERS, a small English-speaking community of partly Caucasoid and partly Negroid descent, dependent primarily on cultivation, fishing and some animal husbandry.

TROBRIANDERS, a Melanesian (Malayo-Polynesian) people inhabiting the Trobriand Isles, and dependent on horticulture and fishing with some animal husbandry.

TROGLODYTE, any person or mythological being who lives in a cave.

TROLLS, large, fearsome, but rather slow-witted supernatural beings who according to Scandinavian folklore, lived in mountain caves or the deepest recesses of the forest.

TROPISM, a response to a stimulus such as light or gravity involving growth or locomotory movement (also called taxis) toward or away from the source of the stimulus.

TROUSERS, bifurcated protective leg coverings which may have been invented as early as the Upper Paleolithic by the Cro-Magnons, who inhabited Europe during the Würm glacial period. Trousers became the universal costume for males throughout Northern and Eastern Europe during the subsequent Mesolithic period, and proved to be a particularly convenient attire for the horse-riding pastoralists of Eastern Europe and Western Asia.

TROY, the city referred to in Homer's Iliad, today represented by a large mound or tell (q.v.) overlooking the Turkish Dardanelles. First excavated by Heinrich Schliemann in 1871, the site at Hissarlik has revealed 9 successive cities, the earliest of which, commonly known as Troy I, dates from the late fourth millennium and represents a small settlement occupying about 1.25 acres. Troy II contained a number of megaron-shaped palaces and a considerable amount of goldwork, thus reflecting an increasing prosperity possibly due to Troy's strategic position controlling the Dardanelles, which would enable its rulers to impose a toll on all commerce passing from the Black Sea to the Aegean and vice versa. Troy II was sacked and destroyed, as were three successive Bronze Age cities erected on the same site. Troy IV was a prosperous trading city, as evidenced by the presence of Mycenean pottery and other foreign products. Dated at between 1800 and 1300 B.C., the city covered a total of five acres, and was protected by imposing walls, within which grey Minyan Ware and the skeletal remains of horses suggest affinities with the Greeks who were settling the Aegean at this time. Troy IV was destroyed by an earthquake, and it was Troy VII that was apparently sacked by the Homeric Achaeans (circa 1260 B.C.), in their campaign to recover the abducted Helen. Troy VII was finally destroyed during the 11th century B.C., just as iron was beginning to replace bronze, with the possibility that this time the attackers were the Dorians who took over much of the Peloponnese and many of the Aegean Islands. Although temporarily rebuilt by a Greek colony in 700 B.C., thereby providing the archeological remains known as Troy VIII, Troy was finally destroyed following the decline of the ninth and last city with the collapse of the Roman empire.

TRUKESE, a Malayo-Polynesian-speaking people inhabiting Truk, in the Central Caroline Islands of Micronesia, dependent on horticulture and fishing.

TRUMPET, a wind instrument which produces a particularly loud, blaring noise, being so shaped that it concentrates the vibrant sound made by the trumpeter who blows into the narrow end. Trumpets were widely used by the Celtic peoples of Europe in warfare, and a modified form of trumpet, known as the bugle, remained in European military use into the present century.

TRUNNIONS, projections on the end of a stone or metal blade, which enable the blade to be secured to a shaft.

TSAMAI, an East African Cushitic-speaking people, related to the Konso and dependent on horticulture and herding.

TSETSE FLY, a blood-sucking fly, common in Central Africa, which carries a variety of diseases harmful to horses and cattle, and also, in the case of sleeping sickness, to men. The tsetse fly was of considerable ecological importance in protecting the rain forest of Africa from destruction at the hands of the expanding Negro horticulturalists. Modern pesticides have now been developed to suppress the tsetse, and the rain forests they protected are now fast disappearing as the Bantu population expands and new villages proliferate.

TSIMSHIAN, a Northwest American Indian people, primarily dependent on fishing with some hunting and food-gathering, whose language belongs to the Penutian family.

TSUMA, an Arawak God represented as a white man.

TSWANA, a Bantu-speaking Negroid people related to the Sotho and largely dependent on horticulture and cattle-herding.

TUALCHA MARA, an Arunta marital arrangement whereby a boy becomes engaged to marry a daughter of a particular female – who in effect becomes his mother-in-law before his future bride has been born.

TUAREG, Hamito-Semitic Berber nomads of the Sahara.

TUCUNA, a South American Indian people speaking an Arawak-related language, who are dependent on fishing, horticulture, and some food-gathering.

TUINA, a superior Samoan king controlling several distinct districts or peoples.

TUKULOR, a West African Fulani people of mainly Negroid type, dependent on horticulture and pastoralism. Some authorities believe that they reveal a Hamitic admixture.

TULA, the capital city of the Toltecs. Originally associated with Teotihuacan, but more recently identified as the Tula site in the present-day state of Hidalgo, it was founded in the 10th century A.D. The remains reveal a stepped pyramid surmounted by a temple carved with a frieze of warriors and a plumed feathered serpent representing Quetzalcoatl, together with carvings of jaguars and eagles in relief on the face of the pyramid. Tula was destroyed by conquest in A.D. 1168.

TULAFAE, a Samoan 'talking chief' (q.v.).

TULE SPRINGS, a site near Las Vegas, Nevada, where charcoal dated by the radiocarbon method at 25,000 B.P., was at first presumed to indicate human occupation. However, subsequent excavations found no confirmatory evidence to support the possibility of human occupation at this early date, although definite evidence of human occupation as early as circa 11,000 B.P. was uncovered.

TULLISHI, a Kordofanian-speaking (Niger-Congo) people of the Nuba group, largely dependent on horticulture, animal husbandry and some hunting.

TUMBAGA, an alloy comprising copper, gold, and silver, found in a natural state in both Central and South America, where it is used to manufacture ornamental jewelry.

TUMBUKA, a Bantu-speaking Negroid people of the Bemba-Lamba group, largely dependent on horticulture and some hunting.

TUMPLINE, a length of cord or other material attached to a load carried on the back. The tumpline passes over the forehead as a means of supporting and maintaining the load in position.

TUMULUS, a common term for a burial mound equivalent to a barrow, cairn or kurgan.

TUMULUS CULTURE, the term broadly used to refer to an assembly of Bronze Age cultures, mostly located in central and eastern Europe between the period 1500 to 1200 B.C. These generally reveal burial in a stone box or chamber covered by a round barrow or mound. Inhumation is more common, but cremation urns are sometimes found. Burials are accompanied by a wide variety of bronze equipment, sometimes amounting to a hoard. Swords with flanged hilts, daggers, spears and other military equipment reflect the warlike nature of the Tumulus Culture people. The main center of the Tumulus Culture may be identified in Bavaria and generally covered the area formerly occupied by the Unetiče culture but also extended into North Germany and across the Rhine into Alsace. Cremation appears to have become increasingly popular during the course of the Tumulus Culture, until it finally became the predominant custom, and the Tumulus Culture was replaced by the Urnfield Culture of the Late Bronze Age.

TUN, the Mayan term for a year, which was regarded as comprising 360 days.

TUNDRA, the term used to refer to the vast plains which surround so much of the Arctic Circle. Because of the severe climate their subsoil remains permanently frozen, and the tundra lacks trees, bushes and grass, although the surface soil is usually covered by mosses and lichens. These mosses and lichens provide only a poor living for animals, since the ground on which they live is generally frozen in winter, and submerged under watery marshes in the hot summers.

TUNEBO, a South American Indian people speaking a Chibchan language. The Tunebo live in western Colombia and are dependent on horticulture, fishing, and some hunting and gathering.

TUNGUS LANGUAGES, a group of languages spoken in Eastern Siberia, which are related to the Manchu language. (See SIBERIANS).

TUNICATA, a group of protochordates or simple marine chordate animals. Tunicata are distinctive in that they lack a notochord (q.v.) but possess gill slits.

TUNISIANS, a North African people of Hamito-Semitic origin, who today speak Arabic.

TUPAIA, a three shrew, the fossil remains of which have been found as early as the Mesozoic. Although arboreal, and classed as primates, the living Tupaia have claws like terrestrial mammals instead of flat nails like most of the primates.

TUPI-GURANI LANGUAGES, a South American Indian family of languages including Siriono, Mundurucu, Camayura, and Tapirape on the Matto Grosso, and Tupinamba and Cayua on the Atlantic Coast.

TUPIK, the Eskimo name for a skin tent.

TUPILAQ, the soul or ghost of a dead person in the Eskimo culture, which is generally feared rather than revered since the Eskimos are not ancestor-worshipers (q.v.).

TUPINAMBA, a South American Indian people who speak a Tupi language and occupy the Brazilian coastlands: formerly dependent on horticulture, hunting, fishing and food-gathering.

TURBAN, a long length of cloth wound around the head, commonly worn by various Hindu and Moslem peoples.

TURIRI, see TAURI.

TURKANA, a Negroid Nilotic-speaking people of the Karamajong group, primarily dependent on horticulture and cattle-herding with some food-gathering and hunting.

TURKS, today absorbed into the Caucasoid population of Anatolia, the Ottoman Turks were originally a Turkic immigrant pastoral people who overran the Byzantine Empire and established their own Ottoman Empire. Their language, which is of Altaic origin, remains the official language of modern Turkey.

TURMERIC, a plant which produces a red colored dye which is used by orthodox Hindus to apply distinguishing caste marks to their foreheads.

TURNAK, an Eskimo shaman's guardian spirit.

TURU, a Bantu-speaking Negroid people of the Rift group, largely dependent on horticulture and animal husbandry.

TUTANKHAMEN, an 18th dynasty pharaoh of Egypt, whose name has become well-known in modern times mainly because his tomb in the Valley of the Kings, although disturbed by grave robbers, survived largely intact and provided a rich wealth of information and artifacts when excavated in 1922. Although his tomb may have been poorer than that of many of the more famous pharaohs, it nevertheless astonished the world with its evidence of the richness and artistic profusion of Egyptian culture, and also of the elaborate rituals associated with the Egyptian royal burials. The mummified corpse of the pharaoh, with its head covered by a magnificent gold mask, lay in a cask of pure gold, weighing over a ton, which in turn was enclosed within two outer casks of gilded wood. Other rooms in the tomb contained statues, furniture, and chariots. In his life, Tutankhamen succeeded Akhenaton (q.v.), and suppressed the monotheism of the latter while re-establishing the worship of Amen and the many other Egyptian gods.

TUTELARY SPIRIT, a guardian or house spirit believed to protect the members of a household.

TUTULUS, a decorated, circular bronze ornament, worn on the waist by the women of Denmark and other parts of Northern Europe during the Bronze Age.

TWANA, a coastal Salish, Northwest American Indian people, whose language belongs to the Mosan division of the Algonquin-Mosan phylum, and who are dependent primarily on fishing with some hunting and food-gathering.

TWILLING, a style of basket-making in which a single strand is drawn alternately over two vertical strands and then under the next two vertical strands. This process is repeated, leaving a small space between each strand.

TWINE, any form of yarn twisted together with the strands going in opposite directions.

TWINING, a form of basket-making in which a pair of strands are drawn horizontally across a pair of vertical strands, but the two horizontal strands are woven in and out alternately, crossing over each other between each vertical strand. This gives the basket considerably greater strength.

TWINS, some societies welcome twins as an occasion for rejoicing and as an augury of good fortune, while others fear twins, and as in the case of many Australian aboriginals put one or both to death.

TYPOLOGY, the classification of artifacts into groups which resemble each other in form, type and style of manufacture, such a group being known as a 'type series'. The distribution of various type series, both geographically and through time, is an essential element in the work of the archeological analyst in his attempt to interpret the historical and pre-historical significance of the artifacts uncovered by excavation. Similarities can be explained either by generic descent, in which modifications have occurred in two different series derived from a common ancestral cultural tradition, or else by diffusion implying the transmission of the same cultural idea from one society to another. The term is also used by linguists, but in this case the concept of typological method is applied to any classification of languages based on their structural similarities and dissimilarities, rather than on the basis of shared generic origins.

TYR, (1) the Norse god of war who gave his name to our modern day of the week – Tuesday. (2) a major Phoenician city located on a small island off the coast of Lebanon which is now joined to the mainland. Tyr was the parent city from which Carthage was colonized. It survived, despite being sacked first by Nebuchadnezzar in 574 B.C. and again by Alexander the Great in 332 B.C. Alexander the Great appears to have destroyed the city very thoroughly, after a successful siege in which he was obliged to build a causeway to connect the island to the mainland, and excavations have so far revealed little surviving evidence of the pre-Alexandrian city.

TYROLEANS, the Tyroleans are a Southern Germanic people, divided since World War I between the North Tyrol (Austria) and the South Tyrol (Italy).

U

UAXACTUN, a major Mayan ceremonial center, located in present day Guatemala, revealing pottery from the pre-Classic period. A later temple platform reflects Olmec art forms, but most of the surviving structures belong to the Classic Mayan period between the 3rd and 10th centuries A.D.
UBAID, TELL AL', a tell site located close to the ancient city of Ur which is important for the evidence which it has provided of underlying pre-Sumerian cultures, from which the Sumerian civilization appears to have evolved. In common with almost all other Sumerian cities, the later Ubaid city overlays an earlier Stone Age horticultural settlement revealing painted pottery of a greenish color decorated with dark brown or black geometrical designs. The Ubaid Neolithic culture appears to have covered the entire Mesopotamian region prior to the appearance of copper and bronze and the emergence of the more sophisticated Sumerian civilization. At the Ubaid site, the transition from the Neolithic pre-Sumerian culture to the more highly evolved Sumerian civilization is apparent not only architecturally in the transition from the early Neolithic temple sites, which may be regarded as prototypes of the Sumerian temples, but also in the appearance of copper statues and mosaic lion-headed eagles, bulls and stags around 2600 B.C. – a time contemporary with the appearance of the first dynasty at nearby Ur.
UDAKEA, a two-ended drum used in India, shaped rather like an hour-glass.
UGARIT, an archeological site located in Ras Shamra on the Syrian coast, revealing a long chronology from the early Neolithic through the Chalcolithic and Bronze Ages until the 12th century B.C., when the city was finally destroyed by the Peoples of the Sea. Excavations reveal commercial relations with Egypt, Achaean Greece and the Hittite empire, as well as evidence of the worship of Baal and Astarte. Cuneiform scripts indicate that the language was Semitic, being related to Phoenician and Hebrew, while documents from the 15th and 14th centuries B.C., written in a cuneiform script adapted to alphabetic usage, considerably clarify our information regarding the Canaan culture.
UGARITIC, an early 28 letter alphabet used by the inhabitants of the city of Ugarit in Syria, which may have contributed to the development of the alphabet as used by the Phoenicians.
UGORSK, one of the Ugric group of languages.
UGUBU, a bow designed for use as a musical instrument.
UINTAH UTE, an American Indian people inhabiting the Eastern Great Basin, who speak a Shoshone (Uto-Aztec) language. The Uintah Ute depend for their livelihood on hunting, food-gathering and fishing.
UKRAINIANS, an East Slavic, Caucasoid people, who speak a language closely related to Russian and have traditionally been dependent on agriculture and herding for their livelihood.
ULAWANS, a Melanesian (Malayo-Polynesian) people, largely dependent upon horticulture, fishing and some animal husbandry.
ULITHIANS, a Malayo-Polynesian people of Micronesia, who are dependent on horticulture, fishing and some animal husbandry.
ULLYINGA, a pointed wooden instrument used by Australian aboriginals during ritual ceremonies for the evulsion or removal of teeth.
ULNA, one of the bones of the forearm which articulates with the humerus and the wristbone.
ULOTRICHOUS, possessing frizzly hair.
ULTIMOGENITURE, a custom under which the parental household property passes to the youngest member of the family. Ultimogeniture was customary in Celtic society, where older male children each received a share of the family property and established new households when they married, leaving the youngest son to inherit the parental household on the death of the father.
ULTRABRACHYCRANIC, extremely broad-headed, i.e., possessing a cranial index of excess of 90.
ULTRADOLICHOCEPHALIC, extremely long or narrow-headed, possessing a

cranial index of less than 64.9.

ULU, a knife comprising a semi-circular blade fitted into a wooden handle, usually carried by Eskimo women.

ULUNAIKA, stones of discoid shape used in a Hawaiian bowling game.

UMATILLA, North American Indians who speak a Penutian language of the Sahaptin-Nez Percé group, and were formerly dependent on fishing, food-gathering and hunting.

UMBILICAL CORD, the cord joining the mammalian fetus to the maternal placenta, ejected with the placenta following the birth of the child. Many primitive peoples hold the umbilical cord in great respect: some carefully preserving it for the remainder of the child's life, others disposing of it by some traditional ritual procedure.

UMIAK, a flat-bottomed boat constructed of a wooden frame covered with walrus hide, the umiak differs from the kayak in being open and less maneuverable.

UMOTINA, a South American Indian people living in inland Brazil, the Umotina speak a language related to Gê, and are dependent on horticulture, hunting, food-gathering and fishing.

UNCIAL, an elaborate tedious style of handwriting, common in Europe between the 3rd and 8th centuries A.D., which was eventually replaced by miniscule writing.

UNCLE, CROSS, the mother's brother.

UNCLE, PARALLEL, the father's brother.

UNCOMPAHGRE UTE, an American Indian people inhabiting the Eastern Great Basin, the Uncompahgre speak a Shoshone (Uto-Aztec) language and were formerly dependent on hunting, food-gathering and fishing.

UNCTION, the act of being anointed in a magico-religious ceremony with some kind of oil or other liquid.

UNDERWATER ARCHEOLOGY, the increasing sophistication of underwater swimming and diving techniques has recently led to an upsurge in underwater archeology. While earlier attempts to recover artifacts from inland lakes, wells, or from submerged offshore sites had formerly to be made by dredging, divers using aqualungs have recently recovered the contents of many Greek, Roman and Carthaginian ships wrecked in the Mediterranean as well as of Spanish galleons wrecked in the Caribbean.

UNDERWORLD, an underground location in which the souls of the dead were believed to gather according to Egyptian, Greek and many other western religions. The entrance was frequently guarded, and the souls of newly-deceased persons required either a guide or else magical equipment or formulae to gain entrance.

ÚNETIČE, a term used to refer to the early Bronze Age Indo-European culture which extended from Bohemia, Moravia, Hungary, Austria, Bavaria and Switzerland. The earliest phase is dated around 2000 B.C., while the Classical Únetiče lasted from 1800 to 1600 B.C. Únetiče bronzes have been found in many places in the North European plain, especially along the banks of the rivers Elbe and Saale.

UNGULATE, a hoofed, herbivorous animal which normally lives on herbs and is particularly suitable for domestication by pastoralists.

UNICELLULAR, any organism consisting of a single cell, e.g., protozoa.

UNICORN, a legendary animal, often associated in Europe with royalty. White in color, the unicorn probably derives from the sacred horses of the Germans and other Indo-Europeans, but is distinguished by a single long horn growing from the center of its forehead.

UNILATERAL KINSHIP, kinship recognized through one parent only. This will be either patrilineal or matrilineal, and usually gives rise to clan groupings.

UNIOVULAR TWINS, identical or monozygotic twins.

UNIVALLATE, a ditch, the earth from which has been raised in a bank running along one side of the ditch.

UNSCHEDULED RITES, magical or religious rituals which are performed in an emergency instead of on regular calendrical dates.

UNTOUCHABLE, the member of a subordinate caste (especially in India) who is considered to be ritually unclean and who literally may not be touched by the members of higher social castes for fear of ritual defilement.

UPANISHADS, the 13 basic books of Hinduism. (See VEDIC LITERATURE).

UR, one of the more important cities of ancient Sumeria, excavated by Sir Leonard Wooley during the years 1922-1929. Underlying the Sumerian city the remains of Ubaid-type Neolithic occupation were uncovered, dating from approximately 4300 B.C. However, the Ubaid deposits were covered by no less than 8 feet of silt, evidence of a major flooding of lower Mesopotamia which may be linked to the Sumerian legend of a Great Flood, later borrowed by the Hebrews for inclusion in the Old Testament. After 2800 B.C., impressive remains of the first Sumerian dynasty at Ur were uncovered in the royal cemetery where the corpse of the deceased king had been laid to rest, accompanied not only by a fabulous collection of jewelry and grave furniture, but also by dozens of royal companions or attendants who had been selected to accompany the soul of their dead king into the afterlife. The third dynasty at Ur, commencing 2100 B.C., was responsible for impressive architectural achievements including a large ziggurat (q.v.) built in honor of the patron moon god Nannar. Although destroyed by the Elamites and again by the later Amorites, Ur recovered its prosperity during the 2nd millennium, before going into a final decline in the 6th century B.C., leading to its abandonment in the 4th century B.C.

URAEUS, the snake or asp which appears as a sacred symbol on the headdress worn by the Pharaohs.

URAL-ALTAIC LANGUAGES, a phylum of languages comprising two separate families known as Uralic and Altaic. There is some dispute regarding the closeness of the relationship linking the Ural-Altaic families, and the Uralic group seems to be almost as closely related to Indo-European as to Altaic. However, considerable affinites do exist and the concept of an Uralic-Altaic phylum is still accepted. (See ALTAIC and URALIC).

URALIC, a language of the Ural-Altaic phylum, spoken mainly in Europe and Western Asia. The three major branches of the Uralic family comprise the Finnic group, notably Lapp, Finnish and Estonian; the Ugric group, today represented by the Magyar language of Hungary; and the Samoyed group, including a number of minor languages spoken in Northern Russia and Northwestern Asia.

URANIUM-LEAD DATING, a method of dating which may be applied to very ancient geological formations by measuring the rate of disintegration of uranium into lead. The half-life of uranium is 4,560,000 years, and although it is possible by this process to assess the age of the earth at slightly less than 5 billion years, and also to date rock formations of the earlier periods, the method cannot be applied to recent strata.

URARTU, a state which flourished between the 9th and the 7th century B.C. in the mountain valleys of Eastern Anatolia, with a population closely related to the Hurrians.

URBAN, referring to the social conditions characteristic of densely populated areas, generally characterized by numerous segmentalized or secondary social contacts.

URDU, a modified form of Hindustani (q.v.) spoken in Pakistan and also among many Indian Moslems. Urdu contains a number of Arabic and Persian words, and came into existence as a lingua franca when Arabic and Moghul rulers dominated Northern India.

UREA, as excreta, resulting from protein breakdown, urea is produced mainly by vertebrates, although it is also found in plants. With the present human population explosion and consequent increase in domestic animals used as a food supply by this human population, the disposal of the enormous quantities of urea now being produced by mammals has become a serious ecological problem.

URIAL, a species of sheep which was domesticated circa 4000 B.C. from wild

URN, a term which may be applied to any broad, deep pottery vessel. (See also CINERARY URNS).

URNFIELD CULTURE, a term used to refer to a group of local European Bronze Age cultures whose members buried their dead in cinerary urns, each in an individual grave. The earliest evidence of the large Urnfield cemeteries is to be found in Hungary dating from the end of the 3rd millennium B.C., but by the 14th century B.C., Urnfields and accompanying Bronze Age artifacts were widespread throughout East-Central Europe, covering much of present-day Poland and Czechoslovakia. From this area, the practice of cremation and urn burial appears to have spread northwards into Germany and westwards into Western Europe, and was carried by the Terramare people into Northern Italy. Urnfield burials, and the accompanying artifacts and pottery, are found on the Rhine by the 11th century B.C., and had reached Southern France by 750 B.C., this evidence reflecting an expansion of the Celtic culture. The practice of cremation and the Urnfield complex appear to have come to an end in Northern and Central Europe, at the time of the spread of the use of iron from the Hallstatt area in the 7th century B.C., and the Greeks, Etruscans and Latin peoples abandoned cremation in favor of inhumation prior to the rise of Roman Classical civilization.

URUK, referred to in the Bible as Erech, and represented by the modern town of Warka, Uruk was one of the major cities of ancient Sumeria, located some 30 to 40 miles northwest of the city of Ur. As in other cases evidence of the preceding Ubaid culture can be found beneath the Sumerian city, so that there is clear archeological evidence of a steady transition from the Ubaid Neolithic into the Copper and Bronze Age civilizations of the Sumerian period. Excavations at Uruk have also revealed the earliest evidence of Middle Eastern writing in the form of pictographic tablets, in which simplified pictures, each representing a complete idea, were inscribed on soft clay tablets which were subsequently baked. Uruk was the seat of the hero king of Sumerian mythology Gilgamesh, who was in fact the fifth king of Uruk. Both the city and its surrounding land were regarded as the property of the god Anu, whose temple was constructed on a large ziggurat. Although losing some of its earlier preeminence during Babylonian times, Uruk survived as as important city for some 4000 years, until the end of the Parthian empire.

URUS, an extinct, wild ox which formerly inhabited the north European forests.

URUYA, a Peruvian term for a rope stretched across the gorge of the river as a track for a basket. Similar devices are found in other parts of the world, including the Himalayas.

USIAI, a Melanesian (Malayo-Polynesian) people from the Admiralty Isles, primarily dependent on horticulture with some food-gathering and animal husbandry.

USUFRUCT, the concept of ownership in use seems to be very widespread among preliterate peoples, representing the sense of ownership which emerges, with the full support of custom, as a result of constant use by a particular individual or family. Our modern concept of property appears to have evolved out of usufruct.

USURY, the practice of loaning money for a fee, or what is today known as interest. Strongly kinship-oriented societies seldom permit the concept of usury between kinsmen, and in such societies money-lenders (where they exist) are usually aliens.

UTENSIL, an object used for preparing or storing food or some other material.

UTO-AZTECAN LANGUAGES, a phylum of language which includes the Nahuatlan, Piman, Shoshone and Taracahitian families. Notable amongst these are Aztec, Papago, Pima and Huichol.

UVEANS, a West Polynesian people dependent on horticulture and fishing.

UZBEG, a Turkic-speaking,cultivating people of Turkestan.

V

VALDIVIA, a culture located on the coast of Ecuador, which first appeared early in the 3rd millennium B.C., and flourished until around 1400 B.C. The Valdivian pottery provides us with some of the earliest examples of pottery manufacture found in the New World, and its close resemblance to the Jōmon pottery of Japan has encouraged theories of Oceanic migration from the Indonesian area, to Taiwan, to Japan (prior to the arrival of the Bronze Age Japanese-speaking peoples), and the eastern coast of Siberia (where definite evidence of Jōmon type coastal settlements can be found), the West Coast of North America, to Ecuador on the Northwestern Pacific coast of South America.

VALLEY OF THE KINGS, an arid and rocky valley in Upper Egypt, near Thebes, which was used as a royal cemetery during the period of the New Kingdom. The tombs of the pharaohs were cut into the limestone cliffs bordering the valley, separate stone temples being constructed close to the river for the performance of the rituals necessary for the well-being of the royal soul in the afterlife. It was in the Valley of the Kings that the tomb of Tutankhamen, the only royal grave to have substantially escaped the attention of grave robbers before being excavated by trained archeologists, was discovered in 1922.

VAMPIRE, in Slavic folklore, vampires are corpses which leave their graves at night to feed upon the blood of living beings. Victims of vampires were believed in turn to become transformed into vampires. A vampire was recognizable by its protruding canine teeth, and once identified could be destroyed by impaling its body to the ground with a wooden stake.

VANUA LEVU, a Melanesian (Malayo-Polynesian) people inhabiting the Fiji Islands, formerly dependent on horticulture, fishing, food-gathering and some animal husbandry.

VARVE COUNTING, a method of dating by counting the layers of sediment deposited annually in springtime in glacier-fed lakes. Since the coarser grains of sediment settle first and the finer elements (such as clay) settle later, the sediments accumulated in layered bands of levels. This enables the age of any strata of sedimentation in which fossils or artifacts have been found to be precisely stated. (See DATING SYSTEMS).

VASE, an open container, usually made of pottery, glass, or stone. Vases were of great importance during the Neolithic and early metal ages since they were used to store both solids and liquids. Being made of durable materials, and frequently decorated according to local styles, their remains provide invaluable material for archeological research.

VEDDAH, a largely Australoid people who are believed to have been the pre-Dravidian inhabitants of much of Southern Asia, and who today survive only in hybrid form. The evidence indicates that the Veddas of Ceylon are probably the least hybridized of the surviving Veddoids, although Veddoid genes entered into the composition of many present-day peoples of Southern Asia. The Veddahs lived in caves or bark huts and subsisted by hunting and food-gathering. However, the Veddah language is of borrowed Indic origin being related to Singhalese. The evidence indicates that the Veddahs of Ceylon are probably the least hybridized of the surviving Veddoid peoples, although genes of the Australoid Veddoid type have entered into the composition of many present-day peoples of Southern Asia.

VEDIC, the form of speech in use among the Indo-Aryans, shortly after their arrival in India, from which Classic Sanskrit later developed.

VEDIC LITERATURE, the sacred literature of the Aryans which was originally transmitted orally, but came to be written down between the 11th and 8th centuries B.C., by which time it had undergone modification at the hands of the increasingly important Brahman priestly caste. There were four Vedas: the *Rig Veda*, the *Yajur Veda*, the *Sama Veda* and the *Artharva Veda*, all comprising hymns of praise to the gods and sacrificial ritual tests and magical spells. Each of the Vedas in turn comprised certain specific parts: namely the *Sanhita*, comprising the *Mantras* and *Ganas* (hymns and prayers); the *Brahmanas*, comprising guidance for the performance of Vedic ceremonies; the *Upanishads* or philosophical discourses; and the *Aranyakas*, intended for contemplative studies by Brahmans who have retired from active performance of their religious duties to contemplate on the philosophical interpretation of the Vedas. There is ample evidence that the original four Vedas date from a period long before the Indo-Aryans left a colder or at least more temperate northern home to invade India. In addition to the four Vedas, the Vedic sacred writings also included the *Upa Vedas* which dealt with medical, musical, military, architectural and artistic formulae; the *Ved-Angas* concerned with grammar, astronomy, pronunciation and the *Upangas*, comprising epic poems, legendary histories, philosophical, legal and ritual traditions. The *Upangas* comprise a class of writings known as the *Itihasas*, which include the famous *Ramayana* and *Mahabharata*; the *Puranas*, which recount the stories of the gods and their deeds; and the *Dharma sastras* or *Laws of Manu*. An additional and late aspect of the *Upangas*, known as the *Tantras*, constitute an attempt to equate the old Indo-Aryan beliefs with the aboriginal animism of the indigenous inhabitants. Other sacred writings of the ancient Brahmanistic Hindu religion are the *Sutras* and *Parisishtas*, which are in effect a collection of summaries of notes written in later times for the guidance of those seeking to study the sacred literature.

VELAR, a guttural sound produced by raising the back part of the tongue to meet the soft palate, as in the sound of a *k* or hard *g* in the English language.

VELLUM, a form of fine parchment manufactured from animal skin.

VELLUS, the name used to describe the very fine down-like short hairs as found on the human forehead and on the face of females.

VENDA, a Bantu-speaking Negroid people related to the Sotho and largely dependent on horticulture and cattle herding.

VENDETTA, a blood feud (q.v.) persisting between two or more different kinship groups through several generations.

VENDIDAD, the first part of the *Zend Avesta* (q.v.).

VENETIC, an extinct peoples from whom Venice derives its name, who seem to have spoken an Indo-European language closely related to the Italic group.

VENTANA CAVE, an archeological site in Arizona comprising a rock shelter which reveals a lengthy and well-stratified tradition of prehistoric occupation. The lower levels show evidence of occupation by a hunting people, as exemplified by the bones of the extinct American horse, bison and other animals. These are overlaid by artifacts associated with the Desert Culture (q.v.) and finally with those of a people of the Hohokam Culture (q.v.).

VENUS FIGURINES, highly stylized figurines portraying naked women with broad hips and large breasts, usually made of clay but sometimes carved from stone or ivory. The head in particular is stylized, with no attempt to reveal facial features, some authorities having interpreted the blankness of the face to imply a hood-like mask or virtual face-covering. The earliest Venus figurines were associated with Upper Paleolithic Gravettian and Upper Perigordian sites across Europe from the Pyrenees to Russia, but similar figurines are also associated with the Old European Neolithic civilization of the Balkans, and may well be ancestral to the cult of the 'Great Mother' goddess, widespread in the Aegean and Mediterranean, prior to the introduction of the Indo-European pantheon of Sky-Gods.

VERTEBRAL COLUMN, the chain of bones, linked by cartilage, which surrounds the spinal cord. In most vertebrates, the vertebrae are attached to the skull at the anterior end, and conclude in a tail at the posterior end. The vertebral column replaces the notochord (q.v.) at an early stage of vertebrate embryonic development.

VERTEBRATES, chordates (q.v.) which have evolved a vertebral column (q.v.). Vertebrates first evolved as marine organisms (e.g., fish) from coelenterata via marine invertebrate chordates. The first cerebellum or elementary brain appeared among marine vertebrates in the Paleozoic period.

VERTESSZÖLLOS, a site some thirty miles from Budapest in Hungary. Here very significant fossil remains were discovered which reflect an essentially Homo sapiens subspecies now identified as Homo sapiens paleohungaricus, but sometimes classed with the Swancombe and Steinheim remains as Homo sapiens steinheimensis. Vertesszöllos fossils date from the Mindel glacial period, possibly as early as 750,000 years B.P.

VERTEX, the highest point of the human skull.

VERULAMIUM, originating as a Brythonic Celtic settlement in East Britain, Verulamium was developed into a major city under the Romans, which covered some 200 acres and was complete with forum, theater and defensive walls. Although destroyed by Queen Boadicea in her ill-fated revolt against the Romans, Verulamium was rebuilt and remained prosperous throughout the period of Roman occupation. Surviving the Saxon conquest, it was subsequently renamed St. Albans, following the revival of Christianity.

VESTA, the Roman goddess of the hearth fire.

VESTIGIAL REMNANT, any organ or tissue which has greatly diminished in functional significance or even totally lost its former biological purpose as a result of evolutionary change. In many cases, however, vestigial organs retain important functions at earlier stages of embryonic development.

VIENNA SCHOOL, see KULTURKREIS.

VIETNAMESE, see ANNAMESE.

VIGESIMAL COUNTING, a system of numbering based on units of twenty instead of units of ten. Found among the Ainu, this system may be a survival of an older tradition, possibly dating back to the Upper Paleolithic. It has been suggested that the number twenty was selected because the number of fingers total twenty digits.

VIKINGS, the term Viking has been variously interpreted, sometimes as 'the people of the fjords (or inlets)' but more commonly as 'the people who lived in wicks ' or fortified settlements. The Vikings first came into prominence in the 7th century A.D. and remained active until the 12th century A.D., during which time they first raided and then settled large areas along the Atlantic coastline of Western Europe, penetrating the Mediterranean and even sailing down the West African coast. Vikings from Sweden similarly penetrated the major rivers of the Baltic into Russia, carrying their boats overland to the Dnierp, so as to reach the Black Sea from whence they attacked Constantinople, the capital of the Eastern Roman Empire. Devoted to the pagan traditions of their ancestors, they demonstrated an intense animosity against Christianity, and delighted in destroying monastic settlements and churches. Vikings were responsible for colonizing Iceland at the beginning of the 10th century, and for establishing settlements in Greenland and on the northeast coast of America. The evidence of the Icelandic sagas also refers to explorations and settlements on the North American coast, which appear to have carried them at least as far south as Newfoundland – and possibly further, since they reported the discovery of fruits which could be used for the manufacture of wine and applied the term Vinland to the North American coast.

The river- and sea-faring ability of the Vikings was based on the various improvements which they made to the ancient Indo-European river boats. These comprised shallow longboats, originally devised by Proto-Indo-Europeans for use on the rivers of the Pontic Steppes, probably also ancestral to the boats used by the Peoples of the Sea (now believed to have been Indo-Europeans) who settled the islands of the Adriatic coast of Yugoslavia. The transatlantic voyages were accomplished by a shortened, broader version of the longboat, equipped with a heavy keel, which was capable of weathering all but the most violent North Atlantic storms.

Sociologically, the Vikings preserved into the Iron Age the social structure and traditions of the Heroic (Bronze) Age. The Vikings were by no means uncouth. Archeological evidence as well as literary evidence indicates that they were well-equipped technologically, that they paid considerable attention to their dress and personal appearance, and that they developed refined traditions of etiquette and even their poetry exhibits a love of flowers and romantic beauty as well as of war.

VILLA, a term used to refer to the large country estates of the landowners of Imperial Rome, who in contrast to the yeoman subsistence farmers of the Republican period, owned large slave-worked plantations, growing produce for the market. The term is always restricted to a more elaborate type of residence, usually possessing decorative wall plaster, underfloor heating and a built-in drainage system.

VILLAFRANCHIAN, a period of relatively cold climate which spanned the Pliocene-Pleistocene boundary, and may have stimulated more rapid evolution in the development of intelligence among certain of our hominid forebears, as well as evolutionary changes in other life forms.

VILLAGE, a rural community comprising a group of individual households, small enough for all the members of the community to know each other. Villages first appeared as a result of the adoption of horticulture or fishing as a means of subsistence, and in all except contemporary western societies, the members of a village are usually a closely-knit group of kinship-related persons, sometimes even belonging to the same clan or even comprising a single extended family. (See also ZADRUGA).

VILLAGE COMMUNITY, a 'village community' may be distinguished from a 'house community' (q.v.) by the degree to which the private ownership of property has evolved. Although grazing and hunting lands may continue to be held in common, all cultivated land has generally been apportioned to separate families, and goods that are produced by the individual household are generally regarded as being the property of that household – in contrast to the house community, in which produce is shared among all members of the kinship group.

VILLANOVIAN, an Iron Age culture which was localized in Northern Italy, in the area of modern Tuscany and Bologna, named after an archeological site at Villanova, close to Bologna. The Villanovian culture may have derived from the Terramare (q.v.), and the Villanovians were probably ancestral to the peoples of Italic speech. Although they used iron weapons, the Villanovians still made extensive use of bronze, and their settlements reveal a distinctive type of burnished pottery, decorated with meandering lines, grooved bands and swastika (q.v.) sun symbols. Although settlements were moderately large, the Villanovians do not appear to have constructed large towns or cities, and those that lived in Tuscany were either displaced or subjugated by the Etruscans (q.v.) between the 8th and 6th centuries B.C.

VINČA, a large tell site close to the modern city of Belgrade revealing advanced late Neolithic and Chalcolithic cultures which evolved out of the earlier Starčevo Neolithic around 5500 B.C. and persisted until around 3500 B.C. when the area was overrun by Indo-Europeans. The name has also been given to a total culture complex centered on the Danube around Belgrade, which formed a part of the Old European (q.v.) Balkan civilization, examples of the Old European linear script being common on Vinča pottery.

VINICULTURE, the cultivation of the grape-vine for the purpose of producing alcoholic beverages. European viniculture certainly dates from the Bronze Age, but probably extends further back into the Neolithic.

VIRGIN BIRTH, the idea that a human female can conceive as a result of contact with persons or objects possessing magico-religious properties is widespread in a number of primitive societies. In Indo-European antiquity, many heroes were sired by gods who mated with mortal mothers, but in such cases the concept of virgin birth is inappropriate, since cohabitation with an anthropomorphic god was precisely claimed. By contrast, the Christian belief in the birth of Jesus, through the impregnation of Mary by the Holy Ghost, was rooted in the much more primitive belief of magical 'virgin birth'.

VIRILOCAL, see PATRILOCAL.

VIRUSES, a group of disease-producing parasites which are unable to multiply except with the aid of the genetic material contained in the tissues of the host organism. Extremely small in size, they are invisible under most microscopes and are small enough to be able to pass through filters which would detain bacteria.

Indeed, bacteria may also suffer from virus attacks. There is considerable debate as to whether viruses, which are incapable of reproducing without the agency of host material, should be classified as living organisms, since they appear to represent a primitive level of evolutionary development midway between non-living and living matter.

VISION, COLOUR, the ability to see colours first evolved among certain fossil primate species, and is today characteristic of all simian and anthropoid primates. However, due to a sex-linked genetic defect, some 5% of contemporary living male hominids are colour-blind, the percentage varying considerably between different races and populations and being highest among those nations which have led a sedentary, agricultural life for several millennia. The implication appears to be that while natural selection still operates against colour-blindness among hunting populations, colour-blindness is not a fatal handicap in sedentary societies.

VISION, STEREOSCOPIC, an ability which developed among primates, whereby the eyes are able to focus upon a single object, making possible three dimensional vision and with it the measurement of distance.

VIVIPAROUS, a term used to describe animals whose embryos develop within the maternal organism, which consequently gives birth to live offspring, e.g., placental mammals.

VODUN, see VOODOO.

VOICED SOUNDS, sounds which are produced as a result of the vibration of the vocal cords as for example *b*, *d*, or *z*.

VOICELESS SOUNDS, sounds produced without any vibration of the vocal cords, e.g., *t*.

VOLTAIC LANGUAGES (also GUR), a subfamily of the Niger-Congo linguistic family which includes Songhai, Dogon, Tallensi, Konkomba, Mossi, and Birifor.

VOLUTE, an ornamental spiral, resembling the shape of a scroll.

VOODOO (also VODUN), a set of religious beliefs, still popular among many Caribbean Negro populations, which combines elements of West African (Dahomean) magico-religious cults with the worship of a pantheon of supernatural beings largely borrowed from Catholicism.

VOTIVE DEPOSITS, votive deposits represent offerings made to the gods, and usually take the form of objects deposited in sacred sites such as caves, lakes, peat bogs or rivers.

VOTIVE TABLET, a tablet inscribed with a dedication recording the fulfillment or intention to fulfill a religious oath or obligation.

VOWEL, a sound produced without any blockage of the outgoing air by friction or closure of the passage.

VUGUSU, a Bantu-speaking Negroid people of the East Nyanza area, largely dependent on horticulture and animal husbandry.

VULGATE, an early Latin translation of the scriptures, usually referring to the version produced by Jerome in the 4th century A.D.

W

WADADOKADO (HARNEY VALLEY PAIUTE), a Shoshone-speaking Uto-Aztec North American Indian people of the coastal Great Basin, dependent on food-gathering, hunting and some fishing.

WADJAK, fossil remains, comprising two nearly complete skulls with jaws and teeth, found at Wadjak in central Java in 1889/1890 are Neanderthaloid in type. Many features of the skulls resemble those of living Australoids, so that Wadjak man is usually regarded as proto-Australoid. The skulls date from the late Upper Pleistocene.

WAGON, correctly speaking, the term wagon should be applied to four-wheeled vehicles. Two-wheeled animal-drawn vehicles are described as 'carts' or (if light-weight) chariots (q.v.).

WAHLUND EFFECT, a term given to the genetic pattern which results from protracted inbreeding within an originally hybrid population.

WAICURI (also GUAICURI and WAIUORI), an American Indian people of Baja California who speak an isolated language, related to Pericu, which may have affinities with Hokan or Yuman.

WAIWAI, a South American Indian Carib-speaking people, dependent on horticulture, and some hunting, fishing and food-gathering.

WAKE, a meeting of the family, relatives and in some societies the friends of the deceased, on the occasion of a burial. Traditional rituals are completed in honor of the departed, and generous hospitality is provided to all who attend the ceremony.

WALAPAI, a Hokan-speaking, Plateau Yuman, American Indian people, dependent on food-gathering and hunting.

WALDALGESHEIM, an important archeological site in Kreis Kreuznach, Germany, revealing a La Tène Iron Age chariot burial which indicated the penetration of Celts into the Germanic Rhineland. The rich grave furniture includes gold and bronze ornaments and equipment, and is dated around the latter part of the 4th century B.C.

WALLACE'S LINE, a deep channel in the sea dividing the islands of Borneo and Bali from the Celebes, Lombok, Timor, New Guinea, Australia, New Zealand and related islands. Continentral Drift (q.v.) appears to have separated the land masses to the southeast of Wallace's Line from those to the northwest, which latter were probably united with the mainland of Asia during pluvial (q.v.) periods of the Pleistocene. As a result quite different species of plants and animals are to be found on opposite sides of the line, no placental mammals being found southwest of Wallace's line prior to the immigration of hominids some 10 to 15 thousand years ago.

WALLOONS, the French-speaking inhabitants of Southern Belgium.

WAMPUM, beads used as both money and as ornaments among North American Indians. Wampum beads were customarily made from white and purple quohog shells, hollowed so as to facilitate arrangement as a necklace or as decorations on a belt.

WAND, a stick or length of bone believed to contain supernatural powers. Usually incised with ritual designs, the wand may have a very ancient Paleolithic origin, and is believed to be ancestral to the sceptre carried by the Indo-European kings.

WANDOROBO, see DOROBO.

WANINGA, a group of spears, tied together with human hair and covered with colored feathers, which serves the same purpose as a churinga (q.v.).

WANTOAT, a Papuan people from East Papua, dependent on horticulture with some hunting and animal husbandry.

WAPISHANA, a South American Indian people, living in southern Venezuela and speaking an Arawak language, who are dependent on horticulture, hunting and fishing.

WAR, a situation which develops when two opposed societies resort to violence in an attempt to determine the outcome of a dispute and to impose their own wishes on each other. Simpler hunting and gathering peoples cannot afford the luxury of a continuing war, but occasionally come into conflict when drought, hunger or population pressures cause one group to invade the territory of another. Among horticultural and fishing societies, who generally lack the resources required for the support of a prolonged war, raiding by war parties – in a maneuver somewhat analogous to a hunting expedition – frequently becomes as much a pastime as a necessity, and may even become a cultural obligation in response to magico-religious requirements, as in the case of head-hunting among the Nagas and the raids conducted by the Aztecs to procure prisoners for sacrifice. Organized and persistent modern warfare is a 'luxury' only possible among peoples with a developed agricultural or industrial economy, who are able to support and maintain professional armies.

WAR PATH, an expression derived from a Northeastern Woodland Indian term

for a military raiding expedition.
WARI, see HUARI.
WARKA, see URUK.
WAROPEN, a Melanesian people of Northeast New Guinea, largely dependent on food-gathering, fishing, horticulture, hunting and animal husbandry.
WARP, in basketry or cloth-weaving, the parallel foundation threads over and rhrough which the weft or cross thread is passed.
WARRAU, A South American Indian people generally regarded as Arawak but not satisfactorily identified linguistically. The Warrau occupy the Orinoco delta in Venzuela, and are dependent upon hunting, fishing and food-gathering.
WASHO, an American Indian people located in inland California, who speak a language usually classified as Hokan, and are dependent upon food-gathering, hunting and fishing.
WASSAIL, traditional songs sung at drinking parties in medieval and post-medieval Germanic Europe. Originating as toasts (q.v.) set to music, the wassail invariably comprise songs of goodwill in honour of kings or national heroes, or in honour of the friends and relatives of the participants. Thus the wassail are survivals of an ancient Germanic ritual, whereby alcoholic beverages were drunk to honour the gods, or to commend kinsmen and allies to the care and protection of the gods.
WATAP, a fiber derived from the split root of a spruce, pine or other tree, and used by Algonquin Indians as a thread for the making of baskets and the sewing together of pieces of birch bark for tipi coverings.
WATER LAWS, an appreciation of the need for laws to provide ecological regulation is revealed in many early civilizations. Both the Code of Hammurabi and the laws of Ancient Rome included provisions for the protection and regulation of rivers and canals, recognizing the significance of running water and sometimes even of the sea itself, as natural elements vital to the survival of the community as a whole.
WATERMELON, the fruit of a trailing vine which was probably indigenous to Africa, and spread from thence to Spain, and from Spain to the New World, as well as eastwards to the Middle East and Southern Asia.
WATTLE AND DAUB, a form of construction comprising a framework of thin interwoven wooden sticks plastered with mud or clay.
WATUSSI, an unusually tall, Northern Bantu herding people.
WAWI, a term used in the Gilbert Isles to refer to a local form of Black Magic.
WEAVING, a technique which is similar to basketry, but employs softer materials and produces a more pliable product, known as cloth.
WEFT, the vertical threads which interlace with the warp (q.v.) in basketry and cloth-making.
WEI, a Chinese dynasty dating from 368 to 557 B.C., known for its unglazed but pigmented pottery.
WEIR, any fence or obstruction constructed across a stream of flowing water for the purpose of catching fish. A small opening left in the weir is filled by a deep basket, which entraps fish to pass through the weir.
WELL, any hole in the ground which accumulates water by diffusion from the subsoil.
WELL, ARTESIAN, a narrow well penetrating deeply into a layer of subsoil, in which the pressure of water is sufficiently high to force a column of water up to the tube to reach the surface. Artesian wells derive their name from the district of Artois in France, where they have been in use for several hundred years.
WELSH, a Brythonic Celtic people, traditionally dependent on cattle-herding and agriculture. Although influenced by Roman culture and influenced by Christianity at an early date, the Welsh or Cymric language has survived as a living language to the present day, and early written Welsh documents provide us with much knowledge of the 'British' culture of pre-Christian times. Early Welsh society was strongly organized on kinship lines and highly stratified with kings, princes, and druids occupying the central roles. The history, laws, and religious beliefs were memorized in poetry and song, providing the basis of a rich musical

tradition.

WENDS, a Germanic term for the Slavic occupants of Western Poland during the early Middle Ages. (See SLAVIC LANGUAGES).

WEREWOLF, a man believed to be capable of transforming himself into a wolf. The old European belief in werewolves who hunted human prey at night may be derived from ancient memories of secret societies such as the Isawyiia of Morocco and the Leopard Men of West Africa, who attire themselves in the skins of animals to kill and consume human meat.

WERGILD (or WERGELD), an old Germanic term, literally translated as 'man money', which refers to compensation paid by the relatives of an offender to the relatives of a man who is injured or slain.

WESSEX, a West Saxon kingdom established early in the 6th century A.D. by the Saxon King Cedric, who claimed descent from Woden. Under King Alfred, Wessex not only repulsed the attacking Danes, but succeeded in becoming the dominant nation in a united English confederacy.

WESSEX CULTURE, an early Bronze Age Celtic culture associated with numerous barrows, which at first covered inhumations but later covered the funerary remains of cremations. Commencing around 1700 B.C., the culture of the period known as Wessex I utilized an arsenical copper alloy, but that of Wessex II, dating from 1550 to 1400 B.C., employed a regular bronze made from copper alloyed with tin. The people of Wessex appear to have maintained trading relations over large areas of Europe, their artifacts reflecting contacts with Mycenaean Greece as well as with the peoples of the eastern Baltic.

WESTERN APACHE, a Southern Athabascan-speaking, North American Indian people, dependent primarily on hunting, food-gathering and horticulture.

WESTERN NEOLITHIC, a term sometimes used to distinguish the Cortaillod, Windmill Hill, Almeria, and similar Atlantic Neolithic cultures. These were possibly the creation of an Atlanto-Mediterranean people, as distinct from the Neolithic traditions of the First Northern and Danubian Valley cultures.

WHALING, a form of basket making which involves twining with a group of three wefts.

WHARE WANANGA, a Polynesian school or workshop in which craftsmen are taught the secrets of their trade.

WHEAT, two different species of wild wheat appear to have been domesticated during the Neolithic. These were Einkorn (q.v.) and Emmer (q.v.).

WHEEL, an artifact possessing a circular or round circumference, adapted to a rotary motion. The earliest wheels were invented in the Neolithic, being constructed from solid pieces of wood, and were used both for transportation purposes (wheeled vehicles replacing the earlier sledges dragged along the ground on runners) and also in pottery-making, as the potter's wheel (q.v.). Spoked wheels, lighter and therefore more useful for transportation purposes, first appeared around the beginning of the 3rd millennium B.C.

WHEEL, PERSIAN, a wheel equipped with buckets, still used to lift water from wells and rivers into irrigation channels in many areas throughout the Middle East and Egypt.

WHEEL, POTTER'S, a round turntable developed in the Neolithic to improve upon the earlier hand-shaping pottery techniques. Damp clay can be easily shaped into symmetrical bowls, vases or receptacles when rotated on such a wheel or revolving table.

WHEEL, PRAYER, a small wheel inscribed with sacred prayers and phrases, popularly used by Buddhists as an aid to the recitation of ritual texts.

WHIPPING RITUAL, the practice of flogging a wrongdoer for the purpose of driving out the evil spirits supposedly responsible for his or her misbehaviour. Initiates to secret societies may also be required to undergo ritual flogging in order to purify their souls of evil or unclean forces, as was the practice among the Hopi (q.v.).

WHITE KNIFE SHOSHONI, a Shoshone-speaking Uto-Aztec North American Indian people of the Coastal Great Basin, dependent on food-gathering, hunting and some fishing.

WHITE RACE, see CAUCASOID.
WHORL, see DERMATOGLYPHIC MARKINGS.
WHORL, SPINDLE, the small flywheel, frequently made of stone or pottery, fitted to a spindle to ensure that it moves at a regular speed. Spindle wheels were invented in the late Neolithic, shortly after the development of sophisticated cloth weaving techniques, and frequently survive as archeological evidence of weaving long after the rest of the wooden weaving equipment has decayed.
WICHITA, Muskogean-Siouan-speaking North American Indians of the Caddoan group, the Wichita occupied the Great Plains and were traditionally dependent on horticulture practiced in the river valleys, supplemented by hunting and food-gathering.
WICKER WORK, a form of basketry in which the warp is made from rigid material but the weft is made from a flexible thread.
WICKIUP, a North American Indian dwelling, comprising a grass hut, shaped like a beehive. The wickiup is somewhat similar to the grass hut of the Nuer and other African people.
WIFE-LEASING, the principle, typically among the Todas of Southern India, whereby husbands (or groups of husbands in a polyandrous society) may permit other men to have sexual access to their wives, in return for a specific payment an agreed-upon gift or some other benefit.
WIFE-LENDING, a custom common to certain societies whereby guests, friends or relatives may be permitted sexual access to the host's wife as a gesture of goodwill or hospitality.
WIGWAM, a conically-shaped hut used by Northeastern Woodland American Indians, comprising a framework of wood covered by bark or matting.
WIITOKA, a craving for human flesh, sometimes experienced by Ojibwa, Cree, and also Eskimo individuals, who nevertheless fear that if they yield to the craving they will become cannibal ogres. In times of severe famine, the Eskimos and certain North Canadian Indians living in severe environments have been known to resort to cannibalism for self-survival, but the act is generally regarded with repulsion, and has not been legitimized by magico-religious sanctions.
WIKMUNKAN, an aboriginal people from Northeastern Australia, dependent on hunting and gathering supplemented by some fishing.
WILL-O'-THE-WISP, a light caused by burning marsh gases, reputed in Celtic folklore to represent a supernatural being, the sight of which was an ill-omen.
WILTON, the name given to an African culture derived from the Mesolithic culture of Europe, which survived among the Capoid population of eastern and southeastern Africa, until these were supplemented by immigrant and warlike Bantu horticulturalists equipped with an Iron Age culture.
WIND INSTRUMENT, a class of musical instruments of varying degrees of complexity, ranging from the simple reed flute to the trumpet and organ. In most wind instruments sound is produced when a player blows into or across the instrument held to his mouth. The discovery of prehistoric wind instruments has contributed greatly to the study of anthropomusicology, since the manner of their construction provides evidence regarding the musical intervals and scales known to the society which produced them.
WINDMILL HILL, a British Neolithic culture, named after an impressive causeway camp close to Avebury in Wiltshire, England. The earliest phases of the Windmill Hill culture date from the latter part of the 3rd millennium B.C., and the Windmill Hill site, occupying the crown of a hill on the Wiltshire Down, comprises three more or less parallel ditch and mound earthworks, encompassing a long barrow, and a later Bronze Age cemetery of round barrows. Although the Windmill Hill culture was formerly regarded as covering the entire Neolithic stage of British prehistory, it is now customary to distinguish the Windmill Hill from the earlier Neolithic, as evidenced by the Hembury campsite, and to identify it with the Middle Neolithic, characterized by the introduction of long barrows, polished flint axes, and leaf-shaped arrow-heads into Britain. The Late Neolithic, which followed the Windmill culture, is also regarded as a separate phase, distinguished by the presence of beaker pottery.

WINNEBAGO, Muskogean-Siouan-speaking North American Plains Indians of the Siouan group, occupying the Great Plains and dependent on horticulture, practiced in the river valleys, and supplemented by hunting and food-gathering.
WINNOWING BASKET, a shallow basket-tray used for tossing grain so that the wind can blow away the chaff.
WINTU, a California Penutian-speaking people dependent on food-gathering, hunting and fishing.
WISCONSIN GLACIATION, the name given to the last North American glaciation, which probably corresponded to the Alpine Würm glaciation (q.v.).
WISHRAM, an Oregon Penutian-speaking Indian people, mainly dependent on fishing with some hunting and food-gathering.
WITCH, a person skilled in the control of supernatural powers, usually female, who uses these powers for evil purposes.
WITCHCRAFT, the ability to control the fate of other persons by magic. Witchcraft is usually exercised by professional witches or witchdoctors, who hire out their services to individuals seeking to revenge themselves on their enemies, but in many societies, such as the Haida of Northwestern America, individuals who know the necessary secret formulae and ritual may attempt witchcraft for their own purposes.
WITCH DOCTOR, a man who attempts to cure illnesses, believed to be of supernatural or magical origin, by the use of magic.
WITCH-SOUL, the Azande and many other tribes of Central Africa believe that certain individuals inherit a witch soul, which can be dispatched at will to bring harm to their enemies.
WITOTO, a South American Indian people, speaking a language probably related to the Tupi group, who are dependent on horticulture, fishing, and some hunting and gathering.
WIYOT, a Northwestern California Algonquin-speaking people, dependent on food-gathering and some hunting.
WODAABE FULANI, a Niger-Congo-speaking people related to the pastoral Fulani, and primarily dependent on animal herding supplemented by some horticulture.
WODEN, the Anglo-Saxon form of the Norse Odin, the Allfather of the Germanic gods, who gave his name to Wednesday.
WOGEO, a Melanesian-speaking people of Northeast New Guinea, largely dependent on horticulture, fishing, food-gathering and some animal husbandry.
WOLFF'S LAW, the biological principle by which an organ may become enlarged as its functions increase, but become atrophied when the importance of these functions decreases.
WOLOF, a Negroid West African Senegalese people, dependent primarily upon horticulture, animal husbandry and some fishing. Wolof belongs to the Atlantic group of the Niger-Congo families (q.v.).
WONGAIBON, an aboriginal people from southern Australia, dependent wholy on food-gathering, hunting and some fishing.
WOODHENGE, a henge-type earthwork containing six concentric rings of wooden posts, clearly of religious significance, located two miles northeast of Stonehenge (q.v.). Pottery found at Woodhenge indicates that it belongs to the Late British Neolithic.
WOODLAND CULTURE, a general term used to refer to a culture widespread in the wooded eastern part of North America, involving the use of horticulture, the construction of burial mounds, and the manufacture of a distinctive form of pottery decorated with patterns made from an impressed cord or fabric. Localized in the heavily forested areas of the eastern part of North America, the Archaic Woodland culture appeared around 1000 B.C., and eventually evolved into the Hopewell culture (q.v.), which represented the peak of Woodland achievements. The southern portion of the Woodland culture was modified by substantial influences from the Mississippi culture (q.v.), but the older Wood-

land tradition survived in the northeast, albeit in a somewhat decayed condition, until well after the arrival of the first European settlers.

WOODSKIN, a type of canoe, from 15′ to 30′ in length, constructed by the South American Guyanas from a single piece of bark, carefully removed in one piece from the 'purpleheart' tree.

WOOF, see WEFT.

WOOMERA, an Australian aboriginal name for a spear-thrower, known in the Americas as an 'atlatl'.

WORK-OF-WORKS, a vast encyclopedia compiled under the direction of the Ming emperor Yung-lo, comprising nearly 23,000 volumes.

WOVOKA, a Paiute Indian prophet who preached that the dead Indian warriors of the past would return to help their descendants drive out the white man. The historical Ghost Dance movement (q.v.) of the end of the 19th century was largely a response to Wovoka's prophecies.

WRAITH, the ghostly double of a living person, whose appearance is generally regarded as an omen of approaching death.

WREATH, a ring made from the flowers or leaves of sacred plants. In the European tradition, wreaths were frequently worn as crowns on festive occasions, as for example the ring of ivy worn by a victor at the Olympic games in ancient Greece, the ring of oak leaves worn on the head of a victorious Roman general, or the ring of mistletoe worn by Scandinavians to celebrate the Yuletide festival. Long floral wreaths worn around the neck are also an ancient tradition in India, having probably passed from there to the Malayo-Polynesian world.

WRITING, any conventional system of visual symbols designed by men to convey information or ideas. It is possible that the earliest script may have evolved in linear form in the Old European civilization of the Balkans around 5000 B.C. Pictographic writing, comprising a number of symbols representing standardized pictorial impressions of specific objects, is in use in Sumeria and Egypt during the early 4th millennium B.C., and also appears to have evolved independently in China around the 2nd millennium B.C. as well as among the Maya of Central America some 2500 years later. In Egypt, pictographs evolved into hieroglyphs (q.v.), whereas in Sumeria they were replaced by wedge-shaped cuneiform (q.v.) inscriptions. An alphabet comprising symbols which represented only the consonants was used by the Phoenicians around 1000 B.C. Although the Greeks were using a distinctive Linear B script as early as 1400 B.C., the Phoenician script was adopted into Greek usage around 800 B.C., being then substantially modified by the Greeks who added signs to depict the vowels. Cretan or Minoan Linear A, dating from the later part of the 3rd millennium B.C. has not yet been deciphered. The Chinese script is still essentially rooted in pictographic symbols, with some concession to phonetic principles, while Japanese writing uses symbols, similar to the pictographic signs of the Chinese adapted for phonetic usage. Early writing on wax plates was accomplished with the aid of a stylus (q.v.), and similar instruments were used for writing on clay tablets. A split reed pen was used for writing on papyrus, with an ink made from soot mixed with gum, or from cuttlefish juice. A more durable ink was obtained later from a mixture of oxide of iron and gallnuts. The bark of the lime tree was frequently used in Greece, and animal skins, parchment and vellum came into later use. Private correspondence in the Greek and Roman world was usually on wax tablets, set into a wooden frame. European languages were written from left to right, Semitic from right to left, Chinese from top to bottom.

WRITING, CURSIVE, any simplified form of script intended for speedy handwriting, in which groups of individual characters making up a word are linked together.

WRITING, LINEAR, any system of writing which uses straight lines or stylized symbols which cannot be interpreted as pictographs. The script used among the Minoans and Myceneans was a linear script which may be related to the linear symbols of the Old European civilization, now believed to be the world's oldest script – a series of linear symbols inscribed on ritual pottery found in Neolithic sites in the Danube valley and adjacent Balkan area from the 6th millennium

onwards.
WUNDU, a purification ritual in which Muslims wash with water before reciting their five daily prayers to Allah.
WURLEY, a South Australian aboriginal shelter.
WURM, the last of the four major Alpine glaciations of the Pleistocene.
WUTE, a Negroid Central African Niger-Congo-speaking people, mainly dependent on horticulture supplemented by some animal husbandry and hunting.

X

XAM, a Khoisan-speaking Bushman people of Southwest Africa, largely dependent on food-gathering and some hunting.
XANTHOCHROI, a term used by von Eickstedt to refer to blond, fair-haired North European Caucasoids.
XANTHODERM, a term used by von Eickstedt to refer to Mongoloid or yellow-skinned races.
X-CHROMOSOME, the x-chromosome determines female sex when combined with another x-chromosome received from the male sperm cell, but when combined with a y-chromosome, the resultant zygote will develop as a male.
XENOGRAFT, see HETEROGRAFT.
XERXES, an Achaemenid Persian king who destroyed the city of Babylon following a rebellion by its inhabitants, but was defeated in the attempt to conquer Greece by the destruction of his fleet in a naval battle fought against the Greeks at Salamis in 480 B.C.
XHOSA, a Bantu-speaking Negroid people of Southern Africa, largely dependent on horticulture and cattle-herding.
XIUHCOATL, the cult of the plumed serpent or fire snake, practiced by the Aztecs at their capital of Tenochtitlan.
XYLOPHONE, a primitive musical instrument comprising a series of pieces of wood of varying length which, when beaten, produce sounds of different tone.

Y

Y-CHROMOSOME, Y-chromosomes are carried only in the male sperm cell. When combined with an X-chromosome in the fertilized female egg cell, the Y-chromosome ensures that the fertilized egg will develop into a male child.
YABARANA, a South American Carib-speaking Indian people, dependent on horticulture with considerable hunting, fishing and some food-gathering.
YAGUA, a South American Indian people speaking a Peban language, probably related to the Carib family and dependent on hunting, horticulture and some fishing.
YAHGAN, a South American Indian people who formerly lived on Tierra del Fuego, but are now virtually extinct. Their language was related to Alacaluf, and they depended on fishing supplemented by some primitive hunting and food-gathering.
YAJUR VEDA, see VEDIC LITERATURE.
YAKA, a Bantu-speaking Negroid people living in the lower Congo, who are largely dependent on horticulture with some domestication of animals and hunting.
YAKO, a Bantu-speaking Negroid people of the West Africa Gross River area, dependent mainly on horticulture with some hunting and food-gathering.
YAKUTS, see SIBERIANS.
YAMI, a Malayo-Polynesian-speaking people of the Muong group, largely dependent on cultivation and fishing with some animal husbandry.
YANA, a Northeastern California, American Indian, Hokan-speaking people, dependent on food-gathering, hunting and fishing.
YANG, the Taoist concept of a basic male component of the universe, complementary to 'yin' (q.v.).

YANG-SHAO, a highly developed Neolithic culture, formerly located around the central area of the Hwang-Ho River. Excavation reveals relatively large unprotected settlements comprising circular houses, hand-made pottery, and flaked and polished stone tools. Millet and pork were the main sources of food, and burial was by inhumation of the body in a trench grave.
YANZI, a Bantu-speaking Negroid people of the Kasai group, largely dependent on horticulture, hunting and fishing.
YAO, a Bantu-speaking Negroid people of the Yao-Makonde group, largely dependent on horticulture and fishing.
YAPESE, a Micronesian-speaking (Malayo-Polynesian) people inhabiting the Pacific island of Yap, who are largely dependent on horticulture and fishing, with some animal husbandry.
YAQUI, a Northwest Mexico Indian coastal people who speak a Uto-Aztecan language, and are primarily dependent on horticulture supplemented by some food-gathering, hunting and fishing.
YARMOUTH INTERGLACIAL, the name given to the North American interglacial period which probably corresponded to the Alpine Mindel-Riss interglacial.
YARURO, a South American Indian people living in Venezuela around the Middle Orinoco River, and dependent on horticulture, hunting, fishing and food-gathering. Their language remains essentially unclassified.
YATENGA MOSSI, a Negroid West African Voltaic people, largely dependent on horticulture and some food-gathering.
YAVAPAI, a Hokan-speaking, Plateau Yuman, American Indian people, dependent on food-gathering and hunting.
YAYOI, a farming culture, largely dependent on rice, introduced into South-Western Japan around 250 B.C., at a time coinciding with the arrival of Bronze Age horse-riding Japanese warrior invaders who came from the Asian mainland.
Y-CHROMOSOME, y-chromosomes are carried only in the male sperm cell. When combined with an x-chromosome in the fertilized female egg cell, the y-chromosome ensures that the fertilized egg will develop as a male.
YGGDRASIL, the world Tree of Life (according to the Nordic Eddas, an ash) grew in a sacred grove, close to a fountain guarded by elves. Evil in the form of the dragon Nidhoff lay at the foot of Yggdrasil, an eagle sat on the upper branches, and the squirrel Ratatosk inhabited its boughs. The Celtic Hy-Brasil may be analogous to Ydddrasil.
YIDDISH, a language derived from a mixture of Medieval German with various Hebrew and Slavic components, commonly spoken by East European or Ashkenazim Jews. Yiddish appears to have developed from the German of early medieval Bavaria, modified in vocabulary and pronunciation by Hebrew influence. It remains a living language to this day.
YIN, a Taoist Chinese word for the basic female element in the universe. (See also YANG).
YOKUTS, a Penutian-speaking California Indian people.
YOMBE, a Bantu-speaking Negroid people living in the lower Congo, largely dependent on horticulture and some hunting and fishing.
YONI, the symbol of the female generative power, central to a Hindu cult, which has many adherents in India and Tibet. Possibly of ancient Paleolithic origin, like the mother goddess of Europe and Western Asia, the 'yoni' symbolizes the earth and fertility, and is frequently represented by an oval or circle, suggesting the vulva. The 'yoni' and the phallic 'lingam' (q.v.) are sometimes portrayed jointly to symbolize the combined male/female principles of the universe.
YORUBA, a coastal Nigerian Negroid cultivating people who speak a Kwa language.
YUAN, the Yuan dynasty reigned in China from A.D. 1280 to 1368, the period being notable for its decorated porcelain with a distinctive underglaze of cobalt blue.
YUCATEC MAYA, a Central American Mayan people, primarily dependent on

agriculture supplemented by some fishing and hunting.
YUCCA, a South and Central American plant, closely related to the lily, whose roots may be soaked in water to produce soap-like suds.
YUCHI, North American Woodland Indians who speak an Iroquois (Muskogean-Siouan) language, and are largely dependent on horticulture with hunting, fishing and food-gathering.
YUKAGHIR, a small population occupying probably the most severe climatic region in the world in the tundra southeast of the Siberian Lena River. Their Paleo-Asian language and way of life date at least from the Upper Paleolithic, and the language has no known affinities. The people are Mongoloid in appearance, and resemble the Tungus. Subsistence was traditionally based on hunting of reindeer (customarily ambushed at river crossings), fishing and some food-gathering, but reindeer herding has replaced reindeer hunting in recent times.
YUKI, a Northern California people, speaking a Hokan language of the Pomo-Yuki group, who are dependent on food-gathering, hunting and fishing.
YUKUT, a Turkic-Altaic-speaking people who live in the tundra region of North Siberia and depend mainly on animal-herding with some hunting, fishing and food-gathering.
YULETIDE, a North European festival celebrated with songs, banquets and joyful ceremonies at the time of the winter equinox. Many of the traditional 'Christmas' rituals, such as mistletoe and the yule-log, now often criticized by Christian clerics, derive from those of the pagan Yule. (See also CHRISTMAS).
YUMA, an American Indian people, speaking a language of the Hokan family, on the Colorado River, who are dependent on horticulture, fishing, hunting and food-gathering.
YUNGUR, a Negroid Niger-Congo-speaking people of the Adamawa-Eastern group, mainly dependent on horticulture with some animal husbandry and hunting.
YUPA, a South American Indian people speaking a Carib language, dependent on horticulture, food-gathering and some hunting.
YURAK, a Samoyed, Uralic-speaking people of the North Eurasian tundra, dependent mainly on reindeer herding, hunting and fishing.
YUROK, a Northwestern California Algonquin-speaking people, primarily dependent on food-gathering and fishing with some hunting.
YURT, a portable tent, constructed of felt stretched over a light framework of wood, which is widely used among Mongol pastoralists of the Asian steppelands in the course of their summer migrations.

Z

ZADRUGA, a prehistoric type of village settlement which survived in the Balkan area of Europe from the Neolithic to the beginning of the present century. The village comprises a single patriarchal extended family sharing all property, labor and agricultural produce. Each nuclear family, however, possesses its own house. The village activities are directed by a hereditary village headman who presides over an assembly comprising all adult male heads of nuclear families.
ZAGROS MOUNTAINS, the range of mountains which separates the high plateau of Iran from the low alluvial plains of Mesopotamia. It was in the valleys of the Zagros that wheat and barley were first domesticated.
ZAPAROAN, a South American language related to Tupi.
ZAPOTEC, a people who resided in the valley of Oaxaca in Mexico, whose main capital was located at Monte Alban. The Zapotec culture first appeared around A.D. 300, but in the 14th century the Oaxaca Valley was partially settled by invading Mixtecs. The Aztecs also dominated much of the valley of Oaxaca, but as the area was never fully subjugated the Zapotec language has survived to the present day.
ZAZZAGAWA, a Chad-speaking (Hamitic-influenced) Hausa people, largely dependent on horticulture with some animal husbandry and food-gathering.

ZEBU, the humped cattle of Africa, probably descended from the same stock as the Brahman cattle of India, and certainly not indigenous to Africa.
ZEMI, a divinity, sometimes represented in human and sometimes in animal form, of the Arawak Indians of Central America and Jamaica.
ZENAGA, Semitic-speaking Bedouin Arabs of North Africa, mainly dependent on animal herding and some horticulture.
ZEND, the sacred language of the Zoroastrians. (See also AVESTA).
ZHOB, an archeological site located in Northern Beluchistan (Pakistan), which has given its name to a local Chalcolithic culture. Black painted pottery and pottery figurines of females and of humped cattle resembled similar artifacts found in pre-Indus Valley strata at Harappa as well as certain artifacts recovered from Tepe Hissar in Northern Iran, which latter have been dated around the 4th and 3rd millennia B.C. It is therefore possible that the Zhob culture represents a geographical stage in which the culture of the Zagros mountains diffused eastwards across Iran into Beluchistan, and from thence into the Indus valley, to become the basis of the later Indus Valley high civilization.
ZIGGURAT, a large rectangular mound, constructed from a series of steps or stages, erected by the Sumerians as a basis on which their temples could be constructed. These temples contained anthropomorphic figures housing the spirit of the local city god, who was believed to own all the land, buildings and people who lived therein.
ZINJANTHROPUS, otherwise known as Australopithecus boisei. Zinjanthropus remains were found by Mary Leakey in 1959 in Bed I at Olduvai in association with Oldowan tools, and have been dated at 1.75 million years ago in the lower Pleistocene. Characterized by extremely robust jaws, and elements of a sagittal crest, Zinjanthropus boisei (sometimes called 'nutcracker man') possessed powerful mandibles. Similar fossils also found at Olduvai have also been classed as Zinjanthropus.
ZINZA, an East Lacustrine, Bantu-speaking Negroid people, mainly dependent on horticulture and some animal husbandry.
ZITHER, an East European musical instrument, the strings of which are adjusted parallel to the resonator and equipped with accurate tuning devices. Formerly used in religious ceremonies.
ZIWIYEH, an archeological tell site situated close to Lake Urmia in Northwestern Iran, in which a hoard of gold, silver, ivory and other valuable items was found, dating from the 7th century B.C., and believed to be the work of a local people known as the Mannai. The craftsmanship reveals strong similarities to that of the Scythians, as well as influences from Assyria and Luristan.
ZŁOTA, a cemetery in southern Poland revealing both Neolithic and Chalcolithic burials. The presence of battle-axes, globular amphorae and Corded Ware pottery suggests Indo-European origins, although most of the dead were laid in contracted positions in simple graves.
ZODIAC, a division of the celestial bodies into 12 major areas, each named after a specific cluster of stars. The study of the heavenly movements was used by the Babylonian priests, and especially the Chaldaeans, as a means of divination and is still used for this purpose by many Hindus in contemporary India. (See also ASTROLATRY and ASTROLOGY).
ZOMBIE, according to the Vodun magico-religious traditions of the Caribbean, a zombie is a person whose soul has been stolen by a magician, and whose body is therefore soulless and ready to carry out any instructions the magician may care to give it.
ZOROASTRIAN RELIGION, the worship of Ahura Mazda, the Wise Lord who symbolized goodness and light, in opposition to Agra Mainyu or Ahriman, the spirit of darkness, was the first major religion portraying the struggle between Good and Evil as a major principle of doctrine. Zoroastrianism represented an emergent monotheism which grew out of the old Aryan religion, and was soon accepted by all Aryan states throughout Iran. The Magi or Zoroastrian priests recognized the pantheon of Aryan gods only as courtiers or lieutenants of Ahura Mazda.

ZULU, a Bantu-speaking Negroid people of Southern Africa, largely dependent on horticulture and cattle herding.
ZUNI, an Aztec-Tanoan-speaking North American, Western Pueblo (Shoshone-related) people, dependent primarily on horticulture, with minimal hunting and some food-gathering.
ZYGION, the most lateral point on the zygomatic arch.
ZYGOMATIC ARCH, an arched bone formation linking the upper jaw to the ear aperture, usually large in mammals with strong jaw muscles but smaller in primates as a result of a decrease in the size of the jaws.